"This book offers a comprehensive, interdisciplinary insight into the concept of intellectual capital and its role in socio-economic growth and development as new sources of competitiveness are sought. The authors offers a unique perspective to intellectual capital integrating international management, international human resource management, strategic management and elements of international political economy, thus making it a captivating read."

Anna Visvizi, Deree College – The American College of Greece

"In the era of Big Data, Analytics and Artificial Intelligence, Intellectual Capital remains the key resource and enabler of innovation and sustainability. I recommend this book as a leading edition in covering the emerging convergence of IC and Information Technology."

Miltiadis D. Lytras, Research Professor, Deree College – The American College of Greece; Distinguished Scientist, King Abdulaziz University, Kingdom of Saudi Arabia

Intellectual Capital in the Digital Economy

This book presents a global view of digital and knowledge-based economies and analyses the role of intellectual capital, intellectual capital reports and information technology in achieving sustained competitive advantages in the globalized economy.

Intellectual Capital in the Digital Economy reviews the state of the art in the field of intellectual capital and intellectual capital reports, exploring core concepts, strengths and weaknesses, gaps, latest developments, the main components of intellectual capital, the main sections of the reports, and indicators of each component. It presents experiences from pioneering companies and institutions in measuring intellectual capital around the world. It incorporates an interdisciplinary and cross-sectorial approach, offering a comparative view of intellectual capital reports elaborated in different regions of the world. This book presents case studies and experiences on the building of intellectual capital reports in organizations. In addition, the book discusses the benefits and challenges of building intellectual capital reports in smart economies and societies.

This book is of direct interest to researchers, students and policymakers examining intellectual capital and the knowledge-based economy.

Patricia Ordóñez de Pablos is a professor in the Department of Business Administration in the Faculty of Economics and Business at the University of Oviedo, Spain. She is Editor-in-Chief of the *International Journal of Learning and Intellectual Capital* (IJLIC), *International Journal of Asian Business and Information Management* (IJABIM) and the book series Routledge Advances in Organizational Learning and Knowledge Management.

Leif Edvinsson is a key pioneering contributor to the theory and practice of Intellectual Capital (IC). He was the world's first director of IC in 1991, and is Cofounder and Founding Chairman of the New Club of Paris. In 2000 he was appointed to the world's first professorship on Intellectual Capital at Lund University, Sweden. In 2015 he was appointed to the Advisory Board to JIN – the Japan Innovation Network, and in 2016 he was appointed to the Advisory Board of the Norway Open Innovation Forum. In 2006 he was promoted to Chair Professor in Intellectual Capital at the Hong Kong Polytechnic University.

Routledge Advances in Organizational Learning and Knowledge Management

Series Editor: Patricia Ordóñez de Pablos, University of Oviedo, Spain

Strategic topics such as Organizational Learning (OL) Knowledge Management (KM), and Intellectual Capital (IC) are gaining greater interest both from the academic community and organisations in the highly competitive environment of today's economy. The influence of innovation and learning present a competitive advantage for firms, universities, organizations and regions.

The main goal of this book series is to bring together a selection of new perspectives from leading researchers on topics such as knowledge management and learning in cities and regions; knowledge management and intellectual capital reporting in universities, research centres and cities; future skills of knowledge workers, gamification and more.

The books in this series will reflect the most up-to-date research by leading experts from around the world, with special attention to new emerging topics. Some of the books will have a specific focus on relevant topics within certain economies/zones (for example, Central Asia, Himalayan Region, Gulf Region, New Silk Route).

1 Intellectual Capital in Organizations
Non-Financial Reports and Accounts
Edited by Patricia Ordóñez de Pablos and Leif Edvinsson

2 Knowledge and Practice in Business and Organisations
Edited by Kevin Orr, Rod Bain, Bonnie Hacking, Clare Moran, Sandra Nutley and Shona Russell

3 Creative Working in the Knowledge Economy
Sai Loo

4 Intellectual Capital in the Digital Economy
Edited by Patricia Ordóñez de Pablos and Leif Edvinsson

For more information about this series, please visit: www.routledge.com/Routledge-Advances-in-Organizational-Learning-and-Knowledge-Management/book-series/RAOLKM

Intellectual Capital in the Digital Economy

Edited by Patricia Ordóñez de Pablos
and Leif Edvinsson

LONDON AND NEW YORK

First published 2020
by Routledge
2 Park Square, Milton Park, Abingdon, Oxon OX14 4RN

and by Routledge
52 Vanderbilt Avenue, New York, NY 10017

Routledge is an imprint of the Taylor & Francis Group, an informa business

© 2020 selection and editorial matter, Patricia Ordóñez de Pablos and
Leif Edvinsson; individual chapters, the contributors

The right of Patricia Ordóñez de Pablos and Leif Edvinsson to be identified as the authors
of the editorial material, and of the authors for their individual chapters, has been asserted in
accordance with sections 77 and 78 of the Copyright, Designs and Patents Act 1988.

All rights reserved. No part of this book may be reprinted or reproduced or utilised
in any form or by any electronic, mechanical, or other means, now known or
hereafter invented, including photocopying and recording, or in any information
storage or retrieval system, without permission in writing from the publishers.

Trademark notice: Product or corporate names may be trademarks or registered trademarks,
and are used only for identification and explanation without intent to infringe.

British Library Cataloguing-in-Publication Data
A catalogue record for this book is available from the British Library

Library of Congress Cataloging-in-Publication Data
A catalog record has been requested for this book

ISBN: 978-0-367-25067-6 (hbk)
ISBN: 978-0-429-28588-2 (ebk)

Typeset in Bembo Std
by Newgen Publishing UK

Contents

List of figures	x
List of tables	xiii
Notes on editors and contributors	xiv
Preface	xxix
PATRICIA ORDÓÑEZ DE PABLOS	

PART I
Knowledge, innovation and the transition to a more circular economy

1

1 The future is digital – insight is key!   3
TRULS BERG

2 Open Innovation 2.0 supporting structural knowledge   7
BROR SALMELIN

3 The World Health Innovation Summit (WHIS) platform
for sustainable development: from the digital economy to
knowledge in the healthcare sector   19
GARETH PRESCH, FRANCESCA DAL MAS, DANIELE PICCOLO,
MAKSIM SINIK AND LORENZO COBIANCHI

PART II
Global outlook and intellectual capital in Asia and Europe   29

4 What drives the development of intellectual capital?
A longitudinal study   31
AINO KIANTO, MIKA VANHALA, PAAVO RITALA AND HENRI HUSSINKI

5 An intellectual capital framework of enterprise innovative
efficiency capability: a Hong Kong study   45
IRENE Y.H. FAN, RONGBIN W.B. LEE AND HALEY W.C. TSANG

viii   *Contents*

6 A comprehensive analysis of the importance of intellectual
   capital elements to support contemporary developments in
   Chinese firms   62
   GANG LIU, AINO KIANTO AND ERIC TSUI

7 Integrated Strategy Development based on intangibles   74
   MARKUS WILL

PART III
Intellectual capital and digitalized economy   95

8 IC Israel reporting: the journey from 1998 into the future   97
   EDNA PASHER, LEIF EDVINSSON, OTTHEIN HERZOG AND LEE SHARIR

9 Intellectual capital and digital technologies in academic
   entrepreneurship: premises for a revolution?   106
   GIUSTINA SECUNDO AND ROSA LOMBARDI

10 Overcoming cognitive bias through intellectual capital
   management: the case of pediatric medicine   123
   FRANCESCA DAL MAS, DANIELE PICCOLO AND DANIEL RUZZA

PART IV
Comparative view on national intellectual capital   135

11 Sustainable National Intellectual Capital in the digital age: a
   global outlook   137
   CAROL Y.Y. LIN AND LEIF EDVINSSON

12 Comparative view on national intellectual capital   163
   MARCOS CAVALCANTI, VALÉRIA MACEDO AND LARRIZA THURLER

PART V
Towards the development of intellectual capital standards
and culture   179

13 The trends of intellectual capital disclosure in the new
   economy: evidence from Australian firms   181
   YIRU YANG

Contents ix

14 Entrepreneurialism: a multi-faceted cultural movement 194
PIERO FORMICA

15 Towards the development of intellectual capital standards 206
RON YOUNG

16 Intellectual capital management scoring: a contribution to the
measurement of intangibles standardization 217
FLORINDA MATOS AND VALTER VAIRINHOS

PART VI
**Future challenges and risks for intellectual capital and
trade on IA and ideas** 233

17 Future challenges and risks for intellectual capital and trade
on IA and ideas 235
KARL MCFAUL

18 The role of blockchain for intellectual capital enhancement
and business model innovation 256
DANIEL RUZZA, FRANCESCA DAL MAS, MAURIZIO MASSARO
AND CARLO BAGNOLI

19 From trade in goods and services to trade in ideas 266
ESKIL ULLBERG

20 Revisiting the intellectual capital research landscape: a
systematic literature review 279
HENRI HUSSINKI, TATIANA GARANINA, JOHANNES DUMAY
AND ERIK STEINHÖFEL

Epilogue 293
LEIF EDVINSSON

Index 296

Figures

2.1	Components characterizing Open Innovation 2.0	8
2.2	Open innovation ecosystem	12
4.1	Research model	35
4.2	Results for the strategic factors	37
4.3	Results for the structural factors	38
5.1	The Intellectual Capital Framework of Enterprise Innovative Efficiency Capability (SCOPE)	47
5.2	Expert weighting on the importance of SCOPE aspects	50
5.3	Sample industry distribution vs. government statistics	51
5.4	Company size distribution	52
5.5	Length of business distribution	52
5.6	EIECI survey results on the 14 aspects	53
5.7	EIECI survey results on the 14 aspects by industry	54
5.8	Background information of the interviewed companies	55
5.9	Results of the four interviewed companies	56
6.1	Research model	65
6.2	Path coefficients and effects of the research model	67
7.1	Structural model of Integrated Strategy Development	76
7.2	Procedural model of Integrated Strategy Development	79
7.3	Strategic Options Portfolio	81
7.4	Schematic overview of ISD analysis results	84
7.5	Overview of fields of intervention and development goals	85
7.6	Allocating actions in target system	88
7.7	Exemplary action roadmap	90
7.8	Exemplary indicators allocated in the target system	91
8.1	*The Intellectual Capital of The State of Israel*, 3rd edition	99
8.2	Holon IC report	101
8.3	Danya Cebus IC report	102
9.1	IC and digital technologies in academic entrepreneurship	114
10.1	The BACRI flow	128
11.1	The relationship between SNIC and GDP per capita (ppp) for 59 countries	144
11.2	The correlation between health and GDP per capita (ppp) for 59 countries	144

11.3	The correlation between public structure and GDP per capita (ppp) for 59 countries	145
11.4	The correlation between education and GDP per capita (ppp) for 59 countries	146
11.5	The correlation between renewal and GDP per capita (ppp) for 59 countries	146
11.6	The correlation between CNC and GDP per capita (PPP) for 59 countries	147
11.7	The SNIC of two Australasian, two North American and four Nordic countries over 18 years	148
11.8	The SNIC of eight major European countries over 18 years	149
11.9	The SNIC of five Asian countries, Israel and UAE over 18 years	149
11.10	The CNC of two Australasian, two North American and four Nordic countries over 18 years	150
11.11	The CNC of eight major European countries over 18 years	150
11.12	The CNC of five Asian countries, Israel and UAE over 18 years	151
11.13	The SNIC and GDP for the top two countries in each of Figures 11.7–11.9	153
11.14	The CNC and GDP for the top two countries in each of Figures 11.10–11.12	153
Appendix 11.1 SNIC model		159
12.1	Timeline of studies on national intellectual capital	167
13.1	The relative emphasis in terms of IC categories	187
13.2	Changes in intellectual capital	188
13.3	Changes in internal capital	188
13.4	Changes in external capital	189
13.5	Changes in human capital	191
14.1	Knowledge in action	197
16.1	ICM – Intangible Capital Model	227
16.2	Structural model for causal relations between IC components compatible with ICM	228
17.1	Economic life-cycles of innovation	237
17.2	Policy innovation framework – prototype version	238
17.3	Policy innovation framework – published version	239
17.4	Business model taxonomy	248
19.1	Trade balance in royalty and services in Sweden	267
19.2	Renewal capital vs. GDP per capita (PPP) for four Nordic countries	269
19.3	Twelve renewal capital indicators for Sweden. A decline in the share of R&D to the economy as a whole can be observed	270
19.4	Renewal capital vs. GDP per capita (PPP) for Sweden, Singapore, Israel and Switzerland	271
19.5	Royalty trade balance vs. intellectual capital (renewal capital)	272
20.1	The distribution between accounting and managerial papers on IC and intangibles	283

xii *Figures*

20.2 The dynamics of the annual number of managerial papers on
IC and intangibles 284

20.3 IC and intangibles articles by continent: 2000–2017 285

20.4 The dynamics of the annual number of managerial papers on
IC per continent 285

20.5 The research trend regarding a single-element vs
multi-element approach on IC 287

Tables

2.1	Differences between innovation approaches are fundamental	9
Appendix 4.1	Measurement items	40
5.1	The fourteen aspects of SCOPE	48
6.1	Data validity	66
6.2	Goodness-of-fit statistics of research model	67
6.3	Results of hypotheses test for research model	67
6.4	Direct, indirect and total effect analysis	68
7.1	Summary of a strategic option in the strategy matrix (excerpt)	82
7.2	Weighting of development goals in the target system	87
7.3	Impact assessment of actions	89
9.1	Digital technologies in the current complex scenario	112
10.1	Bias in clinical medicine according to O'Sullivan and Schofield (2018)	125
11.1	SNIC and its components' score and ranking for 59 countries	140
11.2	Score and ranking comparison between SNIC and NIC	142
11.3	Countries and SNIC components having a high correlation with GDP per capita (ppp)	147
11.4	Correlation table of the selected indicators	155
Appendix 11.2	Indicators of Sustainable National Intellectual Capital (SNIC) model	160
Appendix 11.3	NIC version 2.0 model	161
13.1	Sample selection	185
18.1	The seven design principles	258
19.1	Impact of trade in ideas on intellectual capital in the digital economy	273
19.2	The educational benefits of MOOCs	273
19.3	The career benefits of MOOCs	274
19.4	The 4th Industrial Revolution	274
20.1	Top 20 accounting and management journals according to Google Scholar Metrics	282
20.2	IC elements in the focus of the analysis in accounting and management journals (as a percentage of the total sample)	288

Editors and contributors

Editors

Patricia Ordóñez de Pablos is a professor in the Department of Business Administration in the Faculty of Economics and Business at the University of Oviedo (Spain). Her teaching and research interests focus on the areas of knowledge management, intellectual capital, organizational learning and Asia. She is Editor-in-Chief of the *International Journal of Learning and Intellectual Capital* (IJLIC) and *International Journal of Asian Business and Information Management* (IJABIM), as well as the editor of a number of books (Routledge, IGI-Global, Springer, etc.). She is the Editor in Chief of the book series Routledge Advances in Organizational Learning and Knowledge Management.

Leif Edvinsson is a key pioneering contributor to the theory and practice of Intellectual Capital (IC). He was the world's first director of IC in 1991. He also led the prototyping in 1996 of the Skandia Future Center as a lab for organizational design. In 1998, he was awarded the "Brain of the Year" award, UK by the Brain Trust. He is also listed in *Who's Who in the World*. He is the Cofounder and Founding Chairman of the New Club of Paris. In 2000 he was appointed to the world's first professorship on Intellectual Capital at Lund University. In 2013 he was awarded the Thought Leader Award by the European Commission, Intel and Peter Drucker Association. In 2015 he was appointed to the Advisory Board to JIN – the Japan Innovation Network. In 2016 he was appointed to the Advisory Board of the Norway Open Innovation Forum. He was awarded the KM Award 2017, in Geneva, by km-a.net.

Contributors

Carlo Bagnoli is Professor of Strategy Innovation at the Department of Management, Ca' Foscari University of Venice. Before joining academia, he was the founder and CEO of Logisma Consulting Srl. He received his PhD in Business Economics at Ca' Foscari University of Venice. He was a visiting research fellow at the University of Florida. He is the proponent and scientific coordinator of the Strategy Innovation Hub. He is also the founder and scientific director of Strategy Innovation Srl: a Ca' Foscari University spin-off focused on action research. Among his institutional assignments, he is the Rector delegate for strategy innovation. His research interests include strategy innovation, business strategy, knowledge management, and social and entrepreneurial innovation. His research has been applied in multiple research contexts. He participated in and coordinated several national and European research projects. He has presented several papers at top international conferences and won the Kizok best paper award on SME at the 3rd EIASM Workshop on Intangibles and IC and the third best paper award at the SMS conference, Glasgow. He is Distinguished International Business Scholar, Angelo State University College of Business and Norris Family Endowment for International Business, October 2013.

Truls Berg is a serial entrepreneur, angel investor, inspirator and open innovation evangelist. He is the managing partner of Digital Insight as well as the founder and Executive Chairman of the Open Innovation Lab of Norway where 42 of Norway's leading corporations build their innovativeness. He is also the Chairman of NorBAN (Norwegian Business Angel Network). He is also a popular speaker and a regular columnist in *Computerworld, InnoMag* and *Nettavisen*. He is an avid proponent of the value of Inspiration, Innovation and Insight with diverse experience from Norwegian and international businesses. He has so far contributed to the launch of 12 businesses, including Sybase Norway, Component Software, bWise, Integrate, Comperio, Divine Nordic, Inspirator, Movation and the news channel InnoMag.no. In addition, he has assisted a number of other start-ups. In 2013 he co-wrote the book *Half way to the Future: 5 Mega Trends that Will Change the World*. He is also the author of the book *The Info Ocean: A Survival Guide for the Knowledge Workers of Tomorrow*, which was published in 2008 (Norwegian title: *Informasjonshavet: en overlevelsesguide for morgendagens kunnskapsmedarbeider*). He founded Component Software Group in 1997 (now renamed Affecto) and grew that to 180 employees. He co-founded Comperio, Integrate, Divine Nordic, Inspirator and Movation. He also served as the chairman of the Norwegian Computer Association from 2001 to 2003 and in 2002 he was voted Norwegian Leader of the Year.

Marcos Cavalcanti has a DSc in Computer Science from the Université de Paris XI, and is a professor at the Federal University of Rio de Janeiro – UFRJ. He is a director of CRIE (Reference Center for Business Intelligence, lab for Entrepreneurship and Innovation associated with the Engineering Program of UFRJ). He is an editor of *Revista Inteligência Empresarial* (a business intelligence journal in Brazil) and the coordinator of MBKM (Master's of Business and Knowledge Management) and WIDA (Web Intelligence and Digital Ambience). He is a member of the board of the New Club of Paris.

xvi *Editors and contributors*

Lorenzo Cobianchi, MD, PhD is an assistant professor of Surgery at the University of Pavia. He graduated at the University of Pavia where he also obtained the specialty in General Surgery in 2008. He was a post-doctoral fellow of the University of Miami at the Diabetes Research Institute where he gained experience in translational research, cell transplantation and regenerative medicine. He is involved in clinical and research activity. His areas of interest are: new technologies in general surgery; new integrated approaches for the treatment of pancreatic cancer; regenerative medicine and bioscaffold; new strategies for the treatment of postoperative pain. He is also active in medical student and residency education.

Francesca Dal Mas has a Bachelor's and a Master's degree in Business Administration from the University of Udine, Italy, a Law degree from the University of Bologna, Italy, and a PhD in Managerial and Actuarial Sciences from the Universities of Udine and Trieste, Italy. During her PhD, she was a visiting fellow at the Aoyama Gakuin University of Tokyo, Japan; the Graduate School of Management St. Petersburg State University, Russia; Sapienza University of Rome, Italy; University of Cassino and Southern Lazio, Italy; University of Salento, Italy; Macquarie University of Sydney, Australia; the Hong Kong Polytechnic University, China; and the Sharif University of Technology of Tehran, Iran. She has been working as an independent consultant and lecturer in the field of strategy and knowledge management for 15 years. She is an international assessor for the MIKE – Most Innovative Knowledge Enterprise Award for Italy and Iran. She is a lecturer in Strategy and Enterprise at the Lincoln International Business School and an honorary research fellow at Sapienza University of Rome. She has authored several papers in the field of strategy, intangibles and sustainability. She is a member of Ipazia, the International Observatory on Gender Research, of the International Association for Knowledge Management, and the Intellectual Capital Accreditation Association.

Johannes Dumay is Associate Professor of Accounting and Finance at Macquarie University, Sydney, Australia. Originally a consultant, he joined academia after completing his PhD in 2008. His thesis won the European Fund for Management Development and Emerald Journals Outstanding Doctoral Research Award for Knowledge Management. He researches accounting, intellectual capital, knowledge management, corporate reporting and disclosure, research methodologies and academic writing. He has written over 100 peer-reviewed articles, book chapters and edited books, and is highly cited. He is the Associate Editor of the highly regarded *Accounting, Auditing and Accountability Journal*, and *Meditari Accountancy Research*, and Deputy Editor of *Accounting & Finance*.

Irene Y.H. Fan has more than 30 years of innovative experience in the ICT industry. She developed and managed mobile products and services in Canada and was named DMTS (Distinguished Member of Technical Staff) at Lucent Technologies/Bell Labs. She oversaw the innovation strategy and the Digital Living Lab at the Hong Kong Applied Science Technology and Research Institute. Irene currently serves as the Chief Knowledge Scientist of SCALE InnoTech Limited, visiting Professor of the Bangkok University, and the Associate Editor of the *International Journal of Knowledge and System Science* (IJKSS). She also provides consultation services in technology management, strategy planning, innovation, knowledge and intellectual capital management in the ICT, education, NGO and government sectors. She obtained her PhD in Industrial and Systems Engineering (Knowledge and Technology Management) from the Hong Kong Polytechnic University, and both her Master's and Bachelor's degrees in Industrial Engineering (Operations Research and Management Science) from the University of Toronto.

Piero Formica began his career as an economist at the OECD's Economic Prospects Division in Paris. He is a senior research fellow of the Innovational Value Institute at Maynooth University in Ireland. At the C_LAB (a multidisciplinary laboratory for the development of innovation projects between the universities and businesses) in Veneto, Italy, born out of collaboration between the Universities of Padua and Verona, he conducts experiments for the development of innovative projects by students who attend the lab. He received the Innovation Luminary Award in June 2017 from the Open Innovation Science and Policy Group under the aegis of the European Union for his work on modern innovation policy. He serves on the editorial boards of *Industry and Higher Education, The International Journal of the Knowledge Economy, The International Journal of Social Ecology and Sustainable Development, The Journal of Global Entrepreneurship Research, The South Asian Journal of Management* and *Frontiers in Education*. He writes for the digital edition of the *Harvard Business Review*. He has published extensively in the fields of knowledge economics, entrepreneurship and innovation. *Exploring the Culture of Open Innovation: Towards an Altruistic Model of Economy* (2018) is his most recent published work.

Tatiana Garanina (PhD) is an associate professor at the School of Accounting and Finance, University of Vaasa, Finland. She was previously employed for ten years by the Graduate School of Management, St. Petersburg University, Russia. She has studied in executive education programs at Harvard Business School (USA), Institute of Finance (the Netherlands), and University of Ariel (Israel). She has published over 30 peer-reviewed articles in leading Russian and international academic journals. Her research is focused on corporate governance, intellectual capital, and value-based management. She delivers courses in accounting and financial statement analysis and valuation at all program levels from Bachelor's degrees to executive education programs. Her papers are presented at leading international conferences, such as the European Accounting Association Meeting, American Accounting Association Meeting, Strategic Management Society Meeting, Academy of

xviii *Editors and contributors*

Management Meeting, and others. She has been a member of the EFMD Board of Trustees since 2018.

Otthein Herzog worked from 1977 to 1993 for IBM Germany in software product development, AI research and AI technology transfer. From 1993 to 2009, he held the position of the chaired professor of Artificial Intelligence at the University of Bremen, Germany, where he continued to conduct research. Since 1998, he is Affiliate Research Professor in the Machine Learning and Inference Laboratory, George Mason University, Fairfax, VA, USA. Since 2010, he holds the Wisdom Professorship of Visual Information Technologies at Jacobs University Bremen. In 2015, he joined the CIUC, Tongji University, Shanghai, PRC, as Summit Program Professor of AI for Urban Planning. He is a Fellow of acatech – German National Academy of Science and Engineering, and Fellow of the German Informatics Association where he also chaired the AI Section for six years. His research interests include AI methods for the coordination and optimization of complex processes in Industry 4.0, for Wearable Computing for work processes, and for planning Intelligent Cities. In these fields, he has published more than 270 refereed scientific articles and books including four patents. He was named recently by an independent jury as one of the ten most influential minds of Artificial Intelligence in Germany.

Henri Hussinki (DSc Economics and Business Administration) is an assistant professor of business analytics at the LUT School of Business and Management, LUT University, Lahti, Finland. He researches intellectual capital, knowledge management practices, knowledge management systems and technologies, data science, business model innovation and accounting of intangibles. His research has been published in journals and edited books such as *Journal of Knowledge Management, Journal of Intellectual Capital, Auditing and Accountability Journal, Critical Perspectives on Accounting, Accounting* and *The Routledge Companion to Intellectual Capital*. His research has been awarded the Journal of Intellectual Capital's Highly Commended Paper (Emerald Literati Awards, 2018) and the Teemu Aho Award for outstanding doctoral dissertation in the field of economics and business administration (2016).

Aino Kianto (DSc Economics and Business Administration) is a professor of Knowledge Management in the School of Business and Management at LUT University, Lahti, Finland. Her teaching and research focus on knowledge management, intellectual capital, creativity, innovation and organizational renewal. Her research on these topics has been published widely (altogether almost 150 academic publications) and acknowledged with several international awards (three best paper awards and four mentions for excellence in academic journals). She is known as one of the most prominent academic figures in the fields of Intellectual Capital and Knowledge Management and she has delivered key note speeches and acted as a track chair in several related international conferences. She is the Associate Editor of *VINE Journal* *of Information and Knowledge Management Systems* and is a member of the editorial boards of three other journals (*Knowledge Management Research Practice*; *Journal of Knowledge Management*; *International Journal of Knowledge and Systems Science*). She is also the academic director of the Master's Programme in Knowledge Management and Leadership at LUT University and has had a key role in making this programme the most attractive in the whole university (based on the number of applicants in the year 2019: 713 applicants for 45 student positions, 6.3 per cent acceptance rate). In addition to academia, she also has worked with the Future committee of the Finnish parliament and regularly lectures for companies and practitioners.

Rongbin W.B. Lee is Emeritus Professor, Former Director of KMIRC and Head of State Key Laboratory of Ultra-precision Machining Technology of the Hong Kong Polytechnic University. He has pioneered research and practice in knowledge management in various industrial sectors in Hong Kong which include manufacturing, trading, public utilities and health care, and has conducted research projects in knowledge elicitation and mapping, unstructured information management and organizational learning and innovation. In 2002, he established the Knowledge Solution Laboratory in the Hong Kong Polytechnic University (PolyU) – Microsoft Enterprise Systems Centre, the first of its kind in Hong Kong. He is currently the chief editor of the *International Journal of Knowledge and Systems Science*, co-editor of the *Journal of Information and Knowledge Management Systems* and associate editor of the *International Journal of Learning and Intellectual Capital and Learning*.

Carol Y.Y. Lin (PhD, University of Texas at Austin) is Distinguished Professor in the Department of Business Administration at National Chengchi University. In 2017, she obtained the Outstanding Research Award, conferred by the Ministry of Science and Technology, the most prestigious research award in Taiwan. She has published extensively on strategic HRM, SME management, intellectual capital, corporate social responsibility and social innovation. In addition to over 50 academic referred journal papers and 100 conference proceedings, she has published 14 books in English with Springer New York and Singapore, covering the topics of National Intellectual Capital and the impact of societal and social innovation. She has also held several administrative positions, including the Dean of International Cooperation, Director of Creativity Center, Dean of Student Affairs, Director of International Exchange and Education, and the Founding Director of English Taught International MBA programme (the first IMBA programme in Taiwan). Before changing her career to academia, she served as Customer Service Manager in Singer Sewing Machine Companies for two years, and Office Manager in K-Mart Taipei Purchasing Office for six years.

Gang Liu is a PhD candidate at the Knowledge Management and Innovation Research Center, Department of Industrial and Systems Engineering of

xx *Editors and contributors*

The Hong Kong Polytechnic University. His research interests comprise knowledge management theory, intellectual capital, organizational performance and innovation. His current study examines knowledge management practices and organizational performance relationships in a wholistic perspective.

Rosa Lombardi is Associate Professor of Business Administration at Sapienza University of Rome, Italy, since 1 September 2019. She obtained the Italian National Qualification as Full Professor. She was Assistant Professor of Business Administration from 2014 to August 2019. She received her PhD in Business Administration in 2012. She serves as Editor-in-Chief of the *International Journal of Digital Culture and Electronic Tourism*, as Associate Editor of the *Palgrave Communications Journal*, is an editorial board member of *Meditari Accountancy Research, Management Decision, Corporate Social Responsibility* and *Environmental Management, International Journal of Applied Decision Sciences* and *International Journal of Organizational Analysis* and is a guest editor and reviewer for several international peer-reviewed academic journals. Her research interests cover intellectual capital, intellectual capital reporting, corporate governance, disclosure, management accounting and control systems, evaluation of firms and business networks, decision-making processes, knowledge transfer, strategy and smart technologies, ethics and corruption prevention models. Her research activities have been documented in about 120 international papers. She is the Coordinator of the SIDREA Research Group on "Intellectual Capital, Smart Technologies and Digitalization". She is also the winner of: 2015 EMERALD/EMRBI Business Research Award for Emerging Researchers; and Best Paper Award SOItmC&RTU 2017 by SOItmC & Riga Technical University Conference.

Valéria Macedo is a researcher at CRIE (Reference Center for Business Intelligence, lab for Entrepreneurship and Innovation associated with the Engineering Program of the Federal University of Rio de Janeiro – UFRJ). She is a PhD student at UFRJ in the Information Science Program of the Brazilian Institute of Information in Science and Technology – IBICT. She has an MSc in Business Administration and is a specialist in Knowledge Management with interests in network science, assessment of the economy of intangibles.and impacts on the new knowledge economy. She has many years professional experience in the corporate market of the capital and derivatives market segment, coordinating in the area of professional education and certification, and has implemented projects directed to distance education.

Maurizio Massaro, PhD, is an associate professor in the Department of Management of the Ca' Foscari University of Venice, Italy. Before joining academia, he was the founder and CEO of multiple consultancy firms. He has also served as a research centre vice president in the field of metal analysis. He was a visiting professor at Florida Gulf Coast University (USA) and Leicester University (UK). He enjoys several contacts and research partnerships with universities in the USA, continental Europe, UK, Asia, and Australia. His research interests include knowledge management, intellectual capital, strategy and research methods. His research has been applied in multiple research contexts. He is the representative in Italy for the MIKE – Most Innovative Knowledge Enterprise Award, and he is a member of the Global MIKE study group of the Hong Kong Polytechnic University.

Florinda Matos has a PhD in Social Sciences, Organizational Behaviour Studies from the Technical University of Lisbon, and she has a Master's degree in Business Sciences from ISCTE – IUL Business School, Lisbon. She was a founding member of ICAA – Intellectual Capital Association and, currently, she is its president. In addition, she is an associate researcher of DINÂMIA'CET – IUL – Centre for Socioeconomic and Territorial Studies. She was also a post-doctoral researcher in the area of the Social Impacts of Additive Manufacturing in NOVA.id.FCT and, presently, she is leading the project "KM3D - Knowledge Management in Additive Manufacturing: Designing New Business Models" in a national consortium, funded by FCT – Fundação para a Ciência e a Tecnologia. She is also a member of the scientific committee of several international conferences, where she has participated as organizer, speaker, mini-track chair and reviewer. She has more than 30 published academic articles and scientific papers, book chapters and books related to management, sustainability, knowledge management, intellectual capital management and innovation.

Karl McFaul consults as a strategist, lecturer and innovation project manager on the EU, city and business levels in Europe and beyond building attractive, productive and resilient ecosystems for innovation in the digital transformation of the AI economy. He is a co-founder of Future Navigators and has, together with an international network of expertise on Intellectual Capital (IC) management research in Europe, USA and Asia, developed a unique method and practice of connecting capital assets to scale financial returns with a positive impact on society and the environment. He has recently developed a new framework for policy innovation as a member of the European Commission High-Level Expert Group on the Impact of the Digital Transformation on EU Labour Markets. He is an elected member of the New Club of Paris and the Future Center Alliance. He is a former manager at the European Spallation Source (ESS), a €1.8 billion project constructing the world's most powerful big science infrastructure for materials research. He holds an Executive MBA from Lund University School of Economics & Management and an MFA from the University of Gothenburg. He is a DSDM certified Agile Coach and a pioneer in IoT, VR and digital platform economics from Chalmers University of Technology.

Edna Pasher earned her PhD (1981) in Media Ecology at New York University Department of Communication Arts and Sciences and has served as a faculty member at Adelphi University, the City University of New York, the Hebrew University in Jerusalem, Ben-Gurion Universities at Beer Sheva, the Academic College of Tel-Aviv-Yaffo and the Tel-Aviv University. She founded EP as an international strategic management consulting firm in 1978. The firm provides customized consulting services to organizations in both the private and the public sectors. She was the pioneer and leader of the Innovation and Knowledge management movement in Israel and a member of Entovation International, an international network of management consulting companies specializing in innovation management. In addition she is an active member of the international community of the Intellectual Capital pioneers. She has 24 years of experience in regional and international ICT research and innovation projects funded by the EU using a variety of evaluation methodologies, modelling techniques, quantitative and qualitative analysis. She is a founding partner (1991) and chief editor of *Status – the Israeli Management Magazine*, and a founding partner and chairperson (2015) of ISCI Israel Smart Cities Institute (NGO). She is also a frequent speaker at international conferences. She led the progress of the intellectual report of Israel, Denya Cebus company, Holon's municipality, Tidhar group and has written articles for *Intellectual Capital Journal*, chapters for different books and other publications such as *The Complete Guide to Knowledge Management: A Strategic Plan to Leverage Your Company's Intellectual Capital* and *Exploring the Culture of Open Innovation: Towards an Altruistic Model of Economy*. She is currently working with other professors on a new method for integrating artificial intelligence and Big Data tools to combine in the IC report.

Daniele Piccolo has a degree in Engineering and one in Medicine, both from the University of Udine, Italy. He is the founder and Chief Executive Officer of Nucleode Srl, an innovative start-up company in the field of technology and healthcare based in Gorizia, Italy. He spent some months as a research fellow at the Northwestern University of Chicago, USA, in 2013, and the University of Pittsburgh, USA, in 2015. Besides being an entrepreneur, Daniele is currently a PGY1 Neurosurgery Resident at the University of Padua, Italy. He is the author of some publications linking medicine, technology and management.

Gareth Presch has a Bachelor's degree in public health management and is a social entrepreneur who believes in sharing knowledge. He is the founder and CEO of the World Health Innovation Summit (WHIS), a platform that empowers people and communities to improve their health and wellbeing while generating value. A problem solver and healthcare strategist, he has experience working in public, private and voluntary healthcare settings in the NHS (ehealth) and abroad. Patient focused and quality driven, he is a former Chief Officer of the National Haemophilia Council, a statutory body in Ireland. He has also managed National Clinical Programmes on blood transfusion (establishment of the National Blood Transfusion Committee), haemochromatosis and the endoscopy improvement programme. He is the Expert for UNGSII Foundation on SDG 3 Good Health and Wellbeing, whose mission is to ensure that the world reaches the global goals by 2030. He is also the Co-President of the Romanian One Health Initiative and Vice Chair of the GWI SDG Initiative and is currently a St George's House Leadership Fellow. He has advised and been a member of a number of successful charity fundraising events in the past and continues to support charitable causes locally, nationally and internationally.

Paavo Ritala, DSc (Economics and Business Administration), is a professor of Strategy and Innovation at the School of Business and Management in the Lappeenranta University of Technology (LUT). His key research themes include collaborative innovation, knowledge sharing and protection, coopetition, platforms and ecosystems, as well as sustainable value creation. His research has been published in journals such as *Journal of Product Innovation Management, Industrial and Corporate Change, Industrial Marketing Management, British Journal of Management* and *Technovation.*

Daniel Ruzza has a Bachelor's degree in Business Administration and a Master's degree in Accounting and Finance, both from Venice Ca' Foscari University, Italy. During his Master's degree, he was a visiting student at the Xi'an Jiaotong University of Suzhou, China. In the years 2018–2019, he was a research fellow at the Department of Management of Venice Ca' Foscari University, Italy, as well as Business Analysis at Strategy Innovation, the Ca' Foscari University's spin-off. He is now a full-time PhD student in Management at the Department of Business and Management of the Luiss Guido Carli University of Rome, Italy.

Bror Salmelin is a former adviser for Innovation Systems at the European Commission, where he was responsible for open innovation and modern innovation systems. He has expertise in the intangible economy and value creation, related to policies like innovation policy, productivity and strategy. As creator of the Open Innovation Strategy and Policy Group (OISPG), an industry-led group on strategic priorities for open and service innovation, his focus is on open innovation and societal and industrial commons. He co-created the concept of Open Innovation 2.0, and organized several top-level conferences on the topic. He developed the innovation tool of the European Network of Living Labs, comprising 350 sites throughout the world. Having a technical background in systems and automation, he has led units on Manufacturing, Electronic Commerce and Collaborative Working and became Advisor in Innovation. Before joining the EC in 1998 he was Deputy of the ICT Section in the Finnish Innovation Agency and worked also as diplomat in Los Angeles. He is a member of the New Club of Paris, the Advisory Board for the Innovation Value Institute, Ireland, and was a member of the HLG of European Innovation Systems. He is a frequent speaker at international events due to his insight in modern innovation, innovation ecosystem creation and strategic development.

xxiv *Editors and contributors*

Giustina Secundo is Senior Researcher in Management Engineering at University of Salento (Italy). Her research is characterized by a cross-disciplinary focus, with a major interest towards Intellectual Capital management, Innovation Management and academic entrepreneurship. She has been scientifically responsible for several education and research projects held in partnership with leading academic and industrial partners. Her research activities have been documented in about 150 international papers. Her research has appeared in *Technovation, Technological Forecasting & Social Change, Journal of Business Research, Journal of Intellectual Capital, Knowledge Management Research & Practices, Measuring Business Excellence* and *Journal of Knowledge Management*. She has been a lecturer on Project Management at the Faculty of Engineering of the University of Salento since 2001. She is a member of the Project Management Institute. In 2014 and 2015 she was a visiting researcher at the Innovation Insights Hub, University of the Arts London (UK).

Lee Sharir is a reserve officer in the Israel Defense Forces. During her military service, she served as a research officer and dealt with technological and economic projects in the intelligence corps. She is currently completing a Bachelor's degree in Economics, Management, and Human Resources from Bar Ilan University. She works in the Dr Edna Pasher Group as a project manager and advisor to management, especially in projects that focus on innovation, knowledge management and community building in many organizations in Israel. She is the Head of International Relations at the Research Department of the Israel Smart Cities Institute (NGO) established by Dr Edna Pasher. She is active in the CItyTLV (NGO) which is leading the Israeli eco-system in the field of fintech and leads the Prowoman Bar-Ilan branch to promote women in the Israeli labour market.

Maksim Sinik is a software architect, conference speaker, CTO and Founder at Nucleode Srl, an innovative start-up company in the field of technology and healthcare based in Gorizia, Italy. He strongly believes that the next significant evolution for healthcare lies in technology. He is an open-source software enthusiast. As an expert of the so-called platform companies or "platfirms", he is the lead maintainer and software engineer at HospitalRun, an open-access platform that offers a free downloadable software for hospital management with the aim of providing the most modern hospital information system to less resourced environments.

Erik Steinhöfel studied Industrial Engineering with the specialization in Innovation Management at the University of Applied Sciences Berlin and the University of Technology, Sydney. He leads the Competence Center for Knowledge Management (CCKM) at the Fraunhofer Institute for Production Systems and Design Technology Berlin and is an expert in knowledge management, strategic planning and innovation management. Supporting a wide variety of organizations and developing management methodologies in the frame of several public and industrial projects across Europe, Asia and South America, he refined his expertise in these fields. Nowadays, his main research focus is on business model development in small and medium-sized enterprises.

Larriza Thurler is a researcher at CRIE (Reference Center for Business Intelligence, lab for Entrepreneurship and Innovation associated with the Engineering Program of UFRJ). She has a PhD in Information Science from the Brazilian Institute of Information in Science and Technology – IBICT / Federal University of Rio de Janeiro – UFRJ, and MSc in Communication and an MBA in Strategic Management and Innovation. He professional experience is in project management, communication and knowledge management.

Haley W.C. Tsang is currently a PhD student. She graduated from the Hong Kong Polytechnic University with a Master's of Philosophy and holds a double degree – BEng (Hons) in Industrial and Systems Engineering and BBA (Hons) with a major in Marketing from the same university. Her working experience includes a position in a global financial services company providing risk management and portfolio optimization solutions for major investment houses. She was awarded the "Best Paper and Presentation" in the PhD and Master's Colloquium at the 8th European Conference in Intellectual Capital in Venice, Italy. Her research interests include knowledge management, intellectual capital, risk management and learning sciences.

Eric Tsui is a professor in the Department of Industrial and Systems Engineering of the Hong Kong Polytechnic University. His research interests include knowledge management technologies, blended learning, cloud services and collaborations. He is also the Principal Instructor of two Massive Open Online Courses (MOOCs) on edX covering the topics of Knowledge Management, Big Data and Industry 4.0. He is an honorary advisor to three Hong Kong Government departments and provides consultancy and professional services to many private organizations, and NGOs in Hong Kong, Singapore, Malaysia, Australia, Japan and Brunei. He has BSc (Hons.), PhD and MBA qualifications.

Eskil Ullberg is an adjunct professor at George Mason University, Fairfax, VA, USA, and the head of the Trade in Ideas Program, which is currently at the Institute of Management of Innovation and Technology. His research interest is markets in patents, and how they can leverage the human capital formation, especially for developing countries, through exchange in human ideas. He is a pioneer in studies of markets in patents using experimental economics. Prior to his academic work he worked as a strategy consultant for 20 years for companies and government agencies focusing on the management of risk. His work has been published in academic journals, books and been presented at international organizations including the UN (ECOSOC) and WTO, focusing on maximizing human potential.

xxvi *Editors and contributors*

Valter Vairinhos is a retired Portuguese Navy Officer, where he served as a naval engineer between 1964 and 2009. He has a doctoral degree – in Multivariate Data Analysis – from the Statistics Department of Salamanca University, Spain. Currently he shares his investigation activity between ICLab – ICAA and the Statistics Department of Salamanca University. His main investigative interests are related to graph data mining and the automatic synthesis of results from multivariate data analysis, being the author of a methodology, based in intersection graphs, to generate automatic synthetic descriptions of results from multivariate data analysis and its implementation through a software (BiplotsPMD) where those ideas are put to use.

Mika Vanhala, DSc Economics and Business Administration, is an associate professor in Knowledge Management and Leadership at the LUT School of Business and Management, LUT University, Finland, and post-doctoral researcher at the School of Management, University of Vaasa – Kokkola University Center Chydenius, Finland. His primary research interests are the relationship between HRM practices, organizational trust and organizational performance, as well as intellectual capital and knowledge management in value creation. His research has been published in, for example, *Human Resource Management Journal*, *Journal of Knowledge Management*, *Personnel Review*, and *Journal of Managerial Psychology*.

Markus Will is head of the Fraunhofer IPK Project Office Brazil and the appointed senior researcher for Intellectual Capital Management at the Division Corporate Management of Fraunhofer IPK, Berlin. He completed an apprenticeship in business administration and holds a Master's in communication sciences. In 2011, he successfully completed his doctoral thesis on "Strategic Business Development Based on Intangibles in Small and Medium-Sized Enterprises" at the Technical University Berlin. After working as a junior consultant at Siemens Business Services he moved to Fraunhofer IPK where he was developing and leading various customer projects on change and knowledge management, process optimization and internal communication. Based on his experiences as project manager of the German federal initiative "Wissensbilanz – Made in Germany" and the European Union's pilot-project "InCaS. Intellectual Capital Statement – Made in Europe", he was elected member of the board of the German association for Intellectual Capital Management in 2012. Since 2007, he has been a lead trainer at Fraunhofer Academy and has acted as a management consultant for several large corporations. Today he is responsible for Fraunhofer IPK's management consulting activities in Brazil with a focus on Business Planning and Strategic Management of Innovation Ecosystems.

Yiru Yang is an accounting lecturer at Central Queensland University. Yiru completed her Doctor of Philosophy from the University of Wollongong in 2016. Her thesis focused on studying the underlying earnings reporting quality, equity overvaluation and intellectual capital reporting of Australian

Securities Exchange listed firms. She has presented and published peer-reviewed articles across a range of academic disciplines: intellectual capital, financial and non-financial reporting quality, earnings management and equity overvaluation. Prior to joining Central Queensland University, Yiru had built her experience in teaching various accounting subjects at both undergraduate and postgraduate levels at the University of Wollongong. She believes her teaching strength comes from understanding students' unique requirements and assisting them to achieve as much as they can. She has also gained industry experience in organizations and she is now the shareholder and director of the GP Health Australia Pty, Ltd.

Ron Young is the founder of the Knowledge Associates International group of companies, who are international management consultants with head-quarters in Cambridge, UK. He is acknowledged as a leading international expert in knowledge and innovation management. He specializes in knowledge-driven results for organizations. He contributed to the production of the UK Government White Paper "UK Competitiveness in the Knowledge Driven Economy". He regularly provides keynote presentations and master classes at leading international conferences around the world. He chaired the BSI Knowledge Management Standards Committee, and is a member of the ISO Standards workgroups for Knowledge Management, Asset Management, Quality and Innovation Management. He lecturers on the Global Knowledge Economy and he teaches the Knowledge Asset Management Methodology at leading universities. He consults with the United Nations, World Bank, European Commission and the inter-governmental Asian Productivity Organization (APO). He specializes in developing knowledge strategies, policies, governance models, standards, knowledge systems and knowledge-driven platforms. He works with major multinational corporations, international and national organizations. He was a lead consultant for the European Commission 3 million euro "Know-Net" and "LEVER" collaborative research projects. He is the joint author of several books on Knowledge and Innovation.

Preface

Patricia Ordóñez de Pablos

Introduction

The book analyses the knowledge-based economy and digital economy and explores emergent technologies and tools on the 2020 horizon, post 2020, as well as trends, challenges and risks. Readers will navigate through a rich collection of 20 chapters written by leading international experts on intellectual capital, knowledge management and information technology, enhancing their understanding and insights on key issues for the competitiveness of companies and societies in the coming years,

The book reviews the state of the art in the field of intellectual capital and intellectual capital reports: core concepts, strengths and weaknesses, gaps, latest developments, main components of intellectual capital, main sections of the report, and indicators of each component. It covers experiences from pioneer companies and institutions in measuring intellectual capital around the world. It incorporates an interdisciplinary and cross-sectorial approach and offers a comparative view on intellectual capital reports elaborated in different regions of the world. The book presents case studies and experiences on the building of intellectual capital reports in organizations. In addition, the book discusses the benefits and challenges of building intellectual capital reports in smart economies and societies.

Contents of the book

This book is divided into six sections that address new and emerging topics in the field of intellectual capital in the digital economy in order to achieve sustained competitive advantage, economic growth and prosperity.

Part I: "Knowledge, innovation and the transition to a more circular economy" comprises three chapters addressing topics like Open Innovation 2.0, digital economy in the healthcare sector and the digital future.

Chapter 1, titled "The future is digital – insight is key!" (by Truls Berg), discusses innovation in Norway and explores the cases of two Norwegian companies, Aker BioMarine (a founding member of the Open Innovation Lab of Norway) and Agder Energy. Interesting insights and conclusions are presented.

xxx *Preface*

Chapter 2, titled "Open Innovation 2.0 supporting structural knowledge" (by Bror Salmelin) discusses "the strong connection between modern, open innovation, the methods and ecosystems and the importance of intellectual capital for competitiveness and sustainable development both in societal and economic dimensions".

Chapter 3, titled "The World Health Innovation Summit (WHIS) platform for sustainable development: from the digital economy to knowledge in the healthcare sector" (by Gareth Presch, Francesca Dal Mas, Daniele Piccolo, Maksim Sinik and Lorenzo Cobianchi) examines "the contribution of 'platforms' in a critical sector, that of healthcare, by analyzing the case of the World Health Innovation Summit (WHIS). Results show how 'platforms' like WHIS can contribute to the creation and spreading of knowledge, involving experts, professionals, and people, and reinvesting efforts, value, and money back to the community in a circular way. New technologies can thereby enhance the creation of new sustainable business models and solutions able to increase the social value, thereby allowing the move from a digital economy to knowledge".

Part II: "Global outlook and intellectual capital in Asia and Europe" presents fours chapters addressing several key topics, from intellectual capital from a longitudinal approach and innovative efficiency capability in Hong Kong, to intellectual capital in China and strategy and intangible resources.

Chapter 4, titled "What drives the development of intellectual capital? A longitudinal study" (by Aino Kianto, Mika Vanhala, Paavo Ritala and Henri Hussinki) states that "The beneficial consequences that intellectual capital exerts on various aspects of organizational performance have become well established facts demonstrated in a wide range of empirical studies. However, little knowledge exists on what drives the development of intellectual capital itself. To bridge this gap in the current understanding, this chapter examines the different organizational aspects that enhance or hinder the development of intangible value drivers. It is posited that two key groups of organizational factors are likely to impact the development of intellectual capital: strategic and structural. The theoretical model specifying these and their influence on the essential aspects of intellectual capital is tested with partial least squares (PLS)-based structural modelling, analysing a longitudinal dataset collected via two waves of surveys in 2013 and 2017 from 96 Finnish organizations. The chapter contributes to the literature on intellectual capital from a dynamic-temporal perspective, and helps to inform managers and policy-makers about the strategic and structural factors that influence the development of intellectual capital in organizations".

Chapter 5, titled "An intellectual capital framework of enterprise innovative efficiency capability: a Hong Kong study" (by Irene Y.H. Fan, Rongbin W.B. Lee and Haley W.C. Tsang) states that "efficiency is no longer just measured in maximizing output with minimal resource input. A new knowledge paradigm views efficiency with the innovative use of intangible resources. A composition index of EIECI (Enterprise Innovative Efficiency Capability Index) was developed with Intellectual Capital dimensions. The index was applied in a study of Hong Kong enterprises. The overall score of EIECI for Hong Kong

Preface xxxi

is found to be low. Only 8% of the companies scored 'Good' or 'Excellent'. The tourism sector and the financial services and banking sector have higher rating scores. Hong Kong scored high in transformational leadership, quality of knowledge workers, and agility. However, the companies are weak in the use of data and automation, adoption of gamification, and open innovation as their company strategy. The study further analyzes different industry sectors and identified different characteristics of their respective EIECI. Four enterprises were interviewed on their good practices in innovative efficiency works, such as design thinking, knowledge worker, transformational leadership, and information technology adoption and automation".

Chapter 6, titled "A comprehensive analysis of the importance of intellectual capital elements to support contemporary developments in Chinese firms" (by Gang Liu, Aino Kianto and Eric Tsui) suggests that "to better understand the relevance of intellectual capital for organisational performance in the Chinese context, and in particular the interplay among the different components of intellectual capital and their impacts on organisational performance, this chapter seeks to address the question of how intellectual capital impacts organisational performance in Chinese firms. The present study also seeks to widen the scope of study and to explore the value of intellectual capital from the perspective of two key company stakeholders: employees and customers. Structural equation modelling was used to test seven hypotheses with a data set of 139 Chinese firms. Our findings suggest that human capital significantly affects the market performance of firms via the mediating factors of structural capital, internal relational capital, external relational capital, customer value creation and employee job satisfaction while structural capital has the strongest impact on a firm's market performance. In addition, internal relational capital positively affects employee job satisfaction while external relational capital significantly influences customer value creation. Our study is one of the first to investigate the relationship between intellectual capital and market performance, both directly and as mediated by employee job satisfaction and customer value creation, especially in the context of the world's largest emerging economy, China".

Chapter 7, titled "Integrated strategy development based on intangibles" (by Markus Will) states that "the development towards a knowledge-based economy has already progressed so far that intangible resources already have, in many cases, a greater influence on business success than classical material production factors. In the context of the digital economy, this challenge becomes even more important as competitive differentials on a globalized market will increasingly rely on intangible features rather than 'hard' product functionality or price only. The method 'Integrated Strategy Development' (ISD) aims at enabling small and medium-sized enterprises (SMEs) to design strategies for the development of their business model, systematically integrating the necessary qualitative aspects of intangible assets to meet the needs of the knowledge-based and digital economy. The ISD model has been tested and used in various application contexts where it has proven to be of practical benefit in the strategy definition and the respective implementation planning and monitoring in European SMEs

xxxii *Preface*

from various business sectors. Incremental adaptations of the method were used in further application contexts including the strategic planning and evaluation of applied research institutes in Brazil. The article concludes with further application and development potential of the ISD method for the digital economy".

Next, Part III: "Intellectual capital and digitalized economy" offers three chapters reviewing the building of intellectual capital reports in Israel, the role of digital technologies and intellectual capital in academic entrepreneurship and how intangible resources can help to overcome cognitive bias.

Chapter 8, titled "IC Israel reporting: the journey from 1998 into the future" (by Edna Pasher, Leif Edvinsson, Otthein Herzog and Lee Sharir), explores "the story of the evolution of Intellectual Capital (IC) reporting in Israel from 1998 to the present and the next stage – adding Artificial Intelligence (AI) to IC to navigate ecosystems. Edna Pasher PhD & Associates first adopted the concept of 'knowledge-based organizations', when Prahalad and Hamel published the paper 'The Core Competence of the Corporation' in 1990 and since then our strategic consulting has focused on supporting organizations in identifying their core knowledge for competitive advantage".

Chapter 9, tiled "Intellectual capital and digital technologies in academic entrepreneurship: premises for a revolution?" (by Giustina Secundo and Rosa Lombardi), states "the increasing attention to the third mission of universities is increasing the impact and the social value a university creates in the surrounding environment. In this scenario, a major focus on intellectual capital (IC) management and performance management is required, where IC is considered at the same time as mission and performance in the university context. Simultaneously, digital technologies, such as social media, mobiles, business analytics, Internet of Things, Big Data, Advanced Manufacturing, 3D printing, cloud and cyber-solutions, MOOCs and artificial intelligence, are nowadays permeating all private and public organizations. Digital technologies can enhance the development of IC and strategic assets within the academic entrepreneurship process. However, even if their disruptive role has been widely recognized at the business level, and the IC field reached its cusp in the mid-2000s, new research is needed to understand the potentiality of digital technologies on IC management. In this scenario, our analysis is directed to investigate how emerging digital technologies could impact on the development, management and disclosure of IC in academic entrepreneurship. Findings show a renewed framework based on the 'input–output logic' promotes an understanding of how digital technologies support the creation, management and disclosure of IC in universities. Implications for theory and practices, and avenues for future research to inform this novel field of investigation are discussed".

Chapter 10, titled "Overcoming cognitive bias through intellectual capital management: the case of pediatric medicine" (by Francesca Dal Mas, Daniele Piccolo and Daniel Ruzza) suggests that "intellectual capital as the sum of human, structural, and relational capital is among the key resources for an organization to produce value. However, knowledge as an intellectual resource may show a dark side. Human capital, for instance, is often affected by cognitive bias coming from knowledge and beliefs. Cognitive bias may negatively affect decision-making processes. Bias may be dangerous in all fields. However, the situation can be particularly critical in medicine, where statistics state how up to 75% of all clinical errors are of cognitive origins. The chapter aims at investigating if and how intangibles management can help to overcome cognitive bias. The work employs a case study approach analyzing BACRI, a digital platform in the field of pediatric medicine. BACRI, which stands for 'Critical Child' in Italian, allows identifying young patients at risk who need immediate care. The case study shows how the joint effect of structural capital, human capital, and relational capital is the key to the overcoming cognitive bias, in a virtuous circle. Intangibles management can so limit the dark side of knowledge".

Part IV: "Comparative view on national intellectual capital" presents two chapters offering a global outlook on sustainable national intellectual capital and a comparative view on national intellectual capital

Thus Chapter 11, titled "Sustainable National Intellectual Capital in the digital age: a global outlook" (by Carol Y.Y. Lin and Leif Edvinsson), introduces "the SNIC (Sustainable National Intellectual Capital) model consisting of five components, namely health, public structure, education, renewal and CNC (connectivity and contactivity). The first ten SNIC countries by descending order are: Denmark, Switzerland, Norway, the Netherlands, Singapore, Finland, Sweden, Luxembourg, Canada and UAE. We found that the higher the SNIC, the higher the GDP per capita (ppp), indicating the value of SNIC in explaining GDP growth. Generally speaking, advanced countries show a declining trend in SNIC. Out of the 23 countries studied, only Denmark, Norway, Switzerland, the Netherlands and UAE showed progress in SNIC over the 18 years (spanning 2001–2018). Other than SNIC, innovative capacity has a high correlation with GDP, education, renewal, CNC and cyber security. Three implications are presented: rich countries have great potential to develop SNIC, based on the development of Norway and UAE; small countries have an advantage in developing SNIC, based on the performances of Denmark, Switzerland, Norway, Singapore, Luxembourg and the Netherlands; and CNC alone cannot achieve expected economic performance, since better CNC does not explain better GDP".

Chapter 12, titled "Comparative view on national intellectual capital" (by Marcos Cavalcanti, Valéria Macedo and Larriza Thurler), states that "the effectiveness of the methodologies for measuring socioeconomic indicators, such as Gross Domestic Product (GDP), to gauge the impact of production on global chains, has been questioned by academics, governments and non-governmental organizations in the face of a significant increase in business on digital platforms and the greater importance of intangibles in the economy. This new scenario implies the need for new regulations for economic transactions that impact the world economy, as well as new theories and methods for calculating indicators related to productive factors and human capabilities from data available on the web. Through a review of the literature and existing models for the measurement of national intellectual capital, there were also gaps in the construction of

xxxiv *Preface*

indicators and opportunities in the design of a model that uses open government data platforms for indicators aligned with the measurement of intellectual capital. Also noted are new initiatives in the generation of national intellectual capital, suggesting more systemic applications for the adoption of such metrics in governmental strategic planning and national policies".

Next, Part V: "Towards the development of intellectual capital standards and culture" introduces four chapters that explore intellectual capital standards, the disclosure of intellectual capital in Australia and cultural issues and entrepreneurship.

Thus Chapter 13, titled "The trends of intellectual capital disclosure in the new economy: evidence from Australian firms" (by Yiru Yang), investigates "the trends in IC disclosure in Australian firms. The sample used for this study is based on 574 firm-year observations of Australian Securities Exchange (ASX) 200 listed firms from year 2012 to year 2015. The study finds that IC disclosure has increased from year 2012 to year 2015. Reporting human capital appears to be more in favour, followed by external capital, while reporting internal capital seems to be less in favour compared to the other two categories. The emphasis on human capital may arise from the increasing awareness of safety issues, know-how, and employee diversity. Alliances and other forms of collaborative arrangements are important in Australian firms as Business collaborations was the most reported IC item. Although reporting internal capital seems to be less in favour compared to the other two categories, however, Network systems, Technological processes, and Information systems, under the internal capital category, have increased significantly from year 2014 to year 2015, which suggests that in recent years, Australian firms have tended to adopt the growth of the new economy to apply more efficient technology systems".

Next, Chapter 14, titled "Entrepreneurialism: a multi-faceted cultural movement" (by Piero Formica), proposes that "entrepreneurialism is a multi-faceted cultural movement, a polar star by which to navigate the sea of new-model enterprise creation at the intersection of science and the humanities. It makes the entrepreneurial journey accessible to scientists, artists and humanists, acting as an art form that transplants Brunelleschi's perspective in the art world into the socio-economic sphere. In confronting ignorance born of not knowing the answers to the difficult questions posed by the digital revolution, the techno-humanist panoramic view of entrepreneurialism defies fundamental principles, underpinned by experience, with creative thinking and imaginative perspectives. Transformative entrepreneurship, that which disrupts the status quo by redefining market boundaries and norms so that entirely new markets come into view, stems from the dreams, explorations and discoveries of entrepreneurialism".

Chapter 15, titled "Towards the development of intellectual capital standards" (by Ron Young), asks "why should we even consider moving towards the development of intellectual capital standards? For many people, standards are perceived as a list of strict requirements to comply with, and, on the contrary, much new intellectual capital is developed through non-conformity, non-compliance, co-creativity and innovation, and does not lend itself to strict standard requirements at all. Well, first of all, management systems standards with a main focus on intellectual capital already exist today, and I will outline the key ones in this chapter. Secondly, I propose that we urgently need far more work on international standards for intellectual capital measurements and reporting, to enable the development of a new knowledge economic theory. This will then allow us to better understand and manage the increasingly knowledge-driven global economy for the 21st century. Thirdly, I will share the latest developments for new emerging standards with which I am involved, and concerns that I have, for the need for standards in the future for human and machine intelligence working together. This could even result in a redefinition of intellectual capital in organisations as we know it today, as we continue to move humanity forward in a much safer, healthier, wealthier, happier and most ethical way".

Chapter 16, titled "Intellectual capital management scoring: a contribution to measurement of intangibles standardization" (by Florinda Matos and Valter Vairinhos), affirms that "the increasing gap existing between what organizations state in their annual reports and what is the reality of their intangible assets is reflected in the growing variation between book value and market value. To positively impact future value, organizations require a better understanding of intellectual capital (IC), its impact on performance and what tools are available to identify, measure and manage it. Therefore, the quality of intangible assets management is a highly explanatory indicator of the importance given by the company to the development of its intangible assets and, also, of the reliability and sustainability of the company itself. In this chapter, a review of existing IC measurement methodologies and systems is presented. Moreover, the possibility of building an Intangible Capital Management Scoring System (ICMSS) and what its necessary features would be are examined. This chapter contributes to the discussion about IC measurement and IC management. The former aims to demonstrate the value of existing IC, using a generally accepted definition and a measurement method. The latter, in the context of an organization, is concerned with what actions top-level decision makers should take to guarantee that IC is being developed and that its value increases over time".

The final section of the book is Part VI: "Future challenges and risks for intellectual capital and trade on IA and ideas". It presents four chapters that discuss innovative topics such as blockchain and intellectual capital, trade on IA, trade on ideas and advances in the field of intellectual capital.

Chapter 17, titled "Future challenges and risks for intellectual capital and trade on IA and ideas" (by Karl McFaul), explores how "the digital transformation is reshaping our society and business landscape at a high speed, while our administrative governing bodies are slower in response, adaptiveness and relevance in meeting the needs to develop skilled citizens and a sustainable business life in the AI economy. In 2018–2019, the European Commission brought together a High-Level Expert Group on the Impact of the Digital Transformation on EU Labour Markets to develop a set of policy recommendations that can

xxxvi *Preface*

ensure that the benefits of digital transformation are fairly distributed between different economic sectors, businesses and individuals. One of the outcomes of the group's work was a new *framework for policy innovation* described as 'a guiding framework for thought leadership on the impact of digital transformation on EU labour markets'. This study presents the work, the source material and thinking in the prototyping leading up to the published version of this framework. I hope this study can help policy makers, business leaders, academic workers, as well as citizens, to better understand how technological innovation leads to organisational innovation, how this affects different forms of intellectual capital, and how we can develop new strategic tools for transformational leadership to accelerate humanity in the AI economy".

Chapter 18, titled "The role of blockchain for intellectual capital enhancement and business model innovation" (by Daniel Ruzza, Francesca Dal Mas, Maurizio Massaro and Carlo Bagnoli), discusses how "blockchain is considered as one of the most disruptive technologies, with an estimated growth from USD 1.2 billion in 2018 to USD 23.3 billion by 2023 worldwide. Blockchain has the potential to disrupt all business activities as much as the internet, social media, and mobile technologies did in the past. It enhances the creation of new business models, and forces organizations to work differently. The chapter aims to analyze the potentiality and the effects of blockchain on current and future business models from an intellectual capital perspective, by applying a Structured Literature Review (SRL) on the most recent scientific as well as professional production on the topic. The findings highlight how the design principles of blockchain technology can enhance the intellectual capital of an organization, as well as lead to a business model innovation".

Chapter 19, titled "From trade in goods and services to trade in ideas" (by Eskil Ullberg), states that "trade is first of all in ideas. No goods are produced that are not first created by a human idea nor services performed without first being organized by people. The value of goods has dominated trade since its beginning and services are now a large part of that. World exports are about 30% of world GDP, up from 10% half a century ago. Less than 2% is in ideas, measured by royalty licensing. However, this trade has grown at 16% per annum in the last decades, twice that of goods and services. Digitalization may replace 40% of trade in goods through 3D printing. The digital economy, reducing risks and transaction costs, enables global trade in ideas, based on impersonal intellectual property rights. This chapter discusses the importance of (i) intellectual capital – including IP rights like patents and copyrights – and (ii) transferring and licensing them enabled by the digital economy for a number of small countries and Nordic countries. This can serve as an example for developing nations. Policies giving incentives to high-risk investments in new knowledge are needed to (i) create basic knowledge, (ii) better integrate science and technology and (iii) develop new productivity-enhancing technology".

Chapter 20, titled "Revisiting the intellectual capital research landscape: a systematic literature review" (by Henri Hussinki, Tatiana Garanina, Johannes Dumay and Erik Steinhöfel), conducts a systematic literature review (SLR) to "provide insights on intellectual capital (IC) research models in terms of their preference for a single IC element or multiple IC elements, as well as how this varies between researchers from different continents. This aspect is critical, as recent literature has stressed that a firm needs an interplay of multiple IC elements to create IC-based value. This SLR is conducted by reviewing all the relevant research papers from the 20 top accounting and 20 top management journals published between 2000 and 2017. The results suggest that European researchers have contributed mostly to the multi-element perspective of IC, while American scholars have had the most notable impact on the single-element studies. These results are discussed by critiquing the current state of the IC literature and by offering transformative ideas for future research directions".

Finally, Leif Edvinsson, in his epilogue, reflects on the National Intellectual Capital and Ranking of Nations, GII – Global Innovation Index and the digital economy.

Patricia Ordóñez de Pablos
The University of Oviedo, Spain
November 2019

Part I

Knowledge, innovation and the transition to a more circular economy

1 The future is digital – insight is key!

Truls Berg

Norway: a small country in a large world

Norway is a small country in a large world, its total population is less than half of London's. Yet, together with its Nordic neighbours, it represents a region that is the world's eighth largest economy, a region that in many areas is leading the way towards the future – a future that undoubtedly will be digital and where insight will be key!

While oil for Norwegians can be described as mother nature's gift and quite probably the best message in a bottle ever to come our way, it is up to today's generation to make the shift to a new era; to a global knowledge-based innovation society where digital technology is being used for the benefit for all and insight into the data helps create a better and more sustainable world.

We Norwegians are not only among the winners in the UN's yearly competition to be the world's happiest country, even though our Nordic friends are fierce competitors, we are also a country with one of the highest percentages in the world of workers in the public sector and the country where one can expect to live the longest. However, taking a long view, this is not an unproblematic combination!

Norway currently has a total of 2.7 million employees. Of these, over 30 per cent work in the public sector, which is twice as many as in most other comparable countries. According to the OECD, the proportion of working Norwegians will in fact fall from 65 per cent to less than 50 per cent by 2025.[1] By 2050, over a quarter of Norway's population will be older than 65 and our pension obligations will explode. In fact, life expectancy now increases by almost five hours per week, every day!

These figures show us all that Greta Thunberg and her generation is right when they point out that we have done a poor job at what is perhaps the most important task every generation is given. Our generation's obligation to hand over to the next generation a world in better shape than we ourselves received it, with better tools to tackle the challenges and with a clear sense of direction.

Why is this?

The missing sense of innovation urgency

The problem is that most businesses as well as the public sector seem to be satisfied with the status quo. There's simply a lack of innovation urgency. That's why we still have over 400 municipalities, half of them with less than 5000 people and over 500 government agencies working in a uncoordinated manner to support this old structure. I'm going to go out on a limb here and suggest that other countries might have some of the same issues.

The challenge lies in establishing systems and mechanisms for working in a structured and coordinated way, thereby learning from each other and doing more of what works and less of what does not.

> It is over a thousand years since Norway was united to a kingdom. But for ICT in the public sector, it is apparently the supremacy of the ness kings that still prevails.
>
> (Minister of Innovation Heidi Grande Røys, 2009)

Unfortunately this quote still applies.

The willingness to fight for the status quo is enormous, the goals are often too vague and implementation plans too ambitious. The good news is that the 42 members of the Open Innovation Lab of Norway are busy rethinking their business models, organization and processes. For most people, this means a radical change in perspective. To succeed in this transformation, it is necessary to develop digital models and new skills, learn new methods of innovation and embrace new forms of leadership. Digital innovation is all about taking advantage of new technological opportunities!

Let's take a look at two of our members.

Aker BioMarine

One of the most forward-thinking is Aker BioMarine, a Norwegian innovator both at sea and onshore and a founding member of the Open Innovation Lab of Norway. The company, which is an integrated biotechnology company that harvests, cultivates and markets Antarctic krill, does a lot of exciting new work. This work has not only given them the acknowledgement of being voted Norway's most innovative company in 2017 by an esteemed jury I had the privilege to chair, in 2018 they went on to become Europe's most innovative company.

One of their mantras is the notion that the traditional, transaction–based sales model is dead. Instead, Aker BioMarine have chosen to invest in interactive, lasting partnerships with their customers. "The goal is simply to become part of our customers' success", explains Matts Johansen, CEO at the company.

Key to this is their open innovation model, which in practice means that the company's product expertise and market insights are shared with the customers. This knowledge transfer ranges all the way from product development, demonstration of krill's health and wellness benefits, expertise in retail and branding techniques.

"We want to be experienced as a partner who contributes with valuable insights, introduces new opportunities in the marketplace, and which guides our customers to growth and product expansion", says Johansen.

The market is young, so innovation and entrepreneurship are important to drive growth in the krill oil market. In recent years, Aker BioMarine has therefore initiated a number of exciting research and innovation projects with the aim of driving the krill category forward. Korea, for example, has quickly become one of the top countries for one of the company's important products.

As Johansen concluded when I asked him why they succeed with digital innovation:

> It is all about courage; daring to explore new arenas and test new concepts. In addition, we have total backing from the board, who has a high tolerance for making mistakes. We probably fail no less than others, but we excel at adjusting fast and often!

That's a key element in succeeding in a volatile and complex world, and it works.

Agder Energy: solving global energy challenges in innovative ways

Agder Energy is an old Norwegian natural power operator that has taken on innovation as a core process in a very profound manner.

Agder Energy's Engene transformer station outside Arendal on the south coast of Norway has become a global example of how cloud technology and machine learning can be used to revolutionize the power industry and the power system we know today.

A meeting between Microsoft and Agder Energy in 2015 marked the start of an innovation project with a shared ambition to develop new solutions to use the power grid in a smarter and more sustainable way. The pilot project has attracted international attention and has been cited by Microsoft as an example of how cloud-based technology can help solve climate and energy challenges. The result is now revolutionizing the industry.

In a proprietary cloud platform, data on production, consumption and batteries are collected and analysed in real time with machine learning and smart algorithms playing a key role. This makes it possible to utilize the power grid in a much more efficient way than today. Instead of adjusting production to demand, they have built a solution that helps adjust the demand for grid capacity. Agder Energy was the runner-up in this year's most innovative Norwegian companies competition and last year they were honoured with a global innovation award in Washington.

The smart combination of old and new resources

We're living in exciting times. New winners pop up and old giants crumble and die. Most things change, but let's remember that something is at least as important as before!

We want the freedom to make wise choices, and we seek leaders to help us achieve our goals.

In the last 200 years, the business sector has in reality been driven by three input factors: people, machines and materials. The dawn of the innovation age has given us three new resources: information, interest networks and ideas. These new factors are not only pollution-free and renewable, they also share the wonderful benefit of increasing value when used effectively.

Information used properly saves lives, reduces costs, provides new opportunities and improves our everyday lives in many ways. Simply put, there are two types of businesses out there now: those who train hard every day to get better, and the ones who talk a lot and show up with high heels and a box of popcorn and still expect to win the marathon. They will find it very hard to succeed in a digital future where insight is key, and inspired employees realizing that innovation is a core process will outrun them every step of the way.

Note

1 OECD Economic Surveys: Norway 2019. www.oecd-ilibrary.org/economics/oecd-economic-surveys-norway-2019_c217a266-en.

2 Open Innovation 2.0 supporting structural knowledge

Bror Salmelin

Introduction

In this text I illustrate the strong connection between modern, open innovation, the methods and ecosystems and the importance of intellectual capital for competitiveness and sustainable development both in societal and economic dimensions.

Open Innovation was coined by Henry Chesbrough in early 2000, but was focused very much on collaboration and cross licensing of intellectual capital, knowledge across firms. Very soon, by combining some of the ideas of Bill Mitchell, Henry Chesbrough and Eric von Hippel, the European concept of Living Labs emerged, and was developed into a European innovation policy instrument, which was formalized in 2006 as the European Network of Living Labs (ENoLL).

The idea of ENoLL was (and is) to create open innovation cities and sites where innovation happens faster and the success rate would be higher than by using traditional methods like in-house laboratories, user pilots and testbeds. Not only geographical but also thematic networks were encouraged.

The key idea is to have all the innovation actors in active roles, integrating and reflecting the ideas leading to scalable markets, products and services. Of importance here was the notion of active co-creation involving users seamlessly in the process, i.e. focusing on structural intellectual capital growth and sharing.

Very soon after the concept emerged the practical framework was created by using Open Innovation 2.0 (OI2) to describe the process and approach. OI2, with Open Innovation Ecosystems (OIE), created a fertile ground for creating new products and services in an environment providing a safety net for ideation, innovation and scale-up.

This development coincides strongly with the work done by Carol Yeh-Yun Lin and Leif Edvinsson[1] in measuring the impact of intellectual capital on competitiveness of nations and regions. Especially their findings on the importance of structural intellectual capital highlights the potential of OI2 as a key strategic approach for innovation.

Open Innovation 2.0

Open Innovation 2.0 is a new innovation approach formulated by Martin Curley and Bror Salmelin in their paper "Open Innovation 2.0: A New Paradigm", published in conjunction with the Irish European Union Presidency conference Open Innovation 2.0 held in Dublin in May 2013. The paper identifies critical elements in the new approach, clearly differing from the previous approach based on cross-licensing knowledge to create open innovation.

The key components are based on 20 interlinked elements (Figure 2.1) from which, in this context, the following are highlighted:

OI2 is a mash-up parallel process where the public policy maker needs to create the framework for this interaction (mash-up) to happen. OI2 is genuinely intersectional as innovation often happens in crossroads of technologies and applications and is not a linear extrapolation from the past.

To speed up the scalability all stakeholders need to co-create the solutions/find the innovations together, in real-world settings. Only then do we have a strong driver to create new markets and services and are we able to scale up successes quickly. There is inherent buy-in in this kind of innovation environment. On the other hand, by involving end users as co-creators upfront and seamlessly do we quickly see the less successful experiments and prototypes failing; "failing fast, scaling fast" is actually one of the strongest advantages of Open Innovation 2.0.

All this leads to a quadruple helix innovation model where the triple helix model (research, industry, public sector) is complemented by the people component. Indeed, in this model the citizens are not seen as passive objects of new

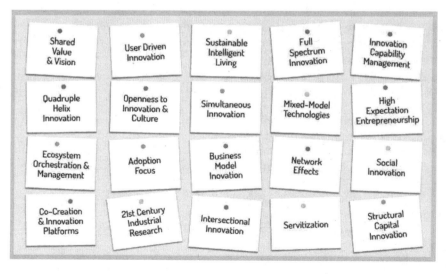

Figure 2.1 Components characterizing Open Innovation 2.0.

products or services but as active agents contributing seamlessly in the whole innovation process.

Importantly, taking both the quadruple helix approach and interdisciplinarity into account we enter the innovation ecosystem model. The cluster model for innovation is outdated because it still reflects the sectorial approach. We see in many regions of Europe how the cluster approach has been successful in industrial sectors, for example in Germany and Northern Italy. However, the cross-fertilization beyond traditional value chains to value networks and further value constellations is increasingly important.

The paradigm changes from closed innovation to open innovation and furthermore to Open Innovation 2.0 which can be illustrated by Table 2.1.

As can be seen from Table 2.1, the innovation pyramid is also turned upside-down; instead of having the traditional top-down view, the innovation power is with the crowd, and those actors who can best take advantage of this change will be the winners in innovation capability.

When assessing if we are focusing strongly "enough" on modern innovation we need to draw attention to the following key elements of Open Innovation 2.0:

Innovation ecosystems instead of clusters. Our activities have been traditionally oriented, and still are strongly clustered, i.e. the players are from rather homogenous sectors when we need increasingly multidisciplinary problem solvers. For example, the PPP approach strongly supports the existing clusters, but the component of creating new industries in Europe is rather weak. We have a strong responsibility to create "not-yet-existing" industry in Europe. We cannot copy, for example, the US/Silicon Valley patterns as we then leave our key competencies underused.

Quadruple helix co-creation rather than triple helix. When creating the "new" it is essential to have the users as active co-creators and not only as objects as is the

Table 2.1 Differences between innovation approaches are fundamental

Closed innovation	Open innovation	Open Innovation2.0
Dependency	Independency	Interdependency
Subcontracting	Cross-licensing	Cross-fertilization
Solo	Cluster	Ecosystem
Linear	Linear, leaking	Mash-up
Linear subcontracts	Triple helix	Quadruple helix
Planning	Validation, pilots	Experimentation
Control	Management	Orchestration
Win–lose game	Win–win game	Win more–Win more
Box thinking	Out of the box	No boxes!
Single entity	Single discipline	Interdisciplinarity
Value chain	Value network	Value constellation

case in triple helix innovation. Users and societal capital together along with stretching the boundaries of societal acceptance of proposed solutions is essential. This relates also to policy issues like security, identity management, privacy etc. Users and user communities are diverse and their skills levels are unique assets in European innovation.

Cross- and interdisciplinary innovation. This aspect is rather weak in most of public research programmes. Some horizontal activities are merging like start-up support and STARTS in the European context, but still the programme is very much constructed within a sandbox architecture. Spill-over cross-disciplinary interactions (igniting positive collisions) are rather rare and seldom planned into the design of strategic objectives. Due to the evaluation system it is also rather difficult to bring projects together creating a complementary project portfolio where these collisions reinforce each other. Likewise, it is rather difficult to have at the end a project selection which coherently supports prioritized policy areas. The new framework research programme of the EU looks a lot more promising than the past ones in this respect.

Enabling more uncertainty in the project design. According to some proposers in governmental programmes, evaluation scores have suffered in cases where experimentation and prototyping (Experimentation and Application Research – EAR) methods have been suggested, as then the project delivery was not precisely described – which actually is impossible if there is uncertainty due to the method. Launching several competing prototypes/experiments and progressing with the successful and scalable one, killing off the failing ones, also means resource reallocation in the project when it is progressing. Now it seems that the *evaluators appreciate precise, well-defined, linear project plans with clear deliverables in a fixed timeline.* But one can ask if that is creativity, research and development involving high ambitions and delivery. This experimental, cross-disciplinary approach is effectively building intellectual capital to be shared.

Experimentation and rapid prototyping in real-world settings. The EAR methodology was suggested already in early 2000s by the EAC (Esprit Advisory Committee). This approach was based on strong user involvement to see the feasibility of the proposed results. In some degree this approach is used but rather mildly as most still speak about piloting, which means a de facto linear innovation model. Early prototyping and co-creation are not specifically encouraged, even if it would be essential for the creation of the "new". This should be strongly emphasized in project design.

Fail fast – scale fast. Publicly funded programmes have not (yet?) seen projects where upfront the design is based on several rapid prototypes of solutions from which the best ones are brought forward and scaled up – and the failures are killed off at an early stage. This relates also to the evaluation criteria (as before) of the projects as reallocation of the resources in this way in projects (or project portfolios) does not follow the traditional way projects have been managed. The culture of risk avoidance rather than risk management dominates. However, if all of the projects fulfil their objectives then the objectives have far too low an ambition level and the best performance is not pushed for!

Creation of open engagement platforms. This relates very strongly to the very recent digital developments with IoT, the cloud, Big Data, blockchain etc. The Digital Single Market (DSM) with open platforms is a critical enabler for open pan-European business platforms. In Europe there are good examples of elements moving to this direction of engagement platforms, for example FIWARE, where the platform is offered for used in various applications, for example in the smart city context. The same approach needs to be reinforced in the IoT, cloud and Open Data approaches, in the way that all these platforms are treated functionally like one, open, mixed technology platform, enabling the creation of new solutions and business models. Open engagement platforms enable affordable prototyping and experimentation, also in real-world settings, and can be critical when fostering the growth of new enterprises. We should *not* treat these technology-oriented platforms as separate, but integrate them to be open application platforms in various areas. Open engagement platforms are strong drivers for new industries, and the DSM is a prerequisite for these on a pan-European scale.

However, the platforms need to be integrated functionally on a metalevel, in order for businesses to use them as easily as children use Lego building blocks; with standardized interfaces, interoperable functionality and clear rules, for example related to IPR. Only then can we move towards industry and societal commons, which both are essential for future developments. The industrial and societal commons are again an essential and good showcase for the importance of structural intellectual capital for sharing, thus providing possibilities for higher value offerings from all stakeholders together.

Open Innovation Ecosystems (OIE)

- Open stands for openness, curiosity, interlinking of different stakeholders, technologies and challenges.
- Innovation is making things happen, beyond ideation; scalability, and creating entirely new approaches. Innovation speed and success attracts talent and inwards investment, both intellectual and financial.
- Ecosystems means involving all stakeholders in a quadruple helix manner, in order to build interdependencies and the courage to drive a common agenda. It goes beyond sectors, clusters or PPP, involving all the ingredients needed in a mash-up process.

What is important is that a culture is built to enable seamless interaction between the projects and the actors in ecosystems, that a regionally new co-creative culture is created and that also new kind of courage is fostered in experimenting and bringing the results into the real world.

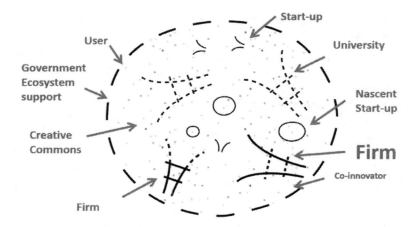

Figure 2.2 Open innovation ecosystem.

The ecosystem has processes for interaction which are based on trust and sharing values. This is essential, as Open Innovation Ecosystems are much more than a collection of individuals, organizations operating under strict rules. Basic principles like trust need to be in place, guidelines as well, but this means also that the challenge within ecosystems is to provide safety nets allowing serendipity to happen simultaneously. Process design for open interaction becomes critical.

In Figure 2.2 the heterogeneity of competencies are shown by the different dots, combining together into competencies, more or less organized. A firm is an example of a well-organized form of collaboration, but increasingly we have expertise (or problem ownership; quadruple helix in mind!) regrouping project by project, based on their competencies.

Public support for the ecosystems is important not only in funding (and, for example, the precommercial procurement of innovative solutions) but also as one important participant in creating the rules in the ecosystem, in increasing trust, and in increasing the open mind sets of all participants in their various, simultaneous roles. As an example, a citizen can be a professional, distributing his skills towards several problem solvers, but at the same time he can be a problem owner longing for some solutions, etc. Each of us has multiple simultaneous roles in these ecosystems, roles which can be simultaneously public and private, as problem owner or solver (contributor).

Open innovation environments call for a research, development and innovation (RD&I) methodology based on the courage to experiment, trial, scale-up and daring to fail small, but not big.

The new innovation drivers (Open Innovation 2.0) call for new types of mind setting where the involvement of all stakeholders in a collaborative, co-creative culture is key. The quadruple helix model, where the research community, industry, public sector and citizens are all active actors, creates a win–win situation as it is targeted to create new markets and the fast upscaling of the successful solutions.

Having the OIE as a goal to attract talent, financial resources and ideas to be experimented with and prototyped in the real world leads to the need to engineer and design the portfolio of activities to create a winning game by sharing, not closing. Open Innovation Ecosystems create strong interdependency and a drive to make things happen. They have the possibility to drive the change by merging the technology enablers like ICT with societal change.

Now it is up to the quadruple helix innovation community to tackle the challenge and experiment with the future; to scale up successes.

The research institutions/community is bringing new seed into the innovation system which interacts with the real world (users) via research, technology, development and innovation (RTDI). The users based on this interaction act as a piloting and experimentation environment creating new markets for policies, products and services. Cyclic innovation can also be initiated by the co-creativity of the users. What is important is that we have the fast cycle of new market creation where users and industry are the key. In addition, we have longer cycles where infrastructures (conditions for innovation) are created, where the public sector has an important role to foster new seed to grow, to make infrastructure investments, and to create favourable conditions for frictionless processes in the faster innovation cycle.

Focus in this framework is on the creation of the "new" but of course the users' behaviour strongly affects the old existing markets in their renewal.

In Figure 2.2. I also tried to explain that depending on the sector the balance between the various quadruple helix players is different, especially when we see the research and techical development (RTD) component in creating the "new" (industries, services, products).

I approach collective innovation from the OIE perspective. It is important to note, that innovation needs multiple elements to be successful, i.e. scalable to the real world. It needs ideas based on knowledge, for that knowledge to spark(le) in interdisciplinary collisions and to be scaled to real-world settings.

Collective intelligence is the "commons", i.e. the structural knowledge and processes which constitute the basis upon which value is built through innovation. Modern innovation happens in complex environments and is often interdisciplinary, meaning that one single player is not enough to bring the ideas to market. And very often the innovation process does not only create the value offering, but also entirely new markets with the users.

Here we come to an important component in modern innovation ecosystems. We need to consider all quadruple helix components to be actively present and contributing to commonly agreed values. The quadruple helix consists of the public sector, private sector, academia and citizens (civic society), all in active roles. Too often the citizens are seen as just users, i.e. in a very passive role from an innovation perspective.

14   *Bror Salmelin*

To enable structural intellectual capital to grow, which is essential for success and competitivity, the trust and mobility between the four player groupings need to be in place. Without common values, and commonly agreed (behavioural and compensational) rules a sharing economy is not possible, nor are genuinely open innovation ecosystems where additional value is built on shared commons.

It is also essential to look at the new professions and the new roles people need to have to be able to form effective innovation paths as illustrated by Piero Formica in many of his speeches and works. We need orchestrators, who lead the value-shaping process like the conductor of an orchestra who determines how the masterpieces are to be performed. We need curators who are responsible for consistency and quality of knowledge in given areas like curators in art exhibitions. And we need bridgers who bring the curated contents together under the commonly played masterpiece. Bridgers need to be T-shaped persons, with broad knowledge and curiosity about "everything" and with extrovertism and courage to link together very wide competencies. And, finally we need to have systems designers who enable this interaction to take place in the ecosystems in a highly spontaneous manner.

When speaking about collective innovation we need to see beyond the existing clusters, existing organizational formats to highly dynamic value constellations, organizations that can capture the dynamics of combining competencies based on the task needed to be performed. We see value propositions driving the innovation field, not the organizational formats we see too often happening today.

In the late 1990s we spoke about holonic enterprises and fractal factories as well as virtual enterprises quite a lot. They were conceptual then, but modern technologies like clouds, Big Data, blockchain etc. are now enabling the flexible and safe combination of competencies and sharing the value created in a fair manner. This, together with highly distributed operational models and technologies (3D printing for example), enable collective innovation not only on a product level but also at the organizational and societal levels.

Participative innovation where citizens are actively involved can be driven also by public organizations: some good examples of participatory budgeting are already in place in some advanced cities, but there is still long way to go. This also raises the question of how the participatory co-creative process is orchestrated. The municipality, like the citizens, needs to learn how to play together for a common future. In these kinds of environments, it is extremely important to have safety nets, stopping catastrophes from happening by mistake.

The power of co-creativity in an environment which builds common values and operating processes among all quadruple helix participants in OIEs will dominate the innovation landscape in the mainstream in the rather short term, due to complexity and the need for the inclusion of all "brains" to increase both success rate and speed of innovation. Trust, new roles and organizational forms and experiment-friendly real-world settings are essential to ensure high-quality

Open Innovation 2.0   15

and high-value results to be shared and to be built on, for a common future. Everyone participating in the common ecosystem has simultaneously multiple roles and will have a fair share of the created value, provided that the players are able to create a common playing ground for all in the collaborative innovation scene. This culminates in the question: How to share better to create more together?

From Living Labs to Open Innovation Ecosystems

The starting point when developing Living Labs in the European context was openness. Openness in sharing platforms for services but also an open mind set for collaboration among all stakeholders. The thinking stems from the early 1990s when the hot topic was virtual and holonic enterprises, which were as a group creating both agile and scalable structures for operations – by sharing common operating architectures and by collaborating strongly on a task-driven basis. Good examples of holonic/fractal/virtual enterprise theories were developed, for example, in the IMS (Intelligent Manufacturing Systems) initiative among the leading industrial economies in the 1990s. Scaling up this thinking we come very close to the foundations of Living Labs by adding to it the public and societal components.

Combining the approach by von Hippel about user-driven concepts and co-creativity in innovation processes with the approach of open innovation introduced by Chesbrough in 2003, we come to the two fundamentals of modern innovation theory. The definition of open innovation by von Hippel focuses on the creation of public goods while the one introduced by Chesbrough builds on sharing, cross-licensing and in that way being a market- and product-driven approach.

Open platforms, sharing and the seamless interaction of all stakeholders is essential in Living Labs. The quadruple helix approach has thus been central as an innovation model from the very beginning and onwards.

Open Innovation Ecosystems are increasingly becoming the synthesis of Living Labs and open innovation processes. We see a real new paradigm evolving when combining these. Open innovation has become much more than the cross-fertilization of ideas between organizations, it has become a flow of colliding ideas, raising sparks for new innovations in real-world settings.

Following the research of Lin and Edvinsson there are clear indications that intellectual capital, and especially structural intellectual capital, drives competitiveness and innovation. This means in turn that from an innovation policy perspective the interaction fluidity is a critical feature of any successful innovation system.

Fluidity in this context means frictionless interaction, experimentation in the real world, and a lot of unexpected, unplanned collisions of ideas, problems and of course competencies, providing the spark. It is not only about single, excellent components in the system, it is centrally about collisions and connectivity.

16   Bror Salmelin

The cross-fertilization of ideas is nothing new as such, but what ecosystem thinking does is embed diversity and serendipity in the innovation process more systematically than ever before.

It is important to move from clusters to ecosystems in our innovation system design. There is nothing wrong with clusters, but they tend to be rather mono-lithic, focusing on one only sector. Of course, the clusters reinforce the sector they work in, but have the tendency more towards improving, extrapolating than to creating something new. Hence the emphasis on modern innovation systems needs to be increasingly on the "in-between" areas where creation of the "new" is likely, and as a consequence, fast growth.

To substantiate the potential for new market creation end-users need to become active drivers together with the other stakeholders in jointly cre-ating the "new". The quadruple helix innovation model gives clear roles to all stakeholders, including the users as active agents from the very beginning. Earlier the users were objects in the process, not co-creators. By taking the users actively on board we see immediately which solutions can be scaled up and which will fail for various reasons. Scaling up the emerging successes quickly is key to maintaining the dynamics in the innovation system. There are also indications that those organizations which cut failing projects at an earlier stage will be more successful in the longer run.

Again, we come to the ecosystem when we think about where the experi-mentation and early prototyping is to be done. In real-world settings one can at an early stage see the potential and also identify the paths for fast entry into full-scale markets. Seamless user involvement is thus essential. It is important also to understand that properly designed innovation ecosystems provide a safety net from ideation to the market. Failing fast also often means failing small, and experimentation and early prototyping in turn means faster results to be brought to the market, even incrementally.

Business model experimentation in these OIEs is also essential. Due to the dynamics of the economy and technology it is rarely possible to write old-fashioned extensive business plans. Often it is enough to have a business model idea and then develop it continuously and further in real-world settings, to finally see what works and what does not. Fast adjustment and experimentation are the way forward.

Here legislation can also play a remarkable role if it is a catalysing one. Restrictive legislation again is a strong hindrance for business model innov-ation. A proper legal framework is one of the most important factors for the fluidity of the innovation space mentioned above.

Innovation has moved from linear processes to mash-up processes where diversity, speed and experimentation are the fundamentals.

We have moved from closed innovation to open innovation and further towards Open Innovation 2.0, which highlights the interaction, fluidity and mash-up nature of innovation processes, including all stakeholders in quadruple helix innovation.

Conclusion

Living Labs and Future Centers are good examples of innovation hubs, which are multistakeholder places where the cross-disciplinary ignition of ideas happens, and where by OI2 principles a large mix of projects interact. Engagement platforms, frictionless experimenting and all stakeholder involvement are critical to attract both intellectual and financial capital to those hubs. Smart cities/Living Labs can become those kinds of innovation ecosystems, but besides regional ones there can and should also be thematic ones.

However, the word "smart" is very restrictive by nature in this context. It nowadays places a lot of weight on technology-driven environments with (IoT-based) sensors, data processing and – in a certain manner – control. Hence the Japanese approach of "wise places" is much closer to the thinking of Open Innovation Ecosystems, as the interactions within happen based on mutual, common values and fostering common learning and development based on sharing. The human, societal and value-based approach is essential for sustainability in all senses.

Open Innovation Ecosystems can be regional or thematic, or both. They are built on strong interaction between the competencies, as illustrated in Figure 2.2 by the different dots. The ecosystem itself has tens or more projects (funnels in Chesbrough's sense) which can be more or less leaking ones which broaden the competence base of each action. The funnels in this context represent development projects, not organizational boundaries. Spill-over effects to the whole ecosystem from the projects should increase the societal but also knowledge structural capital enabling the continuous rise of the value proposition of the new activities.

Sharing infrastructures but also experience and knowledge is a key of the trust to be built within the ecosystem itself. Trust is highly important because of the interdependence of all stakeholders in this mutual win–win process. Cross-fertilization and sharing do not happen without trust.

For structural intellectual capital to be fully exploited requires the infrastructures as well. We also need recent technology developments (IoT, cloud, Big Data, blockchain etc.) to be integrated, following the same meta-architecture to industry and societal commons, enabling fast and easy propositions for new value creation by and with all stakeholders in the Open Innovation Ecosystems. Some good developments are visible but the architecture of the metalayer is still not yet standardized.

In ecosystems it is, as previously stated, very important to allow collisions to spark the real innovations, even disruptive ones. Hence the creation process requires courage to design a governance structure for the ecosystem to let it grow organically. The prototyping and experimentation of policies is one of the important components in this development too.

Living Labs, networked society, democratizing innovation, open innovation, disruptive innovation are also examples of the many words which are

18 *Bror Salmelin*

fluently used without often thinking about the reality behind them. The reality is, however, in the courage to change the behaviour, including the governance structures to create something new. The reality is also to turn these buzzwords into a functioning innovation ecosystem with new dynamics.

ICT provides connectivity and the shared space of knowledge, meaning that the new paradigm of OIE is more achievable than ever before. In this rich connectivity we need to see the new role of all players partaking in the spirit of quadruple helix innovation and moving with the dynamics needed to create an experimentation and prototyping culture. This culture reveals the options for success earlier and significantly reduces the risk for big failures too.

Living Labs with Open Innovation 2.0 seems to be the key for success and speed, as well as inclusion of all in the innovation process.

Let's create the future based on common values, together.

More valuable reading can be found in, for example, the publications by OISPG and the European Commission, for example at https://ec.europa.eu/digital-single-market/en/news/open-innovation-publications.

Living Labs and the European Network of Living Labs provides information including a newsletter here: https://openlivinglabs.eu.

Note

1 See, for example, the Open Innovation Yearbooks published by the European Commision, 2009–2018, at https://ec.europa.eu/digital-single-market/en/news/open-innovation-publications.

3 The World Health Innovation Summit (WHIS) platform for sustainable development

From the digital economy to knowledge in the healthcare sector

Gareth Presch, Francesca Dal Mas, Daniele Piccolo, Maksim Sinik and Lorenzo Cobianchi

Introduction and objective of the study

Several new technologies have been introduced in the last decade to the design, production, and sales of products and services. From augmented and mixed reality to artificial intelligence, from robotics to big data analytics, new technologies have enabled faster and more efficient innovation through the creation of new products, services, processes, new ways of communication and opportunities to increase the business (Bagnoli *et al.*, 2019; Fletcher, 2015; Kagermann, 2015). Technology, in general, is becoming cheaper and more accessible, and this leads to previously unknown possibilities, fostering progress, bringing opportunities for organizations to expand their horizons and knowledge (Dal Mas *et al.*, 2019; Toniolo *et al.*, 2019). The introduction of such technologies fosters the development of new strategies (Amit and Zott, 2001; Schlegelmilch *et al.*, 2003; Teece, 2010) as well new business models (Biloslavo *et al.*, 2018; Nielsen *et al.*, 2018; Teece, 2010), meaning the way an organization creates, captures, and distributes value (Osterwalder, 2004; Osterwalder *et al.*, 2014).

One of the most successful business models enhanced by the introduction of such technologies is that of platform companies (Gawer and Cusumano, 2014) or so-called "platfirms" (Troiani *et al.*, 2016) as new digitally enabled business models. The phenomenon is so relevant that literature defined it as a new industrial revolution. According to Troiani *et al.* (2016, p. 2),

> after the era of the machines that have boosted physical power, the digital revolution has extended the power of human intelligence and its ability to influence the surrounding environment. The organizational and business model of platform-companies lies in fact at the heart of contemporary enterprises that are growing faster, immediately expanding to a global level and revolutionizing the logics on which entire industries have been based for decades.

One of the most known examples is Airbnb, which has extended its economic value from nothing to over \$24 billion in only nine years, more than any hotel chain in the business, including Marriott and Hilton.

However, the concept of value has been evolving over time. While once it was limited to a dimension of economic or financial value for the shareholders, it has now embraced a wider concept, which includes the wealth and well-being for the society and the environment (Dal Mas, 2019; Edvinsson *et al.*, 2005; Grafstrom and Edvinsson, 1996; Massaro *et al.*, 2018). Sustainability has hence become a central topic in a modern society which is facing global climate problems, poverty, pollution, and a lack of basic healthcare services in several areas of the planet. In 2015, the United Nations established the 17 Sustainable Development Goals (SDGs) as the commitment that all countries must meet. The SDGs call for massive economic and social changes that allow businesses to run in order to satisfy the needs of consumers while taking sustainability into the picture. This includes a lower consumption of resources, especially non-renewable ones, respect for nature and the earth, and attention towards social issues such as equality and inclusion. These new perspectives call for new sustainable business models (Boons and Lüdeke-Freund, 2013; Seelos and Mair, 2005, 2007; Tukker, 2004). Zott *et al.* (2011) state how adopting a sustainable business model can help businesses to create value not only for customers but also for other stakeholders, society, and the natural environment. The value is thereby captured and distributed across a broad set of stakeholders. The new technologies can be seen as powerful allies for sustainable business models to reach the goals, by helping to provide sustainable products, services, as well as transparent and sustainable supply chains (Linton *et al.*, 2007; Seuring and Müller, 2008).

Sustainability is taking advantage of the platfirm business thanks to the so-called cross-side network effect, that can help to create value by gathering people together to foster and share ideas (Ruutu *et al.*, 2017). One of the most well-known examples is Wikipedia, where people can contribute to the general knowledge of society by creating and double-checking content that is freely available to everyone, making knowledge quickly accessible free-of-charge even to the poorest countries of the world. The required characteristics to provide a successful platfirm strategy are to attract people, facilitate the exchange of knowledge among them, allowing the recombination of knowledge creating a feedback loop where the users that find interesting knowledge remain and contribute further.

Interestingly enough, those business models have proven to be very successful in the healthcare sector. An example is the Health Information Exchange (HIE) platform, which provides the capability to electronically share clinical information among different healthcare information systems. HIE aims to facilitate the access and the retrieval of clinical data to provide safer and more timely, efficient, effective, and equitable patient-centered care (Moore *et al.*, 2012; Yaraghi *et al.*, 2015). One more example is Hospitalrun,[1] an open-access platform founded in 2012 that offers free downloadable software for hospital management, to provide the most modern hospital information systems to less-resourced environments, especially those in the least developed countries. Hospitalrun, which is being used by thousands of hospitals and clinics in countries including Kenya, Nigeria, and India, was initially established with the cooperation of C.U.R.E. clinics,[2] a non-profit, humanitarian relief organization. Therefore, platfirm business models have been proven to be an interesting option to develop sustainable models, especially in the healthcare sector.

This chapter aims to contribute to this research stream by presenting the case of World Health Innovation Summit (WHIS),[3] a preventive healthcare platform developed with the aim of empowering people to improve their health and well-being by facilitating community engagement generating shared value.

The WHIS project

Introduction

The WHIS project was created in 2015 by Gareth Presch, a healthcare manager with 20 years of experience working in the sector in Ireland and the UK. During his work in eHealth and District Nursing in Cumbria, UK, Gareth noticed the massive pressures on the system and the high level of staff turnover due to these increased pressures. People were constantly leaving due to high stress and other factors. Delivering high-quality patient-centered care cannot be met if the organizations are continuously losing staff. The organization would also struggle to attract staff if the values were not right. Cumbria has had problems recruiting and retaining staff, which is well-publicized.

Gareth started from the concept that people attract people, so he came up with the idea of a community for patients, clinicians, managers, voluntary sector, education, and the business community, which was later called "the World Health Innovation Summit" (WHIS) to attract thought-leaders to Cumbria. The idea was to support these leaders to disseminate their knowledge through the platform and peer-reviewed journals, and that would help attract staff while showcasing the region as a great place to live, work, and invest.

However, very quickly after the first event, Gareth and his staff realized there was more to it. The technology could help the idea evolve from a simple community to a platform to provide opportunities to support people in improving their health and well-being (prevention) that could be applied to any healthcare economy in the world.

Aims and scope

WHIS is aiming to empower people to improve their health and well-being while addressing the challenges faced by the health service. Those challenges lie in an aging population (Börsch-Supan *et al.*, 2005), rising levels of obesity, and other lifestyle diseases (Wilkinson and Pickett, 2006), all set against an 18 million worker shortfall in healthcare staff (Limb, 2016).

The idea is that there are opportunities to create a new preventative model that supports people's health and well-being through the WHIS platform, through effective community engagement and sharing knowledge that delivers well-being for the citizens while creating new opportunities and ecosystems to support the implementation of the UN Sustainable Development Goals, generating value shared that can be recycled and used to regenerate existing and new communities worldwide.

The platform allows everyone to collaborate and to break silo-working through system thinking: from linear to circular, dis-connection to interconnectedness, silos to emergence, parts to wholes, analysis to synthesis, and isolation to relationships. WHIS is the answer to this: a platform for collaboration with a focus on preventative healthcare. Indeed, according to the Institute for Global Health Sciences of the University of California – San Francisco (Duff-Brown, 2017), diseases like obesity, cancer, etc. could cost $47 trillion by 2030 despite the advancement of research in integrated care, including in oncology (Cobianchi *et al.*, 2016; Peloso *et al.*, 2017; Zhang *et al.*, 2019). WHIS provides the opportunity to bring together people from many different industries, whose new ideas and different perspectives create new opportunities and value through knowledge transfer.

WHIS plans to become the world's leading platform for health and well-being as it can be shared and scaled to support any community and bring value. WHIS has followers and leaders in several countries around the world, such as the UK, Ireland, UAE, Thailand, Nigeria, Kenya, Switzerland, the United States, to name a few. WHIS is partners with the United Nations Global Sustainable Index Institute, the foundation leading the implementation of the 17 UN Sustainable Development Goals in cities around the world.

The primary value of WHIS is trust, with the motto "Trust is the Oil of the Future". WHIS grows by attracting like-minded individuals who understand that what WHIS does is for the common good, combining thought and emotional leadership. WHIS provides the methodology and the value proposition, while the actors take ownership and generate the income streams locally, nationally, and internationally.

Knowledge sharing and knowledge recombination

The WHIS model is based on combining human, social, and structural capital (Edvinsson *et al.*, 2005; Edvinsson and Malone, 1997; Grafstrom and Edvinsson, 1996), creating a knowledge transfer platform that exists to support the health economies around the world. The WHIS platform works around five main pillars: WHISKids, WHISatwork, WHISSeniors, WHISGreen, WHISTech. Every WHIS pillar is driven by a specific value proposition that supports knowledge transfer to benefit people's health and well-being in the specific area. The platform aims are connecting people, inspiring and influencing positive change. WHIS provides a platform to develop new ideas, prototype at a local, national, or international level. From pregnancy, creative arts, and design thinking new models and ideas that add community value can be developed through the platform.

Building a community focused on health issues, the platform makes knowledge and ideas globally scalable. All the social prescribing programs that are already on the platform can be shared everywhere in the world. WHIS can take them from being a local initiative to having worldwide reach. The WHIS team has held summits and activities right across the UK (Newcastle, Carlisle, Nottingham, Blackpool, Manchester, Birmingham, Leicester, among others), Thailand and Greece. The programs and wellness activities (wellness retreats) have been tested in Cumbria. Additionally, to create engagement, WHIS has launched a magazine (*WHISInspire*), and WHISTalks, with various other initiatives to support people's health and well-being in development.

The platform can be defined as a social business, aiming to generate income streams to then reinvest money back into local communities (Porter and Kramer, 2006). Once overheads are covered, the profits are reinvested back into the community. The objectives are to improve people's health and well-being while creating a new ecosystem through a sharing and circular economy. An independent report has demonstrated that every £1 invested in the activities will generate £36 in terms of social return on investment back to the local community.

Successful case studies

One of WHIS' most successful stories has been WHISKids, a program for school children that focuses predominantly on mental health and well-being. From the work in Cumbria and teaming up with a local innovative program for all ages, My Way Code, WHIS codeveloped a primary schools program which helps children aged 4–11 years understand emotions and physical symptoms and what they can choose to do to be more healthy mentally and physically. A couple of thousand children have gone through the program in Cumbria over the last couple of years. WHIS takes accountability into high consideration, and always measures its work. The results of WHISKids are impressive. The children have so far self-reported the distance traveled in their understanding of their mental health and well-being as being increased by an average of 20%. Middlesbrough Football Club is soon going to apply the WHISKids methodology to football, and more sports and clubs are on the agenda (rugby, cricket, golf, and others). WHISKids can be seen as an example of knowledge sharing and codesign with local partners to bring innovative solutions at scale.

Other programs developed by WHIS to support people are: WHISatwork (stress management in the workplace, ...), WHISSeniors (falls prevention, quality of life, loneliness, ...) WHISTech (artificial intelligence, robotics, virtual reality, ...) and WHISGreen (energy, waste, and water). New programs are being developed, including a Cancer Wellbeing program, Creative Arts, Design Thinking, and a Global Pregnancy Wellbeing program. All programs are based on health education, health promotion, and disease prevention.

24   *Gareth Presch et al.*

These programs and services will have a positive effect on people and communities over the short, medium, and long term and this is all down to the WHIS platform.

WHIS and the UN SDGs

In September 2015, 193 heads of state pledged their commitment to implement the 17 Sustainable Development Goals at the United Nations. The UNGSII FOUNDATION was created to assist and accelerate the implementation process, with the mission to ensure that the world reaches its goal, at the latest, by 2030. WHIS is a partner with UNGSII for the SDG 25 + 5 Cities Leadership platform.[4] This is an ambitious program conceived by the UN Director-General Michael Møller and Heildelberg Mayor Prof. Eckhart Würzner. The project has identified 25 cities and five indigenous communities from around the world to become lighthouses, where experts in their field will come together and help those cities deliver the SDGs by 2030.

WHIS is working on the SDG 3 "Good health and well-being", supporting the 25 cities working with institutions, universities, and city councils to support them and see what can be done to implement the SDGs. WHIS disseminates information about healthy living and welcomes any support and knowledge sharing, merging, for instance, post-operatory recovery with physical activities and, for example, park walk (Ireland *et al.*, 2019).

In addition to the 25 cities, WHIS is also setting up what is being called Hubs, cities that will become incubators for new ideas and new programs that can be prototyped, proven, and then scaled to the 25 cities. WHIS plans to bring in leading experts to work on creating these solutions, to be subsequently tested out. As part of that, WHIS is also working on the creation of the next generation health and well-being centers, a mix of clinical, physical, and emotional well-being services.

Discussion and conclusion

In conclusion, we would like to start from the premise that inspired this work. New technologies have brought the development of a knowledge economy. Knowledge is a key resource, and it is peculiar since it does not consume resources with its use. Rather, the opposite occurs, it increases its value the more it is used.

The case of WHIS represents an interesting example in the healthcare sector, one of the most influenced by new technologies and continuous innovation and research (Christensen *et al.*, 2000; Currie and Guah, 2007; Iacopino *et al.*, 2018; Lucas, 2015; Mascia and Di Vincenzo, 2011; Muzio and Faulconbridge, 2013). The platform aims to develop new programs in the healthcare and well-being field, gathering together the most brilliant minds in the area, allowing medical doctors, nurses, educators, psychologists, managers, and other experts to share their ideas and knowledge through the web and on the ground. The galaxy of ideas enables the development of programs devoted to specific users (school-aged children, older people, mothers-to-be, cancer patients, to mention a few) that can be directly prototyped and tested into communities and cities, but also in hospitals, clinics, hospices, schools, and any other organization.

The more the programs are used, the more data and cases are collected, and the process leads to a continuous improvement of the models and protocols. New and meaningful jobs can be created and healthcare professionals and experts that are dealing with new cases allow the accumulation of new knowledge, to further refine the programs. New ideas can be generated, from innovative ways to recover from surgery to older adults' wellness programs, from pregnancy and breastfeeding to raising public awareness towards organ donation.

Best practices, as well as successful programs like WHISKids, can be exported to other countries and cities, involving more professionals and users. Again, the more the protocol is used, the more it can be refined, increasing its impact and the overall value of the process and leading to new opportunities (for instance, refined educational programs or classes to be implemented into schools, universities, or hospitals). Innovation and ideas can come from everywhere, and platforms like WHIS allow those ideas to be prototyped, shared, create training and employment, and scaled in a successful way.

The platform or "platfirm" allows, first, the attraction of talents that can share ideas and incorporate them in new business models that can be spread all over the world through community engagement that can be shared digitally. Moreover, the use of a social business model for WHIS allows the development of a broader concept of value. Not only does the value generated by the community applying for the projects return at a greater value in terms of impact and well-being, but the overall profit realized by the platform is reinvested, creating an endless virtuous circle. WHIS represents a positive example of a cross-side effect where buyers, producers, professionals, and social actors operate together to find new solutions. Technology allows the spreading and increasing of knowledge at no extra cost, with a turbo effect on its impact.

In concluding our work, we want to highlight how new technologies can allow the development of new solutions and new ways of increasing the social value thanks to the knowledge economy, especially in critical sectors like healthcare. The future of business will be aligned to social value as we can move from the digital economy to knowledge.

Notes

1 Website: https://hospitalrun.io.
2 Website: https://projectcure.org/clinics.
3 Website: www.worldhealthinnovationsummit.com/.
4 Website: www.ungsii.org/sdg-cities.

References

Amit, R. and Zott, C. (2001), "Value creation in E-business", *Strategic Management Journal*, Vol. 22 No. 6–7, pp. 493–520.

Bagnoli, C., Dal Mas, F. and Massaro, M. (2019), "The 4th Industrial Revolution and its features: Possible business models and evidence from the field", *International Journal of E-services and Mobile Applications*, Vol. 11 No. 3, pp. 34–47.

Biloslavo, R., Bagnoli, C. and Edgar, D. (2018), "An eco-critical perspective on business models: The value triangle as an approach to closing the sustainability gap", *Journal of Cleaner Production*, Vol. 174, pp. 746–762.

Boons, F. and Lüdeke-Freund, F. (2013), "Business models for sustainable innovation: State-of-the-art and steps towards a research agenda", *Journal of Cleaner Production*, Vol. 45, pp. 9–19.

Börsch-Supan, A., Hank, K. and Jürges, H. (2005), "A new comprehensive and international view on ageing: Introducing the 'Survey of Health, Ageing and Retirement in Europe'", *European Journal of Ageing*, Vol. 2 No. 4, pp. 245–253.

Christensen, C.M., Bohomer, R. and Kenagy, J. (2000), "Will disruptive innovations cure health care?", *Harvard Business Review*, Vol. 78 No. 5, pp. 102–112.

Cobianchi, L., Peloso, A., Vischioni, B., Panizza, D., Fiore, M.R., Fossati, P., Vitolo, V., *et al.* (2016), "Surgical spacer placement prior carbon ion radiotherapy (CIRT): An effective feasible strategy to improve the treatment for sacral chordoma", *World Journal of Surgical Oncology*, Vol. 14 No. 211, pp. 1–9.

Currie, W.L. and Guah, M.W. (2007), "Conflicting institutional logics: A national programme for IT in the organisational field of healthcare", *Journal of Information Technology*, Vol. 22 No. 3, pp. 235–247.

Dal Mas, F. (2019), "The relationship between intellectual capital and sustainability: An analysis of practitioner's thought", in Matos, F., Vairinhos, V., Selig, P.M. and Edvinsson, L. (Eds.), *Intellectual Capital Management as a Driver of Sustainability: Perspectives for Organizations and Society*, Springer, Cham, pp. 11–24.

Dal Mas, F., Piccolo, D., Cobianchi, L., Edvinsson, L., Presch, G., Massaro, M., Skrap, M., *et al.* (2019), "The effects of artificial intelligence, robotics, and Industry 4.0 technologies: Insights from the healthcare sector", *Proceedings of the First European Conference on the Impact of Artificial Intelligence and Robotics*, Academic Conferences and Publishing International.

Duff-Brown, B. (2017), "Non-communicable disease could cost global economy \$47 trillion by 2030", https://globalhealthsciences.ucsf.edu/news/non-communicable-disease-could-cost-global-economy-47-trillion-2030.

Edvinsson, L., Hofman-Bang, P. and Jacobsen, K. (2005), "Intellectual capital in waiting: A strategic IC challenge", *Handbook of Business Strategy*, Vol. 6 No. 1, pp. 133–140.

Edvinsson, L. and Malone, M. (1997), *Intellectual Capital: Realizing Your Company's True Value by Finding Its Hidden Brainpower*, HarperCollins, New York.

Fletcher, D. (2015), "Internet of Things", in Blowers, M. (Ed.), *Evolution of Cyber Technologies and Operations to 2035*, Springer, New York, pp. 19–32.

Gawer, A. and Cusumano, M.A. (2014), "Industry platforms and ecosystem innovation", *Journal of Product Innovation Management*, Vol. 31 No. 3, pp. 417–433.

Grafstrom, G. and Edvinsson, L. (1996), *Accounting for Minds: An Inspirational Guide to Intellectual Capital*, Skandia, Stockholm.

Iacopino, V., Mascia, D. and Cicchetti, A. (2018), "Professional networks and the alignment of individual perceptions about medical innovation", *Health Care Management Review*, Vol. 43 No. 2, pp. 92–103.

Ireland, A.V., Finnegan-John, J., Hubbard, G., Scanlon, K. and Kyle, R.G. (2019), "Walking groups for women with breast cancer: Mobilising therapeutic assemblages of walk, talk and place", *Social Science and Medicine*, Vol. 231 No. June, pp. 38–46.

Kagermann, H. (2015), "Change through digitization: Value creation in the age of industry 4.0", in Albach, H., Meffert, H., Pinkwart, A. and Ralf, R. (Eds.), *Management of Permanent Change*, HHL Leipzig Graduate School of Management, Leipzig, pp. 23–45.

Limb, M. (2016), "World will lack 18 million health workers by 2030 without adequate investment, warns UN", *British Medical Journal*, Vol. 354, p. 15169.

Linton, J.D., Klassen, R. and Jayaraman, V. (2007), "Sustainable supply chains: An introduction", *Journal of Operations Management*, Vol. 25 No. 6, pp. 1075–1082.

Lucas, D.P. (2015), "Disruptive transformations in health care: Technological innovation and public policy reforms in the hospital industry", *International Journal of Interdisciplinary Organizational Studies*, Vol. 9 No. 1, pp. 1–22.

Mascia, D. and Di Vincenzo, F. (2011), "Understanding hospital performance: The role of network ties and patterns of competition", *Health Care Management Review*, Vol. 36 No. 4, pp. 327–337.

Massaro, M., Dumay, J., Garlatti, A. and Dal Mas, F. (2018), "Practitioners' views on intellectual capital and sustainability: From a performance-based to a worth-based perspective", *Journal of Intellectual Capital*, Vol. 19 No. 2, pp. 367–386.

Moore, T., Shapiro, J.S., Doles, L., Calman, N., Camhi, E., Check, T., Onyile, A., *et al.* (2012), "Event detection: A clinical notification service on a health information exchange platform", *Amia Annual Symposium Proceedings*, pp. 635–642.

Muzio, D. and Faulconbridge, J. (2013), "The global professional service firm: 'One firm' models versus (Italian) distant institutionalized practices", *Organization Studies*, Vol. 34 No. 7, pp. 897–925.

Nielsen, C., Lund, M., Montemari, M., Paolone, F., Massaro, M. and Dumay, J. (2018), *Business Models: A Research Overview*, Routledge, New York.

Osterwalder, A. (2004), *The Business Model Ontology: A Proposition in a Design Science Approach, Business*, PhD Thesis, University of Lausanne, Switzerland.

Osterwalder, A., Pigneur, Y., Bernarda, G. and Smith, A. (2014), *Value Proposition Design: How to Create Products and Services Customers Want*, John Wiley & Sons, Hoboken, NJ.

Peloso, A., Viganò, J., Vanoli, A., Dominioni, T., Zonta, S., Bugada, D., Bianchi, C.M., *et al.* (2017), "Saving from unnecessary pancreaticoduodenectomy. Brunner's gland hamartoma: Case report on a rare duodenal lesion and exhaustive literature review", *Annals of Medicine and Surgery*, Vol. 17, pp. 43–49.

Porter, M.E. and Kramer, M.R. (2006), "Strategy and society: The link between competitive advantage and corporate social responsibility", *Harvard Business Review*, Vol. 84 No. 12, pp. 78–92.

Ruutu, S., Casey, T. and Kotovirta, V. (2017), "Development and competition of digital service platforms: A system dynamics approach", *Technological Forecasting and Social Change*, Vol. 117 No. April, pp. 119–130.

Schlegelmilch, B.B., Diamantopoulos, A. and Kreuz, P. (2003), "Strategic innovation: The construct, its drivers and its strategic outcomes", *Journal of Strategic Marketing*, Vol. 11 No. 2, pp. 117–132.

Seelos, C. and Mair, J. (2005), "Social entrepreneurship: Creating new business models to serve the poor", *Business Horizons*, Vol. 48 No. 3, pp. 241–246.

Seelos, C. and Mair, J. (2007), "Profitable business models and market creation in the context of deep poverty: A strategic view", *Academy of Management Perspectives*, Vol. 21 No. 4, pp. 49–63.

Seuring, S. and Müller, M. (2008), "From a literature review to a conceptual framework for sustainable supply chain management", *Journal of Cleaner Production*, Vol. 16 No. 15, pp. 1699–1710.

Teece, D.J. (2010), "Business models, business strategy and innovation", *Long Range Planning*, Vol. 43 No. 2–3, pp. 172–194.

Toniolo, K., Masiero, E., Massaro, M. and Bagnoli, C. (2019), "Sustainable business models and artificial intelligence: Opportunities and challenges", in Matos, F., Vairinhos, V., Salavisa, I., Edvinsson, L. and Massaro, M. (Eds.), *Knowledge, People, and Digital Transformation: Approaches for a Sustainable Future*, Springer, Cham, pp. 113–128.

Troiani, F., Sica, R. and Scotti, E. (2016), "Welcome to the era of platform-companies", *Harvard Business Review Italia*, Vol. July, pp. 2–3.

Tukker, A. (2004), "Eight types of product-service system: Eight ways to sustainability? Experiences from suspronet", *Business Strategy and the Environment*, Vol. 13 No. 4, pp. 246–260.

Wilkinson, R.G. and Pickett, K.E. (2006), "Income inequality and population health: A review and explanation of the evidence", *Social Science and Medicine*, Vol. 62 No. 7, pp. 1768–1784.

Yaraghi, N., Ye Du, A., Sharman, R., Gopal, R.D. and Ramesh, R. (2015), "health information exchange as a multisided platform: Adoption, usage, and practice involvement in service co-production", *Information Systems Research*, Vol. 26 No. 1.

Zhang, J., Liang, W., Liang, H., Wang, X. and He, J. (2019), "Endpoint surrogacy in oncological randomized controlled trials with immunotherapies: A systematic review of trial-level and arm-level meta-analyses", *Annals of Translational Medicine*, Vol. 7 No. 11, pp. 1–12.

Zott, C., Amit, R. and Massa, L. (2011), "The business model: Recent developments and future research", *Journal of Management*, Vol. 37 No. 4, pp. 1019–1042.

Part II

Global outlook and intellectual capital in Asia and Europe

4 What drives the development of intellectual capital?

A longitudinal study

Aino Kianto, Mika Vanhala, Paavo Ritala and Henri Hussinki

Introduction

With the advent of the globalized knowledge-based economy, intangible resources, such as multi-skilled employees, sophisticated information systems and well-handled customer and societal relationships, have become important drivers of value creation for organizations. These intangible value drivers are often grouped under the larger concept of 'intellectual capital' (Edvinsson and Malone, 1997; Sveiby, 1997). In recent years, an increasing number of studies have shown that intellectual capital strongly influences the performance of organizations (Subramaniam and Youndt, 2005; Buenechea-Elberdin et al., 2018; Cabrilo et al., 2018; Hussinki et al., 2018), regions (Pöyhönen and Smedlund, 2004; Bounfour and Edvinsson, 2005) and nations (Lin and Edvinsson, 2010; Käpylä et al., 2012; Seleim and Bontis, 2013) alike.

However, there has been little research to date about the different organizational aspects that enhance or hinder the development of such intangible value drivers. In other words, what kinds of organizational antecedents lead to increases in various aspects of intellectual capital? To bridge this gap in the literature, the current paper seeks to discover what drives the development of intellectual capital in firms.

We posit that two key groups of organizational factors are likely to impact the development of intellectual capital: strategic and structural. In the rest of this chapter, we explain the essential aspects of intellectual capital and the strategic and structural factors that could potentially influence it. Then we use longitudinal data, collected via two waves of surveys in 2013 and 2017 from 96 Finnish organizations, to examine the observed development of intellectual capital variables. These data on intellectual capital development were then combined with data on the strategic and structural characteristics of these companies, drawn from the survey datasets and public databases. We used partial least squares (PLS)-based structural modelling to examine the causalities between the strategic and structural aspects and intellectual capital development. Our results contribute to the literature on intellectual capital from a dynamic-temporal perspective and will help inform managers and policy-makers about the strategic and structural factors that influence the development of intellectual capital in organizations.

Theoretical background

The components of intellectual capital

The resource-based view of the firm maintains that an organization's competitive advantage is based on the valuable, rare, inimitable and non-substitutable (VRIN) resources and capabilities that the firm governs (Barney, 1991). The knowledge-based view of the firm, on the other hand, argues that intangible factors, such as knowledge and a firm's capabilities to manage it, are likely to possess the VRIN qualities and can thus be sources of sustained competitiveness (Grant, 1996). Based on these arguments, the academic debate about the value of intangibles has flourished over the last few decades. In addition to theory development, a plethora of empirical studies have examined the nature, composition and performance drivers of intangibles.

Typically, the value-creating intangibles have been coined under the heading of intellectual capital (Edvinsson and Malone, 1997; Sveiby, 1997). Intellectual capital of a firm consists of three elements: human capital, structural capital and relational capital (e.g. Bontis, 1998; Petty and Guthrie, 2000; Inkinen, 2015).

Human capital includes the value-creating capacities embedded in and available through the people working for a company. These relate to the skills, knowledge and capacities of organizational agents and their motivation, attitudes and various types of personal characteristics, such as creativity and self-efficacy beliefs (Edvinsson and Malone, 1997; Sveiby, 1997; Bontis, 1998). An organization's stock of employee competencies, experience, knowledge and social and personality attributes forms the basis from which it can effectively and efficiently solve problems and realize its strategic goals.

Structural capital refers to those aspects of an organization that support employees in their work, such as information systems, tools, facilities, databases and documents (Edvinsson and Malone, 1997), as well as 'softer' enabling factors like organizational culture and values, leadership philosophy and collaboration climate (Roos et al., 1997; Sveiby, 1997). Structural capital is thus not dependent on or carried by individual employees, and, from an organization's perspective, is arguably a more collective and stable resource than human capital. The conversion of human capital to structural capital is therefore considered paramount for securing an organization's long-term competitiveness (Sullivan, 2000).

Finally, an organization's relational capital can be divided into two main types: internal and external relational capital (Inkinen et al., 2017). Internal relational capital includes the extent and quality of relationships among the actors within an organization (Tsai and Ghoshal, 1998). These relate to the relationships among employees, relationships between employees and their supervisors and managers at various levels of the organization and relationships between organizational units and functions (Nahapiet and Ghoshal, 1998; Yang and Lin, 2009). External relational capital, in contrast, refers to the knowledge and value available through the relationships that a firm has with its key external stakeholders, such as customers, suppliers and distributors (Cabrita and Bontis,

What drives the development IC? 33

2008); in some firms, relationships with funding institutions and an investment community can also be highly significant. An organization's image and brand also are crucial facets of its external relational capital (Roos et al., 1997; Bontis, 1998).

Drivers of intellectual capital

As noted previously, while there is a significant volume of academic literature on intellectual capital, most studies have concentrated on either the identification and reporting of current levels of intellectual capital in firms or on the influence of intellectual capital on various types of organizational performance indicators. Very little is known about how firms' intellectual capital changes over time and what kinds of factors explain any changes. We therefore tackle this topic in this exploratory study and argue that, in an organizational context, there are two main types of change factors: those associated with an organization's strategic choices, and those associated with its structural characteristics.

Strategic choices are related to four key issues. First, organizations exhibit varying degrees of knowledge intensity, which reflects the relative importance of knowledge resources (as opposed to other types of resources) as the inputs in a firm's productive processes (Starbuck, 1992). In knowledge-intensive firms, a firm's main activities are based on intangible resources, and intellectual capital and its management mechanisms are key sources of competitive advantage (Autio et al., 2000).

Second, another crucial facet of strategic choice concerns a firm's research and development (R&D) intensity. R&D investments are a fundamental way to create new knowledge (Youndt et al., 2004), and their magnitude in any given firm reflects the importance attached to rapid learning and the application of new knowledge (Bierly and Chakrabarti, 1996). This choice is manifested in the resources that a firm allocates to speeding up learning processes, such as the proportion of manpower directed to R&D activities.

Third, an organization's strategic choices also include the extent to which it focuses on tacit and/or codified knowledge as sources of value. Hansen et al. (1999) conceptualized this as a choice between personalization and codification. Personalization is a knowledge strategy that seeks to link people to each other to foster the 'person-to-person' sharing of tacit knowledge. Codification, on the other hand, seeks to capture and store knowledge in an explicit form for subsequent transfer and reuse by others within the organization. The choice between these two strategies is not necessarily mutually exclusive, and most organizations mix personalization and codification in different proportions (Scheepers et al., 2004)

Fourth and finally, an organization can direct its activities toward producing either products or services for the market. A firm's degree of servitization is firm- rather than industry-dependent because firms operating within the same industry can choose the extent to which they concentrate on product or service output. There is some evidence that the relative importance of particular

34   *Aino Kianto et al.*

types of intellectual capital may differ for service- versus production-oriented companies (Kianto et al., 2010). A service orientation has also been found to influence the managerial mechanisms of knowledge governance that yield the most beneficial results (Kianto and Andreeva, 2014). Consequently, this strategic choice factor is also expected to impact the development of an organization's intellectual capital over time.

Moving on to *structural features*, first, company size may impact an organization's willingness and ability to develop its intellectual capital. Larger organizations may need to formalize their activities by developing standardized guidelines and codes of conduct to build various elements of intellectual capital. This is also linked to the classic problem of the 'liability of smallness' (Freeman et al., 1983), in which small firms often need to invest a lot of resources in survival and may not be able to develop their intellectual capital as systematically as larger firms.

Second, the financial resources available for an organization's use are another important structural factor. Profitable firms have more opportunities to innovate and to invest in the development of intellectual capital than do firms that have not been able to generate a profit (Surroca et al., 2010). Thus, we propose that the financial resources an organization has in its use could also function as an explanatory factor for the development of intellectual capital.

Third and finally, the technological level of an industry is likely to impact an organization's need to develop intellectual capital (Buenechea–Elberdin et al., 2017, 2018). For example, firms that operate in high-technology industries deal with more complex knowledge than firms that operate in low-technology industries, and this is also reflected by higher levels of intellectual capital among high-technology firms. In addition, high-technology industries require a faster pace of knowledge renewal.

Figure 4.1 visualizes these arguments and demonstrates the overall research model of the present study.

Methods

Sample and data collection

In order to test the model with true causal logic (i.e. time lag between independent and dependent variables), we utilized two datasets that we collected in 2013 ($N = 259$) and 2017 ($N = 221$) from Finnish firms with at least 100 employees. The data for independent variables (strategic and structural factors) were collected in 2013 and the data for dependent variables (the change in intellectual capital) were collected in 2013 and 2017. After merging the two datasets, we ended up with a cross-industry dataset of 96 companies, as this was the number of firms that responded to both surveys. In both data collection phases, all firms were contacted by telephone by an external research company and the person in charge of the firm's human resources was asked to respond to the questionnaire.

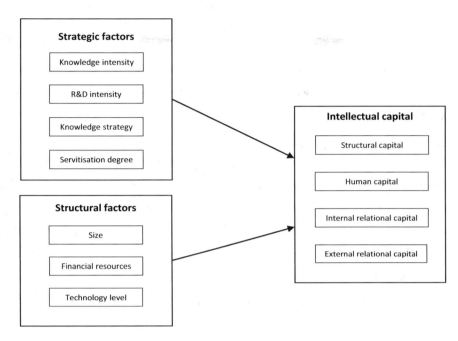

Figure 4.1 Research model.

A key-informant technique was used to collect data from one respondent per company. The most heavily represented industries in our dataset were manufacturing (37.2%) and wholesale and retail trade (18.1%), followed by transportation and storage (8.5%), services (8.5%), professional, scientific and technical activities (7.4%) and construction (7.4%). Most respondents held key positions related to issues of intellectual capital: 71.9% of them were human resources directors or managers, 11.5% other directors or managers, and 7.3% managing directors.

Measures

Item wording and scale response anchors for all measures are presented in Appendix 4.1.

Independent variables. Independent variables were categorized as the strategic and structural factors that drive the development of intellectual capital in organizations. Four strategic factors were assessed: *knowledge intensity* was measured as the proportion of tangible versus intangible resources used by a company in its operations; *R&D intensity* was reported by respondents as the percentage of R&D staff compared to all company employees in 2012 (we used a natural logarithmic transformation of the variable for the analysis); *knowledge strategy* was reported by respondents as the extent to which tacit versus codified knowledge functioned as the source of the company's competitive ability; and *servitization degree* was measured as the proportion of products versus services in the company's net sales in 2012.

Three structural factors were assessed in our survey: *company size* was operationalized as both the number of employees and sales turnover; *financial resources* were measured by a company's return on assets (ROA) and return on equity (ROE) in 2013; and *technology level* was assessed by assigning companies to high-technology or low-technology groups based on the Statistical Classification of Economic Activities in the European Community. Data concerning structural factors was obtained from the Amadeus database.

Dependent variables. The scales for the four dimensions of intellectual capital (human, structural and internal and external relational capital) were based on work by Inkinen et al. (2017). The measurement items in both surveys were identical, with the only difference being that the 2013 survey utilized a 5-point Likert-type scale while the 2017 employed a 7-point scale. On all scales, respondents were asked to assess how different statements regarding the dimensions of intellectual capital applied to the organization they represented. Human, internal relational and external relational capital were assessed by three items while structural capital was assessed by four. For each dependent variable, we calculated the change in intellectual capital dimensions by subtracting the 2013 levels from the 2017 levels after adjusting the data to account for the different Likert-type scales used in 2013 and 2017. This adjustment was done by converting the 7-point scale used in 2017 to a 5-point scale that corresponded to the 2013 scale.

Control variables. We used the 2013 levels of intellectual capital for each dimension as control variables in order to control for the possibility that initial levels of intellectual capital could affect their change rate.

Results

We used Partial Least Squares (PLS) for the analyses (version 3.2.7 of SmartPLS; see Ringle et al., 2015) and followed the process suggested in the literature (see, e.g. Hair et al., 2014). According to Hair et al. (2014), PLS-based structural modelling can be utilized with smaller sample sizes, and a sample size of 96 was determined to be enough for our research model. The first step was to assess the reliability and validity of the measurement models. We then used the structural model to test our hypotheses.

Measurement model

To test the measurement model, we assessed both internal consistency and discriminant validity. According to a series of tests, the model demonstrated good validity and reliability for the operationalization of the concepts of intellectual capital.

First, the construct reliabilities (CR) for all of our constructs were above the recommended threshold of 0.7 (Bagozzi and Yi, 1991). Second, the factor loading of each item was high and statistically significant, indicating that they were all related to their specific constructs and thereby verifying the relationship posited among the indicators and constructs. Third, the measure of average variance extracted (AVE) exceeded the cut-off point of 0.5 (e.g. Fornell and Larcker, 1981) for all of our intellectual capital constructs. Fourth and finally, the tests of discriminant validity showed that each construct's AVE was greater than the squared correlation between other constructs (i.e. the shared variance between a given construct and other constructs in the model). In addition, we tested discriminant validity using the Heterotrait-Monotrait (HTMT) ratio by following the procedure suggested in the methodological literature (e.g. Henseler et al., 2016; Hair et al., 2017). The results showed that the HTMT values for all pairs of constructs were under the threshold value of 0.90; furthermore, based on a computed bootstrapping procedure, all HTMT values were also significantly different from 1. These results indicated that the constructs in the model differed from each other. See Appendix 4.1 for the factor loadings, CRs and AVEs.

Research model

Our model was able to explain about 46% of the variance in human capital over time, 43% for structural capital, 27% for internal relational capital and 53% for external relational capital. The statistically significant paths are presented in Figures 4.2 and 4.3; for clarity, strategic and structural factors are presented separately.

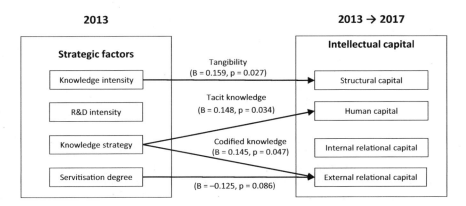

Figure 4.2 Results for the strategic factors.

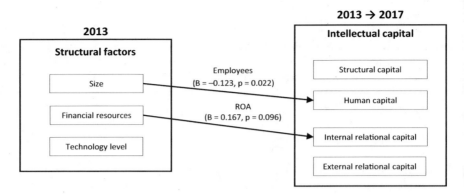

Figure 4.3 Results for the structural factors.

Model results suggest that three of the four strategic factors functioned as drivers of intellectual capital development: knowledge intensity, knowledge strategy and servitization degree. First, regarding knowledge intensity, resource tangibility was connected to changes in structural capital ($B = 0.159$, $p = 0.027$). Second, in terms of knowledge strategy, both tacit and codified knowledge resources had positive effects on intellectual capital: the paths from tacit knowledge to changes in human capital ($B = 0.148$, $p = 0.034$) and from codified knowledge to changes in external relational capital ($B = 0.145$, $p = 0.047$) were both positive and statistically significant. Third, higher degrees of servitization led to negative changes in external relational capital ($B = -0.125, p = 0.086$).

In addition, two of the three structural factors influenced changes in intellectual capital. First, a company's size had a negative effect on human capital: the path from number of employees to changes in human capital was negative and significant ($B = -0.123, p = 0.022$). Second, a company's financial resources, and more specifically its ROA, had a positive effect on changes in internal relational capital ($B = 0.167, p = 0.096$).

Discussion

Our study used a unique longitudinal dataset that was collected through two rounds of surveys in 2013 and 2017. The use of longitudinal data allowed us to examine changes in the levels of intellectual capital of 96 Finnish firms over a four-year period, as well as to examine factors that might explain why some firms were able to increase their intellectual capital over time while other firms' intellectual capital decreased. We divided our analysis into two types of antecedents: strategic and structural factors.

The strategic factors included four important antecedents that we expected to play roles in the development of firms' intellectual capital. First, we examined knowledge intensity in terms of a firm's key tangible and intangible resources. Our results showed that firms with high tangibility (i.e. those that rely heavily on property, equipment and machinery in their operations) significantly increased their structural capital during the four-year study period. This was in contrast to firms that relied more heavily on intangible resources (e.g. information, expertise, contacts and processes) which witnessed reduced levels of structural capital during the study period. Interestingly, this indicates that knowledge-intensive firms, which could benefit greatly from structural capital (e.g. well-functioning information systems and databases), are not necessarily as prone to utilizing them as firms that are already good at utilizing other types of tangible resources. In addition, this finding suggests that knowledge-intensive firms, which are at the forefront of the digital revolution, may find it difficult to be satisfied with their structural capital (e.g. information systems, collaboration tools and databases), as it is difficult for these firms to keep up with the requirements and demands of modern knowledge-workers.

Second, we found no relationship between a firm's R&D intensity (the share of R&D staff out of all company employees) and the change of any of the four dimensions of intellectual capital. This suggests that R&D investments do not explain how well a firm can develop its intellectual capital; R&D investments are instead demonstrated by a firm's improved products and services.

Third, we examined firms' knowledge strategies (Hansen et al., 1999) and whether firms' competitive abilities were based on tacit or codified knowledge. We found that firms relying on tacit knowledge-based strategies improved their human capital while firms relying on codified knowledge improved their external relational capital. These findings provide strong support for the distinctive merits of both strategies. One the one hand, tacit knowledge is likely to improve employees' and teams' skills and competence over time. Since tacit knowledge is embedded predominantly in a firm's employees, firms that rely on it as their primary source of competitiveness cannot survive without improving their human capital. On the other hand, focusing more on codified knowledge helps firms to develop their external relationships and collaborations, given the easier transferability and the coordination benefits it offers in inter-organizational exchanges (Mowery et al., 1996; Simonin, 1999).

Fourth, we examined whether a firm's degree of servitization (the proportion of net sales from services vs. products) influenced changes in its intellectual capital. We found that servitization led to decreases in firms' external relational capital. This may be due to the difficulties that service-oriented firms face in trying to establish external relationships. Service businesses typically rely on intangible, heterogeneous and perishable features (see, e.g. Ritala et al., 2013), which may make it more difficult for them to engage external actors in comparison to firms that operate with more concrete products.

We also examined three structural factors that we hypothesized might influence firms' abilities and willingness to develop their intellectual capital. Among these, we found that firm size (the number of employees) had a negative effect on firms' levels of human capital, whereas financial resources (and more specifically their ROA) increased their levels of internal relational capital. The finding that larger firms' human capital decreased while smaller firms' increased over the four-year study window can perhaps be explained by external factors. Between 2013 and 2017, the wider European economy did not perform very well, and, as part of the European market, larger Finnish firms may have suffered disproportionately to smaller firms that were less tied to the wider markets; their relative levels of human capital over this period may reflect this. In addition, the finding that a firm's ROA contributed to its development of internal relational capital can be understood as a source of necessary 'slack' – in other words, as a resource that helps a firm's employees and departments increase the frequency and quality of their communication and collaboration efforts. Conversely, when financial resources are tight and a firm lacks a positive ROA, it might not be able to invest in internal processes and collaboration, needing instead to focus on operational optimization and profit generation.

Overall, our findings provide interesting insights into how strategic and structural factors affect changes in firms' intellectual capital. These findings improve the field's understanding of different types of firms' abilities to develop their intellectual capital. As such, our study provides a unique contribution to the literature on intellectual capital by exploring the antecedents of changes in several dimensions of intellectual capital over time. We expect that the results will be useful for intellectual capital scholars and practitioners and will provide new research avenues for future studies to explore. Our results also complement those of previous research that examined the development of strategic management activities related to intangibles (Kianto et al., 2013). Future studies should examine more systematically how firms' strategic choices allow them to develop different dimensions of intellectual capital and how this eventually relates to value creation and firm performance. Another potential subject for future research is further exploration of how different strategic and structural drivers influence the development of other types of intellectual capital elements, such as renewal, trust or entrepreneurial capital (Buenechea-Elberdin et al., 2017; Inkinen et al., 2017).

Appendix 4.1

Measurement items

Concept	Item
Knowledge intensity	In your evaluation, to what extent do tangible resources (such as machinery, equipment and property) and intangible resources (such as information, expertise, contacts and processes) represent the resources your company uses in its operations? (1 = operations are completely based on tangible resources, 10 = operations are completely based on intangible resources)
R&D share	The proportion of research and development staff of all employees in 2011 (estimate)

Concept	Item
Knowledge strategy	To what extent can the following be described as the sources of your company's information-based competitive ability? (1 = not at all, 5 = very much)
Tacit	Tacit knowledge and special expertise represented by teams and individuals
Codified	Documented information and standardized expertise that can be reproduced quickly and efficiently
Servitization	In 2012, our company's net sales consisted of: (1 = 100% product sales, 10 = 100% service sales)

Concept	Item	Factor loadings		CR		AVE	
	To what extent do the following statements apply to your company (1 = completely disagree, 5★ = completely agree); (★ 7 in 2017)	2013	2017	2013	2017	2013	2017
Human capital	Our employees are highly skilled at their jobs	0.827***	0.858***	.87	.87	.68	.69
	Our employees are highly motivated in their work	0.749***	0.806***				
	Our employees have a high level of expertise	0.896***	0.829***				
Structural capital	Our company has efficient and relevant information systems to support business operations	0.620***	0.727***	.83	.84	.56	.56
	Our company has tools and facilities to support cooperation between employees	0.715***	0.576***				
	Our company has a great deal of useful information in documents and databases	0.843***	0.869***				
	Older documents and solutions are easily accessible	0.792***	0.798***				
Internal relational capital	Different units and functions within our company – such as R&D, marketing and production – understand each other well	0.647***	0.816***	.81	.91	.59	.78
	Our employees frequently collaborate to solve problems	0.851***	0.912***				
	Internal cooperation in our company runs smoothly	0.797***	0.909***				

Concept	Item						
External relational capital	Our company and its external stakeholders – such as customers, suppliers and partners – understand each other well	0.805***	0.764***	.87	.88	.70	.70
	Our company and its external stakeholders frequently collaborate to solve problems	0.869***	0.928***				
	Cooperation between our company and its external stakeholders runs smoothly	0.833***	0.813***				

*** Statistically significant at 0.005 significance level.

References

Autio, E., Sapienza, H.J. and Almeida, J.G. (2000) 'Effects of age at entry, knowledge intensity, and imitability on international growth', *Academy of Management Journal* 43(5), 909–924.

Bagozzi, R.P. and Yi, Y. (1991) 'Multitrait-multimethod matrices in consumer research', *Journal of Consumer Research* 17(4), 426–439.

Barney, J.B. (1991) 'The resource based view of strategy: Origins, implications, and prospects', *Journal of Management* 17(1), 97–211.

Bierly, P. and Chakrabarti, A. (1996) 'Generic knowledge strategies in the US pharmaceutical industry', *Strategic Management Journal* 17(S2), 123–135.

Bontis, N. (1998) 'Intellectual capital: An exploratory study that develops measures and models', *Management Decision* 36(2), 63–76.

Bounfour, A. and Edvinsson, L. (2005) *Intellectual Capital for Communities*, Oxford: Elsevier Butterworth-Heinemann.

Buenechea-Elberdin, M., Kianto, A. and Sáenz, J. (2018) 'Intellectual capital drivers of product and managerial innovation in high-tech and low-tech firms', *R&D Management* 48(3), 290–307.

Buenechea-Elberdin, M., Sáenz, J. and Kianto, A. (2017) 'Exploring the role of human capital, renewal capital and entrepreneurial capital in innovation performance in high-tech and low-tech firms', *Knowledge Management Research & Practice* 15(3), 369–379.

Cabrilo, S., Kianto, A. and Misic, B. (2018) 'The effect of IC components on innovation performance in Serbian companies', *VINE Journal of Information and Knowledge Management Systems* 48(3), 448–466.

Cabrita, M.D.R. and Bontis, N. (2008) 'Intellectual capital and business performance in the Portuguese banking industry', International Journal of Technology Management 43(1–3), 212–237.

Edvinsson, L. and Malone, M. (1997) *Intellectual Capital: Realising Your Company's True Value by Finding Its Hidden Brainpower.* New York: HarperCollins.

Fornell, C. and Larcker, D.F. (1981) 'Evaluating structural equation models with unobservable variables and measurement error', *Journal of Marketing Research* 18(1), 39–50.

Freeman, J., Carroll, G.R. and Hannan, M.T. (1983) 'The liability of newness: Age dependence in organisational death rates', *American Sociological Review* 48(5), 692–710.

Grant, R.M. (1996) 'Toward a knowledge-based theory of the firm', *Strategic Management Journal* 17(S2), 109–122.

Hair, J.F., Hult, G.T.M., Ringle, C. and Sarstedt, M. (2017) *A Primer on Partial Least Squares Structural Equation Modeling (PLS-SEM)*, 2nd edn, Thousand Oaks, CA: Sage Publications.

Hair, J.F., Sarstedt, M., Hopkins, L. and Kuppelwieser, V.G. (2014) 'Partial least squares structural equation modeling (PLS-SEM): An emerging tool in business research', *European Business Review* 26(2), 106–121.

Hansen, M.T., Nohria, N. and Tierney, T. (1999) 'What's your strategy for managing knowledge?', *Harvard Business Review* 77(2), 106–111.

Henseler, J., Hubona, G. and Ash Ray, P. (2016) 'Using PLS path modeling in new technology research: Updated guidelines', *Industrial Management & Data Systems* 116(1), 2–20.

Hussinki, H., Ritala, P., Vanhala, M. and Kianto, A. (2018) 'Intellectual capital profiles and financial performance of the firm', in J. Guthrie, J. Dumay, F. Ricceri and C. Nielsen (eds.), The Routledge Companion to Intellectual Capital, New York: Routledge, pp. 450–462.

Inkinen, H. (2015) 'Review of empirical research on intellectual capital', *Journal of Intellectual Capital* 16(3), 518–565.

Inkinen, H., Kianto, A., Vanhala, M. and Ritala, P. (2017) 'Structure of intellectual capital: An international comparison', *Accounting, Auditing & Accountability Journal* 30(5), 1160–1183.

Käpylä, J., Kujansivu, P. and Lönnqvist, A. (2012) 'National intellectual capital performance: A strategic approach', *Journal of Intellectual Capital* 13(3), 343–362.

Kianto, A. and Andreeva, T. (2014) 'Knowledge management practices and results in service-oriented versus product-oriented companies', *Knowledge and Process Management* 21(4), 221–230.

Kianto, A., Andreeva, T. and Pavlov, Y. (2013) 'The impact of intellectual capital management on company competitiveness and financial performance', *Knowledge Management Research & Practice* 11(2), 112–122.

Kianto, A., Hurmelinna-Laukkanen, P. and Ritala, P. (2010) 'Intellectual capital in service- and product-oriented companies', *Journal of Intellectual Capital* 11(3), 305–325.

Lin, C.Y.Y. and Edvinsson, L. (2010) *National Intellectual Capital: A Comparison of 40 Countries*, New York: Springer.

Mowery, D.C., Oxley, J.E. and Silverman, B.S. (1996) 'Strategic alliances and interfirm knowledge transfer', *Strategic Management Journal* 17(S2), 77–91.

Nahapiet, J. and Ghoshal, S. (1998) 'Social capital, intellectual capital, and the organizational advantage', *Academy of Management Review* 23(2), 242–266.

Petty, R. and Guthrie, J. (2000) 'Intellectual capital literature review: Measurement, reporting and management', *Journal of Intellectual Capital* 1(2), 155–176.

Pöyhönen, A. and Smedlund, A. (2004) 'Assessing intellectual capital creation in regional clusters', *Journal of Intellectual Capital* 5(3), 351–365.

Ringle, C.M., Wende, S. and Becker, J. (2015) SmartPLS 3, Boenningstedt: SmartPLS.

Ritala, P., Hyötylä, M., Blomqvist, K. and Kosonen, M. (2013) 'Key capabilities in knowledge-intensive service business', *The Service Industries Journal* 33(5), 486–500.

Roos, J., Roos, G., Dragonetti, N.C. and Edvinsson, L. (1997) *Intellectual Capital: Navigating the New Business Landscape*, Basingstoke: Macmillan Business.

Scheepers, R., Venkitachalam, K. and Gibbs, M.R. (2004) 'Knowledge strategy in organisations: Refining the model of Hansen, Nohria and Tierney', *The Journal of Strategic Information Systems* 13(3), 201–222.

Seleim, A. and Bontis, N. (2013) 'National intellectual capital and economic performance: Empirical evidence from developing countries', *Knowledge and Process Management* 20(3), 131–140.

Simonin, B.L. (1999) 'Ambiguity and the process of knowledge transfer in strategic alliances', *Strategic Management Journal* 20(7), 595–623.

Starbuck, W.H. (1992) 'Learning by knowledge-intensive firms', *Journal of Management Studies* 3(4), 262–275.

Subramaniam, M. and Youndt, M.A. (2005) 'The influence of intellectual capital on the types of innovative capabilities', *Academy of Management Journal* 48(3), 450–463.

Sullivan, P.H. (2000) *Value Driven Intellectual Capital: How to Convert Intangible Corporate Assets into Market Value*, New York: John Wiley & Sons.

Surroca, J., Tribó, J.A. and Waddock, S. (2010) 'Corporate responsibility and financial performance: The role of intangible resources', *Strategic Management Journal* 31(5), 463–490.

Sveiby, K.E. (1997) *The New Organizational Wealth: Managing & Measuring Knowledge-based Assets*, San Francisco, CA: Berrett-Koehler.

Tsai, W. and Ghoshal, S. (1998) 'Social capital and value creation: The role of intrafirm networks', *Academy of Management Journal* 41(4), 464–476.

Yang, C. and Lin, C. (2009) 'Does intellectual capital mediate the relationship between HRM and organizational performance? Perspective of a healthcare industry in Taiwan', *International Journal of Human Resource Management* 20(9), 1965–1984.

Youndt, M.A., Subramaniam, M. and Snell, S.A. (2004) 'Intellectual capital profiles: An examination of investments and returns', *Journal of Management Studies* 41(2), 335–361.

5 An intellectual capital framework of enterprise innovative efficiency capability

A Hong Kong study

Irene Y.H. Fan, Rongbin W.B. Lee and Haley W.C. Tsang

Introduction

Efficiency in running a business is essential for enterprises. Traditional efficiency emphasizes maximizing output with the minimum input of resources, elimination of redundant processes, and keeping a lean working force. Striving for maximum efficiency forms the basis of industrial engineering and scientific management as pioneered by Taylor (1911) as well as the advocating of business process reengineering two decades ago (Hammer & Champy 1990). However, the pitfalls of reengineering have been addressed and well reported in the literature (Nwabueze & Kanji 1997; Al-Mashari & Zairi 1999). Nevertheless, efficiency improvement is still a fundamental concern in business operations.

With the emergence of the digital economy, we have witnessed a paradigm shift in how business is done nowadays. There have been revolutionary changes in the management landscape. Gradually we have moved away from the resource paradigm to the knowledge paradigm of producing products and services, and innovation has been identified as the driving force for value creation and the future survival of an organization. There is a growing awareness that competitive advantage and sustainability are directly linked to the learning and innovation of organizations. Both innovation and the efficient use of resources to deliver an output still constitute the core business. There are many ways to measure output and input. The output can be broadly defined as the extent the business goal is achieved. It can be measured in terms of tangible output such as value added and corporate revenue, and intangible value such as quality of service provided and the number of people benefited. In intellectual capital studies, the value added in terms of human capital, structural capital or relational capital is also an output. For example, the Value-Added Intellectual Coefficient (VAIC) proposed by Pulic (1998) is an indirect measure of the efficiency of value added. Consequently, the input to achieve an optimal output is more complex in the digital economy as the input is no longer confined to traditional resources of labor, land, and monetary values.

Being a service-oriented economy with the service sector accounting for 93% of the Gross Domestic Product, Hong Kong is an excellent place for this study on the interplay between efficiency and innovation. Moreover Hong

Kong is Asia's most dynamic metropolitan city, well known for its business efficiency. The Institute for Management Development (IMD) in 2017 ranked Hong Kong first out of 63 economies based on four indicators: economic performance, government efficiency, business efficiency, and infrastructure (IMD 2017). In terms of innovation, according to the recent 2018 WIPO Global Innovation Index GII study, Hong Kong has been ranked 14th in the world (Dutta et al. 2018).

Efficiency vs. innovation

The traditional perceptions of innovation and efficiency are paradoxical. Christensen contends that the obsession with efficiency is killing "empowering" innovation (Nisen 2012). He is referring to the fact that current business focuses only on streamlining bottom–line savings and additional profits but ignores the long-term effects of missing disruptive innovations. Martin also argues that "a superefficient dominant model elevates the risk of catastrophic failure" (Martin 2019). James (2019) simply said, "Efficiency is the Enemy of Innovation." Relatively there are few firms able to balance these two emphases (Sarkees & Hulland 2009). In fact, innovation and efficiency do not have to be competitive if we view them through the complexity lens.

Due to advances in ICT, e-business and widespread use of social media, improvement in efficiency nowadays can only be brought about with the use of the latest smart technologies and latest management know-how. Even in the consumer service sectors, many traditional industries such as catering, retailing, logistics, loan services, and insurance seek increasing use of the mobile web, artificial intelligence, big data and internet of things (IoT) to enhance their business efficiency. The purpose of this study is twofold: firstly to identify the factors in people, technology, and processes that can contribute to raising efficiency based on a well-established intellectual capital framework, and secondly, to conduct a survey in industry on the capability of enterprise to sustain efficiency through the measurement of an Enterprise Innovative Efficiency Capability Index (EIECI). Innovative efficiency is different from innovation efficiency. The latter refers to the efficiency of innovation, whereas the former refers to the attainment of efficiency through the innovative use of knowledge (which is an intellectual asset), not by reducing the input of traditional resource alone. The knowledge is seen here as a catalyst (not an input resource) which can raise efficiency without diminishing marginal return.

Measurement of innovative efficiency capability

Composition of the EIECI

To assess Hong Kong's capability to sustain our business efficiency through innovative means, we have developed the Enterprise Innovative Efficiency Capability Index (EIECI). EIECI is a composite index that measures the capability of performing efficient work in an enterprise in an innovative way, that is not by cutting input resources. Efficiency was traditionally measured as a useful output over input (effort, resources, energy). However, this treats efficiency and innovation as opposites. In reality, the two are not competitive nor merely causal but have a complex relationship.

The innovative efficiency capability of organizations leverages the complexity theory and the Intellectual Capital (IC) framework (Fan 2012). IC is defined by Andriessen and Stam (2004: p. 10) as "all intangible resources that are available to an organization, that give a relative advantage, and which in combination can produce future benefits." Researchers and practitioners have put in a great effort to identify how the combination of intangible resources can gain value and improve efficiency.

IC comprises three basic elements: Human Capital (HC), Structural Capital (SC) and Relational Capital (RC). HC refers to the knowledge, skills, experience, and capability that an individual owns and contributes to the organization. SC encompasses process, strategy, culture, infrastructure, and systems. RC deals with the relationship with external entities such as customers, suppliers, and partners. We regard IC as the input, the building of which is essential to build up our capability to sustain our efficiency in business and organizations.

The capability factors arrive through two steps: a comprehensive literature review and an expert view based on the Delphi methodology. Five strategic dimensions under the IC framework are identified that are most relevant to efficiency sustainability in the digital economy. The five dimensions are Strategy (S), Customer-centric (C), Office Environment (O), Process (P), and Empowered Employee (E) dimensions (Figure 5.1). They are composed of their respective sub-dimensions, a total of 14 aspects (Table 5.1). An Enterprise Innovative Efficiency Capability Index (EIECI) is thus measured for each enterprise on their scores (from 0 to 1) in these 14 aspects. An overall EIECI

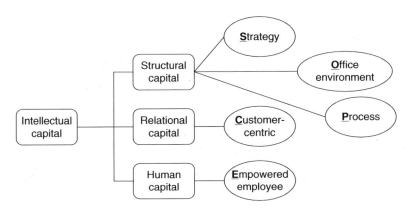

Figure 5.1 The Intellectual Capital Framework of Enterprise Innovative Efficiency Capability (SCOPE).

48 *Irene Y.H. Fan et al.*

Table 5.1 The fourteen aspects of SCOPE

5 Dimensions (SCOPE)	14 Aspects
Strategy	Business Model Innovation
	Open Innovation
	Gamification
	Agility
Customer-centric	Customer Communications & Services
	Service Design Thinking
Office Environment	Smart Office
	Creative Space
Process	Automation
	Use of Data
	IT Adoption
	Knowledge System Adoption
Empowered Employee	Knowledge Worker
	Transformational Leadership

score (out of 100) is calculated to yield an integrated rating of the innovative efficiency capability.

Components of the EIECI

Strategy (S) is one of the three dimensions of Structural Capital this study measures. Strategy is the art and science of planning and using resources for their most efficient and effective use to achieve a desirable future. Modern strategic planning adopts Business Model Innovation, Open Innovation, Gamification methods, and Agility. Business Model Innovation uses new and unique concepts to realign resources, processes, and profit formula with a new customer value proposition. Open Innovation is the use of purposive inflows and outflows of knowledge to accelerate internal innovation, and expand the markets for the external use of innovation, respectively (Chesbrough 2004). Crowdsourcing, open competition, and incubator programs are some examples of Open Innovation. Gamification uses game mechanics and elements in non-game contexts to motivate people's engagement. Companies use gamification to motivate employees and promote customer engagement and loyalty. Agility looks at ways that organizations seek to approach their operations and resources in a flexible, responsive manner when facing changes in the internal and external environment.

Customer-centric (C) measures Relational Capital. Customer Communication and Services measure how creative the organization leverages advanced communication, social media, and mobile marketing technologies and tools. Service Design Thinking measures the aspects of customer focus and co-creation of products or services. The purpose of service design is to design according to the needs of customers or participants so that the service is user-friendly, competitive, and relevant to the customers (Service Design Network 2008).

Smart Offices can create an enhanced user experience that helps to increase productivity, attract and retain talent, support well-being, and promote corporate brand values. Smart buildings can also use space more flexibly and efficiently, reducing costs, and lessening environmental impact (British Land 2017). Besides the physical smart office, the use of office as a Creative Space is also vital for innovative efficiency. It refers to the creative and collaborative working environment that encourages interaction and collaboration among staff as well as with customers and partners. The Smart Office and Creative Space form the Office Environment (O) dimension of the EIECI.

Process (P) is another critical dimension for innovative efficiency. Automation of business processes and decision-making improves the efficiency of the operation of an organization significantly. The ability to collect, analyze, and use the enormous data volume that can be managed internally and externally is crucial in today's business world. The adoption of advanced Information Technologies in business operation, communication, and collaboration is indispensable. In a Knowledge Economy, the utilization of Knowledge System to conduct knowledge storage, organization, and sharing is also critical.

Finally, Empowered Employee (E) forms the last dimension of EIECI and measures the critical elements of Human Capital in two ways. Peter Drucker (1999) suggested that "the most valuable asset of a 21st-century institution will be its knowledge workers and their productivity." Knowledge Workers manage themselves to capture, generate, use, and share their knowledge to accomplish their work. On the other hand, Transformational Leadership is required to enable the Knowledge Workers to manifest their full potential by coaching and encouraging them.

Weighting of the capability factors

Ten international industry and academic experts were invited to weight the importance of different dimensions and aspects of the EIECI. The weighting among the five SCOPE dimensions does not differ significantly, but they do represent the expert view in order of importance. The essential factor is Employee, followed by Customer, Process, Office, and Strategy. The expert weighting with respect to the 14 aspects is shown in Figure 5.2. The expert opinion of importance has been used for weighting factors in calculating the EIECI scores.

The study of EIECI in Hong Kong industry

Methodology

The study adopted the pragmatic paradigm and was based on two approaches: (1) pragmatic research that allows the integration of quantitative and qualitative

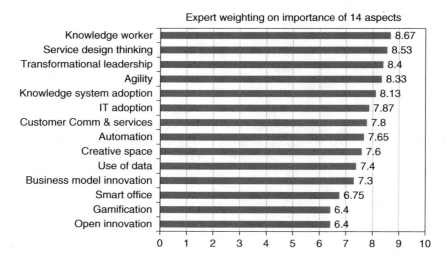

Figure 5.2 Expert weighting on the importance of SCOPE aspects.

methods, (2) multi-case method that enables a more in-depth and thorough understanding of the research problem with context. A quantitative study in the form of a survey was conducted, and then a qualitative study followed to validate the findings. To be specific, the whole study was divided into two stages. In stage 1, based on previous knowledge and research results on organizational innovation capability, a composite index was developed to measure the innovative efficiency capability based on a multi-dimensional systemic model. A survey was constructed based on this index model, which was then validated with selected enterprises. In stage 2, selected enterprises were invited to participate in the study. The data collected were analyzed with a standard statistical package to generate descriptive data, which was then consolidated as an analysis report on the innovative efficiency capability of the participating enterprises. By participating in this study, enterprises could gain a new perspective on and quick evaluation of their business efficiency and inspiration about technological innovations and best practices.

Survey

An online web-based survey was launched on May 8, 2017. The collection of survey responses took place between May 8 and June 13. Each enterprise who returned the survey received an individual report on their EIECI index. A random validation was done by calling 5% of the sample to check their answers on the phone. Based on the 100 samples collected, the data was aggregated and analyzed for the overall and sector-based analyses.

The study was based in Hong Kong, and only enterprises in Hong Kong were selected for distribution of the online survey. The study asked to which

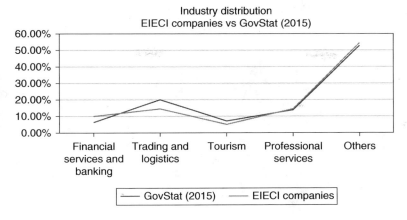

Figure 5.3 Sample industry distribution vs. government statistics.

industry each participating companies belonged. A total of 19 different industries were reported which were categorized into 6 groups as below:

(i) Financial Services and Banking
(ii) Trading and Logistics
(iii) Tourism
(iv) Professional Services and other producer services
(v) Manufacturing
(vi) Others

The sample distribution is very similar to the Hong Kong industry distribution when comparing the sample with the HKSAR government data in Four Key Industries (Census and Statistics Department of HKSAR 2017) (Figure 5.3). Manufacturing has been grouped with other industries for comparison purposes.

Company size

The questionnaire used the OECD classification for Size of Enterprise: micro enterprises (fewer than 10 employees), small enterprises (10 to 49 employees), medium-sized enterprises (50 to 249 employees), and large enterprises (250 or more employees). The sample was 66% small to medium sized enterprises (SMEs) and 34% large enterprises (Figure 5.4). When compared to Hong Kong statistics, the classification was adjusted to match the definition of HKSAR classifications. For the manufacturing sector enterprises with fewer than 250 people were classified as SMEs, whereas for the non-manufacturing sector SMEs constituted enterprises with fewer than 50 people. Consequently the sample

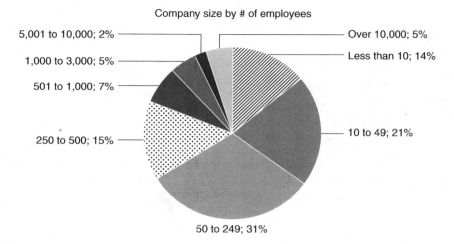

Figure 5.4 Company size distribution.

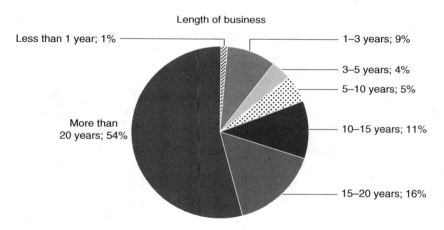

Figure 5.5 Length of business distribution.

was 60% large enterprises and 40% SMEs. The Hong Kong statistics reported that the SME percentage of Hong Kong industries is over 98%. The differences were likely caused by the SME to large enterprise ratio of the database used.

Length of business

The sample included more businesses with an extended period of operation (Figure 5.5). Over 81% of the sample had been in operation for over 10 years.

Only 10% of the organizations were businesses that had been operating for under 3 years.

Survey results

The EIECI overall score was 42.24 (D Grade). This implies, on average, the companies have low innovative efficiency capability. They are inferior in some of the aspects of innovative efficiency capability and need to act to avoid lagging the competitors. Over 72% of the respondents scored "Low" or "Insufficient." Only 8% of the respondents scored "Good" or "Excellent." This demonstrates the room for improvement for Hong Kong industry on innovative efficiency capability is high.

Among the five dimensions of SCOPE, Empowered Employee scored the highest with 0.67. The other four dimensions all scored in the range 0.37–0.39. A further breakdown of the 14 aspects is depicted in Figure 5.6. Transformational Leadership and Knowledge Worker scored highest, followed by Agility. The bottom three aspects are Open Innovation, Gamification, and Use of Data.

Among the four pillar industries, Manufacturing and Other Industries and Financial Services and Banking stand out as 10% scored "Excellent." Tourism had 20% scored "Good," moreover this was the industry category that had the highest combined percentage for "Excellent" and "Good." Manufacturing, on the other hand, had the highest score for "Insufficient" and "Low."

The study further analyzed the different results of the industry sectors in SCOPE and the 14 aspects (see Figure 5.7). It is noted that Tourism outperformed the other industries in all dimensions except Process. Financial Services and Banking had the best result in Process and came second or third in all other dimensions. Trading and Logistics rated the lowest in Office Environment

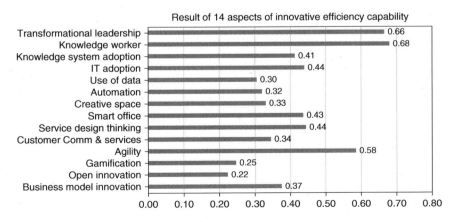

Figure 5.6 EIECI survey results on the 14 aspects.

	Financial services and banking	Trading and logistics	Tourism	Professional services and other producer services	Manufacturing	Others	Overall
EIECI index	45.70	38.05	48.08	37.20	38.02	45.75	42.24
Strategy	0.38	0.35	0.42	0.32	0.32	0.41	0.37
Customer-centric	0.41	0.29	0.56	0.34	0.36	0.42	0.39
Office environment	0.42	0.34	0.47	0.35	0.34	0.41	0.39
Process	0.45	0.32	0.34	0.30	0.32	0.40	0.37
Empowered employee	0.68	0.65	0.76	0.63	0.64	0.69	0.67
Business model innovation	0.44	0.34	0.41	0.39	0.30	0.38	0.37
Open innovation	0.19	0.20	0.24	0.12	0.18	0.28	0.22
Gamification	0.29	0.17	0.32	0.14	0.13	0.33	0.25
Agility	0.53	0.61	0.65	0.53	0.58	0.60	0.58
Customer comm&services	0.38	0.26	0.52	0.23	0.30	0.40	0.34
Service design thinking	0.44	0.34	0.60	0.47	0.43	0.46	0.44
Smart office	0.46	0.37	0.51	0.43	0.42	0.45	0.44
Creative space	0.38	0.29	0.43	0.26	0.26	0.37	0.33
Automation	0.45	0.27	0.21	0.24	0.26	0.36	0.32
Use of data	0.40	0.25	0.30	0.21	0.22	0.37	0.30
IT adoption	0.46	0.41	0.49	0.39	0.42	0.46	0.44
Knowledge system adoption	0.49	0.36	0.37	0.38	0.39	0.43	0.41
Knowledge worker	0.67	0.66	0.79	0.63	0.65	0.70	0.68
Transformational leadership	0.69	0.63	0.72	0.62	0.62	0.69	0.66

Figure 5.7 EIECI survey results on the 14 aspects by industry.

and Customer-centric. Professional Services and other producer services and Manufacturing were both mid-stream. Neither the "Other" industry category, which is not among the traditional four pillar industries, nor Manufacturing had a very balanced rating, running second or third in all dimensions. A closer look at the 14 aspects of EIECI reveals that all industries had higher capabilities in the Human Capital category – Knowledge Workers with Transformational Leadership. This confirms the quality of human resources in Hong Kong. Agility also stood out as another high capability.

The Financial Services and Banking industry led in some areas: Automation, Use of Data, Knowledge System Adoption, and Business Model Innovation. This echoes the understanding of Hong Kong as one of the world's key financial hubs. Tourism led in 8 out of 14 aspects: Knowledge Workers, Transformational Leadership, IT Adoption, Smart Office, Creative Space, Agility, Customer Communication and Services, and Service Design Thinking. Particularly in the Customer-centric related aspects, Tourism has a significant lead compared to other industries, except in the aspect of Automation, for which it had the lowest score. The highest ratings in the remaining two aspects, Open Innovation and Gamification, went to the non-traditional non-manufacturing industries. Education Services scored high in both aspects. Other leading industry categories included Information and Communication; Retail, Accommodation and Food Services; Public Administration, Social and Personal Services. It is worth noting that Professional Services and Other Producer Services, as one of the four pillars of Hong Kong industry, ranked lowest in the overall EIECI score in 3 out of 5 dimensions (Strategy, Process, Empowered Employee) and 8 out of 14 aspects. Trading and Logistics, another pillar, had three of the lowest scores, in Service Design Thinking, Smart Office, and Knowledge System Adoption.

Interviews and good practices

Four enterprises were also interviewed to collect data regarding their good practices in innovative efficiency works. Among the sample, two enterprises earned a relatively high EIECI score. Both were from the industry of Professional Services and Other Producer Services. They excelled in most of the aspects measured in EIECI and outperformed their peers in the same industry. Their good practices were identified and further analyzed to verify and demonstrate the EIECI dimensions.

The backgrounds of the companies are compared in Figure 5.8.

Their scores are compared as depicted in Figure 5.9.

Service design thinking and gamification

Company A scored full marks in the Service Design Thinking aspect. Company A, being an engineering consultancy firm, regards themselves as designers. They aim to provide total solutions/design to clients, meaning that they strike for a holistic solution instead of a sub-optimal one. They take into account as many aspects as possible in formulating the best way to fulfill clients' needs. To equip staff with the necessary skills, they set up systematic training. For junior to middle-level staff, a three-day design school is organized twice every year. There is a new theme for the design school each time, and to encourage staff to think out of the box not all the themes are directly related to the daily operations. The latest one was on Collective Sensemaking to Innovation (CSI). The acronym of this theme, CSI, is the same as that of "Crime Scene Investigation," and the storyline behind the games/tasks were similarly about crime. For example, one survival game was designed with the idea that participants would understand that if they could not innovate faster than others, they would not survive in the market. In another activity, the competition was to win the "Amazing Race." Participants had to go to various checkpoints to collect as many essential pieces

Company code	Industry	Company size (No. of employees)	Year of history	Listed or non-listed	MAKE award winner?*
A	Professional services and other producer services	~2600	~40 years	Non-listed	Yes
B	Financial services and banking	Over 2,800	~25 years	Non-listed	No
C	Real estate	~8,000	~35 years	Listed	No
D	Professional services and other producer services	~15000	~50 years	Non-listed	Yes

Figure 5.8 Background information of the interviewed companies.
* MAKE Award stands for Most Admired Knowledge Enterprise Award.

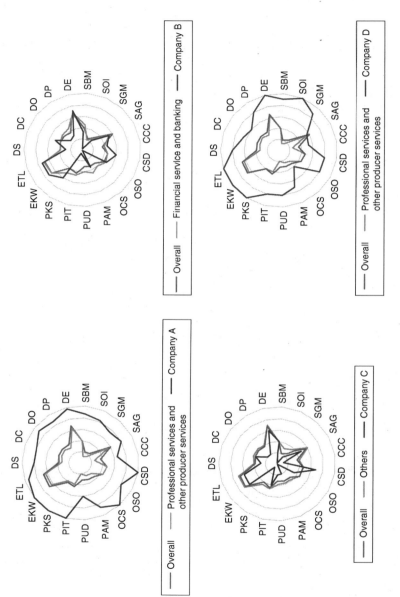

Figure 5.9 Results of the four interviewed companies.

of evidence as possible and as fast as possible. This was designed to challenge the participants physically and mentally. For senior staff, there is also a two-day conceptual design mastery course. Moreover, for staff who will soon be promoted to the "Director" grade, training on innovation is provided as is training on how they can help the company win in services.

Company D recently launched the use of "badges" for contracted staff. As long as they completed their job satisfactorily within the contract period, they would obtain "badges." With these "badges," they became the approved workers of the company. They could then add these "badges" to their profiles on professional networking websites like LinkedIn to increase their credibility. The company also plans to roll out a similar program for permanent staff. They are also actively exploring the feasibility of other online/electronic games for training purposes.

Knowledge worker

Company D has a town hall meeting regularly to update employees about the recent projects and future plans of the company during which there is also a discussion session. They organize a two-day event to recruit potential candidates through challenging activities coached by their staff. Such types of activity are planned to be held for internal employees as well. There is also a program to encourage staff to submit their innovative ideas. A panel consisting of various management-level staff would assess the feasibility of the ideas. The winners will receive awards, and the selected ideas will be implemented in the company. The company also has a corporate university for staff training and development. A new large learning center for training will also be in use soon.

Unlike other corporate universities which focus on soft skills training, Company A also operates a company university which aims to train up staff's soft skills as well as technical skills. There are three levels of corporate training in Company A: (1) Continuous Professional Development (CPD); (2) Master Module; and (3) Doctoral Module. For the CPD, topics will be about the latest trends/updates from the market or project teams. For the Master Module, Company A collaborates with various universities (e.g. MIT, University of Cambridge, Boston University) to operate a one-year Master's degree course for their staff as well as clients. Another Master Module on machine learning will be run next year because Company A plans to replace routine work with machine learning. For the Doctoral Module, they will sponsor high-performing staff to pursue a Ph.D. Moreover, they operate over 40 skills networks (equivalent to Communities of Practices, CoP) for all skills leaders to share their knowledge.

Company C scored the second highest in the Knowledge Worker aspect. The company offers a certain amount of subsidy for each employee to take courses/programs of their choice, which may or may not be directly related to their the nature of their job. This is very different from the practices of other companies. Furthermore, they invite external experts or even competitors to share their experiences and insights and, in turn, give seminars to other organizations, like government departments, as knowledge sharing. One point to note is that they do not have a program internally to train up staff as they usually hire experienced staff / qualified professionals who have a certain level of knowledge already.

Transformational leadership

Company B scored the highest in the Transformational Leadership aspect. Company B does not follow the conventional top–down approach for the management of the company. It prefers a flexible management style, meaning that it provides a set of guidelines/instructions for employees to follow while still allowing a certain flexibility. The degree of flexibility given depends on the nature of the departments. For example, for departments related to projects, more flexibility is allowed while for those concerned with underwriting or compliance, there are more restrictions. Also, the company encourages staff to share their ideas, a practice their staff have become used to. They can share their new ideas verbally, through email, or during regular meetings. Once the company receives these ideas, certain staff members are responsible for filtering out ideas and exploring their feasibility (similar to a pre-project study).

Company D has great leaders who are willing to support projects initiated by staff as long as the proposed projects make commercial sense. There is a knowledge culture program for employees to share best practices. Recently they launched a new program helping employees build their personal brand. Employees are required to develop their profile on the internal platform and specify their special knowledge/skills, and what and how they have contributed to the company in the past so that others can locate and approach them in case needs arise. This internal platform is also connected to LinkedIn. An innovative feature of this program is that the marketing department helps promote the employees on social media, making them famous for specific knowledge not only internally but also externally. With this program, the company hopes to encourage the personal development of staff and raise their awareness of the importance of building their own brand.

Open innovation

Company A offers internal funding to various research projects (either internal projects or joint projects with external parties like universities and think tanks). There are currently around 500 research projects running globally. They also embrace the concept of open innovation and are very willing to share their knowledge with partners. Activities like open forums are frequently held to facilitate the exchange of ideas. For example, recently, an open forum on social innovation was held in a university in Hong Kong.

Use of data

Company D has the technology needed to capture and analyze useful data. There are many regulations and restrictions regarding the use of data. The company is still exploring the best way to optimize the use of data.

As the government has imposed strict guidelines on insurance practitioners, Company B is very sensitive to any use of customer data. They make customers' privacy their priority. They protect the customer data the best they can and therefore prefer not to use the data for further analytical purposes. At the same time, the top management team of Company B has changed a few times over the past years. A substantial amount of resources will be needed to integrate different types of data into a single database with a standard format before analysis can be done.

Company C, in general, does not have an IT system to capture market intelligence data and does not utilize any significant data technique to make predictions or corporate policy decisions. They are lacking experience in using big data. Applications and location sensors are now available in some shopping malls, but big data analysis is not adopted. They mentioned, however, that such a big data approach would be useful for future property development and rental market analysis, for example, locating stores in a shopping mall to suit the needs/preferences of customers.

Information technology adoption and automation

Company A is undergoing a digital transformation process. For example, they use dashboards to monitor the usage of their printing and scanning system. An app was developed to aid visualization of the designs. Users can use the app to scan a drawing, and the app will return either a static view (3-D view) or even a dynamic view of the design. They also make use of laser scanning technology to facilitate the building design. How to fully utilize AI (Artificial Intelligence), VR (Virtual Reality), and MR (Mixed Reality) techniques is also a priority task. They also help clients transform digitally.

Company B obtained a low score in the Information Technology Adoption aspect. There is no software specifically for business process management, customer relationship management, or video conferencing, though they are currently implementing a collaboration tool for multi-channel communication. Also, they do not utilize any big data, data mining, or data analytics techniques. They considered the possibility of adopting the big data approach before but found that substantial resources are required for enhancement of the existing system. Even the present customer portal captures some customer data, but analysis of these types of data is rare. For artificial intelligence (AI), they do not regard it as very useful for the company because, for example, customers prefer to talk with a real person instead of a computerized assistant on issues like insurance claims.

Company C has a rather low score in the Automation aspect. The company has a "Document Management System," but not every department adopts such a system. Some management staff prefer hard rather than soft copies as they claim that the uploading and downloading time is extended. Moreover, the drawings of building designs are quite large in size, and without suitable equipment, viewing them electronically would not be convenient or even possible. Also, they use prefabricated façades for some building projects in which standardized parts are available in the design, but no automatic construction method is deployed at their construction sites. They are also testing a "paperless" approach in their office, but it is still in the infancy stage.

Further involvement of various departments to streamline the administrative procedures leading to paperless operation will be required. At construction sites, such a paperless approach is rather difficult because dust is everywhere, which do not suit the use of electronic devices. Some of their competitors in the industry are already using a mobile application to facilitate construction management. The feasibility of such an approach in the company is worth exploring.

Company D has used mobile technologies to automate some daily processes. For example, booking a meeting room and staff appraisal can also be conducted using a mobile phone. There are still processes that are not yet automated. For instance, staff still have to submit an expense claim in hard copy form.

Conclusion

From the survey of 100 companies in various sectors of Hong Kong industry, it was found that the Tourism and the Financial Services and Banking sectors have the highest rating scores. This is in line with the fact that these two are among the top four key industries in the Hong Kong economy. In terms of the 14 components surveyed, these companies rated themselves highest in Leadership, quality of Knowledge Workers, and Agility. The factors which received the lowest ratings were Use of Data and Automation; also weak were the adoption of Gamification and Open Innovation as their company strategy. The findings, though expected, clearly indicate the areas where enterprises need to pay more effort to build up their structural capability to sustain future business efficiency.

Both innovation and efficiency are essential for enterprises, industries, and countries for the long term and for sustainable development. The conventional quantitative measurement of efficiency ignores the complexity and systemic reality between input and output of innovation. This project aims to develop a comprehensive index that examines the performance of enterprises on their capability to sustain their business efficiency in the changing digital economy. Enterprises who participated in the study benefited through an understanding of the critical sustainability factors and identified possible ways to improve.

Acknowledgment

The authors wish to thank Fuji Xerox (HK) for the financial support to launch this study in Hong Kong and the companies who took part in the study.

References

Al-Mashari, M. & Zairi, M. (1999), "BPR implementation process: an analysis of key success and failure factors," *Business process management journal, 5*(1), pp.87–112.

Andriessen, D. & Stam, C. (2004), "The intellectual capital of the European Union/measuring the Lisbon Agenda," Center for Research in Intellectual Capital, Holland University of Professional Education, Alkmaar.

British Land (2017), *Smart offices: a 2017 vision for the future*, British Land. http://officeagenda.britishland.com/assets/pdfs/smart-offices.pdf.

Census and Statistics Department of HKSAR (2017), *Hong Kong monthly digest of statistics*, May 2017. A Feature Article. www.statistics.gov.hk/pub/B10100022017MM05B0100.pdf.

Chesbrough, H. (2004), "Managing open innovation," *Research-technology management, 47*(1), pp.23–26.

Drucker, P.F. (1999), "Knowledge-worker productivity: the biggest challenge," *California management review, 41*(2), pp.79–94.

Dutta, S., Reynoso, R.E., Garanasvili, A., Saxena, K., Lanvin, B., Wunsch-Vincent, S., León, L.R. & Guadagno, F. (2018), "The global innovation index 2018: energizing the world with innovation," *Global innovation index 2018*, p.1.

Fan, I.Y.H. (2012). A study of the relationship between intellectual capital and innovation performance based on complexity theory, doctoral thesis, Hong Kong Polytechnic University, Hong Kong.

Hammer, M. & Champy, J. (1990), "Introduction to business process reengineering," *Industry week, 1*, Harvard University, USA.

The Institute for Management Development (2017), *The 2017 IMD world competitiveness ranking*, viewed May 16, 2019, www.imd.org/globalassets/wcc/docs/release-2017/2017-world_competitiveness_ranking.pdf.

James, G. (2019), "Efficiency is the enemy of innovation," Inc.com, viewed May 16, 2019, www.inc.com/geoffrey-james/efficiency-is-enemy-of-innovation.html.

Martin, R.L. (2019), "The high price of efficiency," *Harvard business review, 97*(1), pp.42–55.

Nisen, M. (2012), "Clay Christensen: why our obsession with efficiency is killing innovation," *Business insider*, December 12. www.businessinsider.com/clay-christensen-our-obsession-with-efficiency-is-killing-innovation-2012-12.

Nwabueze, U. & Kanji, G.K. (1997), "A systems management approach for business process re-engineering," *Total quality management, 8*(5), pp.281–292.

Pulic, A. (1998), "Measuring the performance of intellectual potential in knowledge economy," in *2nd McMaster World Congress on Measuring and Managing Intellectual Capital by the Austrian Team for Intellectual Potential*, pp.1–20. Hamilton, Ontario, Canada. https://pdfs.semanticscholar.org/708b/ebbe69caebcd281c5e18425cc645cee9816d.pdf

Sarkees, M. & Hulland, J. (2009), "Innovation and efficiency: it is possible to have it all," *Business horizons, 52*(1), pp.45–55.

Service Design Network (2008), "What is Service Design?," *Service design network*, viewed August 17, 2018, www.service-design-network.org/intro/.

Taylor, F. (1911), *The principles of scientific management*, Harper & Brothers, USA.

6 A comprehensive analysis of the importance of intellectual capital elements to support contemporary developments in Chinese firms

Gang Liu, Aino Kianto and Eric Tsui

Introduction

The knowledge-based approach to organisational competitiveness has emerged as a key perspective for understanding organisational performance, and intellectual capital is now widely seen as a key driver of organisational success and competitive advantage. Intellectual capital refers to the possession of the knowledge, applied experience, organisational technology, customer relationships and professional skills that provide a company with a competitive edge in the market (Edvinsson and Malone, 1997). While there exists widespread agreement that intellectual capital significantly impacts organisational performance (e.g. Roos et al., 1997; Al-Ali, 2003; Kamukama et al., 2011; Hussinki et al., 2017; Buenechea-Elberdin et al., 2018; Cabrilo et al., 2018; Iqbal et al., 2019; Kengatharan, 2019), the significance of intellectual capital in emerging economies, such as China, is less well understood (Kanchana and Mohan, 2017; Kianto et al., 2018).

Since the Chinese economic reforms and open-door policy of 1978, China's economy has grown dramatically. It is now the second-largest global economy after the United States (Claus and Oxley, 2014) and is predicted to surpass the United States in economic aggregate around 2020 (Fouré et al., 2012). China's unprecedented economic success over the past several decades has primarily depended on economies of scale in labour-intensive industries rather than on knowledge-based approaches such as invention and innovation (Fan, 2014). However, it is important for China to transform its economic growth patterns from a tangible resource-based economy to a knowledge-based model in which many of the tasks and activities involve knowledge-intensive decision-making.

In response, the Chinese government has proposed the national priority codenamed 'Made in China 2025' that aims to upgrade the manufacturing capabilities of Chinese firms to smart factories and the development of smart homes and smart cities (Li, 2018). While machine automation underpins a key part of the 'Made in China 2025' motive, human skills are needed to harness and analyse the data collected from deployed sensors and equipment, as well as to leverage the use of cloud-based inter- and intra- collaboration systems for

IC in the development of Chinese firms   63

distributed processing and to apply collective wisdom. Indeed, the term 'cyber-physical systems' (Lee et al., 2015) has been created to describe integrated systems that can sense and execute appropriate responses to an operating environment with pre-programmed human input that uses real-time analyses of data collected from functioning equipment and the external environment.

To better understand the relevance of intellectual capital for organisational performance in the Chinese context, and in particular the interplay among the different components of intellectual capital and their impacts on organisational performance, this chapter seeks to address the question of how intellectual capital impacts organisational performance in Chinese firms. Previous studies on the intellectual capital-performance relationship have tended to focus on either financial or innovation performance indicators (e.g. Bontis et al., 2000; Kianto et al., 2013; Liu et al., 2017). The present study seeks to widen the scope of study and to explore the value of intellectual capital from the perspective of two key company stakeholders: employees and customers. This study therefore not only provides new data on intellectual capital in an emerging economy but also deepens the field's understanding of intellectual capital's benefits for both employees and customers.

Literature review and hypothesis development

According to Sullivan (2000), intellectual capital is defined as the hidden value of an organisation that can be transformed into profit. Intellectual capital can be broadly divided into three categories: human capital, structural capital and relational capital (Kwee, 2008). Human capital is related to the skills, competence and knowledge of an organisation's employees (Sveiby, 1997) and cannot be owned by an organisation (Edvinsson and Malone, 1997; Stewart, 1997), while structural capital concerns knowledge that remains in the possession of an organisation when individual employees leave (Sveiby, 1997). Finally, relational capital refers to the relationships among all the stakeholders of an organisation (Kwee, 2008), and can be further classified as internal relational capital and external relational capital. Internal relational capital refers to all relational capital within an organisation, whilst external relational capital refers to all relational capital between an organisation and its external stakeholders, such as vendors, customers and governments.

However, although it is widely believed that a firm's employees, and their knowledge, are the firm's most important resources. Evidence about the relationships among the different intellectual capital elements is varied and somewhat contradictory. For instance, some studies have reported significant positive relationships among human capital, structural capital and relational capital (Bontis et al., 2000; Wang and Chang, 2005), while others have found such relationships to be insignificant (Zhang and Wan, 2006; Cheng et al., 2010). Empirical studies on the relationship between firm performance and intellectual capital, including human capital, structural capital and relational capital, have also reported inconsistent results, with some studies indicating that all are relevant to firm performance (Zhang and Wan, 2006; Kamukama et al., 2010) and others have found that only some components of intellectual capital exert an impact on organisational outcomes (e.g. Chu et al., 2011). In addition, the indicators used to measure firm performance have varied between studies, making comparisons difficult. In particular, the relationships among relational capital, customer value creation and employee job satisfaction are still poorly understood. Further research on these relationships is therefore necessary (Liu and Lee, 2016), and in the present study, we set out to evaluate seven novel hypotheses.

First, since employees are responsible for developing a firm's structural capital (Kianto et al., 2017), hypothesis 1 (H1) is that there is a positive relationship between human capital and structural capital.

Second and third, since structural capital (e.g. business processes, collaboration tools, databases) facilitates communication between employees, suppliers and customers, hypothesis 2 (H2) is that there is a positive relationship between structural capital and external relational capital, and hypothesis 3 (H3) is that there is a positive relationship between structural capital and internal relational capital.

Fourth, customer value creation is a competitive advantage that can distinguish a firm from its competitors (Ulaga, 2001; Wang et al., 2004). Since external relational capital is an indicator of a firm's relationships with external stakeholders, hypothesis 4 (H4) proposes that there is a positive relationship between external relational capital and customer value creation. Further, although many studies have investigated the relationship between a firm's intellectual capital and its financial performance, relatively few studies have assessed firms' market performance directly. For example, Hussinki et al. (2017) argued that a firm's superior market performance could result from higher intellectual capital and knowledge management practices, but clear quantitative relationships are missing. It is possible that customer knowledge and collaboration significantly affect a firm's marketing effectiveness (Taherparvar et al., 2014; Fidel et al., 2015). Therefore, our hypothesis 6 (H6) is that there is a positive relationship between a firm's customer value creation and its market performance.

Since support and encouragement from colleagues could improve employee job satisfaction and therefore performance (Kianto et al., 2016), hypotheses 5 (H5) is that there is a positive relationship between a firm's internal relational capital and its employees' job satisfaction. Additionally, ever since the Hawthorne studies of the late 1920s and 1930s, it has been believed that employee job satisfaction significantly impacts individual job performance (Petty et al., 1984) and therefore ultimately impacts firm performance (Robbins et al., 2013). Hypothesis 7 (H7) therefore seeks to test the assumption that there is a positive relationship between a firm's employee satisfaction and the firm's market performance.

Figure 6.1 presents this study's research model.

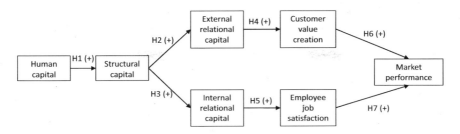

Figure 6.1 Research model.

Research methodology

To address these research questions, a questionnaire validated in previous studies (Hussinki et al., 2017; Hussinki et al., 2018) was used to collect data from Chinese firms. The original English questionnaire was translated into Chinese and then retranslated back into English to check for translation errors, and prior to implementation the questionnaire was preliminarily distributed to several firms in order to identify and rectify any misunderstandings. The primary sample was drawn from a list of companies in a database of Ningbo University alumni or collaborators. An Internet-based survey was also conducted across China to supplement the data collection.

In total, we received 139 valid responses, thereby meeting the requirement of sufficient sample size for data analysis. Around one third (34%) of respondents were managers and directors, while the rest held various other professional positions within their companies. The majority (66%) of respondents were from the city of Ningbo, while 14% were from Shenzhen, 6% were from Shanghai and 2% were from Beijing; the rest were from other cities. Large firms (>1000 employees) and medium-sized firms (300–1000 employees) each accounted for about 22% of respondents, while small firms (<300 employees) accounted for another 14%; the remaining firms did not specify their size.

Empirical results

Structural equation modelling was used to test each of the seven hypotheses. Since a multivariate normal distribution of data underlies the maximum likelihood method in structural equation modelling path analysis, it was first necessary to test if our data were approximately normally distributed. The assessment of normality was conducted by AMOS (version 21). All of the variables' skewness and kurtosis values were within the recommended range, indicating that the data were approximately normally distributed and could be used in maximum likelihood structural equation modelling estimations.

66 Gang Liu et al.

Table 6.1 Data validity

Construct	Item	SE (≥0.5)	AVE (≥0.5)	CR. (≥0.7)
Internal relational capital	IRC01	0.749	0.5910	0.8116
	IRC02	0.702		
	IRC03	0.848		
External relational capital	ERC01	0.864	0.7211	0.8857
	ERC02	0.807		
	ERC03	0.875		
Structural capital	SC01	0.735	0.6077	0.8226
	SC02	0.776		
	SC03	0.825		
Human capital	HC01	0.743	0.6061	0.8217
	HC02	0.811		
	HC03	0.780		
Market performance	MP01	0.841	0.5992	0.8158
	MP02	0.649		
	MP03	0.818		
Customer value creation	CV01	0.802	0.5951	0.9112
	CV02	0.810		
	CV03	0.806		
	CV04	0.723		
	CV05	0.724		
	CV06	0.730		
	CV07	0.798		
Employee job satisfaction	EJS01	0.832	0.7246	0.8402
	EJS02	0.870		

Scale reliability was assessed by calculating alpha values using SPSS (version 21); the values ranged from 0.809 to 0.913, indicating sufficient reliability of all the scales. The validity of the data was assessed using average value extracted (AVE) and composite reliability (CR) measures (see Table 6.1). AVE measures the amount of variance that is captured by a construct in relation to the amount of variance due to measurement error; all of our AVE values were above 0.5, indicating that our selected constructs could explain most of the data variance (Fornell and Larcker, 1981). Similarly, valid CR measures should be 0.6 or higher (Bagozzi and Yi, 1988), and all of our CR values above 0.8 (as shown in Table 6.1), indicating that the validity of our data was well within acceptable ranges.

The fit statistics ($\chi 2$ = 429.964, df = 244, p = 0.000, $\chi 2/df$ = 1.762, RMSEA = 0.074, SRMR = 0.0688, NNFI = 0.904, CFI = 0.915), as shown in Table 6.2, indicated that our model demonstrated an acceptable level in total fit. The data also demonstrated support for each of our seven hypotheses: we found that human capital was fundamental to increasing structural capital (H1; C.R. = 7.894, $p<0.001$); that structural capital positively influenced both internal relational capital (H2; C.R. = 9.835, $p < 0.001$) and external relational capital (H3; C.R. = 9.255, $p<0.001$); that external relational capital was also positively

Table 6.2 Goodness-of-fit statistics of research model

Fit index	$\chi 2$(freedom)	p	$\chi 2/df$	RMSEA	SRMR	NNFI	CFI
Result	429.964(244)	0.000	1.762	0.074	0.0688	0.904	0.915
Recommended cut-off value	/	p≥0.01	≤3	≤0.08	≤0.1	≥0.9	≥0.9

Table 6.3 Results of hypotheses test for research model

	Estimate	S.E.	C.R.	p	Result
HC → SC	0.930	0.118	7.894	***	Supported
SC → ERC	0.781	0.084	9.255	***	Supported
SC → IRC	0.892	0.091	9.835	***	Supported
ERC → CVC	0.864	0.097	8.942	***	Supported
IRC → EJS	0.742	0.085	8.742	***	Supported
CVC → MP	0.573	0.111	5.174	***	Supported
EJS → MP	0.290	0.101	2.871	0.004**	Supported

*** $p<0.001$ (two-tailed) ** $p<0.01$ (two-tailed) * $p<0.05$ (two-tailed)
Note: HC: human capital; SC: structural capital; ERC: external relational capital; IRC: internal relational capital; CVC: customer value creation; EJS: employee job satisfaction; MP: market performance.

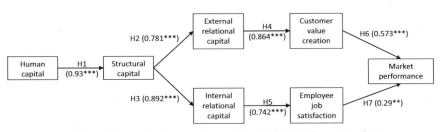

*** p<0.001(two-tailed); ** p<0.01 (two-tailed); * p<0.05 (two-tailed); n.s: not significant

Figure 6.2 Path coefficients and effects of the research model.

related to customer value creation (H4; C.R. = 8.942, $p < 0.001$); that internal relational capital was beneficial to employee job satisfaction (H5; C.R. = 8.742, $p < 0.001$); and that better market performance was associated with customer value creation (H6; C.R. = 5.174, $p<0.001$) and employee job satisfaction (H7; C.R. = 2.871, $p < 0.01$). Model results are detailed in Table 6.3 and Figure 6.2.

Human capital, structural capital and customer value creation exerted a stronger influence on market performance than internal relational capital and external relational capital. Our results moreover suggested that market performance could grow by magnitudes of 0.538, 0.579 and 0.573, respectively, if human capital, structural capital and customer value creation were increased by

68 Gang Liu et al.

Table 6.4 Direct, indirect and total effect analysis

Effect	Dependent Independent	SC	IRC	ERC	EJS	CVC	MP
Direct effect	Human capital	0.930	0	0	0	0	0
	Structural capital	0	0.892	0.781	0	0	0
	Internal relational capital	0	0	0	0.742	0	0
	External relational capital	0	0	0	0	0.864	0
	Employee job satisfaction	0	0	0	0	0	0.290
	Customer value creation	0	0	0	0	0	0.573
Indirect effect	Human capital	0	0.829	0.726	0.616	0.627	0.538
	Structural capital	0	0	0	0.662	0.675	0.579
	Internal relational capital	0	0	0	0	0	0.216
	External relational capital	0	0	0	0	0	0.495
	Employee job satisfaction	0	0	0	0	0	0
	Customer value creation	0	0	0	0	0	0
Total effect	Human capital	0.930	0.829	0.726	0.616	0.627	0.538
	Structural capital	0	0.892	0.781	0.662	0.675	0.579
	Internal relational capital	0	0	0	0.742	0	0.216
	External relational capital	0	0	0	0	0.864	0.495
	Employee job satisfaction	0	0	0	0	0	0.290
	Customer value creation	0	0	0	0	0	0.573

a magnitude of 1. However, among all intellectual capital components, internal relational capital had the greatest influence on employee job satisfaction in terms of both direct and indirect effects, while external relational capital had the most impact on customer value creation. Detailed results of the direct, indirect and total effect analyses are shown in Table 6.4.

Discussion

Few studies have evaluated the benefits of intellectual capital investment in the context of China as it enters the 'Industrial Internet' (also sometimes called the Industry 4.0) era. The key overall finding of this study is that intellectual capital investments yields various types of performance-related benefits for Chinese companies, lending strong empirical support to the national 'Made in China 2025' campaign.

Intellectual capital includes a number of different components, of which we found structural capital to have the strongest impact on a firm's market performance. In this respect, our findings echo those of Chu et al. (2011) and Kianto et al. (2018), which found that structural capital is an especially prevalent intangible value driver in the Chinese context. However, it should be noted that those studies only assessed the direct impacts of intellectual capital components and did not consider the components' interrelationships and conversions. The present study thus complements and extends previous knowledge by demonstrating the interrelationships among human capital, structural capital, internal relational capital and external relational capital.

Contrary to the findings of Bontis et al. (2000), our research model indicated that structural capital in Chinese firms plays a mediating role between human capital and internal relational capital as well as external relational capital, suggesting that structural capital is beneficial for building both stronger internal relational capital and external relational capital. In fact, we found that information technology tools, business processes and other components of structural capital can facilitate a firm's both internal (internal relational capital) and external (external relational capital) relationships organisations. In practice, this can be interpreted to mean that a Chinese firm's success depends not only on its strong internal knowledge, process management and information technology, but also on its employees' abilities to identify, develop, deploy and operate new products and services in the newly developing smart factories, homes and cities. A firm's ability to harness the collective wisdom of both its employees and its partner organisations is crucial to its success, and collaborations of this nature can enhance the firm's dynamic capabilities.

It has also been previously suggested that human capital is fundamental for firm performance (Bontis et al., 2000; Wang and Chang, 2005; F-Jardón and Martos, 2009), and the results of this study suggest that human capital significantly affects the market performance of firms via the mediating factors of structural capital, internal relational capital, external relational capital, customer value creation and employee job satisfaction. By demonstrating that human capital is also crucial to intellectual capital in the Chinese context, this study confirms the findings of studies conducted in other regions (e.g. Bontis et al., 2000; Wang and Chang, 2005; F-Jardón and Martos, 2009). In the 'Made in China 2025' context, human capital is manifested as the acquisition of new skills and competencies among workers who often need to make knowledge-intensive decisions, as well as among workers who need to work cooperatively with machines (e.g. robots) to solve problems.

Our findings also indicated that market performance was improved by both employee job satisfaction and customer value creation, with the latter having an especially large impact. The improved market values of firms with higher customer creation values are easily understood, since they reflect the reality that customers and markets are inseparable; as more customers consume a firm's products or services, the probability of better market performance for the firm thus increases. In the context of the 'Made in China 2025' campaign, success is typically measured by customer experience (i.e., how a customer assesses the value they receive from a service) rather than by customer satisfaction (i.e., a customer's explicit feedback on provided services). Our findings also indicated that the role of employee job satisfaction for market performance, although smaller than that of customer value creation, is nonetheless nontrivial and should not be underestimated. Moreover, while external relational capital most strongly promotes customer value, internal relational capital is the key driver of employee job satisfaction. Thus, taken together, our results suggest that managers should pay attention to building mutually beneficial collaborative networks both within their firm and with key external stakeholders (Nahapiet and Ghoshal, 1998).

Although we believe our results to be valuable, all studies have some limitations, including the present one. First, as is common among organisational-level studies that are based on individually reported data, there may be some doubt as to whether the survey answers provided by individual respondents accurately reflect firm-level realities (Ferraresi et al., 2012). Second, most of our samples came from eastern China, where the economy is more robust than in western China. Although Chinese culture, rules and regulations overlap both regions, the geographic distribution of our sample may limit the generalisability of our results across China, and future studies should seek to observe whether relevant differences exist between eastern and western China. Third, firms of different sizes, ages and capital structures and in different industries have distinct operating characteristics, especially in terms of intellectual capital management (Molodchik et al., 2019); future research should therefore give more consideration to the diversity of firm types.

Despite these limitations, however, this research contributes to theory development in a number of ways. Our findings demonstrated associations between the intellectual capital components of human capital, structural capital, internal relational capital and external relational capital in the context of the world's largest emerging economy, China. Our study is also one of the first to investigate the relationship between intellectual capital and market performance, both directly and as mediated by employee job satisfaction and customer value creation. In sum, we found that firms that create more human capital, structural capital, internal relational capital and external relational capital have higher levels of customer value creation and employee job satisfaction, and are therefore likely to outperform their competitors in the Chinese market.

In addition to this study's theoretical contributions, it also suggests some managerial implications. Corporate talent development programmes are necessary for employees to improve their skills and expertise, especially given the national urgency assigned to the 'Made in China 2025' campaign. Moreover, we found an indirect association between investments in information technology systems (structural capital) and knowledge management, suggesting that organisations should implement knowledge management systems to facilitate knowledge sharing, collaboration and problem-solving among employees. Finally, and unsurprisingly, our results suggest that firms aiming to achieve better market performance should pay attention to improving employee job satisfaction and delivering superior customer experiences.

This study also provides some suggestions for policymakers. Employee training should be a focus not only of Chinese firms but also of the government, which should invest in education in order to boost the supply of knowledge workers who are capable of working in the 'Made in China 2025' world that the government envisions. At the same time, the government should investigate policies to attract foreign knowledge workers to China. The government should also consider providing financial incentives for firms to invest in knowledge management systems and technologies, particularly for small and medium-sized enterprises, in order to improve their structural capital. Finally, the government should support the establishment of industry alliances, which could facilitate corporate collaborations, as well as the establishment of training centres to teach workers needed skills and competencies.

Acknowledgements

The authors of this study would like to thank the Hong Kong Polytechnic University Research Committee for the provision of a scholarship (project code: RUNQ) to conduct this research.

References

Al-Ali, N. (2003) *Comprehensive intellectual capital management: Step-by-step*, Danvers, MA: John Wiley & Sons.

Bagozzi, R.P. and Yi, Y. (1988) 'On the evaluation of structural equation models', *Journal of the Academy of Marketing Science* 16(1), 74–94.

Bontis, N., Chua Chong Keow, W. and Richardson, S. (2000) 'Intellectual capital and business performance in Malaysian industries', *Journal of Intellectual Capital* 1(1) 85–100.

Buenechea-Elberdin, M., Kianto, A. and Sáenz, J. (2018) 'Intellectual capital drivers of product and managerial innovation in high-tech and low-tech firms', *R&D Management* 48(3), 290–307.

Cabrilo, S., Kianto, A. and Milic, B. (2018) 'The effect of IC components on innovation performance in Serbian companies', *VINE Journal of Information and Knowledge Management Systems* 48(3), 448–466.

Cheng, M.-Y., Lin, J.-Y., Hsiao, T.-Y. and Lin, T.W. (2010) 'Invested resource, competitive intellectual capital, and corporate performance', *Journal of Intellectual Capital* 11(4), 433–450.

Chu, S.K.W., Chan, K.H. and Wu, W.W.Y. (2011) 'Charting intellectual capital performance of the gateway to China', *Journal of Intellectual Capital* 12(2), 249–276.

Claus, I. and Oxley, L. (2014) 'The Chinese economy, past, present and future', *Journal of Economic Surveys* 28(4), 595–599.

Edvinsson, L. and Malone, M.S. (1997) *Intellectual capital: Realizing your company's true value by finding its hidden brainpower*, New York: Harper Business.

F-Jardón, C.M. and Martos, M.S. (2009) 'Intellectual capital and performance in wood industries of Argentina', *Journal of Intellectual Capital* 10(4), 600–616.

Fan, P. (2014) 'Innovation in China', *Journal of Economic Surveys* 28(4), 725–745.

Ferraresi, A.A., Quandt, C.O., dos Santos, S.A. and Frega, J.R. (2012) 'Knowledge management and strategic orientation: Leveraging innovativeness and performance', *Journal of Knowledge Management* 16(5), 688–701.

Fidel, P., Schlesinger, W. and Cervera, A. (2015) 'Collaborating to innovate: Effects on customer knowledge management and performance', *Journal of Business Research* 68(7), 1426–1428.

Fornell, C. and Larcker, D.F. (1981) 'Evaluating structural equation models with unobservable variables and measurement error', *Journal of Marketing Research* 18(1), 39–50.

Fouré, J., Bénassy-Quéré, A. and Fontagné, L. (2012) 'The great shift: Macroeconomic projections for the world economy at the 2050 horizon', G-MonD Working Paper n23.

Hussinki, H., Kianto, A., Vanhala, M. and Ritala, P. (2018) 'Happy employees make happy customers: The role of intellectual capital in supporting sustainable value creation in organizations', in F. Mathos, V. Vairinhos, P.M. Selig and L. Edvinsson (Eds.) *Intellectual capital management as a driver of sustainability: Perspectives for organizations and society*, Cham: Springer, 101–117.

Hussinki, H., Ritala, P., Vanhala, M. and Kianto, A. (2017) 'Intellectual capital, knowledge management practices and firm performance', *Journal of Intellectual Capital* 18(4), 904–922.

Iqbal, A., Latif, F., Marimon, F., Sahibzada, U.F. and Hussain, S. (2019) 'From knowledge management to organizational performance: Modelling the mediating role of innovation and intellectual capital in higher education', *Journal of Enterprise Information Management* 32(1), 36–59.

Kamukama, N., Ahiauzu, A. and Ntayi, J.M. (2010) 'Intellectual capital and performance: Testing interaction effects', *Journal of Intellectual Capital* 11(4), 554–574.

Kamukama, N., Ahiauzu, A. and Ntayi, J.M. (2011) 'Competitive advantage: Mediator of intellectual capital and performance', *Journal of Intellectual Capital* 12(1), 152–164.

Kanchana, N. and Mohan, P.R.R.R. (2017) 'A review of empirical studies in intellectual capital and firm performance', *Indian Journal of Commerce & Management Studies* 8(1), 52–58.

Kengatharan, N. (2019) 'A knowledge-based theory of the firm: Nexus of intellectual capital, productivity and firms' performance', *International Journal of Manpower*, https:// doi.org/ 10.1108/IJM-03-2018-0096.

Kianto, A., Andreeva, T. and Pavlov, Y. (2013) 'The impact of intellectual capital management on company competitiveness and financial performance', *Knowledge Management Research & Practice* 11(2), 112–122.

Kianto, A., Garanina, T. and Andreeva, T. (2018) 'Does intellectual capital matter for organizational performance in emerging markets? Evidence from Chinese and Russian contexts', in J. Guthrie, J. Dumay, F. Ricceri and C. Nielsen (Eds.) *The Routledge companion to intellectual capital*, New York: Routledge, 463–480.

Kianto, A., Sáenz, J. and Aramburu, N. (2017) 'Knowledge-based human resource management practices, intellectual capital and innovation', *Journal of Business Research* 81, 11–20.

Kianto, A., Vanhala, M. and Heilmann, P. (2016) 'The impact of knowledge management on job satisfaction', *Journal of Knowledge Management* 20(4), 621–636.

Kwee, K.C. (2008) 'Intellectual capital: Definitions, categorization and reporting models', *Journal of Intellectual Capital* 9(4), 609–638.

Lee, J., Bagher, B. and Kao, H.A. (2015) 'A cyber-physical systems architecture for Industry 4.0-based manufacturing systems', *Manufacturing Letters* 3, 18–23.

Li, L. (2018) 'China's manufacturing locus in 2025: With a comparison of "Made-in-China 2025" and "Industry 4.0"', *Technological Forecasting & Social Change* 135, 66–74.

Liu, G. and Lee, R. (2016) 'Knowledge management practices and firm market performance: A structural equation modelling approach', *Knowledge Management Forum* 1(2), 145–155.

Liu, G., Tsui, E. and See-To, E. (2017) 'Flourish or perish: An empirical study of the telecommunication equipment vendors from an IC perspective' in E. Tomé, G. Neumann and B. Knežević (Eds.) *Theory and Applications in the Knowledge Economy*, 529–544.

Molodchik, M.A., Jardon, C.M. and Bykova, A.A. (2019) 'The performance effect of intellectual capital in the Russian context: Industry vs company level', *Journal of Intellectual Capital*, 20(3), 335–354.

Nahapiet, J. and Ghoshal, S. (1998) 'Social capital, intellectual capital, and the organizational advantage', *Academy of Management Review* 23(2), 242–266.

Petty, M., McGee, G.W. and Cavender, J.W. (1984) 'A meta-analysis of the relationships between individual job satisfaction and individual performance', *Academy of Management Review* 9(4), 712–721.

Robbins, S.P., DeCenzo, D.A. and Coulter, M.K. (2013) *Fundamentals of management: Essential concepts and applications*, Upper Saddle River, NJ: Pearson.

Roos, J., Roos, G., Dragonetti, N.C. and Edvinsson, L. (1997) *Intellectual capital: Navigating the new business landscape*, Basingstoke, England: Macmillan Business.

Stewart, T.A. (1997) *Intellectual capital: The new wealth of organizations*, New York: Doubleday/ Currency.

Sullivan, P.H. (2000) *Value driven intellectual capital: How to convert intangible corporate assets into market value*, New York: John Wiley & Sons.

Sveiby, K.E. (1997) *The new organizational wealth: Managing and measuring knowledge-based assets*, San Francisco, CA: Berrett-Koehler Publishers.

Taherparvar, N., Esmaeilpour, R. and Dostar, M. (2014) 'Customer knowledge management, innovation capability and business performance: A case study of the banking industry', *Journal of Knowledge Management* 18(3), 591–610.

Ulaga, W. (2001) 'Customer value in business markets: An agenda for inquiry', *Industrial Marketing Management* 30(4), 315–319.

Wang, W.-Y. and Chang, C. (2005) 'Intellectual capital and performance in causal models: Evidence from the information technology industry in Taiwan', *Journal of Intellectual Capital* 6(2), 222–236.

Wang, Y., Po Lo, H., Chi, R. and Yang, Y. (2004) 'An integrated framework for customer value and customer-relationship-management performance: A customer-based perspective from China', *Managing Service Quality: An International Journal* 14(2/3), 169–182.

Zhang, B. and Wan, W. (2006) 'An empirical research on the effects of intellectual capital investment and intellectual capital on business performance', *China Soft Science* (7), 137–146.

7 Integrated Strategy Development based on intangibles

Markus Will

Background and purpose of Integrated Strategy Development

As the Fraunhofer IPK study on intangible assets in German companies (cf. Will 2015, Alwert et al. 2010) suggests, the development towards a knowledge-based economy has already progressed so far that intangible resources already have a greater influence on business success than classical material production factors. This is true for all sectors and size classes, although this phenomenon is particularly important in the services sector. In the context of the digital economy, this challenge becomes even more important as competitive differentials on a globalized market will increasingly rely on intangible features rather than "hard" product functionality or price only.

Against this background, also small and medium-sized enterprises (SMEs) must increasingly deal with the targeted development of sustainable competitive advantages, which can only be achieved through the specific bundling of intangible assets into core competencies that are difficult to imitate. This requires the development of so-called knowledge-based business models, that is the strategic orientation of business activities towards certain intangible resources and customer values with the aim of achieving unique selling propositions in the market or at least a promising competitive position and survival in the mid- to long-term perspective.

Integrated Strategy Development (ISD) aims at enabling SMEs to design strategies for the development of their business model, systematically integrating the necessary qualitative aspects of intangible assets to meet the needs of the knowledge-based and digital economy. The method supports in detail the following management tasks through a structured communication process based on SME-suitable workshop concepts and analytical tools:

- Explication and documentation of existing strategies and strategic options.
- Development and review of strategic goals with regard to logical consistency.
- Analysis of internal and external influencing factors, in particular intangible assets, in relation to specific strategic objectives.
- Derivation and prioritization of fields of action, development goals and measures for corporate development in the sense of strategic goals.

- Systematic alignment of current and planned measures with strategic objectives.
- Continuous control of measures and monitoring of implementation success.
- Further development of strategies over time and adaptation to new (internal and external) circumstances and framework conditions.

In principle, the ISD method is applicable to all sectors and size classes of SMEs. On the one hand, it can be used for the holistic and continuous planning of corporate development, for example in regular strategy meetings for the further development of the company as a whole or of a specific business area. On the other hand, it can be used modularly for specific use cases and questions from the point of view of the individual company, for example:

- Make specific strategic decisions, for example "Should we open a new business segment or launch a new product on the market and are we capable of doing so?"
- Implement decisions that have been made operationally, for example "What do we have to do to successfully launch the business segment or product?"
- Ensure strategic alignment of planned/ongoing measures, for example "To what extent do our measures support market entry in the new business area or the launch of a new product?"

Model of Integrated Strategy Development

ISD is a practical method to support the strategic business development of SMEs. Strategic Corporate Development refers to the intentional control of an organizational change process with the aim of ensuring sustainable competitive advantages and the economic survival of an enterprise. A strategy, defined as a consistent bundle of goals and measures, is thus the means by which the desired corporate development is controlled.

In order to operationalize the Strategic Corporate Development and transform it into a promising strategy, it is necessary to define the elements that are to be changed by the strategy (content). The focus of ISD lies on intangible resources and customer values, which contribute to the development of sustainable competitive advantages. On the other hand, the dynamic process of change needs to be structured in order to enable its systematic control (process).

The following structural model of ISD was designed under the consideration of balancing completeness and complexity reduction at the same time. It summarizes the essential content and process considerations of the ISD (see Figure 7.1). In the vertical perspective of the model, all essential content dimensions of a corporate strategy are depicted. They are also referred to as analysis levels of the ISD. In the horizontal perspective, on the other hand, the process of strategy development is presented on the basis of essential intermediate results of strategy development, which encompass both aspects of strategy formulation and strategy implementation.

76 *Markus Will*

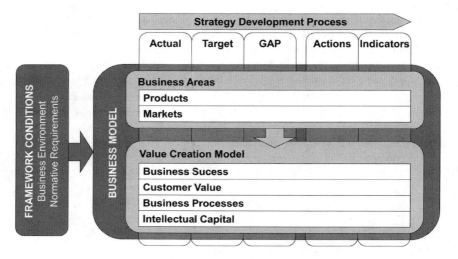

Figure 7.1 Structural model of Integrated Strategy Development.
Source: Own illustration.

In principle, *framework conditions* limit the opportunities for corporate development. This includes on the one hand the opportunities and risks arising from current developments in the *business environment*, that is from trends on the customer and supplier markets, as well as from the competitive situation and technological, social and political/legal trends in the wider environment of the company. On the other hand, *normative requirements* of the company owners and possibly other stakeholders must be taken into account, which may include overriding goals of the company's development, such as certain profit or growth targets as well as other general restrictions.

Based on these framework conditions, the *business model* of the respective company is developed. The business model is described in the ISD method using the following elements: on the one hand, the *business areas* are to be defined as homogeneous product-market combinations for the respective company (see Hungenberg 2008). Therefore, "products" and "markets" form the first two elements of the business model and summarize which product/service (should) provide which benefits for which target groups. On the other hand, the "architecture of goods and services provision" and the "revenue model" (see Stähler 2002) have to be determined, that is the way in which the organization, by using resources in business processes, produces and provides the product/service defined in the business segment for the respective target groups and at the same time generates economic returns. In ISD, the architecture of goods and services provision, including the revenue model, is referred to as the *value creation model*. In line with ISD's focus on content, value creation for customers and thus differentiation in the market is increasingly driven by intangible factors (see Welge and Al-Laham 2001). Therefore, intangible assets must be explicitly included in the value creation model from both the internal resource perspective and the external market perspective. *Business processes* form the connecting element between the internal intangible resource base – *intellectual capital* – and the intangible *customer values* from an external market perspective. The *business success* level, in turn, links the value creation model to the framework conditions defined above (requirements of owners and stakeholders, opportunities and risks in the business environment) and to the desired development of the business areas by operationalizing the overriding economic and strategic goals. In this way, the value creation model makes it possible to specifically identify the drivers of the company-specific knowledge-based business model and convert them into promising strategies.

In this way, the intangible resource base is tied to the higher level of the corporate strategy by linking intellectual capital with the specific business of the respective company, that is its products and markets, via the different levels of the value creation model. This ensures a practice-oriented and consistent concept for the management of SMEs, which does not present the intangible assets as detached or additional objects that "still" have to be managed, but rather as indispensable prerequisites for the creation of goods and services and successful market cultivation and thus, as an integral part of the entire business model. Company-specific configurations of intellectual capital that are difficult to imitate can be condensed into "core competencies" (cf. Prahalad and Hamel 1990) as the internal part of a knowledge-based business model. Customer values that are relevant to competition and differentiation can, on the other hand, be summarized as "value proposition" (see Weinstein and Johnson 1999) in the sense of a "value promise" of the respective business area to the customers.

In the dynamic perspective of the organizational change process, the ACTUAL state of the business model and thus, the initial situation of the respective company is described first. Based on the given framework conditions, the TARGET, that is the desired state of the business model, is then described at a defined point in time in the future, usually with a time horizon of 3–5 years. This results in the GAP, that is the strategic difference between TARGET and ACTUAL. While ACTUAL and TARGET describe static states of an organizational system at different points in time, the GAP summarizes its dynamic change in the form of strategic development goals. *Actions* can be derived from the GAP to close the strategic gap over time. *Indicators* make it possible to monitor the desired change in the sense of the strategy on the basis of quantitative measures.

While the description of ACTUAL, TARGET and GAP structures the *strategy formulation* at all content levels of the business model, the planning of suitable actions and the definition of suitable metrics support the systematic *strategy implementation*. This complies with the methodological principle of integrating strategy formulation and operational implementation.

In summary, ISD aims to answer the following questions in order to arrive at a consistent overall picture that establishes clear guiding principles and goals for actions in line with the strategy:

Business areas (products and markets)
- In which business areas (product–market combinations) are we active?
- How does value creation work for the customer?
- How do we intend to develop and expand the existing business areas in the future?
- Which strategic goals result from the desired development of the business segments?

External view of the value creation model (customer values and business success)
- Where are our main competitive advantages?
- How can we differentiate ourselves from competition in the defined business areas in the future?
- How do we determine that we are achieving our strategic goals?

Internal view of the value creation model (intellectual capital and business processes)
- Where are our internal strengths and weaknesses?
- Which business processes and intangible resources must we develop how in order to achieve the strategic goals?

Implementation of ISD

In order to systematically answer these questions, the procedural model of ISD summarizes the individual methodological steps into three main phases (cf. Figure 7.2).

Each phase creates a useful intermediate result. Depending on the specific application and requirements or already existing intermediate results, the individual phases can also be applied modularly and "stand-alone". ISD is based on the workshop procedure of the German methodology for Intellectual Capital Statements, "Wissensbilanz – Made in Germany" (see Alwert et al. 2008). A strategy team, consisting of representatives of the management and, if necessary, other key persons, goes through the steps in a structured series of workshops. The strategy team is guided by an appropriately trained moderator who is responsible for the systematic implementation of the procedure.

Since a detailed description of all steps, including the instruments and tools used, is not possible within the scope of this article, selected partial results of the three phases of ISD are presented in the following overview. For better illustration, the application example of a German IT service provider is used. For a complete description of the method, the interested reader is referred to Will's dissertation (cf. Will 2012). Practical guides with more detailed descriptions of individual methodological modules and analysis tools can be found in Will and Wuscher (2014) and Alwert and Will (2014).

Integrated Strategy Development 79

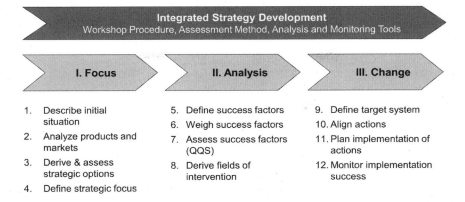

Figure 7.2 Procedural model of Integrated Strategy Development.
Source: Own illustration.

The starting point of the integrated strategy development process is always an internal or external *trigger*. Possible triggers are:

- Significant deviations from the ongoing performance and success monitoring result in a strategic need for action, for example revenue losses in certain market segments.
- New internal requirements, for example new overall objectives, are set by owners or other stakeholders.
- New external requirements, for example changed market conditions, make it necessary to review and, if necessary, adjust the strategy.
- A cyclically defined strategy process is initiated by the management on a regular basis (e.g. annually).

"Focus" Phase

The objective of Phase I "Focus" is to reach a consensus within the strategy team on the strategic option to be focused upon, that is to define as clearly as possible the various strategic options for action arising from the company's current business model and current developments in the business environment.

This result can already serve as a first guideline for the further management decisions of the individual members of the strategy team. The benefit is that the decision-making scope of the individual managers is given clear guidelines so that decisions can be made at future, unforeseeable decision points without complex coordination processes in the sense of a common objective.

For the further procedure of ISD, this first focus sets the overall objectives and determines the questions to which the further analysis and implementation planning of the strategy refer. This means that the success factors to be defined

80 *Markus Will*

in Phase II must logically derive from these overall objectives and answer the question: What do we need to achieve these overall objectives?

Phase I "Focus" is divided into four logical steps:

Step 1: Describe initial situation
Step 2: Analyse products and markets
Step 3: Derive and asses strategic options
Step 4: Define strategic focus

Key questions, templates and simple analysis tools support these four steps (see also Will and Wuscher 2014). First, some basic data of the company are collected and the existing general company objectives as well as relevant developments in the business environment are queried (step 1). With the help of portfolio analyses based on the so-called "BCG matrix" (see Alwert and Will 2014) existing products and markets are presented in a structured manner and evaluated with regard to their current contribution to earnings and future growth potential (step 2). Then, for example with the help of the so-called "Ansoff Matrix" (see Ansoff 1957), various strategic options are systematically derived and evaluated in the next step (step 3).

The chances and risks of the respective option are discussed in the strategy team on the basis of the available data and information collected so far. The opportunities and risks inherent in an option must be reflected on the one hand in the opportunities and threats in the business environment (result from step 1) and on the other hand in the initial situation of the company, that is the existing business areas and the existing revenue model with its specific growth potential (result from step 2). A further portfolio presentation serves as a visual aid to support the discussion in the strategy workshop: the "Strategic Options Portfolio" (StratOp-Portfolio). In the StratOp-Portfolio (see Figure 7.3), minimum and maximum values are plotted as an optimistic and pessimistic assessment of the opportunities and risks of a strategic option and result in an area that represents the extent of uncertainty in the strategic option evaluation in the strategy team: the larger the area, the greater the uncertainty about the actual business development resulting from the option in question.

The assessment of the opportunities of a strategic option is operationalized by the sales potential that can be generated in the best-case scenario (upper value on the Y axis) and in the worst-case scenario (lower value on the Y axis). The risk side should include not only the cost and effort of measures to directly implement a strategic option (e.g. the development of a new product as an investment), but also possible consequential costs or even financial damage that could result from failure or incorrect implementation. Here, too, an estimate for the "best case" and the "worst case" must be discussed in the strategy team and the corresponding minimum and maximum values defined on the X axis.

In principle, the interesting options lie to the left or above the dotted diagonal, as the opportunities outweigh the risks. The relative distances between

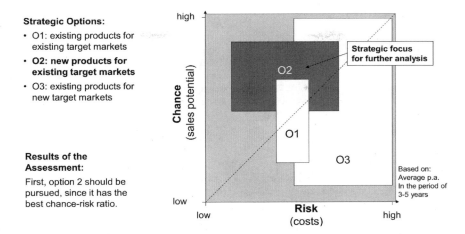

Figure 7.3 Strategic Options Portfolio.
Source: Own illustration.

the opportunities and risks of the individual options are decisive. In a positive extreme case, a strategic option can be evaluated so clearly in terms of its opportunity/risk ratio that it can be located as a point or very small area as far to the left as possible at the top of the StratOp-portfolio. If the measures for implementing this strategic option can be derived directly from this analysis, the next phase of the status quo analysis can be skipped and directly transferred to Phase III for planning the actions.

As a rule, however, strategic options are characterized by a certain degree of uncertainty and the risk of failure. Therefore, in the following analysis phase, it will be determined how the required success factors, from market-related success factors to the necessary business processes and intangible resources, are positioned today with regard to a specific strategic option. From this detailed assessment of strengths and weaknesses, the decisive development actions can then be derived in order to systematically increase the chances of successfully implementing a strategic option and minimize the risks. From a methodological point of view, the analysis in Phase II has the task of reducing the existing uncertainty, and thus the area size of the relevant strategic option in the StratOp-Portfolio. An iteration between phases I and II is conceivable, for example, in which an analysis is first carried out for each interesting strategic option in order to reduce the planning uncertainty at the outset and to develop a better basis for decision-making for or against a particular strategic option.

Finally, a selection of a strategic option as well as a summary of this focused option as the TARGET state on the business model levels "product" and "market" is made. Mirrored at the ACTUAL status, the GAP – that is the gap

82 Markus Will

Table 7.1 Summary of a strategic option in the strategy matrix (excerpt)

Analysis Level	ACTUAL	TARGET	GAP
Markets	In the Western European market for high-quality software solutions for large companies, we offer our customers individual solutions for their document. management.	In the pan-European market for document management systems, we occupy a leading position in quality and customer service.	Expansion to include new markets in Eastern Europe with a focus on the need for high-quality, customer-specific solutions.
Products	We cover the entire range of services for document management systems from concept creation to technical implementation and on-site service.	We cover the entire range of services for on-site installed document management systems as well as the hosting of databases for our customers.	Extension of the product portfolio with hosting offers.

Source: Own illustration

between the ACTUAL status and the desired TARGET status of the company's business areas — results (step 4). A respective excerpt of the strategy matrix is shown in Table 7.1, using the example of an IT service provider.

This summary of the analysis results produced so far should be adopted in the strategy workshop and forms the basis for defining the strategic focus that will be needed as input for the analysis in the next phase.

"Analysis" Phase

The aim of the second phase is to define the influencing factors (success factors) that are essential for achieving the strategic goals defined in Phase I and to evaluate them in terms of their importance and current characteristics. This results in a strength–weakness profile of the success factors, from which the fields of intervention can be derived, which are central to the implementation of the selected strategic option and which are covered by corresponding actions in the third phase.

During the analysis, the moderator must ensure that the following rules are adhered to by the strategy team:

- All team members have equal rights (everyone has one vote).
- Each team member is a representative of his/her area of responsibility or department (reflected assessment: how do my colleagues and employees see it?).

Integrated Strategy Development 83

- Each team member evaluates from the point of view of his area with regard to the overall organization.
- The strategic objectives set out in Phase I are the evaluation yardstick or benchmark.
- The entire spectrum of given scales should be used to illustrate relative distances.
- Objective arguments must be exchanged and documented, that is the own evaluation must be justified and discussed.

Phase II is divided into four logical steps that build on each other:

Step 5: Define success factors
Step 6: Weight success factors
Step 7: Assess success factors (QQS)
Step 8: Derive fields of intervention

After the strategic goals at the business model levels "product" and "market" have been defined in Phase I, the influencing factors at the levels "business success", "customer values", "business processes" and "intellectual capital" for achieving these goals are defined in Phase II (Step 5), their influence on the strategic goals is weighted (Step 6) and their current status is evaluated (Step 7). The proven assessment procedure of the European methodology for Intellectual Capital Statements (see European Commission 2008) is used in the dimensions quantity (Qn), quality (Ql) and systematics (Sy) – the so-called QQS assessment. The overview shows the "Management Portfolio" diagram, displaying the relative development potential of each success factor (represented by "bubbles" in the diagram) for all four analysis levels of the value creation model. Supplemented by the QQS bar charts, all essential analysis results can be displayed in condensed form (see Figure 7.4). Printed as a poster, for example, this overview serves the strategy team for a structured discussion of the strategic need for action at each analysis level. The aim is to prioritize the fields of intervention with the greatest need for action.

In principle, fields of intervention may refer to success factors from all analysis levels of the value creation model, which are to be improved by targeted development actions in the sense of the strategic objectives (strategic need for action). In the interests of effective and efficient management of actions, however, a few fields of action should be prioritized at each analysis level.

For this purpose, the development potential of the respective success factors in the strategy team is discussed on the basis of the "Management Portfolio". In principle, two options for action can be considered:

- Stabilize strengths, that is maintain relatively strong success factors with high weighting (top right in the portfolio) actively at the good level or continuously optimize them.

84 *Markus Will*

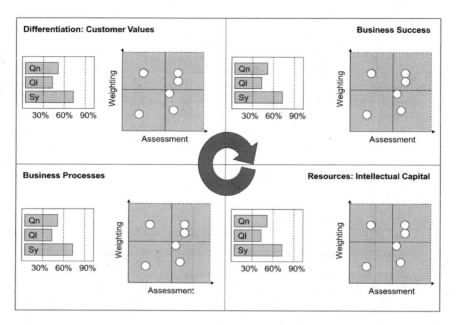

Figure 7.4 Schematic overview of ISD analysis results.
Source: Own illustration.

- Compensate weaknesses, that is systematically improve and develop relatively weakly developed success factors with a high weighting (top left in the portfolio).

Priority is given to defining those success factors as fields of intervention that have a relatively high significance and at the same time a relatively large potential for improvement. This corresponds to the second option (to compensate weaknesses). Justification: if two factors are of equal importance, greater effects can be achieved for the factor with the greatest potential for improvement in accordance with the marginal benefit principle. However, it must be considered which option is strategically advantageous and whether there is an additional need for action in the already well-developed factors in order to keep them at the current level or improve them incrementally.

On this basis and with the help of the improvement potentials recorded in step 7, the concrete challenges in the fields of intervention are discussed in the strategy workshop and defined as development goals per field of action (step 8). A development goal is a desired (positive) change in a success factor that contributes to closing the gap between the ACTUAL state and the TARGET state. Once a consensus has been reached in the discussion on the fields of intervention and the changes to be aimed for and the results have been recorded in

Differentiation: Customer Values				Business Success		
ID	**Field of intervention**	**Development goal**		**ID**	**Field of intervention**	**Development goal**
PD1	Product quality	Reducing complaints		BS1	Financial success	Increasing sales growth
SD2	Delivery time/ -loyalty	Increasing adherence to delivery dates		...	...	...
...	...	...				

Business Processes				Resources: Intellectual Capital		
ID	**Field of intervention**	**Development goal**		**ID**	**Field of action**	**Development goal**
BP1	Distribution	Increasing productivity of distribution		HC3	Employee motivation	Stabilizing motivation in development department
...	...	...		SC1	Cooperation, knowledge transfer	Improving communication between project teams
				...	...	...

Figure 7.5 Overview of fields of intervention and development goals.
Source: Own illustration.

the overview (see Figure 7.5), the development goals per field of intervention are finally described.

The result of Phase II "Analysis" is then a complete description of the development goals at the four levels of the value creation model in the context of the strategic objectives defined in Phase I at the business area level. Therefore, the descriptions of the individual development goals should be linked to the overall objectives. The following question must be answered: What is the benefit for the company as a whole or for the individual business areas against the background of the defined strategic objectives if the individual development goal is achieved?

The complete list of the development goals described is the basis for the target system and serves as a guideline for the derivation of targeted development actions in the next phase.

"Change" Phase

The aim of Phase III is to develop the fields of intervention identified in Phase II in accordance with the strategic objectives defined in Phase I. In order to systematically control this development, a consistent target system is defined. On the basis of this target system, suitable development actions can be derived and prioritized, their implementation can be planned and their success and impact can be measured and evaluated. The resulting monitoring system supports the systematic monitoring and continuous control of strategic corporate development.

Phase III is divided into four logical steps that build on each other:

Step 9: Define target system
Step 10: Align actions
Step 11: Plan implementation of actions
Step 12: Monitor implementation success

The strategic objectives derived in Phase I (at the "Product" and "Market" levels) and the development goals developed in Phase II (at the Business Success, Customer Values, Business Processes, Intellectual Capital levels) are transferred to a consistent target system by recording the ACTUAL and TARGET status and the GAP in the form of development goals at all levels of the business model and checking them for consistency and completeness (step 9). The development goals may be weighted for further prioritization. This can be done either by an impact analysis, supported by the so-called impact matrix (see Alwert et al. 2008), or alternatively on a scale of 1–10 (see Table 7.2).

On this basis, the next step is to collect and evaluate proposals for actions in a structured manner (step 10). In order to visually support the discussion on the potential impacts and benefits of a proposed action in the workshop, the previously developed proposal for action can be allocated in the target system. Here, too, a poster with the target system, visualized as an impact network, is a good way to support the workshop procedure in this step (see Figure 7.6).

The aim of this sub-step is to achieve a common understanding of the scope and objectives of the respective actions before they are systematically evaluated. In order to prioritize proposed actions in the next step in line with the strategy, their impact on the achievement of the key development goals is evaluated and summed up. The expected contribution of the individual action to achieving the respective development goal is estimated on a scale of 0–3, whereby indirect impacts can also be taken into account. In principle, negative impacts are also conceivable if one action supports one development goal but obstructs or counteracts another.

To assess the contribution to the goal, the strategy team discusses in the workshop how high the respective contribution is to be assessed. The row total indicates the contribution of the individual action to all development goals (column "Total target contribution"). By multiplying the respective target contribution by the previously defined weighting points per development goal, a weighted utility value per action can also be calculated. The higher this value, the greater the target contribution of the respective action must be evaluated and prioritized accordingly. The list of actions collected is sorted in descending order according to this utility, so that a ranking is made according to the size

Table 7.2 Weighting of development goals in the target system

	Business success		*Definition*	
Results	Sales growth		In order to achieve our vision of being the leader in our market segment, we need to ensure a growth in revenue of 20% p.a.	
	Return on sales		For the necessary reinvestment in the growth we need a return on sales of at least 10%.	

	Fields of intervention	*Development goals*	*Definition*	*Weighting*
Markets	Product quality, customer loyalty	Reduce complaints	The product quality perceived by the customer should be further optimized at a high level in order to increase customer loyalty (or avoid emigration) and to save costs by fewer complaints.	6
	Delivery reliability	Increasing adherence to delivery dates	Not only delivery dates with high priority, but also low-priority delivery dates promised to the customer should be adhered to 99%.	1
Processes	Distribution	Increase productivity of distribution	In distribution, the sales volume must be increased in order to enhance the internal capacity utilization of the existing capacities so that it can be built up accordingly.	10
Resources	Cooperation and knowledge transfer	Improving communication between project teams	Cross-departmental cooperation and communication in project teams should be more structured (uniform, systematic, automated) and transparent (comprehensible) in order to increase efficiency and ultimately save time and costs.	3
	Employee motivation	Stabilizing motivation in development department	Overloading of individual employees should be reduced by better portability of tasks. For this, a uniform process understanding within the department has to be established.	1

Source: Own illustration

88 *Markus Will*

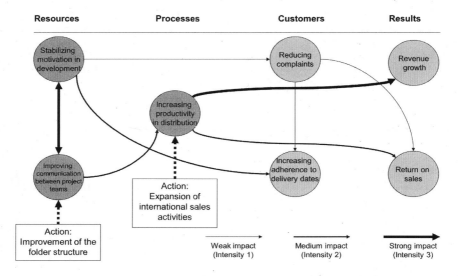

Figure 7.6 Allocating actions in target system.
Source: Own illustration.

of the expected target contribution. The result is recorded in the prioritization matrix (see Table 7.3).

The methodical goal of this step is, against the background of limited corporate resources, to generate efficiency through the greatest possible strategic benefit at the lowest possible cost. On the basis of the prioritization matrix and the discussion of the strategically most important effects of the actions, the strategy team makes the final decision as to which actions are to be planned and implemented in the next step (step 11).

For strategic and clear control of the actions prioritized and selected in the previous step, several actions can be bundled into strategic programmes and brought into a logical-temporal sequence. The result of this step is a roadmap of the strategic programmes with defined points in time for measuring and monitoring the success of the actions and the achievement of the objectives (see Figure 7.7). This enables a continuous and systematic control of strategic programmes, aligned to the previously defined development goals. On the basis of this rough planning, ISD offers further support for the implementation of the actions in the form of processes and templates for internal detailed planning as well as for regular reporting and measurement of the implementation success (for further details see Alwert and Will 2014).

On the level of the single action, step 11 of the ISD procedure also produces an action plan or a respective planning order for each prioritized action. The strategy team then takes over the control function at the strategic level with a view to the company as a whole and the overall structure of the target system,

Table 7.3 Impact assessment of actions

Action	Contribution to development goals					
	Increase productivity of distribution	*Reduce complaints*	*Improve communication between project teams*	*Stabilize motivation of development department*	*Total goal contribution*	*Utility value (weighted)*
Weighting of development goals	10	6	3	1		
Sum of the effects of the actions	5	12	17	15		
Expansion of sales activities on international markets	3	0	0	0	3	30
New product group added to the product portfolio	2	1	0	0	3	26
Keeping professional competence up to date	0	3	1	1	5	22
Optimization of processes by means of IT and documentation	0	1	3	3	7	18
Avoidance of complaints and reduction of the reject rate	0	3	0	0	3	18
Improvement of the folder structure	0	1	3	2	6	17
Optimization of the ERP system	0	1	2	3	6	15
Professionalization of project management for internal projects	0	0	3	2	5	11
Introduction of a uniform discussion process	0	0	3	2	5	11
Introduction of appraisal interviews	0	1	1	1	3	10
Library	0	1	1	1	3	10

Source: Own illustration

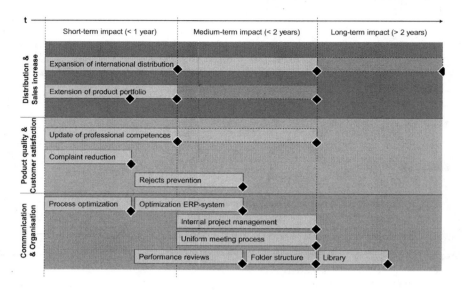

Figure 7.7 Exemplary action roadmap.
Source: Own illustration.

while individual action teams, each with one action manager or project manager, are responsible for the operational implementation of actions. If the detailed planning is also handed over to the action team and its project manager, the latter must deliver a detailed action plan as a result to the strategy team. On this basis, the strategy team decides on the implementation and assigns a corresponding implementation order to the respective action team. This triggers a document-supported workflow which is supported throughout ISD by document templates.

In order to support the management of strategic corporate development at the overall level, an indicator-based monitoring system is then set up (step 12), which connects the previously derived development goals with a few relevant key performance indicators and target values, which are continuously compared with the actual values in order to monitor the implementation success (see Figure 7.8).

The indicators and target values derived in this way can now be integrated into any existing monitoring or controlling system that the company is already using for management purposes. The compatibility of ISD with relatively common instruments, such as the Balanced Scorecard, also supports this integration. Whether transferred into the company's own action or project management system or not, ISD always provides a collection of checklists and templates for the final methodological step in order to support the continuous control of the actions in a continuous workflow, whereby the indicators serve

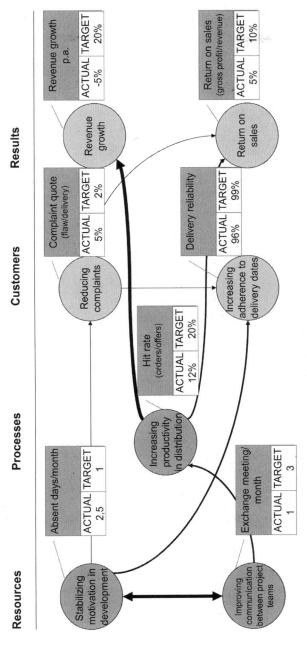

Figure 7.8 Exemplary indicators allocated in the target system.
Source: Own illustration.

92 Markus Will

the ongoing monitoring of the achievement of objectives. ISD thus enables a structured process from strategy formulation and strategic analysis to implementation planning and continuous strategic control in a suitable manner for SMEs. Simple logical steps can be processed flexibly to achieve an optimal cost–benefit ratio for the user.

Application examples and future potential in the digital economy

The model of the ISD has been used in various application contexts where ISD has not only proven to be useful in the strategy definition and the respective implementation planning and monitoring in European SMEs from various business sectors, but thanks to the flexible adjustment of the system boundaries it is also applicable to parts of large organizations, like a department, a business area or even a specific strategy or strategic programme relying on several units of an organization which may be represented in one virtual organizational system. Furthermore, the central methodological modules of ISD have already been tested and well proven in practice by several pilot projects on Intellectual Capital Statements in Europe, for example "Wissensbilanz – Made in Germany" (cf. Alwert et al. 2008).

In an adapted form, the ISD method has served as a basis in other application fields, for example in the business and implementation planning of a national network of applied R&D institutes in Brazil as well as for a respective management evaluation system to regularly check and analyse the institutes' performance and management maturity on a strategic level. Using the ISD model and its elements to structure and systematize the strategic management process of each institute's directorate and management team, a selected set of ISD modules and tools were partly adapted to the strategic context and requirements of applied research, technological development and innovation, and simplified for use in a highly dynamic environment. Also in this context, ISD has proven to provide a logical structure and clear methodological guideline that supports the collaborative elaboration of strategies, their implementation and monitoring, especially supporting the Brazilian R&D network's strategy to focus on industry-oriented research, using a business-based operational model of the institutes (to be detailed in upcoming publications).

As an outlook for further application and development potential in the digital economy, ISD may be used as a mental framework that provides a logical structure to (a) turn big data into strategic, decision- and action-relevant knowledge, and (b) cluster and allocate existing software devices, analytical tools and apps according to their use in specific steps and levels of the strategic management process. This includes:

- Selecting and defining the right set of Key Performance Indicators (KPIs), based on the strategic objectives and actual challenges of a company or organization.

Integrated Strategy Development 93

- Ensuring the relevance of measured data and providing an individual strategic interpretation context for this data.
- Tackling the challenge of an enormous amount of data being captured in the digital economy that needs to be analysed and assessed, by providing the relevant strategic topics, questions and requirements to be answered by the data.
- Processing and aggregating data and analysis results for certain decision-making or planning tasks within the context of strategic management.

As a result of such an approach, ISD may serve as the framework to design a digital representation of the company's individual business model and specific strategy. Enhanced by embedded real-time data and by management functions for analysis, planning and monitoring according to the ISD steps, analysis levels and modules, this development may lead to the construction of a "Management 4.0" system, providing data-based support in the strategic management process for the involved actors at the top and middle management levels, that is the "strategy team" of the respective company or organization.

Tackling these challenges of the digital economy and the so-called "Industry 4.0" by bringing sense, logics and structure from a strategic management viewpoint into the rapidly growing data repositories may also help to link the technological opportunities of the digital age with the existing concepts of knowledge management and the learning organization. In the end, the advancements in digitalization and connectivity on a global market should become the basis to turn any company into a real learning organization, constantly analysing its outputs and performance to constantly optimize operations and adjust strategic routes – based on real-time data from various sources, systematically processed and aggregated according to the organization's individual strategic needs.

References

Alwert K, Bornemann M, Meyer C, Will M, and Wuscher S (2010) *Wissensstandort Deutschland – Deutsche Unternehmen auf dem Weg in die wissensbasierte Wirtschaft.* Berlin: Fraunhofer IPK.

Alwert K, Bornemann M, and Will M (2008) *Wissensbilanz – Made in Germany. Leitfaden 2.0.* Berlin: German Federal Ministry for Economics and Technology Germany.

Alwert K, and Will M (2014) *Leitfaden Maßnahmen managen. Zusatzmodul zum Leitfaden 2.0 zur Erstellung einer Wissensbilanz.* Berlin: Fraunhofer IPK.

Ansoff H I (1957) Strategies for diversification. *Harvard Business Review*, 35, 5: 113–124.

European Commission (2008) *InCaS: Intellectual Capital Statement – Made in Europe.* European ICS Guideline. Online: www.incas–europe.org.

Hungenberg H (2008) *Strategisches Management in Unternehmen. Ziele - Prozesse - Verfahren.* 5th revised and extended edition. Wiesbaden: Gabler.

Prahalad C K, and Hamel G (1990) The Core Competence of the Corporation. *Harvard Business Review*, 68, May–June: 79–91.

Stähler P (2002) *Geschäftsmodelle in der digitalen Ökonomie. Merkmale, Strategien und Auswirkungen.* 2nd edition. Lohmar: Eul.

Weinstein A, and Johnson W C (1999) *Designing and Delivering Superior Customer Value: Concepts, Cases, and Applications*. Boca Raton, FL: St. Lucie Press.

Welge M K, and Al-Laham A (2001) *Strategisches Management. Grundlagen – Prozesse – Implementierung*. 3rd edition, Wiesbaden.

Will M (2012) *Strategische Unternehmensentwicklung auf Basis immaterieller Werte in KMU – Eine Methode zur Integration der ressourcen- und marktbasierten Perspektive im Strategieprozess*. Stuttgart: Fraunhofer Verlag.

Will M (2015) Intellectual Capital Statement as a Strategic Management Tool: The European Approach. In: Ordónez de Pablos P, Edvinsson L (Eds.) *Intellectual Capital in Organizations: Nonfinancial Reports and Accounts*. New York: Routledge.

Will M, and Wuscher S (2014) *Leitfaden Strategische Ziele entwickeln. Zusatzmodul zum Leitfaden 2.0 zur Erstellung einer Wissensbilanz*. Berlin: Fraunhofer IPK.

Part III

Intellectual capital and digitalized economy

8 IC Israel reporting

The journey from 1998 into the future

Edna Pasher, Leif Edvinsson, Otthein Herzog and Lee Sharir

Introduction

In this chapter we tell the story of the evolution of Intellectual Capital (IC) reporting in Israel from 1998 to the present and the next stage – adding Artificial Intelligence (AI) to IC to navigate ecosystems.

Edna Pasher PhD & Associates first adopted the concept of "knowledge based organizations" when Prahalad and Hamel published the paper "The Core Competence of the Corporation" in 1990 and since then our strategic consulting has focused on supporting organizations in identifying their core knowledge for competitive advantage.

In 1995, Edna first met Leif Edvinsson at a GDI conference on Knowledge Management in Zurich, organized by Betty Zucker, and invited both of them to the very first exposure of the new concepts in Israel. The response of the participants in the event was very enthusiastic to the surprise of Leif Edvinsson, who found himself surrounded by them as they hope to get hold of the first IC report of Skandia!

This started our IC joint journey in Israel.

Following his success with IC in Skandia, Leif developed the first IC report for Sweden, and Edna and Leif collaborated to create the first IC report for Israel.

Again Israelis became very excited, and we translated together *The Hidden Value in the Desert* (The title we gave the IC Israel Report) into English. One copy, which I gave a friend who was at that time working in the Israeli embassy in Madrid, created interest in the worldwide Israeli diplomatic Israeli to whom we happily distributed copies. The IC Israel report became a very effective tool in visualizing the competitive advantage of Israel in the global market.

This unexpected overwhelming success in 1998 led to an interest in the local Israel community as well. We recounted the story at our annual Knowledge in Action events, and as a consequence knowledge management became a new movement in Israel. (Two more national IC Israel reports were later funded by the Israel Chief Scientist.)

The next step in the Israel IC evolution was IC reporting on a municipal level. Holon, a city close to Tel Aviv, was suffering from negative immigration.

98   *Edna Pasher et al.*

New cities were built close by that attracted the citizens of Holon. The new mayor, Moti Sasson, appointed a new municipality CEO and they together led a revolution that made the city attractive again! They promoted Holon as "The city for children" and translated this bold vision into an innovative strategy and projects which made it by 2011 "The Most Admired Knowledge City" in the world and its mayor one of *Monocle* magazine's top 10 "movers and shakers" mayors.

We were invited to contribute a city IC report to this successful innovative journey, visualizing the intangible assets of Holon (in Hebrew only). Following this, a private company in the construction sector – Danya Cebus – decided to experiment with the IC model.

Itamar Deutser, the CEO was preparing the company for an IPO and liked the idea of having a tool to visualize the intangibles of the company. Our IC report made the market value higher! Another construction company, Tidhar, followed a few years later. We managed to engage the whole company in the process.

Unfortunately, however, innovation takes a long time to scale up, and all of these reports remain only pilot projects: after 21 years we have not yet been successful in scaling up the tools as we had originally hoped! But we never give up, and we are now prototyping a new concept – adding AI to IC – with the help of Otthein Herzog, who has joined us in this exciting journey. We hope this innovation will help us to scale up IC reporting in the new environment – the economy of ecosystems!

Stage 1: IC of the country

The Intellectual Capital of the State of Israel

Figure 8.1 depicts the third edition of the report *The Intellectual Capital of The State of Israel*, funded by the Israel Chief Scientist.

The first IC report of Israel, published in September 1998, presented the hidden values and the key success factors of Israel. As the State of Israel entered its 51st year, it was already one of the most developed countries in the world: Israel was the only country in the world in which the population had increased by 330% while having to fight periodic wars. This growth had dramatically narrowed the gap between Israel and the developed countries.

The findings revealed Israel's achievements during the first 50 years of its existence as a state in different areas including education, science, international relationships, communication and computer infrastructure.

The IC report was based on data and information collected from written material such as professional literature, newspaper and magazine articles, as well as discussions, brainstorming sessions and interviews with key figures from diverse fields. The project included an extensive representation of the younger generation's perspective since they are Israel's source for future affluence and growth.

IC Israel reporting 99

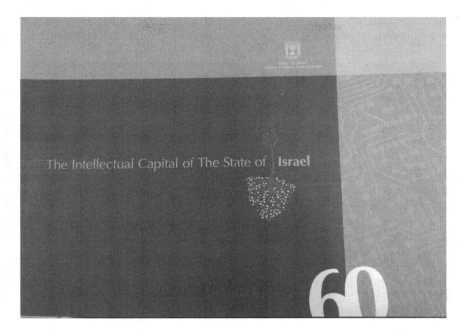

Figure 8.1 The Intellectual Capital of The State of Israel, 3rd edition.

The process

We decided to base the Israel IC report on a comparison of Israel with other developed countries, and not with developing countries, since developed countries are those that serve as role models for Israel and with which Israel competes on the international markets.

The project had four phases:

Phase 1: Creating a vision of Israel to serve as the benchmark for the study
Phase 2: Identifying the core competencies needed to realize this vision
Phase 3: Identifying the key success factors for each core competence
Phase 4: Identifying the indicators for each key success factor

Phase 1: Creating a vision of Israel

The vision of Israel used in this report was crystallized through brainstorming sessions and interviews with leading figures in various fields: life sciences, social sciences, urban planning, accounting, business management and many more disciplines and perspectives.

We involved young people as well and asked them questions about what they wished to see in the future of the county. The vision incorporated elements of

100   *Edna Pasher et al.*

the Israel 2020 program, which had been formulated by a team of leading experts and included four alternative planning directions for Israel's future.

In addition a "peace scenario" was prepared which assumed a lasting peace between Israel and its neighbors. As a result of the peace process the team envisioned accelerated economic growth.

The vision of Israel that emerged in our study of its IC was the substantiation of Israel's position as a developed, modern, democratic and pluralistic nation – attractive to the world's Jewry, investors, tourists and it's own citizens.

Our conclusions were:

First, Israel should strive to enhance the quality of life for all its residents. This must include an effort to increase equality among the various sectors in the society and to decrease socio-economic disparities. Similarly, the country must eliminate verbal and physical violence and increasing crime. It must do this while building a culture based on tolerance and mutual respect.

Second, the country must make itself attractive for future generations by continuing to develop its knowledge-based industries, scientific research, and technological development. These are in fact the country's front lines of its future progress.

To achieve these goals, Israel must nurture peaceful relations with its neighbors in the Middle East.

Stage 2: IC of a city

Holon: visualizing the transition into the City of Children (Figure 8.2)

We know that many cities around the world are eroding and that stagnation is one of the main problems they face. These cities have reached the point where they no longer renew their services, improve their infrastructures or invest in human capital. The result is a process in which citizens are leaving the city where they went to school, grew up and felt at home.

The IC report can help a city to reposition itself based on its existing advantages and thereby exploit them for its own benefit.

After establishing a steering committee in the Educational and Cultural Administration of the city of Holon, there need arose to launch the project in all parts of the administration, and to motivate and commit the employees to take an active role in the process. "Knowledge Cafés" were organized for employees, managers and other stakeholders in order to enable effective brainstorming sessions with large groups of people. The sessions focused on evaluating what should and what should not change at Holon, how to contribute on an ongoing basis to the renewal and revitalization of the city, and on which areas the city should focus in which it should invest. The Knowledge Café discussions resulted in a finer definition of the Educational and Cultural Administration's vision. This vision led to the commitment of municipality employees to specific goals. These goals incorporated fostering a highly qualified creative and professional team with a high degree of freedom to initiate, design and implement their goals in a unique way.

Figure 8.2 Holon IC report.

Phase 2: Identifying the core competencies

Having created and defined Holon's vision, the second phase in the process was initiated to identify the core competencies needed to realize the vision. This phase was accompanied by interviews with many different city personnel and city residents dealing with different issues and questions. As a result, 14 different competencies were found to exist.

Phase 3: Identifying the key success factors

The next step was to measure Holon's Educational and Cultural Administration Intellectual Capital: Financial Capital, Human Capital, Process Capital, Market Capital, Renewal and Development Capital.

It was discovered that Holon had invested significantly more in education, culture and the environment than other municipalities. Holon's initiatives, actions and interactions thus allowed the exchange, evaluation, update, development and creation of knowledge.

In conclusion, Holon used the Intellectual Capital Report as a tool to assess and visualize the overall ability, potential and actions of the Educational and Cultural Division, a process that has helped stave off the emigration of Holon's inhabitants to other urban areas.

102 Edna Pasher et al.

Phase 4: Identifying the indicators for each key success factor

In order to make the key success factors measureable each of them needs to be characterized by a set of measurable indicators, e.g., for the environment key success factor, indicators would include, for instance, air quality indices, the amount of green area in a city, and water quality. In this way, key success factors become comparable for different cities, and can be analyzed by Big Data Analytics over extended periods of time.

Stage 3: IC of a company

Danya Cebus going public with an IC report as a supporting tool (Figure 8.3)

The initiative to create an intellectual capital report for the Israeli construction company Danya Cebus originated from its CEO's vision to visualize the hidden values and assets of the company in order to leverage its business activities.

There were, in addition, several other reasons for creating such a report:

1 Forming a supplementary management tool for strategic planning purposes.
2 Defining an effective tool for assessing the company's value in preparation for an IPO.
3 Creating an innovative marketing channel for the company and its activities.
4 Identifying and effectively managing the company's intangible assets and core competencies.

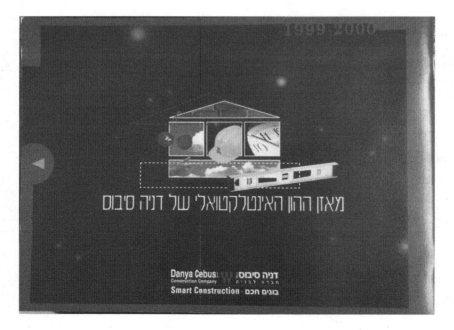

Figure 8.3 Danya Cebus IC report.

As part of the company's pioneering spirit, its management decided to produce an IC report and to become the first construction company in the world to produce such an IC report.

The first phase for the preparation of the Danya Cebus IC report was the formation of a steering committee headed by the CEO. The purpose of the steering committee was to manage the process of preparing the report.

The second phase was to launch the project in all parts of the organization and to motivate and commit the employees to take an active role in the process. Therefore, a Knowledge Café involving more than 40 employees and managers was conducted, facilitated by us. The outputs of the group discussions in the Knowledge Café included the definition of Danya Cebus' vision and values.

In the next phase several strategic workshops were conducted with the steering committee. The aim of these workshops was to finalize the list of the company's key success factors for future growth, and their measurement indicators. The heterogeneous makeup of the steering committee enabled each participant to suggest various indicators, based on his/her unique perspective derived from their professional functions. This enriched the workshop discussions and consequently led to better outputs.

Finally the relevant information and knowledge about the different indicators was collected and analyzed from the company's existing database. This enabled completion of the formulation of an in-depth IC report for Danya Cebus.

Lessons learnt from our IC Israel journey

- It seems that in Israel, *the public sector is more open to innovation* than the private sector, trying new methods and tools to improve its work while the private sector is willing to adopt methods only after they have proven to be effective.
- The IC report can make a real difference by *engaging all stakeholders*, focusing on the vision and the goals of the entity described (country, city, company), and raising awareness of the intangible assets that had not been measured before.
- *A periodical display* of an organization's competencies will increase the market value of the company and diminish stock fluctuations in the market that are rooted in reasons irrelevant to an organization's capacity.
- An IC report can serve as a central management tool enabling a systematic examination of an organization's competencies and *navigating their development to succeed in the future*.

The future

An interdisciplinary approach to IC & AI in innovation ecosystems: adding Artificial Intelligence methods to improve IC reports

One of the key challenges of ecosystems is the scaling up of start-ups. Over the past decades, a lot of effort has been invested in this direction. The result is an overwhelming number of new startups created every year. However, many of

104   *Edna Pasher et al.*

these ventures do not survive their early stage and close down before they have exhausted their potential. It takes innovative measures to address this challenge. Contrary to conventional methods, mostly based on financial potential, the use of intellectual capital measures should allow for the discovery of the venture's innovative potential, even if the economic benefit is yet unclear.

This section will describe IC measures in order to identify high-potential innovations, mainly in high-tech industries.

The IC methodology can both *detect high potential innovation combined with high-tech capabilities* and the IC of the ecosystem at different maturity levels.

The enhancement of an ecosystem's infrastructure by raising awareness of its IC potential will lead the ecosystem to become more ambitious and to build on emerging market success for future growth and sustainability.

IC comprises the intangible value of a business, covering its people (human capital), the value relating to its relationships (relational capital) and everything that is left when the employees go home (structural capital), of which intellectual property (IP) is but one component.

By adopting an innovative approach that adapts the IC Navigator to startups, scaleups and complete ecosystems, and enhancing it using state-of-the-art data analytics it is possible to identify the most effective key performance indicators (KPIs) to follow in each of the focal areas: human capital, structural capital and relational capital. This can be prototyped at all levels – the startups, the scaleups and the ecosystem – to focus efforts and allocate investments where the probability for success is the highest. Such an IC navigating tool compares very favorably against using only financial indicators, which cover the past, but in a fast-changing environment reveal very little about the potential for future growth. The IC Navigator is like a compass – a method that helps design a roadmap to realize a vision for a city or a region as quickly as possible.

Innovation happens on a micro level in SMEs but can only thrive and grow with macro support in the ecosystem or at the political level. Therefore, we provide tools and directions to define and support those qualitative factors which lead to sustainable growth via innovation. To this end, it is most important to unveil the interdependencies between IC reports on individual startups and scaleups and the macro/political perspective at the ecosystem level.

As most strategies stumble in the implementation phase and entrepreneurial ecosystems are difficult to manage, the selection of appropriate metrics and their interrelations are a decisive factor. Focusing on metrics that are imperfect or not meaningful can have a serious impact, leading management to make poor decisions that hurt the ecosystem members.

In innovation ecosystems we implement the concept, the model and practice of IC, defined, as above, as the intangible value of a business (or also an ecosystem, in the future), covering its human capital, relational capital and structural capital. An IC report is a balanced and holistic picture of both financial and intangible assets along with its *potential future value*.

We develop the IC model to measure and manage innovation ecosystems based on the definition of influence factors and KPIs applied to startups, scaleups and ecosystems. These KPIs are based on structured, unstructured, quantitative and qualitative data and are evaluated using the "Wissensbilanz Toolbox" and complemented by data analytics classification methods based on Open Source systems. Special emphasis is placed on the determination of the interrelationships between the different levels. The navigation tool approach is *adaptive* to all levels: the individual entrepreneurs, the startups, the scaleups, the innovation ecosystem and the countries and regions supporting them. The tool can be used ultimately as a guide for the realization of visions and goals.

Bibliography

Albats E and Fiegenbaum I (2016). *Key Performance Indicators of Startups: External View.* Manchester: The International Society for Professional Innovation Management (ISPIM). Retrieved from https://search.proquest.com/docview/1803692176?accountid=14136

Cavalcanti AFDR (2019). *A Method for Documenting the Goals and KPIs of Accelerators and Startups* (Doctoral dissertation, Carleton University)

Edvinsson, L (2002). *Corporate Longitude.* Pearson

The Intellectual Capital of The State of Israel [online]. http://economy.gov.il/Publications/ Publications/DocLib/IntellectualCapitalOfIsrael_Nov2007.pdf

Kemell KK, Wang X, Nguyen-Duc A, Grendus J, Tuunanen T, and Abrahamsson P (2019). 100+ Metrics for Software Startups: A Multi-Vocal Literature Review. arXiv preprint arXiv:1901.04819

Knowledge Café methodology: www.theworldcafe.com/

Lin YC and Edvinsson L (2019) *National IC Yearbook.* Springer; New Club of Paris

Pasher E (2005). The Intellectual Capital Report of Danya Cebus: Smart Construction. In Abdul Samad K (ed.) *Knowledge Management in the Construction Industry: A Socio-Technical Perspective.* IDEA. pp. (53–66)

Pasher E, Levin-Sagi M, and Hertzman H (2011). Knowledge Cities. In Carrilo FJ (ed.) *Holon: Transition into City of Children.* pp. (113–121)

Pasher E and Shachar S (2005). Intellectual Capital for Communities. In Bounfour A, Edvisson L (eds.) *The Intellectual Capital of Israel.* Routledge. pp. (139–150)

Prahalad CK and Hamel G, (1990). The Core Competence of the Corporation. *Harvard Business Review,* Vol. 68, Issue 3, pp. 79–91

9 Intellectual capital and digital technologies in academic entrepreneurship

Premises for a revolution?

Giustina Secundo and Rosa Lombardi

Introduction

In the university context intellectual capital (IC) is considered at the same time as mission and performance (Secundo et al., 2010). The growing attention to IC in universities is due in part to the role universities play in the knowledge-based society (Secundo et al., 2015; Secundo et al., 2018a) in part to the institutional transformations universities have experienced in recent years. Specifically, it has been widely argued that universities are vital actors in the knowledge-based society because of their contribution in shaping human capital (Pérez and Sanchez, 2007) with knowledge, competencies, abilities and expertise.

Moreover increasing attention to the third mission, besides the traditional teaching and research mission, is further increasing the impact and social value a university creates in the surrounding environment (Etzkowitz, 1983; Etzkowitz and Leydesdorff, 2000; Clark, 2004). In this scenario, entrepreneurial universities (Etzkowitz, 1983; Etzkowitz and Leydesdorff, 2000; Jongbloed et al., 2008; Lombardi et al., 2017; Lombardi et al., 2019) answer to the requirements of third mission achievement and stakeholder engagements, including also teaching and research (Clark, 1998; Lambert, 2003; Burritt et al., 2017). However, the renewed mission of entrepreneurial universities requires a major focus on IC management and performance management (Lee, 2010; Sangiorgi and Siboni, 2017).

Intellectual capital (IC) has been defined as "intellectual material, knowledge, experience, intellectual property, information … that can be put to use to create [value]" (Dumay, 2016, pp. 169). Thus, for most universities, IC is considered to be the main driver of value creation (Sangiorgi and Siboni, 2017; Secundo et al., 2016; Secundo et al., 2018b) and at the same time the main output (Secundo et al., 2010). At the European level, the increasing attention on and application of IC frameworks for performance measurement is also a consequence of the neoliberal transformation universities embraced in recent years to become more autonomous, efficient and competitive (Leitner et al., 2014).

Simultaneously, in the last years there has been an increasing trend of studies supporting the advent of digital technologies; different classifications and characteristics form the basis of the organizations' competitiveness (Giones and Brem, 2017; Nambisan et al., 2017; Rippa and Secundo, 2018; Secundo et al.,

2018; von Briel et al., 2018). Digital technologies, such as social media, mobiles, business analytics, Internet of Things, Big Data, Advanced Manufacturing, 3D printing, cloud and cyber-solutions, MOOCs and artificial intelligence are nowadays permeating all organizations, manufacturing or service, private or public (Fischer and Reuber, 2011; Greenstein et al., 2013; Fitzgerald et al., 2014). Digital technologies provide a lot of potentiality for business, entrepreneurship and management; they can enhance the development of the IC and strategic assets both in public and private organizations and in the market and society (Yoo, 2010).

At the university level, the different categories of digital technologies can enhance IC development, management, measurement and disclosure. Universities are extensively using websites and social media to communicate their IC (Bisogno et al., 2014; Low et al., 2015) and to demonstrate the value they are creating for society (Secundo et al., 2018a). Moreover, 3D printing can be adopted to realize and prototype research projects, thus contributing to the development of structural capital. Furthermore, all the business analytics could improve the performance measurement through IC indicators; Secundo et al. (2017a) argue that the available Big Data can support the development of IC in all its components: human capital, social capital and structural capital.

However, even if the disruptive role of digital technologies has been widely recognized at the business level, and even if IC research reached its cusp in the mid-2000s, new research is needed to understand the potentiality of digital technologies in IC management. In this scenario, our analysis is directed to investigate the impact of new digital technologies in the university scenario adopting the IC lens. Specifically, this chapter has the purpose to understand how digital technologies support the creation and the disclosure of IC in universities using a renewed framework. The research question to which we try to provide an answer is:

RQ: How could the emerging digital technologies impact on the development, management and disclosure of IC in academic entrepreneurship?

Thus, the research question is answered using the Rippa and Secundo theory framework (2018) as an interpretative lens to understand why and how a university, in accomplishing its mission in the form of academic entrepreneurship, derives value from digital technologies. Our findings reveal that a renewed framework based on the "input–output logic" promotes an understanding of how digital technologies support the creation, management and disclosure of IC in universities. Our chapter is novel because it provides results that advance support for IC and digital technologies in universities and is directed to the academic community and policymakers.

The remainder of the chapter is organized as follows: first it examines the relevant literature; it then presents the findings and posits the possible premises for a revolution; and finally it presents a discussion, conclusions and the path towards the revolution.

Literature review

IC in the academic entrepreneurship setting

While initially conceived as an institution with a teaching mission, in recent years, the university has been assuming a "third mission" (Molas and Gallart, 2005; Laredo, 2007): contributing to society and economic development more directly (Etzkowitz and Viale, 2010) and so integrating the traditional teaching and research mission. Now universities are being required to operate in a more entrepreneurial way (Gibb and Hannon, 2006), commercializing the results of their research, spinning out knowledge-based enterprises (Kirby, 2006) and enhancing the diffusion of innovation in increasingly knowledge-based societies (Etzkowitz, 2004). In this strategic role, knowledge assets and IC underpin the core drivers of value creation and need to be appropriately managed and measured (Marr et al., 2004) to assess the impact at the economic and social level.

IC can be conceived of as intellectual material, knowledge, experience, intellectual property and information that can be put to use to create value (Dumay, 2016). Moreover IC is considered valid for universities to meet the new management challenges they currently face as well as to diffuse their intangible resources and activities to stakeholders and society at large (Sanchez et al., 2009). As such, in recent years there has been a rising application of IC research in universities and a myriad of IC measurement frameworks have been proposed (Sanchez et al. 2009; Dumay, 2014).

For such purposes, universities play a determinant role and are being encouraged to see the advantages, both for their internal management and for their relations with society, of identifying and managing IC (Sánchez et al., 2009). As Secundo et al. (2015, p. 419) outline: "in research centres and universities, the key issue at stake is the effective management of intangible assets and IC, which constitutes the largest proportion of universities' assets". Similarly, Ramírez-Córcoles and Manzaneque-Lizano (2015) argue for European universities to present information on IC. Therefore, an IC research (ICR) agenda is relevant for universities seeking to understand how intangible and intellectual assets contribute to their mission and performance. In the IC literature, several definitions of IC have been proposed. As Pike et al. (2006, p. 233) outline, a significant obstacle when talking about IC is the absence of an agreed-upon definition. The term IC and the terms intangible assets, intellectual assets and intangibles are often used synonymously (Dumay et al., 2017a). Some studies stress the importance of IC in the progress of new ventures (Peña, 2002; Baum and Silverman, 2004) emphasizing its influence in entrepreneurial firms' successes, as it contributes to the creation of value and facilitates the ability to reach goals and objectives.

The term "intellectual capital" is usually employed as a synonym for intangible assets which can be transformed into economic value. Yet, there is no commonly accepted unified definition for IC. In a university setting, IC can play a crucial role (Sangiorgi and Siboni, 2017) and the term in this context incorporates the institution's non-tangible, financial or non-physical assets, including processes, capacity for innovation, patents, tacit knowledge of staff and their abilities, talents and skills, the recognition of society, and networks of collaborators and contacts (Burritt et al., 2017). The three main IC components (Guthrie et al., 2017) align with universities as follows (Ramírez and Gordillo, 2014: 175):

- Human capital (HC): the explicit and tacit knowledge of university students and staff (e.g. teachers, researchers, managers, administration and service staff), acquired through formal and non-formal education processes.
- Structural capital (SC): the explicit knowledge embodied in the scientific and technical outputs the university develops. It may be divided into: organizational capital – the operational environment derived from the interaction between research, managerial processes, organizational routines, corporate culture and values, internal procedures, quality and scope of the information system; and technological capital – the technological resources available at the university, such as bibliographical and documentary resources, archives, technical developments, patents, licences, software, databases.
- Relational capital (RC): refers to the value generated through the university's internal and external relations. This includes its relations with public and private partners, position and image in networks, brand, partnerships with the business sector and regional governments, links with non-profit organizations and society in general, collaborations with national and international networks and alliances, and reputation.

The weight, role and intrinsic meaning of each IC component differ depending on the university's profile, mission and vision, and national context (Secundo et al., 2016). These differ based on the types of universities. Those universities defined as research-intensive emphasize the critical role of researchers (HC), the publication record of researchers (SC), and networks with prestigious universities (SC). Entrepreneurial universities focus on staff with a commercial mindset that is involved in business-oriented activities (HC), the creation of spin-offs (SC) and partnership agreements with the private sector (RC). Teaching universities will concentrate on attracting quality staff and students (HC), developing graduate and post-graduate programmes (SC) and partnership agreements with prestigious universities for student mobility (RC) (see Secundo et al., 2016). These three IC components cannot be considered independently of each other, as they are inextricably linked and mobilized through universities' strategies and activities (Vagnoni and Oppi, 2015; Catasús, 2017).

In this scenario, developing IC means an "awareness and understanding [of] IC's potential for creating and managing a sustainable competitive advantage" (Secundo et al., 2016) in achieving the organizations' mission and objectives in the long term. Simultaneously, IC development was initiated through the slogan to make "the invisible visible by creating a discourse that all could engage in. Mission accomplished" (Petty and Guthrie, 2000), and allows for the recognition and specification of a primary step in the university's IC maturity.

Disclosing IC means: "the revelation of information that was previously secret or unknown" (Dumay and Guthrie, 2017, pp. 30), and interest in investigating the IC disclosure (ICD) practices of universities is on the rise (Cuozzo et al., 2017; Lombardi and Dumay, 2017; Sangiorgi and Siboni, 2017) as more and more top university managers are beginning to discover its benefits (Secundo et al., 2018a; Ndou et al., 2018). As a result of the "Bologna Process", and the idea of creating a European research space, most recent studies of ICD focus on the European context (Secundo et al., 2018a).

Managing IC means that specific indicators supporting decision-making processes by organizations represent a way to deal with IC. In this perspective, IC management mainly derives from "qualitative IC measurement models emphasizing the utility of IC in decision making" (Kujansivu, 2009) and it is a mission for universities and higher education (HE) institutions as they are created and funded with the purpose to build the workforce of tomorrow, stimulate organizational and technological innovation, and enhance the network of relationships which cross-fertilize industrial and academic expertise. The distinction between measurement and management is justified as follows: "one of the two approaches, the measurement approach, has aimed at providing a number expressive of the IC value, while the management approach, aimed at using the IC indicators derived from strategy for decision-making purposes, [and both have] emerged as different ways of dealing with IC (Habersam & Piber, 2003)" (Veltri et al., 2014). Universities are directed to proactively manage and measure the IC components.

However, IC measurement and management models are of several types (Edvinsson & Malone, 1997; Roos et al., 1997; Sveiby, 1997; ARC, 2000; DATI, 2000; Meritum report, 2002) and the application of the collective intelligence approach within universities supports the management of IC involving internal and external stakeholders adopting the ecosystem perspective (Secundo et al., 2016). Thus, the measurement of IC should move towards IC management defining paths of an organization's value creation based on knowledge (Veltri et al., 2014). In this scenario, many experiences exist in the European context including, for example, the INGENIO project to improve the knowledge management and value creation in universities (Sánchez and Elena, 2006; Bezhani, 2010). Managing IC is not simply "yet another management tool" (Secundo et al., 2015, p. 429) because IC should be at the core of the decision-making process (Secundo et al., 2015). In this way, IC can be developed especially to improve relational capital along the value chain (Bornemann and Wiedenhofer, 2014).

In light of previous consideration, the investigation is directed to understand how it is possible to benefit from digital technologies in such processes using IC components by universities adopting an ecosystem approach.

Digital technologies for IC

The utilization of digital technologies represents a thrilling development path for individuals and organizations among which universities, entrepreneurial universities and education institutions are playing a relevant role. Thus, digital technologies under several tools could improve IC development, management, measurement and disclosure by universities demonstrating the value creation for society (Secundo et al., 2017b; Secundo et al., 2018a).

Adopting the IC perspective, digital technologies and connected infrastructures have a strong potential for business models, innovations and entrepreneurship of universities (Lombardi et al., 2017) at a worldwide level. Thus, in the current scenario promoting academic entrepreneurship needs huge channels of value (Chang, 2017), involving increasingly all stakeholders in its context and re-shaping its boundaries (Dumay and Garanina, 2013; Dumay et al., 2018). The adoption of digital technologies tools by universities is especially analysed through the ecosystems in which they operate and survive to create social, economic and intangible values.

Additionally, significant literature (Nambisan, 2017; Rippa and Secundo, 2018) recognizes and systematizes digital technologies and infrastructures and their role in the academic entrepreneurship perspective. Particularly, Nambisan (2017) identifies as digital technologies the following three connected emerging blocks: (i) digital artefacts, (ii) digital infrastructures and (iii) digital platforms. Digital artefacts are directed to provide products and services to end-users and are composed of digital components, applications or content (Kallinikos et al., 2013). Digital artefacts assume several forms and sources. They are included in software and hardware devices as well as for instance in smartphones and other devices, in apparel, home appliances and toys.

Digital infrastructure is the digital tool and system of a socio-technical nature that supports the communication and/or computing capabilities (Ciborra, 2000; Nambisan, 2017; Rippa and Secundo, 2018) in innovations processes and in end-to-end activities in company systems. It is defined as a socio-technical process that identifies digitalization (Tilson et al., 2010) and establishes relationships is entrepreneurship and performance achievement. Thus, digital infrastructure is composed of several components, for instance, online communities, additive manufacturing, cloud computing and data analytics.

Digital platforms are services and/or architectures hosting complementary offerings (Parker et al., 2016; Rippa and Secundo, 2018; Tiwana and Konsynski, 2010), including also artefact components. Generally, the presence of a platform leader guides the modular platforms and value creation using codebase from software-based systems (Nambisan, 2017). They are also composed of modules identified as adjunct software subsystems linking platforms to several functions. Digital platforms are able to manage information technology capabilities through specialist frameworks answering to users' needs and allowing for utility sharing. Table 9.1 summarizes the main digital technologies for IC in the university context.

112 *Giustina Secundo and Rosa Lombardi*

Table 9.1 Digital technologies in the current complex scenario

Digital technologies

Artefacts	Infrastructure	Platforms
Blockchain	Apps, Mesh apps and service architecture	Additive manufacturing
Storytelling	Big Data and learning analytics	Artificial intelligence and machine learning
Business portfolio	Cloud computing	Intelligent things
Virtual and augmented reality	Social media	Internet of Things
Conversational system		Drone technology

Source: Our elaboration.

The underlying assumption behind our research is to consider that digital technologies tools could leverage the way academia is pursuing entrepreneurship processes with a pervasive effect on the rationale, processes and forms of academic entrepreneurship as well as on the stakeholders involved towards the achievement of university entrepreneurship goals (Rippa and Secundo, 2018).

Big Data and IC for universities

Since the ubiquity of Big Data, an emerging line of research has appeared in the IC research space (Secundo et al., 2018). Big Data currently represents a hot topic for researchers and practitioners (Laney, 2001; De Mauro et al., 2016; Erickson and Rothberg, 2014). It encompasses the enormous amounts of digital data from various sources that can be analysed to gain invaluable insights (Morabito, 2015). There are six main dimensions that characterize Big Data: volume, velocity, variety, veracity, variability, and value (Laney, 2001; Gandomi and Haider, 2015).

Secundo et al. (2017a) argue that the "available data and information within the sphere of Big Data can support the implementation of IC in all its components", especially, in fourth-stage IC research (Secundo et al., 2018a), where the role of IC cannot be confined within a single organization. By developing new approaches, strategies and infrastructure to acquire, store and manage the data continuously created in the entire ecosystem, Big Data can be a relevant contributor to shifting the focus of IC from organizations to the ecosystems in which they operate to create knowledge and achieve value on a wider scale (Secundo et al., 2017b). Within the university context, one of the main sources of Big Data is online media channels, such as websites, online reports, and, in particular, social media (Fortunato et al., 2017; Dutta, 2010) as used by students, alumni, future students, faculty and staff. Specifically, social media is a useful and rich channel of communication for information between organizations and their stakeholders (Chua, 2011). Social media is defined as "a group of Internet-based applications that build on the ideological and techno-logical foundations of Web 2.0, and that allow the creation and exchange of user-generated content" (Kaplan and Haenlein, 2010, p. 61). ICD could benefit from different digital technologies and among these from social media thanks to the creation and exchange of information instantaneously by allowing inter-active communication and relationships with all the stakeholders (Dumay and Guthrie, 2017).

In addition, evolutions in technology, Big Data and the way society communicates are shifting ICD practices from traditional media to online channels, like websites, Facebook and Twitter (Cuozzo et al., 2017; Dumay and Tull, 2007; Lombardi and Dumay, 2017). Some universities are using websites and social media extensively to communicate their unknown IC information (Bisogno et al., 2014; Low et al., 2015), going beyond regulated and voluntary reporting. Since online media channels are among the main sources of Big Data, the information disclosed through these channels could be a relevant contributor to ICD (Fortunato et al., 2017). They generate a massive, variable and valuable amount of data from a variety of sources (Secundo et al., 2017a) that could be leveraged for ICD, even if this is not intentionally disclosed as IC (Garanina and Dumay, 2017). As argued by Secundo et al. (2017a), Big Data currently available can support the practices of IC management, in the aim to overcome the hesita-tion for sharing IC information (Cuozzo et al., 2017; Schaper et al., 2017).

IC, digital transformation and academic entrepreneurship: premises for a revolution?

Through an integration of the findings from the literature studies on IC management within the university context, a process-based model has been developed to allow those universities and higher education systems involved in the achievement of the third mission (social engagement and regional devel-opment) through the implementation of academic entrepreneurship activities to take advantage of the emerging digital technologies in the creation, man-agement, measurement and disclosure of IC. The framework is based on an input–output logic which considers tangible and intangible aspects related to academic entrepreneurship. The innovativeness of the framework relies on its adaptation to different universities and higher education systems approaching an "Entrepreneurial Orientation" in the emerging scenario of the digital dis-ruption (Lombardi, 2019). Figure 9.1 illustrates the new framework.

Here, moving from the Rippa and Secundo (2018) framework, the main components of our proposed framework organized in input, output, process and value creation and digital technologies adopted will be described.

Intellectual capital (IC). IC represents the input and the main output of the frame-work described as follows: human capital (HC) refers to the intangible value that resides in the individual competencies of people (staff, students, professors, technicians, researcher, external stakeholders); structural capital (SC) comprises

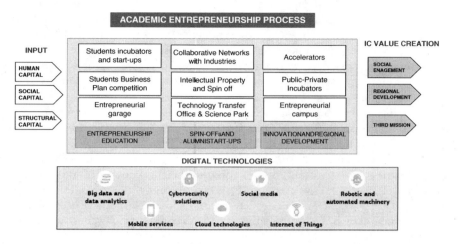

Figure 9.1 IC and digital technologies in academic entrepreneurship.
Source: Our elaboration.

the resources that are found in the organization itself, i.e. what remains when academic staff and students leave (value, processes, research projects' results, databases); relational capital (RC) refers to the intangible resources and capabilities able to generate value linked to the university's internal and external relations in terms of contact, agreements, sponsorship, collaborations.

Academic entrepreneurship process. The input is transformed into output by leveraging the following processes characterizing academic entrepreneurship: entrepreneurship education (entrepreneurship garages; student business plan competitions); spin-offs and alumni startups (collaborative networks with industry and alumni; intellectual property and spin-offs; technology transfer office & science park); innovation and regional development (accelerators; public–private "incubators"; entrepreneurial campus).

Academic entrepreneurship output. The most relevant output of the academic entrepreneurship process includes a large spectrum of entrepreneurial activities: large-scale science projects, creation of technology park, contracted research, consulting, patenting/licensing, spin-off firms, industry training courses, publishing academic results, producing highly qualified graduates. These outputs are developed and managed thanks to the disruptive role of the digital technologies that allow the power of the collective intelligence to be engaged with the academic context.

Digital technologies for IC. Digital technologies, such as social media, mobiles, business analytics, Internet of Things, Big Data, Advanced Manufacturing, 3D printing, cloud and cyber-solutions, MOOCs and artificial intelligence

IC in academic entrepreneurship   115

nowadays permeate all organizations, manufacturing or service, private or public (Fischer and Reuber, 2011; Greenstein et al., 2013; Fitzgerald et al., 2014). This wave of digital technologies enables the creation, development and management of all the IC and intangible assets created through the academic entrepreneurship process. For example, social Big Data allow students and alumni to be in contact with the university as regard current and future educational activities; 3D printing allows faculty and students to develop and realize the prototype of their projects; robotics is a novel technology supporting R&D activities within joint public–private laboratories; business plan development in collaboration with interested stakeholders is supported by the adoption of e-learning platforms.

IC value creation. The investigation of IC value creation dynamics of academic entrepreneurship cannot be afforded without taking into consideration its impact at the internal and external level. There is increasing difficulty in measuring and managing the strategic impact of IC when we move from the internal level (university) to the external one (environment) (Figure 9.1) (Elena-Perez et al., 2011). As regards value creation at the university level (internal level), it can be expressed in terms of quality assurance, an internal assessment report and international ranking (Secundo et al., 2015). These aspects allow the consideration of, first, IC development as a mission for universities and HE institutions as they are created and funded with the purpose to build the workforce of tomorrow, stimulate organizational and technological innovation, and enhance the network of relationships which cross-fertilize industrial and academic expertise. Second, IC is a metric of performance and the intangible report may well represent for HE and research organizations what the balance sheet and the income statement are for business companies. As regards value creation at the regional level and society as a whole (external impact), it can be expressed in terms of regional development and social engagement and finally third-mission achievement (Trequattrini et al., 2018). IC management of academic entrepreneurship allows universities to implement the general recommendation defined in the EU guide "Connecting Universities to Regional Growth" (Goddard and Kempton, 2011), i.e. the active engagement of universities and other HE institutions in regional innovation strategies for smart specialization, in cooperation with research centres, businesses and other partners in civil society. A collective intelligence approach as recommended by Secundo et al. (2016) is fully accomplished thanks to the wide adoption and assimilation of digital technologies by the university's community.

Discussion, conclusion and the path towards the revolution

The increasing interest in digital technologies and connected infrastructures is revealing thrilling insights, especially the real impact on several organizations' dimensions among which IC development, management, measurement and disclosure in universities worldwide. In this perspective, our chapter answers the research question "How can emerging digital technologies impact the development, management and disclosure of IC in academic entrepreneurship?" by proposing an innovative framework based on "input–output logic" and considering tangible and intangible aspects related to academic entrepreneurship. Thus, our framework proposition relies on its adaptation to different universities and higher education systems approaching an "Entrepreneurial Orientation" in the digital technologies revolution (Lombardi, 2019).

Interestingly, our analysis proposes the investigation of the impact of new digital technologies in the scenario of universities adopting the perspectives of IC components. Through the Rippa and Secundo (2018) framework, we discovered the main components of our new framework organized as input, output, process and value creation and digital technologies. Particularly, our main components are the IC dimensions, academic entrepreneurship processes, academic entrepreneurship output, digital technologies for IC, and IC value creation. Thus, our renewed framework mainly moved from the need to adopt new management and reporting tools, which incorporate IC (Sánchez and Elena, 2006) in the university context, even if several difficulties are experienced when trying to implement "business" thinking typical of the academic entrepreneurship activities in existence (Lombardi et al., 2017). Additionally, the measurement of IC should move towards IC management to identify the paths of an organization's value creation based essentially on knowledge creation and sharing (Veltri et al., 2014).

In this scenario, universities should use the IC of their academic, professional and public policy networks responding to social concerns, such as ethical and environmental issues. Thus, patents, publications, research and business researches or spin-offs are, for example, some of the results of IC component interaction. From here, universities create, transform and transfer knowledge, aligning it to their vision and mission using, in recent years, digital technologies to demonstrate the value creation for society (Secundo et al., 2018; Ndou et al., 2018). Examples include:

- websites and social media to communicate their IC (Bisogno et al., 2014; Low et al., 2015);
- mobile services and cloud technologies to provide and share information;
- social Big Data to provide students and alumni connection with the university for educational activities;
- 3D printing to provide faculty and students the opportunity to develop and realize the prototype of their projects;
- robotics to support R&D activities within joint public–private laboratories.

Thus, our renewed framework based on the input–output logic emphasizes the dynamic relationship among the three components of IC and their strategic impact on value-creation dynamics in academic entrepreneurship, proposing different categories of digital technologies to enhance the IC development, management, measurement and disclosure. Additionally, it provides critical examination of how IC in the university context requires a tailor-made framework to adapt all requirements deriving from a different stage of IC maturity.

Our framework is aligned to the need to recognize and develop IC as well as to assume IC as a management technology (Guthrie et al., 2012), especially when universities attempt to manage IC for the first time using different digital technologies. Following the maturity of IC stages in universities, the adoption of digital technologies could increase the value-creation dynamics at an internal and external level in the ecosystem scenario. Lastly, the ICD provided by universities is supported by digital technologies among which a special role is played Big Data analytics allowing for IC reporting (Lombardi and Dumay, 2017). The online media tools (e.g. websites, online reports and social media pages) used to inform and disclose IC to stakeholders in a timely manner (Dumay, 2016) represent relevant disclosure channels (Dumay and Tull, 2007; Lombardi and Dumay, 2017) for the university's IC.

Thus, the contributions of this chapter focus on recognizing a renewed framework to systematize digital technologies and IC components in the university scenario expanding existing literature. Beyond the theoretical implications for academia, this study carries practical implications for university managers. Our framework reveals that one of the benefits of IC development, management, measurement and disclosure for universities using digital technologies is in demonstrating their role and contribution to society, especially from an ecosystem perspective.

The main limitations of this chapter derive from the absence of empirical evidence. Future research is directed to collect data within the universities scenario demonstrating in practice how our renewed framework enhances IC development, management, measurement and disclosure through digital technologies and the adoption of connected infrastructures. Future research efforts might also focus on comparing the differences between IC and digital technologies in public and private universities.

References

Austrian Research Centers (ARC) (2000) Wissensbilanz 1999 Seibersdorf. [Online document] http://www.arcs.ac.at.

Baum, J.A. and Silverman, B.S. (2004), "Picking winners or building them? Alliance, intellectual, and human capital as selection criteria in venture financing and performance of biotechnology startups", *Journal of Business Venturing*, 19(3), 411–436.

Bezhani, I. (2010), "Intellectual capital reporting at UK universities", *Journal of Intellectual Capital*, 11(2), 179–207.

Bisogno, M., Citro, F. and Tommasetti, A. (2014), "Disclosure of university websites: Evidence from Italian data", *Global Business and Economics Review*, 16(4), 452–471.

Bornemann, M. and Wiedenhofer, R. (2014), "Intellectual capital in education: A value chain perspective", *Journal of Intellectual Capital*, 15(3), 451–470.

Burritt, R., Guthrie, J., Evans, E. and Christ, K. (2017), "Expanding collaboration between industry and business faculties in Australia", *Academic Leadership Series*, 8, 9–26.

118 *Giustina Secundo and Rosa Lombardi*

Catasús, B. (2017), "The relevance of IC indicators", in J. Guthrie, J. Dumay, F. Ricceri and C. Nielsen (Eds), *The Routledge Companion to Intellectual Capital: Frontiers of Research, Practice and Knowledge*, London: Routledge, 492–504.

Chang, S.H. (2017), "The technology networks and development trends of university–industry collaborative patents", *Technological Forecasting and Social Changes*, 118, 107–113.

Chua, A.Y. (2011), "How Web 2.0 supports customer relationship management in Amazon", *International Journal of Electronic Customer Relationship Management*, 5(3–4), 288–304.

Ciborra, C. (2000), "A critical review of the literature on the management of corporate information infrastructure", in *From Control to Drift: The Dynamics of Corporate Information Infrastructures*. Oxford: Oxford University Press, 15–40.

Clark, B.R. (1998), *Creating Entrepreneurial Universities: Organisational Pathways of Transformation*, Oxford, New York and Tokyo: IAU Press/Pergamon.

Clark, B.R. (2004), "Delineating the character of the entrepreneurial university", *Higher Education Policy*, 17(4), 355–370.

Cuozzo, B., Dumay, J., Palmaccio, M. and Lombardi, R. (2017), "Intellectual capital disclosure: A structured literature review", *Journal of Intellectual Capital*, 18(1), 9–28.

Danish Agency for Trade and Industry (DATI) (2000), A Guideline for Intellectual Capital Statements: A Key to Knowledge Management. [Online document] http://efs.dk/download.pdf/viden.uk.pdf.

De Mauro, A., Greco, M. and Grimaldi, M. (2016), "A formal definition of Big Data based on its essential features", *Library Review*, 65(3), 122–135.

Dumay, J. (2014), "Reflections on interdisciplinary accounting research: The state of the art of intellectual capital", *Accounting, Auditing & Accountability Journal*, 27(8), 1257–1264.

Dumay, J. (2016), "A critical reflection on the future of intellectual capital: From reporting to disclosure", *Journal of Intellectual Capital*, 17(1), 168–184.

Dumay, J. and Garanina, T. (2013), "Intellectual capital research: A critical examination of the third stage", *Journal of Intellectual Capital*, 14(1), 10–25.

Dumay, J. and Guthrie, J. (2017), "Involuntary disclosure of intellectual capital: Is it relevant?", *Journal of Intellectual Capital*, 18(1), 29–44.

Dumay, J., Guthrie, J., Ricceri, F. and Nielsen, C. (2017a), "The past, present and future for intellectual capital research: An overview", in J. Guthrie, J. Dumay, F. Ricceri and C. Nielsen (Eds), *The Routledge Companion to Intellectual Capital: Frontiers of Research, Practice and Knowledge*, London: Routledge. 1–18.

Dumay, J., Guthrie, J. and Rooney, J. (2018), "The critical path of intellectual capital", in J. Guthrie, J. Dumay, F. Ricceri and C. Nielsen (Eds), *The Routledge Companion to Intellectual Capital: Frontiers of Research, Practice and Knowledge*, London: Routledge, 21–39.

Dumay, J. and Tull, J. (2007), "Intellectual capital disclosure and price sensitive Australian stock exchange announcements", *Journal of Intellectual Capital*, 8(2), 236–255.

Dutta, S. (2010), "What's your personal social media strategy?", *Harvard Business Review*, 88(11), 127–130.

Edvinsson, L. and Malone, M.S. (1997), *Intellectual Capital: Realising Your Company's True Value by Finding Its Hidden Brainpower*, New York: Harper Business.

Elena-Pérez, S., Saritas, O., Pook, K. and Warden, C. (2011), "Ready for the future? Universities' capabilities to strategically manage their intellectual capital", *Foresight*, 13(2), 31–48.

Erickson, S. and Rothberg, H. (2014), "Big Data and knowledge management: Establishing a conceptual foundation", *Electronic Journal of Knowledge Management*, 12(2), 108–116.

IC in academic entrepreneurship   119

Etzkowitz, H. (1983). "Entrepreneurial scientists and entrepreneurial universities in American academic science", *Minerva*, 21(2), 198–233.

Etzkowitz, H. (2004), "The evolution of the entrepreneurial university", *International Journal of Technology and Globalization*, 1(1), 64–77.

Etzkowitz, H. and Leydesdorff, L. (2000), "The dynamics of innovation: From National Systems and 'Mode 2' to a triple helix of university–industry–government relations", *Research Policy*, 29(2), 109–123.

Etzkowitz, H. and Viale, R. (2010), "Polyvalent knowledge and the entrepreneurial university: A third academic revolution?", *Critical Sociology*, 36(4), 595–609.

Fischer, E. and Reuber, A.R. (2011), "Social interaction via new social media: (How) can interactions on Twitter affect effectual thinking and behavior?", *Journal of Business Venturing*, 26(1), 1–18.

Fitzgerald, M., Kruschwitz, N., Bonnet, D. and Welch, M. (2014), "Embracing digital technology: A new strategic imperative", *MIT Sloan Management Review*, 55(2), 1.

Fortunato, A., Gorgoglione, M., Messeni Petruzzelli, A. and Panniello, U. (2017), "Leveraging Big Data for sustaining open innovation: The case of social TV", *Information Systems Management*, 34(3), 238–249.

Gandomi, A. and Haider, M. (2015), "Beyond the hype: Big data concepts, methods, and analytics", *International Journal of Information Management*, 35(2), 137–144.

Garanina, T. and Dumay, J. (2017), "Forward-looking intellectual capital disclosure in IPOs: Implications for intellectual capital and integrated reporting", *Journal of Intellectual Capital*, 18(1), 128–148.

Gibb, A. and Hannon, P. (2006), "Towards the entrepreneurial university?", *International Journal of Entrepreneurship Education*, 4, 73–110.

Giones, F. and Brem, A. (2017), "Digital technology entrepreneurship: A definition and research agenda", *Technology Innovation Management Review*, 7(5), 44–51.

Goddard, J. and Kempton, L. (2011), *Connecting Universities to Regional Growth: A Practical Guide*, Brussels: EU.

Greenstein, S., Lerner, J. and Stern, S. (2013), "Digitization, innovation, and copyright: What is the agenda?", *Strategic Organization*, 11(1), 110–121.

Guthrie, J., Ricceri, F. and Dumay, J. (2012), "Reflections and projections: A decade of intellectual capital accounting research", *British Accounting Review*, 44(2), 68–92.

Guthrie, J., Dumay, J., Ricceri, F. and Nielsen, C., Eds. (2017), *The Routledge Companion to Intellectual Capital: Frontiers of Research, Practice and Knowledge*, London: Routledge.

Habersam, M. and Piber, M. (2003), "Exploring intellectual capital in hospitals: Two qualitative case studies in Italy and Austria", *European Accounting Review*, 12(4), 753–779.

Jongbloed, B., Enders, J. and Salerno, C. (2008), "Higher education and its communities: Interconnections, interdependencies and a research agenda", *Higher Education*, 56(3), 303–324.

Kallinikos, J., Aaltonen, A. and Marton, A. (2013), "The ambivalent ontology of digital artifacts", *MIS Quarterly*, 37(2), 357–370.

Kaplan, A.M. and Haenlein, M. (2010), "Users of the world, unite! The challenges and opportunities of social media", *Business Horizons*, 53(1), 59–68.

Kirby, D. (2006), "Creating entrepreneurial universities in the UK: Applying entrepreneurship theory in practice", *Journal of Technology Transfer*, 31, 599–603.

Kujansivu, P. (2009), "Is there something wrong with intellectual capital management models?", *Knowledge Management Research & Practice*, 7(4), 300–307.

Lambert, R. (2003), *Lambert Review of Business–Industry Collaboration*, Norwich: HMSO.

Laney, D. (2001), "3-D data management: Controlling data volume, velocity and variety", Application Delivery Strategies by META Group Inc. available at http://blogs.gartner.com/doug-laney/files/2012/01/ad949-3D-Data-Management-Controlling-Data-Volume-Velocity-and-Variety.pdf (accessed 20/04/2017).

Laredo, P. (2007), "Revisiting the third mission of universities: Toward a renewed categorization of university activities?", *Higher Education Policy*, 20(4), 441–456.

Lee, S.H. (2010), "Using fuzzy AHP to develop intellectual capital evaluation model for assessing their performance contribution in a university", *Expert Systems with Applications*, 37(7), 4941–4947.

Leitner, K.H., Curaj, A., Elena-Perez, S., Fazlagic, J., Kalemis, K., Martinaitis, Z., Secundo, G., Sicilia, M.A. and Zaksa, K. (2014), *A Strategic Approach for Intellectual Capital Management in European Universities: Guidelines for Implementation*, UEFISCDI Blueprint Series No. 1, Bucharest: Executive Agency for Higher Education, Research, Development and Innovation Funding.

Lombardi, R. (2019), "Knowledge transfer and organizational performance and business process: Past, present and future researches", *Business Process Management Journal*, 25(1), 2–9.

Lombardi, R. and Dumay, J. (2017), "Guest editorial: Exploring corporate disclosure and reporting of intellectual capital (IC): Emerging innovations", *Journal of Intellectual Capital*, 18(1), 2–8.

Lombardi R., Lardo A., Cuozzo B. and Trequattrini R. (2017), "Emerging trends in entrepreneurial universities within Mediterranean regions: An international comparison", *Euromed Business Journal*, 12(2), 130–145.

Lombardi, R., Massaro, M., Dumay, J. and Nappo, F. (2019), "Entrepreneurial universities and strategy: The case of the University of Bari", *Management Decision*, DOI 10.11.08/MD-06-2018-0690.

Low, M., Samkin, G. and Li, Y. (2015), "Voluntary reporting of intellectual capital: Comparing the quality of disclosures from New Zealand, Australian and United Kingdom universities", *Journal of Intellectual Capital*, 16(4), 779–808.

Marr, B., Schiuma, G. and Neely, A. (2004), "Intellectual capital: Defining key performance indicators for organisational knowledge assets", *Business Process Management Journal*, 10(5), 551–569.

Meritum Report (2002), *Guidelines for Managing and Reporting on Intangibles*, Meritum.

Molas-Gallart, J. (2005), "Defining, measuring and funding the third mission: A debate on the future of the university", *Coneixement i Societat*, 7(January–April), 6–27.

Morabito, V. (2015), *Big Data and Analytics: Strategic and Organizational Impacts*, Cham: Springer International.

Nambisan, S. (2017), "Digital entrepreneurship: Toward a digital technology perspective of entrepreneurship", *Entrepreneurship Theory and Practice*, 41(6), 1029–1055.

Nambisan, S., Lyytinen, K., Majchrzak, A. and Song, M. (2017), "Digital innovation management: Reinventing innovation management research in a digital world", *MIS Quarterly*, 41(1), 223–238.

Ndou, V., Secundo, G., Dumay, J. and Gjevori, E. (2018), "Understanding intellectual capital disclosure in online media Big Data: An exploratory case study in a university". *Meditari Accountancy Research*, 26(3), 499–530.

Parker, G., Van Alstyne, M. and Choudary, S.P. (2016), *Platform Revolution: How Networked Markets Are Transforming the Economy – and How to Make Them Work for You*, New York: W.W. Norton.

Peña, I. (2002), "Intellectual capital and business start-up success", *Journal of Intellectual Capital*, 3(2), 180–198.

IC in academic entrepreneurship   121

Pérez, S.E. and Sánchez, M.P. (2007), *Governing the University of the 21st Century: Intellectual Capital as a Tool for Strategic Management*, Madrid: Universidad Autonoma de Madrid.

Petty, R., and Guthrie, J. (2000), "Intellectual capital literature review: Measurement, reporting and management", *Journal of Intellectual Capital*, 1(2), 155–176.

Pike, S., Boldt-Christmas, L. and Roos, G. (2006), "Intellectual capital: Origin and evolution", *International Journal of Learning and Intellectual Capital*, 3(3), 233–248.

Ramírez, Y. and Gordillo, S. (2014), "Recognition and measurement of intellectual capital in Spanish universities", *Journal of Intellectual Capital*, 15(1), 173–188.

Ramírez-Córcoles, Y. and Manzaneque-Lizano, M. (2015), "The relevance of intellectual capital disclosure: Empirical evidence from Spanish universities", *Knowledge Management Research & Practice*, 13(1), 31–44.

Rippa, P. and Secundo, G. (2018), "Digital academic entrepreneurship: The potential of digital technologies on academic entrepreneurship", *Technological Forecasting and Social Change*, 146, 900–911.

Roos, J., Roos, G., Dragonetti, N.C. and Edvinsson, L. (1997), *Intellectual Capital: Navigating in the New Business Landscape*, Basingstoke: Macmillan.

Sánchez, M. and Elena, S. (2006), "Intellectual capital in universities", *Journal of Intellectual Capital*, 7(4), 529–548.

Sánchez, M., Elena, S. and Castrillo, R. (2009), "Intellectual capital dynamics in universities: A reporting model", *Journal of Intellectual Capital*, 10(2): 307–324.

Sangiorgi, D. and Siboni, B. (2017), "The disclosure of intellectual capital in Italian universities", *Journal of Intellectual Capital*, 18(2): 354–372.

Schaper, S., Nielsen, C. and Roslender, R. (2017), "Moving from irrelevant intellectual capital (IC) reporting to value-relevant IC disclosures: Key learning points from the Danish experience", *Journal of Intellectual Capital*, 18(1), 81–101.

Secundo, G., Del Vecchio, P., Dumay, J. and Passiante, G. (2017a), "Intellectual capital in the age of Big Data: Establishing a research agenda", *Journal of Intellectual Capital*, 18(2), 242–261.

Secundo, G., Dumay, J. and Del Vecchio, P. (2018), "Guest editorial. Intellectual capital and Big Data: A managerial revolution or a reality?", *Meditari Accountancy Research*, 26(3), 354–360.

Secundo, G., Dumay, J., Schiuma, G. and Passiante, G. (2016), "Managing intellectual capital through a collective intelligence approach: An integrated framework for universities", *Journal of Intellectual Capital*, 17(2), 1–23.

Secundo, G., Lombardi, R. and Dumay, J. (2018a), "Intellectual capital in education", *Journal of Intellectual Capital*, 19(1), 2–9.

Secundo, G., Margherita, A., Elia, G. and Passiante, G. (2010), "Intangible assets in higher education and research: Mission, performance or both?", *Journal of Intellectual Capital*, 11(2), 140–157.

Secundo, G., Massaro, M., Dumay, J. and Bagnoli, C. (2018b), "Intellectual capital management in the fourth stage of IC research: A critical case study in university settings", *Journal of Intellectual Capital*, 19(1), 157–177.

Secundo, G., Perez, S.E., Martinaitis, Ž. and Leitner, K.H. (2017b), "An intellectual capital framework to measure universities' third mission activities", *Technological Forecasting and Social Change*, 123, 229–239.

Secundo, G., Perez, S.E. and Žilvinas Leitner, K.H. (2015), "An intellectual capital maturity model (ICMM) to improve strategic management in European universities: A dynamic approach", *Journal of Intellectual Capital*, 16(2), 419–442.

Sveiby, K.E. (1997), "The intangible assets monitor", *Journal of Human Resource Costing and Accounting*, 2(1), 73–97.

Tilson, D., Lyytinen, K. and Sørensen, C. (2010), "Research commentary. Digital infrastructures: The missing IS research agenda", *Information Systems Research*, 21(4), 748–759.

Tiwana, A. and Konsynski, B. (2010), "Complementarities between organizational IT architecture and governance structure", *Information Systems Research*, 21(2), 288–304.

Trequattrini, R., Lombardi, R., Lardo, A. and Cuozzo, B. (2018), "The impact of entrepreneurial universities on regional growth: A local intellectual capital perspective", *Journal of the Knowledge Economy*, 9(1), 199–211.

Vagnoni, E. and Oppi, C. (2015), "Investigating factors of intellectual capital to enhance achievement of strategic goals in a university hospital setting", *Journal of Intellectual Capital*, 16(2), 331–363.

Veltri, S., Mastroleo, G. and Schaffhauser, M. (2014), "Measuring intellectual capital in the university sector using a fuzzy logic expert system", *Knowledge Management Research and Practice*, 12(2), 175–192.

von Briel, F., Davidsson, P. and Recker, J. (2018), "Digital technologies as external enablers of new venture creation in the IT hardware sector", *Entrepreneurship Theory and Practice*, 42(1), 47–69.

Yoo, Y. (2010), "Computing in everyday life: A call for research on experiential computing", *MIS Quarterly*, 34(2), 213–231.

10 Overcoming cognitive bias through intellectual capital management

The case of pediatric medicine

Francesca Dal Mas, Daniele Piccolo and Daniel Ruzza

Introduction and objective of the study

According to Resource-Based View theory, organizations need to have access to unique resources to support their strategy. Among these resources, intellectual capital (IC) has been named as one of the most critical ones. Since its first development, IC is defined as the set of intangible assets that the firm owns or has access to (Edvinsson and Malone, 1997). The literature claims that IC has three pillars. The first pillar is represented by human capital (HC), which highlights people's knowledge, skills, and experience (Massaro *et al.*, 2018). The second pillar has been defined as structural capital (SC), the organization's codified knowledge, culture, and database (Massaro *et al.*, 2017). Last, but not least, the literature recognizes relational capital (RC), which represents the power of the internal and external relationships that the organization enjoys (Dal Mas *et al.*, 2019).

Literature has investigated how intangibles management can help the progress of all organizations, be they private or public, increasing their value. The sectors analyzed go beyond the industrial and manufacturing fields, including, for instance, education (Lombardi *et al.*, 2019; Secundo *et al.*, 2018), sports (Gerrard and Lockett, 2018), financial and insurance services (Bontis and Serenko, 2009; Edvinsson and Malone, 1997) among others, coming to nations, cities, and communities (Bounfour and Edvinsson, 2005; Lin and Edvinsson, 2008). The healthcare sector has been widely investigated from an IC perspective (Cavicchi and Vagnoni, 2017; Lytras and De Pablos, 2009; Santos-Rodrigues *et al.*, 2013)

A recent study (Dal Mas, *et al.*, 2019) starts from the market capitalization value pattern over time framework (Edvinsson, 2000) to explain the progress of surgery, which benefits from innovation and intangibles management in several ways. The structural capital injections in terms of new technologies and human capital injections in terms of new skills required and a shift in the role of the surgeon lead to new positive outcomes that benefit from both the new knowledge created as well as a higher efficacy and better use of resources. The outcomes involve an increasing value for several stakeholders, from the patient who gets a better quality service to the hospital or healthcare organization

124   *Francesca Dal Mas et al.*

which reduces its costs and enjoys a better flow of processes, from the physician who gets qualified help and reduces his/her working stress to the whole society that benefits from all data acquired and new knowledge created.

However, sometimes, knowledge can limit success by showing a dark side. The literature recognizes, for instance, the presence of knowledge barriers and difficulties in sharing (Massaro *et al.*, 2014), as well as intellectual liabilities (Giuliani, 2013).

When it comes to one of the pillars of IC, such as HC, we may cite the French Enlightenment writer Voltaire, who once said: "The human brain is a complex organ with the wonderful power of enabling man to find reasons for continuing to believe whatever it is that he wants to believe."Voltaire referred to cognitive bias, which can be defined as the disproportionate weight in favor of or against one thing, concept, person, or group compared with another, usually in a way considered to be unfair. People too often rely on their knowledge and beliefs, limiting the possible options, and often leading to a wrong decision or choice.

Cognitive bias is frequent in any field, and, as said, is often generated by the knowledge that a person has, which limits the will to take a wider portfolio of options into consideration. If cognitive bias is always dangerous in decision making, it becomes particularly critical in medicine, where it can lead to severe negative outcomes. According to medical literature, up to 75% of all clinical errors are of cognitive origins (O'Sullivan and Schofield, 2018). O'Sullivan and Schofield (2018) recognized several kinds of bias in clinical medicine, as summarized in Table 10.1.

According to O'Sullivan and Schofield (2018), several "debias" techniques and tools may be activated to mitigate the cognitive bias effect in clinical practice. Among these, the authors highlight the importance of bias-specific teaching sessions for med students, slowing down from stress, metacognition and considering the alternatives, using checklists, enhancing the knowledge of statistical tools, using new methods (like gaming).

Starting from these premises, our chapter wants to investigate the eventual impact of intellectual capital on cognitive bias, to understand if and how IC management can help in overcoming bias in medicine, considering the newly available digital technologies.

Research method

To carry on our analysis, and thus investigate our research goal, we employ a case study approach (Yin, 2009). According to the literature, case studies are particularly interesting when "the impetus of our research project lies in some broad, familiarizing, questions about a social process" (Swanborn, 2010, p. 24). Case studies help to spread the academic debate among practitioners, who have "preference for case studies and research derived from practice experience" (Bolton and Stolcis, 2003). The use of more qualitative approaches could help to disseminate academic research among practitioners (Dal Mas, Massaro, *et al.*,

Overcoming cognitive bias 125

Table 10.1 Bias in clinical medicine according to O'Sullivan and Schofield (2018)

Availability bias	More recent and readily available answers and solutions are preferentially favored because of ease of recall and incorrectly perceived importance
Base rate neglect	The underlying incident rates of conditions or population-based knowledge are ignored as if they do not apply to the case in question
Confirmation bias	Diagnosticians tend to interpret the information gained during a consultation by someone else to fit their preconceived diagnosis, rather than the converse
Conjunction rule	The incorrect belief that the probability of multiple events being correct is more significant than a single event. This relates to "Occam's razor" – a unifying and straightforward explanation is statistically more likely than multiple unrelated explanations
Overconfidence	An inflated opinion of the own diagnostic ability leads to a subsequent error. The confidence in the judgments does not align with the accuracy of these judgments
Representativeness	Misinterpreting the likelihood of an event considering both the critical similarities to its parent population and the individual characteristics that define that event
Search satisfying	Ceasing to look for further information or alternative answers when the first plausible solution is found
Diagnostic momentum	Continuing a clinical course of action instigated by previous clinicians without considering the information available and changing the plan if required (mainly if that plan was commenced by a more senior clinician)
The framing effect	Reacting to a particular choice in a different way depending on how the information is presented
Commission bias	A tendency towards action rather than inaction. The bias is "omission bias"

2019; Massaro *et al.*, 2016). Moreover, the literature highlights how some managerial issues require deeper insights that are not possible within the traditional statistical analysis (Mouritsen, 2006). To ensure transparency, we tried to be as rigorous as possible in our work and data collection and analysis (Massaro *et al.*, 2019).

The case study is about the BACRI project, carried on by Nucleode Srl, an innovative start-up company in the field of technology and healthcare based in Gorizia, Italy,[1] together with the Pediatric Department of Burlo Garofolo Hospital of Trieste, Italy. "BACRI" is the acronym in Italian for "BAmbino CRItico," which in English stands for "critical child," referring to the health condition of children. We chose to analyze the case of Nucleode since it is an innovative company working in one of the sectors which are most affected by a swift digital transformation, that of healthcare (Christensen *et al.*, 2000; Dal Mas *et al.*, 2019; Iacopino *et al.*, 2018; Lucas, 2015; Mascia and Di Vincenzo, 2011; Snowdon *et al.*, 2015). Moreover, Nucleode can be defined as an intense-knowledge company, fully relying on its IC to carry on its projects. Its HC

126 *Francesca Dal Mas et al.*

involves high-skilled professionals from a variety of fields (medicine, engineering, IT, graphic design, and communications). As a technological company, Nucleode relies on its SC, which is the core of its product development. The company uses its developed technologies as well as top know-how coming from multinational companies like Microsoft. RC is for Nucleode as relevant as the other dimensions of IC. Indeed, the company works closely with hospitals, private clinics, universities, physicians, as well as other organizations in the field of technology and medicine to ensure the best connections and trials to the end users of its products. The context in which Nucleode operates makes it ideal for studying the impact of intangibles management and digital technologies on healthcare and medicine. Data acquisition was made involving several actors of the project, and all information coming out of the data collection was double checked with the company's CEO.

The BACRI project

Introduction

In everyday clinical practice, severe infections are defined as conditions such as sepsis, meningitis, pneumonia, bacterial gastroenteritis, osteomyelitis, and orbital cellulite (Bleeker *et al.*, 2001). Those infections in pediatric age are still associated with high mortality and morbidity rates, not only in the most disadvantaged socio-cultural contexts but also in economically more advanced countries. In Italy, for instance, severe infections are responsible for 1.7% of infant mortality under the age of five (ISTAT, 2014), a fact that has undergone profound changes over the years thanks to the improvement of socio-economic conditions and the role played by primary prevention. Suffice it to say that in 1960, infectious causes were responsible for 41.3% of infant mortality under five years, while in 1930, this percentage reached 69.7% (ISTAT, 2014). Italy is today one of the countries in the world with the lowest infant mortality rate (3.9 deaths per 1,000 live births/year under five years) and the mortality rate for infectious causes is lower than the data reported in other European countries (13.6% of infant mortality between 1–14 years in Belgium[2] (Wilson and Bhopal, 1998).

In children aged 0–14 years, the incidence rate of severe infections is around 1% per year (Van Den Bruel *et al.*, 2006). This means that an outpatient pediatrician will be faced with a severe bacterial infection two to three times a year, numbers much lower than the total non-severe infections that are managed in daily clinical practice. This data, while on the one hand seems to reduce the extent of the problem for the individual pediatrician, on the other increases the probability of not promptly recognizing more serious clinical conditions, which lack the symptoms and warning signs typically associated with a severe bacterial infection ("textbook signs": impaired perfusion, signs of meningeal irritation, cyanosis, petechiae, convulsions) (Van Den Bruel *et al.*, 2005).

For the outpatient pediatrician and the inpatient Emergency Department's pediatrician, it is vital to be able to distinguish children with an acute infectious disease at low risk from those potentially at high risk. An element that makes this distinction even more difficult is the fact that in the early stages of illness, a severe infection may begin with signs and symptoms, not unlike those of an uncomplicated infectious disease. This fact is confirmed by the work of Thompson *et al.* (2006), in which the onset symptoms of bacterial meningitis in the first 4 hours of illness can be totally non-specific (e.g. rhinorrhea and cough), while the signs of meningeal irritation and the petechial rash can appear in an average time of 13–22 hours from the onset of symptoms.

For the pediatrician, the main challenge is therefore represented by the early recognition of those clinical conditions in which, despite the lack of signs and symptoms of high specificity due to severe bacterial infection, a possible evolution in this sense cannot be excluded. Cognitive bias is possible due to the type of symptoms that may occur. The bias may be of several types as recognized by O'Sullivan and Schofield: overconfidence of the physician in quickly formulating a diagnosis, representativeness (especially in those times of the year like winter when many children get low-risk illnesses like flu), or framing (when the initial symptoms may recall a common disease).

In the literature, there are numerous works aimed at identifying signs and symptoms of alarm that can allow the early recognition of a potentially critical child and thus guide the work of the clinician (Van Den Bruel *et al.*, 2006; Hewson *et al.*, 2000; Pantell *et al.*, 2004). Most of the papers presented underline that greater sensitivity and specificity can be achieved by analyzing together more signs and symptoms, according to patient approach models described as "classification trees."

The development of the BACRI project

On the model of the Belgian experience (Van Den Bruel *et al.*, 2006) it was proposed by Professor Egidio Barbi, MD Chair of the Pediatric Department of Burlo Garofolo Hospital in Trieste, Italy, to perform a prospective and multicenter study, which aims to assess sensitivity and specificity achieved by seven variables in identifying a severe bacterial infection in children aged 0–14 years, who do not show signs and symptoms of high specificity due to severe bacterial infection in progress.

The project, which was soon named "BACRI" to recall the aim of understanding the critical health condition of the child under observation, was employed by the start-up company Nucleode Srl. The BACRI platform (Figure 10.1) uses cloud computing technologies for data collection, storage, and export. Cloud computing, intended as a flexible and cost-effective model for the supply of e-Government ICT services, represents a tool for saving and rationalizing IT resources through economies of scale. For these reasons, the use of the cloud is foreseen in the ICT strategies of many countries, and at the European level, the references to cloud computing are multiplied in the strategic documents and the main programs.

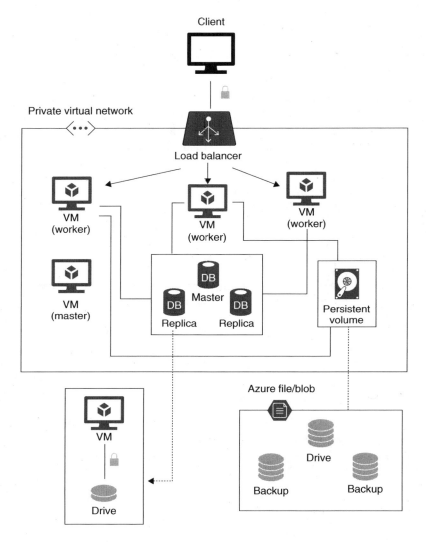

Figure 10.1 The BACRI flow.

The application is a cloud-based system that is online 24/7, and that can be easily accessed without any specific IT knowledge. It is protected from external intrusions and ensures high data privacy levels, according to the Health Insurance Portability and Accountability Act (HIPAA), the ISO 27001 standard and the General Data Protection Regulation (GDPR – Regulation EU2016/679). The platform is built upon micro-service architecture and is constantly monitored and backed up. The data is separated into chunks that are encrypted independently so that, even in the case of intrusion, all the information would not be readable to the attacker. All connections, both from client to server and from server to DB, are secured by the latest TLS protocol.

Personal information and clinical data are entered into the system by out-patient pediatricians or inpatient ER pediatricians through a responsive web interface, usable from a desktop computer, laptop, or mobile phone. During data entry, the system shows anomalous values based on certain parameters such as the patient's age, body temperature, heart rate, and respiratory rate, allowing easy identification of patients at immediate risk. Clinical data is then immediately rendered anonymous and prepared for statistical analysis.

The clinical study, now being completed, is being conducted by among the four most famous hospitals in pediatric care in Italy: the Burlo Garofolo Pediatric Institute (Trieste), the Agostino Gemelli University Polyclinic (Rome), the Giannina Gaslini Pediatric Hospital (Genoa), the ASUIUD (Udine) and by a group of outpatient pediatricians from the Friuli Venezia Giulia and Apulia Regions in Italy.

A first objective of the study is to provide an operational tool (score / flow chart) in which the search for specific clinical variables in a context of first acceptance may allow the early identification of children potentially at high risk, thus reducing the cognitive bias of the physician and helping the operator with a rigorous technological tool.

The secondary objective of the study is to strengthen territory–hospital exchange through work that brings together family pediatricians, hospital pediatricians, and cultural associations of pediatricians in the creation of a net-work of contacts and operational choices, which allows reporting and manage-ment of critical cases.

Other goals include enhancing the general knowledge in pediatric medi-cine by studying the database: symptoms, early diagnosis, coherence, and final diagnosis. Results are scheduled to be published in peer-reviewed journals, presented at medical conferences and congresses, and used during training and lessons to med students and pediatric residents.

Communication and dissemination to families through brochures and leaflets may also be on the agenda once the system gains enough data, to make parents or guardians aware of dangerous situations and the need for immediate care.

Discussion

The BACRI project aims at collecting and analyzing clinical data to enable the early identification of children potentially at high risk. The technological platform relies on the collection of a relevant amount of data, thanks to the involvement of several pediatric hospitals and departments, as well as outpatient pediatricians. The output of the platform can be an aid for the physicians involved, who will be able to formulate a diagnosis overcoming his/her bias due to overconfidence, representativeness, or framing. Indeed, as stated above, knowledge can sometimes represent a danger for HC since human beings can

130   *Francesca Dal Mas et al.*

limit their options due to their bias. SC happens to be immune to human bias. A PC or software will elaborate every single piece of information as if it was a unique one, no matter what has happened before, or how many times a different or similar situation has occurred. SC can then act as a precious help to HC to support the decision-making processes. So, is there a predominance of SC over HC?

The literature has highlighted the dark side of knowledge. Cognitive bias can be defined as one such issue, mainly referring to one of the pillars of IC, such as HC.

The BACRI case is a practical example of SC, which has the aim, among others, to reduce cognitive bias. However, the BACRI platform is something more than SC. Indeed, it is functioning and successful only if HC and RC enter the game as well. The database needs the collection of data, which are inserted by physicians. The pediatricians must make a first analysis of the patients and their symptoms to fill the dataset. The correct identification of symptoms is essential to let BACRI analyze the picture and give a high or low-risk alert. HC is so essential to feed SC, to let it become fully operational.

Moreover, despite BACRI not being artificial intelligence software, the more data are collected, the better analysis can be undertaken. To ensure a massive availability and collection of data, several institutions, hospitals, and pediatricians must be involved. RC is then essential to the BACRI initial team, to ensure that more and more organizations and practices decide to adopt the system and to fill it with data. RC is then strategic when it comes to the dissemination of the results, which, one day, may include families and guardians, who could help to alert the healthcare facility if certain symptoms are shown together. RC is so relevant that may lead to co-production.

A galaxy of intangibles is needed to overcome cognitive bias, with HC, SC, and RC working together and fostering each other.

Conclusion

As stated in the introduction, the IC of an organization is among the key resources to create value. However, sometimes the knowledge connected to IC can show a dark side. Cognitive bias coming from previous knowledge and beliefs often affects HC by limiting the options and leading to wrong decisions. Bias in medicine can be particularly dangerous. The case of BACRI allowed investigating the pediatric sector, in which the early diagnosis of high-risk infections is crucial to saving a child's life. Several times physicians are biased by their past experiences, by the high number of cases seen in the same period, or by the way symptoms show. BACRI, as an SC digital tool, supports physicians in detecting high-risk children, to provide them with immediate care. However, BACRI, as a part of SC, can work properly only if supported by the HC and RC dimensions. The joint effect of SC, HC, and RC is the key to help the overcoming of cognitive bias, in a virtuous circle. Intangibles management is then able to limit the dark side of knowledge.

Notes

1 See the company website www.nucleode.com.
2 See Care-and-Health. The Flemish agency for care and health (agency of the Flemish Ministry for Health and Family). Link: www.zorgen-gezondheid.bc.

References

Bleeker, S.E., Moons, K.M.G., Derksen-Lubsen, G., Grobbee, D.E. and Moll, H.A. (2001), "Predicting serious bacterial infection in young children with fever without apparent source", *Acta Paediatrica, International Journal of Paediatrics*, Vol. 90, pp. 1226–1232.

Bolton, M.J. and Stolcis, G.B. (2003), "Ties that do not bind: Musings on the specious relevance of academic research", *Public Administration Review*, Vol. 63 No. 5, pp. 626–630.

Bontis, N. and Serenko, A. (2009), "A causal model of human capital antecedents and consequents in the financial services industry", *Journal of Intellectual Capital*, Vol. 10 No. 1, pp. 53–69.

Bounfour, A. and Edvinsson, L. (2005), *Intellectual Capital for Communities: Nations, Regions, and Cities*, Elsevier, Burlington, MA.

Cavicchi, C. and Vagnoni, E. (2017), "Does intellectual capital promote the shift of healthcare organizations towards sustainable development? Evidence from Italy", *Journal of Cleaner Production*, Vol. 153, pp. 275–286.

Christensen, C.M., Bohomer, R. and Kenagy, J. (2000), "Will disruptive innovations cure health care?", *Harvard Business Review*, Vol. 78 No. 5, pp. 102–112.

Dal Mas, F., Massaro, M., Lombardi, R. and Garlatti, A. (2019), "From output to outcome measures in the public sector: A structured literature review", *International Journal of Organizational Analysis*, forthcoming.

Dal Mas, F., Paoloni, P. and Lombardi, R. (2019), "Wellbeing of women entrepreneurship and relational capital: A case study in Italy", in Lepeley, M.T., Kuschel, K., Eijdenberg, E. and Pouw, N. (Eds.), *Exploring Wellbeing among Women in Entrepreneurship: A Global Perspective*, Routledge, London, forthcoming.

Dal Mas, F., Piccolo, D., Edvinsson, L., Presch, G., Massaro, M., Skrap, M., Ferrario di Tor Vajana, A., *et al.* (2019), "The effects of artificial intelligence, robotics, and Industry 4.0 technologies: Insights from the healthcare sector", *Proceedings of the First European Conference on the Impact of Artificial Intelligence and Robotics*, Academic Conferences and Publishing International Limited, forthcoming.

Dal Mas, F., Piccolo, D., Edvinsson, L., Skrap, M. and D'Auria, S. (2019), "Strategy innovation, intellectual capital management and the future of healthcare: The case of Kiron by Nucleode", in Matos, F., Vairinhos, V., Salavisa, I., Edvinsson, L. and Massaro, M. (Eds.), *Knowledge, People, and Digital Transformation: Approaches for a Sustainable Future*, Springer, Cham, forthcoming.

Edvinsson, L. (2000), "Some perspectives on intangibles and intellectual capital 2000", *Journal of Intellectual Capital*, Vol. 1 No. 1, pp. 12–16.

Edvinsson, L. and Malone, M. (1997), *Intellectual Capital: Realizing Your Company's True Value by Finding Its Hidden Brainpower*, HarperCollins, New York.

Gerrard, B. and Lockett, A. (2018), "Team-specific human capital and performance", *British Journal of Management*, Vol. 29 No. 1, pp. 10–25.

Giuliani, M. (2013), "Not all sunshine and roses: Discovering intellectual liabilities 'in action'", *Journal of Intellectual Capital*, Vol. 14 No. 1, pp. 127–144.

Hewson, P.H., Poulakis, Z., Jarman, F., Kerr, J.F., McMaster, D., Goodge, J. and Silk, G. (2000), "Clinical markers of serious illness in young infants: A multicentre follow-up study", *Journal of Paediatrics and Child Health*, Vol. 36, pp. 221–225.

Iacopino, V., Mascia, D. and Cicchetti, A. (2018), "Professional networks and the alignment of individual perceptions about medical innovation", *Health Care Management Review*, Vol. 43 No. 2, pp. 92–103.

ISTAT (2014), "La mortalità dei bambini ieri e oggi in Italia (Anni 1887–2011)", Istat, available at: www.istat.it/it/files/2014/01/Mortalita_-sotto_i_5_anni-.pdf.

Lin, C.Y.-Y. and Edvinsson, L. (2008), "National intellectual capital: Comparison of the Nordic countries", *Journal of Intellectual Capital*, Vol. 9 No. 4, pp. 525–545.

Lombardi, R., Massaro, M., Dumay, J. and Nappo, F. (2019), "Entrepreneurial universities and strategy: The case of the University of Bari", *Management Decision*, doi:10.11.08/MD-06-2018-0690.

Lucas, D.P. (2015), "Disruptive transformations in health care: Technological innovation and public policy reforms in the hospital industry", *International Journal of Interdisciplinary Organizational Studies*, Vol. 9 No. 1, pp. 1–22.

Lytras, M.D. and De Pablos, P.O. (2009), "Managing, measuring and reporting knowledge-based resources in hospitals", *International Journal of Technology Management*, Vol. 47 No. 1–3, pp. 96–113.

Mascia, D. and Di Vincenzo, F. (2011), "Understanding hospital performance: The role of network ties and patterns of competition", *Health Care Management Review*, Vol. 36 No. 4, pp. 327–337.

Massaro, M., Dumay, J. and Bagnoli, C. (2017), "When the investors speak: Intellectual capital disclosure and the web 2.0", *Management Decision*, Vol. 55 No. 9, pp. 1888–1904.

Massaro, M., Dumay, J. and Bagnoli, C. (2019), "Transparency and the rhetorical use of citations to Robert Yin in case study research", *Meditari Accountancy Research*, pp. 44–71.

Massaro, M., Dumay, J., Garlatti, A. and Dal Mas, F. (2018), "Practitioners' views on intellectual capital and sustainability: From a performance-based to a worth-based perspective", *Journal of Intellectual Capital*, Vol. 19 No. 2, pp. 367–386.

Massaro, M., Dumay, J.C. and Guthrie, J. (2016), "On the shoulders of giants: Undertaking a structured literature review in accounting", *Accounting, Auditing and Accountability Journal*, Vol. 29 No. 5, pp. 767–901.

Massaro, M., Pitts, M., Zanin, F. and Bardy, R. (2014), "Knowledge sharing, control mechanisms and intellectual liabilities in knowledge-intensive firms", *Electronic Journal of Knowledge Management*, Vol. 12 No. 2, pp. 117–127.

Mouritsen, J. (2006), "Problematising intellectual capital research: Ostensive versus performative IC", *Accounting, Auditing and Accountability Journal*, Vol. 19 No. 6, pp. 820–841.

O'Sullivan, E.D. and Schofield, S.J. (2018), "Cognitive bias clinical medicine", *Journal of the Royal College of Physicians of Edinburgh*, Vol. 48 No. 3, pp. 225–232.

Pantell, R.H., Newman, T.B., Bernzweig, J., Bergman, D.A., Takayama, J.I., Segal, M., Finch, S.A., *et al.* (2004), "Management and outcomes of care of fever in early infancy", *Journal of American Medical Association*, Vol. 291 No. 10, pp. 1203–1212.

Santos-Rodrigues, H., Faria, J., Cranfield, D. and Morais, C. (2013), "Intellectual capital and innovation: A case study of a public healthcare organisation in Europe", *Electronic Journal of Knowledge Management*, Vol. 11 No. 4, pp. 361–372.

Secundo, G., Massaro, M., Dumay, J.C. and Bagnoli, C. (2018), "Intellectual capital management in the fourth stage of IC research: A critical case study in university settings", *Journal of Intellectual Capital*, Vol. 19 No. 1, pp. 157–177.

Snowdon, A., Schnarr, K. and Alessi, C. (2015), "Global trends in health-system innovation", in Singh, V.K. and Lillrank, P. (Eds.), *Innovations in Healthcare Management: Cost-Effective and Sustainable Solutions*, CRC Press, Boca Raton, pp. 11–32.

Swanborn, P. (2010), *Case Study Research: What, Why and How?*, Sage, London.

Thompson, M.J., Ninis, N., Perera, R., Mayon-White, R., Phillips, C., Bailey, L., Harnden, A., *et al.* (2006), "Clinical recognition of meningococcal disease in children and adolescents", *Lancet*, Vol. 367, pp. 397–403.

Van Den Bruel, A., Bartholomeeusen, S., Aertgeerts, B., Truyers, C. and Buntinx, F. (2006), "Serious infections in children: An incidence study in family practice", *BMC Family Practice*, Vol. 7 No. 23, doi:10.1186/1471-2296-7-23.

Van Den Bruel, A., Bruyninckx, R., Vermeire, E., Aerssens, P., Aertgeerts, B. and Buntinx, F. (2005), "Signs and symptoms in children with a serious infection: A qualitative study", *BMC Family Practice*, Vol. 6 No. 36, doi:10.1186/1471-2296-6-36.

Wilson, D. and Bhopal, R. (1998), "Impact of infection on mortality and hospitalization in the North East of England", *Journal of Public Health Medicine*, Vol. 20 No. 4, pp. 386–395.

Yin, R.K. (2009), *Case Study Research: Design and Methods*, Sage, Thousand Oaks, CA, 4th Ed.

Part IV

Comparative view on national intellectual capital

11 Sustainable National Intellectual Capital in the digital age

A global outlook

Carol Y. Y. Lin and Leif Edvinsson

Introduction

The digital age, also called the information age since the 1970s, enables us to transfer information freely and quickly through the internet and email, and to gain information and networking efficiently through Google Search, Facebook, LinkedIn, Instagram and other social media. What are the common characteristics of these communication tools? Unlike land and equipment, they are the intangibles created by human wisdom. Nowadays, ICT (information, communication and technology) has become a yardstick to weigh the advancement of a nation. Countries with more advanced ICT are considered to be more competitive.

Traditionally, economists utilize metrics such as GDP per capita and other similar economic indicators as a measure of a country's growth and progress. In recent years, there has been a shift away from models of productivity that focus on tangible assets – capital, machinery, land, and raw material – to intangible assets such as knowledge, skills, information and innovation. National as well as corporate competitiveness relies more and more on the intangibles, for example, the possession of talented manpower, national/corporate image, government efficiency and networking for sustainability. Particularly in the post–financial–crisis era, it has become clear that countries with higher national intangibles weathered the crisis better and rebounded more robustly than those with lower intangibles (Lin et al., 2013[2014]: 71). The 2008 financial crisis also exhibited the inability of traditional monitoring tools to prevent crisis. As a result, there is a growing need to monitor and analyze trends of national intangibles (Stahle, Stahle and Lin, 2015).

Intangible assets are often synonymous with the term "intellectual capital", which can be defined as the "intellectual material – knowledge, information, intellectual property, experience – that can be put to use to create wealth" (Stewart, 1997 cited from Lin and Edvinsson, 2011). We have been working on intellectual capital research for almost 16 years, with a special focus on national-level intellectual capital (NIC). Over the years, in addition to academic journal papers and conference papers, a total of 13 NIC books have been published promoting the importance of NIC as well as investigating the 2008 global financial crisis from the perspective of NIC (Lin and Edvinsson, 2011; Lin et al., 2013/2014).

This chapter introduces our NIC 3.0 model – Sustainable NIC (SNIC). Although the NIC model is still valid, having been developed through version

138   Carol Y. Y. Lin and Leif Edvinsson

1.0 with 28 indicators and version 2.0 with 48 indicators (Stahle, Stahle and Lin, 2015), we regard it is time to supplement the NIC model with a model for Sustainable National Intellectual Capital (SNIC) in responding to the demand for sustainability and the digital age. At one meeting in Malmo, Sweden in 2013, Leif Edvinsson and I (Carol) talked about the future importance of connectivity and contactivity (CNC). In doing so, we jointly drew the five-dimensional SNIC model as exhibited in Appendix 11.1, with CNC binding the other four dimensions together. This chapter shares the research findings based on our SNIC model, generally for 59 countries and particularly highlighting some outstanding countries in various indicators.

In what follows, we first describe the development of the SNIC model. Second, we exhibit the global SNIC ranking. Third, we show the relationship between SNIC and GDP per capita (ppp). Fourth, we display the general SNIC and CNC profiles of 23 major countries. Fifth, we explain the global profile of digital readiness for the 59 countries. Finally, we conclude this chapter.

The development of the SNIC model

Still based on the NIC 1.0 and 2.0 models of human capital, market capital, process capital and renewal capital, SNIC includes five dimensions, namely health, public structure, education, renewal and CNC (connectivity and contactivity). Public structure is somewhat similar to process capital, education to human capital and renewal capital remains the same. Two new dimensions, "health" and "CNC", have been added. Since SNIC depicts sustainability, we adopted futuristic thinking and substituted market capital for the dimensions of health and CNC, envisioning the issues aroused from rapidly aging societies and the increasingly connected world. Also, with the rationale that when public structure is sound and connectivity is strong, market capital should naturally follow. We drew four interlocking circles (health, public structure, education and renewal) with a ring of CNC to reinforce the linkage of the four circles and forge their relationships, as shown in Appendix 11.1.

With this conceptual model, we have to work on the indicators to make sense of the SNIC model. As with the NIC model, the data source of the SNIC model is from the database of the widely accepted International Institute for Management Development (IMD), which has published the *World Competitiveness Yearbook* for over 30 years. That is, the IMD database provides valid and quality data, which are consistent for annual data updating and cover both qualitative and quantitative indicators suitable for the calculation of intangible assets, as the intangibles cannot be fully represented by simply adding up some objective indicators. Since SNIC is positioned to be a supplement to the NIC model, we tried to use different indicators to achieve a synergy effect for the two models. During the validation process, we selected around 60 indicators out of over 300 IMD indicators, undertook many rounds for statistical testing and eventually retained 44 indicators in five dimensions with good reliability ranging from .81 to .88 and good explaining power of each indicator for each dimension through SEM (structural equation modeling) analysis. Readers can refer to Appendix 11.2 for the selected indicators of the SNIC model.

Sustainable National Intellectual Capital 139

Just as the NIC, the SNIC model utilizes two types of data: data with an absolute value, such as *"trade to GDP ratio"* in the CNC dimension, and data with a qualitative rating by experts, based on a scale of 1–10, such as *"sustainable development"* in the renewal dimension. Out of the total 44 indicators, 30 are subjective in nature, marked "S" in the last column of Appendix 11.2. To integrate quantitative scores and qualitative ratings, all numerical indicators were transformed by taking the ratio of the absolute value relative to the highest value of each quantitative variable and then multiplying by 10 to transform the number into a 1–10 score. Using the aforementioned data analysis methods, SNIC was constructed for the 59 countries in the dataset, covering data from 2001 to the most recent data, some from 2017 and some from 2018.

Global SNIC ranking

Table 11.1 shows the global SNIC ranking of 59 countries based on the most recent data of each indicator. The first ten SNIC countries by descending order are: Denmark, Switzerland, Norway, the Netherlands, Singapore, Finland, Sweden, Luxembourg, Canada and UAE. The top ten countries include four Nordic countries, three other European countries, one Asian, one North American and one Middle-Eastern country. The four Nordic countries have always been at the top of the list of our previous NIC studies (Lin and Edvinsson, 2011; Lin et al., 2013[2014]), with Finland and Sweden usually alternating the top position followed by Denmark and Norway. Interestingly, Denmark is number one and Norway is number three in the SNIC. The results show that Norway has excelled Finland and Sweden in the SNIC, indicating the need for a further study regarding what Norway has done over recent years. It is no surprise that Switzerland and Singapore are still in the top five, since their performance was also outstanding in the NIC model. Luxembourg and the Netherlands are also strong in the intangibles, ranking within the top ten in the 2017 NIC model. Canada and UAE are new members in the top-ten list. In the past, Canada has always lagged behind its strong neighbor, USA, in the NIC; surprisingly it surpassed USA in the SNIC. UAE is the biggest surprise to be included in the top-ten list, advancing from its NIC ranking of 24.

The bottom five SNIC countries include Venezuela (59th), Brazil (58th), Columbia (57th), Ukraine (56th) and Croatia (55th). It is not surprising that these countries are also at the bottom of the NIC rankings with the exception of Croatia. Croatia was ranked 49th in the 2017 NIC. Particularly, there is a message for Brazil, as the other BRIC countries have acceptable SNIC rankings among the 59 countries, with China ranked 33rd, India 41st and Russia 45th. Since intangible assets have become more and more important for developed and developing countries alike, Brazil needs to ponder how not to lag behind the other BRIC countries.

To probe the relationship between the SNIC and NIC models, we have prepared Table 11.2 comparing both their scores and rankings. Readers can refer to Appendix 11.3 for the NIC version 2.0 indicators. The comparison shows very high correlations between the two models, with a score correlation of .949 and a ranking correlation of .952. That means, although SNIC has two new dimensions,

Table 11.1 SNIC and its components' score and ranking for 59 countries

	Health		Public		Education		Renewal		CNC		Overall SNIC	
Mean	6.416		5.465		5.995		5.319		5.197		28.391	
SD	1.212		1.072		1.049		1.096		0.850		4.907	
Country	Score	Ranking	Score	Ranking	Score	Ranking	Score	Ranking	Score	Ranking	Score	Ranking
Argentina	5.63	41	3.90	54	4.55	52	4.06	52	4.19	53	22.33	52
Australia	7.79	10	5.84	27	6.76	14	5.23	31	5.03	32	30.66	21
Austria	7.87	8	6.20	13	6.47	20	6.52	10	6.04	11	33.10	13
Belgium	7.45	14	5.55	32	7.02	10	6.40	12	5.94	14	32.36	15
Brazil	4.91	53	3.58	57	4.06	59	3.77	56	3.92	58	20.23	58
Bulgaria	5.12	50	4.43	49	4.29	56	4.07	51	4.57	47	22.48	50
Canada	8.02	5	6.57	10	7.55	6	6.11	14	5.79	15	34.03	9
Chile	5.69	38	5.95	20	5.36	43	4.49	43	5.08	30	26.58	39
China	5.94	36	5.94	21	5.91	34	5.75	24	5.02	34	28.56	33
Colombia	4.49	57	4.08	52	4.28	57	3.83	55	4.04	55	20.72	57
Croatia	5.65	40	4.04	53	4.77	47	3.52	57	3.95	57	21.92	55
Czech Republic	6.68	28	5.86	25	5.62	40	5.17	32	5.46	21	28.80	32
Denmark	8.38	3	6.81	5	7.67	2	7.43	1	6.52	4	36.80	1
Estonia	6.32	32	5.71	29	6.34	27	5.46	28	5.52	20	29.36	28
Finland	7.96	6	6.35	11	7.45	7	6.55	9	6.04	11	34.35	6
France	7.71	12	5.72	28	6.43	21	5.79	23	4.81	40	30.46	23
Germany	7.84	9	6.05	16	6.37	26	6.33	13	5.35	24	31.93	18
Greece	5.75	37	3.62	56	5.82	36	4.48	44	4.63	46	24.29	44
Hong Kong	6.73	27	6.70	8	6.71	15	5.71	26	6.95	2	32.80	14
Hungary	5.52	45	5.24	38	4.81	46	4.70	39	4.35	49	24.62	43
Iceland	7.94	7	6.22	12	7.29	8	5.94	19	5.95	13	33.34	11
India	4.78	54	5.35	37	5.62	40	4.59	40	4.66	44	25.00	41
Indonesia	4.44	58	5.13	39	4.75	48	4.40	47	4.72	43	23.45	47
Ireland	6.55	30	5.93	23	6.55	19	5.84	20	6.50	5	31.37	19
Israel	7.13	18	5.94	21	7.26	9	7.12	3	5.66	17	33.11	12
Italy	6.98	22	4.44	47	5.68	38	4.99	34	4.80	42	26.89	37

Country												
Japan	7.35	17	5.71	29	5.85	35	5.83	21	5.01	35	29.75	25
Jordan	6.15	34	5.05	41	6.33	28	4.94	37	5.28	25	27.75	35
Kazakhstan	5.59	43	5.49	35	6.15	32	4.82	38	5.08	30	27.12	36
Korea	6.58	29	5.36	36	6.40	23	6.08	16	4.84	38	29.27	29
Lithuania	6.06	35	5.50	34	6.19	31	5.74	25	5.78	16	29.27	29
Luxembourg	7.45	14	6.71	7	6.71	15	6.11	14	7.28	1	34.26	8
Malaysia	6.27	33	6.02	19	6.20	30	5.81	22	5.42	22	29.72	26
Mexico	5.13	48	4.23	50	4.37	54	3.89	54	4.41	48	22.03	54
Netherlands	8.31	4	6.73	6	7.57	5	6.80	5	6.42	6	35.83	4
New Zealand	7.10	19	6.05	16	6.24	29	4.96	36	5.25	26	29.60	27
Norway	8.46	2	6.97	4	7.66	3	6.79	7	6.27	7	36.14	3
Peru	5.13	48	4.70	44	4.71	50	3.45	58	4.21	52	22.20	53
Philippines	5.21	47	4.69	45	5.47	42	4.03	53	4.14	54	23.55	46
Poland	5.34	46	5.01	42	6.02	33	4.58	41	4.84	38	25.80	40
Portugal	6.98	22	5.53	33	6.85	12	5.43	29	5.66	17	30.44	24
Qatar	7.01	21	7.38	2	6.41	22	5.61	27	5.60	19	32.00	17
Romania	4.66	55	4.64	46	4.42	53	4.43	46	4.66	44	22.81	48
Russia	4.95	52	4.44	47	5.67	39	4.45	45	4.28	51	23.79	45
Singapore	7.43	16	7.09	3	7.62	4	6.80	5	6.64	3	35.58	5
Slovak Republic	5.04	51	4.23	50	4.31	55	4.16	49	4.81	40	22.55	49
Slovenia	6.53	31	5.57	31	6.40	23	5.39	30	5.37	23	29.25	31
South Africa	5.60	42	3.41	58	4.75	48	4.31	48	4.29	50	22.35	51
Spain	7.10	19	5.07	40	5.76	37	4.98	35	4.88	37	27.80	34
Sweden	7.74	11	6.09	14	6.98	11	7.38	2	6.13	8	34.31	7
Switzerland	8.50	1	6.66	9	7.81	1	7.12	3	6.09	10	36.18	2
Taiwan	6.78	26	5.86	25	6.59	18	6.51	11	5.17	29	30.90	20
Thailand	5.57	44	5.91	24	5.14	45	5.04	33	5.23	27	26.88	38
Turkey	5.67	39	5.00	43	4.66	51	4.52	42	4.97	36	24.81	42
UAE	6.94	24	7.85	1	6.64	17	6.03	18	6.12	9	33.57	10
Ukraine	4.64	56	3.74	55	5.17	44	4.11	50	3.97	56	21.63	56
United Kingdom	6.89	25	6.08	15	6.38	25	6.06	17	5.18	28	30.60	22
USA	7.65	13	6.03	18	6.81	13	6.72	8	5.03	32	32.23	16
Venezuela	3.48	59	2.46	59	4.09	58	2.68	59	2.81	59	15.53	59

Table 11.2 Score and ranking comparison between SNIC and NIC

| | Total score | | | |
	SNIC 2018		NIC 2017*	
Mean	*28.391*		*23.608*	
SD	*4.907*		*4.380*	
2 Score Correlation		*0.949*		
2 Ranking Correlation		*0.952*		
Country	*Score*	*Ranking*	*Score*	*Ranking*
Argentina	22.33	*52*	17.93	*55*
Australia	30.66	*21*	26.51	*20*
Austria	33.10	*13*	27.49	*16*
Belgium	32.36	*15*	27.04	*17*
Brazil	20.23	*58*	17.35	*57*
Bulgaria	22.48	*50*	20.42	*42*
Canada	34.03	*9*	27.51	*15*
Chile	26.58	*39*	21.99	*35*
China	28.56	*33*	20.86	*40*
Colombia	20.72	*57*	17.83	*56*
Croatia	21.92	*55*	18.94	*49*
Czech Republic	28.80	*32*	23.74	*28*
Denmark	36.80	*1*	30.74	*2*
Estonia	29.36	*28*	24.65	*26*
Finland	34.35	*6*	29.93	*6*
France	30.46	*23*	24.73	*25*
Germany	31.93	*18*	28.21	*12*
Greece	24.29	*44*	19.26	*45*
Hong Kong	32.80	*14*	28.79	*9*
Hungary	24.62	*43*	20.43	*41*
Iceland	33.34	*11*	26.91	*18*
India	25.00	*41*	18.63	*52*
Indonesia	23.45	*47*	18.75	*51*
Ireland	31.37	*19*	28.23	*11*
Israel	33.11	*12*	28.15	*13*
Italy	26.89	*37*	21.94	*36*
Japan	29.75	*25*	26.31	*22*
Jordan	27.75	*35*	19.38	*44*
Kazakhstan	27.12	*36*	21.18	*37*
Korea	29.27	*29*	25.76	*23*
Lithuania	29.27	*29*	24.09	*27*
Luxembourg	34.26	*8*	28.95	*8*
Malaysia	29.72	*26*	23.28	*30*
Mexico	22.03	*54*	18.88	*50*
Netherlands	35.83	*4*	29.95	*5*
New Zealand	29.60	*27*	26.45	*21*
Norway	36.14	*3*	29.43	*7*
Peru	22.20	*53*	19.17	*47*
Philippines	23.55	*46*	18.49	*53*
Poland	25.80	*40*	22.07	*34*
Portugal	30.44	*24*	23.15	*31*
Qatar	32.00	*17*	23.01	*32*
Romania	22.81	*48*	19.69	*43*
Russia	23.79	*45*	19.23	*46*

Sustainable National Intellectual Capital 143

Table 11.2 Cont.

Country	Total score			
	SNIC 2018		NIC 2017★	
Mean	28.391		23.608	
SD	4.907		4.380	
2 Score Correlation		0.949		
2 Ranking Correlation		0.952		
Country	Score	Ranking	Score	Ranking
Singapore	35.58	5	29.99	4
Slovak Republic	22.55	49	20.98	39
Slovenia	29.25	31	23.72	29
South Africa	22.35	51	18.16	54
Spain	27.80	34	22.85	33
Sweden	34.31	7	30.34	3
Switzerland	36.18	2	31.95	1
Taiwan	30.90	20	27.79	14
Thailand	26.88	38	21.18	37
Turkey	24.81	42	19.04	48
UAE	33.57	10	25.51	24
Ukraine	21.63	56	17.26	58
United Kingdom	30.60	22	26.61	19
USA	32.23	16	28.25	10
Venezuela	15.53	59	13.79	59

★ NIC 2017 excluded FC.

health and CNC, and there are only about one out of four overlapping indicators, the ranking of SNIC does not deviate too much from that of NIC.

It is worth noting that three countries (marked in green) have shown great improvement when comparing NIC with SNIC. Canada advanced its ranking from 15 to 9, Norway from 7 to 3, and UAE shows the most remarkable advancement from 24 to 10. Three other countries (marked in red) show regression, Hong Kong from 9 to 14, Sweden from 3 to 7, and USA from 10 to 16. Although the results of the above-mentioned six countries are still in the upper 30th percentile of the total 59 countries, the ebb and flow indicate the need for some attention. For example, why is Canada advancing while USA is regressing? Why did UAE spring up so fast?

SNIC and GDP per capita (ppp)

To show the relationships of SNIC and its components (health, public structure, education, renewal, and connectivity and contactivity) with GDP per capita (ppp) (hereinafter referred to as GDP for brevity), Figure 11.1 to Figure 11.6 are prepared. Figure 11.1 shows a high correlation (.741) between SNIC and GDP (see the coefficient at the left bottom corner), indicating the higher the

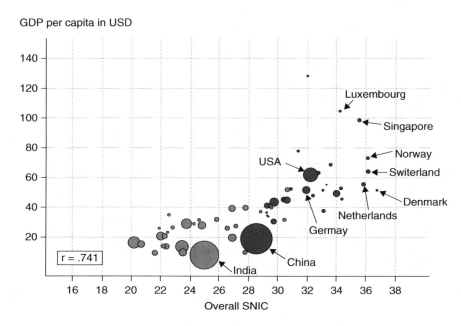

Figure 11.1 The relationship between SNIC and GDP per capita (ppp) for 59 countries.

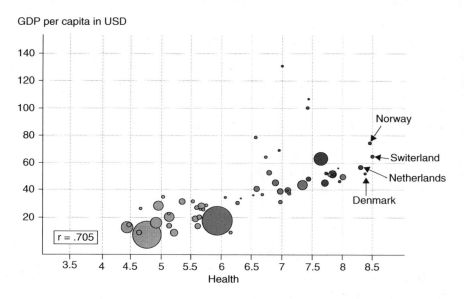

Figure 11.2 The correlation between health and GDP per capita (ppp) for 59 countries.

Sustainable National Intellectual Capital 145

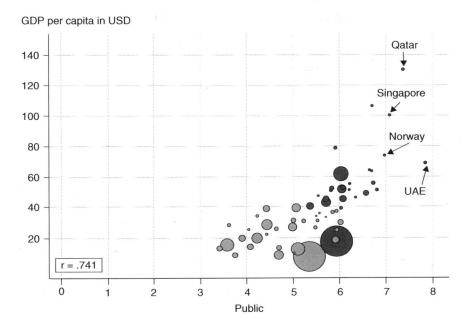

Figure 11.3 The correlation between public structure and GDP per capita (ppp) for 59 countries.

SNIC score the higher the GDP. Countries with higher SNIC scores in the right upper corner are identified with marks, namely Denmark, Switzerland, Norway, Singapore and Luxembourg. Interestingly, most of them are small countries as the size of the bubbles represents population. Four large countries (USA, Germany, China and India) are also identified for readers to know their relative position in the background bubbles for other figures.

Figure 11.2 shows the relationship between the first component, "health", with GDP, indicating a high correlation of .705. Switzerland, Norway, Denmark and the Netherlands have much better health than other countries.

Figure 11.3 shows the relationship between the second component, "public structure", with GDP, indicating a high correlation of .741. UAE, Qatar, Singapore and Norway have a much better public structure than other countries.

Figure 11.4 shows the relationship between the third component, "education", with GDP, indicating a high correlation of .69. Switzerland, Norway and Singapore have a much better education system than other countries.

Figure 11.5 shows the relationship between the fourth component, "renewal", with GDP, indicating a high correlation of .689. Denmark, Sweden, Switzerland, Norway and Singapore have a much higher level of renewal capital than other countries.

Figure 11.6 shows the relationship between the fifth component, "CNC", with GDP, indicating a high correlation of .583. Luxembourg, Hong Kong and Singapore have a much better CNC than other countries.

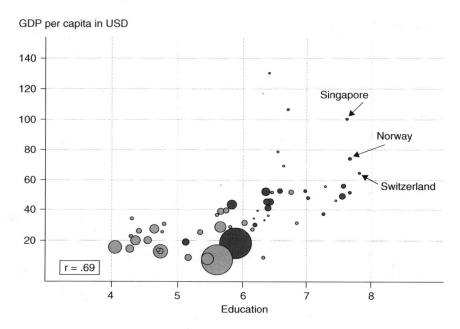

Figure 11.4 The correlation between education and GDP per capita (ppp) for 59 countries.

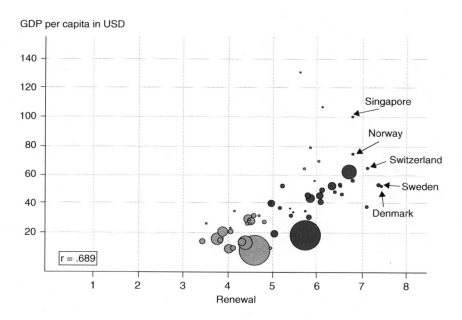

Figure 11.5 The correlation between renewal and GDP per capita (ppp) for 59 countries.

Sustainable National Intellectual Capital   147

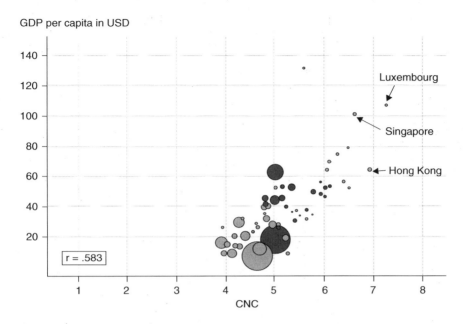

Figure 11.6 The correlation between CNC and GDP per capita (PPP) for 59 countries.

Table 11.3 Countries and SNIC components having a high correlation with GDP per capita (ppp)

Country	SNIC	Edu.	Health	Public structure	Renewal	CNC
Denmark	X		X		X	
Switzerland	X	X	X		X	
Norway	X	X	X	X	X	
Singapore	X	X		X	X	X
Luxembourg	X					X
Netherlands	X		X			
Qatar				X		
UAE				X		
Sweden					X	
Hong Kong						X

Source: Summarized by this study.

Table 11.3 summarizes the results of Figures 11.1–11.6, showing that both Norway and Singapore are selected five times, Switzerland four times, and Denmark three times. In other words, Norway, Singapore, Switzerland and Denmark are the four countries identified as high performers in terms of SNIC vs. GDP.

General SNIC and CNC profile of major countries

Since this chapter focuses on sustainability and the digital age, Figures 11.7–11.12 present the profile of sustainable national intellectual capital (SNIC) and connectivity and contactivity (CNC) of three sets of countries. The first set includes eight advanced countries, namely Australia, New Zealand, Canada, USA, Denmark, Finland, Norway and Sweden. That is, two countries in Australasia, two in North America and four Nordic countries. The rationale of putting these countries together is because their economic development follows a similar path. The second set includes eight European countries, namely Austria, Belgium, France, Germany, Luxembourg, the Netherlands, Switzerland and United Kingdom. The third set covers seven countries, with some known for their advancement in technology. They are Hong Kong, Israel, Japan, Korea, Singapore, Taiwan and UAE.

Figure 11.7 shows that the SNIC of Denmark and Norway has grown over the years, with Norway having the most obvious improvement, moving from the bottom two in 2001 to the top two in 2018. Finland shows the greatest fluctuation, moving from the top position in 2001 to number three, having been overtaken by Denmark and Norway in 2018. Moreover, Finland exhibited the most obvious dip for the years 2007 and 2008, perhaps due to the global financial crisis. Sweden has been up and down over the years, ending with a small decline in 2018. Canada shows a slight decline in 2018, compared to its 2001 score. Australia, New Zealand and USA show an obvious decline and are

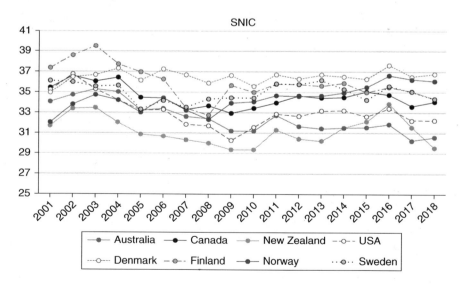

Figure 11.7 The SNIC of two Australasian, two North American and four Nordic countries over 18 years.

Sustainable National Intellectual Capital 149

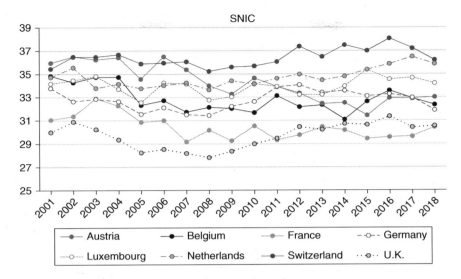

Figure 11.8 The SNIC of eight major European countries over 18 years.

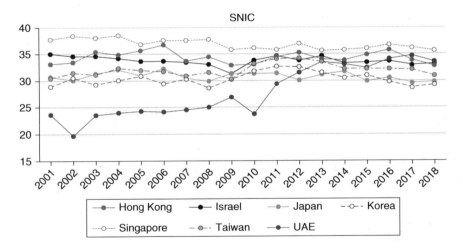

Figure 11.9 The SNIC of five Asian countries, Israel and UAE over 18 years.

the bottom three in 2018. In this set, only Denmark and Norway have shown progress in SNIC over the 18 years.

Figure 11.8 shows that Switzerland became the best performer from 2007 onward, surpassing Austria. The Netherlands is the second best performer in 2018. Although Luxembourg is the third best performer in 2018, it has not shown much progress compared to its 2001 score. Austria has the largest decline,

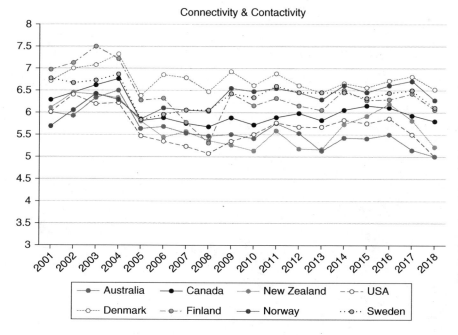

Figure 11.10 The CNC of two Australasian, two North American and four Nordic countries over 18 years.

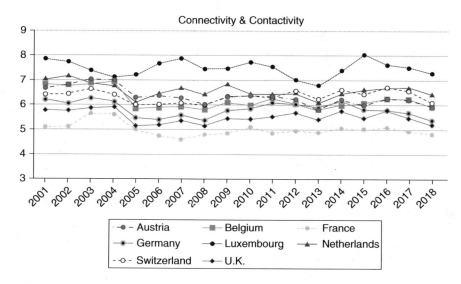

Figure 11.11 The CNC of eight major European countries over 18 years.

Sustainable National Intellectual Capital   151

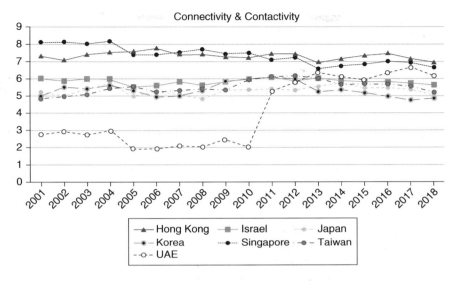

Figure 11.12 The CNC of five Asian countries, Israel and UAE over 18 years.

moving down from the top position in 2001 to number four in 2018. Belgium and Germany also declined over the years. The two large European countries, France and United Kingdom, have remained consistently the lowest ranked two countries over the 18 years. Although they have had some ups and downs, there is little difference between their 2001 and 2018 scores. In this set, only Switzerland and the Netherlands have shown progress in their SNIC over the 18 years.

Figure 11.9 shows that Singapore has consistently been the best performer over the 18 years, even though its SNIC declined somewhat in 2018, compared to its 2001 score. Hong Kong and Israel followed Singapore with a relatively stable path over the 18 years. Japan, Korea and Taiwan are in the third cluster and have shown little progress over the years. Generally, Taiwan leads Japan and Korea in SNIC. UAE shows the most outstanding progress in SNIC over the years, having risen from the bottom to the number two country over the years. In this set, only UAE has shown progress in its SNIC over the 18 years.

In summary, the shape of Figure 11.7 has a clear downward trend, indicating a general decline in SNIC in this set of advanced countries. Figure 11.8 does not show any obvious difference. That is, the countries exhibit only minor fluctuation within the range of 27–37 in the Y-axis over the years, even though several countries have gone up and down. Differently, the shape of Figure 11.9 changes from divergence in 2001 to clustering in 2018, indicating the SNIC of this set of countries has become more alike.

Figures 11.10–11.12 show the progression of connectivity and contactivity (CNC) for the three sets of countries over the years. Figure 11.10 indicates that the CNC of this set of countries exhibit a declining trend, when comparing their development in 2001 and 2018. All eight countries had an obvious dip in 2005 and then stayed relatively stable up to 2018, except that Finland experienced another dip in 2008 due to the financial crisis. Denmark progressed from number three in 2001 to number one in 2018 and Norway progressed from the very bottom in 2001 to the second position in 2018. By contrast, Finland fell from the top position in 2001 to the fourth position in 2018. Other countries changed relatively little in terms of ranking in this cluster. However, Canada performed better than the USA and New Zealand outperformed Australia, which are counterintuitive based on traditional stereotypes.

Figure 11.11 shows that Luxembourg is consistently the best performer and the Netherlands the second best performer over the 18 years. Belgium, in the third position in 2001, was overtaken by Switzerland and Austria and occupies the fifth position in 2018. Over the 18 years the three large European countries, Germany, United Kingdom and France are consistently the bottom three countries in this cluster, with France being the last one.

Figure 11.12 shows that Singapore was the best performer in 2001; however, it was overtaken by Hong Kong in 2011. Israel started at number three in 2001 and was overtaken by UAE, falling to number four in 2018. UAE had the most amazing growth, starting from the very bottom separated by a large gap from all the other countries, yet it gained momentum in 2011 and became number three in 2018, even surpassing Israel. For the rest of the three countries, Taiwan was at the bottom in 2001, yet surpassed Japan and Korea in 2011, continuing in that position through 2018. Over the 18 years, Hong Kong and Singapore declined slightly, while UAE exhibited strong growth and Israel, Japan, Korea and Taiwan all underwent a relatively stable development. As a result, the seven countries are clustered together in 2018 in terms of CNC.

In summary, the first set of advanced countries shows a decline in CNC, ranging between 5.5–7.5 along the Y-axis in 2001 while ranging between 5.0–6.5 along the Y-axis in 2018. This sends a warning that other countries are surpassing them, especially to the USA that became the worst performer in this set in 2018. The second set, composed of European countries, did not fluctuate much over the years, with Luxembourg and France consistently being the best and last performer, respectively. The third set of countries exhibit a divergence ranging between 2 and 8 along the Y-axis in 2001 and narrowing in 2018 to a range between 5 and 7. UAE reveals an obvious pattern of growth in its CNC over the years.

Figures 11.7–11.12 map the status of SNIC and CNC for the three separate sets of countries. In order to get their relative position in the same graph, Figures 11.13–11.14 show the results for the top two countries of each set to show their relative progress over the 18-year period. Figure 11.13 exhibits

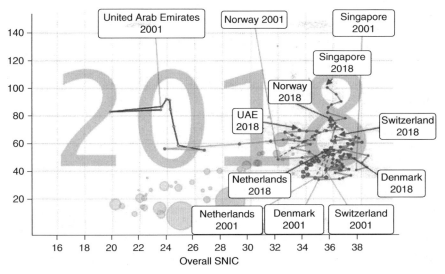

Figure 11.13 The SNIC and GDP for the top two countries in each of Figures 11.7–11.9.

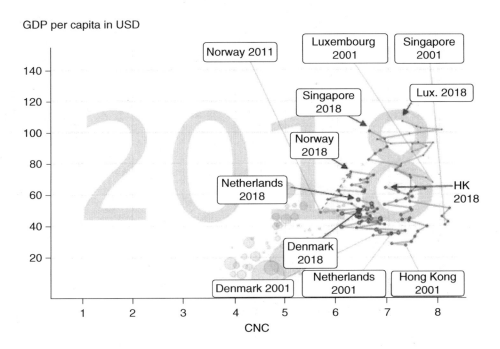

Figure 11.14 The CNC and GDP for the top two countries in each of Figures 11.10–11.12.

the relationship between SNIC and GDP for the top two countries of each set. In terms of SNIC in 2018, the descending order is Denmark, Norway, Switzerland, the Netherlands, Singapore and UAE. The dotted arrows indicate that the higher the SNIC, the higher the GDP growth for Denmark, the Netherlands, Norway and Switzerland over these years. Singapore's SNIC has actually declined, yet its GDP per capita (ppp) is the highest among these six countries. In general, the first set of advanced countries, Denmark and Norway, remain the best performers, followed by the second set of European countries, Switzerland and the Netherlands, and then the third set of Singapore and UAE. Even though Figure 11.7 shows a general decline of the first set of countries in terms of their SNIC, its top two countries, Denmark and Norway, are still ahead of other countries in SNIC in 2018.

Figure 11.14 shows the relationship between CNC and GDP for the top two countries of each set. In terms of CNC in 2018, the descending order is Luxembourg, Hong Kong, Singapore, Denmark, the Netherlands and Norway. Interestingly, different from SNIC, Figure 11.14 indicates that only Norway has a positive relationship between CNC and GDP (indicated by the dotted arrow). The CNC of the other five countries actually has a slight negative relationship with their GDP, meaning better CNC does not explain better GDP. A potential explanation is that these countries already had a relatively high CNC in 2001, and so their GDP growth was not dependent on their CNC development. In other words, CNC has limited explaining power of GDP growth. Different from Figure 11.13, in terms of their CNC in 2018, the second set country Luxembourg and the third set countries Hong Kong and Singapore are ahead of the first set countries of Denmark and Norway.

Global profile of digital readiness for 59 countries

In the SNIC model, four of the indicators are highly related to the digital age, namely, cyber security, internet bandwidth speed, information technology skills and communication technology. Another three indicators, namely, sustainable development, innovative capacity and connectivity, can be considered as the results of the four digital readiness indicators. This section displays their correlations in Table 11.4.

Table 11.4 is the correlation table of the selected indicators to show the digital readiness and the value of those indicators. The correlations exhibited are based on around 1000 observations, with 18-years of data for 59 countries (Appendix 11.4). Item 1, GDP per capita (ppp) in USD, is economic performance; item 2 is overall SNIC; items 3 to 5 cover sustainable development, innovative capacity and connectivity and act like dependent variables to highlight the effect of cyber security, internet speed, information technology skills and communication technology (items 9–12). Items 6 to 8, namely, CNC, education and renewal, are the components of SNIC and can also be viewed as dependent variables

Table 11.4 Correlation table of the selected indicators

	1. GDP per capita	2. SNIC	3. Sustainable Development	4. Innovative Capacity	5. Connectivity	6. CNC	7. Education	8. Renewal	9. Cyber Security	10. Internet Speed	11. Information Tech. skills	12. Commu. Tech.
1												
2	**.741**											
3	.483	**.769**										
4	**.710**	**.860**	**.747**									
5	.637	**.816**	.564	.643								
6	.583	**.902**	**.713**	**.764**	**.797**							
7	.690	**.856**	.656	**.798**	**.776**	.675						
8	.689	**.919**	**.784**	**.896**	**.797**	**.798**	**.796**					
9	.638	**.838**	.664	**.720**	.681	**.778**	**.755**	**.787**				
10	.578	.606	.436	.459	.646	.552	.570	.660	.374			
11	.496	.689	.412	.613	**.787**	.599	**.709**	**.751**	.630	.463		
12	.572	**.775**	.549	.576	**.948**	**.737**	**.708**	**.755**	.689	.506	**.805**	

Note: Correlations above .70 are bold-faced.

156 *Carol Y.Y. Lin and Leif Edvinsson*

We mark the correlations above .70 with bold-face in Table 11.4 to show their importance. Although all the correlations are statistically significant, the degree of their significance varies based on the coefficients. Observing the table vertically, SNIC (.741) and innovative capacity (.710) explain *GDP* growth better than the other indicators; renewal (.919) and CNC (.902) explain *SNIC* the best, followed by innovation capacity (.860), education (.856), cyber security (.838) and connectivity (.816). *Connectivity* has five coefficients over .70, namely, in descending order, communication technology (.948), renewal (.797), CNC (.797), information technology skills (.787) and education (.776). *Innovation capacity* has four coefficients over .70, namely, in descending order, renewal (.896), education (.798), CNC (.764) and cyber security (.720). *Education* has four coefficients above .70, namely, in descending order, renewal (.796), cyber security (.755), information technology skills (.709) and communication technology (.708). *Sustainable development* has three coefficients over .70, namely, in descending order, renewal (.784), innovative capacity (.747) and CNC (.713). *CNC* has three coefficients over .70, namely, in descending order, renewal (.798), cyber security (.778) and communication technology (.737). *Renewal* also has three coefficients over .70, namely, in descending order, cyber security (.787), communication technology (.755) and information technology skills (.751). For the four digital-related indicators (items 9–12), only one coefficient is over .70, i.e., information technology skills, which has a correlation of .805 with communication technology.

Observing the correlation table horizontally, *renewal* (item 8) and *communication technology* (item 12) both have six pairs of correlations above .70, followed by *cyber security* (item 9) with five pairs; *CNC* (item 6) four pairs; and *innovative capacity* (item 4), *education* (item 7) and *information technology skills* (item 11) with three pairs.

The red box of Table 11.4 shows the effect of the four digital age indicators, namely, cyber security, internet bandwidth speed, information technology skills and communication technology. Using a correlation coefficient above .70 as a criterion, apparently cyber security and communication technology have more influence than the other two indicators. Especially, internet bandwidth speed has a relatively low correlation with each of the eight criteria indicators (item 1–8), meaning speed may not be too much of a concern as long as cyber security and communication technology are well taken care of. The relationships of these four digital indicators also have a relatively low correlation with GDP and sustainable development. Viewing the high correlations of SNIC with GDP and items 3–8, very likely the four digital indicators need to be paired with education and transformed to renewal capital in order to have more added value to SNIC and eventually to GDP growth.

Conclusion and implications

This chapter introduces NIC 3.0 – SNIC (Sustainable National Intellectual Capital) model comprising five components, namely health, public structure, education, renewal and CNC (connectivity and contactivity). The SNIC ranking for 59 countries and figures showing the relationship between SNIC, its five components and GDP per capita (ppp) are provided. The profiles of SNIC and CNC for three sets of major countries are also presented. Finally, the global profiles of digital readiness for 59 countries are illustrated.

Our major findings include the following:

1 Unexpectedly, there is a very high correlation of around .95 between SNIC and NIC in the comparison of both scores and rankings. With different sets of indicators, the high correlation between the two models indicates that SNIC can provide valuable information for examining another set of national intangible assets, with a focus on sustainability.

2 Figure 11.1 and Table 11.4 show that the higher the SNIC, the higher the GDP per capita (ppp), indicating the value of SNIC in explaining GDP growth. The message here is strong that investing in enhancing the SNIC will enhance economic performance for developed and developing countries alike. When probing the relationship of the five components of SNIC with GDP, Figures 11.2–11.6 show that public structure has good explaining power with r=.741, followed by health of r=.705. Public structure, such as energy infrastructure, legal and regulatory framework and adaptability of government policy, is important for a country's sustainability. Gradually stepping into aging societies, health condition of citizens shows higher importance than education and renewal for sustainability. CNC has the lowest correlation of r=.583, meaning developing CNC alone is insufficient to bring about expected economic performance.

3 Generally speaking, advanced countries show a declining trend in SNIC. Of the three sets of selected countries (total 23 countries), only Denmark, Norway, Switzerland, the Netherlands and UAE have exhibited progress in SNIC over the 18 years. The countries which have either declined or remained stable may be doing as well as they used to; yet other countries have exhibited rapid improvement and are pushing those formerly good countries downward. However, true sustainability is exhibited by Denmark, Norway, Switzerland and the Netherlands, for they keep on progressing even though they are already very advanced. UAE is the country that performed surprisingly through the data analysis of the SNIC model. Its rapid rise allowing it to catch up with those advanced countries deserves a separate study to determine the reasons.

4 Table 11.4 shows that other than SNIC, innovative capacity has a high correlation of .710 with GDP; it also has a high correlation with three components of SNIC, namely, education, renewal and CNC. Furthermore, it is highly correlated with cyber security as well. This finding is in line with the notion that innovation is the source of future competitiveness. Understanding how to enhance innovative capacity through education and through better CNC may be able to contribute to the accumulation of renewal capital and enhance cyber security.

Implications

Three implications can be drawn from this study; they are described as follows.

1 Rich countries have great potential to develop SNIC

The present in-depth study of the SNIC model reveals two shining countries, Norway and UAE. In NIC research, Norway used to be the laggard of the four Nordic countries, generally coming behind Sweden, Finland and Denmark. In the SNIC model, Norway is ranked number three, behind only Denmark and Switzerland. Further analysis found that Norway ranked second in "health", a new dimension of SNIC, and it advanced in renewal capital as well. UAE ranked first in "public structure" among the 59 countries. As an energy-rich country, it naturally ranks high in energy infrastructure and future energy supply in the public structure dimension. Both Norway and UAE are oil-rich countries engaged in developing a national health system and building sound public structure, which require money. Their good performance in these fields shows the blessings of the rich.

2 The advantage of small countries in developing SNIC

Table 11.3 shows that the countries having a high correlation between SNIC, its components and GDP are all small countries, including Denmark, Switzerland, Norway, Singapore, Luxembourg and the Netherlands. By contrast, large countries, such as France, Germany, United Kingdom and USA, have been declining in their SNIC over the years. Generally, small countries have limited resources compared to large countries; however, they are less cumbersome and more adaptable than the large ones. This finding sends a strong message to the large countries that they should better utilize their bountiful resources to develop the intangibles to prevent themselves from becoming dinosaurs and being outperformed by small countries.

3 CNC alone cannot achieve expected economic performance

This study found a relatively weak correlation between CNC and GDP, indicating that better CNC does not explain better GDP. Although in the digital age, connectivity and contactivity are very important, CNC needs to be linked with other components to become SNIC as shown in the model in Appendix 11.1 for a better result. Clearly, internet bandwidth speed is not a concern; cyber security and communication technology are more important. The results indicate that digital technology needs to be integrated with other operations, such as education and renewal, and then transform itself to other types of intangible assets in order to maximize its benefits.

Sustainable National Intellectual Capital 159

To conclude, this chapter shows the value of SNIC in supplementing NIC in response to the digital age and the requirement for sustainability. The indicators of SNIC contain some future-oriented issues, such as health infrastructure, pension funding, future energy supply, sustainable development, and social responsibility. Responding to this book's main theme of "digital age", the key finding of this study is that, although CNC and digital indicators are important, they need to be integrated and coordinated with other operations, such as public structure, education and renewal, in order to transform itself to other intangibles like SNIC and then to real economic value.

Furthermore, in spite of the implication that rich countries may have greater potential to develop SNIC, three small non-oil-producing countries, Denmark, Switzerland and Singapore, are also outstanding performers in SNIC. Further analysis found that Denmark is number 1 in renewal, number 2 in education and number 3 in health; Singapore is number 3 in both public structure and CNC; and Switzerland is number 1 in both health and education. With limited land and limited natural resources, they remain the top countries over the years. Their national policy in building intangible assets to excel can shed some light for other countries.

Appendix 11.1

SNIC model

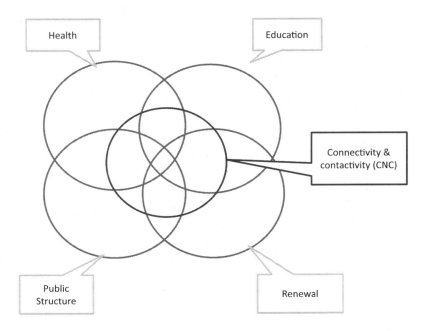

160   *Carol Y. Y. Lin and Leif Edvinsson*

Appendix 11.2

Indicators of Sustainable National Intellectual Capital (SNIC) model

Cronbach's Alpha	Indicator	Subjective indicator
0.84	Healthy life expectancy	
Health	Quality of life	S
	Total health expenditure (%)	
	Health infrastructure	S
	Medical assistance (per physician & per nurse)	
	Health problems	S
	Pension funding	S
0.872	Energy infrastructure	S
Public	Future energy supply	S
	Dependency ratio (age – 15 & 64+ / active population)	
	Credit (credit is easily available for business)	S
	Legal and regulatory framework	S
	Adaptability of government policy	S
	Cyber security	S
	Youth unemployment	
	Personal security and private property rights	S
	Gini index	
0.881	Human development index	
Education	Total public expenditure on education (%)	
	Higher education achievement (%) (WCY)	
	Educational assessment – PISA	
	Educational system	S
	Science in schools	S
	Management education	S
	Language skills	S
	Skilled labor	S
0.874	Internet bandwidth speed	
Renewal	Information technology skills	S
	Technological cooperation	S
	Knowledge transfer	S
	Innovative capacity	S
	Total expenditure on R&D (%)	
	Entrepreneurship	S
	Sustainable development	S
	Public and private sector ventures	S
0.81	Connectivity	S
CNC	Worker motivation	S
(Connectivity and	Flexibility and adaptability	S
contactivity)		
	Social responsibility	S
	Foreign investors	S
	Social cohesion	S
	Trade to GDP ratio	
	Student mobility outbound	
	Communications technology	S

Appendix 11.3

NIC version 2.0 model

Expanded 48 indicators in each type of capital for NIC48 – November 2, 2011

Human capital index	*Market capital index*
1. Skilled labor★	1. Corporate tax encouragement★
2. Employee training★	2. Cross–border venture★
3. Higher education achievement	3. Openness of culture★
4. Pupil–teacher ratio	4. Transparency of government policies★
5. Public expenditure on education	5. Image of your country★
6. 15–64 year-old population	6. Capital availability★
7. Qualified engineers★	7. Trade to GDP ratio (exports + imports)
8. Students PISA performance	8. Current account balance %GDP
9. Human Development Index	9. Investment flows %GDP
10. Gender equality	10. Country credit rating
11. Years of education	11. Investment risk
12. R&D researchers	12. Globalization index

Process capital index	*Renewal capital index*
1. Business competition environment★	1. Business R&D spending
2. Government efficiency★	2. Basic research★
3. Computer per capita + mobile subscribers	3. R&D spending/GDP
4. Internet subscribers + broadband subscribers	4. R&D US$ per capita
5. Convenience of establishing new firms + start up days★	5. IP right protection★
6. Goods and services distribution efficiency★	6. Utility patents/ R&D expenditure
7. Overall productivity	7. Cooperation between corporations and university★
8. Unemployment % + youth unemployment %	8. Scientific articles
9. Consumer price inflation	9. Patents per capita (USTPO+EPO)
10. Health and environment	10. Entrepreneurship★
11. Corruption	11. Development and application of technology★
12. Freedom of speech	12. Venture capital★

★ Data with a qualitative rating based on a 1–10 scale.

Appendix 11.4

List of 59 Countries

Europe – 31 countries
Northern Europe – (Nordic) Denmark, Finland, Iceland, Norway, Sweden
Baltic – Estonia, Lithuania

Western Europe – Belgium, France, Germany, Ireland, Luxembourg, Netherlands, Switzerland, United Kingdom (UK)
Southern Europe – Italy, Portugal, Spain
Southeastern Europe – Bulgaria, Croatia, Greece, Romania, Slovenia, Turkey
Central Europe – Austria, Czech Republic, Hungary, Poland, Slovakia
Eastern Europe – Russia, Ukraine

Americas – 9 countries
North America – Canada, USA, Mexico
South America – Argentina, Brazil, Chile, Colombia, Peru, Venezuela

Australasia – 2 countries
Australia, New Zealand

Asia – 16 countries
East Asia – China, Hong Kong, Japan, Korea, Taiwan
Southeast Asia – Indonesia, Malaysia, Philippines, Singapore, Thailand
South Asia – India
Central Asia – Kazakhstan
Middle East – Israel, Jordan, Qatar, UAE

Africa – 1 country
South Africa

References

Lin, C.Y.Y. and Edvinsson, L. (2011). *National Intellectual Capital: A Comparison of 40 Countries*. New York: Springer.

Lin, C.Y.Y., Edvinsson, L., Chen, J. and Beding, T. (2013/2014) *National Intellectual Capital and the Financial Crisis in … ,* 11 vols. New York: Springer. (Published as eleven volumes, each title completed by the names of the countries in the respective country clusters studied.)

Lin, C.Y.Y., Edvinsson, L., Chen, J. and Beding, T. (2014) *Navigating Intellectual Capital after the Financial Crisis*. New York: Springer.

Stahle, P., Stahle, S. and Lin, C.Y.Y. (2015) Intangibles and national economic wealth: A new perspective on how they are linked, *Journal of Intellectual Capital*, 16(1), 20–57.

Stewart, T.A. (1997) *Intellectual Capital: The New Wealth of Organizations*. New York: Doubleday.

12 Comparative view on national intellectual capital

Marcos Cavalcanti, Valéria Macedo and Larriza Thurler

Introduction

Since the 1990s, theoretical studies and empirical research have been developed focusing on the relevance of intangibles – initially geared to companies and later to territories. Some companies have chosen to adopt such metrics in their organizational strategies to incorporate the indicators into action planning and project evaluation. At the macro level, one-off initiatives have been observed in some countries, such as the United Kingdom, but there are still no governments that have systematically and consistently appropriated indicators to predict economic development and propose policies to become more productive and competitive globally.

Given this context, this chapter aims to make a comparative analysis of models to measure the wealth and economic development of a territory beyond the traditional factors of production, in order to subsidize reflections on the need for new methods from a series of variables that relate to and compose an ecosystem of innovation in the knowledge economy. The comparative analysis will be between indicators developed using statistical data available from governmental and non-governmental bodies.

Unlike the academic models, the analyzed models use tangible (including financial) and intangible asset indicators in an integrated manner, not independently, to determine the competitiveness, capacity for innovation or development of countries based on micro- and macroeconomic principles (Labra and Paloma Sánchez, 2013). This allows a greater dialogue with the Economic Complexity Index (ECI) developed by Hidalgo and Hausmann (2008). Inspired by network science, ECI considers the diversity and complexity of the productive capacities of nations and will serve as a lens for the analysis of the chosen models.

To do so, initially a brief historical retrospective on national intellectual capital and models of intellectual capital measurement will be made to contextualize the evolution from the micro level to the macro level. Subsequently, the ECI developed by Hausmann and Hidalgo will be presented, in order to contextualize the current economic complex scenario and the needs of new indicators. In the sequence, a comparative analysis will be made between the

164   *Marcos Cavalcanti et al.*

models developed by governmental and non-governmental institutions, which have been called Knowledge Economy Indicators in the light of ECI. Finally, the conclusions and suggestions for future studies will be presented.

National intellectual capital

In a historical perspective, intangible assets have become more important than tangible ones for the creation of value, at the micro level, of organizations, as well as macro level of the territory, this being a city, a cluster of innovation and entrepreneurship, or even a country. Thus, tangible assets are currently considered central factors for economic growth and competitiveness for companies and nations. According to a study by Ocean Tomo, the intangible assets of the 500 largest companies accounted for 87% of the total market value of the companies in 2015. In other words, intangible assets such as software, entertainment industry products (music, information, television, movies), consultancies, design, patents and royalties dominate the global market. A World Bank study (2006, 2011) with 100 countries from 1995 to 2005 shows similar results and indicates that intangible capital accounts for 60% to 80% of a country's total wealth.

National intellectual capital includes also non-tangible values of an ecosystem made up of individuals, enterprises, institutions, communities and regions that contribute or can contribute to the aggregation of value, wealth, and consequently the economic development of a nation. There are several definitions for national intellectual capital and there is no unanimity about its components.

Initially, the discussion about intellectual capital focused on the capacity to transform knowledge and intangible resources into economic value in companies, with the first theoretical studies to raise awareness about the subject from the 1990s. In the late 1990s, metrics and applications of empirical research in organizations began to be developed. In this period, studies were also carried out by extrapolating the organizational boundary to include a more comprehensive view of the countries in order to assist in the management of these knowledge resources and to predict national economic performance – this is the first generation of national intellectual capital. The first attempt to measure the intellectual capital of a country was made in the 1990s in Sweden. Since then, many conceptual models were developed, derived from the Skandia Navigator model developed in 1997 by Leif Edvinsson (1997) for the Swedish insurance company, with a focus on human capital and structural capital (Michalczuk and Fiedorczuk, 2018), as well as using the Balanced Scorecard (Kaplan and Norton, 1997) and the Intangible Assets Monitor (Sveiby, 1997).

Starting in the 2000s, the first studies to analyze intellectual capital at territorial level began, with several authors investigating territories or countries, such as Australia, Finland, Israel, Luxembourg, Spain, Sweden, Arabia, Europe and the Nordic countries. The work of Lin and Edvinsson (2011), which analyzed the evolution of 40 countries over a given period, deserves to be highlighted. These punctual investigations can be considered as part of the second generation of national intellectual capital and occurred concurrently with the development of theoretical studies on the subject.

Only more recently do the first movements for the third generation of national intellectual capital begin, suggesting more systemic applications for the adoption of such metrics in governmental strategic planning and national policies. These initiatives also include ways of accounting entry so that data reported by companies can evidence data on intangible assets. They are also proposed at the global level with the possibility of ranking and comparison between countries.

The timeline presented in Figure 12.1 helps to understand the evolution of the three generations of national intellectual capital. The graph does not pretend to cover all the literature on the subject, but only to carry out a collection of relevant studies in order to visualize the progress of the debate on the measurements of the intellectual capital of a territory. Nor are there watertight limits, since the generations overlap many times.

Measuring the intellectual capital of a territory is a complex task, and there is also no consensus on methodology, which makes comparability difficult. Existing theoretical methodologies for measuring national intellectual capital have generally appropriated and adapted the constructs used to measure intellectual capital at an organizational level. Indicators constructed by government institutions and nongovernmental bodies, in turn, are generally based on statistical data, which facilitates comparisons more efficiently and allows analysis over time.

Economic complexity

In the economic world, Marshall (1890), one of the forerunners of the cluster concept, argued that spatially concentrated skill, technology and knowledge favored the existence of a highly productive, innovation-friendly and economically rich environment (Glaeser and Maré, 2001). Nowadays, the new ways of thinking the economy make it possible to use the theory of complex networks to empirically evaluate the probability of a region becoming economically developed by analyzing the complexity of the relations and human capacities available (Diodato et al., 2018; Hidalgo et al., 2018).

Ricardo Hausmann, from Harvard Kennedy School, and Cesar Hidalgo, from Massachusetts Institute of Technology (MIT) identified through network science (Barábasi, 2009) the possibility of mapping the productive chain through the inputs and outputs involved in commercial transactions, that is the net between the financial volume of the import and export of the goods produced in each country. Researchers have identified that this web of relationships makes it possible to assess human productive capacity in a location, region, country and thus identify the level of economic complexity in this environment.

From an economic perspective, this study highlights the relevance of current questions about the inefficiency of economic indicators in measuring economic development. In Hidalgo and Hausmann (2008), indicators of competitiveness,

Year	1st (organization level)	2st (national level)	3 st (global level - Knowledge Economy)
1997	Skandia Navigator (Edvinsson) model was developed in order to measure the intangible assets. Balance Scorecard (Kaplan & Norton) model to evaluation performance form inputs and outputs. Intangible Assets Monitor (Sveiby) a method for measuring intangible assets and a presentation format which displays a number of relevant indicators for measuring intangible assets.		
1999		State New Economy Index (SNEI) (Atkinson et al.) measure states' economic structure in USA.	
2000		Value-Added Intellectual Coefficient (VAICTM) (Pulic) measure of intellectual capital efficiency (ICE).	
2003		Intellectual capital dynamic value (IC-dVAL®) (Bounfour) demonstrate thats is importante do know how IC effectively is linked to national economic growths in different situations: in development or developed economies.	
2004		National Intellectual Capital Index (NICI) (Bontis) constructed the methodology that has been used in studies in different countries. Intellectual capital of the European Union (Andriessen and Stam) publish a report to provide insights into the value of the IC of the 15 countries in relationship to the goals set the European Council in March 2000.	Global Competitiveness Index (GCI) World Economic Forum.
2005		New Framework to Measuring Capital and Technology(Corrado, Hulten and Sichel). Intellectual Capital in the public sector (Bounfour and Edvinsson).	

Year		
2007	Intellectual Capital Index (ICI) (Weziak) – Proposed method of IC measurement is an extension of the proposals of Bontis (2004) and Andriessen and Stam (2004).	Global Innovation Index (GII) (Cornell University, INSEAD, and the World Intellectual Property Organization). OECD Innovation Indicators (Organization for Economic Co-operation and Development). Innovation Union Scoreboard (IUS) União Europeia.
2010		
2011	Integral Analysis (INTAN) (López, Nevado and Alfaro) – Proposed used a model adapted to microeconomic level that takes into account aspects not contemplated by GDP.	
2012	Intellectual Capital for Communities – Nations, Regions and Cities (several authors, edited by Bounfour and Edvinsson) – discuss about new perspectives of understanding value creation and social links, also the best social value from such a capital in the Knowledge Economy	
2014		IMD World Talent Ranking. IMD World Digital Competitiveness Ranking.
2018		EBRB Knowledge Economy Index (European Bank for Reconstruction and Development) Human Capital Project (World Bank) New Framework to Measuring Capital Human (UK Office for National Statistics)

Figure 12.1 Timeline of studies on national intellectual capital.

Source: Prepared by the authors.

productivity, governance and education are insufficient to assess and predict economic growth. Analyzing the country's wealth based on a series of variables in GDP is the same as assessing the health of a child by its weight, say Hausmann et al. (2014): "A more detailed view of development should ultimately concentrate on understanding how nations develop different industries and products, rather than trying to predict how they accumulate capital" (p.2).

During the development of the ECI, Hausmann et al. (2014) analyzed the Global Competitiveness Index (GCI), published since 1979 by the World Economic Forum. The GCI presents what conditions a country offers for the growth of wealth and the living conditions of its population. Thus, the GCI identifies the level of productivity of the country based on calculated averages of a set of determining variables arising from the results released by the industry and public policies adopted in each country. By means of an empirical application the two indicators were compared considering the main information for the evaluation of the growth capacity of an economy. Hausmann et al. (2014) found it more efficient to identify the actual types of industry that a country has and its productive capacity than the set of institutions, policies and factors that determine the level of productivity in the country.

It is worth mentioning that the World Economic Forum's GCI currently contains 12 pillars and seeks to evaluate the productivity and competitiveness ecosystem of the 100 countries that are part of the sample through the following variables: institutions, infrastructure, ICT adoption, macroeconomic stability, health, education, product market, labor market, financial system, market size, business dynamism and capacity for innovation. In 2018, methodological changes occurred in the report with the objective of observing the countries' aptitude in three main aspects relevant to international competitiveness and the 4th Industrial Revolution: (a) to assess the resilience of countries in relation to crises, especially those that impact the financial system to minimize risks and to value macroeconomic stability and workers with their ability to learn and adapt to change; (b) to assess the capacity of innovation ecosystems and their impact at all levels of production, an impact that has been identified in all the evaluated pillars, from the strengthening of institutions that promote innovation to the human factor that encompasses health and education; (c) to assess human development in the pillars that present health and well-being outcomes; of the human skills necessary for the prosperity of the industry, including seeking to evaluate human collaboration, interaction and creativity. The level of methodological complexity for the measurement of the GCI is therefore noted.

The methodology developed by Hidalgo and Hausmann (2008) seeks to model the number of viable variables that a country can produce through its limited capacity and therefore explain the differences in the diversity of products produced in the country through the connection between two variables (import and exporting) connecting countries to products. It should be noted that the studies by Hidalgo and Hausmann (2008) show that the country mixes its products gradually through the addition of skills, that is, the countries with a large productive capacity (with diversified products that do not have ubiquity in other countries) are more likely to add products to their export basket.

As a way of explaining the importance of the diversity and complexity of a country's industrial capabilities and existing know-how to the flow of trade in global markets, Hausmann et al. (2014) have created an atlas of complexity that monitors world economies through a digital platform. The Atlas of Economic Complexity is available on the web and offers visuals and access to the database. Three relevant conclusions can be drawn from the studies by Hausmann et al. (2014):

1 The characteristics of a networked community are: connectivity (it reflects the measure of a community's central location in the product space); proximity (it reflects the distance between two products in the community); geographic space (it refers to the locality of the country and the resources it possesses – specialized knowledge and productive capacity). Thus, a networked community represented by machines, electronics and chemicals tends to be much more complex than the oil or tropical agriculture communities due to the convergence of know-how and the productive environment necessary for the development of the economy. For example, oil as a natural resource can make countries with high convergence in high-income countries, such as Qatar and Kuwait, and countries with low convergence, such as Venezuela, a low-income country.
2 The relevance of the conjunction of formal education and professional training, through experience, intensifies the development of productive capacity (Hanushek and Woessmann, 2008). Thus, it is not enough for years of formal schooling for society to produce, but to raise intellectual capital plus the diversity of productive knowledge in space.
3 The industry that does not have the necessary capabilities to innovate their products in their locality will end up not investing in innovations or it will not diversify its line of products. This scenario makes the process of developing productive knowledge difficult by interactions in local networks, making them dependent on external resources.

Economist Paulo Gala, author of the book *Economic Complexity: A Perspective to Understand the Ancient Question of the Wealth of Nations*, states that ECI reveals Brazil as a poor country, which always been due to the lack of public policies and government incentives aimed at building environments conducive to the development and growth of the industrial sector. According to Gala (2017), Brazil has a medium or intermediate complexity because it has an export agenda made up of more ubiquitous products (oil, coffee, iron ore and sugar, which represent agricultural and extractive activities) than non-ubiquitous ones (planes, cars, auto parts). Balland et al. (2018) have found that complex economic activities are concentrated more in large cities regardless of the technological innovations of communication and the advances in the area of transport of the

21st century. The research took into account scientific publications, industry indicators, occupations and the American historical patent base since 1850.

Recently, academic research explored ECI methodological processes to understand the specific industry's role, specific occupation and location-specific knowledge on growth and survival of new firms in Brazil. Jara-Figueroa et al. (2018) have identified through open data available from the Brazilian government that the specific knowledge of the sector is of the utmost importance for pioneer companies due to the need to hire experienced workers that boost their faster growth and consequently their survival. Jara-Figueroa et al. (2018) also verified that the effects of occupational and school-specific knowledge are not relevant in this process. The analysis performed in a microspace identified that the knowledge measured by years of schooling is not a determining factor in the survival of a pioneer company, but rather to the relation of past and future knowledge of the activity. In addition, management skills and trust relationships based on social capital were identified, demonstrating that these variables should play an important role.

In this moment of reflection, where one seeks to understand the new economic dynamics and the impacts of digital business on development, it may be necessary to verify new alternatives for analysis, new ways of dealing with collected data and, with the use of network science, to reinvent the data capture and analysis of information in a knowledge society that leveraged the economy of intangibles.

The methodologies of the Knowledge Economy Indicators

There is a series of models in the literature that are being disseminated by the academy in order to find ways to measure intangibles in the knowledge economy. These are proposals and initiatives that involve modeling at the organization level using existing theory about intellectual capital and intangible asset frameworks. However, there are still many challenges in building frameworks that reflect the reality of intellectual capital in a region or country, that is, at the national level.

The methodologies developed to date are based on two theoretical bases: models of evaluation of intellectual capital at the organizational level or evaluation models at micro and macroeconomic levels with indicators developed through statistical data available from governmental and non-governmental bodies. Most of these indicators are available in an open database and provide analysis on competitiveness, innovation capacity or development. It is important to highlight that the advances made in the last years with digital transformation and its impact on business can give a new positive and negative direction in the development of intellectual capital, and it is necessary to monitor more and more timely data and information on economic development, productivity and human capital.

This topic seeks to identify existing indicators at the national level and to verify the maturity and usability of these data for the analysis of intellectual capital. For this analysis we will start with the initiative carried out in the study by Labra and Paloma Sánchez (2013) when presenting methodologies developed by international organizations and business schools to rank countries in the perspective of innovation and competitiveness and the knowledge economy with variables that permeate intellectual capital. The current stage and the maturation of these indicators will be evaluated and we will contribute to the study of the researchers with the incorporation of new indicators discovered during our research.

In terms of innovation and competitiveness, we can observe collaboration initiatives between institutions for the construction of rankings, based on the innovation capacity of the countries. The following indicators will be presented: Global Innovation Index (GII),[1] Innovation Union Scoreboard (IUS),[2] OECD Innovation Indicators and Global Competitiveness Index (GCI).

The Global Innovation Index (GII) was first released in 2007 and it is designed to build a ranking based on information from 126 countries with a view to assessing its capabilities and innovation results that impact the economy. The GII is considered a quantitative tool that contributes to the decision making of those involved in the ecosystem due to a better understanding of the factors that stimulate innovation and that result in human and economic development. GII, co-published by Cornell University, INSEAD and the World Intellectual Property Organization (WIPO), is published annually and relies on database collaboration and access from various public and private bodies such as the World Bank, International Governance Indicators, Unesco, Ease of Doing Business Index 2018: Reforming to Create Jobs, Organization for Economic Co-operation and Development (OECD), Program for International Student Assessment (PISA), International Telecommunication Union, Measuring the Information Society 2017, ICT Development Index 2017, ISO Survey, International Labor Organization, ILOSTAT among other quantitative indicators published by several institutions. The methodology is constructed by calculating subscripts with inputs of information on innovative activities of institutions, human capital and research, infrastructure, market sophistication and business sophistication, and with outputs of evidence of results from knowledge, technology and creativity. It is noted that the methodology uses sources of information to collect the data for the 80 indicators, and the entire report is available in full to download on its website.

The European Union formalized the creation of the Innovation Union Scoreboard (IUS) to assess the strengths and weaknesses of innovation and thus to monitor the performance of the European Community member countries at the bloc level with regional analysis from 2010. There is also the possibility of monitoring the evolution of innovation due to the goals set in the United Nations Agenda 2020. It should be noted that the dimensions of analysis and indicators are focused on comparative analyses related to the following factors: human resources, attractive research system and favorable innovation environment, investments and financial support for innovation, activities related

172 *Marcos Cavalcanti et al.*

to innovation and intellectual assets with analyses of the impacts on employment and services and products offered to the market. Various data are collected from public databases such as the OECD, World Bank, European Union, Eurostat and Global Entrepreneurship Monitor among other institutions. The IUS can be accessed online at its website[3] with interactive navigation, including graphs that compare two indicators facilitating cross-analysis. It is worth mentioning that the IUS is directed to the performance and European economic structure, being the focus of analysis the capacity of innovation of the human resources of the population between 25–34 years old with the complete secondary education or coming from doctors, for example, unlike the GII that by its the data collected from basic education through the results of the PISA Exam.

The OECD publishes biennially an innovation indicator based on information from surveys and other data collected from other databases that hold authorization such as Eurostat from the European Community. The country ranking is posted on the website – OECD Innovation Indicators[4] and presents in a segmented form for the manufacturing industry and services. The analysis is based on the perspective of the Oslo Manual with the definition of the four forms of innovation (product, process, organizational or marketing). There are interesting analyses of intellectual capital such as the impact of intellectual property protection and patents and the capacity for innovation versus participation in the public and international market. However, the statistics available online in Excel spreadsheets present a number of countries with missing data. The data contained in the innovation, science and technology reports have already been publicly disclosed; however, several of these reports are currently paywalled.

The GCI, published by the World Economic Forum (WEF), has already been addressed in this study, but it is worth noting that in the scope of competitiveness and productivity this indicator was updated to version 4.0 and includes, besides the traditional components, such as economic and educational, new inputs such as human capital, innovation, resilience and agility. One of the objectives of the GCI is to reflect the complexity of the economic development of the countries with the identification of their current stages of competitiveness. The reports are available online at the WEF website through an interactive tool with results by indicator and country.

The International Institute for Management Development (IMD) annually publishes IMD World Competitiveness Ranking (WCI). It is obtained through a methodology that involves the collection of data from numerous research institutions and governmental and non-governmental statistical agencies. The WCI began to be established in 1996 and has since used criteria aimed at analyzing the competitiveness of 63 countries through four main factors: economic performance, efficiency of governance, business efficiency and infrastructure. Only the annual ranking is disclosed on the site and the study in full is paywalled. Some topics in this report are available for access such as the IMD World Talent Ranking and IMD World Digital Competitiveness Ranking. In relation to Digital Competitiveness, the ranking is constructed through the analysis of three factors: knowledge, technology and future readiness. In the context of knowledge, this indicator seeks to assess the existing infrastructure for talent development, investment in training and education, and R&D innovations that contribute to the process of digital transformation. In the technological context, it evaluates the regulatory processes that allow the efficient performance of the business activities and stimulate the development and agility of innovation. In the context of future readiness, the level of preparation of the economy is verified in order to incorporate the digital transformation in its environment.

With an approach to human development and its possibilities in improving well-being whose impact affects economic growth, the first Human Development report emerged in 1990 with the coordination of the United Nations Development Program. It was found at the time that the Gross Domestic Product (GDP) indicator did not address welfare issues but rather issues related to economic progress, based on trade transactions and country wealth results. After almost 30 years of existence, this report seeks to evaluate the perspective of the life of the human being on his life expectancy, health and creativity, with the knowledge and resources necessary for a decent standard of living based on a productive and valued life in the several countries by means of the publication of a ranking of the Human Development Index (HDI),[5] this indicator being complementary to the other indicators that measure development. The HDI uses data from existing education indexes to assess the knowledge dimension, GNI index to assess the standard of living compared to per capita income and life expectancy index to assess the health and wellness dimension. The GNI index is defined by the World Bank:

> GNI per capita (formerly GNP per capita) is the gross national income, converted to U.S. dollars using the World Bank Atlas method, divided by the midyear population. GNI is the sum of value added by all resident producers plus any product taxes (less subsidies) not included in the valuation of output plus net receipts of primary income (compensation of employees and property income) from abroad.

Finally, in the sphere of the knowledge economy, new initiatives were noted by the World Bank and the European Bank towards the development of new indicators. However, before addressing the new indicators, an indicator that was discontinued by the World Bank but used in several academic studies – including in the study of Labra and Paloma Sánchez (2013) – is highlighted briefly. This is the Knowledge Assessment Methodology (KAM) composed of two indicators: Knowledge Economy Index (KEI) and Knowledge Index (KI). KEI was directed towards the analysis if the environment was conducive to the knowledge being used effectively for development through an aggregate index in four pillars of the knowledge economy: economic incentive and institutional regime, education and human resources, innovation system and ICT. For each of the pillars, composite variables are used as follows: for the educational

174   *Marcos Cavalcanti et al.*

structure, data on primary and secondary education, vocational training, education and lifelong learning institutions; for the technological infrastructure, data reported in national surveys on the use of information and communication technologies; for the economic incentive and institutional regime, analysis of the quality of the laws and policies adopted in the countries for the development of entrepreneurship and incentive to the free flow of knowledge in the countries and, finally, in the scope of innovation, the knowledge coming from the creation of patents and academic research. This indicator was widely used in comparative cross-country research with the evaluation of its tangible and intangible assets in the knowledge economy (Chen and Dahlman, 2006).

The European Bank for Reconstruction and Development (EDRB) developed in 2018 an indicator of the knowledge economy, EBRB KE, based on 46 economies divided into four pillars: (1) institutions for innovation, (2) skills for innovation, (3) innovation system and (4) ICT infrastructure. For each of these pillars, a structure of analysis was conceived, as for example in the competences for innovation, which focuses on the identification of adequate training for the workforce in the private sector which is of great importance in the transfer of knowledge, innovation and development of new technologies. The indicator also foresees the stages of development of the countries: initial, intermediate and advanced. The EBRB KE uses open data sources such as the World Bank, the United Nations Educational, Scientific and Cultural Organization (UNESCO), the International Telecommunication Union, the World Economic Forum and the EBRD (the EBRD-World Bank Business Environment and Enterprise Performance Survey, for example), usually having a one-year lag in its compilation, and also dependent on the regularity of updating the data by the sources used. Collaborating in the debate to find a better way to enter data inputs by companies, a new framework is in studies by the Office for National Statistics (ONS) in the United Kingdom by Martin, Senga and Shilton (2019). The model came about because of the new forms of work, new professions and different types of professional training on job, and the data provided by insufficient organizations for an evaluation of the impact of intellectual capital on economic development.

And, lastly, one of the last initiatives in the construction of an indicator of human capital was presented by the World Bank in October 2018. In the initial phase of the project it is possible to highlight one of the objectives of the index: to have an international metric to evaluate certain components of human capital in various countries.

> The index is designed to highlight how improvements in the current education and health outcomes shape the productivity of the next generation of workers: it assumes that children born in a given year experience current educational opportunities and health risks over the next 18 years. The results of this study are based on the results obtained by the Human Capital Index and the results obtained in this study.
>
> (The World Bank, *Human Capital Project*, p.20)

New data are being collected by the World Bank with the possibility of measuring the level of productivity that a worker born in 2018 may contribute as a future worker.

Final considerations

Following this timely analysis of each of the indicators developed by profit and non-profit organizations, it is observed that there is an open path for the possibility of developing new methodologies that can be adopted in a structured way and that contribute to the evaluation of tangible assets and produced in a country or region by identifying the factors that impact economic development. One can note a concern in compiling rankings, but during this research there was some difficulty in identifying initiatives of this nature in individual countries. It is a fact that there is concern about the indicators of competitiveness and productivity with investments in policies that encourage innovation and entrepreneurship, however, there is clear difficulty in obtaining data updated by statistical institutes, which are used in several reports and in the computation of methodological calculations of the indicators. For example, some of the indicators such as the OECD and IMD reports are not available in free versions, making it difficult for researchers and other academics to gain access to the empirical use and possible effective contribution to the research and development of methodologies. Or, with most of the indicators presented here, they use data collected by secondary sources, depending on their update because they do not collect the data in the primary sources, where they are generated.

While it is possible to check the maturity of some indicators such as HDI, IMD, GCI and IUS, there are still gaps to be met for the measurement of intellectual capital, since the current indicators are designed to achieve diverse objectives, innovation, competitiveness and human development using a variety of data. Even GDP remains one of the most used inputs in the calculation of indicators, even though its efficiency in measuring wealth and economic development has been doubted by several economists (Hidalgo and Hausmann, 2009).

It is important to reflect on what inputs could be captured by common features on the various open government public data platforms of the countries. It is also interesting to look for which, through the new technologies and algorithms, could generate dynamic outputs monitored periodically and used by the countries as subsidies of the policies developed for a scenario closer to reality in search of changes that impact economic development in a more medium term.

And finally, by contributing to this debate, it is still difficult for some emerging or developing countries to make sustained investments in the collection of statistical data that will collaborate to serve as a thermometer of the level of productivity through human capacities. However, initiatives concerned with digital transformation have been identified, such as the initiative of the World Bank Human Capital Indicator project and the indicator of the European Bank for Reconstruction and Development's (EDRB) knowledge economy. Perhaps

176   *Marcos Cavalcanti et al.*

the way to be pursued is how these organizations could take advantage of this moment in which several governments seek to adopt the digitization in several services favoring the obtaining of current and continuous data and seek to design indicators that give transparency to the current reality with relevant information inputs. It is also time to innovate in the way of building indicators, monitoring environments and developing more assertive innovation incentive policies, especially with the coming of digital transformation and its impact on the economy of intangibles.

Notes

1   www.globalinnovationindex.org.
2   https://ec.europa.eu/growth/industry/innovation/facts-figures/scoreboards_en.
3   https://interactivetool.eu/EIS/index.html.
4   www.oecd.org/sti/inno/inno-stats.htm#links.
5   http://hdr.undp.org/en/content/human-development-index-hdi.

References

Balland, P. A., Jara-Figueroa, C., Petralia, S., Steijn, M., Rigby, D. L. and Hidalgo, C. (2018). "Complex economic activities concentrate in large cities". [Online] Available at https://ssrn.com/abstract=3219155 (Accessed: May 30, 2019).

Barábasi, A. L. (2009). *Linked: a nova ciência dos networks*. São Paulo: Leopardo.

Chen, D. H. and Dahlman, C. J. (2006). *The knowledge economy, the KAM methodology and World Bank operations*. Washington, DC: World Bank Institute. [Online] Available at http://documents.albankaldawli.org/curated/ar/695211468153873436/pdf/358670WBI0The 11dge1Economy01PUBLIC1.pdf (Accessed: May 30, 2019).

Diodato, D., Neffke, F. and O'Clery, N. (2018). "Why do industries coagglomerate? How Marshallian externalities differ by industry and have evolved over time". *Journal of Urban Economics* (106), 1–26.

Edvinsson, L. (1997). "Developing intellectual capital at Skandia". *Long Range Planning*, 30(3), 366–373.

Gala, P. (2017). *Complexidade econômica: uma nova perspectiva para entender a antiga questão da Riqueza das Nações*. Rio de Janeiro: Contraponto.

Glaeser, E. L. and Maré, D. C. (2001). "Cities and skills". *Journal of Labor Economics*, 19(2), 316–342. DOI: 10.1086/319563.

Hanushek, E. A. and Woessmann, L. (2008). "The role of cognitive skills in economic development". *Journal of Economic Literature*, 46(3), 607–668. DOI: 10.1257/jel.46.3.607.

Hausmann, Ricardo et al. (2014). *The atlas of economic complexity: mapping paths to prosperity*. Cambridge, MA: MIT Press.

Hidalgo, C. A. and Hausmann, R. (2008). "A network view of economic development". *Developing Alternatives*, 12, 5–10.

Hidalgo, C. A. and Hausmann, R. (2009). "The building blocks of economic complexity". *Proceedings of the National Academy of Science*, 106(26), 10570–10575.

Hidalgo, C.A., Balland, P.-A., Boschma, R., Delgado, M., Feldman, M., Frenken, K., Glaeser, E. et al. (2018). "The principle of relatedness". In Morales, A., Gershenson, C., Braha, D., Minai, A. and Bar-Yam, Y. (Eds.) *Unifying themes in complex systems IX. ICCS 2018. Springer proceedings in complexity*. Cham: Springer.

Comparative view on national IC 177

Jara-Figueroa, C., Jun, B., Glaeser, E. L. and Hidalgo, C. A. (2018). "The role of industry-specific, occupation-specific, and location-specific knowledge in the growth and survival of new firms". *Proceedings of the National Academy of Sciences*, 115(50), 12646–12653.

Kaplan, R. S. and Norton, D. P. (1997). *A estratégia em ação: balanced scorecard*. Gulf Professional Publishing.

Labra, R. and Paloma Sánchez, M. (2013). "National intellectual capital assessment models: a literature review". *Journal of Intellectual Capital*, 14(4), 582–607. https://doi.org/10.1108/JIC-11-2012-0100.

Lin, C.Y. Y. and Edvinsson, L. (2011). *National intellectual capital: a comparison of 40 countries*. New York: Springer Science + Business Media.

Marshall, A. (1890) *Principles of economics. Vol. 1*. London: Macmillan.

Martin, J., Senga, F. and Shilton, S. (2019) *Developing experimental estimates of investment in intangible assets in the UK: 2016*. Office for National Statistics. [Online] Available at www.ons.gov.uk/economy/economicoutputandproductivity/productivitymeasures/articles/experimentalestimatesofinvestmentinintangibleassetsintheuk2015/2016#authors (Accessed: May 30, 2019).

Michalczuk, G. and Fiedorczuk, J. (2018). National intellectual capital taxonomy. *Economics and Business*, 32(1), 89–101.

Sveiby, E. K. A. R. L. (1997). "The intangible assets monitor". *Journal of Human Resource Costing & Accounting*, 2(1), 73–97.

The World Bank (2006). *Where is the wealth of nations? Measuring capital for the 21st century*. World Bank Publications.

The World Bank (2011). *The changing wealth of nations: measuring sustainable development in the new millennium*. Word Bank Publishing.

Visited sites

Corwell, INSEAD and WIPO. *The Global Innovation Index* [Online]. Available at: www.globalinnovationindex.org/gii-2018-report (Accessed: May 30, 2019).

European Bank for Reconstruction and Development (EBRD) *Knowledge Economy Index* [Online]. Available at: www.ebrd.com/news/publications/brochures/ebrd-knowledge-economy-index.html (Accessed: May 30, 2019).

European Commission. *Innovation Union Scoreboard (IUS)* [Online]. Available at: https://ec.europa.eu/growth/industry/innovation/facts-figures/scoreboards_en (Accessed: May 30, 2019).

International Institute for Management Development (IMD). *World Competitiveness Ranking* [Online]. Available at: https://worldcompetitiveness.imd.org (Accessed: May 30, 2019).

International Institute for Management Development (IMD). *World Talent Ranking* [Online]. Available at: www.imd.org/wcc/world-competitiveness-center-rankings/talent-rankings-2018/ (Accessed: May 30, 2019).

International Institute for Management Development (IMD). *World Digital Competitiveness Ranking* [Online]. Available at: www.imd.org/wcc/world-competitiveness-center-rankings/world-digital-competitiveness-rankings-2018/ (Accessed: May 30, 2019).

Organization for Economic Co-operation and Development (OECD). *OECD Science, Technology and Innovation Outlook 2018: Adapting to Technological and Societal Disruption*. OECD Publishing, Paris. https://doi.org/10.1787/sti_in_outlook-2018-en.

Ocean Tomo. *Intangible Asset Market Value Study 2017* [Online]. Available at: www.oceantomo.com/intangible-asset-market-value-study (Accessed: May 30, 2019).

178 *Marcos Cavalcanti et al.*

United Nations Development Programme (UNDP). *Human Development Reports* [Online]. Available at: www.hdr.undp.org (Accessed: May 30, 2019).

The World Bank. *Human Capital Project* [Online]. Available at: www.worldbank.org/en/publication/human-capital (Accessed: May 30, 2019).

World Economic Forum (WEF). *The Global Competitiveness Report* [Online]. Available at: http://reports.weforum.org/global-competitiveness-report-2018/ (Accessed: May 30, 2019).

Part V

Towards the development of intellectual capital standards and culture

13 The trends of intellectual capital disclosure in the new economy

Evidence from Australian firms

Yiru Yang

Introduction

Prior to the mid-1990s, scholars started raising the awareness of intellectual capital (IC), especially from in Scandinavian and northern European academia (e.g. Edvinsson and Malone, 1997; Stewart, 1997; Sveiby, 1997). At that time, IC was recognised as something significant that should be measured and reported to create and manage the sustainable competitive advantages of firms (Guthrie et al., 2012). In this growth, various terms, such as intangible resources, intangible assets, knowledge assets and intangibility, have been used interchangeably to cover the concept of IC (Bontis, 2001; Joshi et al., 2013).

In recent decades, the term IC has been used as an instrument of value-creation. Interdisciplinary researchers have investigated how the capital market reacted towards the potential for IC to create firm value (Guthrie et al., 2012; Mavridis, 2005). Guthrie and Petty (2000c) suggest that IC is used as the foundation for the creation and use of knowledge with the intent of enhancing a firm's value. Therefore, IC essentially refers to the ability to translate organisational knowledge into value. Examples of this include a firm's ability to forge and maintain positive relationships with suppliers, customers, and other stakeholders and also the ability to innovate and implement new initiatives. Definitions of IC that emerged from the management accounting literature share a similar theme, which generally refers to the collective knowledge of organisational members that can be used to increase the value of a firm. In sum, IC is generated by or developed from unique organisational designs, innovations, and human resources that can be used to determine a firm's value (Edvinsson and Malone, 1997; Guthrie, 2001; Joshi et al., 2013; Stewart, 1997; Tan et al., 2007). To an extent, accounting standards do not provide for a comprehensive measurement and identification of IC in firms, especially knowledge-based firms (Guthrie et al., 2006; Vafaei et al., 2011). Although International Financial Reporting Standards (IFRS) provide financial information in order to provide comprehensive financial statements that enhance the comparability of financial reports,[1] they have nonetheless adopted the conservative measurements of IC, as argued by Ahmed and Goodwin (2007), Goodwin et al. (2008), and Kim and Taylor (2014). These studies acknowledged that the book value of intangible assets in balance sheets lacks relevance because intangible assets in the balance sheet are represented by only a fraction of IC as a whole.

182 Yiru Yang

The rise of the "new economy", which is driven by information and knowledge, has led to an increased interest in intellectual capital (IC) in recent decades (Bontis, 2001; Petty and Guthrie, 2000). In this "new economy" age, only firms that account for their IC can positively influence investment decisions and the value of firms (Bukh, 2003; Bukh et al., 2005; Holland, 2003; Joshi et al., 2013). Firms that do not disclose IC actually generate information asymmetries and a lack of transparency (Aboody and Lev, 1998; Barth et al., 2001; Vafaei et al., 2011), so this deficiency in IC reporting means that financial reporting loses its relevance to some extent (Amir and Lev, 1996; Lev and Sougiannis, 1996). Therefore, allowing for sufficient IC disclosure would enhance the value-relevance of accounting numbers to investors (Barth and Clinch, 1996; Lev and Zarowin, 1999). In recent decades, Australia has undergone a transformation with an increasing focus on new sectors such as niche manufacturing, tourism, information technology, and financial services. It is also experiencing a relative decline in its traditionally strong areas of mining and agriculture (Guthrie et al., 2006). These changes have led to an increasing emphasis on IC among Australian firms.

This chapter attempts to provide a comparative view to reveal the trends of changes of IC disclosures in Australian firms. The sample used for this study is based on 574 firm–year observations of Australian Securities Exchange (ASX) 200 listed firms from year 2012 to year 2015. The result finds that IC disclosure has increased from year 2012 to year 2015. Reporting human capital appears to be more in favour with 46% of total IC disclosure, followed by external capital, which accounts for 29% of total IC disclosure. Reporting internal capital seems to be less in favour with 25% compared to the other two categories. The increasing awareness of safety issues, know-how, and employee diversity may account for this emphasis on human capital, because most ASX200 firms now provide a safety and sustainability section in their annual reports. Among the 33 IC items, Business collaborations was the most reported item. This means the alliances and other forms of collaborative arrangements are important in Australian firms. Although reporting internal capital seems to be less in favour compared to the other two categories, however the Network systems, Technological processes, and Information systems under the internal capital category have increased significantly from year 2014 to year 2015, which suggests that in recent years, Australian firms have tended to adopt the growth of the new economy to apply more efficient technology systems.

The remainder of this chapter is organised as follows: the following section provides a literature reviews. This is followed by the research method, the results, and the conclusion.

Literature review

Development of IC in Australia

Australia provides an ideal ground for IC reporting because it has experienced fast economic growth in recent decades, and is also undergoing a transformation with an increasing emphasis on new sectors such as niche manufacturing, tourism, information technology, and financial services. It is also experiencing a relative decline in its traditionally strong areas of mining and agriculture (Abeysekera, 2007a; Guthrie et al., 1999).

In the early 21st century, Guthrie and his team have focused on the IC disclosure of the largest (by market capitalisation) Australian listed firms, and identified that most of the IC information reported was on external capital, while the reporting of human capital and internal capital were evenly distributed. The main areas of IC reporting focus on technology and intellectual property rights, human resources, and organisational and workplace structure. The studies concluded that the key components of IC were poorly understood, inadequately identified, and inefficiently managed, and were not reported within a consistent framework. Overall, they argued that few Australian firms appear to have taken a conceptual approach to reporting their IC (Guthrie et al., 1999; Guthrie and Petty, 2000a, 2000b, 2000c).

In a further study, Guthrie et al. (2006) examined the voluntary disclosure of IC attributes for 50 listed Australian firms and 100 listed Hong Kong firms using year 2002 data. Twenty-four items included in three categories (nine relating to internal capital, nine to external capital and six to human capital) were collected using content analysis. Levels of voluntary IC disclosure were found to be low, and in qualitative rather than quantitative form in both countries. The results showed that Australian firms in 2002 disclosed more IC information than Australian firms in 1998 and Hong Kong firms in 2002.

Abeysekera (2007b) has compared the level of IC reporting of large listed firms (based on market capitalisation) in Sri Lanka with the level of IC reporting of large listed firms in Australia using content analysis to capture the IC data. The results suggest that compared to Australian firms, Sri Lankan firms reported more on brand building. Moreover, the human capital disclosure in Sri Lanka was higher than that of Australian firms. He found that the firms in Australia were far more involved in research and development compared to the firms in Sri Lanka, and investors in Australia were willing to support such entrepreneurship. The internal capital disclosure by firms in Sri Lanka was less than in Australia. The author argued that this is due to the Australian government being more supportive than the Sri Lankan government of the entrepreneurial culture in its country, and also the fact that more comprehensive laws were in place in Australia to protect intellectual property rights. In conclusion, IC reporting differences were identified between Sri Lankan and Australian firms, and it is argued that these differences can be attributed to economic, social, and political factors.

All of the above studies empirically examined Australian firm practices in reporting and managing IC. They carried out a content analysis of the top listed Australian firms to understand to what extent these firms report their IC. They applied the content analysis to capture the IC in annual reports by frequency count. Moreover, the authors conducted interviews to provide a greater understanding of how firms identify, measure, manage, and report IC. In their research, the authors used the IC framework developed by Sveiby (1997) and

184   *Yiru Yang*

split IC into three categories: internal capital, external capital and employee competence/human capital.

IC and financial performance in Australia

Evidence about IC and a firm's financial performance in Australia generally supports the belief that IC can enhance a firm's financial performance, and it also carries useful forward-looking financial performance values that are relevant for investors for firm value evaluation.

For example, Joshi et al. (2013) examined the relationship between IC measured by VAIC™ measurement and a firm's financial performance, measured by return on assets (ROA), in the Australian financial sector for the period 2006–2008. The study found that all Australian-owned banks have relatively higher human capital efficiency than capital employed efficiency and structural capital efficiency. The study also found that the size of the bank in terms of total assets, total number of employees, and total shareholders' equity has little or no impact on the IC efficiency of the Australian-owned banks.

Clarke et al. (2011) examined the effect IC efficiency has on firm performance of Australian listed firms between 2004 and 2008. The IC efficiency was measured by VAIC™ measurement, and the firm's financial performance was measured by return on equity (ROE), ROA, growth in revenues, and employee productivity. The results found that there was a direct relationship between IC efficiency and the performance of Australian publicly listed firms, particularly regarding capital employed efficiency and human capital efficiency. A positive relationship between human capital efficiency and structural capital efficiency in the prior year and performance in the current year was also found.

Kim and Taylor (2014) compared the value-relevance of productivity of IC and its components and productivity of book-value of assets based on a sample of 160 Australian listed firms from 2006 to 2010. The study developed models that draw on publicly available accounting numbers and share prices to compute and compare the value-relevance of the productivity of IC (as well as its components of human capital and structural capital). The IC was measured using a components-based direct IC measurement using hand-collected annual reports. The results showed that the productivity of human capital, structural capital, and IC are each positively related to share price, whereas the productivity of total assets at book value is non-significant and tangible assets is negatively significant. The authors concluded that the book value of intangible assets and tangible assets in the balance sheet does not have value-relevance, and intangible assets in the balance sheet represent only a fraction of IC.

Research method

Data and sample selection

The current study used ASX 200 firms from years 2012 to 2015 as the sampling frame. Information related to financial data was obtained from the DatAnalysis

IC disclosure in the new economy   185

Table 13.1 Sample selection

Sample selection	Firm-year observations
Top ASX200 firms	800
Exclusions	
Banks	24
Insurance	16
Diversified financials	36
Real estate	76
Missing data	74
Final sample investigated	574

database. Following Dahmash et al. (2009), firms involved in banking, insurance, diversified financials, and real estate were excluded because they are subject to different reporting requirements. ASX 200 firms were selected as the sample frame because the ASX 200 is recognised as the primary investment benchmark in Australia. ASX 200 firms cover approximately 78% of Australian equity market capitalisation. Moreover, this study has deleted the firms that did not have annual reports and did not have financial information available on the database over the period 2012–2015. After excluding all the missing data, the sample size decreased from 800 firm-year observations to 574 firm-year observations. The detailed sample selection process is shown in Table 13.1.

Content analysis

To capture IC information, this chapter applies the content analysis for 574 annual reports. In analysing the IC content disclosed in the annual reports, this chapter counted the frequency of IC items reported. This chapter conceptualises IC according to Yang's (2018) framework. The IC framework presented was modified so that items likely to be reported by Australian firms will converge better.

The coding framework recorded data from the content analysis using 33 pre-defined IC items including 8 internal capital items (including Intellectual property; Management processes; Technological processes; Information systems; Network systems; Management philosophy; Corporate culture; Financial relations), 11 external capital items (including Brands; Customer satisfaction; Quality standards; Company names; Favourable contracts; Business collaborations; Licensing agreements; Franchising agreements; Distribution channels; Market share; Favourable relations with stakeholders), and 14 human capital items (including Employee involvement in the community; Employee thanked; Employee featured; Employee numbers; Professional experience; Value added by employee; Know-how; Education; Career development; Training programmes; Entrepreneurial spirit, innovativeness, proactive and reactive abilities and changeability; Employment safety; Workplace diversity; Employee welfare).

Overcoming threats to the content analysis

The terms validity and reliability are often expressed in relation to content analysis. The term "validity" is defined as the property of a measure that allows the researcher to say that the instrument measures what he or she says it measures. The term "reliability" is defined as the ability of an instrument to consistently measure the phenomenon it is desired to measure (Abeysekera, 2007a, p.61). According to Milne and Adler (1999) and Guthrie et al. (2004), three main techniques are used to reduce the concerns of reliability and validity in content analysis: by selecting disclosure categories from well-grounded relevant literature, and clearly defining them; by establishing a reliable coding instrument with well-specified decision categories and decision rules; by training the coders and showing that coding decisions made on a pilot sample have reached an acceptable level by other coders. The first two methods can be realised, as this study follows Yang's (2018) IC framework, which clearly defines every IC item. This paper used content analysis on the grounds that the purpose of the analysis was to count pre-determined IC items referred to in the annual reports using Nvivo software. The third technique is difficult to realise due to research-domain restrictions. This is because the conventional reliability test requires a measure of consensus between different coders, which is interpreted by a consensus coefficient. In coding data, another researcher could code the semantic content differently from that recorded in this thesis by this researcher. Abeysekera (2007a) argued that this problem is not due to laxity or carelessness between researchers, but rather because of the differences in objectively driven sensibility and creativity between them. The creative aspect is an accepted factor in semantic content analysis compared to syntactic content analysis. Under semantic rules, words can express different concepts to different people. Since there is no natural language that determines one interpretation of a sentence, the true or correct semantic investigation is directed towards building empirical knowledge rather than normative knowledge (Andren 1980, pp.60–63). According to Abeysekera (2007a), the consensus coefficient has its weaknesses. It can create doubt upon reliable data if the coefficient is low and a high coefficient can seem trustworthy even if it is unreliable because there is a high frequency of false data. A more qualified reliability test can constitute several others by re-coding a random sample of investigated material to identify differences so that an ordinary coefficient can be calculated. However, this method is time consuming and costly. Given the above limitations, the results of the sole researcher's judgement should be trusted, as this seems to be the only feasible way of attaining a measurement of the veracity of data concerning semantic content (Andren, 1980, pp.65–66). Therefore, this study does not require another coder to re-capture IC using content analysis. Nevertheless, the coder has reviewed the annual reports twice. There is a one-week interval period between first time coding and second time coding.

IC disclosure in the new economy 187

Results of the study

Relative emphasis in terms of IC categories

The frequency of reporting by categories of IC (including internal capital, external capital, and human capital) is also to determine whether there is a particular focus on one particular category of capital. Figure 13.1 shows the relative emphasis in terms of IC categories. Reporting human capital appears to be more in favour with 46% of total IC disclosure, followed by external capital, which hits for 29% of total IC disclosure. Reporting internal capital seems to be less in favour with 25% compared to the other two categories. Human capital is emphasised in the light of an emphasis in recent years on increased global competition, so talented people are once more a priority. The increasing awareness of safety issues may also account for this emphasis on human capital, because most ASX200 firms now provide a safety and sustainability section in their annual reports. Moreover, an increasing number of firms reported the diversity of their employees (reporting frequency=564) based on ASX best practice recommendations 3.2, 3.3, 3.4, and 3.5 in corporate governance statement section 4. This increased reporting of human capital may also arise from an increase in employee relations. Most firms (reporting frequency=619) thanked their staff in the chairman's report section of annual reports and also attempted to give special prominence to and reward employees, as shown in the high reporting frequency in the employee featured (reporting frequency=293) item.

The trends of changes of reporting specific attributes

Figure 13.2 shows the changes in the reporting of IC throughout the years from 2012 to 2015. As shown in Figure 13.2, the reporting frequency of IC has increased from 2778 hits in year 2012 to 4119 hits in year 2015. Figure 13.3 shows the trend in internal capital disclosure. The two items disclosed most were Management processes (total reporting frequency=886) and Technological processes (total reporting frequency=831) under the internal capital category.

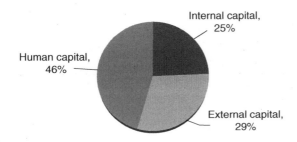

Figure 13.1 The relative emphasis in terms of IC categories.

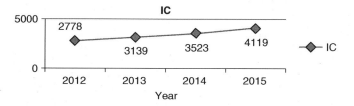

Figure 13.2 Changes in intellectual capital.

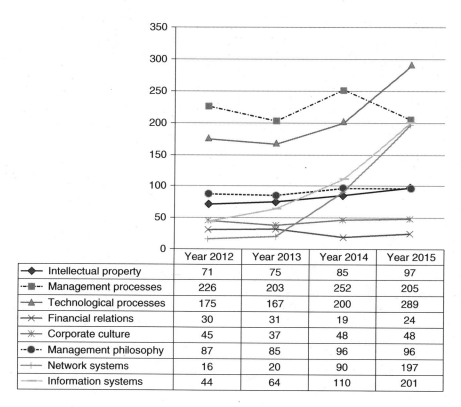

Figure 13.3 Changes in internal capital.

Management processes were most important, which was not surprising because they are principally concerned with relations between people, and are a common way of conducting business that leads to objectives being accomplished. The management processes disclosure decreased slightly in 2013, and then rose up in 2014, but then dropped to a level similar to that of 2013. Intellectual property increased each year from 71 hits in year 2012 to 97 hits in year 2015. Network systems, Technological processes, and Information systems rose dramatically

IC disclosure in the new economy 189

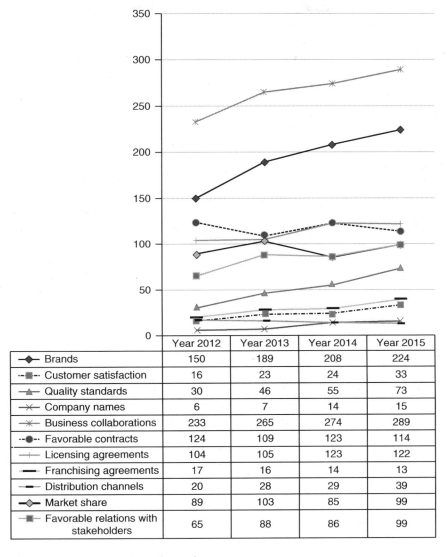

Figure 13.4 Changes in external capital.

from year 2014 to 2015, which suggests that in the new economy, Australian firms pay more attention to more efficient technology systems to adopt the fast growth of the new economy.

Figure 13.4 presents the changes in external capital disclosure. The item disclosed the most was Business collaborations with other partners (reporting frequency=1061). Business collaborations was highest under external capital disclosure because alliances and other forms of collaborative arrangements are important means of implementing firm's growth strategies (Guthrie et al., 2006). The least reported item was Company names (reporting frequency=42). Aside form Franchising agreements and Market share, other external capital items increased from year 2012 to year 2015.

Figure 13.5 shows the changes in human capital disclosure for the sample. Employee safety was the most disclosed item under the human capital category (reporting frequency=821); it increased dramatically from 167 hits in year 2012 to 243 hits in year 2015. The least reported item was Value added by employee, with only 69 hits among the human capital items. As shown in Figure 13.5, all the human capital items increased throughout the reporting period. Know-how and Employee diversity rose significantly from 2014 to 2015. It is suggested that, in recent years, more and more professions have a greater depth of knowledge in the area and a number of experienced staff have become involved in and contributed to Australian firms. Furthermore, Australian firms tend to be equal opportunity employers. They employed people with disabilities and announced that gender diversity is also important.

Conclusion

This chapter examines the trends of changes in IC disclosure in Australian listed firms. The sample for this study is based on 574 annual reports from ASX200 listed firms from year 2012 to year 2015. Using the content analysis, the result of this chapter reveals that IC disclosure has increased throughout the years from 2012 to 2015. It increased from 2778 hits in 2012 to 4119 hits in 2015. Human capital appears to be more in favour of total IC disclosure, which accounts for 46%, followed by external capital. Reporting internal capital seems to be less in favour compared to the other two categories, but Network systems, Technological processes, and Information systems under the internal capital category have increased dramatically from year 2014 to year 2015, which suggests that Australian firms tend to adopt the new economy to apply more efficient technology systems. Human capital is emphasised in the light of an emphasis in recent years on increased global competition, so talented people are once more a priority. Business collaboration was reported the most among IC items. Reporting Employee safety has dramatically increased throughout the sample years in Australian firms. Know-how and Employee diversity rose significantly from 2014 to 2015.

There are several limitations to this study. First, the results of this study may not be applicable to other countries and other non-listed Australian firms, as the study only investigated ASX200 listed Australian firms. Second, the coding framework used in this study comprises 33 IC items. However, other studies have used coding frameworks comprising fewer or more varied IC items. Therefore, when comparing the results of this and other studies, the interpretation of the findings must recognise the differences in approach.

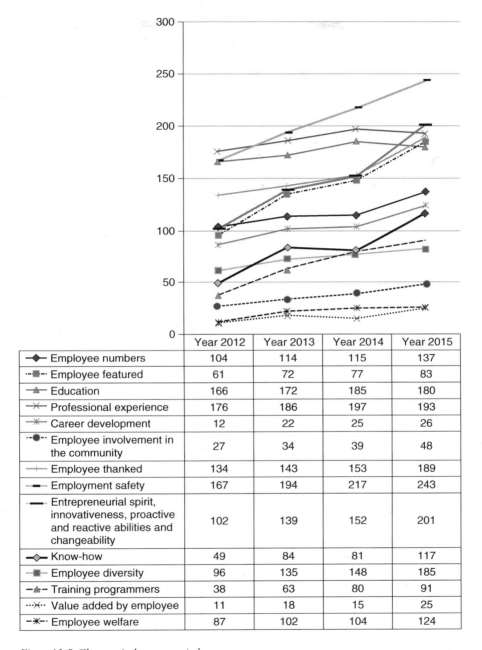

Figure 13.5 Changes in human capital.

Note

1 There have been a few changes concerning IC in the financial statements since the adoption of IFRS. For example, IFRS 3 requires that goodwill is considered to be an asset with an indefinite lifespan, and would therefore not be eligible for amortisation. Instead, the book value of goodwill is subjected to impairment testing at either the level of a cash generating unit (CGU) or a group of CGUs of the consolidated entity. Further, all ICs that do not meet the criteria of control, identifiability, and future economic benefits are to be derecognised as assets and expensed (Vafaei et al., 2011).

References

Abeysekera, I. (2007a), *Intellectual Capital Accounting: Practices in a Developing Country*, Routledge, London.

Abeysekera, I. (2007b), "Intellectual capital reporting between a developing and developed nation", *Journal of Intellectual Capital*, Vol.8, No.2, pp.329–345.

Aboody, D. and Lev, B. (1998), "The value relevance of intangibles: The case of software capitalization", *Journal of Accounting Research*, Vol.36, No.3, pp.161–191.

Ahmed, K. and Goodwin, J. (2007), "An empirical investigation of earnings restatements by Australian firms", *Accounting and Finance*, Vol.47, No.1, pp.1–22.

Amir, E. and Lev, B. (1996), "Value-relevance of nonfinancial information: The wireless communications industry", *Journal of Accounting and Economics*, Vol.22, No.1–3, pp.3–30.

Andren, G. (1980), "Reliability and content analysis", in *Advances in Content Analysis*, ed. K.E. Rosengren, Sage Annual Reviews of Communication Research Vol.9, Sage, Beverly Hills, CA.

Barth, M.E., Beaver, W.H. and Landsman, W.R. (2001), "The relevance of the value relevance literature for financial accounting standard setting: Another view", *Journal of Accounting and Economics*, Vol.31, No.1, pp.77–104.

Barth, M.E. and Clinch, G. (1996), "International accounting differences and their relation to share prices: Evidence from U.K., Australian, and Canadian firms", *Contemporary Accounting Research*, Vol.13, No.1, pp.135–170.

Bontis, N. (2001), "Assessing knowledge assets: A review of the models used to measure intellectual capital", *International Journal of Management Review*, Vol.3, No.1, pp.41–60.

Bukh, P.N. (2003), "The relevance of intellectual capital disclosure: A paradox?", *Accounting, Auditing and Accountability Journal*, Vol.16, No.1, pp.49–56.

Bukh, P.N., Nielsen, C., Gormsen, P. and Mouritsen, J. (2005), "Disclosure of information on intellectual capital in Danish IPO prospectuses", *Accounting, Auditing and Accountability Journal*, Vol.18, No.6, pp.713–732.

Clarke, M., Seng, D. and Whiting, R.H. (2011), "Intellectual capital and firm performance in Australia", *Journal of Intellectual Capital*, Vol.12, No.4, pp.505–530.

Dahmash, F.N., Durand, R.B. and Watson, J. (2009), "The value relevance and reliability of reported goodwill and identifiable intangible assets", *British Accounting Review*, Vol.41, No.2, pp.120–137.

Edvinsson, L. and Malone, M. (1997), *Intellectual Capital: Realizing Your Company's True Value by Finding Its Hidden Brainpower*, HarperCollins, New York.

Goodwin, J., Ahmed, K. and Heaney, R. (2008), "The effects of international financial reporting standards on the accounts and accounting quality of Australian firms: A retrospective study", *Journal of Contemporary Accounting and Economics*, Vol.4, No.2, pp.89–119.

Guthrie, J. (2001), "The management, measurement and the reporting of intellectual capital", *Journal of Intellectual Capital*, Vol.2, No.1, pp.27–41.

Guthrie, J. and Petty, R. (2000a), "Intellectual capital: Australian annual reporting practices", *Journal of Intellectual Capital*, Vol.1, No.3, pp.241–251.

Guthrie, J. and Petty, R. (2000b), "Towards the future: knowledge management and the measurement of intangibles", *Management Today*, January, pp.21–23.

Guthrie, J. and Petty, R. (2000c), "Are companies thinking smart?", *Australian CPA*, Vol.70, No.6, pp.62–65.

Guthrie, J., Petty, R., Ferrier, F. and Wells, R. (1999), "There is no accounting for intellectual capital in Australia: A review of annual reporting practices and internal measurement of intangibles", Paper presented at the OECD Symposium on Measuring and Reporting of Intellectual Capital, Amsterdam.

Guthrie, J., Petty, R. and Ricceri, F. (2006), "The voluntary reporting of intellectual capital: Comparing evidence from Hong Kong and Australia", *Journal of Intellectual Capital*, Vol.7, No.2, pp.254–271.

Guthrie, J., Petty, R., Yongvanich, K. and Ricceri, F. (2004), "Using content analysis as a research method to inquire into intellectual capital reporting", *Journal of Intellectual Capital*, Vol.5, No.2, pp.282–293.

Guthrie, J., Ricceri, F. and Dumay, J. (2012), "Reflections and projections: A decade of intellectual capital accounting research", *British Accounting Review*, Vol.44, No.2, pp.68–82.

Holland, J. (2003), "Intellectual capital and the capital market-organisation and competence", *Accounting, Auditing and Accountability Journal*, Vol.16, No.1, pp.39–48.

Joshi, M., Cahill, D., Sidhu, J. and Kansal, M. (2013), "Intellectual capital and financial performance: An evaluation of the Australian financial sector", *Journal of Intellectual Capital*, Vol.14, No.2, pp.264–285.

Kim, S.H. and Taylor, D. (2014), "Intellectual capital vs the book-value of assets", *Journal of Intellectual Capital*, Vol.15, No.1, pp.65–82.

Lev, B. and Sougiannis, T. (1996), "The capitalization, amortization, and value-relevance of Rand", *Journal of Accounting and Economics*, Vol.21, No.1, pp.107–138.

Lev, B. and Zarowin, P. (1999), "The boundaries of financial reporting and how to extend them", *Journal of Accounting Research*, Vol.37, No.2, pp.353–385.

Mavridis, D.G. (2005), "Intellectual capital performance determinants and globalization status of Greek listed firms", *Journal of Intellectual Capital*, Vol.6, No.1, pp.127–140.

Milne, M. and Adler, R. (1999), "Exploring the reliability of social and environmental disclosures content analysis", *Accounting, Auditing and Accountability Journal*, Vol.12, No.2, pp.237–256.

Petty, P. and Guthrie, J. (2000), "Intellectual capital literature review: Measurement, reporting and management", *Journal of Intellectual Capital*, Vol.1, No.2, pp.155–175.

Stewart, T.A. (1997), *Intellectual Capital: The Wealth of New Organizations*, Nicholas Brealey, London.

Sveiby, K.E. (1997), *The New Organizational Wealth: Managing and Measuring Knowledge Based Assets*, Berrett Koehler, San Francisco, CA.

Tan, H.P., Plowman, D. and Hancock, P. (2007), "Intellectual capital and financial returns of companies", *Journal of Intellectual Capital*, Vol.8, No.1, pp.76–95.

Vafaei, A., Taylor, D. and Ahmed, K. (2011), "The value relevance of intellectual capital disclosures", *Journal of Intellectual Capital*, Vol.12, No.3, pp.407–429.

Yang, Y. (2018), "Do aggressive pro forma earnings-reporting firms have difficulty disclosing intellectual capital", *Journal of Intellectual Capital*, Vol.19, No.5, pp.875–896.

14 Entrepreneurialism

A multi-faceted cultural movement

Piero Formica

Prelude: the invention of a cultural movement

Intellectual capital (IC) is an intangible asset born of a mind accustomed to great things: it embodies the characters of intuition (instinctive feeling), imagination (new ideas not present to the senses) and creativity (original ideas that have value). The culture of which entrepreneurialism is a part intervenes to strengthen that mind. It was Leif Edvinsson, a prime mover and for many the father-figure of the IC evolution, who proposed the form of a tree as an illustrative design for IC, but which places the roots upwards, facing the sky, because the future flowering of the plant depends upon them. Those roots are nothing more than the culture and the relationships interwoven by it, from which arise the abundance and goodness of the fruits of the seasons to come. There is a mental image of this culture that remains a blind spot, however: it is the image of entrepreneurialism, representing a cultural movement that exhibits multiple facets whose common denominator is the interweaving of the human sciences and the natural sciences. Entrepreneurialism heralds a new springtime, with the blossoming of unknown species born of a new knowledge which leads to the acquisition of capabilities, different to those already available, to do new things.

Entrepreneurialism is an art form that, having grasped one or more ideas to open the doors of the future, imagines its transformation into an entity called 'Transformative Enterprise' (Formica and Hixson, 2019). It flourishes when experimenters of non-conformist predisposition meet and interact in informal groups; amateurs and pragmatists, not just academics. If we were to compare the agents of entrepreneurialism to the artistic avant-garde of the early twentieth century, we would see them as Cubists – those who depicted the subject from a multitude of points of view in order to frame it in a broader context. Further, we would attribute to them the characteristics of the Dadaists who rejected the standards of society of the time, believing that imposed societal norms and established expectations had become outdated. The culture of the protagonists of entrepreneurialism gives rise to a constant buzz of creativity that arouses motivations and expectations based on knowledge at the eventide of probability and in the dark night of uncertainty. Furthermore, we would say that those agents constitute a parallel with the cultural movement of the Surrealists to whom we are indebted for representations of illogical scenes, strange creatures, surprising elements and unexpected juxtapositions.

We suffer from both the 'rheumatism of old age' and the 'growing pains caused of over-rapid changes': John Maynard Keynes would surely repeat today these words included in his short essay *Economic Possibilities for Our Grandchildren* (Keynes, [1930] 1932: 358). The cultural movement of entrepreneurialism makes them its own by aggregating scientists and humanists, who partake in a spontaneous process of interactions that transcend existing customs and traditions. In so doing, this alliance imposes a U-turn on society and business. Projects that combine scientific and humanities-based approaches are triggered by ideas which, at first glance, may seem ridiculous and unlikely. Such actions borrow the Aristotelian opinion that a likely impossibility is preferable to an unconvincing possibility (Aristotle, [1996]).

Creative ignorance: entrepreneurialism exceeds the boundaries of received knowledge

If today's knowledge does not reveal what will happen tomorrow, then one must have the courage to take a risk; the risk to prepare oneself to act by practising the culture of creative ignorance. Entrepreneurship embraces this culture with the aim of acquiring new knowledge to do new things.

Creative ignorance is knowledge in action – a cognitive process that leads to a new domain of expertise. As explained by Formica in *The Role of Creative Ignorance* (Formica, 2015: 17), creative ignorance is authentic, conscious (aware of one's ignorance and responding to one's surroundings), intentional (done with intention or on purpose), insightful (the act or outcome of grasping the inward or hidden nature of things or of perceiving intuitively) and perceptive (able to see what others cannot).

The creative ignorant fly as high as Icarus. If the rays of the sun had ever melted the wax used to fasten his wings, the creative ignorant would have detected a design or manufacturing defect and would thus have gone in search of a remedy. Walking into the void of knowledge in the absence of predetermined destinations shapes their ideas. On their way, the creative ignorant discover subtle analogies and, by sagacity and accident, exceed the boundaries set by knowledge maps they possess, thus opening up and connecting previously unknown new routes. In changing trajectories, path creators reveal latent, unexpressed needs of consumers.

Forging communities of the creative ignorant, those who come into conflict with established knowledge maps and mental structures, is a cultural feature of entrepreneurialism. Creative ignorance allows you to see, feel and become aware of something through your senses (intuition). The resulting understanding or interpretation (perception) releases cultural turbulence that disturbs the existing dominant knowledge. These ferments transmute into innovations from which new entrepreneurship emerges.

196 *Piero Formica*

When the new knowledge becomes dominant, one's conviction generates realization that the current state of things is not compatible with discontinuity. Working practices aimed at enhancing the knowledge acquired with incremental innovations provide reinforcement. Facts backed by experience feed confidence in those practices, which require reasonable people who reinforce the rules by repeating them and use data to predict the future in continuity with the past. Thus an army of people, all marching in the same direction, is formed and enlarged. Their attitude is that of Daedalus, who flies to an altitude at which the wax securing his wings will not melt. Outdoing one another is a difficult task: only *ex post* will we realize that, once the ferment of new knowledge has appeared and been consolidated, it is impossible to return to the positions held in the now out-dated domain.

Embedded in the bunker of received knowledge, we do not grasp the new ferments produced by other self-examinations, by metamorphoses of the imagination, which render as useless those ideas accumulated and transferred over time. The earlier experience retained by memory is no longer necessary; it is even harmful. Meanwhile, by cultivating the culture of the impossible and navigating through uncharted waters, experimenters of creative ignorance glimpse opportunities as promising as they appear to be marginal, statistically insignificant events. Their revolutionary ideas are a point of no return. The hitherto dominant position in the realm of conformism is lost once and for all (see Figure 14.1).

Countries that boast of their successes in manufacturing exports, as in the case of 'Made in Italy', are – like Narcissus – in love with their image reflected, in this instance, in the mirror of the received knowledge map. In order not to end up like Narcissus, who gazed upon the muddy waters of the river Styx in the hope of being able to admire his reflection once again, the Italian manufacturers would do well to observe carefully the ugly duckling born from creative ignorance that suddenly changes into a beautiful swan.

From wants to needs: the 'Ba' cultural space of entrepreneurialism

Referring to Japanese theorists Kitaro Nashida, Hiroshi Shimazu, Ikujiro Nonaka and Noboru Konno (see, for example, Nonaka and Konno, 1998), entrepreneurialism embraces the culture of the 'Ba' space, a mental, virtual and physical place in which cooperation between people who do not separate the 'self' from the 'other' brings out unforeseeable and sometimes impromptu creations that reveal and identify the latent needs of consumers.

The passions that manifest themselves in the 'Ba' entertainment space manage to break down the barriers that exist in our minds. These barriers are erected by producers who interrogate the markets using the knowledge maps they have mastered. Together with experts who enrich their maps, they scrutinize and capture the demands of consumers, and meet the specific demands of the most loyal clients. Experts about today's demands and speculating on

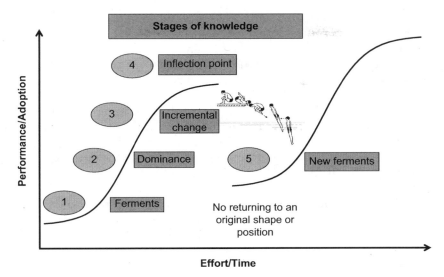

1. Knowledge domain in process.
2. Acquired knowledge becomes dominant.
3. Knowledge enhancement.
4. Yesterday's knowledge does not tell us what is going to happen tomorrow.
5. A new knowledge base.

Figure 14.1 Knowledge in action.

the next tomorrow, they experience a strong and often irresistible tendency to halt innovation at the border of incrementalism, doing what is necessary to safeguard the continuity of the original concepts. Their attitude is a source of light that, while corroborating one's point of view, can deceive, giving rise to looking where it spreads out rapidly; but there is nothing else and little more than improvement of what is already practised with dexterity. As happened to the Nibelungs, the vast treasure consisting of customers and consumers they guard will one day be prey to the Siegfrieds, the visionaries who occupy the 'Ba' space.[1]

There are also barriers built by consumers, either voluntarily or because they are induced by hidden persuaders – advertisers – who entice them to load up their shopping basket of products and services. The barriers raised in spaces reserved for public use portend 'The Tragedy of the Commons' (Hardin, 1968). To have more income and then spend more, everyone grazes more sheep than they should, the collective interest being at stake. It is the consumerist drift that makes the herdsman aggressive, arrogating the right of others to access the common pasture on which there is an increasing number of sheep. Within those barriers, the personal exaltation of happiness, the supreme goal of life, becomes the acquisition of so-called 'positional goods', those conspicuous material goods

198 *Piero Formica*

the demand for which increases as the price rises and the value of which as a status symbol is enhanced until only a few can afford them: the powerful feudal lords, owners of coffers that contain so much, and increasing, wealth.

In the 'Ba' space of entrepreneurialism, individual preferences are not taken for granted. They fall under investigation with regard to the relevance of human values. One wonders about the tendency to sympathize with the joys and pains of others (as did David Hume and Adam Smith); about the altruism that allows the conservation of the human species, while selfishness preserves only the individual (Jean-Jacques Rousseau); about utilitarianism as the pursuit of personal happiness not at the expense of societal happiness (John Stuart Mill). In short, entrepreneurialism promotes entrepreneurship that, by accepting the moral sentiments pleaded by Adam Smith (1761), would not run the risk of being morally corrupted.

The 'Ba' space of entrepreneurialism is therefore a field of experimentation on how to take care of the interests of the company and the entrepreneur without causing harm to others and, in the end, even to themselves, because over time a strongly selfish behaviour has a negative effect on the health of the community to which one belongs. It's like saying that the invisible hand of Adam Smith's *Wealth of Nations* (1761) changes into a visible handshake, so that human beings, as social creatures, can regulate better, and to the benefit of all their relationships.

Along this line of thought, the 'Ba' space separates needs from unrestrained desires, which latter are an incentive to produce an increasing variety of goods and services that causes people trouble. A multi-option society (Gross, 1994) raises questions such as 'did I choose well?' and 'did I lose a better option?'. It is a recurring source of anxiety and concern that ends up prevailing over the pleasure of being confronted with a wide range of choices.

The emphasis placed on needs that reconcile personal interest with the common good gives rise to innovations that generate widespread wealth, with better and cheaper merchandise, transport, communication and utilities, as well as sustainable productivity over time. Both offer access to new experiences that improve the human mind. In the 'Ba' space, the seekers of need move from basic requirements (food, water, personal security and so on) to psychological needs (such as friendship and trust in one's neighbour) and self-realization needs (for example, through collaborative creative activities).

They identify niches in which experimenting with and then implementing customized products and services can take place. In doing so they trigger processes of democratization of consumption and production that mark the birth of an economy of sharing. The aim is to transform markets so significantly that they have a radical impact on people's behaviour.

Re-imagined school: entrepreneurialism as a culture of learner-centred education

Entrepreneurialism ushers a new age of education, moving away from the 'front-loaded' educational system. It is a journey heading towards the re-imagined school, a rebirth of Renaissance learning by forging revolutionary paths for human and relational capital that changes the student's mind. As Virgil wrote 'terraeque urbesque recedunt' (The Aeneid, III, line 72, quoted by Seneca, Epistulae morales to Lucilius, III, 28) – 'leave the cities and the shores behind' (Dryden's 1697 translation – see Virgil, 2009: 92), so the re-imagined school leaves the shore of teaching, with its boundaries restricted by knowledge accrued over time, to reach the far shores of experiential and experimental learning, where passions supported by strong motivation can produce outstanding results. Its characteristics date back to the Renaissance, which ushered in a new narrative that altered the state of the world preparing for the age of experimentation: for instance, with Bacon's method reliant upon experiments (Bacon, [1620] 1902).

Renaissance Man emerged from the medieval wellspring of the desire for received knowledge. The medieval schools headed by scholars (in effect, philosophers and theologians acting as 'schoolmen') were involved in systematizing that knowledge rather than developing a new one. Out of that well Renaissance Man set imagination in motion to journey everywhere, dismissing purely practical ideas (i.e., tried and true) in favour of creative ones – novelties which arouse feelings of uncertainty. Later, in the age of inventions and discoveries between the nineteenth and twentieth centuries, Marie Curie revisited the thread of Renaissance Man with these words,

> Humanity certainly needs practical men, who get the most out of their work, and, without forgetting the general good, safeguard their own interests. But humanity also needs dreamers, for whom the disinterested development of an enterprise is so captivating that it becomes impossible for them to devote their care to their own material profit. Without the slightest doubt, these dreamers do not deserve wealth, because they do not desire it. Even so, a well-organised society should assure to such workers the efficient means of accomplishing their task, in a life freed from material care and freely consecrated to research.
>
> (Curie, 1938)

From the Contamination Labs of the universities of Padua and Verona to the Copernico and Mattei high schools in Bologna, the reimagined school is making progress in the northeast area of Italy, a high-density manufacturing macro-region. A cultural revolution is in process with experimental classes, where teachers guide students along paths to explore and attempt to solve problems. The 'fast food' of mass teaching gives way to the personalization of learning, avoiding the trap of memorization, emphasizing instead trans-disciplinary exploration, practising trans-disciplinary skills, cultivating divergent thinking, testing creative capacities, training in empathic communication and negotiation, and dealing with leadership, all of which constitute a collection of advantages. In Japan, for example, extracting students from the process of committing facts to memory is the goal pursued by a new primary school, the

New International School of Japan (NISJ) in Tokyo. As Shotaro Tani reported in the *Financial Times* in 2017 (*Financial Times*, 2017), the NISJ encourages multilinguistics: more than one language is used at the same time, an essential factor for seeing things from multiple points of view, improving expression and social skills, and preparing young people for careers in which they may have to take on different roles at different times.

Teaching is focused on knowledge maps so that the student is placed in a position to say 'I know'. 'How can I rethink the way I see the problem?'; and 'How many different ways can I solve it?': these are questions that are answered without recourse to complying with the authority of the canons defined in the teaching manuals. Learning prepares the mind to formulate questions rather than to give answers, starting with those that do not admit to being questioned; to cultivate abstruse questions that reveal unusual paths to explore. Learners take pleasure in not finding what they are looking for (Forsyth, 2014), and they are not afraid to confront the uncertainty that comes from the 'unknown unknowns'.[2] In this way facts classified as immutable, fixed once and for all, are challenged and may be proven wrong.

In the learning process, the leading actor is the experimenter who enters the ballroom with light baggage, not burdened with accumulated knowledge, where the questions that are not known dance the can-can, as Mark Forsyth writes in his *The Unknown Unknown* (Forsyth, 2014). It was an Italian writer, Giovanni Papini, who spoke against the school that 'does not invent knowledge but prides itself on transmitting it', anticipating at the beginning of the twentieth century the learning in experimental laboratories which provides a basis for raising, by both students and teachers, unspoken and unprecedented questions, and learning from errors (Papini, 1919).

Transdisciplinarity: the broad cultural space of entrepreneurialism

In a previous study on entrepreneurial renaissance (Formica, 2017), consideration was given to the fusion of humanities and natural sciences that represents the free-thinking of Renaissance Man, as personified in the famous drawing by Leonardo da Vinci of the Vitruvian Man which links art and science in the representation of the human body. Entrepreneurialism seeks to make the entrepreneurial journey a venture among artists, those in the humanities, and scientists, united by their richness of diversity and intensity of interactions. Entrepreneurialism conjures up the representative figures of the Renaissance age, those versatile personalities *à la* Leonardo, the polymaths with vision, free from metaphorical straitjackets of all kinds and engaged in a wide variety of fields.

The culture of entrepreneurialism exists on both sides of human knowledge: namely, science and humanities. By reciprocally invading the other's field, each of these two finds itself in the folds of the other. Subjects dealing with human and social sciences (law, sociology, philosophy, psychology, economics, politics and the like) climb out of the deep hole of their super-specialized knowledge wells; and the same applies to the natural sciences. By crossing all subject spaces, transdisciplinary entrepreneurialism promotes STEAM (Science, Technology, Engineering, Arts, and Mathematics) over STEM (Science, Technology, Engineering, and Mathematics). Thus, integrative thinking drives passions and gives rise to creative thoughts, from which new entrepreneurial styles flourish that intertwine Yin (the moon, the feminine, emotion and creativity) and Yang (the sun, the masculine, rationality and planning). So, Yang companies will not only manifest themselves, concerned about staying in their market by designing strategies and consequent structures: they will also show Yin's face, aiming to discover promising possibilities, to play with emerging ideas that direct them towards other commercial frontiers.

In the transdisciplinary space, one is called upon to experiment by leaving one's mental barn and not to feel upset when the interlocutors express points of view opposed to one's own. In short, you are no longer prey to emotional conflicts. The mind free from prejudices regards the conflict between ideas as personal enrichment: conflict changes from affective to cognitive. The debate triggered by the cognitive conflict between contradictory beliefs and incompatible values becomes an accelerator of ideas that, colliding with each other, will generate new and original ones. The process of collision of ideas is, in short, the beating heart of the experiment. By promoting interaction between individuals of different cultures and disciplines, transdisciplinary experimentation generates the first embryos of innovative business ideas.

Co-working spaces for innovation: the culture of design thinking

The rise of Artificial Intelligence and Digital Transformation is joining Science, Technology, Engineering and Mathematics with the Arts, in a wide embrace. 'Know How to Do' makes a new start by coupling with 'Knowing How to Think, Imagine and Understand'. Creatively combining the 'Four Ways of Knowing' of intellectual capital, the arts act as a catalyst of human-centred use of technology.[3] By maintaining a high propensity for techno-humanities entrepreneurship, entrepreneurialism embeds the culture of design thinking to encourage the generation of ideas that can feed start-ups for generating new values. This requires continuous learning and willingness combined with the ability to advance into the unknown. Innovationists and innovators take over from incrementalists.

To this end, this culture designs co-working spaces, reminiscent of the Renaissance 'bottega' (workshop) of fifteenth-century Florence, perhaps the most famous of which was that of Andrea del Verrocchio (1435–1488) – a sculptor, painter and goldsmith. In those spaces, people were trained as hunters of ideas to be converted into transformative new-venture creations. As at the time of the hunter-gatherers of the Palaeolithic era, hunting and gathering need to be carried out not reluctantly but with enthusiasm; and, as with the

202 Piero Formica

Renaissance bottega, co-working spaces turn ideas into action, foster dialogue, and facilitate the convergence of art and science. Talents are nurtured, new techniques are employed and unique art forms come to light. Painters, sculptors and other artists, and architects, mathematicians, engineers, anatomists and other scientists can meet and work together. The result is entrepreneurship that conceives revolutionary ways of working, of designing and delivering products and services, and even of seeing the world (see, for example, Formica, 2016, 2017).

Entrepreneurialism bears the transformative power of the ideation, that creative process at the intersection of artistic, scientific, business and policy ideas triggered by the social phenomenon that Frans Johansson (2006) called the 'Medici effect', revisiting the driving force of across-the-board innovation attributed to the Medici. In fact, ideation in the Florence of the Medici completes the entire cycle: from the generation of the idea to its realization which, as the Nobel Prize winner Paul Romer, the economist and pioneer of the theory of endogenous growth, would say, comes in the guise of a recipe better than those hitherto produced (Formica, 2017: 14). With this vision, in tandem with the co-working spaces, the culture of entrepreneurship conceives Experimental Lab Communities comprising those from the humanities and social and natural scientists, a kind of super-collider environment where breakthrough ideas and insights occur at the intersection of different disciplines. In the Lab, ideas are being posted looking for problem seekers and problem solvers. The first actively seek out attempts to deal with problems as they arise from the Lab Community ideas; and the latter identify effective solutions by enabling connections that are not immediately apparent of different approaches. Teams of problem solvers and problem seekers are interchangeable. By conducting realistic experiments and/or reproducing the conditions of a situation or process, these teams can make a journey along the business idea spectrum – from learning what the market wants to ascertaining the needs and desires of consumers and developing products their customers may not know they need. The ideas generated through the interactions among stakeholders from different disciplines, who converge and integrate, form an inextricable but productive tangle of artistic, scientific and technical creations.

When the culture of entrepreneurialism lags behind industrial performance: a brief account of the Italian experience

A country that rejects or neglects entrepreneurialism will see its economy stagnate and opportunities shrink. It is not sufficient to have a well-kept garden where you try to plant new entrepreneurial species, as in the case of the northeast region of Italy, the second manufacturing power in Europe behind Germany, with a significant number of companies among the best in Europe in mechatronics engineering and automotive manufacturing. Companies such as Ferrari, Lamborghini and Ducati are owners of a tradition that combines art, craftsmanship and technology. All are engaged in incremental processes, which are improved through experience, with the aim of reducing unit production costs and doing the work more accurately and quickly. Immersed in this reality, the worker takes the bait of technology, but does not see its line.

Italy as a whole suffers a scarcity of transformative entrepreneurship, despite the presence of established and resource-rich companies. Among the wealthy ones, there are more than a few that fear being destabilized by well-funded start-ups which appear as promising monsters and vital mutants. Some of them set their targets higher, aiming at business creation that contributes to the strengthening of their value chains. However, all this is too little, and often too late. The World Bank's data on the ability and ease of doing business for 2016 placed Italy 45th in the world, well below its major competitors (World Bank, 2016). A private survey produced by Corriere della Sera in July 2018, on the work that Italians would like to do shows that they prefer public employment (with 28% of responses, more than in 2016), while only 10% (3% less than 2016) expressed a desire to be an entrepreneur. Even among students, business creation is not a very attractive option. According to OECD data, 6% of the founders of innovative start-ups in Italy were university students, compared to 13.6% in Canada and 9.4% in Germany. Moreover, excessive bureaucracy hampers new entrepreneurs and causes them – an estimated 30% according to the report *Startup Heatmap Europe 2016* – to take routes abroad (European Startup Initiative, 2016).

Epilogue: *Homines Novi*, the protagonists of entrepreneurialism

'Man is only fully a human being when he plays' – so argued Friedrich Schiller, the German dramatist (Schiller, 1793: Letter XV). Entrepreneurialism runs far and wide in the extensive playing fields of human initiative that extends in all directions, being less limited than knowledge. In this representation, which offers a new world, the top players are the *Homines Novi*, those who, contrary to the tradition of the entrepreneurial nobility, open a Renaissance window on wide-ranging cultural fields. As they stride into that landscape, *Homines Novi* move from one near field to another far away. A mental hedgerow cuts off the traditionalists from 'the view of so much of the last horizon' – as the Italian poet Giacomo Leopardi would say (Leopardi, 1819). In a world of specialists, *Homines Novi* are simultaneously classicists and scientists, thus showing they possess Galileo's multi-faceted culture that facilitates interactions. Communication is more difficult and expensive for people who only learn in the areas where they specialize. Richard Feynman, Nobel Prize winner for physics in 1965, condemned extreme specialization as an obstacle to the relations between the varied aspects of human activity. Earlier, in the 1930s, philosopher Bertrand Russell pronounced that knowledge, everywhere, is considered an ingredient of technical ability, losing its value as a good in itself or as a means that opens up a broad and humanistic vision of life in general. Urged by the techno-scientific and humanities-based knowledge of *Homines Novi*, the adherents of entrepreneurialism theorize and implement revolutionary practices, ask impertinent questions and maintain a rule-breaking attitude not detached from fostering a spirit of sharing. The ideas that materialize allow them to perform tasks exhibiting performance superior to that of algorithms.

The cultural movement of entrepreneurialism cultivates intellectual capital which expresses and codifies values that change over time. We are accustomed to measuring everything that is material. However, it is by appraising the intangible assets that we can listen to the melody of culture that links the past and the present to the future. Entrepreneurialism mobilizes three components of intelligence to create resources for use in the exploitation of revolutionary business opportunities. Spatial intelligence grasps the elements that comprise and characterize the playing fields; intuitive intelligence figures out what is not immediately obvious; and interpersonal intelligence triggers collaborative actions.

These three intelligences generate great things years apart, moving the economy from the production of goods to the products of the mind; from mass-produced commodities to personalization of content. In the intellectual economy, the content industry captures the manufacturing industry. The worker who answers questions and then performs tasks is replaced by the ideator who asks questions to escape, as John Maynard Keynes would say, from the old ideas 'which ramify into every corner of our minds' (Keynes, 1935: Preface). *Homines Novi* are path tracers followed by those who fear becoming 'stupid experts' when twin revolutions, one of knowledge and the other of technology, lay bare the worker who doesn't know how to react to the challenges posed by those twins. Thus, revolutionary ideas are revelatory, by posing questions and then discovering original answers which spawn creative activities conceived by the human mind endowed with empathy. The machines never will do it, precisely because they lack the human ability of understanding and sharing feelings.

Notes

1 Nibelung (in Germanic mythology) is 'a member of a Scandinavian race of dwarfs, owners of a hoard of gold and magic treasures, who were ruled by Nibelung, king of Nibelheim (land of mist)'. Siegfried is the hero of the first part of the Nibelungenlied. Source: https://en.oxforddictionaries.com/definition/nibelung (accessed 08 May 2019).
2 The phrase 'unknown unknowns' was coined in 2002 by Donald Rumsfeld, then US Secretary of State for Defense: it occurs, amongst other places, in a press conference he gave to NATO: see www.nato.int/docu/speech/2002/s020606g.htm (accessed 08 May 2019).
3 The Four Ways of Knowing were initially developed by Barbara Carper in the context of nursing practice. See: Carper, 1978.

References

Aristotle ([1996]) *Poetics*, London: Penguin Classics.
Bacon, F. ([1620] 1902) *Novum Organum*, Devey, J. (ed.). New York: P.F. Collier.
Carper, B. (1978) 'Fundamental ways of knowing in nursing', *Advances in Nursing Science*, 12(2) pp. 13–23.

Curie, E. (1938). *Madame Curie: A Biography*, Garden City, NY: Doubleday, Doran, Chapter 23.

European Startup Initiative (2016) *Startup Heatmap Europe 2016*. Available at: www.startupheatmap.eu/ (accessed 08 May 2019).

Financial Times, The (2017) *Special Report: The Race for Talent*. Available at: www.ft.com/reports/race-for-talent (accessed 14 May 2019).

Formica, P. (2015) *The Role of Creative Ignorance: Portraits of Path Finders and Path Creators*, Basingstoke: Palgrave Macmillan.

Formica, P. (2016) 'The innovative co-working spaces of 15th-century Italy', Harvard Business Review, 27 April. Available at: https://hbr.org/2016/04/the-innovative-coworking-spaces-of-15th-century-italy (accessed 08 May 2019).

Formica, P. (2017) *Entrepreneurial Renaissance: Cities Striving Towards an Era of Renaissance and Revival*, Cham, Switzerland: Springer.

Formica, P. and Hixson, N. (2019) 'Incubating entrepreneurialism', Global Peter Drucker Forum, posted 28 March 2019. Available at: www.druckerforum.org/blog/?p=2132 (accessed 08 May 2019).

Gross, P. (1994) *Die Multioptionsgesellschaft*, Frankfurt am Main: Suhrkamp.

Hardin. G. (1968) 'The tragedy of the commons', *Science*, 162(3859) pp. 1243–1248. Available at: https://science.sciencemag.org/content/162/3859/1243 (accessed 08 May 2019).

Johansson, F. (2006) *Medici Effect: What You Can Learn from Elephants and Epidemics*, Cambridge, MA: Harvard Business School Publishing.

Keynes, J.M. ([1930] 1932) 'Economic possibilities for our grandchildren', in: *Essays in Persuasion*, New York: Harcourt Brace, pp. 358–373. Available at: www.hetwebsite.net/het/texts/keynes/keynes1930grandchildren.htm (accessed 08 May 2019).

Keynes, J.M. (1935) *The General Theory of Employment, Interest and Money*, Preface. Available, for example, at: https://cas2.umkc.edu/economics/people/facultypages/kregel/courses/econ645/winter2011/generaltheory.pdf (accessed 08 May 2019).

Nonaka, I. and Konno, N. (1998) 'The concept of "Ba": Building a foundation for knowledge creation', *California Management Review*, 40(3) pp. 40–54.

Schiller, J.C.F. von (1793) *Letters on the Aesthetical Education of Man*. Available at: http://public-library.uk/ebooks/55/76.pdf (accessed 08 May 2019).

Smith, A. (1761) *The Theory of Moral Sentiments* (2nd ed.), London: A. Millar.

Virgil (2009) *The Aeneid*, trans. J. Dryden, Auckland: The Floating Press (Original work published c. 29–19 BCE, translation originally published 1697).

World Bank (2016) *Doing Business 2016: Measuring Regulatory Quality and Efficiency*, World Bank Group Flagship Report. Available at: www.doingbusiness.org/content/dam/doingBusiness/media/Annual-Reports/English/DB16-Full-Report.pdf (accessed 18 May 2019).

General bibliography

Forsyth, M. (2014) *The Unknown Unknown: Bookshops and the Delight of Not Getting What You Wanted*, London: Icon Books.

Leopardi, G., Count (1819) 'L'infinito'. Available at: www.textetc.com/workshop/wt-leopardi-1.html (accessed 08 May 2019).

Papini, G. (1919) *Chiudiamo le scuole*, Firenze: Vallecchi.

15 Towards the development of intellectual capital standards

Ron Young

Introduction

Intellectual capital, in an increasingly knowledge-driven global economy, has to be a key asset, if not the key asset, of the organisation. As well as being an asset of value, intellectual capital is a key driver in both private and public organisations, large and small, towards providing value to citizens, new revenues and profitability, new products and services, customer relationships, quality and productivity. You might say that the intellectual capital employed in an organisation is the grand sum of the knowledge, experiences and expertise available, especially from the employees, together with the knowledge, experiences and expertise embedded in artefacts such as strategies, policies, organisational processes and projects, patents, copyrights, plans, designs, trademarks, documents, tools and technologies. Intellectual capital, well managed, is the driver of innovation. Intellectual capital underpins everything that we do. Everything we see around us today that is made by humans, is a result of successfully developing and applying our intellectual capital and/or our knowledge capital wisely. (An increasing number of organisations refer to the terms intellectual capital and/or knowledge capital, which are in many ways synonymous.)

Why consider standards for intellectual capital?

So why should we even consider moving towards the development of intellectual capital standards? For many people, standards are perceived as a list of strict requirements to comply with, and, on the contrary, much new intellectual capital is developed through non-conformity, non-compliance, co-creativity and innovation, and does not lend itself to strict standard requirements at all.

Well, first of all, management systems standards with a main focus on intellectual capital already exist today, and I will outline the key ones in this chapter. Secondly, I propose that we urgently need far more work on international standards for intellectual capital measurements and reporting, to enable us to move towards a new knowledge economic theory. This will then allow us to better understand and manage the increasingly knowledge-driven economy for the 21st century. Thirdly, I will share the latest developments for new emerging standards with which I am involved, and concerns that I have, for the need for more ethical standards in the future for human and machine intelligence working together. This could even result in a redefinition of intellectual capital in organisations as we know it today, as we continue to move humanity forward in a much safer, healthier, wealthier, happier and most ethical way.

I understand that there are currently over 22,000 ISO standards and over 27,000 active BSI standards (formerly British Standards Institution) covering everything from healthcare and safety, food and agriculture, transportation and aerospace, building and construction, environmental control, information security, broadcast television, video media and music, a wealth of national and international measurements currencies, dates and times etc., just to mention a few, and many more categories across all industry sectors across the world. We have become highly dependant on, and expect the benefits of, international standards in all our daily lives. For example, I find myself writing much of this chapter on a flight back from Asia to London on an Airbus Industries A380 aircraft. For health and safety purposes alone, everything is regulated by international standards – the parts and assembly of the aircraft, the engines, the navigation system and flight planning, communications and air traffic control, fuel quality and minimum fuel requirements etc. Before and during the flight, pilots must comply with minimum flight safety checks throughout, using check-lists which are distillations of aviation wisdom from a growing number of years of new learnings, experiences and innovations. The intellectual capital of the air transportation industry has grown enormously as a result of more global, collective and systematic intellectual capital management during the past 100 years.

Air traffic control systems and real-time weather analysis use international standards for satellite and terrestrial telecommunications. My Apple Mac computer, my iPad and iPhone are all connected by Wi–Fi to the internet, which has also been designed and developed according to international standards. My food and drink, entertainment and on–board hygiene for all passengers must comply with international standards.

These are just a minute number of the standards with which we all comply today and by which we all must live, if we wish to continue to enjoy the same highest level of safety and quality of human life. You might even say, in modern nomenclature, that these standards are becoming a fundamental part of our 21st-century algorithms and digital DNA that are moving us all forward, and many are now even being implemented within increasingly autonomous and intelligent systems.

So, I would like to ask you to think for a moment about the following question. What is the essence of all these standards? I would put to you that the answer is the intellectual capital within our organisations. You may call it intellectual capital, knowledge capital, intangible and tangible knowledge assets, or whatever else you prefer, but international standards are international trading assets, international knowledge sharing assets, tools, guidelines and global good practices, that have been developed over the years by national standards bodies and committees of experts drawn from industry, academia, government, small

208   Ron Young

entrepreneurial businesses and society, who have been collaborating and co-creating. This has all been achieved through consensus-driven decision-making processes within the committees and public consultation.

What key intellectual capital standards exist today?

De facto intellectual capital categories

Well, first of all, a de facto standard has existed for intellectual capital for over 20 years and considers, at least, three categories. Firstly, the 'human capital', the knowledge and expertise embodied in the people that walk in and out of the organisation each day; secondly the 'structural capital', which is embedded and retained in the organisation and often codified and referred to as institutional/organisational memory; and thirdly, the 'relational capital', which is knowledge capital that is developed from sources external to the organisation and is co-created with clients, customers, partners, stakeholders, government etc., through developing trusting relationships, reputation, brand value etc.

But, today, most of us understand 'standards' to be a list of requirements to comply with, which, on the surface, seems hardly a subject for intellectual capital at all. So, let's take a quick look at existing published ISO standards that can make a big difference for the development and management of intellectual capital.

ISO 9001 Quality Management

First, the most successful ISO standard (International Standards Organisation) of all time is the *ISO 9001 Quality Management standard*, with over 1 million organisations certified worldwide. This standard certainly has its roots in manufacturing quality, and zero defects, but it has been successfully used by organisations around the world who want to focus on all types of quality management, not just manufacturing. Today, this standard includes a clause on the importance of organisational knowledge in order to demonstrate quality and business excellence. I would suggest that we think even further, and I say that we should, and could, extend and embed the same principles of quality management to more aspects of the quality of our intellectual capital.

ISO 55000 Asset Management (tangible and intangible)

In 2014 ISO first published the *ISO 55000 Asset Management series of standards*. This series of standards has its roots in managing very tangible assets like infrastructure for road, air, railroad and sea transportation, energy, plant and machinery, hospitals, factories and buildings. To support this, there is a growing community of professional asset managers globally, who manage the physical assets of the organisation by applying this family of standards. But the standard was written to manage both tangible assets and intangible assets. The principles of asset management are very powerful indeed and apply to both types of tangible and intangible assets in full. Within this standard, for example, is a 'strategic asset management plan' requirement, or SAMP, and, alongside this, the notion of managing a portfolio of assets. Intellectual capital management can certainly benefit from the principles of the asset management standard by creating a portfolio of intangible assets to measure and manage, and by creating and implementing a strategic intangible/knowledge asset plan to better achieve organisational objectives. I will say more about the state of the art in measuring intangible assets later in this chapter.

ISO 27000 Information Asset Management

At the same time, in 2014, ISO first published the *ISO 27000 Information Asset Management series of standards*, including cybersecurity. Information can be both a codified tangible digital asset and also an intangible asset, as for example, in spoken communications. Information is the lifeblood of new knowledge creation. I would suggest that the principles of information asset management and security are a fundamental prerequisite to further developing our learning and applying our intellectual capital effectively.

ISO 44001 Collaborative Partnerships

In 2017 ISO first published the *ISO 44001 Collaborative Business Relationship Management standard*. It is now well known in high-performance team research that an effective collaborative team, partnership or community can create and retain new knowledge faster than most other methods. An effective collaborative team can become a thriving natural organic knowledge base for better knowledge retention. And a collection of effective and inter-related individual experts and collaborative teams will morph into a thriving organic knowledge ecology. Again, the principles of effective collaboration are equally fundamental to further developing and applying intellectual capital.

ISO 30401 Knowledge Management

In November 2018, ISO first published the *ISO 30401 Knowledge Management standard* which is the first international standard for the management system for knowledge, and which treats knowledge as an organisational asset that must be managed like any other asset. Effective knowledge management is simply a vital part of intellectual capital management. You might say, knowledge management is meta 'knowledge about knowledge'. I suggest that this new ISO standard must be very seriously considered to be at the heart of effective intellectual management.

ISO 56000 Innovation Management

In 2018 ISO first started to publish the *ISO 56000 Innovation Management series of standards*. This series of standards recognises that knowledge and intelligence have many diverse sources, both inside and outside the organisation, and that these sources will all, collectively and more co-creatively, feed innovation. Today the ISO 56000 series of Innovation Management standards that is being developed includes guidelines, tools and methods for innovation partnership and intellectual property management, strategic intelligence management, ideas management and appropriate measurements.

But that is just a quick snapshot of some key ISO standards today. There are several more standards and developments towards intellectual capital management and measurement.

Integrating ISO standards into one holistic management system

The abovementioned ISO standards that address intellectual capital can of course be implemented individually. But increasingly, many organisations have now implemented several ISO standards. Because ISO have mandated, for several years, that all future ISO standards must be written to comply with the same management systems standard (MSS) template, regardless of the specific topic of focus, it is now possible to integrate these standards into one management system. The aim is to create a more holistic management system for the organisation that requires an integrated and more consolidated management system to manage and audit. More information on this can be obtained from ISO online. The *ISO IUMSS Handbook* (Integrated Use of Management System Standards) is most helpful with integration guidelines.

So, for example, a more knowledge driven organisation could integrate, say, ISO 30401 Knowledge Management standard with ISO 55001 Asset Management standard (focusing on intangible knowledge assets) and ISO 56002 Innovation Management Guideline, as a more powerful knowledge and innovation cluster.

At Knowledge Associates we have developed a multi-dimensional and integrated framework for knowledge and innovation that is part of our implementation education and methodology, and that fully recognises all the ISO standards I have mentioned so far, and the need to implement them at all levels in the organisation – from personal, to team, organisational, inter-organisational and global.

Finally, on ISO standards, I have had the privilege over the years to chair the KMS/1 Knowledge Management Committee for BSI, which is the UK national standards body and mirror committee for the ISO, as well as being a committee and standards liaison member for Asset Management AMS/1 and Innovation Management IMS/1. I am also an active member of ISO international standards development workgroups. This made me realise that the ISO and BSI standards I have mentioned that address intellectual capital must eventually become much more integrated within the organisation as, otherwise, they are at risk of becoming fragmented, closed and even competitive stovepipes of speciality themselves. The intellectual capital of an organisation, by its very nature, must be considered as a whole.

International standards for intellectual capital measurements

IAS 38 Intangible Assets

Since 1998 I have been following the work of the International Accounting Standard Committee and the adoption of *IAS 38 Intangible Assets* by the International Accounting Standards Board (IASB) in 2001. This was subsequently revised in 2004, 2008 and amended in May 2014. The IASB together with the International Financial Reporting Standards (IFRS) work together to provide a common global financial language and reporting of financial accounts for business affairs across international boundaries. This standard should have a major impact on intellectual capital.

I recall that in November 2002 the World Congress of Accountants was held in Hong Kong and the theme of the conference at that time was 'Knowledge Based Economy and the Accountant'. The opening plenum session on day 1 posed the following two key questions 'What are the opportunities and challenges presented by the knowledge-based economy?' and 'How must we redefine "the accountant" and "accounting" for the 21st century?'

Knowledge Asset Management

In 2003 the book *Knowledge Asset Management* was published by Springer. This recorded the essence of two European Commission-funded collaborative research projects Know-Net (EP-28928) and LEVER (IST -1999–20216) of which I was a lead researcher for my Cambridge-based company Knowledge Associates International. The collaborative research budgets totalled 3 million euros. The primary Know-Net research consortium comprised the following companies: Planet Ernst & Young, Knowledge Associates, DFKI, the German Research Centre for Artificial Intelligence and the Centre for Advanced Learning Technologies for the INSEAD business school. We researched as many intellectual capital models and measurements and business excellence models and measurements as we could at that time, including the Baldridge and EFQM models, the Balanced Scorecard and the Skandia Knowledge Navigator, and we further developed a model that better illustrated the ongoing transfer between human capital, structural capital, relational capital and financial capital. We presented these inter-relationships and their inter-dependencies in the book, as a holistic asset management system, and the latest developments and thoughts on measurement of intellectual capital at that time.

Even more so today, the more timeless principles uncovered in this collaborative research work, and published in the book *Knowledge Asset Management*,

212 *Ron Young*

could have a major impact on the way we manage intellectual capital, today and for the future, especially as a series of measurable strategic and operational knowledge assets.

The key question today must be: What are the key knowledge areas and key knowledge assets in our organisation that, if we could better identify, manage, develop, better share and better protect, where needed, measure and report, would make a big difference to achieving our objectives? And the key problem today for many organisations is the loss of critical knowledge and highly valuable knowledge assets as a consequence, due to retirement, rotation, higher mobility of knowledge workers etc.

Intellectual capital measurements for the knowledge economy

It was the late Professor Peter Drucker that first taught me that every several hundred years a major transformation takes place in society due to increasing knowledge. This results in a new radical change in thinking, a paradigm shift, that results in the creation of new institutions, new politics, new social orders and even a new society. I certainly see that happening today, as a more global knowledge- and innovation-driven society. This has especially accelerated since the introduction of the first large mainframe commercial computer systems, almost 60 years ago, and rapid developments since, to personal computing, networks, internet and world wide web, and now, even more smart, mobile and more intelligent cloud-based platforms and knowledge systems. Our ability to now communicate, collaborate, learn, create and manage knowledge, apply critical knowledge assets, and ruthlessly innovate in totally new ways, is upon us. For several years, we have been witnessing the birth and growth of this new global knowledge-driven economy and society.

Yet, despite this miraculous technological revolution, we still manage and measure our global economy using 19th-century industrial thinking and instruments and, at best, 20th-century industrial measurements, based on old and often outdated industrial economic theory. This is simply crazy as much of our economic activity is now driven and based on our intellectual capital management and, as a result, much of our measurements of income, wealth and productivity performance in this area are just missing. Take one very simple and obvious example, using Google search and using social media like Twitter, Facebook and LinkedIn. These tools and technologies enable us to connect to relevant people and information anywhere in the world in seconds, to better learn, cooperate and collaborate as a result. We gain very high-value and substantial benefits from these tools indeed, and many would find it very difficult to live without them as individuals, in teams, as organisations, nations and globally. But because they are new, free and zero-cost items, the economic value is not truly recognised and understood, realised or measured at all. Because information is abundant, its value is not measured properly. The ability to analyse big data and information and turn it into valuable new knowledge and intellectual capital is still not understood well enough, and mainly underestimated, or even ignored, by many. Why is this? Well part of the answer is our failure to have an economic theory that rewards and recognises knowledge and intellectual capital management properly, if at all. Instead, the current industrial economic theory that is inherited from the industrial economy mindset is based on scarcity of physical resources and, therefore, results in excessive competition. Consequently, we fix prices for goods based on the supply and demand of scarce goods. But in a 21st-century, more knowledge-driven economy we realise an abundance, not a scarcity, of information and far more knowledge than ever before. In an industrial economic theory and subsequent accounting system, ownership of goods passes from one entity to another. In a more knowledge-driven economic theory, if I sell my knowledge and intellectual capital to you, I do not lose it but both parties retain it and, actually, the knowledge capital expands in society as it is diffused. In a more knowledge-driven economic theory, we would value collaboration and competition in completely new ways. So, we urgently need better instruments for intellectual capital to measure and report our knowledge capital production and true economic performance and status. In a 19th-century industrial economy, we talk of capitalists (owners of the capital) and the workers (physical labour). Our political system in the UK and internationally still reflects this industrial economy view with political interests protected by our more conservative and labour parties. But in a 21st-century, more knowledge-driven economy, the knowledge worker is both a knowledge capitalist (owner of their own knowledge) and knowledge worker combined, so their political interests are now quite different, and would be better reflected in a more representative sort of 'knowledge political party' based on a new, more knowledge-driven economic theory. Then I believe we will see even more of the major changes and rapid acceleration to a new and better society that Drucker could imagine.

Who should own the data, information and knowledge assets? Will we continue with competitive knowledge hoarding or more collaborative knowledge sharing for benefit? Should we put more emphasis on free, open source, creative commons, knowledge publics and knowledge platforms (knowledge for the common good), often created by more purposeful social and societal not-for-profit entrepreneurs, or should we put more emphasis on privately owned data, information and knowledge assets, with huge rewards for the winners? How should we better manage the ownership and better manage the application of intellectual capital of the United Nations organisations and agencies, individually and collectively, in its quest to meet sustainable development goals within the UN 2030 Agenda? Should these agencies not share their accumulated knowledge based on competition for limited funding? Or does a mixed economy serve us best? A new, more knowledge-driven economic theory will answer such questions and will develop further intellectual property instruments and rights beyond copyrights and patents etc. Then we can more accurately measure the true value of the knowledge-driven goods and services in our national and international economies and better serve our goals for service to humanity. Knowledge flows are likely to continue unabated and far

214 Ron Young

more vigorously across all national boundaries in a digital economy. One thing is for sure, intellectual capital and intellectual capital standards should be at the very heart of a new, more knowledge-driven economic theory, knowledge-driven economy and society.

Redefining intellectual capital for human/machine intelligence

The earlier starting definition that I have given for intellectual capital has served us quite well in the past, for an industrial economy, but, as just discussed, it is about to undergo fundamental, radical and most certainly major disruptive change. This change is primarily because we are in a very deep transformation to a digital economy. Soon, the exponential growth of machine intelligence, with its relentless growth and application, will greatly outpace the growth in human intelligence and application. In certain areas, it already has done so today.

I am convinced that both human and machine intelligences could grow together and strongly work together in new ways to better collaborate, co-create and innovate. And the balance is likely to soon tip even further and transform us from, primarily, people-led productivity, with the support of enabling technologies and tools, to, primarily, digital-led productivity and knowledge platforms, with the support of increasingly empowered people. Digitally driving transformation is inevitable and is well underway. Some even say that if we go beyond the inevitable digital transformation, the creation of a new and more intelligent species is underway.

James Lovelock is one such visionary. Lovelock is one of Britain's most eminent scientists and the originator of the *Gaia Hypothesis* (now Gaia Theory) for planet Earth as a self-regulating organism in 1973. He is an elected Fellow of the Royal Society, with over 200 scientific papers published. In 2019, he published his new book *Novascene: The Coming Age of Hyperintelligence* (2019) and in it he goes even further than I dare say, as he is most convinced that this hyperintelligence will rule the planet within 80 years as the next evolutionary and higher lifeform, for the benefit of all lifeforms. Lovelock informs us that the speed of transmission and development of intelligence in the human brain is based on a conversion speed and interaction of biological systems, synaptic systems and neurons, whereas the digital capability today has the potential to go way beyond our fastest brain conversion and transfer speed. Digital memory, properly managed, far exceeds the performance of human memory. Digital speed, in many areas, far exceeds human cognitive speeds. We are told that, today, digital processing and transfer can be measured to be 10,000 times faster than a human brain. And that is just the logical capability of technology. Parallel processing computing networks today, working together with singular logical computing networks, as a simple analogy to both intuitive knowledge and human reasoning, can learn themselves, make inferences, take decisions and actions. But the big difference is that they can improve at exponential rates.

Ray Kurzweil, Google Chief Technology Officer and author of *The Singularity Is Near: When Humans Transcend Biology* (2005) talks clearly about the linear and exponential growth of human and machine intelligence and the evolutionary algorithms. Kurzweil tells us that exponential growth in machine intelligence is now reaching the level of human intelligence and, in his opinion, will be equal in capacity before 2050.

Coming down to earth a little, to the present day, the new Fourth Industrial Revolution, or Industry 4.0 as it is called, is fully fledged today, and uses new highly disruptive technologies such as robotics, 3D printing, biotechnologies, internet of things, blockchain computing, cloud computing, advanced simulation, systems integration and analytics, to name just a few. These new technologies are being implemented today on platforms that provide 'digital twins' for the entire knowledge lifecycle, from the birth of an idea to maturity of a product and ultimately to product demise, using digital knowledge lifecycle platforms that are connected by the internet of things. In 2017 the UK *Times* newspaper published an article on the 'Internet of Assets' (McClelland 2017). I suggest to you that the 'internet of knowledge assets', a platform that aims to support intellectual capital, is well upon us. At Knowledge Associates we have been prototyping the use of knowledge asset portfolios on a knowledge platform using human and machine intelligence, that we call 'Knowledger' for several years now.

Could you see a digital virtual twin of yourself from birth to death, or for the entire period of working until retirement? Does this notion horrify you or delight you? Most of you are already building one, without knowing, with its foundations in social media today.

Just remember for a moment that machine intelligence is certainly very capable today to be able to read all the standards published and in digital form, in just a matter of seconds!

So, this begs the question, 'Should we redefine intellectual capital management in organisations with increasing human and machine intelligence?'.

IEEE P7000 series of Ethically Designed Autonomous Intelligent Systems

Well, some say that it is more important to first ensure the design of such systems is in the best interests of humanity and to be better able to advance the common good of humanity. The IEEE, the worlds largest technical professional organisation (the Institute of Electrical and Electronics Engineers) have been working on this issue with an aim to ensure that such future automated intelligent systems are designed using international standards to address ethical concerns of design, to better protect humanity. The IEEE launched in 2018 their Ethics Certification Program. For my part, I have become involved and very interested in the development of the *IEEE P7000 Ethical Design for Autonomous Intelligent Systems* standard. I have been following this initiative closely, and the discussions that are taking place around the world, with hundreds of researchers, designers, social scientists and philosophers.

There are several groups working with increasingly ethical considerations and standards for the development, management and application of intellectual

216 Ron Young

capital. A good resource online is from the European Commission, European Group on Ethics in Science and New Technologies, a statement on *Artificial Intelligence, Robotics and 'Autonomous Systems'* (2018).

Moving towards intellectual capital standards

So, what can we practically take away from this quick review of intellectual capital and international standards in the digital economy? I would summarise the three key parts of this chapter as follows. Firstly, why should we even consider moving towards the development of intellectual capital standards? Well, first of all, standards with a main focus on intellectual capital already exist today and I have outlined the key ones. Secondly, I have proposed that we urgently need far more work on new instruments for international standards for intellectual capital measurements and reporting, to enable us to move towards the development of a new knowledge economic theory. We will then better understand and manage the increasingly knowledge-driven global economy during the 21st century and better reflect our true knowledge working performance. From this, I further propose that we consider new knowledge politics to better serve our needs, as both personal knowledge capitalists and knowledge workers. Thirdly, I have shared the latest developments for new emerging standards for the future for human and machine intelligence working together, with a suggestion that we may even need a redefinition of intellectual capital in organisations that embraces human and machine intelligence as a result of the transition to a digital economy.

In conclusion, these are my personal views only, based on my personal research, observations and experiences, and are not necessarily those of the organisations I have mentioned. I fully realise that this chapter on intellectual capital and international standards, now and for the future, has probably led to far more unanswered questions than I have answered and that I have posed. We need more rigorous debate. That is the purpose of this chapter for intellectual capital in the digital economy. I most welcome your feedback, and I would be delighted if we could continue the conversation.

ronyoung@knowledge-associates.com

www.knowledge-associates.com

References

European Commission (2018) *Artificial Intelligence, Robotics and 'Autonomous Systems'*. Brussels: Directorate-General for Research and Innovation.

Kurzweil, R. (2005) *Singularity Is Near: When Humans Transcend Biology*. New York: Viking.

Lovelock, J. (2019) Novascene: The Coming Age of Hyperintelligence. London: Allen Lane.

McClelland, J. (2017) 'Managing intangibles and "internet of assets"'. *Asset Management*, May 17. Distributed and published by Raconteur in association with The Times and The Institute of Asset Management.

16 Intellectual capital management scoring

A contribution to the measurement of intangibles standardization

Florinda Matos and Valter Vairinhos

Introduction

The knowledge economy is increasingly supported by the management of intangible assets. Intangible capital (IC) and performance seem to be associated. To Wang et al. (2016), companies still suffer from the inefficient utilization of their IC, which is not reported. Thus, IC must be identified, measured, managed and monitored (I3M). Although there has been a lot of emphasis on IC, there is no method of scoring intangible capital management. The literature provides a plethora of models for measuring and managing IC, such as Skandia Navigator (Edvinsson & Malone 1997), IAM (Sveiby 1997), IC Index (Roos et al. 1997), or Value Explorer (Andriessen & Tissen 2000), among many others, each providing different advantages and disadvantages in their approaches. It is not surprising that some authors (e.g. Chen et al. 2005; Wang et al. 2016) claim that there is no best or consensus solution for IC measurement. In part, we can explain this fact by evoking the distinctive nature of IC. The literature provides evidence that IC measurement and management practices differ among industries and companies. Studies on this field show that IC in different organizations can be valued in different ways by various indicators or indices. We argue that all contributions that bring more light to the interrelationships between IC elements and IC measurement and management can highlight specific areas of concern for further theoretical research.

This chapter focuses on IC management. In the knowledge economy, companies face the challenge of being both productive and competitive in adverse conditions and stagnant markets. The use of financing from various stakeholders (e.g. shareholders, banks, state) is increasingly complex and limited to companies that have good financial reports. The risk has increased, and funding institutions are frequently subject to regulatory systems that prevent them from financing companies that do not exhibit reliable indicators. However, some of the companies that have better financial reports are often those that quickly descend into bankruptcy. We can remember what happened to companies like Enron and Worldcom, where the use of fraudulent practices made it possible to mislead investors. Also, there are thousands of SMEs (small and medium enterprises) that are annually funded by European Union funds or by state capital that quickly enter insolvency proceedings, and in most situations, creditors cannot recover their investments. Holmen (2005) suggests that the external reporting of IC can close the gap between book value and market value because providing improved information about the "real value" of the company can reduce asymmetries, increase the ability to raise capital by providing a valuation on intangibles, and enhance the company's reputation. Thus, management reports that enable companies to value their IC according to credible scorings has become a fundamental tool to complement traditional financial reports. It has become essential to find effective means to disseminate information on IC, which has to be recognized as a critical element of value creation (Bukh 2003).

There is a consensus in the literature that a significant amount of value can be gained by tracking IC. As our organizations become more knowledge driven, the parameters for measuring performance and growth are changing from efficiency to knowledge. This creates a problem for academics and practitioners related to the fact that knowledge flows and intangible assets are essentially non-financial. As a consequence, proper information on intangibles is lacking, leading to an inability to manage intangibles properly. Edvinsson (2013) challenges us to reflect on alternative ways of thinking, looking into another IC consciousness. Assuming IC as *the future*, which is difficult to measure or even to predict, the author invites academia to see IC as a "systems science, a systematic cross-disciplinary study of how intellectual resources can be identified, nurtured, shared and utilised for the larger good" (Edvinsson 2013, p. 170). Addressing this issue, we present a methodology to obtain an IC management score, to be used as a valid proxy that can be safely used in decision-making processes, where IC is an important issue.

Instead of trying to achieve direct IC measurement, this chapter explores the quality of an Intangible Capital Management Scoring System, captured by the answers from top managers to an appropriate questionnaire and expressed by a score, as a proxy or indicator for the unknown future IC value.

Literature review

The success of any organization in today's economy is driven by intangibles or IC. It is therefore not surprising that organizations require tools and techniques to identify, measure and manage its key value driver. To make successful decisions, management, investors and other stakeholders need information about what drives their organization's value and which elements are the source of that value. As mentioned by McCann and Buckner (2004) it is essential "to gain a better conceptual and operational appreciation of what it means to strategically manage knowledge for sustained competitive advantage" (p. 61).

The IC perspective emerged in the early 1990s as a response to the frustration caused by traditional management tools and their effectiveness to address the issues surrounding the drivers of value creation based on intangible resources. Since then, academics and practitioners have developed a plethora of concepts, principles, models and measures, becoming the focus of significant discussion and enquiry across the management disciplines.

Prior research suggests that the concept of IC is based on the wide recognition that organizational knowledge needs to be managed. IC is an out-of-balance asset that can create value for organizations (Bontis 2001). This definition suggests that IC is always a source of competitive advantage, and that its management should improve business performance. In order to manage and control IC within firms, identifying, measuring and monitoring IC internally is required.

According to Dumay (2009), the traditional frameworks used to manage, measure and report IC needs to be transformed, and the one-size-fits-all approach to IC is unlikely to provide any more answers than it already has. The author argues that one of the problems of the current view of IC measurement is that many of the ideas and terminology of IC that have been developed are the result of past management thinking.

Rooney and Dumay (2016) have stated that there are several quantitative IC frameworks, but that these don't consider the relationship between IC and innovation in the strategic process.

Edvinsson (2013) joins the claims and argues that traditional measurement tools are too limited and do not capture the flow of knowledge, the impact of the flow and the value-creating dimensions over time. IC has increasingly been seen as an integral part of a firm's value creation processes, and investors, analysts and other stakeholders have demanded more reliable and objective information that gives a broader insight into the value creation capacity of IC. An integrated approach to IC management can help us to gain a better understanding of the strategic significance of the organization's knowledge resources and their impact on the value creation process.

Different approaches to IC measurement

The literature presents various methods for measuring IC, which can be used to manage this asset. Some of these methods were attempts made by different companies for their internal use rather than the implementation of a universal measuring method. The following sections present some of the most referenced methods in the literature.

Most influential methodologies to measure IC

Among the best-known methods for IC measurement are Skandia Navigator (Edvinsson & Malone 1997), IAM (Sveiby 1997), Technology Broker (Brooking 1997), and the competence-based strategic management model (Bueno 1998), among many others. Bontis et al. (1999) provide us with a comprehensive review of measures and models. In the following session, we present some of the more relevant methodologies to measure and manage IC.

Intangible Assets Monitor – IAM

Sveiby (1997) developed a model – "The Intangible Asset Monitor" (IAM) – dividing intangible assets into three groups: individual competencies, internal structure and external structure. This method is based on the assumption that the only source of generating profits are individual competencies, efforts of which are reflected in the structure of the internal and external resources of the organization. The external structure includes the relationships with customers and suppliers, alliances, trademarks or aspects of research and development. The internal structure consists of the management of the organization, legal structure, systems, manuals, attitudes, research, development and software. Finally, human capital represents the knowledge, responsibilities and competencies of individuals. In each of the groups, indicators concerning growth, regeneration, effectiveness and stability are additionally distinguished. The total market value of the organization emerges from accountable assets and the three types of intangible assets. The choice of indicators depends on the strategy and should only include some of the indicators measuring each intangible asset.

Skandia's IC Navigator

Skandia's IC Navigator is undoubtedly the most popular analytical model of IC measurement. Based on Sveiby's work, Edvinsson and Malone (1997) proposed a model, "Skandia Navigator", which divides IC into two categories: human capital and structural capital. The origin of Skandia's IC Navigator was an attempt to visualize the hidden value, rather than account for intangibles. Skandia's value scheme contains both financial and non-financial building blocks that combine to estimate the company's market value. While accounting ratios look at the past of an organization, the rating model uses 200 parameters to predict its future value and its capacity for renewal.

Some authors (e.g. Roos *et al.* 1997) consider the contribution of the model relevant, but with limited metrics. This is so because each organization, depending on the importance it gives to the IC, can always create new metrics to measure these intangible assets. The authors also consider that the "Skandia Navigator" has a similar positioning to the accounting balance sheet, since it presents an analysis of intangible assets, at a given moment, and does not visualize the dynamic flows of the organization. It seems that there is no evidence that a better economic performance emerges by using the "Skandia Navigator".

IC - Rating™

Derived from the Edvinsson and Malone (1997) model, IC - Rating™ was introduced by Intangible Capital Sweden AB. The IC - Rating™ methodology is based on the answers to two questions: (i) which parameters does an executive manager need to have insightful knowledge of, to make the right decisions for the future? and; (ii) from where and whom should the executive manager receive this information? The process is based on the collection of data obtained from structured interviews with various stakeholders (managers, employees, customers and suppliers). The information comprises both internal and external elements on the three main components of IC: human capital, structural capital and relational capital.

Using 200 parameters to derive the future value of an organization, the IC – Rating model determines the indices of the IC component as well as an overall index. The calculation of these indices allows visualizing the changes in IC over time. The model correlates the IC with the value obtained by dividing the market value by its accounting value. The model considers three forward-looking perspectives, and in addition to looking at the current effectiveness of the organization, the model looks at efforts to renew and develop itself and the risk against current effectiveness.

The process of IC evaluation has many similarities with the metrics used by the rating scales of companies' financial ratings. The efficiency and renewal are between AAA and D, where AAA corresponds to a very high standard of quality and D means the complete lack of quality. The risk is measured on a scale of four levels ranging from negligible risk (–) to a very high degree of risk (RRR). The methodology is deeply embedded in the theoretical concepts defined by the authors. The mean of each evaluated parameter is calculated to obtain a score for the area (a total of eight areas). The average score for each area will give the average rating of the company, which is transformed into a percentage.

The Value Explorer

The Value Explorer, also known as "KPMG Value Explorer", developed by Andriessen and Tissen (2000), follows a Dutch government project consisting of the creation of an innovation unit, focused on the impact of the knowledge economy on companies.

The model was applied to SMEs in partnership with the consulting firm KPMG. The Value Explorer is a tool for measuring IC, with a five-step approach (Andriesson 2005):

1 Identify IC, making a list of the core competencies of the organization.
2 Make an assessment of value, using a list that evaluates the value, competitiveness, potential for sustainability and robustness of core competencies.
3 Make an assessment of IC by an allocation of part of the expected gains to key competencies.
4 Develop a management agenda based on the results.
5 Make recommendations to management on how to improve the value of IC.

Chen, Zhu and Xie Model

Based on a review of several IC measurement models, Chen *et al.* (2004) designed a measurement model and a qualitative index system of IC, providing organizations with a tool for managing their IC. Due to the intangibility of IC, the authors argue that it cannot be measured with economic variables. Instead of calculating the IC economic value, the model focuses on evaluating the indices and trends of IC. The authors classified IC into human capital, structural capital, innovation capital and customer capital, and the qualitative measuring indices are designed according to their respective content. Indicators were defined for each category and summarized in a single index, by category, by calculating the weighted average.

The *rationale* of this new IC measurement model with its indices is that it enables organizations: (i) to have a more precise and direct understanding of the composition of IC; and (ii) periodically to evaluate its IC developing tendency.

The IC-dVAL® (Intangible Capital Dynamic Value)

The IC-dVal methodology was proposed by Bounfour (2003), linking internal and external perspectives. The model defines a set of metrics to measure IC and dynamically integrates four dimensions of the measurement of intangible assets: inputs, processes, assets and results (outputs). The measurement is made at the corporate level, in various contexts and can also be used at the macroeconomic level, at the country level. The IC-dVal integrates the financial value of assets in the internal business performance, analyzing competitiveness at four levels: resources, processes, intangible assets (intangible capital) and results (outputs).

For the development and implementation of metrics in the overall company performance index, 25 indicators and their weights are considered. The whole company is valued using this index, using the benchmarking approach and analyzing the dynamic value of the IC.

Balanced Scorecard (BSC)

The Balanced Scorecard (BSC) (Kaplan and Norton 1992) aims to measure the organization's performance, based on a set of financial and non-financial indicators. The BSC's set of criteria includes prospective and retrospective measures, i.e. it is assumed that more than evaluating the past, it is crucial to learn for the future. The authors believe that the analysis of organizational results, based exclusively on financial measures, is not enough. Thus, to overcome the limitations, the authors propose that the organization is evaluated on a set of financial, customer, internal business processes, and learning and growth criteria.

The Balanced Scorecard reflects the balance between short- and long-term goals, between financial and non-financial indicators and prospects, and between external and internal performance. The indicators should be developed in line with the context of the company and its strategic objectives.

Although the Balanced Scorecard can also be considered a measurement management system, there is no empirical support to verify the interconnection

Intellectual capital management scoring 223

between financial performance and the capabilities of strategic management. The Balanced Scorecard uses measurement instruments and the management of intangible assets, which lacks some flexibility. There is also some limitation concerning the external environment factors, which limit the analysis of customers, excluding other factors that are determinant for this environment, such as community relations, alliances, suppliers and others.

IC-Index – Intangible Capital Index

The concept of an IC-Index was first proposed by Goran Roos and his colleagues at Intangible Capital Services Ltd. and was first used by Skandia in its IC supplement to the annual report. The model aims to determine a representative index of IC as a percentage value that provides an overview of the financial performance of the organizational IC (Roos *et al.* 1997). Since the index of IC consists of a single global value, it provides a good perception of the utilization degree of intangible assets in the organization. According to the authors, this is a "second generation" model, since it consolidates the various measures of IC in a single measurement and correlates the variation of this measure with changes in market value. In the model, the IC-Index is considered a ranking of indicators for each of the IC components. According to the rankings, in the calculation of the consolidated index of IC, each indicator is assigned a different weight. The final index of IC results from the transformation of the values of the indicators into numbers, usually percentages. The model defines intangible assets as a set of resources or flows that contribute to the processes of value creation in the organization and that do not come from physical or financial assets.

The model is based on two components: human capital and structural capital. Adopting a top-down approach, the model is designed from the organization's strategy. Indices are defined based on the key resources and resource transformations in the navigator. According to Roos *et al.* (1997) the IC-Index has several distinct features: it is an idiosyncratic measure; it focuses on the monitoring of the dynamics of IC; it is capable of taking into account the performance from prior periods; it enables viewing the company from a different external standpoint typically based on the examination of physical assets; it is a self-correcting index, meaning that if the IC-index performance does not reflect changes in the market value of the company, then the choice of capital forms, weights and/ or indicators has not been well made. The model's limitation lies in the fact that an IC-Index is restricted to particular contexts.

Technology Broker

This model was proposed by Brooking (1997) and describes a process for auditing the intangible assets of an organization, considering three alternatives to help estimate the monetary value of IC. The audit methodology identifies and measures attributes of an organization that do not appear on traditional financial statements. The model assumes that the market value of an organization is the sum of tangible assets and IC. The author defines IC as the combination of four assets: market assets, human assets, intellectual property assets and infrastructure assets. The measurement of IC is based on the diagnosis and analysis of responses to questionnaires about the intangible assets of the organization. Brooking (1997) proposes three ways of estimating the monetary value of IC: (i) based on an estimate for the replacement cost of intangible assets; (ii) based on the market value of intangible assets, and; based on the estimated profitability of each intangible asset.

The "Technology Broker" model begins the process of diagnosis with the application of a questionnaire consisting of 20 questions that constitute the IC indicator. The results of this questionnaire make it possible to check the areas of IC that require strengthening. Each component of the model is then examined based on specific audit questions for these variables. In total, the Technology Broker IC audit comprises 178 questions.

After completing the Technology Broker audit, Brooking (1997) proposes three methods to calculate the IC value: cost-based approach (based on the assessment of replacement cost of the asset), income-based approach (assesses the income-producing capability of the asset) and market-based approach (uses market comparables to assess value).

EVA™ and MVA

The Economic Value Added (EVA™) method has its basis in traditional accounting. Economic Value Added (EVA™) was introduced by Stern Stewart as a comprehensive performance measure that uses the variables of capital budgeting, financial planning, goal setting, performance measurement, shareholder communication and incentive compensation to account properly for all ways in which corporate value can be added or lost.

Bontis *et al.* (1999, p. 395) define EVA™ as

> the difference between net sales and the sum of operating expenses, taxes and capital charges where capital charges are calculated as the weighted average cost of capital multiplied by the total capital invested. In practice, EVA™ increase when the weighted average cost of capital is less than the return on net assets and vice versa.

EVA™ is the difference between a company's net operating income after taxes and its cost of capital of both equity and debt.

Market Value Added (MVA), like EVA™, also derives from the concept of economic profit. MVA is the difference between the market value of debt of a company and the capital that lenders and shareholders have entrusted to it over the years in the form of loans (Market Value of Equity), retained earnings and paid-in capital (Total Adjusted Capital). One way to analyze MVA is through the sum of the initial capital invested and the economic profit, residual income or EVA™ accumulated over time.

According to Bontis *et al.* (1999, p. 395), MVA can represent the market's assessment of the net present value of a company's current and contemplated capital investment projects. As such, MVA is a "significant summary assessment of corporate performance".

Exploratory model for an Intangible Capital Management Scoring System (ICMSS)

Several models have been developed in the last 20 years, though problems remain to be solved. One problem with the plethora of frameworks for measuring and managing the components of IC is that no one view, other than the concept of intangibility, has consensus among the various works on the field (Dumay 2009).

Due to the general dependence of IC direct measurement, the proposed models are difficult to apply in real environmental business conditions. It is therefore evident that the models currently available are not flexible enough to be employed in the context of decision making, involving risk evaluation and sustainability related with IC. It is assumed in what follows that some of these problems can be addressed using an ICMSS that allows indirect evaluation of IC, observing and scoring the methods, attitudes and values employed by managers, for the development of the company's IC.

Intangible capital management scoring

A scoring model is a formula that assigns points based on known information to predict an unknown future outcome. Sometimes designed as predictor models, scoring models have been developed and used in the scope of various disciplines (Cooper *et al.* 2001). Credit scoring is probably the most used in the financial domain. The users of scoring models have high praise for them and see them as effective and efficient decision tools. According to Jackson (1983), scoring models have the benefit of combining the financial criteria with the desirable strategic criteria.

As mentioned by Chen *et al.* (2004), the major purpose of IC measurement models is not to measure the financial value of the IC because its financial value is not of too much importance. The significance of an IC measurement model is its ability to offer a tool that provides timely information feedback, which enables managers to modify or adjust their IC strategy accordingly for their sustainable competitive advantage. If managers could find a way to estimate the value of their intangible assets, they could measure and manage their company's competitive position much more easily and accurately (Kaplan & Norton 2004).

Abeysekera (2007) states that the adoption of the international accounting standards of the International Accounting Standards Board (IASB) and the financial statements resulting from them have increased the difference between the book value and the actual value of the organization. Most organizations that disseminate information on intangible assets confine themselves to the use of management reports (Campbell & Abdul Rahman 2010).

The issue of IC management scoring has been explored in the literature – frequently confusing the issues of measurement (obtaining a value for the asset) with the issues of management (how to proceed to develop IC). However, most of the proposed methodologies were not accepted as valid practices for business. An Intangible Capital Management Scoring System (ICMSS) is a classification system for intangible capital management, supported by a methodology to rank companies according to suitable standards and to allow comparisons with each other. This methodology does not try to achieve direct IC measurement but a proxy for it, easily obtained with the direct participation of top managers, avoiding sensible information disclosure. We intend to position a company in the market, ensuring its partners (shareholders, creditors, investors, customers, suppliers, etc.) the reliability in the management of IC and, therefore, its sustainability.

Given the identified emerging need to create systems to improve the kind of information that is provided by traditional accounting systems, we intend to create a scoring model for the management of IC. This study is based on our previous work, the Intangible Capital Model (ICM) (Matos & Lopes 2009; Matos 2013).

The ICM consists of four quadrants: Individual Capital Quadrant, Team Capital Quadrant, Processes Capital Quadrant and Clients Capital Quadrant, divided by 22 parameters: (1) Training / Qualification and Talent Management; (2) Valuation of Know-how and Innovation; (3) Investment in Innovation and Development (ID); (4) Existence of a Policy for Talent Retention; (5) Team Work; (6) Training / Team Qualification; (7) Innovation in Teams; (8) Leadership in Teams; (9) Processes Systematization; (10) Registration of Organizational Knowledge; (11) Existence of Certifications, Environmental and Social Policies; (12) Partnerships; (13) Investment in Innovation and Development in Processes Simplification; (14) Brands Creation and Management; (15) Complaints System; (16) Existence of Awards; (17) Market Audits; (18) Management of the Clients' Satisfaction; (19) Clients' Complaints System; (20) New Markets and Internationalization; (21) New Technologies (22) Networks. The scoring methodology, which positions the companies being evaluated by quadrants and by parameters of the ICM is depicted in Figure 16.1.

To test and verify its rationality an empirical study has been done on the above IC measurement model and its index system, and a detailed analysis has been made of the relationship between the four elements of IC. This chapter presents an ongoing project that is a first attempt to develop a data-driven scoring tool to support the auditing of IC management in the context of Portuguese SMEs. This should be coherent with the ICM model and based on observed data described in Matos (2013), resulting from the answers of top managers to a questionnaire aiming to characterize IC management practices, methods and values in Portuguese SMEs.

Intellectual capital management scoring

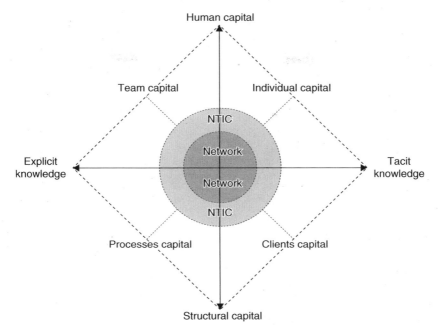

Figure 16.1 ICM – Intangible Capital Model.
Source: Matos (2013).

The research starts from the premise that, subjacent to the manager's supplied answers to the questionnaire – described in Matos (2013) – there is a set of latent (intangible) variables related by a structure, reflecting the management's views on the development of the observed SME's IC, and that this structure is compatible with the specified model.

Figure 16.2 presents one possible model specifying these relations using the Path Modeling (PM) approach to structural equations (Vinzi *et al.* 2010).

Ellipses represent Latent Variables (intangibles) assumed subjacent to the manager's answers. Rectangles represent the 22 observed parameters (Manifest Variables). Latent variables are identified, in what follows, by labels beginning "L", for "Latent" and their meanings are: LNT – Networks and New Technologies; LCI – Individual Capital; LCP – Process Capital; LCC – Clients Capital; LCE – Team Capital; LIC – Intangible Capital.

According to ICM, variable LNT accounts for the general influence that Networks and New Technologies have on IC components and their relationships. This means that LNT is not considered here as another IC component but as an intensifier, facilitator or catalytic effect on IC components and their relationships.

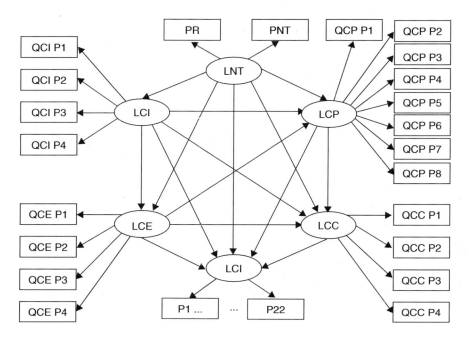

Figure 16.2 Structural model for causal relations between IC components compatible with ICM.

Arrows between two Latent Variables indicate assumed causal (or influence) effects between Latent Variables (LV). For all LV – except for LIC – there are external (observable) or Manifest Variables – MV. In this model, LIC is a second level LV for which there is no MV. Here we follow the usual recommendation for this kind of hierarchical model and assign to it the whole set of MV, associated with the independent LV. See bottom of Figure 16.2.

Estimating the model parameters (numbers associated with each of the arrows) using suitable methodology, it may happen that the assumed causal relations get support from data or not. In general, not all arrows representing relations between LV are supported by data, while others are.

In our case, the model was estimated using Partial Least Squares (PLS), with the methodology specified in Vinzi *et al.* (2010), and implemented in Sanchez (2013) and Sanchez *et al.* (2015), through the R Package Partial Least Squares Path Modelling (*plspm*).

The full results' account will be presented elsewhere. From these results, some findings are: the whole model has a goodness of fit $R^2 = 0.56$, $(R = 0.75)$ and LIC expression as a function of other Latent Components is:

$$\text{LIC} = 0.144 \star \text{LNT} + 0.205 \star \text{LCI} + 0.281 \star \text{LCP} + 0.323 \star \text{LCE} + 0.187 \star \text{LCC}$$

The causal relations specified in the model by the arrows LCI → LCC and LNT → LCC are not supported by observed data (significance > 0.05).

Using the expressions estimating LV in the function of its MV, the SME's scores for each one of the LVs and for LIC are estimated. According to Trinchera and Russolillo (2010), this is a sound and recommended method to obtain scoring functions.

These results are considered encouraging but, given the small data set, further studies with more data are needed.

Conclusion

This chapter shows, through a literature review covering the last 20 years, that some consensus exists regarding IC components (human capital, structural capital and relational capital) and that a large number of methodologies addressing the problem of IC measurement and IC management now exist. In some of those works, the confusion between IC measurement and IC management is frequent. Although a large number of IC measuring methodologies are available, it was observed that few of them have become generally accepted decision instruments used by businesses in issues related to a company's risk and sustainability. In our view, this is caused by the difficulty in implementing direct IC measurement in real environmental business conditions and the consequent lack of flexibility of the resulting instruments. To overcome this difficulty, we have proposed an Intangible Capital Management Scoring System (ICMSS) that uses IC management scores as proxies or indicators for IC measurements in the referred decision-making processes. The creation of this tool can be critical as it will guide companies in the management of their intangible assets and the monitoring of the development of sustainable competitive advantages. However, the creation of a generally acceptable scoring tool is a complex data-driven process, supported by open high-quality data. These studies should continue using significant samples of companies in several countries.

It is argued that this work opens the door to more discussion around IC measurement and constitutes a possible productive way of understanding IC.

Indeed, it is generally accepted that IC means creative capability expressed in innovation and transforming potential, proving that IC is one of the main causes for future financial fluxes and results, not the reverse. From the sustainability point of view, IC is more important than financial power. Consequently, the power to generate future financial benefits depends more on IC than on present financial assets. In this context, the evaluation of the quality of an ICM system is crucial to predict the future behavior, value and sustainability of a specific company or organization.

References

Abeysekera, I. 2007, "Intellectual capital reporting between a developing and developed nation", *Journal of Intellectual Capital*, vol. 8, no. 2, pp. 329–345.

Andriesson, D. 2005, "Implementing the KPMG Value Explorer: Critical success factors for applying IC measurement tools", *Journal of Intellectual Capital*, vol. 6, no. 4, pp. 474–488.

Andriessen, D. & Tissen, R. 2000, *Weightless Weight: Find Your Real Value in a Future of Intangible Assets*, Pearson Education, London.

Bontis, N. 2001, "Assessing knowledge assets: A review of the models used to measure intellectual capital", *International Journal of Management Reviews*, vol. 3, no 1, pp. 41–60.

Bontis, N., Dragonetti, N.C., Jacobsen, K., & Roos, G. 1999, "The knowledge toolbox: A review of the tools available to measure and manage intangible resources", *European Management Journal*, vol. 17, no. 4, pp. 391–402.

Bounfour, A. 2003, "The IC-dVAL approach", *Journal of Intellectual Capital*, vol. 4, no. 3, pp. 396–413.

Brooking, A. 1997, *Intellectual Capital: Core Asset for the Third-Millennium Enterprise*, International Thomson Business Press, London; Boston, MA.

Bueno, E. 1998, "El capital intangible como clave estratégica en la competencia actual", *Boletín de Estudios Económicos*, vol. 53, August, pp. 207–229.

Bukh, P. 2003, "The relevance of intellectual capital disclosure: A paradox?", *Accounting, Auditing & Accountability Journal*, vol. 16, no. 1, pp. 49–56.

Campbell, D. & Abdul Rahman, M.R. 2010, "A longitudinal examination of intellectual capital reporting in Marks & Spencer annual reports, 1978–2008", *British Accounting Review*, vol. 42, no. 1, pp. 56–70.

Chen, J., Zhu, Z., & Xie, H. 2004, "Measuring intellectual capital: A new model and empirical study", *Journal of Intellectual Capital*, vol. 5, no. 1, pp. 195–212.

Chen, M., Cheng, S., & Hwang, Y. 2005, "An empirical investigation of the relationship between intellectual capital and firms' market value and financial performance", *Journal of Intellectual Capital*, vol. 6, no. 2, pp. 159–176.

Cooper, R.G., Edgett, S.G., & Klienschmidt, E.J. 2001, *Portfolio Management for New Products*, 2nd edn, Basic Books, New York.

Dumay, J.C. 2009, "Intellectual capital measurement: A critical approach", *Journal of Intellectual Capital*, vol. 10, no. 2, pp. 190–210.

Edvinsson, L. 2013, "IC 21: reflections from 21 years of IC practice and theory", *Journal of Intellectual Capital*, vol. 14, no. 1, pp. 163–172.

Edvinsson, L. & Malone, S.M. 1997, *Intellectual Capital: Realizing Your Company's True Value by Finding Its Hidden Brainpower*, HarperCollins, New York.

Holmen, J. 2005, "Intellectual capital literature reporting", *Journal of Management Accounting Quarterly*, vol. 6, no. 4, pp. 1–9.

Jackson, B. 1983, "Decision methods for selecting a portfolio of R&D projects", Research Management, vol. 26, no. 5, pp. 21–26.

Kaplan, R.S. & Norton, D.P. 1992, "The Balanced Scorecard: Measures that drive performance", *Harvard Business Review*, vol. 70, no. 1, pp. 71–79.

Kaplan, R.S. & Norton, D. 2004, *Strategy Maps: Converting Intangible Assets into Tangible Outcomes*, Harvard Business School Press, Boston, MA.

Matos, F. 2013, "A theoretical model for the report of intellectual capital", *The Electronic Journal of Knowledge Management*, vol. 11, no. 4, pp. 339–360.

Matos, F. & Lopes, A. 2009, "Intellectual capital management accreditation in Portuguese SMEs", *Proceedings of the European Conference on Knowledge Management, ECKM*.

McCann, J.E. & Buckner, M. 2004, "Strategically integrating knowledge management initiatives", *Journal of Knowledge Management*, vol. 8, no. 1, pp. 47–63.

Rooney, J. & Dumay, J. 2016, "Intellectual capital, calculability and qualculation", *British Accounting Review*, vol. 48, no. 1, pp. 1–16.

Roos, J., Roos, G., Dragonetti, N.C., & Edvinsson, L. 1997, "Consolidating intellectual capital measurements: The IC-Index approach", in *Intellectual Capital: Navigating the New Business Landscape*, Palgrave Macmillan, London, pp. 78–101.

Sanchez, G. 2013, *PLS Path Modeling with R*, Trowchez Editions, Berkeley, CA.

Sanchez, G., Trinchera, L., & Russolillo, G. 2015, "R Package 'plspm': Tools for Partial Least Squares Path Modeling (PLS-PM)".

Sveiby, K. 1997, *The New Organizational Wealth: Managing and Measuring Knowledge-Based Assets*, Berrett-Koehler Publishers, San Francisco, CA.

Trinchera, L. & Russolillo, G. 2010, *On the Use of Structural Equation Models and PLS Path Modeling to Build Composite Indicators*, Universita degli Studi di Macerata, working paper no. 30.

Vinzi, V.E., Chin, W.W., Henseler, J., & Wang, H. (eds.) 2010, *Handbook of Partial Least Squares: Concepts, Methods and Applications*, Springer, Berlin.

Wang, Z., Wang, N., Cao, J., & Ye, X. 2016, "The impact of intellectual capital: Knowledge management strategy fit on firm performance", *Management Decision*, vol. 54, no. 8, pp. 1861–1885.

Part VI

Future challenges and risks for intellectual capital and trade on IA and ideas

17 Future challenges and risks for intellectual capital and trade on IA and ideas

Karl McFaul

Introduction

Prototyping a framework for thought leadership on the impact of digital transformation

"Everything changes and nothing stands still". Attributed to the ancient Greek philosopher Heraclitus (535 BC – 475 BC), this quote serves as a good starting point also in these times for a discussion on how we can navigate in planning, strategising, policy- and decision-making, in the creation of a desirable, probable, of all possible futures. In a world where "change is the only constant", how can we use intellectual capital (IC) as an instrument to reduce risk, discover and evaluate hidden values, orchestrate resources and continuously navigate, adapt and sustainably revitalise our life – as individuals, as organisations and as a society, empowered by technology? How do we estimate the value of a winning strategy, and the tools to develop and implement it? If we would compose a strategic toolbox for our journey into the future of the 21st-century economy, which tools would we bring? These are some questions I would like to raise for further discussion, research and development of new models, methods and business tools based on the material in this chapter.

With leadership and larger investments comes greater responsibility, but the line between fear and courage also becomes thinner. A society in transformation requires not only transformational leadership, but transformational organisations. In terms of collective intelligence, the competitive environment in hierarchical line-organisations provides scarce resources at the top for seeking support, and the market for management consultants has grown big in our times of rapid structural change.

Coming from the world of entrepreneurship, when working for larger institutions – whether academia, research infrastructures, private corporations or political institutions – one might observe a striking difference in how different organisational cultures build and use organisational knowledge – and how differently they approach complex tasks. While business agility, heterarchical (unranked) teamwork, ecosystem innovation and emergent processes come more naturally for SME's in finding their relevant form, the situation changes when organisations grow large, unless they continue to devote resources to management innovation.

Most businesses have a formal methodology for product innovation, and many have R&D groups that explore the frontiers of science. Virtually every organisation on the planet has in recent years worked systematically to reinvent its business processes for the sake of speed and efficiency. However, few companies apply a similar degree of diligence to the kind of innovation that matters most: management innovation (Hamel 2006).

With Gary Hamel's words in mind, in my own work of 2018/2019 for the European Commission High-Level Expert Group (HLEG) on the Impact of the Digital Transformation on EU Labour Markets, I took an initiative together with my colleagues to switch the thinking a bit in our work on developing new policy recommendations for the EU. Instead of thinking "innovation policy", I advocated also for the need of "policy innovation" due to how technological innovation leads to organisational innovation (cf. *ontological design* – what we design, designs us). To prove my point, I had presented for the group my updated and modified version based on a diagram to be found in Christopher Meyer and Stan Davis's book from 2003: *It's Alive: The Coming Convergence of Information, Biology, and Business.*

Our group's task was to develop policy recommendations that could facilitate inclusiveness and cohesion in a time when Europe is facing polarisation in various forms and, when it comes to labour markets, needs to ensure that the benefits of digital transformation are fairly distributed between different economic sectors, businesses and individuals. With the proclamation of the European Pillar of Social Rights in November 2017, the EU highlighted the importance of the rights of its citizens in a fast-changing world.

If technological innovation leads to organisational innovation, consequently, it means that the way work is conducted in the institutions of the European Union will also need to change. To give some insight to the creative process leading us from the diagram in Figure 17.1, to the final version of our framework for policy innovation (Figure 17.3), I have here also provided the prototype (Figure 17.2) preceding our final model, described as a *guiding framework for thought leadership on the impact of digital transformation on EU labour markets* in The Report of the High-Level Expert Group on the Impact of the Digital Transformation on EU Labour Markets (European Commission, HLEG on Digital Transformation, 2019).

To what extent this framework will influence the way the EU in the future develops policies, allocates resources, influences and impacts the future of Europe in the short term and long term remains to be demonstrated. The idea of this framework is to make policy work less *reactively* and instead more *proactively* and with greater relevance in a future, where we will either benefit or suffer from the policies we implement today. Strategy work in large organisations often becomes very academia-centric, relying on doctoral expertise brought in from universities to provide academic legitimacy, research and statistics for evidence-based practice (EBP) in decision-making. Research naturally takes place when

Future challenges and risks for IC 237

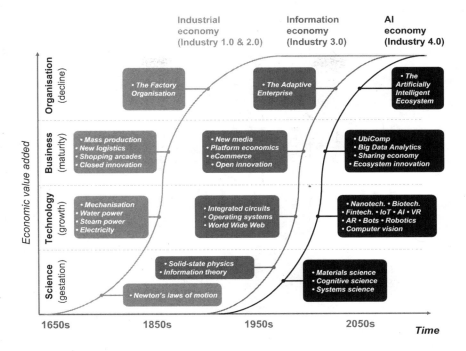

Figure 17.1 Economic life-cycles of innovation.
Source: Karl McFaul, adapted from Meyer, Davis (2003).

things have already occurred in time and space. With things that do not yet exist, but on which we depend – like the future – how do we explore them in order to create and implement relevant policies, if our intention is to put Europe at the forefront of innovation? We came up with the idea that our work on developing policy recommendations should be based not only on research of the past and the present, but also on prototyping scenarios by studying current trends and their possible trajectories into the future, implications they may carry, as well as challenges and opportunities.

Navigating complexity: the domain of emergence

When trying to describe and influence the future, three common approaches are *forecasting*, *envisioning* and *scenario planning*. In planning, the further ahead we try to look and the more complex system whose future we try to predict, the more irrelevant it becomes to work with a plan which tries to make things work under stable conditions. When we're dealing with an increasing number of uncertain factors, we will need other planning tools to identify risks

Directions for policy:

	Trend	Implication	Challenge	Directions for policy:
Society	• *Global labour market* • *Sharing economy* • *The intelligent workspace*	• *Weakening of labor market institutions* • *Downward pressure on real wages* • *Polarization*	**INCLUSION:** • *How do we prevent social polarization in future labor markets?*	**A NEW SOCIAL CONTRACT** • Redistributing the value of digital ownership • A Digital Single Window for employment contributions & taxes • Neutral social protection
Business	• *Platform economics* • *eCommerce* • *Big Data analytics* • *Ecosystem innovation*	• *More entrepreneurs* • *Lower investments In skills from employers* • *Alternative work-relations*	**DECENT WORK:** • *How do we support the creation of quality jobs in the future?*	**NEW LABOUR RELATIONS** • A new Social Dialogue • Equalising treatment of workers with different work arrangements • Preventing occupational safety and health risks
Technology	• *Artificial intelligence* • *Automation/robots* • *Cloud computing* • *Virtual reality and gaming*	• *More labour mobillity* • *Short duration of skills* • *Loss of routine jobs*	**SKILLS:** • *How do we make people employable in the future?*	**A SKILLED WORKFORCE** • Digital skill personal learning accounts • Delivery of training, career guidance and quality assurance • Intermediation to reduce skill gaps (esp. for women in STEM, displaced- or less-skilled workers)

Figure 17.2 Policy innovation framework – prototype version.
Source: Karl McFaul.

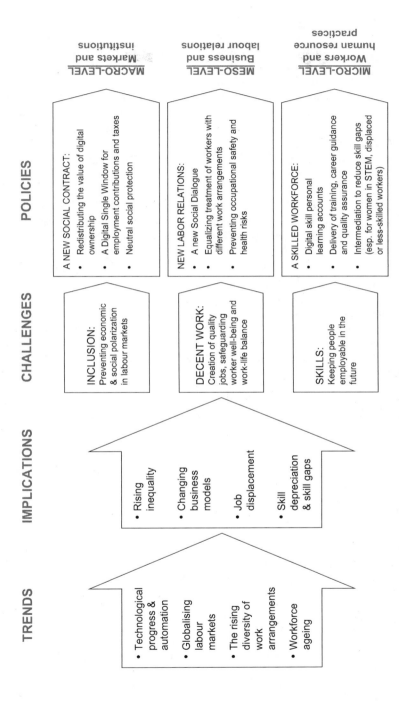

Figure 17.3 Policy innovation framework – published version.

Source: Report of the High-Level Expert Group on the Impact of the Digital Transformation on EU Labour Markets. European Commission (2019).

240   *Karl McFaul*

and opportunities and prepare ourselves for not only one, but several possible futures (Lindgren and Bandhold 2009).

Such a planning tool to aid decision-making, the *Cynefin Framework*, was created in 1999 by Dave Snowden when he worked for IBM Global Services. It can be described as a "sense-making device" that sorts the issues leaders face when making decisions. It presents four different contexts – from *simple*, to *complicated*, to *complex*, to *chaotic* – defined by the nature of the relationship between cause and effect. The purpose is to guide leaders in diagnosing situations in order to act in contextually appropriate ways (Snowden and Boone 2007). This conceptual framework is very useful for understanding how we need to approach work in today's dynamic world of innovation ecosystems, which clearly falls into the domain of complex if not chaotic contexts:

- *Simple contexts* are "the domain of best practice", often few elements involved, characterised by stability and clear cause-and-effect relationships that are easily discernible by everyone. Often, the right answer is self-evident and undisputed.
- *Complicated contexts* are "the domain of experts". Unlike simple ones, they may contain multiple right answers, and though there is a clear relationship between cause and effect, not everyone can see it. This approach often requires expertise. However, entrained thinking is a danger in complicated contexts. It is the experts (rather than the leaders) who tend to dominate the domain. When this problem occurs, innovative suggestions by nonexperts may be overlooked or dismissed, resulting in lost opportunities. The experts have, after all, invested in building their knowledge, and they are unlikely to tolerate controversial ideas.
- *Complex contexts* are "the domain of emergence". Most situations and decisions in organisations are complex because some major change introduces unpredictability and flux. In this domain, we can understand why things happen only in retrospect. Instructive patterns, however, can emerge if the leaders conduct experiments that are safe to fail (cf. prototyping). That is why, instead of attempting to impose a course of action, leaders must patiently allow the path forward to reveal itself.
- *Chaotic contexts* are "the domain of rapid response". In a chaotic context, searching for right answers would be pointless: the relationships between cause and effect are impossible to determine because they shift constantly and no manageable patterns exist – only turbulence. Yet the chaotic domain is nearly always the best place for leaders to impel innovation. People are more open to novelty and directive leadership in these situations than they would be in other contexts.

If human societies, markets and organisations are *complex contexts*, but the work in governing political and administrative institutions is concentrated around an expert-driven approach as described in the *complicated context* in Snowden's framework, then there is a mismatch and probably to a great deal an untapped

Future challenges and risks for IC 241

potential of intellectual capital resources, to drive societal innovation with the greater economy that could be made available through platform economics, community engagement and "wisdom of the crowd".

While technological development allows humans to handle more complexity with greater inclusiveness and cohesion, we see instead an increasing gap (divide) between (1) individuals, who are more or less quick and adept at adopting new innovations, (2) businesses, where some are more capable of building products and services to capture individuals' time and attention, while some others move at a slower pace due to organisational and managerial models that were largely developed in the (first) industrial age, and (3) public policy, which adapts at an even slower pace around income inequality, unemployment, immigration and trade affecting businesses through regulation, taxes and legislation (Bersin, Pelster, Schwartz, and van der Vyver 2017).

How can we close these gaps to avoid the risk of falling into a vicious cycle of less inclusiveness, leading to less cohesion and the greater costs for everyone that come with a broken social contract, polarisation, conflicts, protectionism, less innovation, an economy in decline and a place in stagnation?

If economy emerges in (and depends on) society – and society emerges in (and depends on) our environment, it seems logical to take a holistic view on our individual actions, on our development of new business models, or in policy-making for society at large. The policy innovation framework presented in Figure 17.3 attempts to take such a holistic view on all levels, from individuals on the micro-level, to businesses on the meso-level to society at the macro-level of the system.

In the following, we discuss emerging trends impacting these three levels of labour markets, to explore in further detail the future risks and challenges for intellectual capital – with a special focus on human capital now facing implications and challenges, but also opportunities, as artificially intelligent structural capital is currently emerging, advancing with a disruptive impact on the trade on intellectual assets (IA) and ideas in the global landscape of the 21st-century economy. The reflections on implications, challenges and opportunities have been developed together with my European Commission HLEG colleague Morten Binder, director at HK A-kasse in Copenhagen.

Micro-level: digital impact on human capital

Trends

A well-known observation is that every time technology advances to become twice as powerful, it can be used to build new technology which again doubles in capacity, leading to the exponential nature of technological development and cost reduction described in Moore's law: the number of transistors in a dense integrated circuit doubles about every two years (Moore 1965).

We are currently at the dawn of what could be defined as the *AI economy* (the artificially intelligent economy following on from the industrial and the information economies) and it should be noted that even if the implementation of Moore's law will have an end in terms of physical limitations in how small transistors can be made, this does not mean an end to the continuous exponential development of our technological capability.

In contrast to simply biological life-forms who just survive and replicate (like bacteria), cultural life (like humans) can also design its "software" in terms of knowledge, skills and mind-set. With this intelligence, we are now developing artificially intelligent robots and bots (software robots) that through machine learning and recursive self-learning will be capable not only of surviving, replicating and designing its software, but also of designing and building its hardware – in other words, being able to continue to develop itself as an entirely new life-form (Tegmark 2017).

We have already witnessed the advent of "narrow AI" having the ability to achieve a limited set of goals, for example playing chess or driving a car. In decades or centuries from now, General AI (AGI) is expected to have the ability to perform any kind of cognitive task at least as good as humans can do. After that, Artificial Superintelligence (ASI) is seen as a natural step with general intelligence on a much higher level than that of humans. Even if researchers cannot yet agree on when AI is capable of transforming into AGI and ASI, the technological developments leading this field are already becoming a game changer for business and labour, as automation advances by hardware robots replacing industrial and domestic body labour, and software robots (bots) replacing the cognitive work in information processing tasks.

More powerful technological instruments provide us with new scientific breakthroughs, new knowledge and levels of awareness. This in turn leads to new generational preferences and new ways of learning and productivity. This calls for new forms of ownership in our interactions in business and organisational life.

The forces of change are likely to continue to accelerate and intensify, not least due to the *technological convergence* of AI and:

- *Robotics:* Machines that can substitute for humans and replicate human actions.
- *Networks:* Connecting the physical, digital and social.
- *Platforms and cloud computing:* New business models leveraging networks and intelligence.
- *Blockchain:* An incorruptible digital ledger of economic transactions that can be programmed to record not just financial transactions but virtually everything of value.
- *VR and AR simulation and gaming:* Interactive new worlds for learning, prototyping, testing, working, sports, entertainment and recreation.

Some of the more frequently addressed emerging technologies already having an impact and expected to have even more in the near-term future are:

Future challenges and risks for IC 243

- Sharing economy
- Crowdfunding
- FinTech and cryptocurrencies
- Smart grids, cities and homes
- Wireless energy transfer
- Smart contracts
- Identity management for citizenship, IP protection and monetisation for the individual value creator
- Predictive analytics, prediction markets and "wisdom of the crowd"
- Neighbourhood micro-grids
- Supply chain AI auditing
- Anti-money laundering
- eGovernance

These technologies enable a power shift from centralisation to decentralisation, to disintermediation (no third party) and to distributed self-organised communities. Anyone with online access and basic online skills can socialise, learn, research, innovate, organise, do marketing and business at low or zero cost – as identified or anonymously.

The most striking impact of the digital transformation is the shift from an analogue economy and the value of *tangible assets*, to a digital economy and the value of *intangible assets*. During the last 40 years, the value composition of S&P 500 companies has shifted from ~80% tangible assets to the opposite: ~80% intangible assets (Ocean Tomo 2017). In 2011, four out of the five largest companies by market capital were traditional industrial businesses (Exxon, PetroChina, Shell, ICBC). In 2016, they had all been replaced by digital platform companies (Apple, Alphabet, Microsoft, Amazon, Facebook). At the corporate level, intangible investments (R&D, innovation, knowledge creation and fertilisation, marketing and advertising expenditures) are now unanimously considered the most important sources of performance (Bounfour and Edvinsson 2005).

As digitisation (converting analogue to digital), digitalisation (the application or increase in the use of digital technologies by an organisation, industry or country) and automation transforms *human capital* (competence and skills) into the domain of *structural capital* (the supportive infrastructure, processes and databases of the organisation that enable human capital to function), the future of human capital at work seems to be in the interaction with the organisation's *relational capital* (customers, vendors, stakeholders, advisors, co-creators etc.). With this scenario, the market will demand and increasingly value skills on how to build the nature and quality of relationships, like trust and trustworthiness, norms and sanctions, obligations and expectations, identity and identification (Nahapiet and Ghoshal 1998). This is also what we see in the typical path of change in the task profile of countries, linked to economic development: physical, routine and machine-use tasks are in decline, while intellectual (especially

244 *Karl McFaul*

literacy) tasks, social tasks and ICT use are experiencing steady growth (Macias, Hurley, and Bisello 2016)

Implications

Ownership. Theoretically, the internet is still decentralised (as a distributed system). No one owns all or a considerable portion of the network or infrastructure that connects the World Wide Web. However, from the first stage of the World Wide Web's evolution in the 1990s (Web 1.0 – "the read-only web") to Web 2.0 (the "social web"), the balance of power has become centralised to a few internet giants (for example Google, Facebook, Microsoft, Amazon and Apple) who currently dominate the services that support the internet and who can control and discriminate access, users, data ownership and fair play. At the same time, IPR are essentially government-sanctioned monopolies that immediately create a big incentive for larger publishers to lobby the government in order to strengthen and expand IPR rights, which results in further suboptimal outcomes for digital creativity.

Digital goods have become more central for the economy and an important attribute of digital goods is that they tend to have very low or even zero marginal costs. However, their production (creation) does. This generates an incentive problem in an economy where production is driven by profit. IPR systems come in to solve the incentive problem of zero marginal costs for digital goods, but at the expense of creating two perhaps bigger problems: the need for intrusive enforcement (surveillance) and the drastic limitation of the potential uses (including combinatorial innovation) of digital goods (Eurofound 2018). This has led to a growing movement involving notable internet pioneers and experts in developing the architecture of the new decentralised Web 3.0, where P2P technology enables a more user-centric web allowing individuals to retain complete ownership of our data, identity and digital assets. The Web 3.0 ecosystem already consists of over 3000 variegated crypto coins and over 900 decentralised apps or DApps (a single DApp can mean a team of up to 50 members, each dedicated to disrupting a specific industry). And even though the industry is still in its infancy, the market cap has already exceeded 800 billion (Zago 2018).

Open and transparent access to information is key to facilitate entrepreneurship and to build intellectual capital in the new digital innovation culture. The open source services market is growing exponentially along with crowdfunding and is a driver in post-millennial creativity bringing the licensing models of Free and Open Source (FOSS), Creative Commons (CC) and related applications into the world of work. Open collaboration is now a significant factor in business relations. Among the top 50 most innovative companies internationally surveyed by BCG 2017, the best reported to be supporting open collaboration 77% of the time, compared to just 23% for the not so strong performers.

Labour mobility. The acceleration of change that comes with technological development leads to more transitions on the labour market. Routine jobs are automated, affecting employment in two opposing ways:

- *Negatively:* by directly displacing workers from tasks they were previously performing (displacement effect).
- *Positively:* by increasing the demand for labour in other industries or jobs that arise due to automation (productivity effect).

Besides increasing labour mobility, the duration or "expiration date" of skills is also shortened and workers have to renew their competences frequently during their entire work life. In a global survey of more than 5400 business and IT executives across 31 countries, conducted by Accenture (2017), companies will in coming years begin hiring employees based not only on self-reported experience, but also on behaviours exhibited during previous roles and how individuals handled themselves in certain situations: multinational organisations will introduce employee-facing technologies that are able to identify when a worker is frustrated and then alter the tone and style of feedback or guidance automatically delivered to the worker. Blockchains that manage and verify online data can enable us to launch companies that are entirely run by algorithms, making self-driving cars safer, help us protect our online identities and track the billions of devices on the Internet of Things. New performance-based contracts – taking the form of "if/then/else" between two or more parties – will exclusively be smart contracts that self-govern and self-execute (through Blockchain technology).

Challenges and opportunities

In this context, how do we make people employable in the future? It is a challenge for more formal education systems to catch up on technological progress. As people will shift jobs more frequently, and competencies will have a shorter duration, it will be a challenge to find smart solutions to rapidly fill new vacancies. People without a job might also have difficulties finding a new job due to lack of skills. Furthermore, it might be difficult to test them for a new employer. For some workers, it will not be affordable to invest in training for new jobs, at the same time employers would be reluctant to invest in training when contracts are short. However, in a connected world it is much cheaper and faster to share knowledge than before. We can support people by using the very same technologies, now disrupting the world of work, for new ways of interactive learning. With the ubiquitous access to information and advanced training that people have today at little or no cost (not least *outside* traditional learning institutions) it could be wiser for educational systems to shift from the traditional factory model of schools and universities having an *inside-out* approach in producing expertise, to rather act as learning hubs and

246 *Karl McFaul*

platforms, having an *outside-in* and *user-to-user* approach integrating and facilitating the real-time and real-world development of competence through work and life. A response to the need of more frequent transitions on labour markets could be an evolved system of "self-learning" opportunities with low marginal costs. Learning requires being embedded in work where schools and academic institutions together with vocational education and training (VET) could provide a neutral role for quality assurance (QA) and credentialing in the process of *upskilling* and *reskilling*.

An indication of the importance and urgency when it comes to remodelling our learning systems can be seen in the long-term EU budget 2021–2027, where the European Commission has proposed to strengthen the European Union's social dimension with a new and improved European Social Fund, the European Social Fund Plus (ESF+), with its proposed budget of €100 billion for boosting employability and improving the education and training systems (Lecerf 2018). Among "The European Pillar of Social Rights" (new and more effective rights for citizens, built upon 20 key principles) the first is:

> Education, training and life-long learning – Everyone has the right to quality and inclusive education, training and life-long learning in order to maintain and acquire skills that enable them to participate fully in society and manage successfully transitions in the labour market.

Making use of gaming and simulations will probably disrupt existing recruiting businesses. And more importantly "self-testing" will open a range of possibilities for people looking for new job opportunities. For an inclusive labour market and society in general, it will be important to democratise learning. The future of learning will be life-long and mediated by (Zappa 2012):

- *Digitised classrooms:* Rather than considering IT a standalone tool or skill, digitisation tends to disperse throughout every facet of the classroom (examples: tablets, electronic screens, interactive whiteboards, data projectors).
- *Tangible computing:* Designing "tangible user interfaces" which employ physical objects, surfaces and spaces as tangible embodiments of digital information. Embedding computation in the physical via intelligent objects, the Internet of Things and connectivity with a profound impact on learning mechanisms (examples: reactive materials, reactive furniture, 3D printers, digitally intermediated field trips).
- *Gamification:* Billed as an evolution in grading mechanisms, gamification brings instant feedback to acquired knowledge through achievements and points systems (examples: student-developed apps, educational games, educational programming tools, achievement badges, self-paced learning).
- *Virtual/physical studios:* Bridging the online–offline gap, these future technologies offer a potential future where embodiment is secondary to

information access (examples: eyewear / heads-up displays (HUDs), retinal screens, holography, neuroinformatics, immersive virtual reality).

- *Disintermediation:* Undoing the traditional teacher–student model, these technologies offer a scenario where AI handles personalisation while teachers focus on teaching (examples: telepresence, algo-generated lessons, mobile learning platforms, task-assignment algorithms, S2S teaching platforms, assessment algorithms, student-designed learning mechanics).
- *Opening of information:* Dissemination of information outside the physical silos of schools and classrooms, offering feedback and assessment to students anywhere (examples: portable academic histories, flipped classrooms, inter-school teaching platforms, digitisation of books, open courseware, education app stores, online school communities, video lessons, formal communication backchannels).

Meso-level: digital impact on business and relational capital

Trends

When it comes to firms and the world of business, the most striking change is how the digital transformation has led to a transition from the *pipe* business model, with its linear *value chain* operations from producer to consumer, to the software-enabled non-linear *platform* business model where users (on a platform) create value for other users. Platforms have economic advantages that enable them to grow faster than similar pipeline businesses. This phenomenon alone would lead to significant disruption of traditional industries, as platform businesses displace pipeline businesses at the top of the Fortune 500 rankings. But the era of "platforms-eat-pipelines" is disrupting businesses in many other ways as well. In particular, the rise of the world of platforms is reconfiguring the familiar business process of value creation, value consumption and quality control (Parker, Van Alstyne, and Choudary 2016) (Figure 17.4).

Platforms have moved value creation from *inside the firm* to the ecosystem of supply and demand *outside the firm*. When business moves to platforms, it involves three key shifts: from resource control to resource orchestration; from internal optimisation to external interaction; from a focus on customer value to a focus on ecosystem value.

The internet, the rise of digital platforms and the technological capacity to manage greater complexity and speed of change turn collaborative advantage into the new competitive advantage making organisations move away from using the fewer resources in *closed innovation* to instead adopt the principles of *open innovation* where the future will be even more about *ecosystem innovation* or "open innovation 2.0" (Curley and Salmelin 2018). In the global survey conducted by Accenture (2017), all industries are in coming years expected to have new, dominant market leaders with business structures based on small cores and powerful ecosystems. Incumbent corporations still carrying the burden of legacy bureaucratic models will experience rapid deterioration in market

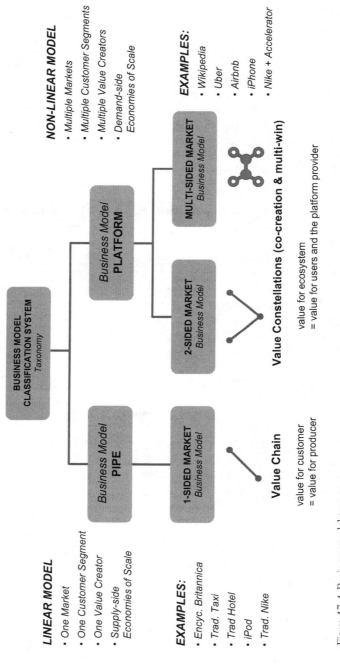

Figure 17.4 Business model taxonomy.
Source: Karl McFaul, adapted from lecture material presented by M. Kärreman, Lund University, 2016.

Future challenges and risks for IC   249

power. Industry leaders from today will have transformed into ecosystem companies spanning multiple markets. The enterprise will lie at the centre of a disruptive ecosystem, holding no physical headquarters and few permanent staff. Their highest-valued asset will be a digital platform. Most S&P 500 companies will be engaged in multiple industry ecosystems, and most will have made public statements about increasing their reliance on ecosystems for future revenue growth. The traditional purpose of industrial-era corporations and management models will be replaced, having been displaced by digitally connected marketplaces. The new normal for businesses with mature digital strategies will be to operate across currently siloed industries such as Tesla does today. For these companies, industry boundaries will vanish, and each new endeavour will amplify disruption.

Implications

The programmability and algorithmic control of production processes makes digital platforms intrinsically much more flexible than previous methods of mechanically controlled devices. Theoretically, an algorithm could be as flexible and adaptable as a human being. This is why the digital revolution could take the automation of labour input in production to the extreme, making human labour redundant (Eurofound 2018). In relation to their revenue, value and societal impact, digital platform companies indicate by their smaller size (in staff numbers) that big corporations cease to become relevant in a world of machine intelligence, distributed fully automated businesses, and democratic human collaboration by open source and open innovation ecosystems. Nobel prize-winning economist Ronald Coase showed in his theory of the firm that there are three costs in the economy: the cost of finding talent, resources and information to create value (cost of search); the cost of getting people to work together in an efficient way (cost of coordination); and the cost of ensuring fair play and the execution of agreements (cost of contracting). These three costs tend to be much lower when something is created inside a company rather than outside. However, when these tasks can now be crowdsourced by users interacting on digital platforms, automated by analytics and AI in combination with peer-to-peer technologies (P2P) eliminating the need of third parties, these costs can now become much lower outside the firm (Zarkadakis 2017).

Lock-in. Digital technologies tend to create demand-side economies of scale, or network effects. This means that the value for consumers of many types of digital goods and services increases with the number of users. This tends to cause *lock-in* (of users), because the cost of switching product or service also grows with the size of the network, to an extent that can effectively make customers entirely dependent on a particular vendor. The very strong concentration of demand-side economies of scale tends to create monopolies (Eurofound 2018).

Unfair competition. The value in digital platform economics is *data and interactions* that can be subject to Big Data analytics for uncovering information including hidden patterns, unknown correlations, market trends and customer preferences

250 *Karl McFaul*

that can help organisations make informed business decisions. If Europe implements regulations that make it more expensive to develop, operate, administrate and use digital platforms – even though the intent is to protect publishers and citizens – this might paradoxically weaken start-ups and strengthen the current internet monopolies.

Disintermediation and deunionisation. Platforms do not only make the role of third parties unnecessary, they also make the traditional line-organisation obsolete. During the last 30 years, since the internet revolution, companies are increasingly adopting and developing new models and methods for organisation and management under the framework of *business agility* – to organise and lead businesses capable of harnessing the power of innovation ecosystems, and to deal with the fast-paced change in today's business environment. This generates new roles and expectations on organisations to provide flexibility, self-organising teams, distributed authority and leadership. Self-organising co-creators, sharing and producing value on digital platforms in innovation ecosystems, does not naturally provide a single representative as an interface for labour market negotiations.

Fewer employees. With the externalisation of labour, platform companies also need many fewer employees. Instead different alternative work arrangements will arise. An example is Airbnb founded in 2008, with USD 21 billion in market capital and 3000 employees, compared to Marriott hotels founded in 1927, with USD 17 billion market capital and 200,000 employees. Although new jobs are created due to technological progress, it is in no way given that workers from declining sectors can fill the gaps in expanding sectors.

Many employers would be reluctant to invest in training their staff when the duration of contracts are shorter, as the expected return on the investment decreases. We might simultaneously see an increase in unemployment levels and "bottlenecks" on the labour market, harming the growth potential of European economies.

Alternative working relations also challenge the legal protection of workers. Who is going to pay the salary, when the (freelance) workers are on sick-leave or parental leave? And how are safety issues connected to the workplace handled in a proper way? It is certainly a risk, that the low qualified workforce will have still more problems keeping their jobs with a reasonable level of pay. But it's not only low-skilled workers who are challenged by robots and AI. Medium- and high-skilled workers will also have to "compete" with machines in the future, although their functional mobility across jobs and sectors is expected to be higher for these groups than others. We can identify a risk, that the next years will result in more polarisation in labour markets, as jobs and revenue are changing owners.

Challenges and opportunities

How do we support the creation of quality jobs in the future? The lower costs for R&D required for digital innovation and productivity, along with connectivity, global reach and exponential potential, will lead to more people engaged in entrepreneurial activity.

Digitalisation creates opportunities for a far more transparent labour market, where jobseekers have much better chances of finding jobs matching their competencies. Competencies need not be tied to the sector where you have your current work experience, as more transparency can lead to higher functional and geographical mobility. This advocates for more experiments like "basic income pilots" to continue and, for example, the development of a new standardisation for credential systems, and a reconfiguration of the "public employment agency" to become a *career incubator* on a European single market.

A better use of "Big Data" could also make it possible to prevent certain "negative social events" (like unemployment, sick-leave and poverty) by predictive analytics, early detection and intervention. Technology can also be used to complement human deficiencies, so people with disabilities can enter the labour market on more equal terms with others.

Macro-level: digital impact on markets and institutions

Trends

With globalisation by digitalisation comes increased competition at a faster speed. As individuals and organisations are connected through global communications, they have huge potential to extend their reach and impact. Change has become so fast and so pervasive that it has an impact on virtually every organisation everywhere, and everyone in them. Appropriate to our times, an acronym has been given to this condition: VUCA. As imagined by the US Army War College and popularised by Bob Johansen in *Leaders Make the Future* (2012, cited in Hughes, Colarelli Beatty, Dinwoodie, 2014), VUCA describes a world that is Volatile, Uncertain, Complex and Ambiguous. Correspondingly, today's strategic leaders must be able to think, act and influence in that environment. Leaders can't ignore the move toward cloud computing and mobile device access that fuels the ability of social networking to significantly influence local, regional and global events (Hughes, Colarelli Beatty, and Dinwoodie 2014). As a response to this, organisations are adopting technologies for navigating the future by predictive analytics as well as developing systems and infrastructure for resilience. As indicated in Figure 17.1 at the beginning of this chapter, *adaptiveness* has become the new art of organisation.

With the increase of mobility, migration and the economy of intangible assets along with urbanisation (the UN estimates 68% of the world's population is projected to live in urban areas by 2050), *talentism* has become a primary focus in organisations, cities and regions. To attract, develop and re-attract talent is key in a world where people are the only differentiator and sustainable advantage as everything else will be commoditised by automation and connectivity. This leads to a human-centric approach in technology, business and organisation.

How globalisation will change European labour markets certainly depends on how we regulate them. It seems to be a reasonable prediction that labour markets, at least for medium- and high-skilled labour, will be greatly influenced by new international competition in the next five to ten years. To understand how the social fabric of society, markets and organisations will transform, we need to look at how individuals are changing their behaviours when adopting the new technology. How will they drive societal transformation in the coming decades and how will they invest time, labour and money?

The rationale for focusing on *millennials* (the generations born after the mid-1980s) is marked by their ever-increasing representation in the workforce. They are the first generations sharing a global culture since their formative years. According to an EY survey made in 2015, millennials, are estimated to make up 75% of the global workforce in 2025. Today they hold USD 17trn of the world's private wealth, and by 2020, that could rise as high as USD 24trn. Looking further ahead, millennials are set to control an even greater share of global wealth, as they are positioned to benefit from one of the largest intergenerational wealth transfers in history (Haefele, Smiles, and Carter 2017). By studying younger generations and their preferences, we can get a hint about where the future is going as they are already shaping their market right now.

Collaborative lifestyles around redistribution markets (pre-owned goods being passed on from someone who does not want them to someone who does want them) and product-service systems (for example car sharing) are empowered by digital platforms and social media, simplifying the practice of the sharing economy, barter economy, the on-demand and gig economy, with peer-to-peer transactions in the exchange of digital and physical goods and services. This allows for a more efficient collective use of resources. A study ordered by the European Commission indicated that the volume of P2P transactions in the EU across five sectors (sales of goods, accommodation rentals, goods sharing, odd jobs and ridesharing) totalled 27.9 billion euros (USD 31.8 billion) in 2015.

Sustainability is also taking over the global agenda as the UN Sustainable Development Goals (UN 17 SDGs) are increasingly in the centre of innovation and talents are attracted to sustainable development. This is driving traditional venture capital into the domain of *impact investing* (financial returns with a positive social and environmental impact), and *impact ecosystems* are emerging as the 21st-century arenas for impact investors to connect with impact entrepreneurs. In the GIIN's 2018 Annual Impact Investor Survey, based on responses from 229 of the world's leading impact investing organisations (including fund managers, banks, foundations, development finance institutions, pension funds, insurance companies, and family offices), respondents collectively manage over USD 228 billion in impact investing assets. This is a fivefold increase since 2013 (Mudaliar, Bass, and Dithrich 2018).

Implications

New arrangements of work in combination with digitalisation make it possible for people to supply their labour internationally. The demand for physical

Future challenges and risks for IC   253

presence will most likely play a lesser role when people are communicating almost entirely through digital channels. If new technology is also shown to be successful in breaking (or reducing) the barriers between languages, could it be the end to national and local labour markets? This has implications for the future labour markets in several ways:

First, labour from third-world countries will have much better opportunities competing with European labour, which will tend to lower real wages in Europe. On the other hand, European labour supply will become more specialised, as the labour market is becoming global.

Second, global labour markets make it difficult to maintain national legal protections on labour markets. A counteracting force could be stronger international institutions enforcing legal and fair competition across national borders.

Third, globalisation will most likely lead to migration pressure between regions. The significance here will depend – among other factors – on the global distribution of wealth and income.

Challenges and opportunities

How do we prevent social polarisation in future labour markets? Inclusiveness needs to start with democratisation of learning, which will require some cures for the current "childhood diseases" of the AI economy – like filter bubbles, platform monopolies and IPR regulations harmful to innovation in the long-tail economy. The current battles over the internet, between governments, big corporations, SME's, academia and citizens, takes place around digital rights, freedom of information, the right to internet access, freedom from internet censorship and net neutrality.

We have to create a new trust among individuals and groups in the digitally empowered society. This happens for example on the sharing economy platforms where users have to be trustworthy and trust each other, relying on the will of other users to share, in order to make an exchange. Platforms in the sharing economy build and validate trusted relationships between members of their community, including producers, suppliers, customers or participants. Organisations are increasingly judged on the basis of their relationships with their workers, their customers and their communities, as well as their impact on society and the environment at large.

Social and environmentally responsible entrepreneurship is a rising trend but still rare and not in parity with the massive amount of capital now going into impact investing. This is an opportunity to create physical and digital meeting arenas, business hubs with incubators and business accelerator programmes for impact investors and societal entrepreneurs to take a lead in the transition to a sustainable business life, supporting the creation of new jobs in a sustainable economy.

With half of the world's population connected via the internet a range of micro-trade opportunities can open which could become a substantial source of income for many people in the future. For an inclusive labour market, labour mobility equipped with a new social contract can become an open "platform of

254   *Karl McFaul*

platforms" for career development, providing quality jobs by matching individuals, skills, demand and supply across multiple places and clusters where social security systems are harmonised between standard employee and non-standard entrepreneurial work arrangements.

References

Accenture (2017), *Technology vision 2017. Technology for people: The era of the intelligent enterprise.* Available at: www.accenture.com/_acnmedia/accenture/next-gen-4/tech-vision-2017/pdf/accenture-tv17-full.pdf.

Bersin, J., Pelster, B., Schwartz, J., and van der Vyver, B. (2017), "Rewriting the rules for the digital age", *2017 Deloitte global human capital trends.* Deloitte University Press. Available at: www2.deloitte.com/insights/us/en/focus/human-capital-trends/2017/introduction.html (Accessed: 6 July 2019).

Bounfour, A., and Edvinsson, L. (2005), *Intellectual capital for communities: Nations, regions, and cities.* Boston, MA: Elsevier Butterworth-Heinemann.

Curley, M., and Salmelin, B. (2018), *Open innovation 2.0: The new mode of digital innovation for prosperity and sustainability.* Cham: Springer.

Eurofound (2018), *Automation, digitalisation and platforms: Implications for work and employment.* Luxembourg: Publications Office of the European Union.

European Commission – Goos, M., Binder M., Ćurković, K., Hieronimus, S., Kirov V., Lehdonvirta, V., McFaul, K., Savona, M., Shaughnessy, G., and Velasco, L. (2019), *Report of the HLEG on the impact of the digital transformation on EU labour markets*, Brussels: European Commission. Available at: https://ec.europa.eu/newsroom/dae/document.cfm?doc_id=58412 (Accessed: 6 July 2019).

Haefele, M., Smiles, S., and Carter, M. (2017), *Millennials: The global guardians of capital.* UBS Chief Investment Office Americas, Wealth Management white paper.

Hamel, G. (2006), "The why, what, and how of management innovation", Harvard Business Review, February. Available at: https://hbr.org/2006/02/the-why-what-and-how-of-management-innovation (Accessed: 6 July 2019).

Hughes, R. L., Colarelli Beatty, K., and Dinwoodie, D. L. (2014), *Becoming a strategic leader: Your role in your organization's enduring success.* 2nd ed. San Francisco, CA: Wiley.

Lecerf, M. (2018), "European Social Fund Plus (ESF+) 2021–2027", *EU Legislation in Progress*, Brussels: European Parliamentary Research Service. Available at: http://europarl.europa.eu/RegData/etudes/BRIE/2018/625154/EPRS_BRI(2018)625154_EN.pdf (Accessed: 6 July 2019).

Lindgren, M., and Bandhold, H. (2009), *Scenario planning: The link between future and strategy.* 2nd ed. New York: Palgrave Macmillan.

Macias, E., Hurley, J., and Bisello, M. (2016), *What do Europeans do at work? A task-based analysis.* Eurofound, Office for the Official Publications of the European Union.

Meyer, C., and Davis, S. (2003), *It's alive: The coming convergence of information, biology, and business*, New York: Crown Business.

Moore, G. E. (1965), "Cramming more components onto integrated circuits", *Electronics.* Available at: https://drive.google.com/file/d/0By83v5TWkGjvQkpBcXJKT1I1TTA/view (Accessed: 6 July 2019).

Mudaliar, A., Bass, R., and Dithrich, H. (2018), *Annual impact investor survey 2018.* Global Impact Investing Network.

Nahapiet, J., and Ghoshal, S. (1998), "Social capital, intellectual capital, and the organizational advantage", *Academy of Management Review*, 23, 2, 242–266.

Future challenges and risks for IC 255

Ocean Tomo (2017), *Intangible asset market value study 2017*. Available at: www.oceantomo.com/intangible-asset-market-value-study (Accessed: 6 July 2019).

Parker, G. G., Van Alstyne, M. W., and Choudary, S. P. (2016), *Platform revolution: How networked markets are transforming the economy – and how to make them work for you*. New York: W. W. Norton.

Snowden, D. J., and Boone, M. E. (2007), "A leader's framework for decision making", *Harvard Business Review*, November. Available at: https://hbr.org/2007/11/a-leaders-framework-for-decision-making (Accessed: 6 July 2019).

Tegmark, M. (2017), *Life 3.0: Being human in the age of artificial intelligence*. New York: Knopf.

Zago, M. G. (2018), "Why the net giants are worried about the Web 3.0", *Medium*. Available at: https://medium.com/@matteozago/why-the-net-giants-are-worried-about-the-web-3-0-44b2d3620da5 (Accessed: 6 July 2019).

Zappa, M. (2012), Infographic: *Envisioning the future of education technology*. Available at: http://mz.wtf/envisioning (Accessed: 6 July 2019).

Zarkadakis, G. (2017), "How AI and Blockchain will change business organization", *Huffington Post*. Available at: www.huffpost.com/entry/how-ai-and-blockchain-will-change-business-organization_b_58cc33f5e4b07112b6472d4a (Accessed: 6 July 2019).

18 The role of blockchain for intellectual capital enhancement and business model innovation

Daniel Ruzza, Francesca Dal Mas, Maurizio Massaro and Carlo Bagnoli

Introduction

Emerging technologies regularly serve as enabling forces for economic, social, and business transformation (Cohen and Ernesto Amorós, 2014). Gartner's "Hype Cycle for Emerging Technologies" places blockchain among the top five technology trends in 2018 (Panetta, 2018). The whole blockchain market size is estimated to grow from USD 1.2 billion in 2018 to USD 23.3 billion by 2023, at an impressive compound annual growth rate (CAGR) of 80.2% during 2018–2023 (Market and Market, 2018). Blockchain is a foundational technology; this means that it is not only a technology that enables the disruption of a traditional business model quickly and with a lower-cost solution, but its potential goes far beyond because it can create new foundations for our economic and social systems (Iansiti and Lakhani, 2017). Many sources support the idea that blockchain has the potential to disrupt all business activities as profoundly as the internet, email, social media, or mobile did (Tapscott and Tapscott, 2016b). Therefore, maintaining a wait-and-see attitude and becoming a late adopter could be costly (Felin and Lakhani, 2018). To stay relevant and compete efficiently, companies will need to provide value in new ways (Ferguson, 2018). No matter what the context is, there is a strong possibility that blockchain will affect every business; the real question is when (Iansiti and Lakhani, 2017).

This chapter analyzes the potentiality and the effects of blockchain on current and future business models from an intellectual capital perspective.

Research method

In our study, we applied a Structured Literature Review (SLR). An SLR is "a method for studying a corpus of scholarly literature, to develop insights, critical reflections, future research paths, and research questions" (Massaro et al., 2016). To identify the current trend on blockchain research, we performed keywords research on Scopus on the title abstract and keywords, limiting the results to the subject area "Business management and accounting". The keywords "blockchain" and "business model" returned 30 results. To enlarge our research, we developed an online analysis searching for papers not published in Scopus,

Blockchain and business model innovation   257

such as practitioners reports and companies' whitepapers. A total number of 47 sources are included in our dataset.

The documents identified in the data acquisition phase were analyzed using the software NVivo. One of the authors coded all the documents identified in a coding structure. Crossing the nodes by developing queries we developed a further analysis of the intellectual capital components.

Blockchain technology

According to Gartner's "Hype Cycle for Emerging Technologies" 2018, blockchain can be placed among the top five technology trends, and it is, therefore, attracting attention from both practitioners and scholars (Panetta, 2018). Blockchain can be defined as a distributed public ledger or database of records maintained by a network of computers that verify any transaction and add it to the public ledger (Morabito, 2017). It is best known as the technology on which Bitcoin is founded (Cong, 2018). Indeed, in the famous whitepaper of Satoshi Nakamoto: "Bitcoin: A Peer-to-Peer Electronic Cash System", it is mainly described as the Bitcoin foundation technology. However, thanks to its characteristics, its capabilities extend far beyond cryptocurrencies. Tapscott and Tapscott (2017) identify three main characteristics. First, blockchain is distributed: it runs on computers provided by a growing number of volunteers distributed all over the world, so there is no central database. Second, it is public: each party on a blockchain has access to the entire database and its complete history (Iansiti and Lakhani, 2017). This implies that there is no need for intermediaries because no single party controls the data or the information, and every party can verify the records of its transaction partners directly. Third, it is encrypted: it uses heavy-duty encryption to maintain security (Tapscott and Tapscott, 2017). In defining the impact of blockchain on business Tapscott and Tapscott (2016a) identify seven design principles essential to understand the blockchain revolution and to give the means to act on it. The seven design principles were first extracted from the Satoshi paper, where they are declared more or less explicitly, and secondarily by practical experience. The design principles, which are summarized in Table 18.1, are useful for the development of software, services, market organizations, governments, and of course, blockchain-based business models.

Business model innovation and disruptive technologies: the role of IC

Blockchain technologies are providing therefore several advantages that can be used to innovate a company's business model. According to Osterwalder and Pigneur (2012), the business model describes the rationale of how an organization creates, delivers, and captures value. The business model definition and the identification of its components have received much interest in the literature. However, it is a static view of the concept (Remane et al., 2017). Due

258   *Daniel Ruzza et al.*

Table 18.1 The seven design principles

Design principle	Means	Implication
1. Network integrity	Validation technique	Acting against the system is made impossible or too expensive
2. Distributed power	Peer-to-peer network	Avoids the concentration of power Ensures the survival of the system
3. Value as an incentive	Remuneration policy: new coins and transaction fees	Aligns the interests and incentives of all the stakeholders Ensures the prosperity of the system
4. Security	Asymmetric cryptography Chain length	Security, speed and personality in transactions
5. Privacy	Trust in the system instead of the actors	It is not necessary to provide personal information
6. Right preservation	Approval of the nodes is required for each transaction Transactions are public	Property rights are guaranteed and applied
7. Inclusion	Reduction of technological barriers to access the blockchain	Expands access to the services offered by the network

to heightening environmental turbulence and transformative developments, recent research has shifted to a more dynamic view of business models (Wirtz et al., 2016). A business model innovation happens when a company modifies or improves one or several elements of its business model (Abdelkafi et al., 2013). Therefore, the business model innovation can be defined as a process that deliberately changes the core elements of a firm and its business logic (Bucherer et al., 2012).

The literature indicates endogenous and exogenous sources of business model innovation (Nowiński and Kozma, 2017). Therefore, a firm should consider the uncertainty and the opportunities in its environment as a potential exogenous source of growth that needs to be exploited (Hitt et al., 2001). Innovative technologies, such as blockchain, may be the primary driver of exogenous business model innovation (Teece, 2010). If we focus on business model innovation as a comprehensive concept, rather than emphasizing any particular business model designs, the resource-based view perspective can be taken into consideration (Schneider and Spieth, 2013). Dasilva and Trkman (2014) argue that business models can be seen as a specific combination of resources which through transactions generate value for the company's stakeholders. Moreover, the resource-based view has increasingly been suggested as an appropriate theoretical framework for research on business models and business model innovation because it identifies the differences between the use of the resources as a source of competitive advantage (Teece, 1984). Besides, Morris et al. (2005) emphasize the business model's innovation potential to mobilize and coordinate the firm's resources. The only way to respond to the disruptive effect of new technologies is to accept them and then find ways to exploit them (Christensen, 1997) as a valuable resource.

Interestingly, while technologies typically represent part of the structural capital, we argue that implementing blockchain to innovate a company's business model requires a comprehensive approach to IC management (Edvinsson, 2000; Massaro et al., 2015, 2017).

Blockchain technology and business model innovation: the impact on structural capital

Structural capital includes processes, systems, structures, brands, intellectual property and other intangibles which are identified as the explicit knowledge of an organization (Massaro et al., 2017). Structural capital has been described as the knowledge that remains in the organization even when employees leave the company (Bontis et al., 2000). The design principles that influence this component of intellectual capital are: "Network integrity" and "Right preservation".

The resources collection process can be done in completely new ways thanks to the combination of the principles "Network integrity" and "Right preservation". To explain how these two principles make it possible, we use the example of financial resources. Thanks to blockchain technology companies can finance themselves in a completely new way: through the Initial Coin Offering. Initial Coin Offerings (ICOs) are a form of fundraising. They are carried out through an open call for funding promoted by organizations, companies, and entrepreneurs to raise money through cryptocurrencies in exchange for tokens instead of shares (Adhami et al., 2018). These tokens can be traded on the aftermarket, and all transactions are verified on a blockchain (Morkunas et al., 2019). The volume of money handled by the ICOs is already remarkable and in continuous growth. In 2017 over USD 5 billion were raised while in the first three quarters of 2018, USD 12 billion were raised (Bussgang and Nanda, 2018). ICOs are a successful tool since they represent a completely new way for start-ups, and companies in general, to gain quick and effective access to financial resources without the constraints and the delays caused by intermediaries (Kastelein, 2017). It also allows raising money without giving up decision-making power as happens with conventional IPOs. Moreover, thanks to the ICOs it is possible to reduce the costs of capital raising, avoiding intermediaries (crowdfunding platforms) and payment agents (banks, credit card circuits) (Adhami et al., 2018).

Moreover, thanks to the combination of the same two design principles – "Network integrity" and "Right preservation" – the authenticity of the intellectual property of the firm as well as the authenticity of the products are guaranteed (Tapscott and Tapscott, 2016a). Indeed, "Network integrity" guarantees that the actors do not try to tamper with the system to violate the property of others. While, thanks to "Right preservation", it is possible to protect the company's intellectual resources more efficiently and effectively. The blockchain allows you to record all information relating to the author, date of creation and description of intellectual property, as well as data relating to the licenses, making counterfeiting practically impossible (Felin and Lakhani, 2018). Consider, for example, the case of patents. Creating a patent is expensive and requires multiple resources and skills. Furthermore, patent protection is characterized by a high risk of litigation. Blockchain technology could solve both these problems, making registration and protection more economical and effective.

Blockchain technology and business model innovation: the impact on relational capital

Relational capital represents all the organization's valuable relationships with customers, suppliers, and external stakeholders and it is based on the idea that firms cannot be considered as isolated systems (Dal Mas et al., 2019; Massaro et al., 2015). Blockchain works as a "digital logbook of transactions" that is innovative and revolutionary thanks to its decentralization, disintermediation, transaction sharing, and tamper-proof qualities (Wang, et al., 2019). Therefore, the implications of blockchain on transactions and relationship management are huge (Queiroz et al., 2019). Among the seven design principles, we identified "Network integrity", "Security", "Inclusion", and "Privacy" as the most influential on this component of the intellectual capital.

Thanks to the "Security" design principle, the supply chain can be disruptive, reducing or eliminating many of the problems connected to it (Hughes et al., 2019). One of the outcomes is shortening the time for transaction execution (Nowiński and Kozma, 2017). Another outcome is the decline in operational costs, which facilitates small transactions (Nowiński and Kozma, 2017). Also, the secure custody chain enables gradual verification of who and how a product has been managed and allows each member of the supply chain to identify where and from whom damage could have occurred (Hughes et al., 2019).

The "Network integrity" and "Security" design principles can change the relation between the company and the customers in different ways. There is no longer the need to trust the counterparty or intermediaries, but trust is placed directly on the system (Tapscott and Tapscott, 2016a). Therefore, it can protect consumers from deceptive counterfeit fraud (Hughes et al., 2019) and reduce the amount of inefficiency and lack of clarity in supply chains by making supply chains more efficient and transparent (Morkunas et al., 2019). Collaboration tools with external partners can change (Wang, et al., 2019). Previously, long-term relational and financial commitments were needed to build a relationship of mutual trust with supply chain actors (Schoenherr et al., 2015). With blockchains, however, trust is incorporated and programmed into the technology platform (Tapscott and Tapscott, 2016a). The point of arrival is that procurement activities can be performed in environments without trust between organizations (Wang, Singgih, et al., 2019). For example, smart contracts are made possible. "Smart contracts are digital agreements that are, ideally, automatically executed once a consensus on an event's outcome is generated on a blockchain" (Cong, 2018). They cannot be seized, stopped, or redirected to a different address. It is only necessary to transmit the signed transaction to any node of the network from anywhere using any support. In this way, they transform the way to do a transaction giving the mathematical certainty that the contract will be executed (Tapscott and Tapscott, 2016a).

"The foundation for prosperity is inclusion, and blockchains can help" (Tapscott and Tapscott, 2016a). The "Inclusion" design principle has the effect of lowering barriers for participation, getting access to target markets that were previously not reachable and therefore creating new customer segments for a business (Morkunas et al., 2019). Participation can be improved in terms of both entrepreneurship and access to work and customers who can have access to companies' offers. Consider the financial sector as an example. Consumers at the bottom of the pyramid don't have access to the basic services because they still can't afford the minimum account balances, minimum payment amounts, or transaction fees to use the system. Today more than 2 billion people do not have access to the financial system. Among these people, money transactions take place in cash. This is not only due to the lack of alternatives, but also because peer-to-peer transactions are preferred. However, mobile banking provides incentives to move from the monetary economy to a mobile digital economy as individuals realize their benefits in terms of theft protection, speed, and accessibility. Blockchain technology is based on the advantages of mobile access and, at the same time, adds transparency, security, responsibility, and trust. Therefore, in countries with limited banking infrastructure and high dependence on liquidity, blockchain could be used as a tool to hold and transfer money (Larios-Hernández, 2017), creating a completely new customer segment.

The trust that is spread into the system makes possible a different relationship not only with customers and suppliers but with all the stakeholders. Consider the example of diamonds. Thanks to the blockchain it is possible to record a diamond's origin and the previous owner's history, which has strong ethical and social implications. Stakeholders have a keen interest in the life of diamonds, which determines the need for the industry to demonstrate authenticity, transparency, and origin. De Beers, the largest diamond manufacturer in the world for the value of its gems, has led the industry's efforts to verify the authenticity of diamonds and ensure that they do not come from conflict zones where the revenues from the gems could be used to finance violence (Lewis et al., 2018). The need to prove that stones are ethically approved is vital for several reasons: as a matter of corporate image; to align the company's behavior with the values of the social context in which it is located; for political issues related to the financing of armed conflicts against governments or financing governments that do not respect the Universal Declaration of Human Rights (Felin and Lakhani, 2018).

Another fundamental issue that blockchain can influence concerns the privacy and security of data and personal information. In this respect, the "Privacy" design principle is the one that is most taken into consideration.

262 *Daniel Ruzza et al.*

Privacy was one of the most dominant issues in 2018, due in large part to the Cambridge Analytica and Facebook scandal. An important theme raised by that scandal is that privacy and security are converging (Burt, 2019). Once, the biggest problem was unauthorized access to our data. The greatest danger was to our digital selves. Today, however, the biggest risk to our privacy and our security has become the threat of unintended inferences, due to the power of increasingly widespread machine learning techniques (Burt, 2019). These inferences may, for example, threaten our anonymity, reveal information about our political leanings or details about our health. By eliminating the need to trust others, the blockchain has eliminated the need to have information about others to the point of not even having to know the true identities of those with whom you are interacting (Tapscott and Tapscott, 2016a). Alternatively, through the blockchain it is possible to regain the control of the information we publish on the web, revealing only the information necessary for each transaction, and obtaining a fair return on information that has value to others (Tapscott and Tapscott, 2016a).

Blockchain technology and business model innovation: the impact on human capital

In an organization, human capital comprises the competencies, skills, experience, and intellectual agility of the employees that possess individual tacit knowledge (Bontis, 1998; Massaro et al., 2018). The design principle that we have identified as the most influential for this building block innovation is "Network integrity".

The blockchain, thanks to the "Network integrity" design principle, can influence human resources. Making it impossible to act against the system, it creates trust and a widespread honesty that allows the companies to get better information about potential contractors and partners in the recruitment process (Tapscott and Tapscott, 2017). With the consent of a potential employee, the company will have access to information whose authenticity is guaranteed by the blockchain. For example, job prospects would not be able to lie about their education or grades because an authority, like the university from which they graduated, entered the data into the blockchain. In a broader perspective a more inclusive world can enhance human capital. When basic services become available to a larger community, the overall human capital that companies can access increases.

Conclusion

Concluding our work, we want to reflect on the main findings of this study and, therefore, develop and address several implications for practitioners, policymakers, and scholars. According to a Deloitte survey on 308 blockchain senior executives at organizations with USD 500 million or more in annual revenue, managers seem to have perceived the urgency and relevance of the advent of blockchain. However, 40% of them have stated that they have little or no knowledge about blockchain technology (Dunker and Krasniqi, 2017). Consequently, our section on "Blockchain technology" aims to fill this gap. The seven design principles identified by Tapscott and Tapscott (2016a), have been integrated with the work of other authors identified in the literature review. These principles represent recurring themes discussed by different authors who have studied blockchain. This knowledge systematization has created a useful structure to understand how blockchain technology works and what are the possibilities to exploit it.

Starting from those principles in our section on "Business model innovation and disruptive technologies" we discuss how the seven principles used to analyze blockchain can in fact impact IC. Security and privacy can be used to increase a company's relational capital and create more inclusive markets. A more inclusive world enhances human capital, providing network integrity within the company and in the overall society. Finally, the use of blockchain can be used to register know-how and patents, providing more straightforward ways to protect intellectual property. In all these changes IC can support the development of new business models, creating a virtuous cycle.

Despite our efforts, this research has some limitations. Even though we adopted a rigid analytical approach, it is unlikely that every available scientific and practitioner publication was included in the literature review we conducted. Moreover, the research on the topic is still in its infancy. Therefore, some interesting future research themes might be developed in the near future without being considered in this study.

References

Abdelkafi, N., Makhotin, S. and Thorsten, P. (2013), "Business model innovations for electric mobility: What can be learned from existing business model patterns?", *International Journal of Innovation Management*, Vol. 17 No. 1, pp. 1–41.

Adhami, S., Giudici, G. and Martinazzi, S. (2018), "Why do businesses go crypto? An empirical analysis of initial coin offerings", *Journal of Economics and Business*, Vol. 100 March, pp. 64–75.

Bontis, N. (1998), "Intellectual capital: An exploratory study that develops measures and models", *Management Decision*, Vol. 36 No. 2, pp. 63–76.

Bontis, N., Chua Chong Keow, W. and Richardson, S. (2000), "Intellectual capital and business performance in Malaysian industries", *Journal of Intellectual Capital*, Vol. 1 No. 1, pp. 85–100.

Bucherer, E., Eisert, U. and Gassmann, O. (2012), "Towards systematic business model innovation: Lessons from product innovation management", *Creativity and Innovation Management*, Vol. 21 No. 2, pp. 183–198.

Burt, A. (2019), "Privacy and cybersecurity are converging: Here's why that matters for people and for companies", *Harvard Business Review*, Vol. 10, pp. 1–6.

Bussgang, J. and Nanda, R. (2018), "The hidden costs of initial coin offerings", *Harvard Business Review*, pp. 1–9.

Christensen, C.M. (1997), *Innovator's Dilemma: When New Technologies Cause Great Firms to Fail*, Harvard Business School Press Books, Boston, MA.

Cohen, B. and Ernesto Amorós, J. (2014), "Municipal demand-side policy tools and the strategic management of technology life cycles", *Technovation*, Vol. 34 No. 12, pp. 797–806.

Cong, L.W. (2018), "Navigating the next wave of blockchain innovation: Smart contracts", *MIT Sloan Management Review*, pp. 1–7.

Dal Mas, F., Paoloni, P. and Lombardi, R. (2019), "Wellbeing of women entrepreneurship and relational capital: A case study in Italy", in Lepeley, M.T., Kuschel, K., Eijdenberg, E. and Pouw, N. (Eds.), *Exploring Wellbeing among Women in Entrepreneurship: A Global Perspective*, Routledge, London.

Dasilva, C.M. and Trkman, P. (2014), "Business model: What it is and what it is not", *Long Range Planning*, Vol. 47 No. 6, pp. 379–389.

Dunker, P. and Krasniqi, M. (2017), "Deloitte survey: Blockchain reaches beyond financial services". Deloitte.

Edvinsson, L. (2000), "Some perspectives on intangibles and intellectual capital 2000", *Journal of Intellectual Capital*, Vol. 1 No. 1, pp. 12–16.

Felin, T. and Lakhani, K. (2018), "What problems will you solve with blockchain?", *MIT Sloan Management Review*, Fall, pp. 32–38.

Ferguson, M. (2018), "Preparing for a blockchain future", *MIT Sloan Management Review*, Vol. 60 No. 1, pp. 15–19.

Hitt, M.A., Ireland, R.D., Camp, S.M. and Sexton, D.L. (2001), "Guest editors' introduction to the special issue Strategic Entrepreneurship: Entrepreneurial strategies for wealth creation", *Strategic Management Journal*, Vol. 22 No. 6/7, pp. 479–491.

Hughes, A., Park, A., Kietzmann, J. and Archer-Brown, C. (2019), "Beyond Bitcoin: What blockchain and distributed ledger technologies mean for firms", *Business Horizons*, https://doi.org/10.1016/j.bushor.2019.01.002.

Iansiti, M. and Lakhani, K.R. (2017), "The truth about blockchain", *Harvard Business Review*, pp. 1–17.

Kastelein, R. (2017), "What initial coin offerings are, and why VC firms care", *Harvard Business Review*, pp. 1–8.

Larios-Hernández, G.J. (2017), "Blockchain entrepreneurship opportunity in the practices of the unbanked", *Business Horizons*, Vol. 60 No. 6, pp. 865–874.

Lewis, B.B., Beers, D. and De Beers, F. (2018), "De Beers turns to blockchain to guarantee diamond purity", Thomson Reuters, pp. 17–20.

Market and Market (2018), Blockchain Market by Provider, Application (Payments, Exchanges, Smart Contracts, Documentation, Digital Identity, Supply Chain Management, and GRC Management), Organization Size, Industry Vertical, and Region – Global Forecast to 2023.

Massaro, M., Dumay, J. and Bagnoli, C. (2015), "Where there is a will there is a way: IC, strategic intent, diversification and firm performance", *Journal of Intellectual Capital*, Vol. 16 No. 3, pp. 490–517.

Massaro, M., Dumay, J. and Bagnoli, C. (2017), "When the investors speak: Intellectual capital disclosure and the Web 2.0", *Management Decision*, Vol. 55 No. 9, pp. 1888–1904.

Massaro, M., Dumay, J., Garlatti, A. and Dal Mas, F. (2018), "Practitioners' views on intellectual capital and sustainability: From a performance-based to a worth-based perspective", *Journal of Intellectual Capital*, Vol. 19 No. 2, pp. 367–386.

Massaro, M., Dumay, J.C. and Guthrie, J. (2016), "On the shoulders of giants: Undertaking a structured literature review in accounting", *Accounting, Auditing and Accountability Journal*, Vol. 29 No. 5, pp. 767–901.

Morabito, V. (2017), "Business innovation through blockchain", https://doi.org/10.1007/978-3-319-48478-5.

Blockchain and business model innovation   265

Morkunas, V.J., Paschen, J. and Boon, E. (2019), "How blockchain technologies impact your business model", *Business Horizons*, https://doi.org/10.1016/j.bushor.2019.01.009.

Morris, M., Schindehutte, M. and Allen, J. (2005), "The entrepreneur's business model: Toward a unified perspective", *Journal of Business Research*, Vol. 58, pp. 726–735.

Nowiński, W. and Kozma, M. (2017), "How can blockchain technology disrupt the existing business models?", *Entrepreneurial Business and Economics Review*, Vol. 5 No. 3, pp. 173–188.

Osterwalder, P. and Pigneur, Y. (2012), *Business Model Generator: A Handbook for Visionaries, Game Changes, and Challengers*, John Wiley & Sons, Hoboken, NJ.

Panetta, K. (2018), "5 trends emerge in the Gartner Hype Cycle for Emerging Technologies, 2018", Smarter with Gartner, August 16.

Queiroz, M.M., Telles, R. and Bonilla, S.H. (2019), "Blockchain and supply chain management integration: A systematic review of the literature", *Supply Chain Management: An International Journal*, https://doi.org/10.1108/SCM-03-2018-0143.

Remane, G., Hanelt, A., Tesch, J.F. and Kolbe, L.M. (2017), "The business model pattern database: A tool for systematic business model innovation", *International Journal of Innovation Management*, Vol. 21 No. 1, 1750004.

Schneider, S. and Spieth, P. (2013), "Business model innovation: Towards an integrated future research agenda", *International Journal of Innovation Management*, Vol. 17 No. 1, DOI: 10.1142/S136391961340001X.

Schoenherr, T., Narayanan, S. and Narasimhan, R. (2015), "Trust formation in outsourcing relationships: A social exchange theoretic perspective", *International Journal of Production Economics*, Vol. 169, pp. 401–412.

Tapscott, D. and Tapscott, A. (2016a), *Blockchain Revolution: How the Technology Behind Bitcoin Is Changing Money, Business, and the World*, Penguin Random House, New York.

Tapscott, D. and Tapscott, A. (2016b), "The impact of the blockchain goes beyond financial services", *Harvard Business Review*, Vol. 10, p. 7.

Tapscott, D. and Tapscott, A. (2017), "How blockchain will change organizations", *MIT Sloan Management Review*, pp. 1–9.

Teece, D. (1984), "Economic analysis and strategic management", *California Management Review*, Vol. 36 No. 3, pp. 172–194.

Teece, D.J. (2010), "Business models, business strategy and innovation", *Long Range Planning*, Vol. 43 No. 2–3, pp. 172–194.

Wang, Y., Han, J.H. and Beynon-Davies, P. (2019), "Understanding blockchain technology for future supply chains: A systematic literature review and research agenda", *Supply Chain Management*, Vol. 24 No. 1, pp. 62–84.

Wang, Y., Singgih, M., Wang, J. and Rit, M. (2019), "Making sense of blockchain technology: How will it transform supply chains?", *International Journal of Production Economics*, Vol. 211 November, pp. 221–236.

Wirtz, B.W., Pistoia, A., Ullrich, S. and Göttel, V. (2016), "Business models: Origin, development and future research perspectives", *Long Range Planning*, Vol. 49, pp. 36–54.

19 From trade in goods and services to trade in ideas

Eskil Ullberg

Introduction

Trade can be said to be first of all in ideas. No goods "grow on trees", they were all first created by a human idea, and no services performed by people are without an idea of making more efficient use of the goods once produced, which can also include many pre-production and production related services. These ideas are today exchanged globally not only in a personal way through intangible assets and intellectual capital inside firms, but also in an *impersonal* way through intellectual property rights between the trading parties. Patents, copyrights, trademarks, design, IC patterns, data and geographic indications today make up this set of impersonal, excludable, tradable and licensable rights.[1] Still, the way we think of – and analyse –trade is essentially as trade in goods or trade in services.

Ideas have always been the driver of economic development and services have always been part of using the goods, but economic organization has been more hierarchical than dynamic until risks[2] and transaction costs have fallen to a level where a new economic structure can emerge, of specialized creators, firms and universities and institutes trading with each other.[3] The digital economy has certainly made more than a "dent" in the management of such risks and the reduction of the transaction costs and therefore changed this dynamic, placing the *already* most valuable assets, the creative ideas, at the forefront of economic policy discussions. This change also places the human capital of nations at the forefront, in particular the hundreds of millions of now highly educated people in developing countries. These countries represent 85% of the world's population and today 60% of the word GDP, the 50/50 break-even point attained already in 2010.[4]

Such changes can already be seen in trade patterns. Based on data from Sweden we find the growth in royalty licensing contributing to 20%(!) of the balance of payments. IT services double that, and financial services ("fintech") are also growing rapidly. See Figure 19.1.

The transition from trade in goods – physical things we can touch – and services – things we do to make productive use of physical things – to trade in ideas changes the world's economic organization as transaction costs come down

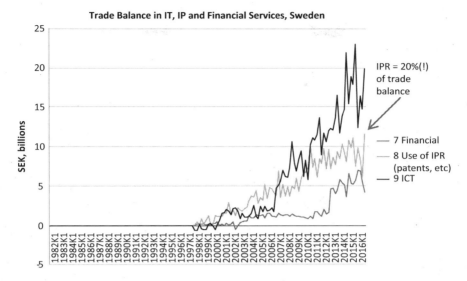

Figure 19.1 Trade balance in royalty and services in Sweden.

partly enabling such change. In addition, the creative art that is made is essentially electronic, also enabled by digitalization, making the "production process" of these ideas also practically global, paving the way for impersonal exchange, based in the potential for the intellectual property *rights* to this created art to be exchanged between trading partners. Such exchange has promises of specialization between creative art partners, yielding productivity gains and economic growth. This *impersonal exchange* thus enables a more efficient *integration* between science (university research) and technology (inventor's creative use of the basic knowledge on nature) (Ullberg, 2012). This integration was the basis for the dramatic economic growth that first took place in the West (North, 1981).

About 85% of the value of companies – who create the ideas, goods and services – currently comes from intangible assets, making book value of companies of limited value. Global billion-dollar valuation start-ups all have huge losses, but the value must come from somewhere: some of it, if not most, may come from the intellectual capital, intellectual property rights like patents and copyrights, customer contracts and other productive assets. The accounting value of intangibles is discussed by Lev (2018) who outlines an agenda for the accounting of intangible assets.

Based on data from the IMF we find that trade in ideas, measured as royalty licensing, is today (2016) about $330 bn or 1.5% of world trade. This is up 50% from 1% ten years ago. The leading actors are the EU (including Switzerland) with 40% of this value, US 39%, Japan 9%, Switzerland (alone) 6%(!) and China and Israel about 0.1% each. This tells a very compelling story, that a country

268 Eskil Ullberg

1300 times smaller, Israel, can have the same realized value as China. Both these nations are "newcomers" to this trade. The leverage of human capital is further made clear by Switzerland with its 6%, another small country who started patenting 130 years ago. If embodied intellectual property (IP) is taken into account, joint ventures, mergers and acquisitions, and other ways such rights are traded, the value may be much higher. This ought to make abundantly clear that when the productive assets traded are based on *human capital*, the size of the country does not matter as much as the size of the people's ideas (Ullberg, 2017).

These values are naturally highly approximative as no public statistics exist that have yet been developed with trade in ideas in mind. See Ullberg et al. (2019b) for an outline of a first statistical framework for trade in ideas. The statistical principles of accounting for trade in ideas, based on international accounting standards for intellectual property rights are discussed in a report and forthcoming book by the author in cooperation with two trade statistics experts.

This chapter addresses key aspects of the impact of the digital economy on the creative arts and trade in ideas. The proposal is essentially that because intellectual property rights can now be transacted and evaluated, the value of the intellectual capital of trading firms and nations can now be effectively realized.

Policy for a complex problem

How can we characterize such a development, and how does the digital economy impact the incentives to shift towards the high-value assets used in trade in ideas?

An improved framework for understanding and approaching intellectual capital (IC) is needed. In a pilot study conducted in 2017, Ullberg, Edvinsson and Lin (Ullberg et al., 2019a),[5] characterize the stock of intellectual capital, giving a brief but strategic overview suitable for an initial policy discussion defining areas of further investigation useful to improve our extant frameworks and theory. To quote American political economist and Nobel laureate Elinor Ostrom (2010):

> To explain the world of interactions and outcomes occurring at multiple levels, we also have to be willing to deal with complexity instead of rejecting it. Some mathematical models are very useful for explaining outcomes in particular settings. We should continue to use simple models where they capture enough of the core underlying structure and incentives that they usefully predict outcomes. When the world we are trying to explain and improve, however, is not well described by a simple model, we must continue to improve our frameworks and theories so as to be able to understand complexity and not simply reject it.

In the pilot study (Ullberg et al., 2019a) the stock of intellectual capital is made up of four different components based on the so-called ELSS model devised by Ståhle, Ståhle and Lin (Ståhle et al., 2015), which is an upgrade to the model created by Lin and Edvinsson (2008). These components refer to human, market, process and renewal *capitals*. It is a *relative* measure across 59 countries, thus indicating the results of strategic *choices* by policy makers, companies and individuals in a competitive world economy. This was illustrated in the pilot study by comparing a number of smaller high-tech nations and Nordic nations.

The human capital component measures higher education, PISA performance and other, in a sense human capital formations. The market capital component focuses on balance of payments and investment positions, and is thus a market access measure. The process capital component focuses on productivity where internet and computer usage are also included. However, productivity gains have been unsatisfactory for more than 50 years. Finally, the renewal capital component focuses on investments in basic knowledge, such as R&D spending/capita, and intellectual property rights. This is most closely related to trade in ideas and in some ways measures the outcomes (results) of the implicit process of the integration of science and technology.

This intellectual capital approach thus suggests that if the digital economy should have any measurable effect on productivity, it must shift incentives for investments towards more "high-yield" assets and these assets must then be used broadly across the world (market access). Measuring the stock of renewable capital over time can thus give us an indication of which countries have had policies that have been effective towards the goal of increasing these assets.

The renewal capital of the Nordic countries is compared in Figure 19.2. We see that Sweden and Finland are losing long-term competitive advantage

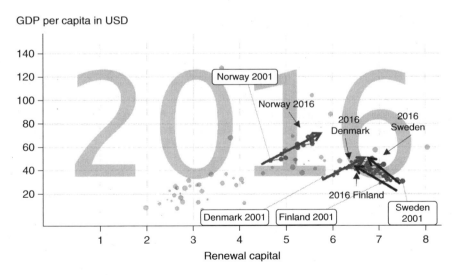

Figure 19.2 Renewal capital vs. GDP per capita (PPP) for four Nordic countries.
Source: Ullberg et al. (2017).

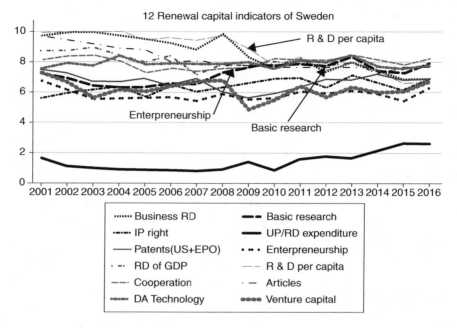

Figure 19.3 Twelve renewal capital indicators for Sweden. A decline in the share of R&D to the economy as a whole can be observed.
Source: Adapted from Ullberg et al. (2017).

and Norway and Denmark gaining in renewal capital. However, all countries continue at about the same rate to grow in GDP terms, i.e. their market capital expands.

The reason for Sweden's decline in renewal capital appears to be a lower R&D/capita, business R&D and academic publications, during the first decade of the 21st century and then a standstill. An uptick in basic research and patenting since 2010 has not compensated for this relative loss of stock in renewal capital (see Figure 19.3). Incentives for investing in R&D and publications have been weak.

The same comparison between small high-tech countries around the world is shown in Figure 19.4. The comparison between these countries shows that Singapore is slightly increasing, Israel is doing a "turn-around" and Switzerland is advancing most in renewal capital (Sweden is the same as in Figure 19.2). The leverage of existing renewal capital is very high in Singapore, high in Sweden and Switzerland, and moderate in Israel (after the turn-around).

As an example, the policies appear to provide fewer incentives to invest in R&D – government or business – as a total share of economic activity in Sweden and possibly Finland than in Norway, Denmark, Singapore, Israel and Switzerland. As all countries expand their economies at about the same pace

From trade in goods to trade in ideas 271

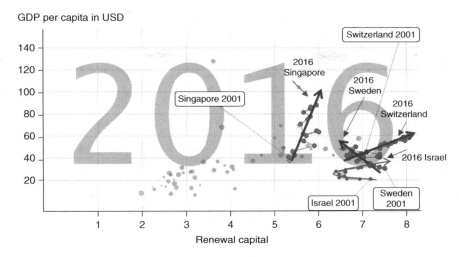

Figure 19.4 Renewal capital vs. GDP per capita (PPP) for Sweden, Singapore, Israel and Switzerland.
Source: Adapted from Ullberg et al. (2017) and Ullberg et al. (2019a).

(except Norway and Singapore, who expand faster), the question of whether the "right" renewal capital is created is obvious.

Trade balance and renewal capital

The net income of these assets to the countries' companies from licensing, given their renewal capital, can be expressed as the royalty trade balance, i.e. the export–import value. The relationship between this trade balance and the intellectual capital (renewal capital) expresses, then, how well these nations turn their renewal capital into economics (see Figure 19.5). Here we see that Sweden tops the returns game whereas Switzerland tops the intellectual capital game among these countries.

Turning these assets into economic use, measured in GDP, and trying to relate that to any impact from the digital economy with better risk management and lower transaction costs is a step towards an effective policy.

A new strategic response

As both the creation of more renewal capital and its use increasingly shifts economic activity to trade in ideas (probably mostly including patents and audiovisual copyrights, but also other intellectual property rights) the countries that are able to use the IP system to link international basic research, international and corporate R&D with the creation of new tradable intellectual property

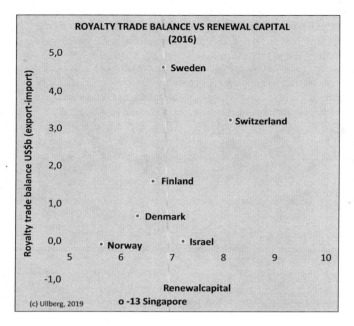

Figure 19.5 Royalty trade balance vs. intellectual capital (renewal capital).
Source: Royalty data (IMF, data.imf.org); IC data (database managed by Prof. J.Y. Lin).

rights will likely benefit from such exchange through specialization. This is done electronically in the digital economy. In addition, trade in goods ("manufacturing") may be replaced upto 40% by 3D printing, according to a study by ING (Leering, 2017), further emphasizing trade in ideas as a transformative activity. This means that the digital economy really ought to focus on the exchange in the ideas themselves. See Table 19.1.

Development and digitalization

The coordination of intangibles is not limited to localized geographies but should be considered global in nature given today's digitalized world. This can be seen as an informal network of collaboration between actors on the basis of history, culture, etc. These informal collaborations, within and between countries, indicate a first step towards new institutional development and learning. This will likely be followed by more regulatory arrangements which may then constitute the new economic, social and environmental system. In a sense, these could perhaps be seen as poly-centric organizations or markets, which would be a form of voluntary cooperation between sovereign government agencies and firms. This can result in more efficient outcomes than centralized government administrations and can be an alternative to fully organized markets with

Table 19.1 Impact of trade in ideas on intellectual capital in the digital economy

Intellectual capital	Digital economy impact	Trade in ideas impact
1. Human	Skills training, research and engineering, MOOCS	The promises of on-line education, training (currently experimental)
2. Market	Transparency, transaction costs, risks, branding, trade data	Very positive; main impact on transaction cost, risks
3. Process	Process efficiency, goods and service distribution	Main impact through development, design, 3D printing, global services
4. Renewal	IP rights, science and tech cooperation, entrepreneurship, venture capital	Direct impact by transferring and licensing IP rights, cooperation between science and tech

© E. Ullberg, 2019

Table 19.2 The educational benefits of MOOCs

Tangible educational benefits	
Any	18%
Completed prerequisites for academic programme	12%
Gained credit toward academic degree	8%

© E. Ullberg, 2019

Source: Based on Coursera survey data presented in Zhenghao et al. (2015).

property rights. An example here is MOOC (Massive Open Online Courses), where universities cooperate on specific classes.

The multiplier effect of digitalization in knowledge sharing far outstrips that of the printing press and the Gutenberg revolution. However, the challenge is in using the vast supply of digitalized information in learning institutions for increased productivity in education. However, this goal of productivity has yet eluded even MOOC players such as Udacity, Coursera, edX and others. Although progress has been made, it appears that it is quite difficult to go beyond rather technical subject matters. However, a recent research study involving a survey of MOOC course completers – comprising a mere 5% of all who sign up for MOOCs (Ho et al., 2014) – showed that 74% reported career benefits (see Table 19.3) and 38% reported educational benefits (see Table 19.2), with people from *developing* countries more frequently reporting benefits from taking MOOCs (Zhenghao et al., 2015).

Business processes appear even more affected by digitalization than education processes, with a corresponding artificial intelligence (AI) shift to design and maintenance. The global free flow of information means that some nations will develop mechanisms to turn such information flows, a kind of intangible,

274 *Eskil Ullberg*

Table 19.3 The career benefits of MOOCs

Tangible career benefits	
Any	33%
Found a new job	26%
Started my own business	9%
Received a pay increase	3%
Received a promotion	3%

© E. Ullberg, 2019

Source: Based on Coursera survey data presented in Zhenghao et al. (2015).

Table 19.4 The 4th Industrial Revolution

1st	*2nd*	*3rd*	*4th*
Mechanization, water and steam power	Mass production, assembly line, electric power	Computer and automation	Cyber physical systems and artificial intelligence

© E. Ullberg, 2019

Source: Adapted from Lejeune (2017).

to better productive use. Business processes are clearly one way to achieve this; Industry 4.0 (see Table 19.4) and AI are also alternatives. Understanding the effects of AI and its productive use in the digitalized economy is therefore one of the proposed projects.

A policy for high-risk high-potential ideas

One key contribution from the digital economy on the creation of intellectual capital is the formation of human capital. When transacted though intellectual property rights – now with more efficient risk management tools such as artificial intelligence and lower transaction costs – this, in turn, enables likely the most valuable intellectual capital with a global reach.

To develop a corporate strategy or government policy to meet the competitive challenges of nations today, new steps have to be undertaken. This area is particularly risky and uncertain. However, risk taking is not something most countries are known for today. Small and rather safe steps, based on proven concepts, often from abroad, are taken in economics, academia and industry. Examples of successes are in the digital music industry, digital payments and digital communication, all of which have global markets, global funding and globally sourced management. However on-line education is still not a success, and the healthcare industry is plagued by costly processes. Policies also appear to closely follow current policies' "pre-defined paths" – rather than reflecting the "path-breaking" moves of inventors and innovators – funded by a banking industry of the last century, including in Sweden and Switzerland where examples include: Ericsson, ABB (ASEA), Atlas-Copco, VOLVO, SKF, Big Pharma and global banking.

This chapter thus backs–up the OECD reports of 2012 and 2016 that were sprinkled with warnings, but, unlike those reports, it does not stop at the analysis. A *future looking strategy* for investment in knowledge building is proposed that can inform policy capable of retaking lost initiatives. Such a goal is needed to structure the activities to take advantage of the promises of trade in ideas. This approach is based on a contribution to the fundamental understanding of the most productive assets today: intellectual capital, as intangible assets, where intellectual property rights are the most valuable.

Countries with cultures of avoiding risk stand in stark contrast with, for example, Israel or Chile, who dash out funds to new high-risk, high-potential projects, with few strings attached except "try it", "learn from it" and "apply again". In Israel, through the chief scientist's office, a decision was made that a 50% success rate was acceptable, with the expectation that these successful projects would yield a ten-fold return. The other 50% – the "failed" projects – would still be expected to lead to a three-fold return, because these scientists, inventors and entrepreneurs would have learnt important skills – for their next attempt![6] Chile has a similar system where funds are used to test new things, possibly contributing to the fact that Chile is considered an "innovation hub" informally coordinating activities across many nations on the Pacific Rim.[7]

From an economic perspective, this solves two problems with respect to risk: trying something new and uncertain when the results may be nil, which will tell *others* (a social gain) what not to do, and since you can apply again even if you "failed", this *rule* (an economic institutional issue) thus incentivizes the long-term learning of the "right stuff" needed to ultimately deliver the ten-fold return! Similar examples of *strategic* use of resources and *incentives to learn* would be critical for many of the small countries mentioned, to break out of the "irons" and catch new winds on the global markets.[8] Extra effort is needed for this purpose.

"Learning by doing" may then not be enough to improve productivity through a creative, inventive and "disruptive" level, only at the current innovation level (Arrow, 1962). To break out of the irons, new creative and inventive ideas are needed, especially in markets that trade in ideas, which are simply too complex to rationalize. Experimenting with new ideas are instead needed and that takes trial and error. Many new ideas, of high potential or impact, must be tried to discover if they are grains that multiply or weed.

A similar problem exists in academia where the confirmation of existing theories, rather than the falsification of theories,[9] is prioritized.[10] This thus leads to a focus on marginal contributions based on existing material, which is publishable and merit building. We all know that this is not how ground-breaking insights – "blue sky" research – come about, but such a risk-averse approach is

276 *Eskil Ullberg*

also found in academia. Theories must be able to be rejected if we are to learn something new and this has to have academic merit as well.

What is missing may thus be the *incentives to learn*. These require the funding of high-risk, high-potential ideas, both academic (science) and industrial (technological inventions). The only way to learn this is by *experimenting* with a large number of ideas. We need to "water the ground", not simply enforce "hard prioritization".[11]

It is the ground and the *seeds of knowledge* that are more important than "picking the winners". One has to let the weeds grow together with the seeds, not risk prematurely ripping up the harvest of what is sown, as we cannot, rationally, say up front which will bring the results. If we accidentally rip up the harvest with the weeds, we reduce the multiplying returns (of what grows), not only the marginal costs (water for the weed). When we know which plants produce, then we tend to them, multiply them, and burn the costly weeds.

We may thus not need a new rational approach to growth, but an age-old understanding of the high risk of not ripping up the future before fruition, justifying such action by employing the rational argument of price (value) equating to marginal cost. In the short term, when all risk is gone, yes (for the sake of efficiency), but in the long term a resounding NO. Growth happens only through individuals, people, humans taking personal risks with money and careers.

Creating a culture of risk-taking would be the medicine for many small countries who wish to be competitive in a global digital economy. *Teaching facts* on the returns gained from watering the fields is then a beginning (Ullberg, 2015b, Chapter 5).

Practically, to reduce risk in order to spur investment in new ideas, I would also propose the "creative company" (Ullberg, 2012), which shifts the incentive from more of the same to more of the new by reducing risk in inventions through: zero taxation, focusing on technology that can be sold, and providing incentives to invest rationally through high capitalization.

Then a research programme on risk-taking should be started, favouring falsification as method and learning by trying new high-risk, high-potential ideas.

Conclusions

This overview and initial discussion of the dramatic shift toward trade in ideas as a main contributor to world trade in terms of value has indicated that in the digital economy we need policies for creating this intellectual capital, perhaps especially impersonally tradable intellectual property rights, like patents and copyrights. This process is a high-risk process as there is no certainty that the new knowledge will be productive or not. Policies that create incentives to invest more in such high-risk assets and trade is therefore key. Falsification of hypotheses must be at the top of the academic agenda, not simply confirming marginal extensions to what we already hold true. The digitalization of trade and finding ways to encourage risk-taking in transacting in the global exchange of ideas and intellectual property rights will result in a broad trade in ideas.

Notes

1 The WTO TRIPS agreement today includes these seven intellectual property rights.
2 The management of risk between entities cooperating to create input to, or produce, new goods or services has now become a more complex issue than a simple "supplier–buyer" relationship in a "linear" manufacturing process of *physical* goods. See "Risk Management" (Ullberg et al., 2002) which discusses five historic steps from an "in house" linear production process to parallelism and real time "cross the globe" services.
3 There are also other reasons, see "The Language of Trust" (Ullberg, 2015a), which analyses the strategies firm licensing patents use to create trust in each other's actions to cooperate.
4 See the work of Michael Spence (e.g. Spence and Leipzig, 2010).
5 This study was funded by VINNOVA, Sweden's innovation agency in 2017 and finalized June 2018. The report is the basis for a forthcoming "Springer Briefs" publication in 2019.
6 Leif Johansson, Swedish industrialist and former president at IVA, the Royal Swedish Academy of Engineering Sciences, during the seminar: "Global Competitiveness and Creativity", Stockholm, 22 November 2017.
7 Personal communication with Ambassador Alejandro Jara, former Vice DG at WTO Legal and Research.
8 Irons: The "trapped" condition a sailing ship finds itself in when the bow of the ship is headed into the wind and the ship has stalled and is unable to manoeuvre.
9 Karl Popper: A theory should be scrutinized by experiments, rejecting classical induction for empirical sciences.
10 Communication with Professor Nils-Eric Sahlin at IVA, 27 November 2017.
11 Leif Johansson, during the seminar: "Global Competitiveness and Creativity", Stockholm, 22 November 2017.

References

Arrow, J.K., 1962. The economic implications of learning by doing. *The Review of Economic Studies* 29, 155–173.
Ho, A., Reich, J., Nesterko, S., Seaton, D., Mullaney, T., Waldo, J., Chuang, I., 2014. HarvardX and MITx: The first year of open online courses, Fall 2012–Summer 2013. SSRN scholarly paper no. ID 2381263.
Leering, R., 2017. 3D printing: A threat to global trade. [WWW document]. ING. https://think.ing.com/reports/3d-printing-a-threat-to-global-trade/.
Lejeune, J., 2017. After the elections: Will the 4th Industrial Revolution be on the agenda of regulators? [WWW document]. Lejeune Association Management. URL www.lejeune.nl/en/whitepapers/after-the-elections-will-the-4th-industrial-revolution-be-on-the-agenda-of-regulators-2/ (accessed 8 November 2017).
Lev, B., 2018. Ending the accounting-for-intangibles status quo. *European Accounting Review*. https://doi.org/10.1080/09638180.2018.1521614.
Lin, C.Y.-Y., Edvinsson, L., 2008. National intellectual capital: Comparison of the Nordic countries. *Journal of Intellectual Capital* 9, 525–545. https://doi.org/10.1108/14691930810913140.

278   *Eskil Ullberg*

North, D.C., 1981. *Structure and Change in Economic History*. New York: W.W. Norton.

Ostrom, E., 2010. Beyond markets and states: Polycentric governance of complex economic systems. *The American Economic Review* 100(3), 641–672.

Spence, M., Leipzig, D., 2010. *The Growth Report: Strategies for Sustained Growth and Inclusive Development*. Commission on Growth and Development, The World Bank.

Ståhle, P., Ståhle, S., Lin, C.Y.Y., 2015. Intangibles and national economic wealth: A new perspective on how they are linked. *Journal of Intellectual Capital* 16, 20–57. https://doi.org/10.1108/JIC-02-2014-0017.

Ullberg, E., 2012. *Trade in Ideas: Performance and Behavioral Properties of Markets in Patents*. New York: Springer.

Ullberg, E., 2015a. *The Language of Trust and Reciprocity in Markets in Patents: A Sociological Analysis of Property Rights on Messages Resolving Uncertainty in Exchange in Ideas*. IP2 Working Paper No. 15016, Stanford IP2 Program.

Ullberg, E. (Ed.), 2015b. *New Perspectives on Internationalization and Competitiveness*. Cham: Springer.

Ullberg, E., 2017. Trade Dialogues: Eskil Ullberg (full lecture). YouTube [WWW document]. URL www.youtube.com/watch?v=boKyIGSk8Pw (accessed 28 February 2019).

Ullberg, E., Edvinsson, L., Lin, J.Y., 2017. *The Swedish IA Gap&Space for Competitiveness in a Global World: Complacency in Economic – Social – Environment Agendas and Strategy to Inform New Policy*. Published by the authors under creative commons license.

Ullberg, E., Edvinsson, L., Lin, J.Y., 2019a. *Intangible Asset Gap in Global Competitiveness: Complacency in Economic, Social and Environmental Agendas*. Cham: Springer Nature.

Ullberg, E., Maurer, A., Magdeleine, J., 2019b. *Statistics Framework for Trade in Ideas*. Geneva: IMIT.

Ullberg, E., Rodriguez, E., Stormby, N., 2002. Risk management: From portfolio strategy to value creating system strategy. *Geneva Papers on Risk and Insurance – Issues and Practice* 27, 467–476. https://doi.org/doi:10.1111/1468-0440.00185.

Zhenghao, C., Alcorn, B., Christensen, G., Eriksson, N., Koller, D., Emanuel, E.J., 2015. Who's benefiting from MOOCs, and why. *Harvard Business Review*. [WWW document]. URL https://hbr.org/2015/09/whos-benefiting-from-moocs-and-why (accessed 15 November 2017).

20 Revisiting the intellectual capital research landscape

A systematic literature review

Henri Hussinki, Tatiana Garanina, Johannes Dumay and Erik Steinhöfel

Introduction

Since the late 1990s, intangible value drivers of the firm, such as intellectual capital (IC), have been the topic of active debate in academic literature and the business press. Interest in intangibles and IC grew to its current level because of changes that took place in economies worldwide, such as the digitalisation of businesses and key knowledge assets, and the servitisation of economies. In addition, practitioner-based academic research (e.g., Edvinsson and Malone, 1997; Sveiby, 1997) managed to convincingly argue about the significant role of IC in the era of the knowledge economy and therefore catch the attention of scholars, managers and policymakers. As a result, a considerable number of academic research papers are being published on the subject.

Because of the growing number of contributions, several literature reviews have tried to recap and summarise the literature. For example:

- Cañibano, García-Ayuso and Sánchez (2000) reviewed pre-2000 literature on accounting for intangibles.
- Petty and Guthrie (2000) conducted a review on measurement, reporting and management of IC.
- Serenko et al. (2010) conducted a scientometric analysis on IC and knowledge management literature published from 1994 to 2008.
- Guthrie, Ricceri and Dumay (2012) identified the performative third stage of IC research.
- Dumay and Garanina (2013) identified the ecosystem-based fourth stage of IC research.
- Inkinen (2015) focused on empirical literature on IC and firm performance.
- Dumay, Guthrie and Rooney (2018) reviewed the critical IC literature to establish whether IC research needed to break free from organisational boundaries and become multidisciplinary.

These literature reviews have provided scholars with progress reports on the intangibles and IC literature and valuable ideas for future research.

This literature review is motivated by a recent paper that demonstrates that even though European and Australasian researchers and scholars differ from their American counterparts with regard to defining IC or intangible resources, their meanings overlap and are mostly focused on the same intangible value drivers of a firm (Cuozzo et al., 2017). Thus, in light of current knowledge, a comprehensive literature review must cover both intangibles and IC literature domains. Since 2000, regions such as Asia and Africa have become increasingly involved; thus, it is important to study the continents side-by-side and determine their scholarly output on IC research. For example, it is already known that European and Australian scholars have focused on the IC concept, whereas American researchers have given more attention to intangible resources, such as brands and patents (Cuozzo et al., 2017). But what about researchers form the other regions? Have they followed the American or European example, or perhaps developed their own approaches to IC research?

The primary objective of this paper is to examine which elements of IC have been researched since 2000 and whether they have been researched as a subset of issues in isolation of each other or as a whole. It is a common argument that different elements of IC, such as human, structural and relational capital, have synergetic relationships and provide benefits for a firm (e.g., create value) in different combinations (Albertini, 2016; Inkinen, 2015). For example, human capital is argued to be the main source of a firm's creativity and competitive advantage (Roslender and Fincham, 2004), but it can be ineffective if there is a lack of structural and relational capital support. In addition, even a high level of structural capital is not enough if a firm does not have knowledgeable employees (human capital) to take advantage of it. Also, knowledge embedded in and available through relationships (relational capital) is better absorbed by a firm with high levels of human capital than a firm with low levels of human capital, whereas structural capital in terms of maintained and updated databases and information systems helps a firm to keep track of and utilise its relational capital.

Thus, another motivating aspect for this study is to learn if the global IC research community has provided a sufficient body of scientific knowledge from the multi-element IC perspective. This is important because it can be assumed that multi-element IC studies provide more valuable insights into IC research and practice than single-element IC studies. Inclusion of accounting and managerial journals is crucial in this type of literature review as both have published numerous papers on IC, with unique and equally important contributions. Accounting scholars are traditionally more interested in intangibles on the company's balance sheet, whereas management scholars have traditionally focused on recognising and utilising IC as a value-driver of a firm.

This SLR takes a novel and multi-disciplinary view of IC by reviewing all the relevant research papers from the 20 top accounting and 20 top management journals published between 2000 and 2017. It provides insights on IC research models in terms of their preference for a single element or multiple elements, by discussing and critiquing the current state of the IC literature and

Revisiting the IC research landscape 281

by offering transformative ideas for future research directions. Next, this paper will provide details of the methodology of the SLR which will be followed by the results, a discussion and conclusions.

Methodology

When conducting a literature review, it is important to choose the correct body of literature, to not bias the results (Massaro, Dumay and Guthrie, 2016). For this reason, a rigorous, structured literature review methodology was applied, as discussed by Massaro, Dumay and Guthrie (2016), to identify relevant articles devoted to research on intangibles and IC in the leading accounting and management journals. The research articles were identified and selected for this study by following a structured six-phase procedure.

Phase 1: The 20 top academic journals in the fields of both accounting and management were chosen. Following the approach of Massaro, Dumay and Guthrie (2016), they were selected based on Google Scholar Metrics, which lists the top academic journals based on citations received in the last five years for a wide variety of categories and subcategories. It also provides a broader coverage of literature sources than Web of Science or Scopus (Harzing and Alakangas, 2016). Based on their quality, relevance and impact, the accounting and management journals listed in Table 20.1 were considered for further analysis.

Phase 2: The individual articles were searched directly via the journals' homepages by using local website search engines. All articles published from 2000 to 2017 were taken into consideration. During an article search, it is crucial to use appropriate keywords to find the right body of literature. Based on the approach of Eccles and Krzus (2010), the following keywords were used to search literature from the journal web pages: "intangible asset★", "intellectual asset★", "intangible capital", "intellectual capital" and "intangible★". After the initial search, removal of duplicates and delimitation based on the year of publication, the number of academic papers was 2,147 and 4,172 for accounting and management journals, respectively.

Phase 3: Based on the title, those articles that did not resonate with the research objectives of this paper were excluded. Thus, if a title did not appear to relate to accounting or managerial research on IC or intangibles, it was deleted from the shortlist. At this point, the number of potentially relevant papers was cut significantly, to 532 for accounting journals and 1,561 for management journals.

Phase 4: The next step was to exclude articles from the shortlist based on the abstracts. At this point, book reviews, discussion articles and editorials/ introductions were excluded because they do not provide research results based on detailed methodological support, which may bias the results of further analysis. As a result, the number of potentially relevant papers was reduced to 349 for accounting journals and 427 for management journals.

Phase 5: Based on observations of the full texts, articles that had only a marginal focus on intangibles or IC were excluded. For example, those articles that

282   Henri Hussinki et al.

Table 20.1 Top 20 accounting and management journals according to Google Scholar Metrics

Top 20 accounting journals	Top 20 management journals
Accounting & Finance	*Academy of Management Journal*
Accounting and Business Research	*Academy of Management Review*
Accounting Horizons	*Entrepreneurship Theory and Practice*
Accounting, Auditing & Accountability Journal	*Harvard Business Review*
Accounting, Organizations and Society	*Industrial Marketing Management*
Auditing: A Journal of Practice & Theory	*Journal of Business Research*
Contemporary Accounting Research	*Journal of Business Venturing*
Critical Perspectives on Accounting	*Journal of Corporate Finance*
European Accounting Review	*Journal of Management*
International Journal of Accounting Information Systems	*Journal of Management Studies*
International Tax and Public Finance	*Journal of Marketing*
Journal of Accounting and Economics	*Journal of Operations Management*
Journal of Accounting and Public Policy	*Journal of Product Innovation Management*
Journal of Accounting Research	*Journal of the Academy of Marketing Science*
Journal of Business Finance & Accounting	*Management Decision*
Management Accounting Research	*Management Science*
National Tax Journal	*Omega*
Review of Accounting Studies	*Organization Science*
The Accounting Review	*Strategic Management Journal*
The British Accounting Review	*Technological Forecasting and Social Change*

Source: https://scholar.google.com/citations?view_op=top_venues&hl=en&vq=bus_accounting taxation.

used intangibles or IC only as control variables in their empirical models or did not reflect the role of intangibles or IC in the interpretation of the results were excluded. The final 325 articles from the 20 top accounting journals and 265 articles from the 20 top management journals reflect a "corpus of scholarly literature, to develop insights, critical reflections, future research paths and research questions" (Massaro, Dumay and Guthrie, 2016) in the fields of intangibles and IC.

Phase 6: NVivo software was utilised to code the abstracts and full texts of the chosen articles. The coding protocol for each reviewed article comprised the following information: name of author/authors, year of publication, country of origin of the first author and the elements of intangibles or IC in focus in each article.

Results

The home country of the affiliated university of each first author was used as a measure for each article's country of origin. Africa was represented by countries such as Egypt and South Africa; Asia included countries such as China, Japan, Singapore and Taiwan; the Americas were represented by the United

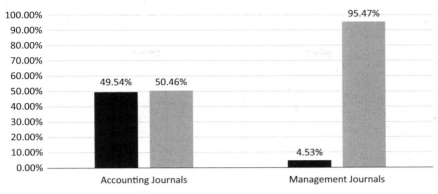

Figure 20.1 The distribution between accounting and managerial papers on IC and intangibles.

States, Canada, Brazil and Mexico; and Europe included several countries from Continental Europe and the United Kingdom. In addition, Australia and New Zealand formed a group of their own.

Next, to establish whether the article was focused on accounting for intangibles or IC, the research perspective of the papers was coded in terms of the elements of intangibles or IC in focus in each article. One group represents those papers that focus on intangibles recognised by different accounting standards (research and development costs, advertising expenses, patents and other capitalised intangibles, etc.), while the second group consists of articles devoted to IC. The distribution of papers based on this coding is represented in Figure 20.1.

The results reflect that accounting journals have published approximately the same amount of papers devoted to both perspectives, while management journals have focused much more on the managerial, non-accounting approach towards IC. To accord with the primary theme of this book, only those papers devoted to the managerial perspective on IC were retained for our analysis, while the sample related to accounting intangibles was reserved for other future research endeavours. During the period 2000 to 2017, there were 164 and 253 papers on IC published in the 20 top accounting and management journals, respectively, which are considered during the following analysis. The publication trend over the years is represented in Figure 20.2.

As can be seen from Figure 20.2, accounting and management journals published approximately the same amount of papers on IC up until 2006. The fact that this changed in 2007 was most likely due to the application of International Financial Reporting Standards (IFRS) in Europe and enhancements of the harmonisation process between IFRS and Generally Accepted Accounting Principles in the United States (US GAAP). At the same

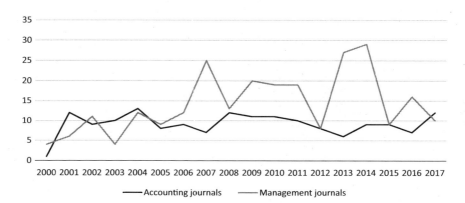

Figure 20.2 The dynamics of the annual number of managerial papers on IC and intangibles.

time, the numbers of papers in management journals reflect a clear trend of increase in 2007. Researchers at that time argued that accounting standards were not capable of capturing the real value of intangible assets, so they started to analyse in detail the non-financial information disclosed in annual reports and other data sources (e.g., Abdolmohammadi et al., 2006; Cerbioni and Parbonetti, 2007). The main topic in post-2006 literature is related to "measuring the unmeasurable" and providing different approaches on investigating "out-of-balance-sheet" intangibles (e.g., Reed, Lubatkin and Srinivasan, 2006; Whitwell, Lukas and Hill, 2007). After 2005, journals from both domains started to publish papers where new approaches to structure IC were introduced. These investigated, for example, reputation (Rindova et al., 2005), customer satisfaction (Aksoy et al., 2008), the efficiency of managerial accounting innovations (Ax and Greve, 2017), environmental disclosures (Middleton, 2015), environmental strategic capital (Clarkson et al., 2011) and ethical capital (McPhail, 2009).

Figure 20.2 shows a surge of management journal papers also after 2008, when the Global Financial Crisis (GFC) hit the world economy. The research papers from that period reflect the importance of IC and its elements for optimising different intra-organisational processes (e.g., Laperche, Lefebvre and Langlet, 2011) and the role of non-financial disclosure for different stakeholders (e.g., Brüggen, Vergauwen and Dao, 2009; Francis, Nanda and Olsson, 2008; Luft, 2009). There was also a sudden increase in the number of published papers from 2012 to 2015, especially in the management journals, a deeper analysis of which showed that during that period there was an increased interest in different group dynamics that help companies to generate IC. Some papers investigate the role of CEO's and board of directors' IC (e.g., Datta and Iskandar-Datta, 2014; Vandenbroucke, Knockaert and Ucbasaran, 2016); some are focused on alliances and networking (Arribas, Hernández and Vila, 2013; Elfenbein and Zenger, 2013) and others investigate group and micro-team dynamics and their

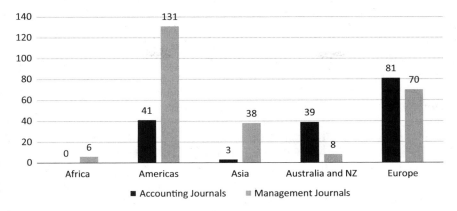

Figure 20.3 IC and intangibles articles by continent: 2000–2017.

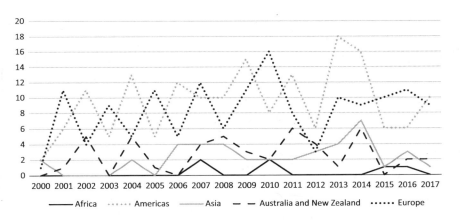

Figure 20.4 The dynamics of the annual number of managerial papers on IC per continent.

role in the company's value creation (e.g., Kemper, Schilke and Brettel, 2013). Moreover, there is also a significant research interest in social capital, with 25% of all papers published in 2012 to 2015 focused on this subject (e.g., Du, Guariglia and Newman, 2015; Purchase, Olaru and Denize, 2014).

The next step of analysis is related to the home country of the author and continent of origin of the publication, which was coded based on the first author's university affiliation. The results are represented in Figures 20.3 and 20.4.

As can be seen from Figures 20.3 and 20.4, the majority of the papers that were published between 2000 and 2017 fall into the categories of the Americas and Europe. Also, it can be noticed that the share of managerial IC papers

286 *Henri Hussinki et al.*

published in accounting journals is higher in Europe than in the Americas, while the trend is the opposite for the papers in management journals. The Americas, mainly represented by researchers from the United States, and Europe, with the highest share of papers being from the United Kingdom, are the leading continents/regions according to the amount of papers published during the observation period. It can also be seen that the authors from Asian universities have increased their research productivity since 2005, publishing significantly more papers, specifically in management, rather than accounting, journals. Besides, it seems that researchers from Australian and New Zealand universities publish their research on IC to a great extent in accounting journals.

The subsequent step of the analysis is devoted to studying which elements of IC were the focus of research during the period 2000 to 2017. This is an especially intriguing step, as contemporary studies (e.g., Albertini, 2016; Inkinen, 2015) strongly suggest that IC elements must interact with each other to create value and improve different performance outcomes in firms (e.g., innovation performance). In other words, IC models that focus only on a single element are essentially missing some critical building blocks and do not necessarily produce as valuable and relevant research results as the multi-element IC models. To make a distinction between multiple-element and single-element taxonomies, papers were coded according to their approach to IC elements. Thus, papers that use the established tripartite framework of IC (human, relational and structural capital), other approaches to IC (e.g., innovation capital, trust capital, strategic capital and entrepreneurial capital – see Inkinen, 2015), the tripartite framework extended with some other elements of IC, and a group of "new approaches", which included some contemporary elements of IC such as reputational capital and environmental capital, were differentiated. The basic coding structure for IC, therefore, was amended each time a new approach emerged or when new multi-element approaches were noticed.

The overall trend regarding single-element versus multi-element approaches is presented in Figure 20.5.

As can be seen in Figure 20.5, multi-element approaches started to dominate after the GFC in 2008, with researchers and managers probably focusing on how investments in different elements of IC could help their companies overcome difficult financial situations and improve intra-organisational processes and performance. The situation changed in 2012 when single-element approaches started to dominate, with particular attention given to human capital and social capital.

The overall data for the accounting and managerial journals are presented in Table 20.2. It is evident that academic research does not obey a universal approach towards the structure of IC. The results reflect that papers published in the accounting journals are more often devoted to a multi-element (66.2%) than a single-element (33.8%) approach. Authors frequently apply the classical tripartite taxonomy of IC and even more frequently extend it with one or multiple further elements of IC to give a new edge to their analysis. This is in contrast to the management journals, where researchers prefer single-element

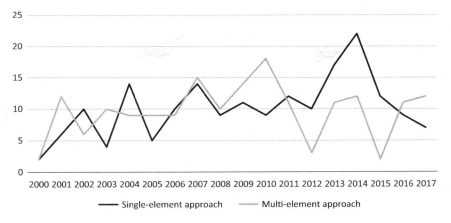

Figure 20.5 The research trend regarding a single-element vs multi-element approach on IC.

approaches to IC (61.4%), with particular attention to social capital (35.0%) and human capital (17.5%). Thus, less than 40% of the papers in these journals are devoted to studying multiple IC elements. Of those multi-element studies, most focus on the classical tripartite model of IC or extended versions.

Summing up the papers from the accounting and management journals, shares of single-element and multi-element approaches to IC are almost equal (51.0% and 49.0%). However, switching the focus to continents provides other kinds of results. The statistics show that researchers representing the Americas are responsible for the majority of the single-element studies on IC (24.5% of the entire sample), with a focus on social capital (10.6%) and human capital (9.8%). This contrasts with the European academics, who write the majority of their research papers on the interrelation between different elements of IC and their combined influence on organisational processes and value creation (22.3%). The "European approach" has also been adopted by Asian (5.6%) and Australian (5.9%) researchers, who more often investigate a multi-element structure of IC and the relationship between different IC elements.

Discussion and conclusions

As the recent academic research has argued, IC creates value for organisations through the interaction of its different elements (e.g., Albertini, 2016; Inkinen, 2015). Thus, the objective of this structured literature review was to explore whether the top-tier academic IC research has provided a sufficient body of scientific knowledge from the multi-element IC perspective. In addition, this paper explored different scholarly traditions with regard to the study of IC, by comparing research approaches of scholars from different continents.

Table 20.2 IC elements in the focus of the analysis in accounting and management journals (as a percentage of the total sample)

IC elements in focus	Accounting journals						Management journals						The whole sample of journals					
	AF	AME	Asia	ANZ	EUR	Total	AF	AME	Asia	ANZ	EUR	Total	AF	AME	Asia	ANZ	EUR	Total
Single-element approach	**0.00**	**10.29**	**0.00**	**10.29**	**13.24**	**33.82**	**1.35**	**33.18**	**7.17**	**1.79**	**17.94**	**61.43**	**0.84**	**24.51**	**4.46**	**5.01**	**16.16**	**50.97**
Human capital	0.00	5.15	0.00	3.68	8.09	16.91	0.90	12.56	1.35	0.00	2.69	17.49	0.56	9.75	0.84	1.39	4.74	17.27
Relational capital	0.00	0.74	0.00	1.47	0.74	2.94	0.00	1.79	0.45	0.00	0.90	3.14	0.00	1.39	0.28	0.56	0.84	3.06
Structural capital	0.00	1.47	0.00	2.21	1.47	5.15	0.00	0.00	0.00	0.00	0.00	0.00	0.00	0.56	0.00	0.84	0.56	1.95
Social capital	0.00	1.47	0.00	2.94	0.74	5.15	0.00	16.14	4.93	0.90	13.00	34.98	0.00	10.58	3.06	1.67	8.36	23.68
Other single elements (brand, innovation, entrepreneurship capital)	0.00	1.47	0.00	0.00	2.21	3.68	0.45	2.69	0.45	0.90	1.35	5.83	0.28	2.23	0.28	0.56	1.67	5.01
Multi-element approach	**0.00**	**12.50**	**0.74**	**13.24**	**39.71**	**66.18**	**0.90**	**16.14**	**8.52**	**1.35**	**11.66**	**38.57**	**0.56**	**14.76**	**5.57**	**5.85**	**22.28**	**49.03**
Tripartite taxonomy (human, relational and structural capitals)	0.00	0.00	0.00	2.94	13.97	16.91	0.00	4.04	4.48	0.00	3.59	12.11	0.00	2.51	2.79	1.11	7.52	13.93
Elements of tripartite taxonomy together with other elements of IC	0.00	2.94	0.00	6.62	12.50	22.06	0.45	7.62	1.79	0.45	3.59	13.90	0.28	5.85	1.11	2.79	6.96	16.99
Other multiple IC elements	0.00	9.56	0.74	3.68	13.24	27.21	0.45	4.48	2.24	0.90	4.48	12.56	0.28	6.41	1.67	1.95	7.80	18.11
Total	0.00	22.79	0.74	23.53	52.94	100.00	2.24	49.33	15.70	3.14	29.60	100.00	1.39	39.28	10.03	10.86	38.44	100.00

Note: Africa (AF), Americas (AME), Australia and New Zealand (ANZ), Europe (EUR)

The results show that, overall, research published in the 20 top accounting and management journals between 2000 and 2017 focused equally on single- and multi-element IC approaches. This finding is positive news for the IC research domain, as around half of the top-tier journal papers have taken the multi-element approach to IC and provided valuable knowledge for their readers. On a more practical level, this means that the more complex multi-element IC models (e.g., Bontis, 1998; Inkinen et al., 2017) have received and will likely continue to receive rigorous scientific testing. This will gradually improve the multi-element IC research models and pave the way for relevant and reliable research output.

However, there are significant differences between the two most prominent groups, the American and European researchers. The Americans have preferred to focus on single elements, while the Europeans have favoured multi-element approaches. The American single-element IC approach overlooks other underlying elements and as such is not able to provide more detailed knowledge about IC-based value creation. However, the advantage of this approach is that it provides a simpler understanding of IC, which may be of benefit to scholars and practitioners who are unfamiliar with IC and intangibles and who may go on to research multiple IC elements after getting familiar with IC and intangibles though single elements. Regardless, this finding prompts a call for broadening the American research focus to multiple-element approaches.

Implications and future research

The findings from this literature review have different limitations. First, only the 20 top management and accounting journals were considered. A second limitation is that the sample papers were analysed without taking into account potential connections with other papers; for example, it is possible that in the American papers, multiple-element approaches to IC were initially pursued, which subsequently led to the application of single-element approaches. Thus, investigating interrelations of contributions might be a promising research opportunity. In this context, it needs to be taken into account that papers reviewed in this study are probably related to contributions that were not published in the 20 top management and accounting journals. Also, a bibliometric analysis might provide reasons for the occurrence of some of the results presented here.

Third, only those contributions from the initial sample that focus on the managerial perspective were included in this study. Thus, a further avenue for research lies in analysis of the contribution of accounting-related papers. This analysis would be valuable because accounting looks deeper into understanding the value of IC and intangibles. In order to manage something, there is always the challenge of measuring it, which in the case of IC and intangibles, has always proven to be a challenge. Accounting has several qualitative aspects that need to be taken into consideration, such as relevance and faithful representation, alongside the enhancing characteristics of comparability, verifiability, timeliness and understandability (IASB, 2018, p. 6). Without considering these characteristics

Henri Hussinki et al.

in either a single- or multi-element approach to IC and intangibles research, the findings may not be complete. Thus, researchers need to extend their research approaches to ensure what is being measured will make a positive contribution to the management of IC.

References

Abdolmohammadi, M., Simnett, R., Thibodeau, J. C., and Wright, A. M. (2006), "Sell-side analysts' reports and the current external reporting model", *Accounting Horizons*, Vol. 20 No. 4, pp. 375–389.

Aksoy, L., Cooil, B., Groening, C., Keiningham, T. L., and Yalçın, A. (2008), "The long-term stock market valuation of customer satisfaction", *Journal of Marketing*, Vol. 72 No. 4, pp. 105–122.

Albertini, E. (2016), "An inductive typology of the interrelations between different components of intellectual capital", *Management Decision*, Vol. 54 No. 4, pp. 887–901.

Arribas, I., Hernández, P., and Vila, J. E. (2013), "Guanxi, performance and innovation in entrepreneurial service projects", *Management Decision*, Vol. 51 No. 1, pp. 173–183.

Ax, C., and Greve, J. (2017), "Adoption of management accounting innovations: Organizational culture compatibility and perceived outcomes", *Management Accounting Research*, Vol. 34, pp. 59–74.

Bontis, N. (1998), "Intellectual capital: An exploratory study that develops measures and models", *Management Decision*, Vol. 36 No. 2, pp. 63–76.

Brüggen, A., Vergauwen, P., and Dao, M. (2009), "Determinants of intellectual capital disclosure: Evidence from Australia", *Management Decision*, Vol. 47 No. 2, pp. 233–245.

Cañibano, L., García-Ayuso, M., and Sánchez, P. (2000), "Accounting for intangibles: A literature review", *Journal of Accounting Literature*, Vol. 19, pp. 102–130.

Cerbioni, F., and Parbonetti, A. (2007), "Exploring the effects of corporate governance on intellectual capital disclosure: An analysis of European biotechnology companies", *European Accounting Review*, Vol. 16 No. 4, pp. 791–826.

Clarkson, P. M., Li, Y., Richardson, G. D., and Vasvari, F. P. (2011), "Does it really pay to be green? Determinants and consequences of proactive environmental strategies", *Journal of Accounting and Public Policy*, Vol. 30 No. 2, pp. 122–144.

Cuozzo, B., Dumay, J., Palmaccio, M., and Lombardi, R. (2017), "Intellectual capital disclosure: A structured literature review", *Journal of Intellectual Capital*, Vol. 18 No. 1, 9–28.

Datta, S., and Iskandar-Datta, M. (2014), "Upper-echelon executive human capital and compensation: Generalist vs specialist skills", *Strategic Management Journal*, Vol. 35 No. 12, pp. 1853–1866.

Du, J., Guariglia, A., and Newman, A. (2015), "Do social capital building strategies influence the financing behavior of Chinese private small and medium-sized enterprises?", *Entrepreneurship Theory and Practice*, Vol. 39 No. 3, pp. 601–631.

Dumay, J., and Garanina, T. (2013), "Intellectual capital research: A critical examination of the third stage", *Journal of Intellectual Capital*, Vol. 14 No. 1, pp. 10–25.

Dumay, J., Guthrie, J., and Rooney, J. (2018), "The critical path of intellectual capital", in J. Guthrie, J. Dumay, F. Ricceri and C. Nielsen (Eds), *The Routledge Companion to Intellectual Capital: Frontiers of Research, Practice and Knowledge*, London: Routledge, pp. 21–39.

Eccles, R. G., and Krzus, M. P. (2010), *One Report: Integrated Reporting for a Sustainable Strategy*, Hoboken, NJ: John Wiley & Sons.

Revisiting the IC research landscape 291

Edvinsson, L., and Malone, M. (1997), *Intellectual Capital: Realising Your Company's True Value by Finding Its Hidden Brainpower*, New York: HarperCollins.

Elfenbein, D.W., and Zenger, T. R. (2013), "What is a relationship worth? Repeated exchange and the development and deployment of relational capital", *Organization Science*, Vol. 25 No. 1, pp. 222–244.

Francis, J., Nanda, D., and Olsson, P. (2008), "Voluntary disclosure, earnings quality, and cost of capital", *Journal of Accounting Research*, Vol. 46 No. 1, pp. 53–99.

Guthrie, J., Ricceri, F., and Dumay, J. (2012), "Reflections and projections: A decade of intellectual capital accounting research", *British Accounting Review*, Vol. 44 No. 2, pp. 68–92.

Harzing, A.-W., and Alakangas, S. (2016), "Google Scholar, Scopus and the Web of Science: A longitudinal and cross-disciplinary comparison", *Scientometrics*, Vol. 106 No. 2, pp. 787–804.

IASB (2018), "*IFRS® Conceptual Framework Project Summary*", London: International Accounting Standards Board.

Inkinen, H. (2015), "Review of empirical research on intellectual capital and firm performance", *Journal of Intellectual Capital*, Vol. 16 No. 3, pp. 518–565.

Inkinen, H., Kianto, A., Vanhala, M., and Ritala, P. (2017), "Structure of intellectual capital: An international comparison", *Accounting, Auditing & Accountability Journal*, Vol. 30 No. 5, pp. 1160–1183.

Kemper, J., Schilke, O., and Brettel, M. (2013), "Social capital as a microlevel origin of organizational capabilities", *Journal of Product Innovation Management*, Vol. 30 No. 3, pp. 589–603.

Laperche, B., Lefebvre, G., and Langlet, D. (2011), "Innovation strategies of industrial groups in the global crisis: Rationalization and new paths", *Technological Forecasting and Social Change*, Vol. 78 No. 8, pp. 1319–1331.

Luft, J. (2009), "Nonfinancial information and accounting: A reconsideration of benefits and challenges", *Accounting Horizons*, Vol. 23 No. 3, pp. 307–325.

Massaro, M., Dumay, J., and Guthrie, J. (2016), "On the shoulders of giants: Undertaking a structured literature review in accounting", *Journal of Intellectual Capital*, Vol. 29 No. 5, pp. 767–801.

McPhail, K. (2009), "Where is the ethical knowledge in the knowledge economy? Power and potential in the emergence of ethical knowledge as a component of intellectual capital", *Critical Perspectives on Accounting*, Vol. 20 No. 7, pp. 804–822.

Middleton, A. (2015), "Value relevance of firms' integral environmental performance: Evidence from Russia", *Journal of Accounting and Public Policy*, Vol. 34 No. 2, pp. 204–211.

Petty, R., and Guthrie, J. (2000), "Intellectual capital literature review: Measurement, reporting and management", *Journal of Intellectual Capital*, Vol. 1 No. 2, pp. 155–176.

Purchase, S., Olaru, D., and Denize, S. (2014), "Innovation network trajectories and changes in resource bundles", *Industrial Marketing Management*, Vol. 43 No. 3, pp. 448–459.

Reed, K. K., Lubatkin, M., and Srinivasan, N. (2006), "Proposing and testing an intellectual capital-based view of the firm", *Journal of Management Studies*, Vol. 43 No. 4, pp. 867–893.

Rindova, V. P., Williamson, I. O., Petkova, A. P., and Sever, J. M. (2005), "Being good or being known: An empirical examination of the dimensions, antecedents, and consequences of organizational reputation", *Academy of Management Journal*, Vol. 48 No. 6, pp. 1033–1049.

Roslender, R., and Fincham, R. (2004), "Intellectual capital accounting in the UK: A field study perspective", *Accounting, Auditing & Accountability Journal*, Vol. 17 No. 2, pp. 178–209.

Serenko, A., Bontis, N., Booker, L., Sadeddin, K., and Hardie, T. (2010), "A scientometric analysis of knowledge management and intellectual capital academic literature (1994–2008)", *Journal of Knowledge Management*, Vol. 14 No. 1, pp. 3–23.

Sveiby, K. E. (1997), *The New Organizational Wealth: Managing & Measuring Knowledge-based Assets*, San Francisco, CA: Berrett-Koehler.

Vandenbroucke, E., Knockaert, M., and Ucbasaran, D. (2016), "Outside board human capital and early stage high-tech firm performance", *Entrepreneurship Theory and Practice*, Vol. 40 No. 4, pp. 759–779.

Whitwell, G. J., Lukas, B. A., and Hill, P. (2007), "Stock analysts' assessments of the shareholder value of intangible assets", *Journal of Business Research*, Vol. 60 No. 1, pp. 84–90.

Epilogue

Leif Edvinsson

> The battle for control of the global economy in the 21st century, will be won and lost over control of innovation technologies.
>
> (Tom Orlik, Bloomberg)

Intellectual capital in the digital economy – aha

In this book there are many great contributions to the perspectives of the book title, on different levels. The above quote is a point of departure for knowledge navigation.

Looking at the position of National Intellectual Capital and the ranking of nations provides a deeper position. Since 2013 Bloomberg has been publishing annually the list of the 10 Most Innovative Economies, based on seven equally weighted metrics – initially analysed for more than 200 countries and ranking 60 countries. See more at www.bloomberg.com/graphics/2015-innovative-countries/.

The top ten Bloomberg Most Innovative Economies in 2019 are

1   South Korea
2   Germany
3   Finland
4   Switzerland
5   Israel
6   Singapore
7   Sweden
8   USA
9   Japan
10 France

The top position is shifting on this list, as well as in comparison with other listings, such as the GII – Global Innovation Index, by WIPO and Insead. See www.globalinnovationindex.org/Home.

The GII was based on 80 metrics for 129 economies in 2019; the GII is moving into its 12th edition. Each year the GII presents a thematic component

294　*Leif Edvinsson*

that tracks global innovation. In the 2019 edition, it analyses the medical innovation landscape of the next decade, looking at how technological and non-technological medical innovation will transform the delivery of healthcare worldwide. It also explores the role and dynamics of medical innovation as it shapes the future of healthcare, and the potential influence this may have on economic growth.

The top ten GII countries for 2019 are:

1　Switzerland
2　Sweden
3　USA
4　Netherlands
5　UK
6　Finland
7　Denmark
8　Singapore
9　Germany
10　Israel

This takes us to the NIC – National IC index by the New Club of Paris, and Dr Carol Lin and Leif Edvinsson. Initially based on 48 indicators, in the four major IC categories (Human Capital, Relational Capital, Organization Capital and Innovation Capital) for 40 countries, since initial research 20 years ago it has expanded to some 60 countries and more available statistical indicators, among others Sustainability National IC – SNIC as well as Health Indicators. See more in Chapter 11.

NIC and SNIC are comprehensive models covering a wide scope of intangibles. GII covers innovation only (with some human capital indicators). In addition, GII ranks over 120 countries, while both NIC and SNIC rank 59 countries. The correlation between them is high. But the trajectory line, rather than actual position, might be the more important barometer for the knowledge navigating of IC! Bruno Lanvin at Insead has also highlighted the shift of position in GII.

Top 10 listed Sustainable NIC countries are:

1　Denmark
2　Switzerland
3　Norway
4　Netherlands
5　Singapore
6　Finland
7　Sweden
8　Luxembourg
9　Canada
10　UAE

Epilogue 295

By looking at these lists several dimensions are highlighted such as taxonomy/distinctions, size of economies, technology culture, global networking infrastructure, political and societal innovativeness.

In the digital economy such ranking might indicate, especially, shifts in position and a valuable basis for IC policy development. This was among others prototyped in Sweden, as stated in Chapter 19. A core insight from this is the importance of

- Structural Capital in the form of societal infrastructure for learning, telecom and health;
- Global packaging of knowledge for trade on ideas, especially as IA – intangible assets;
- Innovativeness in non-technical dimensions such as contractual fabric and societal innovation;

It also highlights the importance of going beyond the Human Capital (HC) dimensions, to look for possibilities for leveraging the HC. This was initially called the IC multiplier (Edvinsson 2002). This and IA also indicate that the core of IC might be in the Relational Capital dimensions, the in-between space of connectivity as well as contactivity. A quest for wisdom is reamplified. Perhaps the evolution of wisdom gamification and training can instil more peacefulness?

Today we can also go deeper digitally, both into collective citizen capability dimensions as well as the brain and neuroscience dimensions.

What part of your brain is the driver of IC aspects? What technology can add to your intelligence as well as sustainability? Which health policy programme will provide the best cultivation of National IC? Circular Economics, Blue Economics or the Wisdom Economics of not knowing? Trade on ideas might take us onto a new chapter of economics, as elaborated in Chapter 19? Much more research, many more case studies and rapid prototyping might guide us to a deeper knowing.

This book is an invitation to navigate deeper and longer into a new economics of IC and IA for wealth creation for future generations.

Happy IC futurizing,

Leif Edvinsson
The World's First Professor of Intellectual Capital

Reference

Edvinsson, Leif (2002) *Corporate Longitude: What You Need to Know to Navigate the Knowledge Economy*. Pearson/Financial Times, London; Bookhouse, Stockholm,

Index

3D Printing 207, 115, 215
academia 112, 117, 181, 276
academic entrepreneurship 108, 111, 112, 113
Accenture 245, 247
accounting 283, 284, 286, 289; balance sheet 220; standards 225, 268
accumulation 25, 157
acquisitions 69, 197, 257
administration 100, 109
advances simulation 215
advertising expenditures 243
Africa 280, 282
Agder Energy 5
agility 53, 60, 173, 235, 250
agreements 114, 249
AI 242, 249
AI Economy 253
Airbnb 20, 250
Aker BioMarine 4
algorithms 175, 204, 245, 247
alliances 182, 190, 220, 284
alphabet 243
alumni 112, 114, 116
Amadeus database 36
Amazon 243, 244
analysts 219
analytical tools 74, 92
analytics 215, 249
annual reports 182, 184, 185, 284
Apple 243, 244
approaches 49, 62, 112
apps 92, 244, 246
artificial intelligence 107
Asia 280, 282
assessment 80, 221, 225, 247
asymmetries 103, 220, 223
attitudes 32, 220, 225
Australian firms 182, 183, 190

Australian Securities Exchange (ASX) 200 firms 182
automation 54, 59, 60, 62

BACRI project 125, 126, 129
balance of payments 260
balanced Scorecard 90, 164, 211, 222
banks 184, 212, 217, 252
barriers 196, 253, 261
Belgium 126, 151, 152
benchmarking approach 222
best practices 25, 50, 58
bibliometric analysis 289
Big Data 14, 112, 113, 115, 117
biotechnologies 215
blockchain 256, 257, 260
Blockchain technologies 257, 259
Bloomberg 4, 293
Bloomberg Most Innovative Economies 293
Blue Economics 295
board of directors 284
book value 181, 184, 218
bots 242
brand value 208
Brazil 169, 283
business accelerator programmes 253
business: analytics 107, 114; areas 76, 78, 80; environment 76, 77, 80, 250; model innovation 258, 260, 263; models 19, 21; processes 76, 78, 222, 236, 274
buyers 25

Canada 139, 143, 203
career incubator 251
case study 124, 125
challenges 5, 21, 245, 253
China 62, 68, 70, 282
Chinese firms 63, 65, 69

Index

circular economy 27
cities 69, 98, 100, 123
classrooms 246, 247
clients 55, 59, 196; capital 227
clinical data 20, 129; practice 124, 126
closed innovation 9, 16, 247
cloud 11, 17, 107, 114; computing 111, 127, 251; platform 5; technologies 5, 18
cloud-based platforms 212
co-creation 9, 10
co-creativity 14
co-creators 8, 9, 16
code of conduct 34
codification 33
coding protocol 282
cognitive bias 124, 127, 129
cohesion 236, 241
collaboration tools 39, 64, 260
collaborative networks 69, 114
collective: innovation 13, 14; intelligence 13, 110, 114
community 13, 21, 33, 97, 115
company size 34, 36
competencies 9, 12, 69
competitiveness 3, 53, 64, 203
composite index 46, 50
connectivity and contactivity (CNC) 138, 152, 158
contracted research 114
control: function 88; variables 36, 282
cooperation 115, 196, 268
core competencies 221
corporate strategy 75, 77, 274
cost-based approach 224
cost of coordination 249
Creative Commons (CC) 244
Croatia 139
cross-fertilize 105, 110
cross-licensing 8, 15
crowdfunding 243, 244
crowdsourcing 48
cryptocurrencies 243, 257, 259
cultural movement 194, 204
culture 275, 276
curators 14
customer satisfaction 69, 185, 284
customer value creation 64, 67, 69
customers 197, 202, 208, 220, 226
cybersecurity 209

Danya Cebus 102, 103
databases 109, 114, 172
debate 32, 165, 174, 279

decision-making 110, 130, 208
Deloitte 262
democratisation 253
Denmark 139, 145, 147, 152
dependent variables 34, 154
development: capital 101; finance institutions 252
devices 60, 92, 245
digital age 93, 137, 154
digital: agreements 260; communication 174; disruption 113; economy 25, 46, 74, 92, 214, 295; future xxix, 6; goods 244, 249; impact 247, 251; infrastructure 107; platforms 247, 249; readiness 138, 154, 157; revolution 19, 39, 249; technologies 107, 111, 249; transformation 173, 214, 236, 243
Digital Single Market (DSM) 11
digitalization 111, 267, 273, 276
digitalized economy 274
dimensions 75, 112, 115, 126
directors 35, 65
disclosure 107, 222, 116, 183, 284
disclosure channels 117
disintermediation 247, 250, 260
disruption 247, 249, 256
disruptive technologies 215, 257, 263
distributors 25
diversity 16, 70, 168, 190, 200
Ducati 202
dynamic flows 220

e-learning platforms 115
earnings 80, 224
Economic Value Added (EVA™) 224
economies of scale 62, 127, 249
ecosystem value 247
Edna Pasher PhD & Associates 98
education: 123, 138, 159, 168; systems 113, 116, 245
efficiency 46
emerging economies 62
emerging: technologies 242, 256; topics iv, xxix; trends 241
employee: job satisfaction 64, 67, 68; relations 187
employers 190, 245, 205
endogenous growth 202
engagement platforms 11, 17
engineering 55, 126, 201, 202
Enterprise Innovation Efficiency Capability Index (EIECI) 46, 47
entertainment 164, 196, 242

298 *Index*

entrepreneurial: campus 114; capital 40, 286
entrepreneurialism 194, 198, 200, 202
entrepreneurs 105, 275
entrepreneurship 195, 261; education 114;
  garages 114
envisioning 138, 237
equality 20, 100
ethical capital 284
Europe 9, 92
European Bank for Reconstruction and
  Development (EDRB) 174
European Commission 211, 216, 246, 252
European economies 250
European Network of Living Labs 7
European Union 171, 172, 217, 236
Eurostat 172
evaluation system 10, 92
experts 24, 196, 207, 209
explicit knowledge 109, 259
exponential growth 214, 215
external relational capital 38, 39
externalisation 250
Exxon 243
eyewear 247

Facebook 113, 137, 244
feedback 69, 246, 247
Ferrari 202
financial: services 53, 54, 60; times 200
Finland 139, 148, 152, 154
Finnish firms 34
FinTech 243
flipped classrooms 247
forecasting 237
foundations 15, 113, 252
Franchising agreements 185, 190
Free and Open Source (FOSS) 244
frontiers 201, 236
functionality 11, 74
future research 109, 117, 263, 279

games 55, 57
gaps 175, 241, 250
GDP 145, 156, 175, 271
gender diversity 190
Germany 9, 145, 202, 294
Global Competitiveness Index (GCI) 171
Global Entrepreneurship Monitor 172
Global Innovation Index (GII) 171, 172,
  175, 293, 294
global market 97, 164
Global SNIC ranking 139
globalisation 251, 252, 253

goodness 194, 228
goods 76, 165, 198, 204
Google 212, 244
governance 168, 172; structure 18
government statistics 51
growth 11, 76, 80, 98
guidelines 12, 34, 209

happiness 197, 198
heads-up displays (HUDs) 247
healthcare sector 20, 21, 24, 216
hierarchical model 228
high education systems 113, 116
high yield assets 269
higher education 110, 113, 269
hits 187, 188, 190
holography 247
Holon 100, 101
Hong Kong 46, 50, 60, 152
hospitals 25, 126, 129, 130
human: assets 224; brains 124, 214;
  capital 32, 47, 64, 109, 190, 241,
  280; capital disclosure 190; capital
  efficiency 184; intelligence 19, 214, 215;
  resources 171, 173, 181, 262; resources
  directors 35
Human Development Index (HDI) 173

IAS 38 Intangible Assets 211
IC: disclosure 182, 183, 187, 190;
  measurement 184, 217; Measurement
  models 110, 221, 225; multiplier 295;
  Navigator 104; report 98, 103; rights
  183, 260
IC-index 223
ICT Development Index 2017 171
ideas 6, 16, 22, 25
identity management 10, 243
IEEE P7000 Ethical Design for
  Autonomous Intelligent Systems
  standard 215
IEEE P7000 series 215
IMD World Competitiveness Ranking
  (WCI) 172
IMF 267
immersive virtual reality 247
inclusion 14, 18, 20, 261, 280
inclusiveness 236, 241, 253
income-based approach 224
incubators 24, 114, 253
independent variables 34, 35
index 46, 222
India 21, 139, 145

Index   299

indicators 103, 110, 138, 170, 171, 172, 222
indices 217, 221, 222
Individual Capital 227
industrial economic theory 213
industrial economy 213, 214
industry 4.0 93, 215; indicators 170
information 137, 156, 157, 168; technology skills 154, 156
Initial Coin Offering (ICO) 259
innovation 4, 5, 46; ecosystem 9, 240; process 9, 13, 15; projects 5
Innovation Union Scoreboard (IUS) 171
Innovative Efficiency Capability Index (EIECI) 46, 47
innovative solutions 23
innovativeness 113
inputs 165, 171, 176
Instagram 137
institutions 245, 252, 253
insurance companies 252
intangible assets 77, 137, 267, 275; capital 217, 222, 226; capital management 217, 226
Intangible Capital Dynamic Value (IC-dVAL) 222
Intangible Capital Management Scoring System (ICMSS) 225, 226, 229
Intangible Capital Model (ICM) 226
intangibles 32, 280, 28; standardization xxxv, 217
Integrated Strategy Development (ISD) 74
intellectual: capital 7, 33, 38, 40, 63, 106, 113, 164, 181, 194, 206, 279; capital report 101; capital standards 208, 216; property instruments 213; property rights 267, 268, 271, 275
intelligent: objects 246; systems 207, 215
interactive whiteboards 246
interdependencies 11, 104
internal assessment report 115
internal relational capital 37, 40
International Accounting Standards Board (IASB) 211
International Financial Reporting Standards (IFRS) 211
International Labor Organization 171
International Telecommunication Union 171
internationalization 226
internet: bandwidth speed 156; monopolies 250; of things 114, 215, 246
intra-organisational processes 284, 286
investors 182, 183, 218

IoT 11, 46
IPR ii, 244
ISD 75, 78
ISO 27000 Information Asset Management 209
ISO 30401 Knowledge Management Standard 209
ISO 44001 Collaborative Business Relationship Management standard 209
ISO 44001 Collaborative Business Relationship Management standard 209
ISO 55000 Asset Management series of standards 208
ISO 56000 Innovation Management series of standards 210
ISO 56002 Innovation Management Guideline 210
ISO 9001 Quality Management 208
ISO IUMSS Handbook (Integrated Use of Management System Standards) 210
ISO standards 208, 210
ISO Survey 171
Israel 97, 98, 100, 152
IT: resources 127; services 260
Italy 9, 126, 202

Japan 11, 199
jobs 25, 245, 250, 252
joint public-private laboratories 115, 116
joint ventures 268

know-how 46, 126, 169, 182
Knowledge Assessment Methodology (KAM) 173
knowledge assets 181, 207, 212, 279
Knowledge Café 100, 103
knowledge creation 116
Knowledge Economy Index (KEI) 173
Knowledge Index (KI) 173
knowledge: intensity 35, 38, 39; lifecycle 215; management 93, 97, 110, 209; management systems 70; maps 195, 196, 200; resources 33, 38, 219; sharing 23, 24, 58, 273; storage 49; strategy 33, 38; transfer 4, 22; workers 39, 49, 212, 216
knowledge-intensive firms 33, 39
Korea 5, 148, 152
KPIs 104, 105
KPMG 221
Kuwait 169

labour markets 241, 246, 253
Lamborghini 202

300　*Index*

latent variables 227
law 200, 241
learning organization 93
legal framework 16
legislation 16, 241
lenders 224
licensing agreements 185
LinkedIn 57, 58
literature view 280, 289
Living Labs 15, 17
logistics 46, 54
longitudinal dataset xxx, 38
longitudinal study xxx, 31
Luxembourg 149, 152, 154, 158

machine learning 5, 242, 262
macroeconomic: levels 170; principles 170; stability 168
management consultants 235
Management Portfolio 83
managers 35, 65
manuals 200, 220
manufacturing industry 172, 204
marginal return 46
market-based approach 224
market capital 269, 270
market: leaders 247; performance 64, 67, 69, 70; value 98, 103, 164, 220, 223
marketing 48, 172, 273
Marriot 20, 250
mathematical models 268
mathematicians 202
maturity 117, 170, 175
measurement 107, 110
Measuring the Information Society 2017 171
medical literature 124
medicine 124, 126, 129
mergers 268
meso-level 241
methodologies 165, 175
metrics 77, 104, 137, 163, 22
Mexico 162, 183
micro-grids 243
Microsoft 126, 243, 244
millennials 252
mixed reality 19, 59
mobility 14, 212, 245, 251
monetisation 243
MOOCs 107, 224, 273
motivation 32, 199
movies 164
multinational companies 120

multiplier effect 273
music 164, 207, 274

national healthcare system 158
National intellectual capital (NIC) 164, 165, 293
Netherlands 139, 158, 294
networking 137, 251, 284
neuroinformatics 247
New Club of Paris 294
New Zealand 148, 152, 283
NIC 137, 294
non-accounting approach 283
non-financial information 284
nongovernmental bodies 165
nordic countries 139, 158, 164, 269
Norway 3
NVivo 257, 282

OECD 51, 171, 175
OECD Innovation Indicators 171
Office for National Statistics (ONS) 174
oil-rich countries 158
online data 245
open courseware 247
open data sources 174
open engagement platforms 11
Open Innovation 7, 9, 48, 58
open innovation ecosystems 11, 15, 17
openness 11, 15
opportunities 4, 253, 258
optimisation 40, 247
organizational: boundary 164; culture 231; knowledge 109; memory 208
output 45, 47, 106
ownership 213, 242, 244

partnership agreements 109
patents 164, 172, 206, 283
Path Modelling (PM) 227
patterns 240, 249, 266
pediatric medicine 129
pension funds 252
performance measurement 106, 107
personalization 33
PetroChina 243
physical: assets 223; labour 213
pilot projects 92, 98
platfirm business 20
platforms 23, 25
polarisation 236, 241, 250
pollution 6, 20
portfolio 80, 83, 124, 209

Index   301

Portuguese SMEs 226
poverty 20, 251
predictive analytics 215, 249
privacy 261, 263
private: company 98; corporations 235; sector 13, 103, 109
productive capacity 168, 169
productivity 168, 174, 184
professional services 51, 54
professions 14, 174, 190
Program for International Student Assessment (PISA) 171
prototypes 8, 10
proxy 2018, 226
psychology 200
Public Administration 54
public: sector 3, 8, 13, 103; structure 138, 157, 158

Qatar 169
Quadruple helix 11, 12, 14
qualitative approaches 124, 125
quality assurance (QA) 246
quality: jobs 250, 254; service 123
quantitative indicators 138, 171
questionnaire 51, 218, 224

R&D intensity 35
R&D investments 33
rating 48, 54
rationale 112, 138, 252, 257
raw material 137
reallocation 10
recommendations 221
reconfiguration 251
recruiting businesses 246
reengineering 45
regions 3, 7, 105, 164, 251, 253, 280
regulations 59, 70, 250
regulatory framework 157
relational capital 32, 47, 64, 109, 247, 260, 263
reliability 36, 66, 186
renewal capital 138, 145, 270
report data analytics 104, 111
reputation 208, 218, 284
research: centres 108, 115; method 124, 182
resilience 168, 172, 251
respondents 35, 36, 56, 65
retail trade 35
retinal screens 247
retirement 212, 215

Return on assets (ROA) 36, 184
Return on equity (ROE) 36, 184
revolution 212, 249
Richard Feynman 203
risks 168, 237, 266, 276
robotics 19, 23, 215
rotation 212

S&P 500 companies 243, 249
scalability 8, 11
scaleups 104, 165
scarcity 203, 213
scenario planning 227
schools 25, 245, 246
science park 114
self-driving cars 245
self-organising teams 250
self-paced learning 246
semantic 186
services 8, 13, 20, 57
servitization 33, 38, 39
shareholders 20, 217, 224, 226
sharing: economy 14, 243, 252, 253; platforms 15
Shell 243
Silicon Valley 9
Skandia Navigator 217, 219, 220
small high-tech countries 270
smart: contracts 243, 260; factories 62, 69; grids 243; solutions 245
SMEs 75, 105, 221
SNIC model 154
social: actors 25; knowledge 107, 170, 285, 287; media 46, 112, 137, 212; polarization 253; responsibility 159
socio-economic conditions 126
sociology 200
software 59, 109, 111, 164, 220, 242
solutions 10, 24, 25
Spain 164
specialized knowledge 169, 201
spin-offs 114, 116
sponsorships 114
sports 23, 123, 242
Sri Lanka 183
stagnation 100, 241
stakeholders 8, 15, 16, 117, 261
standardized interfaces 11
startups 104, 105
statistical tools 124
STEAM (Science, Technology, Engineering, Arts, and Mathematics) 201
steering committee 100, 103

302 *Index*

STEM (Science, Technology, Engineering, and Mathematics) 201
stock 103, 268, 270
strategic level 88, 92
strategic management 40, 93, 223
strategic: option 79, 81, 82; planning 48, 165
strategy 47, 75, 79; formulation 77, 92; implementation 75, 77
StratOp-Portfolio 80, 81
strengths 78, 83, 171
structural: capital 32, 47, 64, 109, 259, 280; factors 31, 34, 36
structured equations 227
student business plan competitions 114
success factors 83, 99, 101
suppliers 47, 64, 181, 226, 253
survey 46, 50, 203; datasets 31
sustainability 20, 159, 229
sustainable development 60, 254, 159
Sustainable National Intellectual Capital (SNIC) 137, 148, 159, 294
sustained competitive advantage 109, 225
Sweden 139, 148

tablets 246
tacit knowledge 39, 109, 262
Taiwan 148, 151, 282
talent 11, 13, 251; development 70, 170, 173
talented people 187, 190
tangibility 38, 39
task-assignment algorithms 247
Team Capital 227
teams 39, 202, 212
teamwork 235
technological: convergence 242; innovation 236
Technology Broker 219, 224
technology park 114
tendency 197, 198, 222
Tesla 249
top–down approach 223, 258
tourism 54, 182, 183
trade 169, 241, 266, 267
training 57, 129, 169, 173
transactions 173, 258, 206
transformation leadership xxxi, 58, 235
transition 216, 253, 253
transparency 125, 176, 182, 261
trends 241, 247, 251

trial and error 275
triple helix 9, 10
turbulence 195, 240, 259
turn-around 270

UAE 151, 152
Ukraine 139
UN 2030 Agenda
UN Sustainable Development Goals 22, 252
uncertainty 10, 80, 200
unemployment 241, 250, 251
United Kingdom 148, 151, 286
universities 106, 107, 109, 110
USA 139, 143, 152, 193
usability 170
users 7, 9, 10, 16

validity 36, 186
value 287; chains 110, 247
value consumption 247
value-creation dynamics 116, 117
value creation model 77, 78, 83
Value Explorer 217
value proposition 17, 22, 48
Value-Added Intellectual Coefficient 40
vendors 63, 243
Venezuela 139, 169
virtual reality 23, 59, 247
vision 99, 100, 103, 109, 116
Vocational education and training (VET) 246
voluntary disclosure 183

weaknesses 84, 171, 186
web 3.0 244
websites 107, 112, 113
well-being 23, 49, 173
WHISKids 23, 25
Wisdom Economics 295
workers 174, 199, 212
workplace 23, 250
World Bank 164, 174, 203
World Economic Forum (WEF) 168, 172, 174
world economy 269, 284
World Health Innovation Summit platform xxii, 21
World Intellectual Property Organization (WIPO) 171

T0388019

THE DIFFERENCE NOTHING MAKES

The Difference Nothing Makes

Creation, Christ, Contemplation

BRIAN D. ROBINETTE

University of Notre Dame Press
Notre Dame, Indiana

University of Notre Dame Press
Notre Dame, Indiana 46556
undpress.nd.edu

All Rights Reserved

Copyright © 2023 by the University of Notre Dame

Published in the United States of America

Library of Congress Control Number: 2022947716

ISBN: 978-0-268-20352-8 (Hardback)
ISBN: 978-0-268-20351-1 (WebPDF)
ISBN: 978-0-268-20573-7 (Epub)

Dedicated to the memory of

Bonnie Lou Robinette,
my mother

and

Michael Jon Gregory Pahls,
my brother in Christ

You formed my inmost being;
you knit me in my mother's womb.
I praise you, because I am wonderfully made;
wonderful are your works!
My very self you know.
My bones are not hidden from you,
When I was being made in secret,
fashioned in the depths of the earth.
Your eyes saw me unformed;
in your book all are written down;
my days were shaped, before one came to be.

Psalm 139:13–16

CONTENTS

Acknowledgments		ix
Introduction		xi
PART 1	Grammar and Contemplation	
ONE	The Difference Nothing Makes	3
TWO	Undergoing Something from Nothing	41
PART 2	Christ as Concentrated Creation	
THREE	Jesus and the Non-Other	81
FOUR	Strange Victory	125
PART 3	Purgation and Union	
FIVE	On the Contemplative Consummation of Atheism	175
SIX	Return to Love	211
Notes		267
Bibliography		297
Index		309

ACKNOWLEDGMENTS

Writing a book often entails sustained labor in solitude, and yet anyone who has engaged in such work knows just how much its very
substance depends upon a host of others. While a great many people
have helped me bring this book to fruition, there are several in particular I wish to acknowledge here.

Thank you to those who provided me critical scholarly engagement in the spirit of friendship at various stages of this book's composition: Grant Kaplan; Ryan Duns, S.J.; Daniel Horan, O.F.M.; Jessica
Coblentz; Chelsea King; Joseph Rivera; Ligita Ryliškytė, S.J.E.; Kevin
Hughes; Andrew Prevot; and Jeffrey Bloechl. To those who provided
me crucial spiritual companionship throughout the writing process:
Martin Laird, O.S.A., and Lama John Makransky. To those who provided me all the above, but especially the joy of unfiltered friendship and conversation: Boyd Taylor Coolman, Rick Gaillardetz, Matt
Petillo, Steve Pope, and Jeremy Wilkins.

A special word of gratitude goes to my wife, Krista, and sons
Trevor and Austin. Thank you for sharing with me the most fulfilling
home life I can possibly imagine.

Early versions of the book's central thesis and themes were presented
at various conferences, workshops, and invited lectures, including
the American Academy of Religion, the Catholic Theological Society
of America, the Boston Theological Society, Theology & Peace, the
College Theology Society, the Centre of Theology and Philosophy,
and the Colloquium on Violence and Religion. Some portions of the

present text first appeared in other publication venues, including "The Difference Nothing Makes: *Creatio ex nihilo*, the Resurrection, and Divine Gratuity," *Theological Studies* 72, no. 3 (2011): 525–57; "Undergoing Something from Nothing: The Doctrine of Creation as Contemplative Insight," in *The Practice of the Presence of God: Theology as Way of Life*, edited by Martin Laird and Sheelah Treflé Hidden (London: Routledge, 2016), 17–28; and "Contemplative Practice and the Therapy of Mimetic Desire," in *Contagion: Journal of Violence, Mimesis, and Culture* 24 (2017): 73–100. All scriptural texts are from the New American Bible Revised Edition.

INTRODUCTION

An Astonishing Claim

Christian theology makes an astonishing claim about our world: creation did not have to be, and yet it is—from nothing. As challenging as it may be for us to imagine, the world we typically take for granted, the only world we actually know, is wholly gratuitous, without necessary existence, and utterly dependent upon an unfathomable God for its very being. While this claim has achieved a formal status in Christian theology—as articulated by the doctrine of *creatio ex nihilo*, or "creation from nothing"—the scope of its significance for Christian imagination and practice is not sufficiently understood.

The central question this book asks is this: What difference does "nothing" make? What does the sheer gratuity of creation mean for our understanding of God? What does it imply about God's intention for creation, for creaturely flourishing amid the impermanence and interdependence of all things? How did this understanding of creation arise within the Christian tradition in the first place, and what role does scriptural testimony play in its subsequent theological development? What does *creatio ex nihilo* imply for our understanding of human-divine interaction? Is it primarily about cosmic origins, or does it also suggest a certain manner of social critique and communal aspiration? How might "creation from nothing" be relevant for addressing the late-modern mood of nihilism, or the sense that "nothing matters"? And, finally, how might this doctrine become a practical and contemplative insight that we can skillfully embody in everyday life?

xi

The basic argument developed in this book is that *creatio ex nihilo* is not a speculative doctrine referring to cosmic origins but a foundational insight into the very nature of the God-world relation, one whose implications extend throughout the full spectrum of Christian imagination and practice. In this sense it serves a grammatical role: it gives orientation and scope to all Christian speech about the God-world relation. It does this by, among other things, characterizing that relationship in noncontrastive terms. God and world do not compete with each other within a spectrum of being. Rather, God is the source and ground of creation's contingent being, its inmost possibility and animating impulse. Creation comes "to be" precisely in and through God's gratuitous act, which means that the more creation truly *is*, the more it reflects its ontological dependence on the Creator.

This is how the privative "from nothing" basically functions. It does not refer to "nothing" as a special kind of "something," as though God creates out of a prior potentiality or cocreative principle. It does not refer to a source alongside God, a numinous force, or some kind of lack in God that creation appears to fulfill. Such speculative approaches, sometimes found in the tradition, may arouse a certain fascination or sense of drama around God's creative act, but usually by attributing some kind of mysterious quality or minimal content to "nothing," when in fact the doctrine denies even this. To this extent, the doctrine of *creatio ex nihilo* functions as a piece of negative theology, not because it means to be obscure, but because it means to remove any concept, intuition, or principle that might mediate between "something" and "nothing." No extradivine necessity is at work in God's creative act, no outside condition is met, no primeval chaos is overcome, no ontological scarcity or unconscious striving in God is satisfied in bringing all things "to be." The difference between there being anything at all, rather than nothing, is absolute—traversable only by the gratuitous act of the Absolute God.

While this noncontrastive relationship can be stated in formal terms, the main burden of the book is to explore the positive content of this relationship, its dynamism and living texture, as well as its more radical implications. Within a Christian theological context, this exploration will be christological in shape, in the sense that Jesus's life, death, and resurrection concretely display the God-creation relationship with maximal clarity and salvific import. It is maximally clear because in Christ the creaturely and the divine are united "hypostatically," in one *person*. It is salvific because it unveils and transforms the deep-seated ways the God-creation relation has become misconstrued or disordered on account of human sin. Human desire, which is originally good and participative of divine life, is susceptible to rivalry, conflict, and violence, and this susceptibility can lead us to cast the God-world relation in contrastive, even agonistic terms. God is thus seen as over against the world, or perhaps associated with a sacral violence underwriting conflict in human relations.

Among the most remarkable features of Christ's life, death, and resurrection is that precisely in the midst of a human failing — a brutal execution — God is revealed as having nothing to do with *our* violence. But more, God is revealed as the One whose self-emptying love enters into the depths of rivalry, conflict, and violence in order to overcome them. This overcoming is not the deployment of an even greater force but, paradoxically, the victory of an inexhaustible and efficacious vulnerability that exposes the roots of conflict and violence. This exposure is simultaneous with the communication of a pacific, pardoning, and divinizing presence. From the perspective of the risen victim, which is one way to characterize the peculiar density of the Easter event, we can begin to envision creation anew, as though for the first time, and perceive with unprecedented clarity that creation is originally given "to be" out of unconditioned goodness and love. Its origin is *agapeic*, not conflictual, and the God-world relation, so far from a matter of competition or rivalry, is the very site of communion. *Creatio ex nihilo*, or our coming into existence "from nothing," is in fact a relation of sheer intimacy with God, and thus our sense of contingency and creaturely poverty, rather than a matter of threat and defensive posturing, can be welcomed and embraced as pure gift, as that which we may freely accept, share with others, and ultimately cherish.

There is a contemplative dimension to this welcoming and embracing of our shared creatureliness. Creation does not have to be, and yet is — gratuitously, freely, wondrously. God summons all things "to be" out of divine freedom, not for God's sake but for the sake of creation itself, without any mediating obstacle or ulterior motive. Creation is *given*. But more, it is *loved* into being. It comes *from*

God. God summons that which is other than God into existence as an expression of God's own fullness of being and love. Creaturely being is thus primordially *received* by us. We can never get to something prior to this original gift. We can never get to its back side, so to speak, for it is who and what we are. Our being thus depends upon God, and this ontological dependence is original and without any other ground. This sense of creation's essential gratuity, if deeply lived into rather than merely thought about, can begin to transform the felt sense of our contingency from one of anxiety-tinged precarity to the welcoming of finitude and our mutual dependence in loving communion. Contemplative practice invites us to "let go" of our defenses and "live into" our creaturely contingency with progressive freedom and deepest acceptance. This acceptance is truly liberating, for rather than struggling to achieve our identity through reactivity, competition, and acquisitiveness, the contemplative way allows us to recognize that with God—and God alone—we do not have to negotiate our existence with a rival; we can wholly trust and live from the One who loves all things into being *ex nihilo*. In characteristically paradoxical fashion, the Christian contemplative path is one of purgation unto union, kenosis unto theosis, nothingness unto fullness.

This paradoxical dynamic achieves its greatest realization in the incarnation, and as I hope to make clear in the unfolding of this book, it is in light of the incarnation that *creatio ex nihilo* gains its fullest content. To give some indication of this, we must first recognize that creation "from nothing," while issuing a certain kind of denial, already implies a positive theological affirmation of enormous consequence. Creation is an act of divine *self*-bestowal. Creation is not just any other, it turns out, but precisely that "other" whose inmost ground and eschatological horizon is God. While in no way annulling the genuine integrity of the created other, the very nature of this difference is such that God imparts God's *self* in establishing it. Creation is just that which comes "to be" when divine life, illimitable in itself, is rendered participable. Because our creatureliness is an act of divine self-donation, our difference from God is in fact the source of our deepest intimacy with God—the event and idiom of God's kenotic outpouring as well as the event and idiom of our ecstatic openness to God. The God-creation relation is therefore not static or thinglike but dynamic and reverberative, a living "betweenness." In being constituted *by* God, creation in all its diversity and emergent possibilities exhibits a vital capacity *for* God. Creation is the unfolding of this relation.

What we call the incarnation, formally speaking, is that event in which God's self-communication coincides utterly with the creaturely capacity to respond in freedom and love. God's kenotic outpouring and creaturely self-transcendence: when these two movements converge in a definitive and unsurpassable way, the very reason for creation—its inner dynamism and eschatological goal—is realized. God's self-communication, already constitutive of creation itself, reaches its climax *in* creation through the incarnation. The Word became flesh. God became human. Without ceasing to be God, God became creaturely not in order to expand divine life—as though this were possible—but in order to shepherd creaturely reality into its fullest fruition. This fruition is not something done passively *to* the creature. Though wholly gracious, it is also the fullest actualization *of* the creature. The difference between God and creation is not eliminated in the Christ-event but preserved and brought into maximal unity-*in*-difference. It is this unity-in-difference that all creation is destined to share, yet it is *in* Christ that this eschatological promise of creation, issued from "the beginning," achieves decisive momentum and irrevocable form. The Christ-event reveals the beating heart of the God-creation relation, its systole-diastole movement, and thus the inmost content of *creatio ex nihilo* really comes to this: we are created *in* Christ (Eph. 2:10). We are created to participate in divine life. God became human so that we might become God, so the patristic axiom goes. Creation and incarnation, though a differentiated historical process, are two aspects of one self-communicating act. Seen retrospectively from the Christ-event, we can say: This is why we were made. This is why we have come "to be." This is how things "shall be." *This* is the difference nothing makes.

PLAN OF THE BOOK

The present book is organized into three main parts, with each part composed of two chapters. Ideally read in sequence, the three parts are relatively self-standing, thematically speaking. While there is an overall progression of argumentation and thematic development from one to the next chapter, each of the book's three parts represents a renewed "take" on creation, Christ, and contemplation. Accordingly, part 1 is more foundational in character and focuses on scriptural resources, philosophical disputation, doctrinal development, and the role of contemplation in theological practice. Part 2 is more christological in bearing as it attempts to show how Jesus's life, death, and resurrection display the inner content of the God-creation relation. Part 3 chiastically corresponds with part 1 in key respects, but now as amplified by the christological focus of part 2. It is also in part 3 that the purgation-union motif of the entire book reaches its greatest pitch.

Part One: Grammar and Contemplation

Chapter 1 takes the form of *disputatio*. It lays out several of the book's main themes by taking up several objections to *creatio ex nihilo* and defending the doctrine as providing crucial insights into the gifted character of creation. Working through biblical, patristic, and philosophical perspectives, and dealing with select postmodern considerations of power and violence, the chapter articulates a noncompetitive account of the God-world relation, which claims that God's unconditioned transcendence is the inmost factor of all created reality. Not only are the divine and creaturely not in rivalry, but the more truly a creature *is*, the more expressive it is of divine reality. Such is the christological "shape" of the God-world relation. The chapter concludes by insisting that *creatio ex nihilo* is not only about cosmic or human origins but also a doctrine that grounds Christian hope in the face of all that diminishes creation. It is eschatological as much as it is protological.

While presuming the narrative and conceptual content of Christian doctrine, chapter 2 underscores (along with Sebastian Moore, Sarah Coakley, Teresa of Avila, Martin Laird, and William Desmond) the contemplative dimensions of a theological inquiry that proceeds by way of "unknowing." Given that *creatio ex nihilo* refers us to our creaturely contingency (i.e., the fact that we do not have to exist, and yet we do), it also invites a patient discovery of the "nothingness"

Introduction xvii

from which we subsist. Contemplation is a way of relaxing into this indefinable, ungraspable mystery, and to this extent it allows us to embrace and even love our contingency rather than deny it or regard it as inimical to human flourishing. It also allows us to resist treating God as a kind of object that competes with or displaces the world. The chapter concludes with a meditation on the inherent goodness of our creatureliness and therefore of the need to grow in our capacities for receiving, deepening, and communicating that goodness with others by way of loving communion.

Part Two: Christ as Concentrated Creation

Part 2 focuses on Christology as "concentrated creation," a phrase taken from Edward Schillebeeckx to name God's eschatological intention for creation. Both chapters draw from the field of mimetic theory in order to explore the creative and destructive potential of human desire. Christology is accounted for here in terms of the pedagogy of human desire, as well as the revelation of the true character of the God-creation relation. Part 2 is the pivot to the book's overall chiastic structure.

Drawing upon the seminal insights of René Girard, along with several of his theological interlocutors, chapter 3 develops a "phenomenology of redemption" by showing how Jesus's life and ministry display the nonrivalrous relationship between God and creation. Focusing on issues of human desire, human conflict, and our propensity toward exclusionary violence, the chapter examines how Jesus's sayings and deeds go to the root of human desire in order to free it from its self-defensive, other-reifying tendencies.

Chapter 4 focuses on Jesus's death and resurrection as the gracious inbreaking of God's love that subverts the mechanisms of power and exclusionary violence from within, revealing once and for all God's noncomplicity in human violence. It develops the *Christus Victor* motif in Christian theology while criticizing certain strains within the Christian tradition that support some version of penal substitution. It also develops the theopolitical significance of this subversion, as it affirms creation in terms of original peace rather than foundational conflict.

xviii Introduction

Part Three: Purgation and Union

Chapter 5 draws upon the Christian contemplative tradition in order to show how the "dark night of faith" is a spiritually patient and discerning way to engage the sense of divine absence that many experience in our post-religious, postsecular age. Drawing upon figures such as John of the Cross and Meister Eckhart, but also more contemporary voices including John Chapman, Charles Taylor, Michael Buckley, and Tomáš Halík, the chapter maintains that the Christian contemplative tradition, along with its understanding of creation from nothing, must incorporate atheistic critique as part of its mystagogical itinerary. It ultimately goes beyond atheism, even radicalizing it in the contemplative journey into divine mystery.

The final chapter of the book highlights *creatio ex nihilo* as an expression of divine love—God's love for finitude, for manifestation, for relationship. Taking seriously the purgative-unitive dynamic of Christian faith, it emphasizes that on the other side of self-emptying and negation lies a return to fullness and affirmation. In extended dialogue with Karl Rahner, Sergius Bulgakov, and other theological exemplars who explore the richly ontological implications of divine self-communication—implications that expressly affirm the cosmicity of the incarnation—chapter 6 brings the book full circle by insisting that God's act of creation is always already ordered toward the incarnation and thus an expression of God's eternal essence as Love. God's love is for the entire community of creation, not just human beings, inasmuch as any contemporary theology of creation must address the ecological dimensions of divine-creaturely communion. The chapter concludes with a meditation on the recovery of our spiritual senses as essential to a faith whose love of God and neighbor is internally related to love of the earth.

PART 1

Grammar and Contemplation

CHAPTER ONE

The Difference Nothing Makes

OBJECTIONS TO NOTHING

"The history of theology is by no means just the history of the progress of doctrine, but also a history of forgetting."[1] So wrote Karl
Rahner in his landmark essay, "Chalcedon: End or Beginning?"
(1951). Written for the fifteenth centenary of the Council of Chalcedon, the essay brilliantly charts a path for overcoming the inadequa-
cies of neo-scholastic theology regnant at the time, especially within
Catholic circles. Treating magisterial pronouncements as fully accomplished propositions that have only to be expounded, such theology
largely failed to grasp the historical character of human understanding, as though by repeating hallowed formulae over time, and with
sufficient confidence, we might be assured of their meaning.

But this is exactly what human understanding is not. "For history is precisely *not* an atomized beginning-ever-anew; it is rather
(the more spiritual it is) a becoming-new which preserves the old,
and preserves it all the more *as* old, the more spiritual this history
is."[2] This phrasing may have a certain Hegelian ring to it, but it is
a basic hermeneutical claim: dogmatic formulations of the past may
indeed be certain kinds of achievements, indispensable attainments
that elicit our admiration and fidelity, but they can only be regarded
as such to the extent that their meaning is constantly *won*, discovered again and again through the hard work of remembering and

3

4   Grammar and Contemplation

reconstruction, approached both as ends *and* beginnings. This is why historical theology and the history of doctrine are crucial for any constructive theology today. "What was once given in history and is ever made present anew does not primarily form a set of premises from which we can draw new conclusions which have never been thought of before. It is the object which, while it is always retained, must ever be acquired anew, by *us*, that is, we who are just such as no one else can ever be in all history."[3]

Rahner's programmatic essay focuses primarily on the christological formulae of Chalcedon, but the same could be said of any doctrinal formulation achieving some normative status in the Christian tradition, including the doctrine of *creatio ex nihilo*. Although "creation from nothing" was never formally promulgated by the Church in discrete form—owing, no doubt, to the rapidity with which it became a default assumption in Christian theology—there is good reason to conclude that the basic grammar it establishes for speaking of the God-creation relation had much to do with orienting the christological formulae that would eventually lay claim to orthodoxy.[4] We are right to suspect an even deeper relation than this, a mutual influence and inner correspondence in which further reflection upon the total meaning and significance of Christ, his resurrection from the dead and qualitatively new presence in the Spirit, put creative pressures on what the earliest Christians imagined creation itself to be—from "the beginning." That is, the very content of creation, as well as the horizon within which it might be imagined, symbolized, and theorized by Christians, took on the distinctive shape and texture it did precisely because of the Christ-event. As Saint Paul puts it in suitably concentrated form:

> He is the image of the invisible God, the firstborn of all creation. For in him were created all things in heaven and on earth, the visible and the invisible, whether thrones or dominions or principalities or powers; all things were created through him and for him. He is before all things, and in him all things hold together. He is the head of the body, the church. He is the beginning, the firstborn from the dead, that in all things he himself might be preeminent. For in him all the fullness was pleased to dwell, and through

The Difference Nothing Makes   5

him to reconcile to all things for him, making peace by the blood of his cross [through him], whether those on earth or those in heaven (Col. 1:15–19)

As all-encompassing as this testimony is, it is not quite possible to draw a straight line from its several references to "the beginning" to the affirmation that God creates all things "from nothing." Multiple mediating factors must be traced before uncovering the peculiar significance of this latter phrase. But it is no less evident that were we to succeed in better understanding the depth and range of significance that *creatio ex nihilo* has for Christian theology, it will require us to unpack the highly concentrated way creation and Christ are envisioned in a passage like this. Such effort would seem a key part of not forgetting in theology.

But what if the doctrine of *creatio ex nihilo* entails its own kind of forgetting? Might it be that when the majority of Christian theologians in the second and third centuries converged upon what can only be described as a strong consensus—as strong a consensus as anyone will find in the early centuries of Christian theology—we have the telltale signs of an eclipse? What if, upon further inspection, the philosophical and theological disputations of the second and third centuries, during which the doctrine of *creatio ex nihilo* was forged, resulted in something like a cover-up, perhaps a misremembering of the biblical sources that the doctrine purported to defend and elucidate? If, in the transition from biblical narrative to doctrinal reflection, we suspect something like a departure, perhaps this will be judged as more or less innocuous, merely a shift from one to another kind of discursive register, one involving little alteration of content, implying no obvious mischief, and mattering little in the end. But if our suspicions are more easily stirred, and if we are inclined to view the inclusion of metaphysics in Christian theology as a kind of a betrayal, as a freezing or conceptual reification of textual traditions that are inherently ambiguous and fluid, then we might conclude that the affirmation of "creation from nothing," along with its emphasis on divine sovereignty and creaturely dependence, is an overreaching piece of ideology. Perhaps the swift convergence around *creatio ex nihilo* in the second and third centuries is less a matter of theological elucidation than it is a lamentable act of metaphysical capture.

6 Grammar and Contemplation

The suspicion that *creatio ex nihilo* represents just this kind of betrayal has gained traction in recent years. Noting as a matter of historical record that its formal development comes subsequent to the biblical tradition, such critics argue that while ostensibly designed to affirm the sovereignty of God and the goodness of matter in the mid-second century disputes with Middle Platonism and gnosticism, "creation from nothing" represents a capitulation to a metaphysical view of God in which power, or omnipotence, serves as its governing predicate. The consequences of this "metaphysical turn" in theology turn out to be disastrous.

In his *The Weakness of God: A Theology of the Event* (2006), John D. Caputo makes precisely this charge. Working in close company with Catherine Keller and Jacques Derrida, among others, Caputo maintains that *creatio ex nihilo* represents the "dream of metaphysical theology" enthralled by the idea of God's absolute dominion over creation and nonbeing, and thus a God who excludes and expels all that evinces liminality, ambiguity, and process—that is, the "chaos" of the deep. With deconstructive sensibilities aroused, Caputo interrogates the scriptural narratives to retrieve disruptive nuances and creative possibilities he believes have long been suppressed in the theological tradition. The work of theopoetics, as he describes his project, eschews the metaphysics of power and opts instead for envisioning God as a "weak force": a God who, rather than bringing all things into being from literally "nothing," creates by eliciting life from the preexistent deep (*tehom*) of the waters, from the fathomless potentiality of the void (*tohu wa-bohu*). Whereas the doctrine of creation *ex nihilo* would suppress indeterminacy in the interests of affirming an ultimate and simple origin to things—with "God" serving as the ultimate power policing creation's boundaries—this alternative, more biblical view embraces the messiness of creation as a "beautiful risk."

A related concern for Caputo is that an omnipotent God is simply not credible in the face of suffering and evil. With occasional appeal to process philosophy and theology, Caputo alerts us to the horns of our dilemma: a God who creates from nothing is responsible for all the world's contingencies, including its many unspeakable horrors, and thus cannot be affirmed as wholly good. The only way we may continue to affirm God's unqualified goodness is if we abandon

The Difference Nothing Makes 7

all "strong theologies" preoccupied with divine omnipotence. God is not simply weak on the basis of willed restraint; God *is* weak, or, is a "weak force" capable only of luring contingent creation through the "event" of invitation. If stirring within the deep is the creative potential for beauty and harmony, so too may *tehomic* energies fragment and destroy. Creation unleashed is an ongoing process that we, along with God, cocreate, enjoy, and endure in hope. The promise of creation is "a promise that keeps its fingers crossed."[5]

The argumentative burden of this chapter is to show that Caputo's characterization of *creatio ex nihilo* is deeply misleading. Though I wish to affirm much of what appeals to Caputo in his theopoetics, not least a view of God as noncoercive love, a God whose creation exhibits genuine contingency and open-endedness, I do not believe he demonstrates that the classical affirmations of *creatio ex nihilo* and divine omnipotence are responsible for all he heaps upon them. On the contrary, these affirmations are precisely what enable us more richly and consistently to envision creation as *gift*. The constructive purpose of engaging Caputo's work in this nexus of issues is that it affords us an opportunity to appreciate the point of *creatio ex nihilo*, which, when taken as an isolated matter of abstract reflection, runs the risk of losing its rich significance within the ecology of Christian discourse. We can engage Caputo's intervention, gratefully but ultimately critically, as a spur for opening up fresh perspectives upon a doctrine that might otherwise go unnoticed. Such is the potential gain of *disputatio*.

I shall proceed in two major steps: first, by showing that *creatio ex nihilo* affirms God's unconditioned transcendence in a way that expressly avoids construing the God-world relationship in competitive (or contrastive) terms. It reflects a basic grammar for speaking of God and creation in a way that names their radical, qualitative difference—a difference that in fact allows us to affirm divine transcendence precisely *as* God's unfathomable nearness. This "difference nothing makes" can also help us appreciate what divine omnipotence might actually mean. It does not mean domination, which is the way Caputo tendentiously frames his analysis of power, and which forces him to set up an untenable dichotomy between "strong" and "weak" theologies. Caputo tends to reverse the terms he opposes, without

8 Grammar and Contemplation

appreciating that it is just this dichotomy that the affirmations of divine transcendence and *creatio ex nihilo* mean to subvert.

Second, I wish to show the internal consistency of *creatio ex nihilo* with the central affirmation of the New Testament—Jesus's resurrection from the dead. This is crucial for the kind of remembering Rahner commends in his essay. The event of Easter, itself an eschatological transfiguration of memory, opened up for Christians a perspective upon God's creativity in a significantly new light. The theology of creation from nothing is logically coherent with, and in Christian theology historically dependent upon, a view of a God who raises to life what has succumbed to the *nihil* of death. A post-Easter imagination, not unmoored metaphysical speculation, underwrites its discovery. By raising Jesus from the dead—this is the definitive manifestation of divine power from a Christian point of view—what is revealed is a God of forgiving hospitality, a God whose boundless generativity is not agonistic or contrastive with creation but pacific, pardoning, and self-diffusive.

Such a view, it must be admitted, will not do much to theoretically explain evil and suffering, which, along with Caputo, I am wont to avoid; but it does constitute the Christian *hope* that evil, suffering, and death do not have the final word. Indeed, despite Caputo's intention to avoid theodicy, his claim that divine omnipotence must be rejected should we wish honestly to face the mystery of suffering does more to explain that mystery than most classical approaches, and without any obvious advantage in motivating us for its practical overcoming.

A Spectrum of Positions

To begin, it will be useful to identify three broad positions one might take in assessing the status of *creatio ex nihilo* and its relationship to the biblical traditions. The first is that *creatio ex nihilo*, as it gained a formal character in the second and third centuries, represents an innovation that imposes something new and largely foreign upon the biblical traditions thought to support it. The genealogies accounting for the historical and ideological factors leading to this imposition may

The Difference Nothing Makes   9

vary in their details, but the basic contention such critics share is that its ascendancy is emblematic of a failure and an eclipse, an ill-fated fall into a metaphysical picture that retrojects a set of considerations about God and cosmic origins that the biblical narratives do not raise and cannot be legitimately enlisted for support.

A second position recognizes the innovative character of *creatio ex nihilo* but views its normative status as consistent with, and elucidatory of, the biblical traditions. The development might be compared to the emergence of the christological dogmas of Nicaea and Chalcedon. If one can grant that the interaction between scriptural traditions and Greek philosophy led to creative syntheses exhibiting both novelty and fidelity in christological reflection—and in fact one sees this interaction already occurring in the New Testament itself—then, similarly, the considerations entailed in the doctrine of creation from nothing need not be thought of as merely late, or fabrications of dubious eisegesis, but providing an interpretive framework that helps us better to understand those scriptural traditions as new questions and insights arise. Even if many of the accounts of creation in scripture remain unclear as to whether God creates *ex nihilo* in any strict sense, once the question of unoriginate matter became live, for example, it became incumbent upon theologians to clarify the point. The doctrine, as formally articulated by Tatian, Theophilus of Antioch, Irenaeus of Lyons, and Tertullian, draws the appropriate conclusion once the issue was posed.

The third (and perhaps most traditional) position is that the postbiblical theologies of *creatio ex nihilo* are not innovative at all but fully continuous with the content of those biblical traditions clearly supporting it. Even if a more technical conceptuality is at work in its later elaboration, the content is the essentially same. The biblical traditions reveal little ambiguity; any fair-minded analysis will show their intent to narrate the act of creation as not dependent upon some prior potentiality or raw material that God fortuitously discovers and against which God must eternally contend. If some of the early church fathers, such as Justin Martyr, taught that God created the world from preexistent, unformed matter, this will be viewed as, say, an uncritical reception of Plato's cosmological speculations in the *Timaeus*, not a valid inference from scripture.

10 Grammar and Contemplation

Caputo (and Keller) clearly opt for the first position, whereas my own view accords with the second, at least in outline.[6] Recent attempts have been made to argue the third, though I shall not consider them here.[7] In taking the second position, it is not essential to my argument that the doctrine's unambiguous affirmation be traced back throughout all the various strata of the biblical canon. Indeed, it is instructive to appreciate its historical emergence, especially as it intertwines with parallel developments in eschatology. As we shall see, protology and eschatology in Christian theology are mutually informative and find in *creatio ex nihilo* a logical meeting place.

Before examining this interaction between protology and eschatology in the biblical traditions, however, we must first deal with some formal considerations of *creatio ex nihilo* as they relate to objections to classical affirmations of divine transcendence and omnipotence. At issue here is the sort of grammar (or rules of speech) operative in such affirmations. My central contention is that if *creatio ex nihilo* is elaborated according to a competitive logic, or as Kathryn Tanner alternatively puts it, a contrastive logic, then its meaning will become irretrievably distorted, with the result that its explicit rejection or modification in favor of presumed alternatives may amount to a subtle acceptance of onto-theological terms, that is, that God and world coexist within a continuum, on the same plane, on a competitive basis, and so on.[8] A more adequate understanding of *creatio ex nihilo*, at least initially, is one that sees in it a systematic denial. Far from making the origin and ground of creation accessible to full comprehension, the statement requires the work of an apophatic discourse that opens up human understanding to the utter gratuity of creation. Formally speaking, nothing is necessary about creation at all.[9] It derives wholly from the incomprehensible mystery of God, whose relationship to creation remains one of loving freedom and fidelity. Rather than implying an agonistic picture that situates God and creation in a relationship of rivalry — such a picture only underwrites the serialization of binary and hierarchically arranged terms (e.g., power/weakness, higher/lower, spirit/body, male/female, active/passive) — *creatio ex nihilo* in fact ruptures such a picture as it emphatically denies that God is "part" of any continuum whatsoever.

The Difference Nothing Makes 11

According to Caputo, however, *creatio ex nihilo* represents a disfigurement of the biblical narratives, one that has turned a more Hebraic vision of creation into "the tale of a pure, simple, clean act of power carried out on high by a timeless and supersensible being, a very Hellenic story that also goes along with a top-down social structure of imperial power flowing down from on high."[10] Caputo would have us take notice of the metaphysician's selective memory that conceals the fragments and unnerving indeterminacies of the creation narratives in their extant form. "We ever-suspicious sacred anarchists, we who have a strong affection for weak theology, suspect foul play."[11] Who is this "we," and how did it ever come to be that "they" buried the bodies?

It is difficult not to notice that Caputo relishes the role of the gadfly, as an exile from a kingdom of orthodoxy that denies him credentials for admission. One might view the constant refrain of "we anarchists" throughout *The Weakness of God* as the seriously playful work of the ironist, since what frequently passes as acceptably orthodox seems decidedly unplayful, far too confident in its ability to trace origins, establish historical continuities, and monitor boundaries. Yet there is a risk that such self-identification makes the work of the ironist more acutely so—that is, not in the way intended—since the rhetoric might only deepen the very "us" and "them" polarization so passionately decried. I point out this recurrent rhetorical feature because it highlights a more basic dichotomization that contributes to the caricature of the doctrine Caputo would deconstruct. The "us" and "them" polarization extends throughout his treatment in the sharply delineated categories of "weak" and "strong," Hebraic and Greek, heterodox and orthodox, and finally creation *ex profundis* and creation *ex nihilo*. One suspects that the terms are set up too conveniently for the sake of argument, and with the consequence that the deconstructionist's professional sensitization to dualities and oppressive hierarchies achieves largely a reversal of terms rather than their fundamental questioning. Consider the following statements:

Divine omnipotence is a concept fulfilled in fantasy, spinning wildly in ideal space, with absolute velocity, while the brutal course of the real world proceeds at a slower, bloodier pace.

12 Grammar and Contemplation

No wonder, then, that the idea of absolute omnipotence did not arise from biblical and historical experience, but rather arose from a metaphysical debate among ecclesiastical theologians in the process of consolidating institutional power who seized upon a biblical idea (*con-capere*) and set it loose into infinity in a way that neither historical nor religious experience could support.

The mainstream orthodox tradition has drummed the primal elements out of the discussion in order to make way for creation ex nihilo, which makes for a cleaner cut, everything black and white, and gives things a firm foundation. The theological tradition thinks that God comes out ahead this way, that God is even greater and mightier, and that God is a greater giver of gifts if God's gift-giving were complete, including both form and matter, exhaustively ex nihilo.[12]

Before looking at the particulars of its historical development, we must notice straight away that *creatio ex nihilo* (and one of its corollaries, divine omnipotence) is objectionable as ideological fantasy, concocted and peddled by a theological elite.[13] It serves as a classic case study in religious neurosis and projection, for by locking God up in a solipsistic bubble of absolute sovereignty it only inures those who maintain it from those harsh realities of history. The biblical traditions do not affirm creation from nothing in the sense articulated in the second and third centuries CE but presume God's creative activity as drawing from *tehomic* depths that have no bottom, no absolute origin, and no lasting determination. Creation is an interminable process of becoming in which God solicits our participation. *Creatio ex nihilo* excludes all meaningful sense of becoming, we are told, for not only does divine creativity operate under such terms by absolute fiat, it also means that the world comes ready-made. Stasis, not dynamism; closure, not openness; force, not invitation is the result of this metaphysically stifling world picture. "My idea," writes Caputo, "which is deeply sympathetic with the critique of omnipotence in process theologians, is to shift the emphasis on the Genesis narratives back from power to goodness, back from being to life, back from a muscle-flexing causal force to a gift-giving word who fashions life out of desert and deep."[14]

The Difference Nothing Makes 13

The choice Caputo sets before us is starkly binary: either theology must come to grips with a view of God who is "weak," and who brings life from *tehomic* depths that have no final master or origin, or theology continues to bury the slippery and stubborn textual bodies in the creation stories that signify those depths in order to maintain the consoling illusion that a cosmic puppet master controls all. Caputo's negative characterization of divine power and sovereignty is here cast in a zero-sum relation with creation: either God is omnipotent, which rules out historical ambiguity and openness within creation, or God is a "weak force," in which case we must learn to accept a vision of creation as an ongoing process we undertake along with God. Or again, either we assert divine omnipotence, which entails an interventionist and "thaumaturgical" view of a God who "suspends or bends natural laws so that in the end things turn out just the way God has planned," or God is more like a "weak force" whose actual existence we can never be quite sure of but whose name harbors the "event" of possibility.[15] "The power of God," writes Caputo, "is the weak force of a word, a meaning, a sense, a solicitation, an invitation, a hermeneutical rather than a physical or metaphysical rule, a call that calls us beyond ourselves and our self-concern, that assures us that the 'world' is not all in all."[16] If there is something attractive about this last statement—and there *is* something attractive about it—the only way it can be consistently affirmed, we are told, is by consigning *creatio ex nihilo* to the scrap heap of metaphysics.[17]

But must we accept this tidy characterization? Are we really at an impasse? Are there no resources in Christian theology, whether ancient or new, that might allow us to hold together the meaning of creation *ex nihilo* and creation *ex profundis* in closest unity, as not at all in competition for claiming our allegiance and inspiring our discourse and practice? Must unconditioned transcendence be fatally at odds with God's nearness? Must omnipotence even be at odds with vulnerability? Along these lines, we might ask whether Caputo's formulation of the problem reflects its own kind of forgetfulness. Might we discover that the manner of framing the problem shares unquestioned premises with modernity's problematization of transcendence and power, and thus despite his attempts to overcome a certain metaphysical picture he remains subtly beholden to it?

14   Grammar and Contemplation

TRANSCENDENCE (AND IMMANENCE) WITHOUT RESERVE

Among the recurrent themes in contemporary theology, criticism of "classical" formulations of divine transcendence figures prominently. Often such criticisms come with the plea that an equal or greater emphasis be given to immanence to balance out some perceived one-sidedness in the theological tradition. Perhaps divine transcendence is thought to dispatch God to a realm of rarefied ideality, some remote space "out there" that leaves God magnificently indifferent to our creaturely drama. Or perhaps the criticism views divine transcendence as a source of oppressive paternalism and thus the wrong kind of involvement in the world, since those who have acquired the privilege of representation can maintain unquestioned authority vis-à-vis others. Talk of God's transcendence becomes code for investing certain persons, cultures, institutions, and religions with the power of normativity. A robust defense of immanence might therefore become strategic for giving expression to a God who is vulnerably involved in the material and historical processes of our contingent existence, for destabilizing and pluralizing "from below" those power relationships that have achieved institutionally sedimented, "top-down" privilege.

Such considerations underscore just how loaded our God-talk is, which is why a central task of theology is to subject to criticism the complex and largely unnoticed ways our discourse about God carries ideological freight. But the almost self-evident link between "transcendence" and divine "apathy" or "tyranny" reflects a fundamental misunderstanding. To put it simply, the problem is not that a greater balance between juxtaposed terms is required, or that a radicalization of immanence (as opposed to transcendence) is necessary to subvert all such "strong theologies." The problem is that all such characterizations of divine transcendence are insufficiently radical.

Creaturely "Distinction" within God

Commenting upon the theologies of divine transcendence in Augustine, Gregory of Nyssa, Pseudo-Dionysius, Thomas Aquinas, and Nicholas of Cusa (among others), Henri de Lubac writes that those who affirm transcendence "do not deny immanence. Indeed, they grasp

The Difference Nothing Makes 15

the idea of transcendence sufficiently to understand that it necessarily implies immanence. If God is transcendent, then nothing is opposed to him, nothing can limit him nor be compared with him: [God] is 'wholly other,' and therefore penetrates the world absolutely. *Deus interior intimo meo et superior summo meo.*"[18] While a statement like this may initially confirm suspicions that transcendence so understood implies domination (nothing can "oppose" or "compare" with God), the statement means to say that the world cannot oppose God because God is not an oppositional reality, that is, not *a* being among beings, not *a* power among powers. To declare God as "wholly other" is to issue a denial of a thoroughgoing sort. God and world are not "one," yet neither are they "two." God and world cannot be identified, yet neither are they two beings constituted by a zero-sum relationship. They are "not-two"—noncontrastive and noncompetitive.

Precisely because God is the incomparable and unconditioned, utterly boundless and unconstrained, God is radically near to creation in its particularity, contingency, and texture: without measure, without opposition, and with no need for a chain of intermediaries in order to be present or efficacious in the world. The infinite "more than" of God is fatally misunderstood if imagined according to a scale of similitude. God and creation stand in a relation of absolute, qualitative distinction—a distinction that comes "to be" through God's free origination. Creation implies a distinction "from" God that, because of its absolute character, remains "in" God.[19] "The difference between God and the world," writes Karl Rahner, "is of such a nature that God establishes and *is* the difference of the world from himself, and for this reason he establishes the closest unity precisely in the differentiation."[20] God grants the world its own sphere of integrity, as other than God, and yet the world wholly dwells within God who remains its (nonobjectifiable) ground. Although on our "side" of this qualitative distinction we might conventionally speak of transcendence as "beyond" the world and immanence "within" it, a more consistent way of putting the matter is that the self-bestowal of the wholly transcendent God is "the most immanent factor in the creature."[21] God is nearer to me than I am to myself, as Augustine declares.

The implications of this theological grammar should not go unnoticed: limited transcendence means limited immanence. If God

16 Grammar and Contemplation

is in some sense regional in relationship to creation—that is, if the distinction is not absolute but categorical—then God would only be somewhere "out there," negatively defined and limited by the world, and so able only to operate "on" or "in" or "with" the world in a local manner. Such a view is in fact characteristic of much Hellenistic thought. Tanner summarizes:

> In Greek and Roman religion and in Greek philosophy to a great extent, divinity refers to a kind of being distinct from others within the matrix of the same cosmos. Divinity characterizes that which is most powerful, self-sufficient and unchanging among beings, providing loci of intelligibility and meaning within an otherwise disordered world. As a distinct sort of being differentiated from others, like any other kind, within the same spectrum of being making up the cosmos, divinity is a predicate determined by commonality and susceptible of difference: it is the sort of thing which can be said to be shared generically with specifying differences of degree.[22]

God and world (and entities within the world) are distinguished according to a valuational hierarchy. God is atop the Great Chain of Being, and divine actuality cascades down the scale to that which is most passive, namely, "matter." As Tanner makes clear, this formulation is contrastive and spatial. We find it in Aristotle, and we find it in Middle Platonism, which formed the philosophical milieu for the debates over *creatio ex nihilo*. In Middle Platonism "divinity is localized as First or Primary Being within a cosmological hierarchy and characterized in an exclusive way that sets it apart from everything else. Divinity and the rest of the world taken as a whole are viewed as logical contraries within a single spectrum; this forces an a priori separation of the two."[23] Such a picture makes the postulation of matter's eternity entirely logical, perhaps even necessary according to its own terms.

The affirmation of God's radical transcendence unsettles this world picture, however. By declaring that God freely originates the whole of created reality, and that there are no preexistent constraints with which God must necessarily contend, whether passive matter, cosmological laws, or *khoral* indeterminacies, *creatio ex nihilo* affirms

The Gift of Being Creaturely

God's relationship to creation as gratuitous. The point has nothing to do with securing for God some tyrannical power, which human beings might co-opt. Rather, it is part of a vision of the God-world relationship that sees no rivalry between them.

The Gift of Being Creaturely

That the biblical narratives speak of God as creator is deeply significant here. Even if scripture is not immediately engaged in the kinds of questions we are considering in this more formal manner, the affirmation of God as creator inclines toward the view of the non-eternity of matter once the question gets explicitly raised. If God is not viewed as "part" of the world in any way, not even its best part, we already have an understanding of God's transcendence that challenges the Hellenistic picture by articulating God's relationship to creation as unnecessary. God does not need the world, nor does God depend on the world in order to be God. Yet God "gives" the world and elects to be intimately involved with those creatures dependent upon God for their very existence. "In Christian belief," writes Robert Sokolowski, "we understand the world as that which might not have been, and correlatively we understand God as capable of existing, in undiminished goodness and greatness, even if the world had not been. . . . The world and everything in it is [therefore] appreciated as a gift brought about by a generosity that has no parallel in what we experience in the world. The existence of the world now prompts our gratitude, whereas the being of the world prompts our wonder."[24] To suggest, as does Caputo, that such a view of God is not available to experience is to miss the difference nothing makes. Sokolowski ventures to say that "the distinction between the world understood as possibly not having existed and God understood as possibly being all that there is" is hardly a matter of abstraction, even if the idea can be abstractly formulated. "The distinction is lived in Christian life"—a point I shall try to make clear later in this chapter and throughout much of the book.[25] But even here we might consider how the simple act of prayer can help nourish the insight that the doctrine of *creatio ex nihilo* enshrines. Rowan Williams elaborates the point with contemplative prayer specifically in mind:

18   Grammar and Contemplation

To say, "I exist (along with the whole of my environment) at God's will, I am unconditionally dependent upon God" means [that] . . . my existence in the world, *including* my need to imagine this as personal, active and giving, is "of God"; my search for an identity is something rooted in God's freedom, which grounds the sheer thereness of the shared world I stand in. . . . Before the literally inconceivable fact of the divine difference and the divine liberty we have no words except thanksgiving that, because God's life *is what it is*, we are. . . . The contemplation of God, which is among other things the struggle to become the kind of person who can without fear be open to the divine activity, would not be possible if God were seen as an agent exercising power over others, bending them to the divine will. Contemplative prayer classically finds its focus in the awareness of God at the centre of the praying person's being—and, simultaneously, God at the centre of the whole world's being: a solidarity in creatureliness.[26]

Williams's account of contemplation entails transcendence (and so immanence) without reserve. While obviously affirming the contingency of creation—creation is "unconditionally dependent" and can be beheld in its "sheer thereness"—Williams also affirms God's radical proximity to creation. Precisely because God's transcendence is illimitable, God is at the "centre of the praying person's being" and the "centre of the whole world's being." This is what the grammar of transcendence is really about; and it is just this grammar that lies at the heart of *creatio ex nihilo*.[27]

One lesson to be drawn from this is the following: those who might plead for a greater emphasis upon immanence in order to correct some perceived imbalance will actually make a more coherent case by deepening our understanding of divine transcendence. The latter includes the former. It is a lesson Caputo seems to have forgotten, or chooses to ignore. To wit: "Indeed, rather than speaking of God's transcendence at all, it might be better to speak of God's inscendence (incendiary inscendence!) or 'insistence' in the world. The essence of God's transcendence lies in God's insistence. . . . I am trying to displace thinking about God as the highest and best thing that is *there* by starting to think that God is the call that *provokes* what is

The Difference Nothing Makes 19

there, the specter that haunts what is there, the spirit that breathes over what is there."[28] Overcoming the onto-theological frame is not best served by denying or limiting God's transcendence, as Caputo seems to imagine. It is served by articulating "the distinction."[29] As Tanner puts it, Christian theology "needs to radicalize claims about both God's transcendence and involvement with the world if the two are to work for rather than against one another." Caputo's position may seem radical in its incendiary insistence, but it is not radical enough. "A contrastive definition [of transcendence and agency] is not radical enough to allow a direct creative involvement of God within the world in its entirety. A contrastive definition does not work through the implications of divine transcendence to the end: a God who transcends the world must also . . . transcend the distinctions by contrast appropriate there."[30]

POWER (AND VULNERABILITY) WITHOUT RESERVE

In light of the noncontrastive account of transcendence above, we can give an account of God's power (or omnipotence) in a similar fashion. Adequately understood, they are two aspects of the same grammar.

Caputo clearly intends to avoid a competitive view of God and creation. "God's transcendence is not to be taken onto-theo-logically as a *summum ens* towering over finite beings," he writes, "nor is it to be taken onto-theo-politically as a sovereign master who supplies the paradigm for the human mastery over everything else. . . . I do not think of God as some super-being who out-knows, out-wills, out-does, out-powers, and out-exists every entity here below, a higher super-entity, a hyper-presence dwelling in a high world."[31] Taken on these terms alone, such statements seem consistent with two fundamental rules Tanner formulates for speaking of divine transcendence and agency. The first, which we have already analyzed, is to avoid any "univocal attribution of predicates to God and world in a simple contrast of divine and non-divine predicates."[32] If God is understood in terms of "being" so that God is, as it were, a very big being standing apart from and over all other beings, God and world will be construed as coexisting within a continuum. Such is a case of onto-theology,

20   Grammar and Contemplation

and it runs roughshod over their absolute, qualitative distinction. It also produces untold confusion in practical and theoretical matters in theology, especially in theologies of grace. If God and world coexist within some kind of continuum, then divine agency is exercised at the expense of creaturely agency, and vice versa. The question of divine will and human freedom becomes an intractable problem.[33]

The second rule therefore follows from the first: "avoid in talk about God's creative agency all suggestions of limitation in scope or manner. The second rule prescribes talk of God's creative agency as immediate and universally extensive."[34] In the same way transcendence and immanence should not be opposed, so must we avoid opposing divine agency and creaturely agency in a manner that suggests reciprocity or mutual exclusion. If we speak of God's agency as limited in some way, either as the result of incapacity or in direct conflict with some other agency, we can no longer consistently speak of God's unconditioned freedom. "Like that of a finite agent, God's influence will be of a limited sort: it may not extend to everything, it may presuppose what it does not produce, it may require the intervening agency of others."[35] This last point should be embraced by one who wishes to avoid thinking of God as a whimsical power who intervenes here and there, or who violently breaks in upon the world in order to subject it to some implacable design. If God is regional vis-à-vis creation, then divine agency will also be regional, with the result that creaturely agency gains its sphere of autonomy to the extent divine agency is uninvolved. Divine power, insofar as it becomes operative in a region where it does not yet reach, will do so in a way that extends, overcomes, appropriates, or cajoles.

The point of this second rule is not to secure for God arbitrary power but rather to show how divine creativity is not at all competitive with the world whose very existence it sustains from within. The *alterity* of God is wholly pacific and generative, limitlessly nurturing and empowering of contingent creation. This is how to understand the abstract idea of "omnipotence." It may be easy to confuse omnipotence with tyranny, but such an understanding "misses the true concept of omnipotence," writes Wolfhart Pannenberg. The "power of God has no precondition outside itself," no "object" against which it must strive, no "antithesis" to which

The Difference Nothing Makes   21

it is tied. "Power" is not a univocal concept that can equally apply to God and creature. A fundamental asymmetry pertains, since the creator God is the one who freely originates and sustains creaturely agency as such. "For this reason," continues Pannenberg, "the scriptures consistently related what they say about God's omnipotence to references to his creative work."[36]

A Theopoetics without Reserve

This last statement is crucial. Christian discourse cannot properly speak of divine power in abstraction from a set of stories that account for God as creator, as redeemer, and as the One who "who gives life to the dead and calls into being what does not exist." This latter expression from Paul's Epistle to the Romans (4:17) finds so many echoes throughout the New Testament that Richard Bauckham has declared it "close to being a definition of God."[37] "God raised the Lord and will also raise us by his power" (1 Cor. 6:14); "the power of God, who raised him from the dead" (Col. 2:12); "who raises the dead" (2 Cor. 1:9); "who raised the Lord Jesus [and who] will raise us also with Jesus" (2 Cor. 4:14); "established as Son of God in power according to the spirit of holiness through resurrection from the dead" (Rom. 1:4; see also Rom. 4:24, 8:11, 10:9; Eph. 1:20; Col. 2:12; 1 Pet. 1:21). There is an intimate relationship in these (and other) passages between God's character, God's power, and Jesus's resurrection. We have here a narrative intervention in an otherwise abstract consideration that gives our discourse a determinative theological shape.[38] Here is a theopoetics without reserve; for rather than denying power to God, which the cross of Jesus disassociated from resurrection might imply, it reframes and reformulates power by revealing its true vocation in the gratuitous offer of reconciled life, even when (and especially when) life has succumbed to violence and unjust death.

I say "theopoetics without reserve" with reference to Caputo's project, for it is here where, after providing a brilliantly suggestive reading of the cross, it stops short of giving an equally suggestive account of how Jesus's resurrection from the dead might creatively reconstruct and rehabilitate the language of power. One cannot but admire Caputo's cross-centered deconstruction: "The power of God

22   Grammar and Contemplation

is not pagan violence, brute power, or vulgar magic; it is the power of powerlessness, the power of the call, the power of protest that rises up from innocence suffering and calls out against it, the power that says *no* to unjust suffering, and finally, the power to suffer-with (*sympathos*) innocence, which is perhaps the central Christian symbol."[39] This "power of powerlessness," so quintessentially Pauline, would seem a creatively subversive way to think of God's activity in the world. It would seem to set up for an incisive understanding of how divine creativity is not reciprocal to the false powers of the world, but is rather a power that is true because it is good, a power that is unlimited because it freely gives itself away and distributes itself so as to reconstitute others in reconciled relation. It seems on the verge of giving a rich account of Jesus's resurrection from the dead, in fact, as the "new creation" that shows how powerlessness so transfigured might provide us a vocabulary for talking about the redemption of "the powers and principalities," even their "participation" in divine life. But this Caputo cannot do. God's "weakness" is not the result of divine freedom. It is incapacity.

Explicitly distancing himself from Paul's presumption of God's unconditional agency (and therefore Paul's reading of the cross in light of the resurrection), Caputo offers a "more radical conception of the weakness of God, of the weak force of God," one that frankly denies God's ability to act "causatively" at all. "God is an event, not in the order of power or being, but in the order of the good."[40] Caputo rejects (not naïvely) the second of Tanner's two rules. He views divine agency not "as immediate and universally extensive," but as a "summons" (a "call," "event," or "lure") that disallows any analogical predication of power to God. "The name of God is the name of an unconditional promise, not of an unlimited power. A promise made without an army to enforce it, without the sovereign power to coerce it. *That* is what I am calling the weak force of God. That force is the power of powerlessness."[41] If such a statement is motivated by concerns with human appropriation and questions of theodicy, we must pause here to consider the implications of systematically disassociating the "order of power/being" from the "order of the good" in this way. I will mention two.

The Difference Nothing Makes 23

Specters of Modernity

The first implication relates to "the distinction" of divine and creaturely freedom previously discussed. If Caputo wishes to say that the only way to affirm divine goodness is by denying that God has the power to act—otherwise we must impute all evil to God, since God could and should prevent it—we might rightly ask whether we can affirm God's goodness if God cannot act. If God is unable to act in the way Caputo suggests, what warrant do we have for declaring God good? How could we distinguish goodness from mere passivity? To be good surely presupposes freedom, and yet it seems difficult to say how God is in any meaningful sense free under Caputo's terms. God might be free *from* the causal mechanisms of the world, but it seems that God is not free *for* involvement in the world. Divine freedom is negatively defined by creaturely agency. To declare God "weak" in a way that presumes limitation to divine freedom is to accept the terms of an onto-theological picture while struggling to avoid them.

As numerous commentators have observed, this apparent dilemma has a distinctively modern pedigree.[42] To situate divine power and creaturely agency in a scenario of contrast is to collapse "the distinction." It makes divine activity appear interventionist when in fact divine and creaturely agency are directly (not inversely) proportional. "There is not an independent causal continuum in which it is puzzling how God could intervene," writes William Placher. "The only causal continuum is one whose every event God sustains. Divine action is not an interruption in or a violation of the normal course of things, but precisely *is* the normal course of things."[43] This is so, not because the course of things follows some predetermined script, but because God positively and continuously *gives* the distinction that makes creaturely becoming possible. To appeal to the distinction between divine and human efficacy in terms of primary and secondary causality, which Placher does, is to affirm that God is continuously involved in the dynamic unfolding of creation as its animating source and ground. Creation has no independent existence. It is given *ex nihilo* by the creator God who positively wills its very existence. The openness and autonomy of creation in its dynamic becoming is contrastive not with divine efficacy, but is the very gift of that efficacy. *Creatio ex nihilo* explicitly affirms the contingency and open-ended "play" of creation. Creation is not self-constituting. It possesses no fixed essences. It is "a reality suspended between nothing and infinity," composed of "relational differences and ceaseless alternations," as John Milbank puts it. Creation from nothing actually gives priority to "becoming and unexpected emergence."[44]

We can say that this "play" of creation is intensified in the contingent freedom of human beings, though it is no less true to say that such freedom remains utterly dependent upon the transcendent God who gives and immanently sustains human freedom as its empowering ground. Divine agency and human agency are not "one," yet neither are they "two." As Rahner explains, "This very difference is established by God himself, and hence something which is autonomous and which alone realizes this radical difference between God and creatures entails no limitation of God's sovereignty. For this difference is not something which happens to him, but rather he alone makes it possible. He establishes it, he allows it, he grants it the freedom of its own self-actualization of this differentiation."[45]

Such a view is obviously in keeping with the Thomistic distinction between primary and secondary causality, but it is hardly exclusive to Thomas. As Placher and Tanner have both shown, it is just this distinction that is regularly presupposed in the so-called classical theological tradition — a tradition that is inaccurately characterized by certain theological revisionists who, rightly working for alternatives to the modern problematizations of human and divine agency, tend to project those problems back onto most premodern approaches. Such anachronistic projections are evident in Caputo's imputation to classical theologies of *creatio ex nihilo* of what in fact are modern problematizations of power, causality, and transcendence.

Narratives of a Vulnerable God

The second implication of unhinging the order of being/power from the order of the good is that it tends to leave power outside the ambit of redemption. Because Caputo frames power (and thus omnipotence) in terms of appropriation, domination, and tyranny, he must drive a distinction between power and goodness so deep that one wonders what positive relationship they could possibly have. If Caputo wishes to help us understand how goodness might itself be a kind of power, though one very different from "the principalities and powers" of this world, the effort is bedeviled by the near total identification of power with violence. This is a great loss, rhetorically and theologically, because it threatens to abandon those very principalities and powers to a realm of ontological violence when in fact Paul understands them to be created by God as *originally* good, as *presently* in a state exhibiting sinfulness, and open to a redeemed *future*.[46] We need not think of these narrative moments in crudely sequential terms, of course, but we must attempt to appreciate how Paul's theology of power, both human and divine, presupposes a broader narrative context whose theology of the cross is triangulated by a vision of original and eschatological peace. A more convincing and rehabilitative theological vision of power is one that affirms this fuller narrative context.

In his *Narratives of a Vulnerable God*, William Placher considers how the Gospels reveal a God whose "strange power" is fundamentally at odds with "power based on fear, power seeking domination, power always edging toward violence."[47] To say "at odds" is not to say reciprocal or retaliatory. God's power is not that sort at all. God's power has nothing to do with the splendid security of a cosmic monarch, but freely gives itself away as the expression of its very essence. What this means is that power based upon fear, domination, and violence is not "real" power at all. It *is* real insofar as its destructiveness is concretely materialized in human relationships, but it is in fact an idolatrous commandeering of true power. Because of the overwhelming pervasiveness of such idolatry it may be tempting to abandon the language of power altogether when speaking of God. The temptation must be resisted. It would amount to a tacit acceptance that power as such is congenitally (and so irredeemably) dominating and quick to violence. To accept this is to accept an upside-down world as right side up. As Placher further points out, renouncing a constructive theology of power makes it difficult to speak of God as creator, sustainer, and redeemer. It immediately renders much of scripture senseless, or worse. (The catena of scriptural passages above would be among the first to drop on the demythologist's cutting floor.) It also raises questions of an ethical sort since, despite Caputo's obvious intentions, it can lead to a fatalism that absconds from political engagement.[48]

Despite the many challenges and ambiguities it faces, positive Christian talk about power needs to reclaim its true vocation, and it can do no better in this rehabilitative task than by radicalizing it. In just the same way that transcendence is not opposed to immanence (as discussed above), so too is divine power in no way opposed to vulnerability. The unconditioned character of divine creativity subverts the binary contrasts of strong and weak. Divine vulnerability is vulnerability without reserve because divine power is not oppositionally structured or rivalrous with the world. God's omnipotence, as understood in Christian theological terms, is very different from what abstract considerations are likely to yield. As Karl Barth reminds us, God's "plenitude of power . . . can assume the form of weakness and impotence and so as omnipotence."[49] "God's power is the power of love," writes Placher, in light of Barth's considerations. It

> does not seek to dominate . . . but acts consistently in love which authentically concerns itself for others. . . . [F]or in freely loving, God is most of all who God is, most exemplifying the kind of power God has. When power means, as so often in human affairs it does, the uneasy quest for domination, then to be moved by another, wounded by another's pain, is experienced as a form of powerlessness, and love is trapped between inaction and the risk of impotence. But the strange power of God reveals such quests for power as a kind of weakness. . . . Vulnerability . . . is a perfection of loving freedom.[50]

The Resurrection in Retrospect

So far, we have considered objections to *creatio ex nihilo* at a more formal level of reflection. In order to meet the criticism that this doctrine makes God out to be some sort of cosmic tyrant whose activity in the world is interventionist, capricious, and dominating, I have tried to show how the doctrine in fact articulates the God-world relationship according to "the distinction," which, rather than resulting in a univocal (and onto-theological) discourse of "transcendence" and "power," requires that we elaborate such terms in a noncompetitive and noncontrastive manner. Only when *creatio ex nihilo* is understood according to this grammar does it gain its enduring and wide-ranging significance in theological discourse. So understood, *creatio ex nihilo* affirms that creation is wholly gratuitous: freely originated by the creator God upon whom it depends for its integrity, and so with whom it does not struggle for self-actualization. Far from being a source of top-down oppression or inbuilt manipulation, the recognition of our utter dependence on such gratuity "is the most liberating affirmation we could ever hear," writes Williams. "With God alone, I am dealing with what does not need to construct or negotiate an identity, what is free to be itself without the process of struggle. . . . God does not and cannot lay claim upon me so as to 'become' God; what I am cannot be made functional for God's being; I can never be defined by the job of meeting God's needs."[51] The striking consequence of this appraisal is that when we understand such divine gratuity as true power—that is, when we allow our discourse of power to be theologically shaped according to "the distinction" in this way—we are uniquely poised to see that "all other powers need to be unmasked or demythologized. The creator's power-as-resource cannot be invoked to legitimize earthly power."[52]

Here is the inner relationship between contemplative awareness and prophetic critique: by becoming attitudinally hospitable to the gratuity of our creaturely origination, and so to our primordial and continual dependence upon a God whose gift of creation comes *ex nihilo*—without any need, without any constraint, with no inner agitation or ulterior motive to augment divine being—not only do we contemplatively enter upon an infinitely pacific otherness who alone accepts us whole in the nakedness of our being, but we also become witness to and transformed by a power that stands as the ultimate index for critiquing every created power. True power—let us not be afraid of this word—is pacific, self-communicating, and empowering of others; it is just this power in which we are invited to participate in a creaturely way. Such an invitation means, as Sokolowski was quoted above as saying, living according to the distinction, which entails allowing our attitudinal horizons, desires, and practices to be

28   Grammar and Contemplation

shaped by and galvanized by the difference nothing makes. With this insight we may now transition from formal to narratival and practical considerations.

Earlier in this chapter I claimed that rather than representing an alien imposition of metaphysics upon the biblical stories of creation, *creatio ex nihilo* is consistent with and elucidatory of them. Even if the second-to-third-century debates over the eternity of matter are the proximate reason for its technical formulation, *creatio ex nihilo* makes explicit in that particular context what a biblical vision of divine creativity and freedom already implies. We can fully acknowledge that there is development in the biblical tradition, and in fact I wish now to trace one of its principal threads. As I wish to make clear, Jesus's resurrection from the dead is, for Christians, the eschatological promise God makes to creation, a promise that is concretely efficacious insofar as it entails the transformation of Jesus's entire creaturely reality (this is what "bodily" resurrection explicitly means). From the perspective of the Easter event—an event which reveals a God who calls unto eschatological life that which has succumbed to the nonbeing and nondoing of death—Christian reflection could come to envision the whole of creation in terms of pure summons. *Creatio ex nihilo* is not a doctrine that arises from fruitless speculation about the first instant of creation, much less some need to secure for God the power of a cosmic tyrant, but rather is an affirmation of how God continuously relates to creation, namely, through the pacific and reconciling freedom of God's very self. It reveals that God's power has nothing at all to do with some interminable struggle with creation. Indeed, if there is a demythologization at work here it is found in the discovery that God has nothing to do with violence or externally imposed necessity. God's relationship to creation is one of original (and eschatological) peace.

Logic and Discovery

It is true that scripture does not explicitly engage the question of "Being/beings" that informs the above discussion of onto-theology. "Incontestably," writes Jean-Luc Marion, "biblical revelation is unaware of ontological difference, the science of Being/beings as such, and hence of the question of Being. But nothing is less accurate than to pretend that it does not speak a word on being, nonbeing, and beingness."[53]

One text to which Marion turns for appeal is Romans 4:17, in which Paul speaks of Abraham's faith to God's call in the same breath as he speaks of the resurrection of the dead. Just as God calls Abraham (and thus Israel) to faith and covenant—the "call" here is utterly uncalled for, based upon no necessity whatsoever—so is the resurrection from the dead a "call" that brings to life that which was not. Nothing compels God to issue this promise or even act upon it once made, and nothing prevents God from bringing the promise into fruition, neither Israel's exile nor the nonbeing of death. The logic is unmistakable: "Abraham is our father in the eyes of God, in whom he puts his faith, and who brings the dead to life and calls into existence what does not yet exist." Marion takes this to mean that faith in the living God cannot be circumscribed within "Being/being." The advent of the call to Abraham, like the call of the dead to life, is one that "crosses being." To say that God is "without being" is to say that God *gives* being. God gives "the distinction." "Being" comes from nothing—nothing other than God who "delivers" it and "puts it into play."[54]

Picking up a similar line of reflection, Williams maintains that the theology of *creatio ex nihilo* finds decisive historic and narrative roots in the event of Israel's return from exile, especially the "second exodus" of the Babylonian exile. We see particularly in Second Isaiah a vision of restoration as the renewal of creation, a second creation that permits a new understanding of creation as such. "Out of a situation where there is no identity," writes Williams, "where there are no names, only the anonymity of slavery or the powerlessness of the ghetto, God makes a human community, calls it *by name* (a recurrent motif in Is. 40–55), gives it or restores to it a territory. Nothing makes God do this except God's own free promise; from human chaos God makes human community."[55] In the gratuity of God's call, what was "not" now "is." Creation is not about the suppression of chaos or any sort of battle with recalcitrant materials. It is "seen as performed by the free utterance of God alone." The point has nothing to do with dramatizing divine power over against something. Indeed, it is to show that creation isn't about power (agonistically framed) at all. "Prior to God's word, there is nothing to impose *on*."

Of course, this understanding of God's gratuitous summons may not lead inexorably to *creatio ex nihilo*, at least as we find it in the second to third centuries; but, argues Williams, it is a "short step to the conclusion that God's relation to the whole world is like this: not a struggle with pre-existing disorder that is then moulded into shape, but a pure summons."[56]

Caputo was earlier quoted as saying that nothing within biblical or human experience could be said to underwrite the theology of divine omnipotence and *creatio ex nihilo*, but here we see how the gratuity of God's call, as well as the narratives of exodus and covenant, provide the historical and narratival resources for just such an understanding.[57] We know from biblical scholarship that the stories of creation were composed subsequent to the events of exodus and covenant, and that only from the point of view of Israel's historic liberation and lived fidelity/infidelity does there emerge a theology of God as creator of the universe. The stories of creation themselves reflect the grammar of exodus and covenant. If, as Williams claims, there is only a short step to the conclusion that God's relationship to the whole of creation is one of pure summons, we can also appreciate that such a step was not taken all at once. David Burrell makes this point when he writes that the Israelites' "preoccupations with the God who calls forth and so redeems a people only slowly gave way to the more cosmic implications of that fact." The theology of creation may be said to exhibit an ongoing process of discovery that radiates from the experience of exodus and covenantal relationship. "Yet when such reflections took place," Burrell adds, "there was no hesitation to affirm this One as both sovereign and free. And the reasons for insisting that this be the case with the creator would plausibly stem from what the experience of redemption had taught them."[58]

To better understand this retrospective movement from soteriology to a reflexive theology of creation, we can usefully make a distinction. On the one hand there is the *logic* of creation from nothing that can be described in formal terms, while on the other there is the process of its *discovery* that arises from lived experience and reflection.[59] If *creatio ex nihilo* reflects a particular logic about the God-world relationship that can be stated in technical language, especially when induced to do so by a particular philosophical and theological dispute, it need not be thought of as divorced from the concrete circumstances that nourish the insight "from below." Of course, it is possible at some later time to declare that *creatio ex nihilo* has always been the biblical view of creation, though such an assessment is clearly mistaken. But it is no less mistaken to ignore those trends in scripture that evidence a process of discovery about the God-world relationship and make those formal terms eminently coherent. This becomes especially clear in the theology of Jesus's resurrection from the dead.

Narratives *in Excess*: Protology and Eschatology Embrace

The belief in the resurrection of the dead is a relative latecomer in Jewish theology. Only in postexilic times do we begin to see its flowering. We can trace the metaphorical elements of resurrection language taking shape in Isaiah, Hosea, Ezekiel, and Zechariah, but only in Daniel (12:2) will we find an unambiguous instance in the canonical Old Testament that affirms (in a metonymical way) personal resurrection from the dead.[60] Intertestamental literature produces more examples, including the memorable scene depicted in 2 Maccabees in which the Jewish martyrs of Antiochus IV are said to await the justice of the general resurrection. What is significant about this example is that it intimately unites resurrection with creation. "I do not know how you came to be in my womb," says the mother to her seven slain sons in the presence of their oppressor. "It was not I who gave you breath and life, nor was it I who arranged the elements you are made of. Therefore, since it is the Creator of the universe who shaped the beginning of humankind and brought about the origin of everything, he, in his mercy, will give you back both breath and life, because you now disregard yourselves for the sake of his law" (7:22–23). The hoped-for resurrection of the dead, which was by the second century BCE a fairly widespread (though not universal) belief among Jews, is directly connected with God's covenantal faithfulness to creation. It therefore bears upon the very character of Israel's God. It enunciates a vision that telescopes eschatology and protology. Resurrection is the (future) fulfillment of creation's (original) vocation, and the deliverance of creation from (present) domination and (the ongoing threat of) annihilation.

32   Grammar and Contemplation

This narrative telescoping is especially characteristic of the New Testament, not least when the Gospel of John speaks of Jesus as "the resurrection and the life" (11:25) and the Logos-made-flesh as the generative principle of creation: "All things came to be through him, and without him nothing came to be" (1:3). Paul too describes Christ simultaneously as the "firstborn of all creation" and the "the firstborn from the dead" (Col. 1:15–18). Christ's resurrection is for Paul not just God's restoration of creation in the midst of its destruction; it instantiates the future fulfillment of creation when God will be all in all (1:28). What is particularly relevant for my purposes here is not to declare, as Pannenberg justifiably does, that Paul's theology provides sufficient scriptural warrant for a theology that affirms *creatio ex nihilo* and divine omnipotence.[61] My interest is what the resurrection reveals about divine creativity. What insight might this central affirmation of the New Testament provide as related to the character of divine power, and might such insight be key to the meaning of *creatio ex nihilo*?

If anything might be summarily said of God raising Jesus from the dead, it could profitably be described as exhibiting a "logic of excess." The character of the Easter event as presented in the New Testament is strikingly consistent with the whole of Jesus's ministry, which, as Paul Ricoeur puts it, "clashes head on with the logic of equivalence that orders our everyday exchanges, our commerce, and our penal law."[62] Jesus's hospitality to those outside centers of power and privilege, his ministry of forgiveness to sinners, his consistent renunciation of violence, his parables that disclose a God whose surprising otherness subverts all earthly claims to domestication and manipulation: these defining features of Jesus's ministry are validated and dramatically reexpressed by the event of Easter, but in a way that now seeks to reestablish communion, through forgiveness, with those who violently expelled Jesus and his Kingdom ministry from their midst. The dynamics of Easter grace is excess upon excess (a "logic of generosity" or "superabundance," as Ricoeur alternatively calls it) because it reveals a power utterly unconditioned by reciprocity and violence.

The resurrection is not an overpowering in any sense. Though it is God's definitive vindication of an innocent man whose violent expulsion typifies the "will to power"—the resurrection is, to be sure,

God's eschatological verdict upon the mechanisms that led to Jesus's crucifixion—the response is not in any way "like unto like." Such a "surprising avenger."[63] Neither is it described in the New Testament as involving displays of bombast. Indeed, the resurrection of Jesus is never (objectively) narrated, only the interpersonal encounters of the risen Christ who imparts shalom, forgiveness, hope, and the possibility of a reconciled community. Consider the stereotypical speeches of Peter in Acts: "Peter said to [those who crucified Jesus], 'Repent and be baptized, every one of you, in the name of Jesus Christ for the forgiveness of your sins; and you will receive the gift of the Holy Spirit. For the promise is made to you and to your children and to all those far off, whomever the Lord our God will call'" (2:38–39). "The God of our ancestors raised Jesus, though you had him killed by hanging him on a tree. God exalted him at his right hand as leader and savior to grant Israel repentance and forgiveness of sins" (5:30–31). In the crucifixion, declares Peter, we have murdered the "author of life" (3:15). Yet this author of life returns to us precisely in the midst of our violence in order to offer us reconciliation with that author, and with each other.

By raising Jesus from the dead, God is revealed as that wholly Other whose creativity is not hemmed in by the nonbeing and non-doing of death. Jesus risen is God's creativity "out of nothing," and so a power that is not negatively structured by anything at all. God's power is revealed as pardoning, self-communicative, and creatively in excess to the self-defensive and self-aggrandizing mechanisms that threaten and destroy creation. Here, more than anywhere else, we see the demythologization of false power at work. As James Alison explains:

> Jesus' resurrection is not revealed as an eschatological revenge, but as an eschatological pardon. It happens not to confound the persecutors, but to bring about a reconciliation.... This permits the definitive demythologization of God. God, completely outside of human reciprocity, is the human victim.... Thus, far from creation having anything to do with the establishment of an order, what is revealed is that the gratuitous self-giving of the victim is identical with, and the heretofore hidden center and culmination of, the gratuitous giving that is the creation.[64]

Drawing upon the work of René Girard, Alison describes the resurrection as the demythologization of God because it reveals definitively that God has nothing to do with violent power. God is not a rival to creation, nor does God form any "sacred" foundation for the sort of scapegoating mechanism that Jesus's death so graphically displays. God's response to such violence reveals true power, which is reconciling and self-donative. God's creativity is "purely gratuitous giving, without motive, with no second intentions, with no desire for control or domination, but rather a gratuity which permits creatures to share gratuitously in the life of the Creator. The relation of gratuity is anterior to what is and has ever been."[65]

Notice the shift in this last sentence: the gratuity of God's relationship to creation as revealed by the resurrection is not ad hoc or some kind of afterthought, but primordially generative of creation—original peace. The peace imparted in the encounters with the risen Christ has nothing to do with the temporary armistice that the suppression of conflict might afford; it is "the primordial peace of the Creator from the beginning."[66] Shalom is anterior to creation. The creaturely "distinction" from God has nothing to do with necessity or some sort of rupture from undifferentiated unity we forever mourn and desperately seek to recapture. The difference of creation from God—this difference nothing makes—is imparted pacifically and generously. To be a creature is original *gift*.

The Johannine and Pauline theologies of creation "in Christ" make just this conjoining of eschatology and protology explicit. The prologue of John's gospel, which, as James D. G. Dunn notes, reflects the "backward extension of the Son of God language—from resurrection . . . to a timeless eternity," articulates a vision of origins that recasts the Genesis account within a post-Easter imagination.[67] "All things came to be through him, and without him nothing came to be" (John 1:3). And, again, in Colossians we see a reframing of creation that looks back (in retrospect) through the resurrection: "He is the beginning, the firstborn from the dead" (1:18). Eschatology and protology here embrace "in Christ," and in this embrace we reach the critical threshold that would be determinative for the affirmation of *creatio ex nihilo* in the patristic period.

The Difference Nothing Makes   35

CREATION IN CHRIST: THE PATRISTIC ELUCIDATION

As Ricoeur has observed, the wisdom Christologies in the Johannine and Pauline literature indicate a theological trajectory that proved crucial for the future of Christian theology.[68] By assimilating the theology of creation within a theology of the Word, so that creation comes to be "in" or "through" Christ, there emerged a shift from a "temporal sense of beginning" toward an "atemporal sense of origin."[69] That is, rather than speaking of God bringing life from prior formlessness (Gen. 1), wisdom Christology of this variety accounts for creation as originating from God's preexistent Word and so as pure summons (John 1). Here there is no temporal "before," no immemorial scene from which creation comes to be, only the gratuitous and pacific summons of the creator God who calls forth the scene as such. These modes of accounting for creation (temporal and atemporal) are not mutually exclusive in the New Testament. In fact, they are intermixed. But it is clear, according to Ricoeur, that the temporal sense of beginning becomes, in these wisdom Christologies, "virtually subordinated" to the atemporal sense of origin.[70]

The significance of this trend for *creatio ex nihilo* is immediately evident, particularly when we observe that the second and third centuries brought to reflection a question not explicitly posed in most biblical accounts of creation, namely, whether the world (or "matter") is eternal.[71] In the encounter with Greek philosophers "who were tenacious advocates of the eternity of the world," patristic theologians quickly and almost unanimously declared the contrary position. They did so, among other reasons, because the thesis of the eternity of the world "seemed to imply the self-sufficiency of the world."[72] By arguing that the world had not always been, that it derives wholly from the freedom of God upon whom it continually depends in intimate relationship, patristic theologians were elaborating a biblical theology of creation while extending the trajectory we find in the wisdom Christologies. Without such continuity it is hard to imagine how *creatio ex nihilo* could become "with astonishing speed the self-evident premise of Christian talk of the creation," as Gerhard May has documented.[73]

36 Grammar and Contemplation

May credits Theophilus of Antioch and Irenaeus of Lyons with providing the classic formulation. Although Tatian was probably the first Christian theologian to explicitly declare in Greek philosophical terms that God created matter (probably in confrontation with Marcionites in Rome), Theophilus was the first to state more fulsomely what *creatio ex nihilo* meant in contrast to the Greek philosophical axiom "Ex nihilo nihil fit."[74] As May explains, in Theophilus we see "the decisive distinction fully grasped and declared between the biblical God creating in omnipotent freedom and the platonic demiurge who is restricted in his creative activity by the precondition of matter and its possibilities. Now with the thesis of *creatio ex nihilo* and the corresponding positive statement that the free decision of God's will is the sole ground of creation, the biblical idea of free creation is properly formulated and validated within the ambit of philosophical thought."[75] This move is hardly arbitrary. If the postulation of the world's eternity was one of the proximate reasons for its explicit formulation, *creatio ex nihilo* in fact gives expression to the biblical emphasis on God's unconditioned freedom and involvement in the world; it exhibits coherence with a view of God "who gives life to the dead and calls into being what does not exist" (Rom. 4:17), and it accords with the vision of creation as having its gratuitous, atemporal origin through God's generative Word. Alas, it is difficult to imagine how patristic theology could have finally arrived at any other conclusion.

May summarizes the emergence of *ex nihilo* theology as a dialectical achievement: it "breaks through principles of philosophical metaphysics" while articulating itself "within the latter's frame of reference and by using its terms."[76] This is a crucial (if subtle) point, for it is here where critics of *creatio ex nihilo* might point to its acceptance in Christian theology as the capitulation to an onto-theological frame when in fact it subverts that frame from within. In the encounter with a world picture that casts God and creation in a zero-sum relation (the demiurge "is restricted in his creative activity by the precondition of matter and its possibilities") the patristic theological response was to account for creation as freely originated by God and thus to characterize the relationship between God and creation in a noncontrastive, noncompetitive way. If it is true that patristic theologians tended to read those scriptural accounts of creation that presume a

The Difference Nothing Makes   37

temporal beginning as though they were speaking of atemporal origin—and so, indeed, there is an interpretive overdetermination at work in the apologetic effort—we should understand that such "concurrence" (Ricoeur) of temporal beginning with atemporal origin in patristic exegesis actually corresponds with identifiable interpretive trajectories in scripture itself.

But there is another fundamental reason for the emergence of *creatio ex nihilo* in patristic theology, which brings us to the problem of evil. Both Theophilus and Irenaeus also spoke of God's free origination of creation in response to the cosmogonic speculations from various "gnostic" groups that located in matter the principle of evil. The Valentinians, for example, affirmed that matter had come into being not as the result of a "sovereign divine act," but as "a byproduct of the fall of Sophia"—Sophia being the last and furthest removed of God's emanations. What so troubled Irenaeus about this picture of world-formation was that it presumed an original violence (a primordial "mistake" or "ignorance") whose overcoming among human beings requires a separative movement from material creation.[77] For Irenaeus, whose idiomatically biblical theology exhibits little interest in freestanding philosophical speculation, creation is wholly contingent, a gift of God's free will, and originally good. Evil is not in any way anterior to, but is parasitical upon, creation. To borrow an illuminating typology from Ricoeur, Irenaeus's is not a "tragic vision" that characterizes the human being as struggling interminably within the agon of life; nor is it one that views the (immaterial) soul as "exiled" in a material order that must be surmounted through spiritual technique or salvific gnosis; rather, it is an "eschatological vision" in which the whole created order, although presently subject to evil, suffering, and the threat of annihilation, looks to a reconciled and transformed future in Christ.[78] It is possible to maintain this eschatological vision without explicitly declaring *creatio ex nihilo*, but it essential to see that the latter's articulation in the second and third centuries in fact exhibits just such a vision and is motivated to safeguard and elaborate it. What stimulates its formulation is the declaration of creation's original goodness—a goodness that is not a necessary emanation of the One or the Good, but a free gift.[79] The point is hardly a matter of empty conjecture. Irenaeus's unpacking of *creatio ex nihilo* in

38 Grammar and Contemplation

fact reflects his soteriological interests. Only within the context of the economy of salvation—covenant, incarnation, and resurrection—does the reflexive theology of origins gain its true significance.[80] To say that creation comes from nothing is, for Irenaeus, effectively to say that the whole of creation is freely originated from divine goodness and summoned to take part in present and future salvation, and that despite (and even in the midst of) the groaning that characterizes creation's ongoing travail, there remains a future for creation that shall bring it into its fullest fruition, precisely *as* creation.[81]

Hope for Creation

This is why I should like to emphasize, to conclude this chapter, that *creatio ex nihilo* is best thought of as a doctrine of hope for creation, not a doctrine that provides an explanation for the world, much less an attempt at theodicy. It is a soteriologically motivated doctrine that declares the penultimacy of evil, sin, and innocent suffering: because they do not have the final word—this is its eschatological vision—neither are they original or anterior to creation. Such an affirmation denies not their present reality but only their ontological ultimacy. It therefore refuses to say that "time and the turmoil are aboriginal, like God, . . . as the ineradicable resistance, indeterminacy, and chance in things with which God must cope." It refuses to characterize God as one who "can do only so much with the raw materials with which he works, that the potter is limited by the clay, that creation is a certain roll of the dice," and so on[82]—statements that, however "poetic," actually do more to explain the existence of evil and suffering than the position advanced here.

While I certainly disagree with the premise that God's unconditioned freedom and agency make God responsible for the evil and innocent suffering in the world—a premise that does not take sufficiently into account the qualitative distinction between divine and creaturely freedom outlined above—I fully recognize that such a position stands squarely in the midst of a mystery that is not made less so by this distinction. To say, as does Placher, that "there is not a single point where God is absent or inactive or only partly active or

The Difference Nothing Makes 39

restricted in action, *and* that there are irrational events that are somehow not caused by God," events we call "sin" or "evil," is actually to highlight the mystery with uncompromising starkness.[83] The appeal to creaturely free will, however necessary at some level, cannot ultimately justify and make comprehensible the excess of evil and suffering in our history. But no more helpful is the attempt to declare God somehow limited by creation—or, more strongly, incapable of causative action. Even if such a maneuver relieves some of the tensions entailed in this mystery, it can make almost no sense of the biblical witness to divine activity in the world, and least of all the New Testament affirmation that God has raised the innocent victim Jesus from the nonbeing of death as the effective promise for the whole of creation.

To the extent that *creatio ex nihilo* is understood not merely as a speculative assertion about the first instant of creation, but as a hopeful doctrine that expresses something fundamental about how God continuously relates to creation, it also allows us to say that "nothing" keeps God from being present to creation in all its contingency and ambiguity. "The very fact that God the Wholly Other is Creator means," writes Edward Schillebeeckx, "that he is also the Ultimate-Intimate One, the One Wholly near at hand."[84] Unconditioned transcendence means unconditioned immanence, and so presence to and solidarity with creatures in the midst of felt separation from God, even death on a cross. This is what Schillebeeckx means elsewhere when he describes the creator God as a God of "pure positivity." The creator God who summons creation "up out of nothing" is the God in whom "negativity cannot have a cause or motive."[85] How can Christians assert this? Or, better, why must Christians assert this? Not from a general theory of God arrived at by unmoored speculation, but from God's liberating and reconciling self-bestowal in the Easter event: "from the 'God of Jesus,' namely from Christian belief in the *resurrection* of Jesus. For it emerges that God transcends these negative aspects in our history, not so much by allowing them as *by overcoming them*, making them as though they had not happened. By nature, and in addition to other aspects and meanings, the resurrection of Jesus is also a corrective, a victory over the negativity of suffering and even death."[86] Schillebeeckx rightly refuses to say that God in any way uses evil or innocent suffering toward some greater purpose, as though God were somehow causatively involved in what destroys creation. Rather, taking Jesus's resurrection from the dead as primordially disclosive of God's character, we can say that God's activity is found in extending reconciliation where there is conflict, healing where there is violence, and eschatological fulfillment where there is death. "Only *in* the overcoming of [evil and innocent suffering] can we say that the negative aspects in our history have an indirect role in God's plan of salvation: *God is the Lord of history.* . . . God wants [our] *salvation*, and in it victory over [our] suffering."[87]

That God can do this, and has done this for Christ, in whom creation has its origin and hope, is an affirmation with far-reaching implications for how we are to live. To affirm that God can be wholly available in our weakness because God's power has nothing at all against which to strive can mean, for those who would inhabit such faith, living from and to a power that is all the more vulnerable because it is all the freer. To affirm that the creator God indwells the grit and grief of our human lives because God's freedom has no need to protect itself can mean, for those who would be "imitators of God" (Eph. 5:1), a willingness to indwell the suffering of others as agents of transformative justice and reconciliation. To affirm that God's relationship to creation is not competitive or rivalristic, but gratuitous and pacific, can mean, for those who would become hospitable to this relationship in prayer and the formation of new behavioral patterns, a shift in desire from the compulsive need to dominate others to the creative liberty of self-donation. To perceive the inner coherence of such affirmations, along with their practical implications, is to begin to understand the difference nothing makes.

CHAPTER TWO

Undergoing Something from Nothing

THE TOUCH OF THE INFINITE

In a remarkable but little-known essay, Sebastian Moore describes the transition from the concept of the infinite to the touch of the infinite as "the most devastating mind-shift conceivable."[1] With reference to the contemplative practice of "unknowing" and its affordance of unobstructed, nonconceptual awareness in prayer, Moore provides a striking account of our creatureliness that gives primacy to the felt reality of our dependence upon the infinite God for our being. "An *experience* of 'without-whom-nothing' is replacing a concept of 'without-whom-nothing.' Through experience, God redeems his self-description from algebra."[2]

The phrase *without-whom-nothing* is a way of invoking the doctrine of *creatio ex nihilo*, and both may be regarded as algebraic expressions helping us to signify a reality that is not so much thinkable as it is undergone. This is not to suggest that the practice of contemplative prayer entails the simple rejection of concepts in our deepening relationship with God. In company with the many exemplars of the Christian contemplative tradition, Moore insists upon the organic relationship between concepts and nonconceptual awareness, between cataphasis and apophasis, between word and silence in the life of prayer, and hence the work of theology. What must be stressed, however, is that the role of conceptualization shifts in tenor and significance, and dramatically so, once the powerful mental habit that keeps God tethered to concepts loosens and finally gives way to the vast, open awareness that manifests itself in contemplative prayer. The one who prays thus begins to learn that, while indispensable, concepts are quite inadequate for knowing God; but more, that God is an "obscure pressure," an "incomprehensible immediacy" working at the very root of the person, ceaselessly inducting us unto new life. Only from such ineffable intimacy can our words about God gain their vitality.

> There is a knowing of God without a concept, that, far from rendering the concept of God otiose, and far from giving us permission for a concept-spurning fideism, gives to that concept a peculiar validity, an edge of meaning, which it would not otherwise have. Conversely, the concept of God gives something to the direct knowledge. For it spells out the absolute and all-conditioning quality that the mystic obscurely knows to be his who is embracing him. . . . [I]t affirms, at the undeniable level of rational philosophic wonder and discourse, that total mastery of God which the mystic obscurely knows at first hand.[3]

In this chapter, I wish to draw upon the Christian contemplative tradition in order to give the doctrine of *creatio ex nihilo* an edge of meaning it would not otherwise have. I want to explore how the deepest insight into our creaturely contingency—our coming "from nothing," or the utter gratuity of God—is in fact a contemplative insight of supreme significance, and that only by freely releasing ourselves through loving dispossession into this gracious "nothing" can we begin to discover, at the felt depths of our being, what it is to be created. As Moore suggestively puts it: "In so far as I experience my self-transcendence *as such*, I am touched by that reality which is the ultimate ratio of my self-transcendence. I am touched by what makes me what and who I am. I experience being created."[4]

If, in the previous chapter, attention was given to the doctrinal significance of creation from nothing from the standpoint of scriptural testimony and philosophical disputation, here it seems needful to newly orient the discussion by exploring how our "coming

Undergoing Something from Nothing   43

from nothing" is a continuous happening that, although not amenable to conceptual representation, can be awakened to, trusted, and ultimately loved. The doctrine of *creatio ex nihilo* is, among other things, an invitation to contemplation. It invites us to look deeply into our creaturely contingency—to peer "all the way down," so to speak—and to notice without flinching that our existence does not depend upon us. We simply do not have to be, and yet we are.

Contemplative inquiry is a way of being patient with this explosive insight—one that we may wish to avoid, alas, but an insight that, if left unattended, impinges upon consciousness by way of anxiety, dread, boredom, or restlessness. While at times disconcerting and painfully purgative, contemplation entails our learning how to become poised in the midst of our creaturely poverty. To be creaturely at all is to be ontologically suspended, to hover over an abyss. It is a "being between," a sharing in the "universal impermanence" of all things. There is, as William Desmond puts it, a "primal porosity" to being a creature, and while such porosity can leave us feeling uneasy or even ontologically queasy, there is "a way of mindfulness" that welcomes this porosity, that allows us to release ourselves in loving trust to it—to become unrestrictedly open to the sheer fact that we are *given* to be.[5]

This welcoming of our contingency, or of our "nullity," is not a matter of vacancy or depersonalization. It does not foster an attitude of nihilism, even though it may seem a hair's breadth away from it, at least from a certain perspective. Indeed, only the contemplative can let in what the nihilist also senses, yet without falling into resentment, despondency, or indifference as a result. It is a "fertile void" that contemplation discovers, a place of continual rebirth wherein we may say yes.[6] "To really know our 'nothingness,'" writes Thomas Merton, "we must also love it."[7]

In the climate of contemplative prayer, we can gain an elemental sense of what being creaturely is and how such creatureliness is not only *not* in rivalry with the unconditioned reality of God but the very site of God's desire to "happen" in us. This by itself should make contemplation central to any serious theological endeavor, but it must be admitted that the ascetical and contemplative roots of praxis and *theoria* are not often foregrounded in the work of theology today as they once were. It is more typical of modern and late-modern works

44 Grammar and Contemplation

of theology to relegate discussion of ascetico-contemplative practice to the study of "spirituality," with the result that texts from the contemplative (or "mystical") tradition are used more rhetorically, by way of illustration, in the expounding of a particular point or issue, rather than as fundamental to its method or manner of approach. My interest in this chapter, however, will be to draw upon contemplative *practice*, and not just celebrated texts imbued with a contemplative sensibility, with the hope of showing how *creatio ex nihilo* can gain a lived sense for us, as something we might wakefully undergo. Approached in this way, the insight into our creatureliness that *creatio ex nihilo* enshrines will be interpretable as something like a way of life, as an itinerary for a way of being in the world, with others, rather than a discrete proposition about a state of affairs determined by a fixed meaning. It is also hoped that, along the way, some of the apparent antinomies encountered in the previous chapter—power and vulnerability, transcendence and immanence, freedom and dependence, and so on—will take on a different set of resonances when situated within a contemplative matrix.

SYSTEMATIC THEOLOGY AND THE WAY OF UNKNOWING

James Alison provides a striking account of the theologian's vocation that captures much what I am suggesting: "The theologian's vocation requires participating on the inside of an act of communication coming from someone who is not an object in the universe. And the notion of the Creator, far from being bad science concerning the beginning of the universe, involves us in undergoing a sense of 'something coming out of nothing.'"[8] To say that creation comes "from nothing" is not so much a statement about an independent state of affairs, as though it were a hypothesis concerning the first instant of the universe. It is an invitation to undergo divine things. It is a way of acknowledging our dependency upon a free Creator who gives all things to be; but more, it is a summons to live out that dependency, wakefully and through the responsible exercise of our freedom, in such a way that we progressively undergo God's self-communicating act of creation. This is hardly the special reserve of

Undergoing Something from Nothing 45

those who call themselves theologians, of course, but Alison reminds us that the work of theology, even in its disciplined and professional aspects, is a vocation that summons those who approach it as a way of life. With reference to Thomas Aquinas, and Dionysius the Areopagite before him, Alison's account of theology as a certain *pati divina* implies far more than the production of ideas that bear reference to that which we call "God," "Christ," or "salvation." It implies a process of change, of being "on the way," so to speak, in which the theologian participates, actively, but with a disposition of deepest welcoming, in a divine happening that is ongoing. It entails an "attitudinal pattern, lived over time" that avails oneself "to a stretched and stressed openness to 'something from nothing.'"[9]

It is precisely here, I submit, where contemplative practice becomes crucial for the work of theology. There are many reasons why this is so, but at least one reason immediately stands out: contemplation is not a discursive strategy that tries to formulate in words, in turns of phrase, in paradoxes, in clashing metaphors, in narrative subversions, or in argument the ungraspable mystery of God. It may accompany all of this, and no doubt is prepared by it.[10] And yet the practice of contemplation—and here I am referring specifically to nondiscursive meditation and prayer—seeks to inhabit that mystery through a long "letting go." Contemplative prayer unsettles our managed impressions and conceptual maps and invites us to discover a more fundamental awareness that cannot be exhausted by any of its contents. It is rather like "free-falling" into an abyss, as Sarah Coakley puts it, but in this case we will find ourselves graciously upheld by an ineffable presence that is always there, as close as closeness itself, but which is usually not noticed by us on account of our many preoccupations, mental chatter, and restless search for identity. In this "formless" way of prayer, which is by no means opposed to discursive approaches of prayer, we release our thoughts and concepts about God in the obscurity of faith, even those that are most ennobling and consoling, and settle into an attentive repose, a living stillness that allows us to become wakeful to the mystery of God in our midst, just as it is.

As a systematic theologian, I am sometimes made achingly aware of the gulf that can separate the work of theology from the contemplative depths of Christian faith. Not that systematic theology as such warrants this charge, but the perception that it does is not uncommon, and more than a few examples lend support to that perception. Often enough, this (real or perceived) gulf is characterized in terms of the disconnect between doctrinal reflection and lived experience—or, just as likely, in terms of the disjunction between conceptually driven "theology" and affectively embodied "spirituality."

I am also aware of various objections to systematic theology that characterize it as anachronistic or, worse, a brand of totalizing thinking that is repressive or distortive of lived reality in some way. Notwithstanding the fact that systematic theology today appears to be in what Coakley calls "a remarkable state of regeneration," a number of common objections to this style of theology, and perhaps theology more generally, can be cited.[11] Coakley herself points to three. The first is that systematic theology is a form of "onto-theology" that lays claim to comprehending God within a system of references, as though God were a kind of object in the world we might grasp or at least extrapolate on the basis of immanent causes and universal principles. The second is related to the first but points to the political implications of a form of discourse that, because it aims for systematic clarity in relating various features of Christian faith in a coherent and compelling way, results in the suppression of marginalized voices and cultural perspectives that would otherwise disrupt its predilection for order. In short, systematic theology tends toward hegemony. The third objection, according to Coakley, assumes a particular feminist and psychoanalytic critique that regards systematic theology as a typically "male" enterprise that seeks to control and master, and which represses or at least subordinates those aspects of life associated with embodiment, affectivity, and the unconscious.

Coakley's own effort in systematic theology, which she describes as the "attempt to provide a coherent, and alluring, vision of the Christian faith," seeks to meet each of these objections, and in the first installment of her multivolume project (the only volume published to date) she does so by working through the doctrine of the Trinity.[12] It is an ambitious project that will be the subject of lively conversation

Undergoing Something from Nothing 47

and debate for years to come as new volumes appear. What is especially promising about her effort, which I intend to develop in my own way here, is her consistent appeal to the ascetico-contemplative life in the work of theology, or what elsewhere she calls its "contemplative matrix."[13]

Systematic theology, on this view, is emphatically not the effort to build a towering, windowless edifice of interlocking propositions that renders God and the Christian life a matter of full comprehension. Neither is its aim for clarity and coherence at odds with a patient sensitivity to lived experience, to the ambiguities and conflicts of interpretation, to the refractoriness of suffering, and to the limits of human knowing. In fact, rightly approached—or, better, when lived into— the work of theology is a self-involving risk undertaken from within a living, breathing community, among diverse voices and cultural perspectives, presupposing a way of life oriented toward that inexhaustible mystery we call "God." Theology is an ascetical and contemplative endeavor, not merely an intellectual one. "It must involve the stuff of learned bodily enactment, sweated out painfully over months and years, in duress, in discomfort, in bewilderment, as well as in joy and dawning recognition."[14]

As unlikely as it may seem to those who find systematic theology objectionable for one or more of the above reasons, such a discipline is in fact an ascetico-contemplative undertaking that knows by unknowing, or, as Coakley puts it, one that proceeds by way of skillful "un-mastery."

> For the very act of contemplation—repeated, lived, embodied, suffered—is an act that, by grace, and over time, inculcates mental patterns of "un-mastery," welcomes the dark realm of the unconscious, opens up a radical attention to the "other," and instigates an acute awareness of the messy entanglement of sexual desires and desire for God. The vertiginous free-fall of contemplation, then, is not only the means by which a disciplined form of unknowing makes way for a new and deeper knowledge-beyond-knowledge; it is also . . . the necessary accompanying practice of a theology committed to ascetic transformation.[15]

It must be said that this view of theology is not exactly new. Though the inclusion of the social sciences and other forms of critical theory does in fact reflect a way of doing theology that opens up new and challenging frontiers, the foregrounding of contemplation in its elaboration is to reclaim the way theology was typically practiced throughout the patristic and medieval eras. Not that all theology ceased to exhibit this contemplative dimension with the rise of modern styles, but it is nevertheless true that only in recent centuries has the "scientific" character of theology shifted in such a way that scripture, creeds, and doctrines might be regarded as an independent body of propositions to which one might intellectually assent, rather than pointers to and resources for an array of virtues and habits of mind enacted in daily life.[16] A similar shift is evident in the history of philosophy as well, as Pierre Hadot has shown, with the effect that premodern philosophy is typically read today for its propositional or argumentative content, to the near exclusion of the art of living it advocates, or what Hadot describes as its "way of life."[17]

While much more could be said about the shifting senses of theology as a scientific discipline—shifts that have contributed to the modern disciplinary distinctions between "theology" and "spirituality"—the main point I wish to emphasize here, in light of Coakley's comments, is that systematic theology, when done well, approaches the mystery of God by way of practical inhabitation, as a reality to be lived into by grace, by participation, and through a ceaseless movement of purgation and transformation lured on by God's inexhaustible self-communication. Such an approach will be different from mere talk "about" God's unknowability. For while it is fashionable today to invoke apophatic styles of theology when stressing the limits of human knowledge, or when characterizing human language as the destabilizing deferral of meaning, a contemplative theology within the Christian tradition will emphasize apophasis as an embodied and communal practice with a trinitarian shape. "For contemplation is the unique, and wholly *sui generis*, task of seeking to know, and speak of God, unknowingly; as Christian contemplation, it is also the necessarily bodily practice of dispossession, humility, and effacement which, in the Spirit, causes us to learn incarnationally, and only so, the royal way of the Son to the Father."[18]

Deep Calls Upon Deep

If the above characterization of unknowing, dispossession, and effacement appears to diminish our creatureliness in any way, as though the "more" of God implies the "less" of our humanity, or vice versa, a point of clarity is in order. As Coakley insists, the radical vulnerability that is characteristic of contemplation is not at all opposed to our creaturely freedom and identity, but is instead the condition for their fuller flowering. "Contemplation is an act of willed 'vulnerability' to divine action. In it, one cooperates with the promptings of divine desire. There is no force; indeed, any force or anger both kill the subtle act of contemplation stone dead. The contemplative steps wilfully into an act of reflexive divine love that is always going on, always begging Christomorphic shape."[19] This "power-in-vulnerability," which for Coakley is critical for addressing a host of nettled issues related to power, agency, and difference, is similar to the point made by Rowan Williams in the previous chapter, which is that with God—and God alone—we are dealing with a reality whose power has nothing at all to do with force; a reality in whom unconditioned dependence and genuine freedom are not opposed; a reality in whose illimitable vastness one can be "lost" so as to be "found." While such *coincidentia oppositorum* may seem little more than wordplay, the truth they are attempting to convey is discoverable in the crucible of contemplative prayer.

Let us recall Williams's statement from the previous chapter that contemplative prayer "classically finds its focus in the awareness of God at the centre of the praying person's being—and, simultaneously, God at the centre of the whole world's being: a solidarity in creatureliness."[20] Here we see that the nondual logic governing our predication of "God" and "world" is a matter of prayerful discovery, not just description. The reason why it can make intuitive sense that God does not displace the world, while being at its center, is because of the nondual, nongrasping awareness that is the hallmark of contemplative prayer. Through repeated acts of availing oneself to God in the simplicity of faith—intentionally, freely, and with a cultivated willingness to let go of one's need to know God through any concept, any need for security, any demand for experience—the contemplative begins to

50   Grammar and Contemplation

discern, at the very source of consciousness and will, a fruitful emptiness that is recognizable as always having been there as the inexhaustible wellspring of creaturely being and freedom.

Belden Lane captures something of this paradoxical freedom-in-relinquishment in his summary of the desert monastic practices of Christian antiquity:

> In the practice of contemplation, one comes eventually to embrace an apophatic anthropology, letting go of everything one might have imagined as constituting the self—one's thoughts, one's desire, all one's compulsive needs. Joined in the silence of prayer to a God beyond knowing, I no longer have to scramble to sustain a fragile ego, but discern instead the source and ground of my being in the fierce landscape of God. One's self is ever a tenuous thing, discovered only in relinquishment. I recognize it finally as a vast, empty expanse opening out onto the incomparable desert of God.[21]

As this quote indicates, contemplative practice takes with absolute seriousness what many of us might theoretically take to be the case, but which can only really be lived into, namely, the incomprehensibility of God. We may readily acknowledge that no idea of God coincides with the reality of God, and we may even be willing to have our images and concepts of God destabilized through the play of paradox, metaphor, and narrative subversion. But such strategies, as helpful and necessary as they are, will likely remain at the conceptual level, and so with the implicit presumption of comprehension, unless they are released through the practice of unknowing. Such unknowing is not a lack of awareness. It is not a matter of blanking out one's affective and cognitive capacities or choking back edifying images and thoughts as they arise. It is, rather, the slow discovery of an awareness that is immeasurably deeper and far more capacious than the discursive activities that ordinarily preoccupy our attention and seem sufficient in representing reality to us. We are perpetually seduced into believing that our affective registrations and conceptual representations of phenomena capture their reality, whether ourselves, other persons, or God. Without being anti-intellectual and anti-realist, contemplative practice unsettles our tenacious grip on things by opening us up to a more fundamental awareness, an abyss of awareness that is always there but which we scarcely notice. We do not cling to this or that content *of* awareness when praying thus, but we abide within the very ground of awareness with simplicity of attention. "Preserve a loving attentiveness to God with no desire to feel or understand any particular thing concerning him," writes Saint John of the Cross, in simple summary of a practice that, when cultivated over time, slowly takes root.[22]

Lane's quote also highlights an important corollary to the incomprehensibility of God, namely, the incomprehensibility of the human person. The suggestive phrase *apophatic anthropology* underscores that contemplative practice entails a thoroughgoing conversion in which we progressively let go of all the usual placeholders and mimetic comparisons that compose our makeshift identities. It calls for a painful but ultimately liberating kenosis, a purgation of the million and one ways our identities are constructed within the warp and woof of human relations, and to which we cleave with deep-seated anxieties. One's thoughts, one's desires, one's needs: through contemplative prayer one learns to free-fall into the vastness of God and slowly surrender the compulsion to form identity in competitive relationship with others, including God.

While such self-emptying can be terrifying for the *ego*—as terrifying as death, which in fact it is—nothing could be more freeing for the *person*. The reason is because of all our vulnerabilities as creatures, none runs deeper than our ontological dependence upon God, with whom there is no vying for being at all. We will discover that God is not some power against which we must strive for existence. God is not a rival to the creature in any way, is not some Big Other with whom identity becomes a matter of contention or negotiation. Because my identity is not something I must attain apart from God, but rather is a gift arising from God's unfathomable depths, I can learn to accept my creaturely poverty and "sink" into my "nothingness" without restraint, resentment, or fear.[23]

Contemplation is not a flight from creatureliness, as some may suppose, but its acceptance. To be creaturely at all is to participate in God's gratuitous creativity, and to venture upon contemplative practice is to become wakeful to that inexhaustible fact. Theologically speaking, contemplative practice concerns the loving mystery of God and our participation in that mystery. It implies nothing other than the process of mystagogy to which all Christians are called by virtue of baptism. It is a way of living into the mystery of salvation that has been granted to us in Christ. By this practice one learns to say yes through the very pores of his or her being, out of depths that are as unsearchable as God's own wisdom (Rom. 11:33). In one respect it is quite accurate to say that this "yes" of prayer is the most fundamental act a human person can make. It is, as Karl Rahner puts it, the "fundamental option" of our lives, this profound allowance of God's creative and reconciling activity within and among us.[24] But in another respect, which is in no sense contrary to the first, this "yes" to God is God saying yes *in* us. As the psalmist says, "deep calls upon deep" (Ps. 42:7). Or as Saint Paul puts it, "the Spirit of God scrutinizes everything, even the depths of God" (1 Cor. 2:10). The Spirit intercedes for us in our weakness with "groans too deep for words" (Rom. 8:26). Contemplative prayer is "in the Spirit," as Coakley notes, for it is a response made possible by an initiative that is not our own but made prior to us, and which pours itself in us as the possibility of our free assent. It is not so much "I" who autonomously prays but

> God (the Holy Spirit) who prays in me, and so answers the eternal call of the "Father," drawing me by various painful degrees into the newly expanded life of "Sonship." There is, then, an inherent reflexivity in the divine, a ceaseless outgoing and return of the desiring God; and insofar as I welcome and receive this reflexivity, I find that it is the Holy Spirit who "interrupts" my human monologue to a (supposedly) monadic God; it is the Holy Spirit who finally thereby causes me to see God no longer as patriarchal threat but as infinite tenderness; but it is also the Holy Spirit who first painfully darkens my prior certainties, enflames and checks my own desires, and so invites me ever more deeply into the life of redemption in Christ.[25]

This "incorporative" (or "reflexive") approach to prayer draws from Romans 8 for one of its scriptural touchstones and stresses the trinitarian movement of God's indwelling. It is not a "conversation

Undergoing Something from Nothing 53

with some distant and undifferentiated deity" but an "answering of God to God."[26] It is not structured by an intentionality that reaches out to God as a quasi-object, mediated through a constellation of concepts, impressions, or sentiments, but instead rests in the subtly expansive awareness of God's desire at work within us. Such nondiscursive awareness does not elide the ontological distinction between God and creature, but neither does it leave our sense of God's "otherness" untouched. The divine "difference" most assuredly remains, as does God's creative liberty, and yet such difference does not reduce to a binary. The Spirit "crosses that ontological twoness transformatively," writes Coakley, "but without obliteration of otherness."[27] Or, just as strikingly, "Twoness, one might say, is divinely ambushed by threeness."[28]

Vast, Open Awareness

I will return to the pneumatological and trinitarian implications of contemplative prayer in the conclusion of this chapter, especially as they provide a distinctively Christian grammar for articulating something of the creature's dynamic relationship with the living God. But here I want to go further into that contemplative unknowing and explore how it allows us to become newly touched, or obscurely affected, by that unique and original relation that gives us our very being, and hence the possibility of our freedom and responsibility. I do so by first discussing some concrete matters related to the practice of this prayer, and then by considering its relevance for discovering, rather than just describing, our differentiating union with God.

By focusing on contemplative practice in this way, I do not mean to isolate it from other forms of practice that make up the Christian life, much less to oppose it to more discursive styles of prayer that draw from scripture, liturgy, iconography, and intellectual reflection. Contemplative practice of the nondiscursive variety should be understood as the ongoing fruit of sensuous, imaginative, and communal engagements with the self-communicating God who became flesh and who, through the resurrection, assumed for all eternity the corporeality of the world. Because of its incarnational texture and eschatological shape, authentic contemplative practice in the Christian tradition can have nothing to do with a suspicion of the body, and it cannot despair of the perceptual, affective, and ideational character of our loving and knowing.[29] What we should rather say is that contemplative practice involves us in relating to the *whole* our experience and relationships in a new way. Contemplation does not add an unusual class of experiences "on top" of everything else, and it does not give anyone a special authority to deliver whispered judgments about God and the meaning of life. What contemplative practice does do is accompany us through a potentially maturating crisis by which we are shown the highly provisional character of our prior experience and certainties about God.

> In the end the contemplative suffers the anguish of realizing that he *no longer knows what God is*. He may or may not mercifully realize that, after all, this is a great gain, because "God is not a *what*," not a "thing." That is precisely one of the essential characteristics of contemplative experience. It sees that there is no "what" that can be called God. There is "no such thing" as God because God is neither a "what" nor a "thing" but a pure "*Who*." He is the "Thou" before whom our inmost "I" springs into awareness. He is the I Am before whom with our own most personal and inalienable voice we echo "I am."[30]

In a telling footnote to this passage, perhaps added later to allay the concerns of a scandalized censor, Thomas Merton insists that contemplative prayer does not undermine the validity of images and concepts in our relationship with God, which have their place, but that in contemplation all "abstract notions of the divine essence no longer play an important part since they are replaced by a concrete intuition, based on love, of God as a *Person*, an object of love, not a 'nature' or a 'thing' which would be the object of study or of a possessive desire."[31] This clarifying point is similar to the one made by Moore above, which is that a concept of "without-whom-nothing" is being replaced by an experience of "without-whom-nothing," and that only through our being touched by the infinite might our concepts about God gain a fresh edge of meaning.

Undergoing Something from Nothing   55

But what can this reference to a "concrete intuition" of God's personhood mean, or our "being touched" by the infinite? Assuming such phrases are not pure nonsense, do they imply that God is an object of experience after all, or that contemplative practice entails the conjuration of special states of consciousness through the deployment of esoteric techniques? While recognizing the difficulties involved in adopting experiential language in connection with apophasis, and with contemplative practice in general—difficulties that cannot be fully addressed here[32]—it is worth pointing out that one telltale symptom of contemplation's onset is the crisis of "experience" itself. By this is meant, in classical contemplative literature, the growing and at times painful realization that what had previously provided consolation and orientation in the life of prayer, in the form of sensations, images, or concepts, begins to dry up and provide difficulties, if not outright obstacles, for prayer's continuation. Previous experiences begin to lose their sweetness, concentration wanes, the heart feels sapped, and prayer itself seems unbearably routine. Tedium or some barely expressible aversion tinctures the very thought of God, with the result that one looks with eagerness for diversion or some means of escape. Perhaps the sense of God's presence grows faint, even withdrawn, such that prior convictions concerning God's constancy, and any dedicated practices or observances sustained by such convictions, begin to buckle and grind. A certain restlessness or torpor, a pervading sense of nothingness, of boredom—or what the ancients broadly called *acedia*—descends like a heavy fog and leaves any former inclination to pray, to meditate, to ruminate over scripture more of a mechanical exercise than a spontaneous act.

As Saint Teresa of Avila counseled her Carmelite sisters in the sixteenth century, it is precisely here, during this "turmoil of mind," when we understand ourselves least, and this lack of knowledge "causes the afflictions of many people who engage in prayer: complaints about interior trials, at least to a great extent, by people who have no learning; melancholy and loss of health; and even the complete abandonment of prayer."[33] While this way of putting it may seem more applicable to a different era, when committed religious life was far more structured and embedded in a culture that could take formal prayer for granted, the symptomatology Teresa outlines

56   Grammar and Contemplation

in this crucial transition in *The Interior Castle* is just as insightful for us now as in her own time.[34] For what the Carmelite Doctor of the Church is pointing to, in the language of medieval faculty psychology, is a capacity of such importance, yet of such subtlety, that its lack of recognition and cultivation is liable to leave even the most committed of aspirants exhausted and confused.

To describe this essentially inexpressible capacity, Teresa offers an analogy. Imagine, she says, two basins of water. One basin receives its water through a system of aqueducts built with remarkable ingenuity. The water flows from its source across a great distance, through channels, down gradations, and over an undulating landscape until finally it provides refreshment. The water pouring forth from the aqueducts is comparable to the consolations derived from discursive forms of prayer, and they depend in part upon the effortful use of our imaginative and intellectual faculties. Because of this mediation and effort, Teresa notes, a certain degree of "noise" inevitably accompanies the basin's replenishment.

As for the second basin, "the water comes from its own source, which is God."[35] Although Teresa confesses that she knows not how this happens, water "overflows" in "the very interior part of ourselves" and "swells and expands our whole interior being producing ineffable blessings."[36] The faculties meanwhile are recollected and absorbed in wonderment, not so much canceled out as serenely rapt, held in restful wakefulness and silently composed as the water wells up from its pacific and searchless depths. It is as though the heart is "dilated" or one's very being "expanded" by a capacity that is at once inmost to the person and yet not a matter of acquisition or manipulation at all. It is sheer gift.[37]

With this analogy Teresa means to alert her readers, especially those encountering difficulties with prayer, to a vast "interior world here within us."[38] Interiority does not mean an inner space of gauzy introspection, and in fact the spatial metaphors of "within" or "above" are interchangeable and ultimately a matter of indifference to her.[39] What concerns her is that her readers recognize the significance of aridity in discursive prayer. Experiences of dryness and desolation *mean* something. Boredom and fatigue in the spiritual life are matters to be interpreted, not brute facts. They are "semiotic phenomena," signs pointing to an unsuspected capacity, precisely in their apparent insignificance.[40] Even the experience of emptiness, which, paradoxically, seems like a lack of experience—or perhaps a crisis within the structure of experience itself—can be viewed as signifying and prompting a new movement in the life of prayer. We should therefore discern in these crises signs of growth, as invitations to venture upon a "wayless" way:

> We belong to Him, daughters. Let Him do whatever He likes with us, bring us wherever He pleases. I really believe that whoever humbles himself and is detached (I mean in fact because the detachment and humility must not be just in our thoughts—for they often deceive us—but complete) will receive the favor of this water from the Lord and many other favors that we don't know how to desire.[41]

It is noteworthy that Teresa concludes this statement with the suggestion that we do not always know how to desire, when it comes to God, or that we must be taught how to desire. On this account, growth in prayer entails something like the restructuring of desire, or desire's transfiguration through a series of crises and new attunements. We must be taught how to desire according to God's own desire, with and after divine desire, and often enough this pedagogical process lures human desire to the very end of its tether, lovingly outstretched toward something like a "blank," as Dom John Chapman memorably puts it. But for those who gently persist in availing themselves in this way, in this outstretching and simplifying practice of desire, a "vague undefinable knowledge of God" awaits in secret: "It grows more and more definite and yet remains just as indefinite: that is to say, the soul becomes more and more definitely conscious of being in the presence of Something undefinable, yet above all things desirable, without any the more arriving at being able to think about it or speak about it—more and more conscious of its own nothingness before God, without knowing how—more and more convinced of the nothingness of creatures, without reasoning on the subject."[42]

The reference to "nothingness" here is by no means a denial of the creature's ontological reality, and we will not find in Chapman's highly practical and justly celebrated letters of spiritual direction any whiff of acosmism or mystical nihilism.[43] What we will find is a phenomenology of the contemplative's growing wakefulness to the fundamental porosity of the creature, and the way this porosity opens us out, should we consent to it, to the unconditioned and gracious reality of God happening in us. The statement reflects the lived sense of our being ontologically "on loan," whose discovery is hardly reason for resignation or despair; on the contrary, it "means an entire confidence, an exultation in being nothing because God is all, which brings the only peace which is true peace."[44]

Again, this nothing/all language might pique all manner of speculative interest, or arouse suspicions of quietism, but a more phenomenological approach can help us appreciate its lived significance. For whereas a representational form of knowing will likely puzzle over how we can grow in an "undefinable" knowledge of anything, the very nature of contemplative awareness is that it progressively releases us from any attitudinal possessiveness that would approach God as a quasi-object of knowledge, or a determinate target toward which our desires might aim. Contemplative practice might well be summed up as a long letting go of desire's acquisitiveness, without desire itself becoming extinguished. It is the free allowance of God's own creative and pacific desire to stretch out in us so that we might desire and live accordingly: from *God's* desire. This deepening immersion into divine life is not the diminishment of creaturely freedom but the growing realization of its fertile ground, and it instills in us, among other things, a practical indifference—or what the contemplative tradition often calls *apatheia* (or "detachment")—to a host of attachments, preoccupations, reactive stances, and fears that constrain and impinge upon our freedom and relationship with others. Teresa insists strongly on this point, noting that among the characteristic effects of contemplative prayer in everyday life is an increased independence from the compulsive "clacking" of one's own discursive faculties and an enflaming of desire to love and serve God with creative abandonment, even in the midst of severe trials. The soul is "not as tied down in things pertaining to the service of God, but has much more freedom."[45]

The key distinction Teresa wishes to make regarding this clacking of the mind is between the flow of thoughts, sensations, and

Undergoing Something from Nothing 59

half-formed imaginings that ordinarily dominate consciousness, on the one hand, and the vast reservoir of open awareness that is not exhausted by that flow, on the other. Whereas ordinarily "the mind flies about quickly" with an unstoppable rush of content, there are moments when our awareness may expand or become dilated in prayer so that it is no longer consumed by that content; it simply remains open in bare attention. The discursive faculties are "suspended" or "recollected," rather like "a hedgehog curling up or a turtle drawing into its shell," leaving the soul poised with quiet expectancy.[46] Here there is no effort or "noise" in the soul, and neither should one "strive to understand the nature of this recollection." With such effortless, unobstructed attention it is good just "to be aware of who God is and that one is in God's presence." Nothing more.

And yet, always more. For it turns out that this simple awareness of God is inexhaustibly rich and expansive. God may not appear as a kind of thing for the mind to grasp or represent in such awareness, but this does not mean that such unknowing is merely a lack. It is abyssal excess.

> Precisely because our deepest identity, grounding the personality, is hidden with Christ in God and beyond the grasp of comprehension, the experience of this ground-identity that is one with God will register in our perception, if indeed it does register, as an experience of no particular thing, a great, flowing abyss, a depthless depth. To those who know only the discursive mind, this may seem a death-dealing terror or spinning vertigo. But for those whose thinking mind has expanded into heart-mind, it is an encounter brimming over with the flow of vast, open emptiness that is the ground of all. This "no thing," this "emptiness" is not an absence but a superabundance.[47]

Martin Laird further notes in this context that various appeals to God's "no-thingness" or "vast, open emptiness" do not imply that God is an impersonal or inert essence—a point to which I will return later in this chapter, given its trinitarian implications. Neither does the reference to our deepest identity hidden with Christ in God elide the Creator-creature distinction. "Far from blurring this distinction it sets it in sharper focus."[48] The reason, he says, has precisely to do with the reality of the Creator-creature distinction itself, which, when approached with a contemplative disposition, can help release some of the conceptual spasms that complicate our attempts to speak consistently about it. If, for example, we approach the Creator-creature distinction by conceptually determining each of its terms, it will be difficult for us to avoid treating "God" and "creature" as though they were two items relating to one another conjunctively ("and"). Or, just as likely, we will relate these terms according to a series of contrasts ("or"), in which case we are bound by a competitive logic that construes God and creature as a zero-sum relation—or, with slightly more sophistication, dialectically. Within the realm of concepts alone we will strain to understand how God could be infinite while also affirming the integrity of finite creatures; we will struggle to explain how God could be unconditionally free while acknowledging that creatures, too, possesses various degrees and modes of agency; we will multiply conundrums in attempting to reconcile notions of divine "power" and "weakness," "presence" and "absence," or creaturely "identity" and "dependence" upon God; and within the realm of concepts alone we will have virtually no way but to imagine divine transcendence in terms of monarchical distance.

"God does not know how to be absent," Laird insists. "The fact that most of us experience throughout most of our lives a sense of absence or distance from God is the great illusion that we are caught up in; it is the human condition. The sense of separation from God is real, but the meeting of stillness reveals that this perceived separation does not have the last word."[49] Here again the insistence on the provisional character of concepts, or the limits of the "thinking-mind," does not lead Laird into a concept-spurning fideism, and yet it does recognize the reifying tendencies of conceptualization that tend to distinguish the thinking subject from the represented object, with the nearly unavoidable result that we imagine God as splendidly (or irrelevantly) "out there." What a contemplative sensibility would have us consider is that the reifying tendencies of conceptualization cannot be resolved by yet another, subtler concept. We cannot think our way out of it. We cannot multiply analogies, spin paradoxes, or crank out

Undergoing Something from Nothing 61

dialectal statements sufficiently to wrest ourselves from the chronic tendency to treat God as yet another item in the universe. Not even the postmodern engagement with mystical and apophatic theologies can do much more than serve as a tentative step toward the actual practice of contemplation, and even then it might only postpone such a step with its fixation on linguistic performance, as though the dazzling display of aporias were a substitute for cultivating interior silence.[50] But with the practice of stillness itself we will find that the reifying tendency that construes God as yet another object of experience—and perhaps a Big Other with which creaturely identity must contend—is relaxed.

It should be noted here that while various traditions of contemplative prayer may recommend certain body postures, watchfulness of breath, or rhythmic recitations of a prayer word or short phrase in order to center one's attention—and to this extent there is a certain skillfulness and habit formation involved—by no means should these practices be regarded as techniques designed for acquiring heightened states of consciousness. Contemplative practice "doesn't acquire anything," writes Laird. "In that sense, and an important sense, it is not a technique but a surrendering of deeply imbedded resistances that allows the sacred within gradually to reveal itself as a simple, fundament fact."[51] This is not a "search for God-as-object-to-be-acquired" but the relaxation of our anxious tendency to buffer ourselves from the fundamental porosity of being.[52] Through the release of our affective defenses and the unclasping our cognitive designs, by unsettling and letting go of the steady stream of sensations, thoughts, and entangled desires that ordinarily structure our experience, the illusion that God is a separable reality may gradually give way to a fresh awareness of what, or rather, *Who* is most fundamentally animating us. "God is the ground of the human being . . . [and so] if we are going to speak of what a human being is, we have not said enough until we speak of God. If we are to discover for ourselves who we truly are—that inmost self that is known before it is formed, ever hidden with Christ in God (Ps. 139:13; Jer. 1:5; Col. 3:3)—the discovery is going to be a manifestation of the ineffable mystery of God, though we may feel more and more inclined to say less and less about God."[53]

That Anything Is at All

To briefly sum up the foregoing, contemplative practice provides an indispensable resource for gaining a lived sense of *creatio ex nihilo*—from the inside. By relaxing into our creatureliness through the surrendering of deeply embedded resistances we may have to it, we do not negate our creaturely identities or capacities for action but allow them to grow open to their ineffable source and ground, to the indwelling Spirit of God who gives us the gift of being and who allows us to respond to that gift in freedom and love. Our creatureliness is "from nothing," which is to say, "wholly from God," and this implies no contradiction with our dignity and efficacy as creatures. We are really and truly "other" than God, and our difference from God is pure gift, not an ontological rupture or emanation from an originally undifferentiated unity we must resent or somehow surmount. The gift of creation means that we are free *for* our creatureliness, for unequivocally saying "yes" to our being at all. This is the *difference* nothing makes.

At the same time, our "otherness" is not a barrier to God's unconditioned reality, and neither is the divine difference properly thought of as alongside or above the world in any spatial sense. Though it is perhaps natural to imagine divine transcendence in just this way, as "out there" or "beyond" the furthest reaches of the empirical universe, we must subject our imagination to scrutiny and free thought from its reifying tendencies. God may infinitely transcend all created reality, but this transcendence is the most immanent factor of our lives, which means that God and creation are neither "one" nor "two" but "not-two." To adopt Nicholas of Cusa's neologism, God is *li non aliud* ("the non-other"): a paradox that expresses in algebraic form an ever-deepening insight available to contemplative inquiry. It is a nondual, nongrasping awareness that is the hallmark of such inquiry, and its cultivation is the way of "knowing by unknowing." This is the difference *nothing* makes.

Perhaps it is easier now to appreciate the fuller significance of Merton's statement above, which is that to really know our "nothingness" we must also love it. The statement is revealing on a number of accounts, but the one I wish to develop further here concerns the relationship it weaves between knowing and loving. To really *know*

Undergoing Something from Nothing 63

our nothingness, Merton suggests—that is, to truly plumb the depths of our contingency, our ontological porosity, the shared poverty of all creatures—we must also *love* it. What difference might this unity of knowing and loving make?

In part 3 we will revisit this question by considering how a contemplative disposition is key for cultivating compassion for all creatures, for the entire community of creation, and how our sense of shared fragility is an indispensable moral and spiritual resource for strengthening our communion with others—our "solidarity in creatureliness," as Williams puts it. But here I wish to explore another aspect of knowing and loving by highlighting the primordial goodness that contemplative awareness senses "deep down things," to invoke Gerard Manley Hopkins's expression. It is a goodness that has no reason to be except for itself; a goodness whose simple excess arouses our astonishment and gratitude; a goodness that imparts itself for the sake of goodness; an agapeic goodness that is "good for nothing."

William Desmond articulates a distinction that will be of crucial significance for the remainder of this book. In *God and the Between*, the third volume of his pathbreaking trilogy, the Irish philosopher offers an account of *creatio ex nihilo* that displays as much systematic rigor as it does contemplative finesse.[54] Noting that the affirmation of "creation" has nothing to do with a scientific hypothesis, as though God were merely an explanation for a succession of causes—an approach that would succeed only in conflating God with a determinate "first being"—Desmond observes that the dominance of instrumental and representational thinking in contemporary discussions of God and creation render both virtually unintelligible.

By *instrumental thinking* Desmond means a "way of mindfulness" that accounts for phenomena primarily in terms of making, producing, manipulating, or putting to use, that is, *techné*. What gains intelligibility and value for instrumental thinking is that which can be concretely rendered as causally efficacious; as that which effects change from one state to another; as that which can be calculated, predicted, and potentially harnessed for its utility, and so forth. By *representational thinking* Desmond means a way of mindfulness that accounts for phenomena in terms of their amenability to explanation and conceptualization. Here, too, concrete determination is of highest value, for to know something by representation means being able to grasp it, to re-present it to oneself or others with stability of concept, to model it, to subsume it within a category, to break it down into constitutive parts, to recompose it, et cetera.[55]

Desmond does not dismiss the role of instrumental and representational thinking in human affairs; in fact, he wishes to rehabilitate such thinking by situating its penchant for univocity within a much broader spectrum of mindfulness, one that includes a rich appreciation for equivocity, dialectic, and what he calls the metaxalogical, that is, "thinking between." Still, the contemporary dominance of instrumental and representational thinking in considerations of whether and to what extent we can say the world is created will leave us blind to the radical significance of the question. Creation "cannot be aligned with any sort of *techné*," he argues. "It is disproportionate to any finite making." But more, "creation shatters all idols." We cannot re-present in concept "what" the act of creation is — i.e., its quiddity — any more than we can render the "thingness" of God in concept. "This means that creator as origin is not a *first being* whence other beings become: the ultimate source of coming to be cannot be a being in that determinate sense."[56] In what sense (or in what senses) can we speak of creation, then?

Desmond is quite aware of various scriptural and theological traditions that have made ample use of images, metaphors, hymns, and narratives to portray the act of creation in terms of making, molding, birthing, summoning, commanding, causing, emanating, and producing; and he is no less aware of the philosophical and theological disputes that precipitated doctrinal clarification in the second and third centuries and the roles that argumentation, dialectic, and conceptual refinement played in them. All of this is to be valued. All of these senses are welcome. All of the overlapping profiles of mindfulness belong to the polyphony of signifying and even "singing" creation. But there is a fundamental distinction, a rupture of imagination and thinking itself, which, when obscured or left unacknowledged, will leave all such efforts susceptible to idolatrous distortion. It is the distinction that arises with a simple, bracing question: Why is there something rather than nothing? Why is there anything at all? From whence the "to be" of things? Not just how things are, or what they are, but *that* they are? Not just this or that process, phenomenon, determinate reality, or nexus of relations, but the whole shebang? *That* it is; that *anything* is; that anything has been, will be, or could be? Why something rather than nothing?

The distinction that breaks open here, and which alone gives the thought of creation its proper and most apophatic form, is the distinction between "coming to be" and "becoming." Desmond puts it this way: "In 'becoming,' the happening is already given as having come to be, and, within the happening of becoming, we can use the notion of cause and effect. But 'coming to be' concerns the ontological arising of happening. It is not a determinate becoming, but rather what determinate becoming presupposes as given it to be at all."[57]

Yet another pass: "The primal givenness of the 'that it is' is not a matter of the 'becoming' or 'self-becoming' of beings. There is a 'coming to be' prior to 'becoming.' The latter presupposes a prior 'that it is,' even granting that this 'that it is' is given with an open promise, and not a static and completed fact."[58]

That anything is "happening" at all rather than nothing: this is the thought that provokes endless astonishment—and not a little vertigo.[59] That anything is underway, that becoming becomes, that relations relate, that events eventuate: all of this presupposes the "coming to be," the "arising out of zero," the "that it is at all," the sheer "givenness of being."[60] For Desmond, the thought of "that it is" implies that becoming is not itself original but *originated*, sourced by a primordial givenness that is not itself "in" the process of becoming. Becoming refers to the "already underway," to the ongoing and dynamic "betweenness" of things. To become is to be "in middle of things," in medias res. It is to be porous to another and swept up in a vast flow of successive, determining relations. In becoming, "one becomes a *determinate something*, out of a prior condition of determinate being and towards a further more realized or differently realized determination of one's being."[61] But the very "coming to be" of anything at all marks an infinite, yawning difference from "becoming"—a difference that no accumulation of becoming could ever "fill up":

> Coming to be, by contrast, is prior to becoming this or that; for one must be, and have come to be, before one can become such

and such. Becoming itself suggests something more primordial about coming to be. Creation is connected with this more primordial coming to be—a coming to be that makes finite becoming itself possible but that is not itself a finite becoming. In every finite being that becomes, which is all beings, there is intimated this prior coming to be which is not a finite becoming: "that it is at all" is here in question, and that it has come to be this at all.[62]

Only with this question in mind—a question that issues forth with endless wonder, if we but allow it—can we begin to speak of creation with sufficient rigor. Properly speaking, when referring to creation we are not talking about a transition from one state to another, from potentiality to actuality, from less to more, from chaos to order, from pliability to determinateness. We are not talking about the realizing of previous possibilities or the molding of eternal, doughlike "matter," as with Plato's demiurge. We are not talking about a cosmic big bang out of quantum fluctuations, the egress of a parallel universe, the disturbance of a steady state, or the like. Rather, we are talking about a "primal givenness," the sheer "coming to be" of anything at all, including all potentiality, all indeterminacy, all openended becoming, and eventuation itself. Instrumental thinking cannot help us here, for every instrumental act presupposes some *thing* upon or through which to work. Instrumental thinking is at home with causes, especially efficient causes, but its usefulness is utterly use*less* when considering the "coming to be" of causal relationships themselves.

And what of representational thinking? At wit's end. For how shall we render "nothing" into a concept? The thought of "nothing" cannot enclose what it thinks. It cannot re-present the "nothing" it intimates. For to ask "what is nothing?" is already to insinuate "something" into it. It is not a "what" at all, and it does not admit of any likeness. No middle term presents itself for the bridging.

Even so, there is wonderment. There is blank astonishment. The thought of "that it is" comes as a shock. We are never done with it. Coming to it again and again, it is just as surprising as the first time. Even though it admits no stability of concept, we *can* ask the question, and asking it induces an upsurge of thought, an overflow of intuition that catalyzes, outlasts, and redeems thought. It is primal astonishment, the ecstasy of thought, the hallowing of mind. Desmond describes the intimation of "nothing"—or the thought of something rather than nothing—as "hyperbolic thought." It "overdetermines" thought, is "in excess" to it, floods its banks. But its excess does not require us to travel great distances to ask it. It needs no academic degree and recognizes no status. It requires no ticket. Children ask it with miraculous spontaneity, leaving their parents to scramble. The question is right in front of us, always there, as close as closeness itself, which is one reason why we so readily overlook it. Understandably so. It's just too much. (Or is it too little?) It doesn't seem to get us anywhere. Things must get done. We must take the givenness of things for granted, it seems, for how could we go about our affairs dumbstruck all the time with the thought that all things are "groundless"? That they (we) need not be at all? That they (we) have not always been and will not always be? That they (we) have no self-subsistence?

We take the incomprehensible *fact* of existence as a matter of fact. Its strangeness seems normal. Of course! We presuppose it, live from it, fugitives from the jaw-dropping thought.

Agapeic Origination

To dwell with the question "Why is there anything at all rather than nothing?" is one kind of contemplative inquiry. The attitudinal hospitality, the patience, the open awareness, the cognitive vulnerability that asking this question really requires: all of this shares in the same kind of mindfulness that contemplative practice classically exhibits, whether of the discursive or nondiscursive variety. Desmond suggests as much, stating that the "porosity of thinking" shares in the "porosity of prayer."[63] "We are simply mindfully dwelling on being as given."[64] Such dwelling is "a kind of philosophical thinking that seems *bestowed*, and not unlike the gifted energy of prayer."[65] Or elsewhere: "Prayer and thought can pass into one another. *Fides quaerens intellectum* might reflect an urge of prayer to become thought, but perhaps equally there is an urge of thought that, at certain limits, becomes porous to the passion of prayer."[66]

Just as Teresa of Avila speaks of the dilation of heart or the expansion of the soul in recollected awareness, an awareness in which the faculties are "suspended in wonder," so do we find in Desmond's account of philosophical thinking a porosity that opens thought to prayerful beholding. Thought itself may "return to zero." It must "be nothing" in order to "be open to everything." We can abandon ourselves to "purposeless admiration at the strange good of other-being, suffered as unutterably precious in its stunning thereness."[67] To be held in wonder, rapt in delight by sheer happening, hollowed out by an elemental rapport with the "to be" of things: such contemplative inquiry brings "refreshment" to thought, "resurrects" it, allows us to say yes again and again and again as though for the first time. Contemplation "introduces rupture into habitual seeing," for by "setting apart" or "purging" the accumulation of perceptual and cognitive habits that powerfully predetermine what is even available to notice, or how to notice, contemplative mindfulness gives us a fresh start, grants access to a beginner's mind, helps us to reawaken with "metaphysical astonishment at the being there of being, in its inward and outer otherness."[68]

Desmond is convinced that such mindfulness provides an indispensable clue for discovering the character of creation itself. Whereas an instrumental and representational style of thinking will imagine creation in terms of "producing" or "fashioning"—or, just as likely, the molding of previous potentialities into new actualities, as from one state of becoming to another—contemplative mindfulness is inclined to sense a great "letting be" in the primordial act of creation. The coming to be of creation is pure gift. It comes from no need at all, no lack. It entails no diremption of the Godhead, involves no struggle among rival forces or deities, requires no intervention into a previous state of affairs. It is not moved by agitation and bears no ulterior motive. It gives no whiff of violence. There is nothing against which it must work, no aboriginal chaos it must order, no obstacle it must surmount, no dragon it must slay. Coming to be "from nothing" means "coming to be for no reason"—no reason other than that it is *good* to be.

It is good that anything is at all rather than nothing, and the sense of astonishment and gratitude that wells up when attuned to that fact

Undergoing Something from Nothing 69

implies that creation issues forth from superabundance, not dearth. Desmond calls this gifting abundance "agapeic origination." In contrast to any will to power that might view creation as "overpowering," creation in the sense of agapeic origination suggests a "nonpossessive dispensation."[69] It allows, releases, renders open, makes possible, nourishes, sustains. It is the opposite of imagining origin as "absolutely possessive," as though God creates and now "owns" creation in order to prop up an unstable, restless "mine." God has no "need" for creation in this sense, does not depend upon it, is not bootstrapped by it, has no "use" for it. And yet God gives creation "to be" from an inexhaustible fullness that freely wishes to communicate existence to that which is other than God, for the sheer goodness of it.

Desmond is quite aware that the technical formulation of creation from nothing does not appear in Genesis, and yet it is manifestly clear in that sacred text, as with the entire canon of scripture, that "the world is not God's self-extension. World is other, and good as other. God beholds that 'It is good.' To behold requires 'standing back.' This is a seeing that says 'yes.' The divine song of esteem is not a song of self, or even a self-congratulation on work well done. The work is well done, but it is the work that is good, deemed and esteemed so by the creator."[70] The coming to be of anything at all comes primordially from God, but not in the sense that it extends from God, as though the world were an externalized project by which God becomes more or less. The goodness of creation is agapeic origination because it flows freely out of a limitless surplus that lovingly "lets be" what is other, for the sake of other. Here there is no explanation for creation that will do. There is no "why," except that goodness gives.

> Why create at all? Because it is good. Creation is not arbitrary fiat. . . . The metaphor of originative speaking is suggestive. God says "Let there be . . . and there was . . ." Creation is an original speaking letting be. Speaking brings the word to existence. The word, speaking, lets being be. A word is not a roar. The roar would be more like the diktat of the despotic divinity. The word, spoken originatively, is the expression of communicative being. The originating word issues from the goodness of generosity. The word is the creative expression of being as agapeic and as

70 Grammar and Contemplation

communicative transcending. Word brings a world to be, word communicates a world, lets it issue into a space of sharing with others.... Wording the between: a sung world—a song not only sung, but a song giving rise to new singers. The originative word would be the primordial "yes" that gives coming to be, a word that is also a blessing with being. We know this elementally in our own being given to be, lived as an affirmation of being that first lives us before we live it. The agapeic "yes" not only blesses with being, it blesses being: It is good to be.[71]

I find this passage extraordinary, worthy of reading aloud, worthy of rumination, an act of prayer. What it communicates can only be "beheld." It does not translate into a hypothesis, even if it provides endless pasture for thought. Indeed, one might go so far as to say that our beholding is to share in God's own beholding. To modify a well-known saying by Meister Eckhart, the eye by which I behold God's "letting be" is the same eye by which God beholds me; my beholding and God's beholding are one beholding—one knowing and one loving.

This disposition of beholding is crucial for approaching contemporary discussions of divine power. Any univocal understanding of power that connotatively links it with coercion or force, or which envisions it in instrumentalist terms, will fatally misapprehend the kind of power that gives all things "to be" from nothing. It will have no sense for creation at all, which is why Desmond insists that the phrase *nonpossessive dispensation* is more evocative. "This is just the opposite of what is divinized in the suggestion of the absolutely possessive God (rather than the blessing 'It is good' such a God might gloat 'I own it, it is mine'). Creation as agapeic origin transcends possession, even self-possession. Its richness is its own willing poverty, in willing to be nothing, that the genuinely other may be endowed as something and as good."[72]

If agapeic origin transcends possession, even self-possession, and if the originating power that gives creation to be is a "willing poverty," or a "willing to be nothing" in order that others may be, then the power of which we speak may, paradoxically, appear a lot like weakness, at least from a certain point of view. To the eye that is not one of beholding, but rather of seizing and representing, the

Undergoing Something from Nothing   71

appearance of agapeic power in our world, to the extent it is even recognized at all, will likely bear the visage of powerlessness, a mere trifle, perhaps a scandal.

> If we are fixed on the magisterial God of despotic power or the erotic sovereign who masters all he surveys, the agapeic God can look impotent, just because it lets be, lets freedom be. Hyper-transcendence is releasing power, hence some will see no power here at all. That is not the fault or default of agapeic service. This reserve makes way, makes a way to allow the power of freedom of what is other to come into its own. Agapeic power is absolving power, releasing others beyond itself, without insistence on the return of the power of the others to itself. It does not bind but unbinds. And it binds by unbinding, in that the deeper bond of agapeic togetherness and service is only thus allowed. Absolute absolving power is an absolving agape, is the absoluteness of the divine together with the relativity of the finite.[73]

Such a statement is unmistakably contemplative in tone, and in coming chapters I shall endeavor to show how the attitudinal "letting be" it displays is indispensable for helping us to interpret the contingent history of creation as God's ongoing gift. God's creative act is not just a matter of origins, or what the theological tradition calls *creatio originalis*, but an act that continuously sustains creatures in being—eliciting, accompanying, and compassionately indwelling creation throughout its history of becoming. The theological tradition specifies this as *creatio continua*, and the phrase makes explicit that God's releasing power is by no means a matter of deistic abandonment, or a one and done deal, but the continuous, covenantal resourcing of creation's open-ended adventure. Creation is not one point in time but the giving "to be" of every existent taking place now, *in* time, from the God who is the "ground of time."[74] Creation is no less *ex nihilo* now than it ever was or ever will be. This is a breathtaking insight, one that happens to be very needful in contemporary discussions of God and creation, and its significance can only be "let in," allowed to seep into our bones, through the porosity of prayer and contemplation.

But there is something else the reader may have detected in Desmond's statement, especially as it refers to agapeic power as "absolving": a power that unbinds and is wholly in service to the finite. Although not explicitly appealing to Christ in this passage, there can be no doubt that its account of power-in-powerlessness is informed by the revelation of the crucified-and-risen One, so much so that the account of agapeic origination would scarcely be possible without it. Or so I maintain. Desmond is, after all, a Christian philosopher, and the assessment of God's power appearing as weakness, so Pauline in character, gives implicit content and tone to Desmond's account of agapeic origination. How else shall we read the statement, appearing on the facing page, that God's compassion entails "entry into all that the finite undergoes, including poverty, abjection, despair, and death. For love of finite life, the agapeic God harrows even hell itself"?[75] Moore is somewhat punchier: "God is all relationship, and this is the antithesis of solitary power. And when we begin to think of God in this different way, we begin to see why it is that the real God, the surprising God, shows up in our power-crazy world naked on a cross, tortured to death by the ruling power as a disturber of what it calls the peace. The disturbing, subversive nature of Christianity begins to appear."[76]

What I am suggesting with these twin statements, and what needs to be more fully developed in part 2, is that when the power of agapeic origin appears in the world of its creation, which it does in Christ—the God-world relation brought into maximal expression, "hypostatically"—the way it appears will be deeply destabilizing to configurations of order premised upon coercion, force, and violent expulsion. To such configurations of power, the appearance of agapeic power in the world can only seem weak; but this weakness is a threat—indeed, its greatest threat. The "weak" presence of God is truly scandalous to the will to power, anarchic of any so-called peace peddled by imperial, exclusionary violence. Herein lies the revolutionary potential of agapeic power. For what it is willing to do in order to "win," which is incomprehensible to those who imagine winning as overpowering, is to "lose" on the behalf of all, including those seized by the will to power. This is absolving power, for it

Undergoing Something from Nothing   73

willingly enters into the false bonds that human beings so often create for themselves, even becoming victim to those bonds in order to free us from those bonds. As the Gospel of John puts it, "A thief comes only to steal and slaughter and destroy; I came so that they might have life and have it more abundantly. I am the good shepherd. A good shepherd lays down his life for the sheep" (John 10:10–11).

Were we to name this new event of creation—an event whose newness is the power of agapeic origination made "flesh," an event that renews creation and makes possible the fullness of life, a future that creation would not otherwise have—we could hardly do better than to borrow a third phrase from Christian theological tradition: *creatio nova*, the "new creation." First formulated by the Apostle Paul, this vision of creation is made possible through the aperture of Jesus's resurrection from the dead, and it implies that any account of creation from a Christian theological perspective must be more than a contemplative beholding, which it must also be. It requires an imaginative work that is responsive to the drama of divine revelation: a perspective that allows us to look "backward" to creation as originating through the Word of God, in the Spirit, and "forward" to the future fulfillment of creation in Christ, through the Spirit, when God shall be "all in all" (1 Cor. 15:28).

Divine Reflexivity

In drawing this chapter to a conclusion, I return to the trinitarian character of contemplative prayer in the Christian tradition and briefly explore how the incorporative or reflexive dynamism it exhibits provides Christian theology one of its most crucial and precious clues for formally articulating something of the God-world relation. There is a primal grammar to this prayer, even in the depths of contemplative silence, and this grammar is indispensable for shaping Christian speech as well as enkindling its imagination and life-practice. Above all, it opens us up to the mind-blowing, heart-stopping realization that the "difference" between God and creation, while absolute and nonreciprocal, is utterly agapeic, generous, and pacific because "difference" is originally and eternally *in* God. The ontological difference that God establishes in giving creation "to be" is a difference of supreme relation because that difference is the overflow of relationship infinitely realized in the triune God. To put it another way, the difference *of* creation is a difference that has its origin *within* the relation of divine persons. Creation is not "outside" of God, as it were, but a happening within the infinite "spaciousness" that God's relational life *is*.

Perhaps this point seems unduly speculative, but let us reexamine a statement already quoted from Coakley regarding the trinitarian shape of contemplative prayer. It is worth quoting again at length:

> Strictly speaking, it is not "I" who autonomously prays but God (the Holy Spirit) who prays in me, and so answers the eternal call of the "Father," drawing me by various painful degrees into the newly expanded life of "Sonship." There is, then, an inherent reflexivity in the divine, a ceaseless outgoing and return of the desiring God; and insofar as I welcome and receive this reflexivity, I find that it is the Holy Spirit who "interrupts" my human monologue to a (supposedly) monadic God; it is the Holy Spirit who finally thereby causes me to see God no longer as patriarchal threat but as infinite tenderness; but it is also the Holy Spirit who first painfully darkens my prior certainties, enflames and checks my own desires, and so invites me ever more deeply into the life of redemption in Christ. In short, it is this "reflexivity in God," this Holy Spirit, that makes incarnate life *possible*.[77]

Notice here that divine life is not a static essence prior to relationship but rather the pure realization *of* relationship. Whatever else we might want (and hope) to say about God, we will find ourselves outside the regulative framework of Christian speech if we assume that "relation" and "unity" are binaries in God. The same holds true for "desire" and "plenitude," "activity" and "rest," "power" and "tenderness," "source" and "reception," and so on. A nonbinary logic is needed. A nondual, noncompetitive—let's call it "trinitarian"—grammar is required that enables our speech about God to operate within minimally sufficient parameters. And while all of this is true for God *in se* (the "immanent Trinity"), it is also true of God's relation to creation (the "economic Trinity").

Without confusing the immanent and economic Trinity, Coakley would have us foreground the role of the Holy Spirit for understanding the God-world relationship.[78] The Spirit is no mere "go-between," much less an "add-on" to the prior unity of Father and Son. Rather, the Holy Spirit "is intrinsic to the very make-up of the Father-Son relationship from all eternity; the Spirit, moreover, is that without which there would be no *incarnated* Son at all, and—by extension— no life of Sonship into which we, too, might enter by participation. The Spirit, then, is what interrupts the fallen worldly order and infuses it with the divine question, the divine lure, the divine life."[79] The crucial insight here is that whereas some models of the Trinity tend to construe the economic relations of Father, Son, and Holy Spirit in a linear fashion, so that the Father sends the Son, and then later the Spirit in order to "extend" the revelation of Christ, a more incorporative and reflexive approach—one patterned after Romans 8, for instance, or the Gospel of John[80]—regards the Holy Spirit as "the primary means of incorporation into the trinitarian life of God, and as constantly and 'reflexively' at work in believers in the circle of response to the Father's call."[81] The incarnation of the Son is enabled by the Spirit, and in and through that same Spirit we are enabled to grow ever more deeply into the life of the Son, by adoption, and cry out "*Abba*, Father" (Rom. 8:15).

This "outgoing" and "returning" movement is perfectly realized *in* God, and yet creation itself participates in this movement, ecstatically and historically. Paul makes the cosmic scope of this participatory movement explicit in the same passage when he declares, "For creation awaits with eager expectation the revelation of the children of God" (8:19). As Coakley observes, this account affirms that the whole of creation is "an adventure into God in which the Spirit *leads* by surprise, adventure, purgation and conviction."[82] Without annulling the difference between God and creation, the incarnation of the Son, through the Spirit, destabilizes any account of difference that depends upon a competitive logic. "In the cosmological disturbance of the incarnation the Spirit destabilizes even that 'certainty' of ontological difference afresh, not by demolishing the utter ontological distinction, but by reinvesting it within participative mystery. In and through the Spirit, such 'fixities' of our human thinking are ever challenged and queried; in and through the Spirit we are drawn to place our binary 'certainties' into the melting pot of the crucible of divine—not human—desire."[83] Put more succinctly, "what the 'Trinity' *is* is the graced ways of God with creation, alluring and confirming that creation into the life of the 'Son.'"[84]

This alluring and confirming activity of the triune God will be of particular interest in the coming chapters. But it bears stressing here, by way of transition to that task, how God's creative act of endowing creation with the gift of difference is truly gratuitous because *differing* is infinitely (and pacifically) realized *in* God. The most comprehensive reason why we can dare to say that creaturely otherness is good, theologically speaking, is because it is grounded by, and expressive of, the sheer positivity of relation within divine life itself, as its "overflow." "Belief in creation from nothing," writes Williams, "is one reflective path towards understanding God as trinity; and belief in God as trinity, *intrinsic* self-love and self-gift, establishes that creation, while not 'needed' by God, is wholly in accord with the divine being as being-for-another."[85]

Hans Urs von Balthasar likewise observes that the deepest possible resource for affirming the Other as "absolutely good," rather than as a privation, rival, or threat, is the trinitarian grammar that names the One God as Father, Son, and Holy Spirit. Among the myriad expressions of which such grammar is capable, most fundamentally it implies that the fullness of unity is the fullness of *relation*, and that the creator God who gives all things "to be" does so precisely out the utter self-donation that God eternally *is*. God's own life is infinitely realized relationship, an eternal and inexhaustibly fecund "to-and-fro" of *ekstasis* and *enstasis*, or what classical trinitarian theology refers to as *circum-cessio*.[86] With the insights of Gregory of Nyssa, Thomas Aquinas, and Bonaventure in mind, Balthasar maintains that God's "letting be" of creation is in fact an economic expression of the Father's eternal "letting be" of the Son, in the "return" of the Spirit, such that creation itself may be said to issue forth *within* God—not as an "extension" of God, but within the relational "spaciousness" of God. God need not "withdraw," as it were, in order to

Undergoing Something from Nothing 77

endow creation with the dignity of difference, as some contemporary theologies of creation suppose. Because unity and difference are not opposed but infinitely realized in God, creation can be said to "happen" within divine life itself.[87] The doctrine of the Trinity "implies that the creaturely 'other-than-God' is plunged into the uncreated 'Other-in-God' *while maintaining* that fundamental 'distance' which alone makes love possible."[88]

PART 2

Christ as Concentrated Creation

CHAPTER THREE

Jesus and the Non-Other

Concentrated Creation

My overall aim in part 1 was twofold: first, to retrieve the doctrinal grammar of *creatio ex nihilo* as it reflects and shapes the Christian understanding of the God-world relation, particularly in response to recent criticisms of that doctrine; and second, to explore something of the lived significance of "creation from nothing" as a reality we might awaken to, and in a sense verify, in the crucible of contemplative prayer. This interplay between doctrinal reflection and contemplative inquiry provides a preliminary response to criticisms that *creatio ex nihilo* is merely an abstract piece of speculation bearing little or no relation to concrete human life, or that its affirmation is really a projective fantasy that valorizes sovereign power in an ideologically fraught manner. By attending to narrative trends in scripture, key issues in theological disputation, and deepening insights afforded by prayer, I hope that a number of the objections raised in chapter 1 have been addressed sufficiently to show just how fruitful this doctrine really is for Christian imagination and practice.

But much more must be said about *creatio ex nihilo* and its relationship to Christian imagination and practice, and in part 2 I am particularly concerned with exploring further its christological and soteriological significance. In part, this significance has to do with the classical dogmas of the faith, since, as numerous commentators have observed, the Chalcedonian formulation of the hypostatic union of natures is internally coherent with the doctrine of creation. Indeed, they exhibit the same logic. To affirm that Jesus is fully human *and* fully divine, and that his human and divine natures are united in one person (*hypostasis*)—united yet not confused, undividedly and inseparably in two natures (*physes*)—is to articulate in yet another, now christologically focused way the noncompetitive relationship between God and creation.[1] For although the christological councils were concerned with more clearly defining the relationship between the mystery of Christ and the mystery of God, they were, by implication, a rather concentrated and vivid way to articulate the God-world relation as such.[2] They did so "maximally," which is to say, by "encompassing both sides of the Creator-creature distinction."[3] In the incarnation, writes Karl Rahner, "We can verify here, in the most radical and specifically unique way the axiom of all relationship between God and creature, namely that the closeness and the distance, the submissiveness and the independence of the creature do not grow in inverse but in like proportion. Thus Christ is most radically [human], and his humanity is the freest and most independent, not in spite of, but because of its being taken up, by being constituted as the self-utterance of God."[4]

This christological axiom means explicitly that Jesus's humanity is not canceled out or displaced by God's self-communication in him. His creatureliness is not "a vaporous and empty apparition which has no validity of its own," but in fact "has the most radical validity, force and reality," precisely because the hidden God is manifest in him.[5] The positive interplay between divine and creaturely freedom is intelligible only if we understand that God is not a rival to the creature in any way, and we are taught this noncompetitive logic quite clearly in the doctrine of the incarnation, which in formal terms declares that God can, without ceasing to be God, "become" a creature, and thus assume a finite, conditioned reality for God's self. Because divine transcendence is unconditioned, and so not a "kind" of being at all, God can become a creature of this contingent, evolving world—flesh (*sarx*), a human being (*anthropos*), born of a woman (Gal. 4:4)—without obscuring or destroying the integrity of the creature.[6] Indeed, *only* a wholly unconditioned God could become a creature without

Jesus and the Non-Other 83

in any way displacing the creature or diminishing the creator. The unequivocal affirmation of Christ's divinity thus enables us to affirm his full humanity, and this double affirmation is key in opening up for us the true nature of the God-world relation.[7]

I will return to these more formal considerations of christological dogma later in chapter 4, but here I wish to explore something of their lived significance by first focusing on how Jesus's life, death, and resurrection open up for us a liberating experience of the generous power that gives all things "to be." That is, I wish to plumb the inner relationship between the unconditioned generosity of God who creates from nothing and the way that generosity shows up in our world in Jesus. Perhaps this will seem an unusual relationship to stress, and yet were we unable to trace this relationship with sufficient clarity it is doubtful whether *creatio ex nihilo* should be regarded as vital to Christian faith after all. It is my contention here that, so far from being a speculative add-on, the doctrine of creation from nothing gains its historical and soteriological content in the Christ-event, for it is the crucified and risen Jesus who most transparently discloses in our history the utterly free, nonrivalrous, and redemptive love of God who gives all things "to be." There is a hermeneutical circle at work in this contention: by looking *through* the Christ-event, so to speak, a moment of supreme eschatological significance is allowed to guide and inform a perception of divine creativity that has been active from "the beginning," and which promises a future for creation that is not easily deducible from the present. Even if implicitly, the Christian way to behold our creatureliness is through a christological aperture. Such perception is demonstrably at work when Saint Paul declares in the same breath that Christ is "the first born from the dead" and the one in whom "were created all things in heaven and on earth" (Col. 1:15–18). It is evident when the Gospel of John affirms, "All things came to be through him, and without him nothing came to be" (John 1:3). In both formulae Christ is recognized as "concentrated creation," to borrow a felicitous phrase from Edward Schillebeeckx, for in him we perceive "creation as God wills it to be."[8]

What is most striking about the way God's creative will shows up in our world is that it does not necessarily seem like power at all. In fact, it may very well appear to us as weakness, at least if our understanding of power is predetermined by notions of force, prestige, appropriation, and iron-clad security. Little wonder, then, that when the creative Word of God appears within such a system of coordinates it is perceivable only under the aspect of contradiction, as "foolishness" and "infirmity." The Philippians hymn captures this paradoxical quality quite precisely as it describes the manifestation of Christ in kenotic terms. Whereas a cosmic despot maintains power through a series of relationships rooted in subordination—a merely regional transcendence enclosed within a violent-sacral order—the appearance of Christ assumes the "form of a slave, coming in human likeness; and found human in appearance, he humbled himself, becoming obedient to death, even death on a cross" (Phil. 2:6–8). As Paul notes elsewhere, "Power is made perfect in weakness" (2 Cor. 12:9).

What needs clarification is that such weakness is not without its own peculiar efficacy. The "self-emptying" of God in Christ is not the absence of power; it is its radical incidence—or better yet, it is true power, and the signature of its efficacy is "unbinding" and "unloosing," of "setting captives free." Such gracious efficacy is the precise point of Paul's discussion of "the principalities and powers" that the cross and resurrection unmask and throw into confusion (Eph. 6:12). The power of empire, the power of acquisition, the power of prestige, even the power of death: all are shown to have no *real* power in the end. The principalities and powers are deflated by the cross, outwitted and subverted by a gracious operation in which the Logos of God freely assumes the form of a slave. God inhabits the place of human infirmity, becomes identified with the poor, the naked, the ousted, the subjected—the scapegoat. What was once thought to be the highest or most powerful within an implacable social system is demystified and exposed as vanity. As Stanislas Breton puts it, the self-emptying of God in Christ reveals "the literally enormous distance between the true God who is Nothing and these diversely named principalities that share among themselves the empire of being."[9] This distance means that the true God, who is No-thing other than the crucified God, cannot be implicated in any power based upon violence and prestige. God is not the highest term in any sacred-social order, circumscribed therein. Indeed, compared to such, Christian faith can only (and rightly) be described as atheistic.[10]

We should immediately notice that this subversion of the principalities and powers does not entail their mere reversal. It is not, as Friedrich Nietzsche supposed, merely *ressentiment* that plots its secret revenge. If the Word has become a slave, this does not mean that the slave may now replace (and thus vengefully imitate) the master! Such would only keep a system of reprisals and cyclical violence neatly intact. Jesus's death on the cross does not occasion any reciprocal response to the violence that led to it. "Father, forgive them, they know not what they do" (Luke 23:34). God's response to power-as-force is not tit for tat. It is not the exertion of an even greater force. And neither is the resurrection of Jesus from the dead a display of apocalyptic retribution. The God of kenotic love does not mimic or enter into war with the principalities and powers but instead freely loses the battle on our behalf. Having unleashed their worst, the principalities and powers are exposed as having no genuine power at all, for they cannot finally exhaust the power of God's unlimited dispossession.[11] The creative freedom of God that summons all things from nothing is the creative freedom that raises Jesus from the *nihil* of death in order to reveal the "strange power" of God and to emancipate those locked into interminable cycles of rivalry, dominance, and exclusionary violence. In this way, the life, death, and resurrection of Jesus is an invitation to discern what divine creativity in the human life-world concretely looks like, enfleshed and with a human face that calls us to participate in its gratuitous unfolding.

Discerning readers will likely recognize the influence of René Girard in this overture to part 2. Themes of human rivalry, cyclical violence, scapegoating, and *ressentiment* are among the most obvious clues, but so too the characterization of Christ's ministry, death, and resurrection in terms of a confrontation with the principalities and powers through God's loving act of self-emptying. This is by no means to suggest that such an account is unique to Girard's work, as though the basic themes herein are not fully available in the New Testament and subsequent theological tradition. And yet, Girard's interdisciplinary forays into literary theory, cultural anthropology, and psychology afford an array of penetrating insights into these classic themes, not least for the way they highlight the entanglements of human desire and the dynamics of conversion. As Robert J. Daly puts it, Girard's

86   Christ as Concentrated Creation

work represents something like a "phenomenology of redemption," in the sense that it sheds light on the processes of psychosocial transformation that the Christ-event makes possible.[12] What is happening, anthropologically speaking, when undergoing salvation? Without reducing salvation to a theory, or a one-size-fits-all account, can we begin to articulate in psychological, interpersonal, and cultural terms how the entanglements and conflicts of human desire are loosened up and freed by Christ so as to enable genuine human flourishing? How might God's redemptive love, as expressed in Christ's life, death, and resurrection, be understood as inducing seismic shifts in our perceptual and affective horizons, and not just ideationally? How is the Christ-event the paradigmatic expression of the God-world relation, insofar as Christ is the God-man, and for that reason the catalytic moment, still very much unfolding, whereby God's original purpose for human beings breaks through the accumulated blockages and distortions in our history so as to reveal what creation is *really* like? For this to happen, God's creative intention must reach us at the level of desire, and precisely in those places where human desire is most susceptible to illusory attachments and false transcendence, that is, idols.

This chapter and the next, which together serve as part 2 of this book, draw extensively (though not uncritically) from the work of Girard and from several theologians in conversation with his work. It does so with the conviction that Girard's account of human desire is indispensable for a contemporary theology of redemption that wishes better to understand how Jesus opens up for us a liberating discovery of God's nonviolence. Or, to put it more positively, the fuller implications of Girard's "mimetic theory," so called, are uniquely poised to show how God's nonviolent, nonrivalrous (i.e., noncompetitive) relation with creation, which the Christ-event displays, constitutes an enactment of *original peace*; that however much the content of human history seems maligned by rivalry and violence, as though intrinsic to our nature and therefore unavoidable, these realities are in fact misdirected distortions of our basic goodness. What Jesus's life, death, and resurrection reveal with eschatological potency — as concentrated creation — is that creation, as it is willed "to be" by God, is primordially *good*. By assuming our creatureliness in full measure, and so by entering unreservedly into the fullest depths of human experience, including those places that seem most destitute of meaning and communion, God not only reveals to us the inherent goodness of our coming to be from nothing, but also affirms that this goodness shall prevail despite all that appears contradictory to it. The original goodness of creation assumes here an eschatological thrust, a promissory momentum that allows us to affirm, along with Saint Paul, that while creation may presently groan in travail, it is destined for a fulfillment in which God will be "all in all."

Strong Protagonism, Weak Presence

I wish to flesh out the preceding overview by first outlining the interplay between freedom and vulnerability in God's self-communication in Christ. James Alison, whose work substantially develops Girard's seminal insights, provides an incisive way to do this—by characterizing God's "strong protagonism" as efficacious in the "weak presence" of the crucified and risen Jesus.

"The starting point of Christian theology," Alison writes, "is that the weak and vulnerable presence of that man who allowed himself to be despised and executed was a dense, powerful and deliberate act of communication, flowing not from some sense of party spirit, but from the Creator of everything that is."[13] He continues:

> The sole condition of the possibility of Christian theology is the return, three days after this scenario, of the silenced, dead victim. He reveals himself, with no trace of rancour, and with all the power of one who forgives those who were accomplices to his lynching, to have been the true protagonist of the scene. So, there begins to irrupt into our midst the strange sensation that what had seemed to us to be most solid and dependably from God [i.e., group solidarity achieved through the expulsion of an impure "other"] was nothing more than quicksand, and that all the strength and solidity of the immovable rock has been made present to us in the vulnerability of the despised one.[14]

The above formulation has much to do with first principles in Christian theology, for it highlights the *coincidentia oppositorum* in the basic event from which Christian faith flows. The Creator of everything that is, and who therefore is *the* protagonist of creation ("Let there be . . ."), is revealed in the midst of a specific human failure ("Crucify him!"). God, the very source and ground of creation, whose unconditioned generativity is not in rivalry with the world, nevertheless shows up in our world under the sign of weakness, contradiction, and obscurity. "He was in the world, and the world came into being through him, but the world did not know him" (John 1:10). God's act of self-communication in Jesus amounts to the deliberate inhabitation of that "no place" of shame and abandonment, the unmitigated curse of his death on the cross (Gal. 3:10). This deliberate inhabitation is not to be imagined as divine complicity in the mob violence that rendered Jesus's subjectivity into a defenseless and despised object, as though God sanctioned the brutal execution of Jesus. (Nothing could be more anti-Gospel than to construe the matter this way, even if certain theories of atonement in Christian theology, as well as some popular presentations of the faith, suggest as much.) No. God is not party to the mechanisms of violent expulsion that so often prop up our tenuous social and cultural identities. The voice of the true God is not discernible in the roar of the maddening crowd. It is discerned in the waning voice of the one who becomes victim to the crowd, expelled as "other" to social constructions of reality that have no ear to hear them. By occupying the place of no place, and by eschatologically amplifying the waning voice of the victim, God unveils (*apocalypsis*) what is usually hidden from our view and redirects us toward an alternative kind of social reality—one not founded upon any exclusionary violence whatsoever but which is "favourable to our growth, our becoming and our flourishing as human beings."[15]

It may seem preposterous that God's intention for creation could in any way be disclosed from such human failure, but in order to see how this might be the case we need first to understand that Jesus's death by violent expulsion was no accident. It was the consequence of death-dealing dynamics in the human life-world that Jesus explicitly sought to transform. God's strong protagonism in Jesus throughout his ministry was so existentially threatening to those powers and

Jesus and the Non-Other 89

identities premised upon prestige, acquisition, domination, and exclusionary violence that Jesus was virtually bound, though he accepted this outcome freely, to become the target of their defensive ire. Jesus's ministry pressed directly upon the pressure points of these dynamics, provocatively yet nonviolently, with the hope that they might be released and transformed by the creative sociality that the living God invites us to inhabit. Such a mission was quite dangerous, clearly, because it upset and threw into confusion identities premised upon strong in-group/out-group dualities. It actively traversed settled social boundaries, blurring the pure/impure dichotomies that often result in some being lost or forgotten. "For the Son of Man has come to seek and to save what was lost" (Luke 19:10). Though by no means anarchist or antinomian, Jesus's ministry was nevertheless revolutionary for the way it boldly announced and symbolically enacted an alternative social reality. It called for a way of human relating not founded upon the production of victims. "Did you never read in the scriptures: 'The stone that the builders rejected has become the cornerstone'" (Matt. 21:42; Ps. 118:22–23). Animated by a source experience of the Father's overflowing abundance that seeks out those most vulnerable to expulsion—the poor, the lame, the blind, the ritually impure, and a host of other "lost sheep" scattered through Israel's (and humanity's) landscape—Jesus's ministry was at the same time a prophetic indictment of those cultural habits and social powers that produce or simply allow the vulnerable to exist. To be sure, dichotomies such as these were not unique to Israel, and we might even say that they are endemic to human socialization wherever we find it; but it was precisely Israel's vocation to be "salt for the earth" and a "light for the world" for the way it responded to God's call to justice and mercy within its own house—not just for its own sake but for the sake of the world (Matt. 5:13–16).[16] Like so many of the prophets before him, Jesus was engaged in a criticism immanent to Israel's original vocation. The call to repentance, or metanoia, threading his ministry was intended as a renewal of Israel's vocation, as a new "gathering" of those who were lost, and this meant abandoning one social reality for another.[17]

To gain an initial sense for how Jesus's ministry worked to disrupt in-group/out-group (pure/impure) distinctions, consider the following résumé of this would-be messiah: his frequent table-fellowship with sinners, tax collectors, and a host of others considered beyond the pale; his breaking of purity laws in order to show that the Sabbath was made for human flourishing, not for burdensome precepts that only some could fastidiously keep; his insistence that purity is a matter of personal intention, not outward ritual performance, heredity, or office; his healing and touching of those who, on account of their physical infirmities, were unable to participate fully in Jewish life and worship; his forgiveness of sins, which, among other things, short-circuited a crucial mediating function of the Temple and its administrative class; his admonishment of the disciples for their rivalrous positioning around the table; his public association with and touching of women; his intervention into the stoning of a woman caught in adultery, thus subverting the scapegoat mechanism at work within it; his welcoming of children and the "little ones" to whom the Kingdom belongs; his announcement of beatitude for the poor, the meek, the persecuted, those who mourn, and those who hunger and thirst for righteousness; his portrayal of the reviled outsider (the Samaritan) who extended God's mercy to a victim when a priest and Levite refused—this in response to the question, "And who is my neighbor?"; his portrayal of the Father's compassion galloping out to embrace the prodigal son who finally had come home; his advocacy of fearless speech that brings darkness to light; his call to forgive debts; his trenchant criticisms of wealth and the hoarding of possessions; his sharp criticism of Temple administrators for placing harsh burdens upon ordinary Jews; and, not least, his highly provocative demonstration in the Temple courtyard as he overturned money-changing tables and the seats of the dove sellers during the Passover season, which was (rightly) perceived as a direct challenge to the Temple and the administrative class beholden to Roman imperial power.

Surely such words and acts of "creative maladjustment" were sufficient to make Jesus a marked man.[18] He deliberately drew out into the light those social patterns and mechanisms dependent upon in-group/out-group polarization, which contributed to exclusionary violence in various ways, but with the consequence that he would himself become subject to their reactive charge. As Girard puts it, "Jesus appears as a destructive and subversive force, as a source of contamination that threatens the community. Indeed, to the extent that he is misunderstood he becomes just that. The way in which he preaches can only make him appear to be totally lacking in respect for the holiest of institutions, guilty of hubris and blasphemy, since he dares to rival God himself in the perfection of the Love that he never ceases to make manifest."[19] Though by no means seeking out victimhood, the Gospels portray Jesus as coming to accept that his ministry would ultimately result in his expulsion; that he would become the victim of his own people. This, in part, is what accounts for the apocalyptic admonishments that grow with the rising tide of opposition to his ministry. "Jerusalem, Jerusalem, you who kill the prophets and stone those sent to you, how many times I yearned to gather your children together, as a hen gathers her young under her wings, but you were unwilling! Behold, your house will be abandoned, desolate. I tell you, you will not see me again until you say: 'Blessed is he who is comes in the name of the Lord'" (Matt. 23:37–39). Again, nothing in the Gospels suggests that Jesus wished to become a scapegoat, and yet the entire thrust of his life-ministry was a loving agitation of those deeply nested mechanisms of exclusionary violence within his society, with the result that those mechanisms turned squarely upon him. "Exactly these forces which he had laid bare now confronted him," writes Raymund Schwager. "He was found guilty of blasphemy, condemned by lies, and brought violently to his death. . . . Through his message of the basileia he himself had awakened the forces which concentrated against him, and he lured them out of their hiding-place by his judgment speeches. He was no accidental scapegoat, as is usually the case."[20]

THE SUGGESTIBILITY OF DESIRE

It should be clear from this account thus far that God's strong protagonism in Jesus has nothing to do with passivity or inertia. It is not as though God lacks efficacy in him, or that Jesus's total obedience to the Father diminishes his human freedom in any way. Jesus is not less human or less real for being fully transparent to the One whom he called "Abba." What Jesus is totally empty of is not his humanness, but rather any *rivalry* with the Father. In him there is no blockage of the primordial goodness that gives all things "to be."

"The Other," writes Alison, "the Father, is absolutely constitutive of who [Jesus] is. Yet, because there is no appropriation of identity over against the Other who forms him, the complete dependence on the Other rather than being a limitation or a source of diminishment is exactly what enables the creative flow of life bringing about life to be made manifest and, being made manifest, to be made actual."[21] We should recall here Rahner's formulation above, drawn exactly along Chalcedonian lines: Jesus is most radically human, the most free and creatively independent, precisely because he is the most radically open (or "empty") to the self-utterance of God constituting him. Emptiness and fullness, like obedience and freedom, grow in direct (not inverse) proportion.

Here we can begin perceiving how Jesus's identity is not defined by any appropriation whatsoever. It is not structured by any "against-ness" toward divine creativity. It throws up no resistance to the ceaseless inflow of the Godhead. "Who, though he was in the form of God, did not regard equality with God something to be grasped" (Phil. 2:6). Jesus's relatedness to God is nongrasping and nonreifying. It bears no trace of opposition or self-clinging. "The Father and I are one" (John 10:30). "Everything that the Father gives me will come to me, and I will not reject anyone who comes to me, because I came down from heaven not to do my own will but the will of the one who sent me" (6:38–38). Or again: "My Father is at work until now, so I am at work" (5:17). Alison notes that these and similar passages in John's gospel characterize the whole of Jesus's life as an "uninterrupted participation in the bringing into being of the fulfillment of creation, something only the Father can do of himself." What the Father wills to bring about in creation from the beginning is finally allowed to break through completely in a human person, to be made manifest and concrete in the uninterrupted consent of Jesus. This is what it means to say "there is no rivalry between him and the Father: they are an entirely interpenetrating reality."[22]

To better appreciate the importance of nonrivalrous desire in the above formulation—and therefore why Christ's "pacific desire," as Alison alternatively calls it, is so central to God's self-communication in him—it is necessary to flesh out Girard's understanding of human desire in some detail. Doing so leads us immediately to unpack the most fundamental insight in all of Girard's work, namely, that human desire is "mimetic," or imitative.

In short, our desires are *borrowed* from others. With this single insight, which at first may seem underwhelming or unwelcome, Girard offers a perspective that at once sheds light on why our remarkable capacities for cooperation as a species are so intimately linked with our capacities for violent conflict. The dynamics that enable such far-reaching creative sociality among human beings, the likes of which are unparalleled in any other species we know, are the same dynamics that lend themselves so readily—one need not say inevitably—to our destruction. Because of the way we are constituted, the worlds of difference that distinguish pacific belonging from rivalrous conflict rest upon the thinnest of margins. Because we *desire according to the desire of others*, as Girard puts it, the deep sense of mutual inwardness that makes us who we are, as human persons, can precipitously shift into a suffocating struggle to distinguish "self" from "other"—or, just as likely, "us" and "them"—with the result that we tear ourselves and each other apart. All beings are relational, ontologically speaking, but in the case of human beings, this relationality assumes a deeply affecting intimacy, a penetrating "we-centricity" whereby all "selves" and "others," however inviolable in dignity, are nevertheless mutually constituted and conditioning. We are inextricably linked to one another at the level of desire, even when we imagine our desires as uniquely our own. Indeed, it is precisely this tendency toward "ownness," in the mode of grasping, that lies at the root of human conflict and violence. To better appreciate this relational matrix of human desire, but more, to grow into patterns of life whereby possessiveness yields to pacific relationality, is key to genuine human flourishing. It is, in fact, to participate in *divine* desire.

Natural Born Empathizers

According to Girard, human desire is understood as mimetic insofar as what it desires, that is, its "object," is informed and mediated by the desires of others. In contrast with an individualistic understanding of the self's origination, which views desire as spontaneously and privately formed within the secret depths of the self, a mimetic approach regards human desires, including those that seem most particular to us, as borrowed from others who model them for us and who become our cohorts or potential rivals in their pursuit.[23]

Mimesis does not refer here to a conscious process whereby we reflexively choose to imitate this or that model, though this sometimes happens. Mimesis is largely preconscious. Our desires are "suggested" to us by others, as the Shakespearean insight goes. Objects that elicit interest from us, and that command our attention to pursue, gain the aura of desirability because others pursue them. The desiring gaze cast by the other at an object alerts us to its now-transfigured appearance. Desirability lies not in the object alone or what we take as its inherent properties, even if it seems this way to us, but rather in the significance others confer upon it. Objects light up within a perceptual-volitional field and gain the definition they have for us on account of the social other. When wanting to play with this toy or drive that car; when finding this pair of jeans in style or that hat; when choosing to drink seltzer water or go organic; when seeking this occupation or that prestigious degree; when yearning for this parental recognition or that peer-group belonging: when we desire something, anything, whether the object occupies a physical space (toy, car, jeans) or constitutes a nonphysical reality (coolness, distinction in taste, admiration, power, belonging), that desire is triangulated from the desires of others who are our mediators and models.

I desire according to the desire of the other, as the Girardian axiom goes. The desires we typically assume as linear in structure (figure 1) are in fact bound up with the social other, and thus triangular in structure (figure 2). Even those appetitive desires (e.g., hunger, thirst, sexual impulse) that seem most instinctive and oriented to basic needs can be, and often are, thoroughly recruited by symbolic values

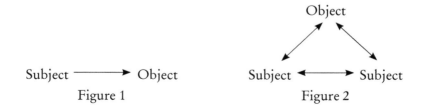

Jesus and the Non-Other 95

and social distinction so as to take on qualitatively new valences in human experience. Our desires deeply implicate us in one another, in ways we scarcely notice. It is as though we are bent upon misidentifying the real source of our desires; we regard them as uniquely our own when we have alighted upon them through the eyes of others.

Since Girard first began to formulate his views on mimetic desire in the 1960s, a significant body of research has emerged from the cognitive and behavioral sciences situating imitation at the heart of human development. Summarizing much of the research from developmental psychology, comparative psychology, neurophysiology, cognitive science, and social psychology, Scott Garrels writes,

> Far from being the simple and mindless act that we typically associate it with ("monkey see, monkey do"), imitation is now understood as a complex, generative, and multidimensional phenomenon at the heart of what makes us human. In fact, imitation may very well be the basis for not only how we learn, but also how we understand each other's intentions and desires, establish relational bonds, fall in love, become jealous, compete with one another, and violently destroy each other, all the while operating largely outside of our conscious awareness.[24]

This interdisciplinary interest in human imitation represents a dramatic shift that has been underway since the late 1970s. Prior to that, human imitation was not very well understood or was regarded as a subset skill in childhood development. To refer just to psychology, William James made several important but isolated observations on the subject, whereas Sigmund Freud gave it almost no importance in his psychoanalytic theory. Jean Piaget granted it more significance in his developmental psychology, but like many others before him he regarded imitation as a skill an infant acquires after the first year of life as it gradually breaks out of its naturally "solipsistic" state. But the presumption that infants are born "asocial" or "radically egocentric" turns out to be one of the "most pervasive scientific myths" about human nature.[25] As Andrew Meltzoff explains, recent research has turned this erroneous view on its head:

The findings from developmental science suggest that preverbal human infants immediately register similarities between self and other. This is not a derived, complex, or cognitively advanced analysis of the social world. There is an intrinsic identification that infants feel before they can speak. This felt connection colors infants' first interactions and interpretations of the social world and impels human communication and social development. Other people are viewed as "Like Me" from the start. This is the newborn's first glimpse of humanity. It is not derived, but basic—not the culmination of moral sentiments, but the foundation of them.[26]

In other words, intersubjectivity is generative of the nascent self. Affective rapport with others forms the very basis of ordinary human development. We are natural born empathizers.

Empirical studies of neonatal imitation demonstrate that newborns are able to mirror the facial and manual gestures of others within the first hour of life.[27] Long before neonates know they have a face, and as a condition for any such awareness, they are capable of affective and sensorimotor correspondence with the gaze of others. "Self-other connectedness and communication exists at birth. Humans imitate before they can use language; they learn through imitation but don't need to learn to imitate."[28]

No less significant is the way infants are able to follow the gaze of another toward an external target. A mother's glance refers the infant to some object, bathing it in the light of her attention, endowing the object with various qualities through her bodily and verbal gestures. Citing Girard's characterization of an object's "transfiguration" resulting from the other's attention, Meltzoff writes that infant studies show how "an inanimate object takes on a special valence when it is looked at by a social other. It is as if having the adult shine her social spotlight on an inanimate object leaves a trace on it, an invisible mark. Such is the power of eyes, that being visually touched by the look of a social other transforms the object from a boring blob to an object of desire that cries out, 'Look at me! Value me!'"[29]

Michael Tomasello describes this as "the nine-month revolution." Whereas previously the infant relates dyadically with other persons and objects, by around nine months new behaviors emerge that "are triadic in the sense that they involve a coordination of their interactions with objects and people, resulting in a referential triangle of child, adult, and the object or event to which they share attention."[30] "Joint attention," as it is now commonly referred to in the literature, closely corresponds to Girard's characterization of desire as triangulated, in that objects elicit notice and value through shared attentional energy.

Importantly, this capacity for following the gaze of others toward an external object is a prelude to grasping the *intentions* of others. Between nine and eighteen months children can understand what another person intends to do with an object when the attempt is unsuccessful. For example, when an adult tries and fails to pull two toys apart, the young child can see through the surface activity and discern the frustrated intentions of the actor. Without prompting, the child will attempt to complete the failed task, which shows that imitation is not the mimicry of perceived behavior but the grasping of *intended* behavior.[31] This is a truly momentous development. In philosophical terms, the child has acquired a "theory of mind," for he or she is able to discern the intentionality within or behind exhibited behavior, including when there is a disjunction between intention and behavior. It also means that the child is now capable of imitative learning, for he or she is able to "tune in" to the intentions of others as the basis for discovering what objects, cultural artifacts, and behaviors are for, and with it a newfound capacity for gradually building upon and modifying them. Imitation creates the possibility for interpersonal and cultural novelty. As Tomasello explains, imitative learning inducts children into human culture by allowing them to become agents of it. In grasping themselves and others as intentional agents,

> a whole new world of intersubjectively shared reality begins to open up. It is a world populated by material and symbolic artifacts and social practices that members of their culture, both past and present, have created for the use of others. To be able to use these artifacts as they were meant to be used, and to participate in these social practices as they were meant to be participated in, children have to be able to imagine themselves in the position of the adult users and participants as they observe them. Children

now come to comprehend how "we" use the artifacts and practices of our culture—what they are "for."[32]

Tomasello persuasively argues, on the basis of his extensive work with primates in comparative psychology, that imitative learning is key to the distinctive evolutionary path of our species. This is not to say that nonhuman primates do not imitate or have cultures, but it *is* to point out that compared to our nearest evolutionary neighbor, with whom we share 98 percent of our genetic material, *Homo sapiens* exhibits a species-unique mode of cultural transmission through imitative learning, as well as a capacity for placing oneself "in the mental shoes" of another, by which instructed and collaborative learning become possible. We imitatively learn from and through others.[33] The result is a "cumulative cultural evolution" that includes a vast array of human artifacts and social practices transmitted over time. Such is "sociogenesis." Through countless modifications of artifacts and practices, whether by individuals or groups, a "ratchet effect" emerges whereby culture produces constantly new environments for human life.[34]

Imitation is "the meta-skill that enables all other skills," writes Iain McGilchrist, for it is how we acquire any skill at all.[35] Arguably the most important adaptation in the evolution of our species, the capacity for imitation massively accelerates the accrual of transmitted skills from one generation to the next. Rather than requiring genetic mutations for specific skills to develop, the selection for imitation proved extraordinarily advantageous in its flexibility. By enabling learned behaviors, early hominids could cultivate a virtually limitless range of skills from one another, modify and build upon them over time, and meanwhile generate an emergent cultural field, or *habitus*, that serves as a kind of "second nature."[36] Skill imitation does not require conceptual analysis, or even language for that matter, and in fact it long precedes anything like abstract thought. "Skills are intuitive," writes McGilchrist, "'inhabited' ways of being and behaving, not analytically structured, rule-based techniques."[37] Imitation is thus an embodied and empathic activity. By it we do not merely copy the behaviors of others, as though through mechanical reproduction, but we imaginatively inhabit the *intentions* of others—another's

Jesus and the Non-Other

aspiration or attentional focus—thereby taking on as our own the perspective of others in mimetic proximity.

The We-Centricity of the Self

One of the far-reaching implications of mimetic desire concerns the inherently relational nature of what we call the "self." Vittorio Gallese puts it well, stating that the self is constitutively and pretheoretically "we-centric." Any lingering Cartesianism that might struggle to understand how we could move from the ego-self to the other suffers from a fatal misrecognition of the self's primordial givenness as being *from* and *with* the other. The other is "co-originally given as the self. Both self and other appear to be intimately intertwined because of the intercorporeity linking them."[38] Gallese makes the point in dialogue with mimetic theory, phenomenology, and recent research on "mirror neurons," which he codiscovered along with his Italian colleagues at the University of Parma in the mid-1990s.

A distinct group of neurons first discovered in macaque monkeys, and later found extensively in human beings, mirror neurons automatically "mirror" the goal-directed motor actions perceived in others. When, for instance, a macaque monkey observes another monkey reaching for food, the very motor sequence that would be involved if the observing monkey performed the action itself is activated in its brain. Just by observing, the monkey participates through simulation in the goal-directed actions performed by others. The same action simulation occurs in humans, though to a far greater extent and with massive affective and ideational content. It is believed by many neuroscientists today that mirror neurons play a significant role in human empathy.[39] Empathy in this sense is not a process of inferring the state of another but a precognitive identification with another. We laugh when others laugh, cry when others cry, feel pain when others feel pain, and get angry when others get angry. We vicariously participate in sporting events, dramatic enactments, musical performances, and social scripts—all simply by witnessing them. The actions, emotions, and sensations of others become meaningful for us because we simulate and share them.[40] We discover ourselves in "we-centric spaces" that give us "implicit certainties about the other. This implicit and pre-theoretical, but at the same time contentful state enables us to directly understand what the other person is doing, why he or she is doing it, and how he or she feels about a specific situation."[41]

While the significance of mirror neurons continues to be assessed, the striking interdisciplinary convergence upon the role of imitation in human life cuts at the heart of a dominant assumption held among many in the modern West: the autonomy of the self. If modern Western societies foster a sense of selfhood as prior to relationship, a self whose inwardly constituted "me" extends "outwardly" into the world through expression and instrumental activity—this is what Charles Taylor dubs as the "buffered self"[42]—studies of human imitation from a variety of fields reveal just how porous selfhood really is. This is not to suggest that human persons are not free, or that mimesis renders individuation illusory. Imitation plays a vital role in the embodied and contextual freedom of human persons. "Imitation gives rise, paradoxically as it may seem, to individuality," writes McGilchrist. "That is precisely because the process is not mechanical reproduction, but an imaginative inhabiting of the other, which is always different because of its intersubjective betweenness."[43] Selfhood is more helpfully described as a highly interdependent reality that arises in the dynamic exchange with others. We are "interdividuals," as Girard puts it[44]— emergent from a vast realm of alterity and inhabited by innumerable others (familial, peer, social, cultural, etc.) whose desires and comportments we tacitly mirror, appropriate, negotiate, and creatively refashion in the tentative project of personal becoming. The self is hardly an atomized ego, not even when we experience extreme alienation, but "in the first instance a real but malleable construct which is a symptom of the way *this body* has been brought into being, and is held in being, by the relationships which preceded it. We are well on the way," continues Alison, "to being able to understand the scientific underpinnings which configure the reality seen more often by poets and mystics than by our recent philosophical and psychological tradition—'Hypocrite lecteur, mon semblable, mon frère'—or the sense we occasionally glimpse that, just beneath the surface of the way 'I' behave consciously, there are others acting speaking, desiring, through me."[45]

Jean-Michel Oughourlian similarly describes selfhood as arising "between" others who remain mutually implicated and constantly

Jesus and the Non-Other 101

"exchanged" through perception, language, and culture.[46] Mimesis "both individualizes us and universalizes us, binds us and at the same gives us liberty."[47] Such "universal mimesis," which Oughourlian likens to a gravitational force in human relationships, does not diminish as persons pass from childhood to adulthood; it only becomes more complex and nuanced, even to the point where we can learn to obscure or manipulate the borrowed character of our desires. Even so, "what one customarily calls the 'I' or 'self' in psychology is an unstable, constantly changing, and ultimately evanescent structure.... We must give due recognition to the interchangeability, the porosity, and the constant interaction between the self and the other."[48] This observation does not lead Oughourlian to declare the self an illusion, such as one finds among some "neuro-nihilists" today, though it does mean that what we often take the self to be, namely, an independent and stable reality, is indeed something illusory that we construct, reify, and tenaciously cling to in the effort to maintain identity, both individually and in groups.[49] Often in such cases we are misrecognizing the source of our desires.[50] We attribute them principally to ourselves when others suggest them to us. Such *méconnaissance* can often be innocuous in everyday life, but it may also lead to conflict with others, especially when we pursue our desires and perceived identities in proximity to others. A mimetic feedback loop can arise wherein two or more persons find themselves struggling against one another in the pursuit of a common object of desire and therefore a contested identity. The mimetic attraction that bonds persons together through shared intentionality and interests can be the very force that sets off rivalry and eventually violence. The we-centricity of the self, it turns out, is structurally ambivalent.

THE GENESIS OF RIVALRY

With a Tug of "Mine"

One of the unsettling corollaries to this understanding of desire is the light it sheds upon the rivalry and conflict that often arise from mimesis. To put it simply, the very mimetic attraction that draws persons together through shared intentionality is highly susceptible to conflict and even violence. That is, a positive feedback loop can abruptly arise whereby two or more persons (or groups) find themselves struggling against one another in pursuit of a common object of desire. Girard provides a schematic account of how such conflict typically occurs:

> If the appropriative gesture of an individual named A is rooted in the imitation of an individual named B, it means that A and B must reach together for one and the same object. They become rivals for that object. If the tendency to imitate appropriation is present on both sides, imitative rivalry must tend to become reciprocal; it must be subject to the back and forth reinforcement that communication theorists call a positive feedback. In other words, the individual who first acts as a model will experience an increase in his own appropriative urge when he finds himself thwarted by his imitator. And reciprocally. Each becomes the imitator of his own imitator and the model of his own model. Each tries to push aside the obstacle that the other places in his path. Violence is generated by this process; or rather violence is the process itself when two or more partners try to prevent one another from appropriating the object they all desire through physical or other means.[51]

The above scenario sets the triangularity of desire into motion, in this case a conflictual motion wherein subjects A and B are entangled by mutual attraction. Though each is ostensibly preoccupied with the object — it is the object itself that appears to them desirable — what makes the object desirable is the attention and significance the other subject invests in it. At this point, subjects A and B might come to share the object out of mutual benefit, or one subject may freely release the object to the other's possession, thus preempting conflict, but so often the attempt of one subject to appropriate the object only arouses a greater appropriative urge in the other, and vice versa. Girard describes this as a shift to "acquisitive desire."

This dynamic is easily observable in children who struggle over the same toy. Though dozens of toys may be within arm's reach, children readily gravitate toward the toy within *each other's* reach. Why is this? What is it about the human animal that makes what the other has

Jesus and the Non-Other 103

(or is) so essential to the way we desire (or wish to be)? Mere aggression cannot account for it. Neither can scarcity. As parents know only too well, any effort to supply an abundance of toys cannot prevent the reciprocal fascination and eventual conflict children arouse in each other. The triangulated toy only *seems* scarce to the children whose desires are mutually transfixed. It may even seem like the only toy in the universe, but only because everything else recedes into the background of their joint attention. With a tug of "mine," the other child suddenly feels piqued and reciprocates the action, thus intensifying the appropriative urge between them. As both struggle over the same toy, each child models desire for the other while at the same time becoming the obstacle to the other. They are model-obstacles for one another, in effect saying "imitate me, don't imitate me" or "desire what I desire, don't desire what I desire." This deep ambivalence is what Girard means by the "double bind" of acquisitive desire. Each child desires the same toy, but in desiring it they encounter each other as the obstacle to its attainment. In the encounter with each other as an obstacle, the object becomes even more desirable. Because the object is just out of reach, each child grasps all the more. Resistance intensifies desire, rendering the object "hyper-real" or "metaphysical," in the specific sense in which Girard uses these terms.[52]

Anyone who has witnessed children struggling over the same toy knows what usually results from it. It may be shocking for parents to watch their beloved child push, hit, or bite other children or call them hurtful names in the attempt to wound or eliminate the model-obstacle of their desire. *From whence does such violence spring?* parents ask themselves in disbelief. Augustine posed the same question in a well-known passage from his *Confessions*: "I have personally watched and studied a jealous baby. He could not yet speak and, pale with jealousy and bitterness, glared at his brother sharing his mother's milk. Who is unaware of this fact of experience? Mothers and nurses claim to charm it away by their own private remedies. But it can hardly be innocence, when the source of milk is flowing richly and abundantly, not to endure a share going to one's blood-brother, who is in profound need, dependent for life exclusively on that one food."[53] Scarcity is not the issue here. The milk flows abundantly enough to satisfy the needs of both infants, and yet the presence of another arouses an appropriative urge that, barring some intervention on the part of the mother or wet-nurse, leads to tantrums. Hence the statement: "So the feebleness of infant limbs is innocent, not the infant's mind."[54]

The mobility of desire is a chief concern for mimetic theory, for it highlights its volatility and the need to channel or give it structure lest it lead to indiscriminate conflict. In the case of the two children struggling over the same toy, if not for the intervention of a third party whose exteriority to the mimetic conflict allows for some resolution ("learn to share," "take turns," "play fair," "go to the other room," etc.), events can take an ugly turn indeed. Soon enough the object of desire disappears as the children become wholly absorbed in each other. Having become undifferentiated in the exchange of pushing and shoving, the conflict reaches a crisis that might conclude with one simply overpowering the other, or with both reeling from the blows each has received, no longer aware of what they were fighting over in the first place. Their struggle has reduced them to a "pure state of reciprocity."[55]

While the above scenario depicts mimetic rivalry within the context of infancy and early childhood, the basic dynamics are operative in all stages of human life, both interpersonally and in groups. This is one of the extraordinary feats of Girard's work, namely, that it illuminates such a broad range of human behavior with such parsimony. But it is also what is so disconcerting about the theory, for it shows just how pervasive conflict really is in human life.

Double Trouble

The view that mimetic desire is at the heart of so much human conflict may not be easily admitted in our contemporary context. One reason for this is that modern individualism is in thrall with the notion that childhood imitation gives way to adult independence and uniqueness. Girard begs to differ. "The mimetic quality of childhood desire is universally recognized. Adult desire is virtually identical, except that (most strikingly in our own culture) the adult is generally ashamed to imitate others for fear of revealing his lack of being. The adult likes to assert his independence and to offer himself as a model to others;

Jesus and the Non-Other 105

he invariably falls back on the formula 'Imitate me!' in order to conceal his own lack of originality."[56] As this quote suggests, it is not that adults grow out of mimetic desire so much as they are better able to cloak and manipulate it. Marcel Proust's depiction of a boardwalk stroll at Balbec masterfully illustrates the point: "All these people . . . pretending not to see, so as to let it be thought they were not interested in them, but covertly eyeing, for fear of running into them, the people who were walking beside or coming towards them, did in fact bump into them, became entangled with them, because each was mutually the object of the same secret attention veiled beneath the same apparent disdain."[57]

Notice the layered webs of mimetic comparison at work here as those strolling the boardwalk expertly conceal their fascination with each other. To show too much interest in others would be to give up the game, for then their secret would be revealed. Instead, they maintain the pretense of their own originality through mutual disdain, and with it the illusion of uniqueness and superiority. Though insults and stones are not hurled, the mimetic rivalry simmers all the same.

Girard argues that this "double mediation," wherein each rival becomes a model-obstacle for the other, lies at the heart of interpersonal and social ressentiment. The dynamic is one of attraction-repulsion. On the one hand, mutual fixation brings two or more parties into increasing proximity *with* one another, while, on the other, each party struggles to differentiate *from* the other in the assertion of originality. Ironically, the more each party attempts to differentiate from the other, the more they become *like* the other. This is one way to read the paradox of mass conformism in individualistic societies. In an era whose unquestioned imperative is to be different, to be unique, to be a standard-bearer, we trip over ourselves for the newest fashion, whether sartorial, artistic, or intellectual. To have unique tastes and preferences, to exhibit alternative styles, to be a revolutionary, an entrepreneur, to transgress boundaries and go where no one else has gone before: none of this actually extracts us from our mimetic entanglements, for it is precisely the desire to be imitated, that is, to be recognized, to be admired, perhaps "idolized," that drives the aspiration for originality in the first place. Girard names this drive to distinction "negative mimesis."[58] In the effort not to do what others do, constant mimetic comparison with others turns out to be just as necessary.[59] Such is the "romantic lie" that underwrites so much of what modern Westerners take individuality to be, which is to sacralize difference from others in order to be "authentic." It is an illusion, Girard insists, because it not only misrecognizes the fact that our desires are always borrowed from others, including the desire to be unique, but also falsely sets up the project of becoming an individual (which is not the same thing as becoming a *person*) by way of relentless interpersonal and social antagonisms. We must constantly strive over and against others in order to achieve our tenuous identities, and this binds us ever more tightly into patterns of mimetic entanglement with others.

This is one of the chief lessons that all great dramatic representation reveals to us, both tragic and comic. Often in such representations the object of triangular desire turns out to be "nothing" in the end. As with the title of Shakespeare's great comedy, the struggle that results when two or more parties find themselves mutually absorbed over prestige and honor turns out to be "much ado about nothing." Like the infants whose escalating conflict renders the object increasingly invisible—they no longer know what they were fighting for—the conflict over prestige and honor, and the resentments and hostilities that ensue when such "metaphysical" objects are not obtained, renders persons and even entire groups increasingly undifferentiated. They become "doubles."

Girard notes the pronounced tendency among dramatists and novelists, including Shakespeare, Proust, and Dostoevsky, to focus on the vortexlike momentum of doubles, but he also notes their frequent appearance in ancient myth and literature. Two classic examples include the founding of Rome, in which Romulus slays his twin brother, Remus, and the first murder in Genesis, in which Cain slays his brother, Abel. Both murders are the culmination of mimetic rivalry, though it is notable that whereas the Roman myth portrays the victorious brother as a sign of Rome's strength, Genesis highlights Abel's innocence. His blood cries to God from the ground (Gen. 4:10). Moreover, God protects Cain with a sign to prevent the cyclical violence of revenge (4:15). Both stories point to a murder as a founding moment. In the former it is the founding of Rome; in the latter it is the founding of the first city (and hence of civilization). But the emphasis of perspective could not be more different. In the former it is the victor's

Jesus and the Non-Other 107

perspective that is taken; in the latter the slain victim is declared innocent while the persecutor is recognized as a potential future victim.

Consider yet another schematic account by Girard of mimetic rivalry and the violence that ensues, but now substitute subjects A and B with groups, or even entire nations, whether defined by social, ethnic, political, or religious affiliation.

> If desire is allowed to follow its own bent, its mimetic nature will almost always lead it into a double bind. The unchanneled mimetic impulse hurls itself blindly against the obstacle of a conflicting desire. It invites its own rebuffs, and these rebuffs will in turn strengthen the mimetic inclination. We have, then, a self-perpetuating process, constantly increasing in simplicity and fervor. Whenever the disciple borrows from his model what he believes to be the "true" object, he tries to possess that truth by desiring precisely what this model desires. Whenever he sees himself closest to the supreme goal, he comes into violent conflict with a rival. By a mental shortcut that is both eminently logical and self-defeating, he convinces himself that the violence itself is the most distinctive attribute of this supreme goal! Ever afterward, violence and desire will be linked in his mind, and the presence of violence will invariably awaken desire.[60]

Girard highlights a tipping point that is easily reached in mimetic conflict, a threshold that, when crossed, turns violence into the goal of desire itself. In this monstrous situation violence assumes an infallible logic. It can justify anything, even the most horrific of acts. One's cause becomes utterly self-authorizing, and what it authorizes is extermination. In the absence of a braking mechanism that might channel or redirect the escalation of reciprocity, the parties will find themselves "battling to the end." Such is the logic of war.[61]

Journalist Chris Hedges depicts this logic with harrowing detail in his *War Is a Force That Gives Us Meaning.* Describing the self-authorizing cause of war as a process of mythmaking, he notes that persons and groups who would ordinarily not recognize themselves as engaging in violent behaviors, and who would be appalled to observe them in others from a distance, can become so ensconced in their causes as to invent meanings where they do not exist and justify actions so heinous as to defy belief. Referring to a broad range of conflicts over the past several decades, including in the Balkans, Northern Ireland, Rwanda, Israel-Palestine, and Iraq, he writes that in "mythic war we imbue events with meanings they do not have. We see defeats as signposts on the road to ultimate victory. We demonize the enemy so that our opponent is no longer human. We view ourselves, our people, as the embodiment of absolute goodness. Our enemies invert our view of the world to justify their own cruelty. In most mythic wars this is the case. Each side reduces the other to objects — eventually in the form of corpses."[62] Hedges further notes that the ferocity of conflict often grows in proportion to the proximity of those engaged in it. "Nationalist and ethnic conflicts are fratricides that turn on absurdities. They can only be sustained by myth. The arguments and bloody disputes take place over tiny, almost imperceptible nuances within the society — what Sigmund Freud calls the 'narcissism of minor differences.'"[63]

In the case of the Balkans, for instance, the conflict among Bosnians, Serbians, and Croatians, and the claims to sovereign identity within such mimetically compressed space, reached a tipping point of violent differentiation from the other, with the terribly ironic consequence that the parties became undifferentiated in reprisals. "The Serbs, Muslims, and Croats struggled, like ants on a small hill, to carve out separate, antagonistic identities. But it was all negative space. One defined oneself mostly by what the other was not."[64] Hedges catalogs several ways "minuscule differences" could "give neighbors the justification to kill those they had gone to school and grown up with," including differing words or inflections in the language that all parties in fact shared, or varying customs and culinary traditions that from an outsider's perspective bear such close resemblance as to be indistinguishable. But even more intractable were the competing claims to victimhood.

All groups looked at themselves as victims — the Croats, the Muslims, the Serbs. They ignored the excesses of their own and highlighted the excesses of the other in gross distortions that fueled

Jesus and the Non-Other 109

the war. The cultivation of victimhood is essential fodder for any conflict. It is studiously crafted by the state. All cultural life is directed to broadcast the injustices carried out against us. Cultural life soon becomes little more than the drivel of agitprop. The message that the nation is good, the cause just, and the war noble is pounded into the heads of citizens in everything from late-night talk shows to morning news programs to films and popular novels. The nation is soon thrown into a trance from which it does not awake until the conflict ends. In parts of the world where the conflict remains unresolved, this trance can last for generations.[65]

Hedges highlights the trancelike character of conflict, which in this case was fueled by the sacred status of being the other's victim. Notwithstanding the fact that there *are* real victims and injustices in such conflicts, the vicious reciprocity that turns such claims into snowballing violence depends upon and intensifies a collective hallucination that dehumanizes the other. The enemy not only becomes "irrational" but a "monster," a "barbarian," the epitome of "evil." The effect of such language is that it allows each party not to notice its own implication in the conflict. The terrible means "we" must sometimes resort to are justified because this is what the monstrous "they" unfortunately necessitate. Meanwhile, a thick haze of self-deception obscures the fact that our desires are awakened by the other, whom we mirror, and upon whom we readily project our inner discords.

A U.S. citizen, Hedges sees all the telltale signs of this projective fantasy in his own country's fight against global terrorism. By embracing the mantle of "civilization" against "extremists," or more aggregately "the axis of evil," genuine self-knowledge and self-criticism become extraordinarily difficult to obtain. Indignation, which so often is righteous, obscures the capacity to notice in oneself the very evil deplored in the other, as well as any complicity in the conditions that make such enmity possible. The abstractions that our labels of others produce, and which must be produced in order to keep the cause mythically pure, blocks the perception that we are reciprocally bound with our so-called enemy, our mimetic doubles. As a consequence, "We will never discover who we are. We will fail to confront the capacity we all have for violence. And we will court our own extermination. By accepting the facile cliché that the battle under way against terrorism is a battle against evil, by easily branding those who fight us as the barbarians, we, like them, refuse to acknowledge our own culpability. We ignore real injustices that have led many of those arrayed against us to their rage and despair."[66]

This analysis is very close to Girard's own, though mimetic theory makes more explicit some of its crucial features. The most important is that the escalation of extremes exhibited by human violence can only be adequately understood if conflictual mimesis is seen as its inner dynamism. While gross injustice and poverty are indeed major factors in conflicts the world over, as well as their consequences, it is remarkable that human animals, unlike other animals, are so prone to exterminate one another, even when basic material conditions are met. We fight over prestige and out of resentments, not merely resources. "Human violence is different," writes Paul Dumouchel, "because of its 'runaway' character. Conflict breeds conflict and violence only leads to more violence. Human violence easily gets out of bounds and out of hand, unless it is checked by some external sanction."[67] The reason for this runaway character is that we are more intensely mimetic than other animals.

Aristotle had it right when he declared that among living creatures, human beings are the most mimetic of all.[68] What he did not recognize is that this intensified capacity for imitation, while allowing for friendship and emulation of virtuous behaviors, is precisely why human beings are the most susceptible to extreme violence among living creatures. Friendships quickly turn into rivalries and our emulation of others readily slips into resentment, conflict, and reciprocal violence. "Humans take offense and seek revenge. When aggressed, they may flee in the moment, but they usually, sooner or later, come back for more. They care not only about the *damage* they have suffered, but also about the *affront*." The reason for this depth of wounding, which can breed hostilities and reprisals lasting hundreds of years, and over countless generations, is that "we humans are more interested in each other than are other social animals. This *reciprocity of Other-interest* is both an expression of, and the means by which is realized the *greater interdependence* that exists between us."[69]

Jesus and the Non-Other   111

Beyond Reciprocity

"Come, Follow Me"

With this summary account of mimetic desire in place—an account we will continue to build upon—it is possible to begin perceiving anew the striking way Jesus's life, death, and resurrection reveal the nonrivalrous, pacific reality of God. To recall William Desmond's phrase from the previous chapter, we can begin to see more concretely how Jesus's invitation to *follow* him is in fact an invitation to inhabit the "nonpossessive dispensation" that characterizes God's primordially creative act. Through the process of discipleship, which is nothing if not a pedagogical process of conversion, we are being drawn into the inside of this creative act. We are being summoned to receive, but also participate in, the "absolving power" of God that exhibits itself as "agapeic service." The key to this transformation is *desire*.

In chapter 1 I referred to the process by which the earliest Christians began perceiving creation afresh in light of Jesus's resurrection from the dead. By looking "backward" through the Easter event it became possible, and eventually necessary, to articulate God's originally creative act as "from nothing"; that in the same way Jesus is raised from the *nihil* of death, so too is God's creativity without any presupposition or mediating obstacle whatsoever. No power, not even the power of death, stands finally opposed to the divine creativity that gives all things "to be." The peculiar density of the Easter event set into motion a dramatic reframing of all prior understandings of creation, so much so that we find in the New Testament the conjoining of protology and eschatology in Christ. Jesus Christ is confessed as the "first born of the dead" (eschatology), but also the one "through whom all things were made" (protology). Creation is thus eschatology in retrospect, or—what amounts to the same thing—eschatology has to do with what creation was meant to be, "from the beginning."

For all the wide-ranging implications this telescoping of protology and eschatology has for the Christian understanding of creation, it bears just as much upon how we are to understand the nature of the Christian scriptures. The resurrection of Jesus from the dead sparks and sustains a process of interpretation whereby his life and death are

112 Christ as Concentrated Creation

read in a significantly new light, and vice versa. The great *novum* of Easter reawakens in the disciples all that Jesus said and did during his lifetime, to which they were also witnesses, and allows them (along with the primitive Christian movement) to remember him in a new way. As crystallized in the Road to Emmaus story, which brilliantly portrays the grieving disciples coming to "relearn" all that they thought happened during Jesus's lifetime—"Then they said to each other, 'Were not our hearts burning [within us] while he spoke to us on the way and opened the scriptures to us?'" (Luke 24:32)—the New Testament as a whole can be described as a process of relearning Jesus from the qualitatively new perspective afforded by Easter. The Gospels are therefore the textual traces of "reading backwards" into Jesus's historical ministry, and indeed the whole of scripture, from the perspective of the resurrection.[70]

One obvious consequence of this retrospective interpretation is that it endows all that Jesus said and did with divine authority. By raising Jesus from the dead, God has not only vindicated an innocent victim from the exclusionary violence that crushed him but also eschatologically ratified the content of Jesus's life, his teachings, his symbolic enactments, his ministry of healing, and his prophetic judgments. Peter's reference to Jesus being "raised to the heights by God's right hand," along with many parallel references in the New Testament, signifies this investment of authority quite emphatically. "Therefore let the whole house of Israel know for certain that God has made him both Lord and Messiah, this Jesus whom you crucified" (Acts 2:36). Because it was *this* man from Nazareth whom God raised from the dead, we can be assured that God's will was fulfilled *in* him. We can have confidence that our faith in Christ expresses our faithfulness to God. But more, we can entrust ourselves to the way of Jesus Christ (John 14:6). The resurrection thus has the effect of conferring upon Jesus unprecedented exemplarity. He is presented as the model whose imitation is nothing less than the imitation of God. The "form" of Christ is just what God's creative desire looks like when it assumes human flesh. We are not left to conjecture how divine creativity would manifest itself in the concrete shape of a human life. It is given to us in Christ, the Lord, the "image of the invisible God, the firstborn of all creation" (Col. 1:15). Christ therefore is God's great

Jesus and the Non-Other 113

act of persuasion, which in the medium of our creatureliness entices us to participate in God's own creative desire.

The Gospels are not mere repositories of information that may or may not attract historical curiosity at a later time. Neither are their narrative forms incidental to the content they convey. They are textual performances that would shape how their readers come to know and desire. They are testimonial and exhortatory, and this because the central figure of them is *modeling* a particular way of life, even if that way of life is costly. "Then Jesus said to his disciples, 'Whoever wishes to come after me must deny himself, take up his cross, and follow me. For whoever wishes to save his life will lose it, but whoever loses his life for my sake will find it'" (Matt. 16:24–25). Clearly this reference to the cross is inspired by an interpretation that reads backward into Jesus's ministry from the perspective of his death and resurrection, which is not to say that Jesus did not know (or could not have known) he would suffer the ordeal of crucifixion. There is an interpretive "fusion of horizons" at work here that allows us to hear in condensed form the call to discipleship that echoes the pre-Easter Jesus as well as the luring presence of the crucified-and-risen One who continues to summon others to a "christomorphic" way of life.

As Gerhard Lohfink observes, variations of the verb *to follow* (*akolouthein*) appear more than eighty times in the Gospels alone.[71] The discipleship portrayed in them implies much more than the rabbinical formation that would have been common at the time. "Jesus . . . did not conduct an established educational operation in rabbinic style; instead, being his disciples meant following him into always-changing situations. But within this constant change, accompanied by its eschatological pressure, there took place a daily exercise, a daily inculcation of the new community of discipleship—involving, for example, the rule that disciples had to forgive one another seventy-seven times a day, that is, constantly (Matt. 18:21–22)."[72] Imitation therefore proves fundamental to the content of Jesus's ministry. He was modeling a way of life for others to follow—a pattern of desire, an imaginative horizon, an attitudinal and behavioral orientation—and this modeling was so important to Jesus's overall aim that he could say, "Whoever is not with me is against me, and whoever does not gather with me scatters" (Matt. 12:30). Jesus's summons to

114 Christ as Concentrated Creation

a particular way of life was not a take-it-or-leave-it proposition. It called for decision. "There can be no neutrality toward Jesus, only for or against. Whoever does not decide *for him* has already decided *against him*."[73] This call to decision was even weightier for the way it implied a decision for or against the renewal of Israel itself. "Since this is about the eschatological gathering of Israel, the choice for or against Jesus is also a decision for or against the salvation of Israel. Anyone who does not gather with Jesus now, in this crucial eschatological situation, stands in the way of the salvation and redemption of the people of God."[74] Because Jesus put forward a way of life to be imitated, provocatively and in closest association with Israel's vocation—"Come after me, and I will make you fishers of men" (Mark 1:17)—it elicited followers just as readily as did adversaries. It mimetically set into motion, with rippling and eddying effect, a spectrum of responses that revealed their fundamental stances toward him and his ministry, whether in the mode of acceptance or rejection. And given the way mimetic desire swiftly alters between attraction and repulsion, or involves a volatile combination of the two, the intensity of Jesus's call to discipleship readily made him the object of both approbation and refusal among those who encountered the decisional urgency of his message, until finally they *all* turned on him, or at least abandoned him during his most desperate hour.

Creative Renunciation

Earlier in this chapter I outlined in broadest strokes the remarkable consistency with which Jesus's Kingdom of God ministry sought to destabilize in-group/out-group (pure/impure) distinctions. Through his various symbolic actions, his miracles of healing, his unsettling questions, his parabolic instructions, his prophetic denunciations, and even his strategic silences, Jesus consistently exhibited a way of life that was creatively maladjusted to any social construction premised upon rivalry and exclusionary violence. His was a ministry that tenaciously, if lovingly, agitated those deeply nested mechanisms in his society premised upon securing identity through the expulsion of some residual and unwanted "other." We can hardly produce a single line from the Gospels that does not display, in some form or another,

Jesus and the Non-Other 115

a counterfactual imagination calling into question some piece of conventional wisdom, some taken-for-granted construct of social reality that regards violence as in any sense normal or willed by God. This is so much the case that we might even define the genre of a gospel as an alternative world of imagination intending to defamiliarize, subvert, and ultimately transform any background understanding that depends upon or leads to the production of victims.

Given this sharp focus on the dynamics of exclusionary violence in the Gospels, it should not surprise us to learn that Jesus commanded his disciples to renounce violence in all its forms. This condition for discipleship may seem quite obvious upon a cursory reading of the Gospels, however difficult it may be to heed in all its practical implications, but we will likely miss the true significance of this renunciation if we do not see in it something more than a moral injunction. To unpack this deeper significance, let us consider the core of Jesus's teaching on violence as crystallized in the Sermon on the Mount.

> You have heard that it was said, "An eye for an eye and a tooth for a tooth." But I say to you, offer no resistance to one who is evil. When someone strikes you on [your] right cheek, turn the other one to him as well. If anyone wants to go to law with you over your tunic, hand him your cloak as well. Should anyone press you into service for one mile, go with him for two miles. Give to the one who asks of you, and do not turn your back on one who wants to borrow.
>
> You have heard that it was said, "You shall love your neighbor and hate your enemy." But I say to you, love your enemies, and pray for those who persecute you, that you may be children of your heavenly Father, for he makes his sun rise on the bad and the good, and causes rain to fall on the just and the unjust. (Matt. 5:38–45)

As Girard observes, the proclamation of the Kingdom of God comes with a categorical renunciation of violence and reprisal in all its forms.[75] This may seem an unremarkable statement at first, given how accustomed we are to hearing platitudes about Jesus's call to love enemies, but Girard insists that Jesus exhibits a keen perception into the logic of violence itself, and the deception it fosters, as well as a path for renouncing it. To renounce the reciprocity of violence is to become open to another kingdom. "This is the Kingdom of love, which is also the domain of the true God, the Father of Jesus, of whom the prisoners of violence cannot even conceive."[76]

One of the reasons why the logic of violence is so difficult to penetrate is because very few people ever suppose they initiate it. We almost always imagine it as triggered by others, by our opponents who have provoked us first with insult, threat, or injury. Our involvement in violence, to the extent we even recognize it as such, is usually one of reprisal, legitimately conducted out of a sense of resistance or self-protection. On such terms, any categorical call to renounce violence is usually taken to mean the renunciation of its provocation, not its reciprocation, with the predictable result that very little changes in human affairs. What Jesus stresses more than anything else, however, is the complete renunciation of *reciprocity*, of being caught up in the mimetic replication of insult or violence endured, even when reprisal seems to us quite natural or justified. Jesus's focus is squarely on the imitative character of violence: its extreme sensitivity to contagion and the way conflict abruptly consumes rivals into vortices of reciprocity. Nonresistance to the wicked is not about condoning oppression, much less becoming a doormat to the oppressor. (Such impassiveness could hardly explain why Jesus would arouse so much resistance in his ministry, assuming he took his own teaching seriously.) Rather, nonresistance means refusing to act *reciprocally* to the oppressor, to be moved by its seemingly inexorable momentum. This is the renunciation not of desire as such but only of acquisitive and conflictual desire. It is, in fact, a form of positive mimesis — of nonviolent imitation of the Father — and it is this form of imitation that lies at the heart of the Gospels:

> In the Gospels, everything is imitation, since Christ himself seeks to imitate and be imitated. . . . Christ says: "Imitate me as I imitate the Father." The rules of the Kingdom of God are not at all utopian: *if you want to put an end to mimetic rivalry, give way completely to your rival*. You nip rivalry in the bud. We're not talking about a political program, this is a lot simpler and more

Jesus and the Non-Other   117

fundamental. If someone is making excessive demands on you, he's already involved in mimetic rivalry, he expects you to participate in the escalation. So, to put a stop to it, the only means is to do the opposite of what escalation calls for: meet the excessive demand twice over. If you've been told to walk a mile, walk two; if you've been hit on the left check, offer up the right. The Kingdom of God is nothing but this, but that doesn't mean it's easily accessible.[77]

The unqualified renunciation of vengeance and reprisal—or what Girard, borrowing from Simone Weil, calls "creative renunciation" (*renoncement créatur*)[78]—is not merely a strategic approach for avoiding conflict in human relations. It is rooted in a source experience of the Father's unconditional love that, as we receive it, progressively releases us from a life preoccupied with mimetic comparisons and reactivity within the human life-world. The God of Jesus Christ is not implicated in our violence, as the Gospels make clear, and neither can God be legitimately identified with any group defined by reciprocity, whether friendly or hostile. This is the bracing significance of Jesus's claim that the Father "makes his sun rise on the bad and the good, and causes rain to fall on the just and the unjust": "For if you love those who love you, what recompense will you have? Do not the tax collectors do the same? And if you greet your brothers only, what is unusual about that? Do not the pagans do the same? So be perfect, just as your heavenly Father is perfect" (Matt. 5:45–48).

In one stroke Jesus diagnoses and deconstructs the all-too-human tendency to identify God with our projections. The Father cannot be parlayed into any social agenda based upon human reciprocity, even when that reciprocity seems to us quite friendly and righteous. By insisting that the Father sends down rain to fall on the righteous and wicked alike, Jesus is breaking with any functional equivalency between God and the highest term of "our" social group. He is disentangling the name *Father* from any context that would annex it to a form of human belonging based upon some definitional contrast with others. God cannot legitimately become the platform for our in-group, or for any closed society, whether tribal, national, ideological, or religious, because God is the God of all.[79]

This is why Alison, following Girard, insists that the Sermon on the Mount is not about morals, that is, setting forth a code of behaviors, but more fundamentally about *desire*. Jesus is offering an alternative between two modes of desire, one determined by the dynamics of the social other and another that desires according to God's desire. He is outlining a pattern of desire "which is *not in any way at all* run by what the other is doing to it; which is not in reaction in any way at all, but is purely creative, dynamic, outward going, and able to bring things into being and flourishing."[80] Jesus is making available to us an understanding of how human desire is typically formed, but also revealing to us a different pattern of desire for our liberation. By pointing out that we naturally love those who love us, and that even tax collectors (i.e., those socially reviled) readily form bonds of friendly reciprocity with others who share mutual interests, Jesus is drawing attention to the very normal way we are culturally formed. "He knows that we are reciprocally-formed animals; he seems to understand that we are ourselves radically imitative creatures who are very seriously dependent on what others do to us, for what we do."[81] Friendly reciprocity may seem quite innocuous, and in any number of instances we can say that this very ordinary form of human sociality is inevitable and fruitful. Neither Alison nor Girard is suggesting that we simply reject ordinary ways of human sociality. But both are keen to point out that lurking within every form of human belonging defined by reciprocity is the fact that soon enough we become dependent upon the social other for our "identity-building kit." "So, you love those who love you, and become more and more dependent on their approval, which means that you allow your behaviour to be shaped by their expectations, and find yourself automatically tied into having shared attitudes of contempt for those whom they despise."[82] That is, you become ever more deeply defined by an in-group that contrasts itself, sometimes subtly, sometimes sharply, and often unconsciously, with various out-groups. Your tenuous identity, or who you take yourself to *be*, becomes a seemingly stable reality through a matrix of contrastive social relations. The "lack of being" that gives you an underlying sense of anxiety, or the lack of security that the volatility of desire induces, can be shored up for a while and assume the aspect of solidity, of "substance," to the extent you gain

Jesus and the Non-Other   119

definitional contrast with others who do not share your interests, or speak the way you speak, or look the way you look, or believe what you believe, or vote the way you vote, or occupy the same social class, or enjoy the cultural distinctions to which you aspire. That is, our sense of "I," just as our sense of "we," is so often constructed out of a host of rivalries.

And, of course, no greater definitional contrast is possible than that which our *enemy* affords. "Give people a common enemy, and you will give them a common identity. Deprive them of an enemy and you will deprive them of the crutch by which they know who they are."[83] This depressing anthropological truth need not define the human species as such, but recent research on human altruism makes clear that a great deal of human solidarity has been generated in our species' history through this very means, or what some researchers call "parochial altruism."[84] Warmth of feeling and generosity toward those within our social groups is often positively correlated with enmity toward outsiders. You and I can achieve a greater, more stable and sovereign sense of "we" to the extent that "they" are deemed antagonistic toward us. You and I may even feel an intoxicating sense of kinship, to the extent that I would sacrifice myself for you, and you for me, so long as we have a common enemy between us. The friendly reciprocity that defines our in-group can be strengthened and made to seem like transcendence itself (e.g., something sacred, an eternal bond, the glory of "sacrifice") precisely through the hostile reciprocity we share toward our enemy. As a way of generating human solidarity, it is one of the oldest tricks in the book.

I will return to this deep-seated anthropological problem (or what we will thematize as "sin") in the following chapter, for it is key to understanding the socially transformative power of Jesus's death and resurrection—a power made perfect in weakness. But here we should observe that Jesus's Sermon on the Mount, and indeed the entire thrust of his life-ministry, is a sustained invitation to be inducted into a way of desiring that is not governed by reciprocity of this sort. By commanding his disciples to "love your enemies and pray for those who persecute you," Jesus is calling for a way of loving that is not dependent upon what the other is doing. It is a love that is disinterested or indifferent, as Alison puts it, not in the sense of being withdrawn or uncaring, but in the sense of being *toward* the other in a way that is not determined by whether the other returns or even acknowledges such love. "So be perfect, just as your heavenly Father is perfect."

Jesus and the "Other Other"

If reciprocity, whether friendly or hostile, tends to be the way we are formed by the social other, usually without our conscious awareness, then the pattern of desire into which God ceaselessly draws us, should we become available to it, is one of creative indifference to such reciprocity. I stress *creative* indifference because, so far from resulting in a dispiritedness or callous unconcern for others, such desire is a vital outflowing of compassionate regard that seeks the other's flourishing—for the other's sake. Such *agapeic* desire is therefore an expression of a creative liberty, rather than a solipsistic retreat, and it shares in, while also making manifest, the divine generosity that gives all things "to be." As we become available to God's unconditional generosity and love, and as we become increasingly dispossessed of the acquisitiveness that binds us in an array of interpersonal and social antagonisms—all of them attempts to seize and secure our "being"—we become participants in God's own freedom.

Jesus reveals God as "the Other other," writes Alison, for "God is able to be *towards* each one of us without ever being *over against* any one of us. God is in no sort of rivalry at all with any one of us; he is not part of the same order of being as us, which is how God can create and move us without displacing us."[85] The apparent tautology of the "the Other other" is actually quite illuminating, for it can remind us through a kind of rhetorical jolt that God is not "other" to us by way of simple contrast, as though God and creation formed a mutually external boundary. God is not "other" like that. God's otherness is *so* Other, we might say, as to not be "other" at all. Like Nicolas of Cusa's appeal to the "non-other" (*non aliud*), which likewise stresses the noncontrastive, nondual relation of God and creation, the "Other other" means to name the ineffable intimacy of God's boundless transcendence, without which creation would not be. God is the

Jesus and the Non-Other 121

"without-which-nothing," to recall Sebastian Moore's phrase from chapter 2, and so in no way should we imagine God and creature as situated within a spectrum of being. Indeed, it is "less inappropriate to say that 'God isn't' than that 'God is,' since the verb 'to be' inescapably has as its reference the universe of existing things amongst which we are, and which are at the same level as us."[86] This is why it is so challenging to speak of God's strong protagonism, for we are inclined to imagine it alongside or competing with (i.e., on the "same level as") created protagonisms.

Precisely because God is not an agent among agents, as though competing with others in a negatively defined space, God is able to be for each of us without being rival to any one of us. And this, Alison notes, is a central feature of the radical monotheism that emerges in Jewish and Christian history, namely, "that of an 'I Am' who is not in any sort of rivalry with anything," and who is "teaching us to see ourselves as a 'we' not over against a 'they,' but as part of a 'they' which is becoming a 'we' in the degree to which we come to perceive our similarity with our neighbour and thus, from being peripheral objects, come to share in the first person narrative which is Creation out of nothing and over against nothing at all, just delight."[87] Alison is working with a very dense insight here. The God who creates from nothing and who gives all things their existence out of sheer gratuity ("just delight") is the God who communicates by way of total self-emptying in order to draw us into living out of this gratuity, out of this "nothing," with no hoarding of being, without clinging to our individual selves or group identities, but with the freedom of radically inclusive love. The "I Am" who creates beyond all necessity and with no motive except to love what bears the dignity of otherness is the "I Am" who invites us to discover ourselves as part of a dramatic unfolding wherein we might learn, however slowly and painfully, to live into a "we" without boundaries. And this means, among other things, our becoming purged of false forms of solidarity that depend upon the mechanisms of expulsion, rooted as they are in acquisitiveness and rivalry. This is why Alison insists that living into this invitation "is going to look remarkably like a loss of identity, a certain form of death," because it will mean "breaking through the strong-seeming, but ultimately fragile, dichotomies of 'in group' and 'out group,' 'pure' and 'impure,' 'good guys' and 'bad guys' which are quite simply the ambivalent functions of our cultural identity."[88] Such dichotomies may promise a kind of stabilization of otherwise fragile identities, and even a form of transcendence that seems to hold our social worlds in place, but in fact all such dichotomies exhibit the logic of exclusionary violence.

And here is precisely why the concrete shape of Jesus's life, death, and resurrection is so decisive in revealing who the creator God really is. Recalling Alison's account of Jesus's identity as wholly constituted by the "Other other," by the creative beneficence of the Father, we can now better glimpse the immense significance in pointing out that in Jesus there is no rivalry with God at all. In him there is no clenching of being, no sequestering of identity. In him there is no grasping at God as "something to be grasped" (Phil. 2:6). Jesus is wholly empty of any acquisitiveness or identity built upon prerogative. This is not at all to say that Jesus is without desire, or that something essentially human is suppressed in him. Rather, Jesus's human desire is perfectly imitative of, and wholly transparent to, the Father who eternally bestows him from within. "Jesus answered and said to them, 'Amen, amen, I say to you, a son cannot do anything on his own, but only what he sees his father doing; for what he does, his son will do also'" (John 5:19). As Alison explains, "Jesus' identity is entirely dependent on that of the Father and is brought into being as a human in a quite specific way: the perfect imitation by the Son of the Father. . . . Because there is no rivalry between Father and Son . . . the Father's creative expansion is able to flow directly into the Son's creative imagination such [that] the Son can bring that expansion into being in the midst of humanity."[89] We should again recall here the noncompetitive logic articulated by Rahner: Jesus is the most fully human not in spite of, but because of his utter openness to God's self-utterance.

But perhaps we can now begin to perceive anew why this perfect imitation of the Father made Jesus susceptible to being rejected and eventually expelled from the very human community he never ceased to love. It was as though the fullness of his humanity was too much to bear, too costly to accept. The kind of humanity Jesus continuously

Jesus and the Non-Other 123

displayed and the kind of we-centricity into which he was inviting those who would follow him destabilized by overflowing the limited and frequently distortive frames of human belonging to which we typically cling, not least because that invitation so steadfastly seeks after those who are lost or excluded as a result.

That Jesus would eventually find himself an object of scorn and violently expelled by powers unable to tolerate a revolutionary ministry premised so exactly upon their exposure: this is not surprising. In this very precise sense Jesus is indeed a "weak presence" because, compared to the reactivity and violence inhering such powers, which he consistently refused to imitate, his voice grows increasingly imperceptible until it is finally vanquished. What requires clarification concerning the seeming contradiction between strong and weak protagonism in Jesus, however, is that there is nothing intrinsically weak about God's self-manifestation in the crucified Jesus. It is not as though God were lacking in some capacity. It is, rather, that God's strong protagonism manifests *as* a weak presence, phenomenologically speaking, because its self-giving love is utterly nonreciprocal to the diverse and gathering powers implicated in Jesus's execution. As Jesus answered Pilate, "My kingdom does not belong to this world" (18:36). It is not as though God exercises self-restraint or undergoes some mythical process of self-divestiture in the event of the cross. No speculative Good Friday is needed to fathom why the unconditioned generosity of God shows up in our world in the vulnerability of a silenced, dead victim. It only appears like weakness to us when compared to the outwardly impressive but ultimately mendacious forms of power that traffic in rivalry and force and depend upon the expulsion of some "other" in order to persist. In point of fact, Jesus's ministry and acceptance of his death exhibit a revolutionary freedom because they flow so directly out of a power that is willing to absorb the death-dealing hostility of those threatened by such love. This is true power.

What *is* surprising, however, and what constitutes the enduring spark of Christian faith itself, is that it will become evident shortly following Jesus's execution that it was precisely God's strong protagonism at work in him all along, including in his death; "behind the one who occupied the place of the victim with the waning voice, the

124   Christ as Concentrated Creation

implausible account and the weak presence, there was a power and a benevolence that were reaching out to us *before we could even begin to imagine them.*[90] No less surprising is how it became possible to recognize this power and benevolence in the midst of such human failure—through the *return* of the crucified as God's offer of reconciliation and eschatological peace. "Behold, I make all things new" (Rev. 21:5; Isa. 43:18–19).

CHAPTER FOUR

Strange Victory

VIOLENCE CONCEALED

In the previous chapter we began unpacking René Girard's analysis of human desire as mimetic. Accordingly, a vast array of our desires is borrowed from the desires of others, even when we attempt to cloak our desires or differentiate ourselves from others through negative imitation. The selves we imagine ourselves to be, while indeed the bearers of freedom and inherent worth, are not freestanding monads but instead are malleable, interdependent expressions of an interpersonal and social other that forms our perceptions and shapes our behavioral patterns, which we creatively rework and model for others. Such modeling is largely a precognitive process, so much so that we often "misrecognize" the true source of our desires, claiming for ourselves sole authorship when in fact a host of others suggest them to us. This *méconnaissance* does not mean that we are mindless replications of a social conglomerate or incapable of exercising freedom within the warp and woof of social relations; neither does it deny the inviolable mystery and responsibility in the task of becoming human, though it does stress that this process is far more porous and we-centric than is often supposed.

Because imitation is the way we come to have anything like a self at all—again, it is not despite mimesis but because of it that we accede to the creative task and responsibility of personhood—it turns out that we are highly susceptible to self-deception and conflict with others. To be sure, mimesis is a fundamental good; it is what makes shared intentionality, cooperation, and cultural formation possible. Even when it leads to conflict, Girard insists that mimetic desire is "intrinsically good, in the sense that far from being merely imitative in a small sense, it's the opening out of oneself."[1] Our mimetic capacities render us ecstatic beings, and dramatically so. Ours is an "extreme openness," for it enables the "desire for God"[2] — a point to which we must return.[3] And yet this very potential for openness, this capacity for creative and loving transcendence with and among others, can devolve into a myriad of suffocating enclosures or flex into the "deviated transcendence" of violence as desire gains an acquisitive edge and fixates upon rivalrously charged objects.[4] In one sense, this is the anthropological meaning of "sin" in Christian theology: the substitution of creative and pacific desire with appropriative and acquisitive desire. What might have been the occasion for fruitful cooperation, or even creative renunciation, becomes instead the scene of conflict. This conflict can run very deep, it turns out, for acquisitive desire always wants more than the object of desire; it wants to "*acquire the being* of his or her model. At such times, I want 'to be what the other becomes when he possesses this or that object.'"[5] Acquisitive mimesis, in contrast to creative mimesis, must displace the other who awakens its desire.[6] Its manner of being is agonistic and appropriative, constantly buffeted by mimetic comparisons and arousing all manner of "passions," for example, jealousy, fear, anger, snobbery, resentment, self-loathing, despair, and hatred. Little wonder that rivals become so absorbed in each other, particularly when trying to differentiate from one another, and little wonder that violence among human beings has a runaway character to it: once they find themselves in some sort of mimetic crisis, rivals are easily swept into conflicts that, barring some braking mechanism or outlet that might discharge the rivalrous tension, snowballs and regenerates itself through the reciprocity of slights, affronts, and eventually blows.

If the analysis of desire as mimetic constitutes the first major plank of Girard's mimetic theory, his account of scapegoating and its effects constitutes the second. We have already become acquainted with this second aspect of Girard's thought in the previous chapter, but in the present chapter I wish to draw this crucial feature out more explicitly in light of Jesus's death and resurrection, with the ultimate aim of showing how the Christ-event in its entirety opens up for us an indispensable and transformative experience of the God-world relation. The resurrection of the crucified Jesus *reveals* by unveiling or unmasking those false forms of order and transcendence that trade upon illusion and fear, and that keep us beholden to destructive patterns of relating to one another. Revelation in this sense has little to do with discrete information "about" God but instead entails a divine pedagogy that invites us into a process of "undergoing God." The christological dimension of this transformative process is key, for it is the Creator's way of reaching out to us in those places where we are most susceptible to deceitful and damaging forms of human belonging. Such is the "strange victory" of the cross.

Scapegoating and Its Effects

The following quotation is yet another schematic account provided by Girard, but this time in reference to the way human beings have often coped with mimetic conflict, namely, by projecting discord upon some expelled "other" in order to achieve a cathartic unanimity.

> By a scapegoat effect I mean that strange process through which two or more people are reconciled at the expense of a third party who appears guilty or responsible for whatever ails, disturbs, or frightens the scapegoaters. They feel relieved of their tensions and they coalesce into a more harmonious group. They now have a single purpose, which is to prevent the scapegoat from harming them, by expelling and destroying him. . . . Mimetic attraction is bound to increase with the number of those who converge on one and the same antagonist. Sooner or later a snowball effect must occur that involves the entire group minus, of course, the one individual, or the few against whom all hostility focuses and who become the "scapegoats," in a sense analogous to but more extreme than our everyday sense of the word "scapegoat." Whereas mimetic appropriation is inevitably divisive, causing the contestants to fight over an object they cannot all appropriate

together, mimetic antagonism is ultimately unitive, or rather reunitive since it provides the antagonists with an object they can really share, in the sense that they can all rush against that victim in order to destroy it or drive it away.[7]

While the word *scapegoat* has permeated our contemporary lexicon sufficiently for most people to be at least vaguely familiar with the basic dynamics Girard describes here, it is worth observing that the English word was first coined by William Tyndale in the sixteenth century to refer to the atoning ritual outlined in Leviticus 16.[8] Accompanying other practices on the Day of Atonement, this particular ritual enacted the purgation of the community's impurity by symbolically transferring it to a goat that was subsequently driven out of the city. After the high priest placed his hands upon the goat and confessed the sins of the people of Israel, the goat was led to a remote place in the desert ("to Azazel") in order to bear and expel the collective sins of the people. With the punishable object now symbolically transferred to a distant and uninhabitable place, the members of the community were reconciled to each other, and the whole community to God, and restored again to its original vocation as bearer of the divine image.

It may be difficult for us to imagine why such a practice developed or how it could have produced the reconciling effects it did for the community. We are even less likely to comprehend why sacrificial practices of all sorts, including sacrifices of humans and animals, are so ubiquitous in archaic cultures. Still, we are all more or less familiar with the remarkable recurrence of that phenomenon we now call scapegoating and the way it depends upon the production of some victim in the pursuit of a group's agenda or internal cohesion. It is such a common trope in our contemporary discourse, in fact, as to have achieved a default ethical critique of something obviously deceptive, even if we almost never recognize ourselves doing it to others. We immediately think of scapegoats as innocent victims produced by crowds or mobs on the lookout for an expedient cause or explanation for their own dysfunction. And this is the basic dynamic that Girard describes: as mimetic tensions give rise to discord within groups, no matter their scale, such tensions can be canalized and projected outward onto a surrogate perceived as responsible for those tensions. The surrogate bears the brunt of group's joint attention, attracts its conflictual energies, and through its expulsion serves to reestablish functional unanimity within the group. To adopt the language of self-organizing systems, when groups encounter disequilibrium due to conflictual pressures building up among members, equilibrium can again be restored and in-group identity reestablished when some liminal object, an "outsider," becomes the target of its collective charge.[9] This is how human beings have often coped with the runaway conflict that mimetic desire can unleash, especially in archaic cultures: through the braking mechanism of convergent enmity upon a scapegoat victim who absorbs and placates the in-group's volatile energies.

We can perhaps better appreciate the force of Girard's analysis of archaic cultures and the role the "violent sacred" plays in them by first considering the stereotypical patterns of scapegoating and its effects in more familiar contexts. For example, we might think of the way two brothers can suddenly find their internal conflicts resolved by ganging up on a third party, perhaps the neighborhood scoundrel who lives down the street. Whereas previously the brothers were fighting among themselves over a triangulated object, say, a bicycle or a baseball glove, their conflictual energy can be vented and transferred onto an outsider who is perceived as a threat to their brotherly bond. As is so often the case, family discords can be assuaged for a time when internal animus is directed toward a nonfamilial other.

Or we might think of a group of adolescent girls who find their mimetic comparisons with one another alleviated by contrasting themselves with the "gross" girl. For want of belonging to each other, they hurl insults at, publicly shame, and obsessively torment another girl whose body type or family background is not quite like theirs. Social media these days are regularly weaponized for the purposes of "cyberbullying."[10] Or consider the proliferation of high school cliques in general and how in-group identities are achieved through strong juxtapositions with other groups (e.g., the jocks, the geeks, the goths, the preps, the thespians, the skateboarders). All of them deeply yearn for belonging, and many of them find it by imitating the styles of dress, musical preferences, speech patterns, and behaviors that broadcast their group's distinction. Each of these groups works to contrast with other groups, and yet they may all discover a new-found unanimity when collectively contrasting themselves against the "loner" or "outcast," the kid whose shyness, disability, funny looks, or accent—whose liminal "weirdness"—sets the boundary for everyone else's "normalcy." He or she, of all kids, is the most vulnerable to bullying and social scorn.

We can detect this all-against-one dynamic in a broader range of social and political phenomena as well. Consider the way immigrant populations are usually greeted by established populations: with anxiety and suspicion. Despite the fact that all of us are ontologically migratory, our tenacious grip on group identity is easily threatened when confronted at home with cultural strangeness. Immigrants are frequently perceived as threats to a nation's imagined linguistic and cultural purity and thus are vulnerable to mistreatment and strategies of containment or exclusion. The scapegoat function of the immigrant is especially likely to be engaged when societies experience collective anxiety over a sense of loss—loss of jobs, loss of values, loss of religious or national prestige, and so on. The desperate search for causes readily fixates upon the cultural stranger, who is variously accused of freeloading, importing crime, diluting the culture, or encroaching upon state territory.[11] A structurally similar process is clearly at work when the values of civilization are thought to be eroding due to the presence of homosexual persons. In many parts of the world homosexuals are libeled, shamed, persecuted, and made to suppress their "sick" and "deviant" behavior for fear that society's venerable institutions and customs will collapse. Even today it is not uncommon to hear that such behavior is to blame for natural disasters, otherwise known as "acts of God."[12]

Or consider the way capital punishment has often served a society's need to ritually purge itself of moral stain. Granted that any civil society needs laws and appropriate punishments in the service of the common good, the state-sponsored (and of course eminently "humane") execution of the criminal who is already locked up for life, with no further potential for inflicting harm upon society, serves to pacify a collective urge for restoring balance to a disrupted social fabric. Not surprisingly, the number of those on death row in the United States is disproportionality Black, poor, and illiterate. As James McBride points out, "It is evident that some categories of persons in society-at-large are statistically more likely to be assigned to the class of the condemned. . . . Although these figures may reflect racial and class bias in the nation as a whole, the presence of the marginalized on the list of the condemned helps to emphasize the difference rather than the similarity of the surrogate victim and to prevent the spillover of violence into mainstream white, predominantly middle-class communities."[13] McBride concludes his Girard-inspired analysis by arguing that the death penalty reveals "the numinous character of public execution, embraced by the state for the expiation of violence in the American body politic."[14]

This numinous character is what Girard means by describing scapegoat violence as "sacred." It is a form of transcendence—a false transcendence, to be sure, but one that provides persons and groups a bulwark against insecurity and loss of social differentiation. It is a "founding" violence, in effect, because it helps to establish an order for social relations, or reestablish them in the midst of social crisis. But, as Girard also stresses, its effectiveness as an ordering principle depends upon an almost impregnable deception. Those engaged in scapegoating do not view themselves as scapegoaters at all. In fact, the very essence of the scapegoat mechanism is that it deflects attention away from those so engaged: "Since cultural eclipse is above all a social crisis, there is a strong tendency to explain it by social and, especially, moral causes. After all, human relations disintegrate in the process and the subjects of those relations cannot be utterly innocent of this phenomenon. But, rather than blame themselves, people inevitably blame either society as whole, which costs them nothing, or other people who seem particularly harmful for easily identifiable reasons. The suspects are accused of a particular category of crimes."[15]

When surveying the testimony of history, literature, and ancient myth, many of the easily identifiable reasons why victims are thus accused have to do with what distinguishes them from the group. Sometimes these distinctions can be subtle, sometimes more pronounced,

132   Christ as Concentrated Creation

but in general they are identified with a harmful moral quality deemed responsible for social crisis. In some cases, the victims of scapegoating are authority figures or persons of privilege (kings, fathers, or a wealthy elite), while in others they are the defenseless and weak (widows, children, and the elderly). Sexual crimes frequent the list, as do transgressions of social taboos. Religious crimes such as heresy or acts of profanation have also made persons susceptible to victimization. Girard refers in this latter context to the feverish pursuits of heretics and witches during times of social unrest and natural disaster, or the recurrent persecution of Jews throughout history, including during the Black Death, when Jews were accused of poisoning the water supply. Physical markers also tend to make persons easy targets of persecutory violence. "Sickness, madness, genetic deformities, accidental injuries, and even disabilities in general tend to polarize persecutors."[16] There is a sense of disorder and miscreation that groups experience when confronted with physical and intellectual disabilities, as though they were something to purge in order to immunize the social body. And notice what most drives such persecutory measures—fear of the group's contingency, that is, lack of substantial "being." "If a disability, even as the result of an accident, is disturbing, it is because it gives the impression of a disturbing dynamism. It seems to threaten the very system. . . . Difference that exists outside the system is terrifying because it reveals the truth of the system, its relativity, its fragility, and its mortality."[17]

While many more examples of scapegoating and its effects could be adumbrated, from interpersonal to more broadly social and political forms, we cannot fail to mention those that take on an unspeakably grand scale, such as the genocides and mass atrocities of the twentieth and twenty-first centuries.[18] Millions upon millions of women, men, and children have been killed, raped, tortured, and displaced from their homes on account of their perceived threat to the nationalistic, ethnic, racial, and ideological purity. As is so often the case with these mass organized slaughters, the attempt is made to purge a group of its internal ambiguities and discords through the expulsion of an "alien" or "impure" element that symbolically bears them. In the case of the Holocaust, which has come to epitomize the horrifying machinations of modern, state-generated sacrifice, Jewish people, along with political dissidents, homosexuals, and disabled persons living under Nazi occupation, were made to bear the collective hostilities of a people dreaming of mythic distinction. The Third Reich's program of ethnic and cultural purity gained its galvanizing force through an obsessive preoccupation with an "infecting" presence requiring containment and eventually extermination. Disturbingly similar dynamics are observable in the many other genocides and mass atrocities that have scarred the last century of global history, with major examples extending from the Ottoman Empire's massacre of ethnic Armenians to the killing fields of Cambodia, the civil wars in El Salvador and Rwanda, and the ethnic cleansing campaigns of Bosnia and Darfur. The pattern is disturbingly consistent, much of it hinging upon an anxious drive to contain or eject an unsettling unlikeness in the pursuit of identity. Miroslav Volf describes this drive as the "will to purity," though it could just as easily be dubbed the "scapegoat mechanism":

> The blood must be pure: German blood alone should run through German veins, free from all non-Aryan contamination. The territory must be pure: Serbian soil must belong to Serbs alone, cleansed of all non-Serbian intruders. The origins must be pure: we must go back to the pristine unity of our linguistic, religious, or cultural past, shake away the dirt of otherness collected on our march through history. The goal must be pure: we must let the light of reason shine into every dark corner or we must create a world of total virtue so as to render all moral effort unnecessary. The origin and the goal, the inside and the outside, everything must be pure: plurality and heterogeneity must give way to homogeneity and unity. One people, one culture, one language, one book, one goal; what does not fall under this all-encompassing "one" is ambivalent, polluting, and dangerous. It must be removed. We want a pure world and to push others out of our world; we want to be pure ourselves and eject "otherness" from within ourselves. The "will to purity" contains a whole program for arranging our social worlds—from the inner worlds of our selves to the other worlds of our families, neighborhood, and nations. It is a dangerous program because it is a totalitarian program, governed by a logic that reduces, ejects, and segregates.[19]

The Creative Murder

To round out our consideration of scapegoating and its effects, I turn to Girard's bold thesis regarding human culture more generally and the role sacred violence plays in it. This focus rightly earns him the title of anthropologist, which he consistently accepts as the most adequate description of his work. Though mimetic theory has proven highly interdisciplinary and enormously suggestive for theological engagement, Girard himself remains principally concerned with the way mimesis leaves the human species susceptible to runaway violence, and hence self-destruction, and how the mechanism of scapegoating functioned in primitive human societies to channel and redirect that violence as a self-regulating protection. We can put the main problem he addresses in the form of a question: If what distinguishes the human animal from other animals is its greatly enhanced capacity for imitation, then how, if such mimetic proximity also makes cyclical and retributive violence a clear and present danger for early hominids, could we have survived our origins? In other words, what were the cultural and symbolic mechanisms that prevented the adventure of hominization from imploding?[20]

It must be stated right away that Girard's response to this question, unsettling as it is, does not mean that human culture *had* to develop the way it did. As Rowan Williams reminds us, dialogue with Girard on the question of human origins "is not to bind ourselves to a mechanistic account of what culture and language 'really' are."[21] If the biblical traditions are witness to anything, it is that culture and language are not "really" a matter of generative violence. Peace is primordial, creation a gift: this is the testimony that scripture overwhelmingly gives, however counterfactual it can seem in human experience. Nevertheless, there is sufficient evidence, both direct and indirect, to suggest that forms of exclusionary violence, including human sacrifice and its ritual reenactments, regularly served to canalize volatile tensions within early hominid groups and establish a "sacred order" that supported their perpetuation. Though not a metaphysical or logical necessity, such mechanisms have proven historically (i.e., contingently) effective in the fragile transition from biological to cultural evolution.

Strange Victory 135

Girard postulates that buried in the fledgling origins of human culture is a crime scene—or, more precisely, a constellation of crime scenes dispersed over vast stretches of time. Based upon the stereotypical patterns of mimetic conflict and scapegoating observable in the kind of phenomena described above, but also the striking recurrence of those patterns in ancient myths and cosmogonies depicting the origins of social order through a generative violence (e.g., rivalry between gods, the slaying of chaos through sacrifice, the dying and rising of gods and kings), Girard maintains that the all-minus-one dynamic of scapegoat violence appears to have served as a bulwark against contagious and potentially catastrophic rivalry within early hominid groups. Through occasions of targeted violence against single victims or a few victims—victims who were regarded as the cause of social unrest—groups were able to "resolve" their conflicts and maintain their tenuous identities sufficiently to grow in social complexity. Scapegoating thus served as a medicinal violence, in that it inoculated the group against its own violent contagion. Hence the double sense of the *pharmakon* in Greek: it is both a "poison" and a "cure." The scapegoat (*pharmakos*) appears in Greek myth, tragedy, and cultic practices as both the cause and remedy of social unrest.[22]

What Girard asks us to imagine are scenarios in which the periodic death of victims produced purgative and pacifying effects for surviving groups. Just as in tragic theater where, as Aristotle explains, the relentless woes and brutal death of the tragic hero induces catharsis for the audience, so can we imagine the cathartic effects of a lynching for those party to it. The brutalized victim, now lifeless, becomes the site of group fascination, inspiring both dread and awe. The *mysterium tremendum et fascinans* described by Rudolf Otto gains here concrete, historical form as those witness to the victim's death are drawn to its unreal spectacle.[23] The collective hostilities of the group are now mysteriously assuaged, confirming that the one lynched was indeed the culprit. The cathartic effects only reinforce the deceptive transference of the group's hostilities to the victim. Here is group delusion in its most unassailable form. But at the same time, and quite paradoxically, the victim's expulsion is also cause for renewed unanimity within the group. The victim is thus both guilty *and* salutary:

guilty as the perceived cause of the social crisis, salutary as the miraculous source of renewed social peace. Girard summarizes the Janus-faced dynamic as follows:

> One must postulate a mimetic crisis of such duration and severity that the sudden resolution, at the expense of a single victim, has the effect of a miraculous deliverance. The experience of a supremely evil and then beneficent being, whose appearance and disappearance are punctuated by collective murder, cannot fail to be literally *gripping*. The community that was once so terribly stricken suddenly finds itself free of antagonism, completely delivered. It is therefore comprehensible that such a community would be henceforth wholly animated by a desire for peace, and bent on preserving the miraculous calm apparently granted to it by the fearful and benign being that had somehow descended upon it. The community will thus direct all future action under the sign of that being, as if carrying out the instructions it had left.[24]

Notice that Girard is interested here in the supreme significance of ritual in archaic societies. Scapegoat violence does not, by itself, make cultural institutions. Ritual reenactments, prohibitions, taboos, social differentiations, and a host of learned practices are ingredients essential to any emergent cultural field for a species as mimetic as we are. It is also important to emphasize that primitive human cultures are about much more than resolving conflict and violence, even if Girard is right that the dominance of ritual in them confirms that "primitive societies are obsessed with the undifferentiation or conflictual reciprocity that must result from the spread of mimetic rivalry."[25] What Girard draws our attention to, and with greater focus than is usually the case among cultural anthropologists, is that while a great diversity of inhabited skills and cultural artifacts are part and parcel of early hominid evolution, there are abundant clues to a "cultural sickness," or what in theological terms we can name as "sin," that has parasitically accompanied our species through history.[26] Lying buried within the cultural fields of our ancestors, amid the many creative and remarkable achievements to which we are also heirs, are the bodies of victims, both real and ritually memorialized, whose liminal status as "dangerous," "strange," or "contaminating" marks the sacred boundary from which in-groups might subsist.

Though we cannot go back in time in order to observe directly the initial stutter steps of hominid evolution—and for this reason our evidence must remain indirect and circumstantial—Girard takes seriously the dynamics that many ancient myths report. Whereas today we may view these myths as bizarre, prescientific accounts of cosmic and human origins that, at best, are interesting for their "metaphorical" or "poetic" value, Girard asks us to read them for what they actually tell us: that the production of emissary victims, along with the ritualized reenactments of human and animal sacrifice, regularly provided a kind of cultural infrastructure on which archaic societies could stabilize and regenerate themselves.

> When we examine the great stories of origin and the founding myths, we notice they themselves proclaim the fundamental and founding role of the single victim and his or her unanimous murder. The idea is present everywhere. In Sumerian mythology cultural institutions emerge from a single victim: Ea, Tiamat, Kingu. The same in India: the dismemberment of the primordial victim, Purusha, by a mob offering sacrifices produces the caste system. We find similar myths in Egypt, in China, among the Germanic peoples—everywhere.
>
> The creative power of this murder is often given concrete form in the value attributed to the fragments of the victim. Each of these is identified as producing a particular institution, a totemic clan, a territorial subdivision, or even the vegetable or animal that furnishes the community its primary food. The body of the victim is sometimes compared to a seed, which must decompose in order to germinate. This germination is the same thing as the cultural system damaged by the preceding crisis or the creation of an entirely new system, which appears often as the first one ever created, as a sort of invention of humanity.[27]

Girard observes in this context that a great comparative anthropologist such as Mircea Eliade could point out the frequent recurrence of a "creative murder" (*meurtre créateur*) in many of the founding myths the world over but never venture to explain why this might be the case.[28] What most interests Girard, however, is not just anthropological description but explanation, and he finds it most compellingly formulated in the following way: the *meurtre créateur* is so recurrent in these founding myths because it frequently "worked."[29] By enacting a targeted violence against *one*, a greater, more indiscriminate violence among the *many* could be averted. Polarization between the one and the many creates in-group unanimity. This is the dark secret lying buried within many of our cultural achievements as a species, both past and present, and it is one we would very much like to ignore.

Violence Revealed

When Girard's thesis on scapegoat violence first appeared in 1972 under the title *La Violence et le sacré*, it caused a stir in France and beyond, not least because it seemed to a number of its readers, approvingly, to expose the violent origins of archaic religions (and presumably all religions) with unusual focus and explanatory range. One favorable review appearing in *Le Monde* heralded it as "the first authentically atheistic theory of religion and the sacred."[30] Such reception was not entirely wrong to situate Girard in company with the likes of Karl Marx, Sigmund Freud, and Friedrich Nietzsche, those whom Paul Ricoeur dubbed "the masters of suspicion."[31] As Robert Hamerton-Kelly explains, Girard's theory "becomes a deconstructive 'hermeneutic of suspicion' in the sense that by exposing the cogs and levers of the sacrificial machine it dispels the mystery and enables us to withdraw cooperation."[32] Mimetic theory can be understood as an effect and instrument of disenchantment, if by "enchantment" we mean the "sacred order" that scapegoat violence generates. The aura of collective transcendence and in-group unanimity at the expense of a victim (or outsider) is subject to demythologization when it becomes the object of research and analysis, and to this extent Girard sees his work in continuity with "secularizing" forces long underway in those cultures where awareness of scapegoating and its effects grows.[33]

What some of those initially enthusiastic of Girard's work missed, however, and one of the reasons why his work remains controversial in the academy today, is that Girard imagines not that he has unearthed the disturbing secrets of human culture through an ingenious theory of his own devising, or with the help of anthropologists and ethnologists who have much to contribute in its elaboration, but rather that the deceptive dynamics of scapegoating were decisively laid bare by the scriptural traditions of Judaism and Christianity. What makes the process of scapegoating more visible to us today than ever before, such that it could even become an object of anthropological investigation, is the influence of those cultures impacted by the biblical traditions and the way those traditions expose, demystify, and destabilize sacral structures over time. Any theorization concerning the mechanism of scapegoating, but more generally any critical stance that gives privileged place to victims of social systems, is indebted to the remarkable sea change that has occurred, and is still occurring, as a result of the biblical traditions that take the perspective of the victim as its organizing hermeneutic. This is true even when the Bible is summarily dismissed as mythical or ethnocentric, as is common among secular humanists today. It is *by* these traditions that we have become sensitized to the expelled "other" in an unprecedented way. "Our society is the most preoccupied with victims of any that ever was," claims Girard. "No historical period, no society we know, has ever spoken of victims as we do. . . . We are all actors as well as witnesses in a great anthropological first."[34]

Much to his surprise in the early part of his career, Girard noticed that when he compared biblical texts to many other myths of cosmic and human origins, the former appeared stubbornly resistant to theoretical assimilation. Like many anthropologists and ethnologists working in the early and mid-twentieth century, Girard expected to find patterns in the creation stories, etiologies, prohibitions, and rituals of the Hebrew and Christian scriptures similar to those found elsewhere. He also supposed that the dying and rising of Christ was, as Sir James Frazer postulated in his famous *The Golden Bough*, structurally parallel to other myths of dying-and-rising gods and largely indistinguishable from other texts enshrining, but also concealing the truth of, scapegoating and its effects.[35] The death of the victim purges the community of its discord and mysteriously restores to it unity and peace. The victim thus "lives on" through the ritualized remembrance of the peace he or she brought, and because of this takes flight in the community's collective imagination as a hero, a god, or a mediator of the gods. This is, in essence, the construction of "the sacred" within many archaic societies, and it is a form of limited, therapeutic violence that keeps at bay a greater, indiscriminate violence.

There are indeed tantalizing parallels to be drawn in comparative analysis, but what most struck Girard was the remarkable trail of instances wherein the biblical texts *reverse* the perspective of the reader from the one usually taken in other myths, with the effect of making visible what is otherwise concealed by them. It was an insight he would develop at length in his *Des choses cachées depuis la fondation du monde* (*Things Hidden Since the Foundation of the World*), which is a reference to Matthew 13:35 ("I will announce what has lain hidden from the foundation [of the world]"). Girard regularly stresses in this work that the Bible's similarities with other mythologies are precisely why its differences stand out all the more significantly. The differences subvert mythic forms "from within."[36] They share similar patterns while frequently reversing and reframing their interpretive stances. If myths of cosmic and human origins typically "incorporate the point of view of the community that has been reconciled to itself by the collective murder and is unanimously convinced that this event was a legitimate and sacred action," then by comparison the central themes and narrative plots of the Bible involve "inverting the relationship between the victim and the persecuting community."[37] For Girard, this reversal lies at the heart of what Christian theology means by "revelation," for it "unveils" (*apocalypsis*) what is otherwise hidden from us, namely, the veiled violence that generates false transcendence, which is to say, idolatry.

This is not to say that the Bible is always consistent in this process of unmasking, as though every narrative and interpretive strand appears unequivocally opposed to "myth" in the specific sense defined by Girard. In fact, it is precisely through the Bible's internal contradictions and ambiguities that we see a genuinely historical process of discovery at work—a pedagogical process culminating in the Gospels whereby an increasingly consistent and penetrating understanding of God's noninvolvement in our violence becomes possible. This may seem an odd thing to say, given the amount of violence portrayed in the Bible, but as Mark Heim points out, the Bible's laser focus on violence has everything to do with what we are in the process of being liberated *from*, which is precisely what many sacred myths tend to obscure. The Bible's narratives are no more violent than other founding narratives, whether of archaic or modern vintage, but only more explicit about the extent to which our "good" violence turns out to be persecutory violence. We do not see our "reconciling violence" as violence at all, for it usually assumes the veil of euphemism and sublimation. We do not actually face the victims of our violence, but this is what the Bible demands we do.

> What is violence doing in the Bible? It is showing us the nature of the mimetic conflict that threatens to destroy human community. It is showing us the religious dynamic of scapegoating sacrifice that arises to allay such crisis. It is letting us hear the voices of the persecuted victims and their pleas for revenge and vindication. It is showing God's judgment (even violent judgment) against violence, and most particularly, God's siding with the outcast victims of scapegoating persecution. The Old Testament is an antimyth. It is thick with bodies, the voices of victims and threatened victims. This landscape is either the product of an idiosyncratic, bloodthirsty imagination or the actual landscape of history and religion. If the latter, then what is remarkable is not that the scriptures describe it, but that we should think it normal not to.[38]

This antimyth thrust of the Old Testament is on display in most of its defining moments, including the story of the first murder, where the blood of Abel declares its innocence from the ground while YHWH protects his murdering brother from cyclical revenge. It is masterfully portrayed in the story of Joseph and his jealous brothers, whose novelistic form takes shape as a failed scapegoat plot, concluding with the would-be victim offering pardon and blessing to his persecutors.[39] It is evident in the Exodus narratives that highlight YHWH's compassionate solidarity with the enslaved Hebrew people, whose escape from their Egyptian oppressors leads them through a wilderness of trials in order to establish a covenantal, counterimperial way of life.[40] It suffuses the entire prophetic tradition and its

142   Christ as Concentrated Creation

passionate criticisms of Israel's moral laxity, preoccupation with royalty, and the tendency to substitute cultic practices for compassionate concern for the poor, the widow, and the orphan. It is grippingly at work in the Book of Job, another failed scapegoat story that insists upon Job's innocence before his accusers, his so-called friends, who try to convince him that his misfortunes stem from some hidden transgression.[41] The perspective of the persecuted is found in many of the psalms as well, including where the psalmist expresses grief over false accusations and lamentation in the face of unjust suffering.[42] It is no less explicit in the "suffering servant" motif in Second Isaiah and the stark figure of the innocent victim who bears the iniquities of his own people for their benefit.

"Throughout the Old Testament, a work of exegesis is in progress, operating in precisely the opposite direction to the usual dynamics of mythology and culture."[43] This implies that the Hebrew Bible reflects a dynamic process of interpreting itself, of challenging and reframing the various (and sometimes contradictory) images of God within the tradition. It testifies to a diverse range of experiences within Israel's many-layered history, and this requires that those who read it in its extant form do so with attentiveness to the way its major themes unfold polyphonically, in fits and stops, even as it trends unmistakably toward the perspective of the victim. The Bible from this point of view is revelatory not because it magically intervenes all at once into human history from an ahistorical plane, beyond the fray of how human beings are culturally formed, but because it reflects and clarifies, precisely within that fray, the way the people of Israel are slowly being inducted into an understanding of God that is unbound by human rivalry and violence. This gives revelation a dramatic character, for it arises within the push and pull of human culture, in sustained dialogue with the self-communicating transcendence of God in a historically mediated fashion.[44]

This dramatic work of exegesis achieves its definitive breakthrough in the Gospels. Thoroughly indebted to the narrative traditions preceding them, and without eclipsing those traditions—Girard strongly denies that this view implies supersessionism, much less anti-Semitism[45]—the Gospels provide the hermeneutical key that clarifies and maximally intensifies their antimythic thrust. Framed from beginning to end with the perspective of a scapegoat victim in its sights, the Gospels portray the life, death, and resurrection of a man who mimetically attracted followers and opponents ("Come, follow me"), and who on account of the kind of ministry he pursued—one explicitly dedicated to the breakdown of in-group unanimity formed at the expense of the stranger—ended up violently expelled by those whose identities were directly threatened by that ministry. And yet, Jesus's innocence is never in question: "Jesus is presented to us as the innocent victim of a group in crisis, which, for a time at any rate, is united against him. All the subgroups and indeed all the individuals who are concerned with the life and trial of Jesus end up by giving their explicit or implicit assent to his death: the crowd in Jerusalem, the Jewish religious authorities, the Roman political authorities, and even the disciples, since those who do not betray or deny Jesus actively take flight or remain passive."[46]

The reversal of this perspectival focus is so thorough in the Gospels, so hermeneutically unswerving, that they are essentially inviting all hearers of the "good news" to imagine *themselves* as complicit in the all-against-one dynamic resulting in Jesus's execution. It is not "those people" who have done this, or who continue to do this, but "we" who do it. In this very precise sense, it is not so much we who are reading the Gospels as they are reading *us*. They are summoning the hearer to conversion, to a way of life liberated from rivalry and exclusionary violence, and they do this by diagnosing and confronting us with the veiled mechanisms by which we typically live.

Girard calls our attention to the stereotypical form that Jesus's crucifixion takes and the striking similarities it bears with the sacrificial violence (or the "creative murder") found in mythic portrayals the world over: "There is not an incident in it that cannot be found in countless instances: the preliminary trial, the derisive crowd, the grotesque honours accorded to the victim, and the particular role played by chance, in the form of casting lots, which here affects not the choice of the victim but the way in which his clothing is disposed of. The final feature is the degrading punishment that takes place outside the holy city in order not to contaminate it."[47]

Noting again that such similarities led some ethnologists in the nineteenth and twentieth centuries to question the historical veracity of the Gospels, as perhaps their authors fabricated its narrative contents from motifs circulating in the wider culture—a hypothesis still sometimes advanced today—Girard flips the premise on its head and insists that these widely circulated motifs testify to real, yet veiled violence, and that it is the Gospels that help us to see them for what they are. The mythic form is not mythic because it is unhistorical. It is only too historical. It is mythic because it conceals the truth of the persecutory violence at its root, which is that its victims are unjustly made to bear and discharge the collective animus of the group. This is what the Gospels subvert by showing that it is the group, not the scapegoat, which stands as guilty.

> For there to be an effective, sacralizing act of transference, it is necessary that the victim should inherit all of the violence from which the community has been exonerated. It is because the victim genuinely passes as guilty that the transference does not come to the fore as such. This piece of conjuring brings about the happy result for which the lynching mob is profoundly grateful: the victim bears the weight of the incompatible and contradictory meanings that juxtaposed, create *sacredness*. For the gospel text to be mythic in our sense, it would have to take no account of the arbitrary and unjust character of the violence which is done to Jesus. In fact the opposite is the case: the Passion is presented as a blatant piece of injustice. Far from taking the collective violence upon itself, the text places it squarely on those who are responsible for it.[48]

By "arbitrary" Girard does not mean random. For while it is true that many scapegoats *are* victims of happenstance, or gain their strangeness vis-à-vis the group on the basis of characteristics they neither control nor fully understand, the occasion of Jesus's crucifixion has everything to do with the kind of ministry he freely initiated, which in effect drew the dynamics of scapegoating upon himself. Nothing about this goading process suggests a reckless or suicidal intention, but it does indicate an acute awareness on Jesus's part of the mechanisms that lead to social exclusions and false in-group unanimity, which when destabilized is virtually bound to react in its characteristic form. It is just this kind of semiautonomous "power" with which Jesus is contending throughout his ministry, but always in a way that remains nonreciprocal to that power, accepting all along the cost such a ministry would exact from him and trusting to the bitterest end that his fidelity to God's reign would be vindicated.

STRANGE VICTORY

"I Am Jesus, Whom You Are Persecuting"

Williams offers a concise summary of the basic Christian story that captures several elements of the foregoing analysis: "[It] tells us that the most fundamental and generative subject or energy or resource we can imagine [i.e., God] is beyond rivalry; it demonstrates this in the enactment of a human life in which arbitrary violence is both exposed for what it is and accepted without retaliation, so that we see that we do not need exclusionary sacrifice after all; and it thus establishes a form of human solidarity that does not depend on the identification of a scapegoat and the closing of boundaries against the stranger."[49] Williams makes explicit here the inner relationship between the unconditional generosity of God who gives all things "to be" and the way such unconditioned generosity manifests itself in Jesus. There is a telescoping of perspective here that situates Jesus at the center of a vision opening out unto the illimitable transcendence of God. The concrete form of Jesus's life, death, and resurrection is unsurpassably "iconic" in disclosing this transcendence, and it does so not by way of static reference points but through the movement and texture of a life that assumes a particular shape and historical incidence. The fact that this living icon of God was the victim of exclusionary violence is cause for endless astonishment and not a little trepidation, for it reveals once and for all that the source and ground of all that is cannot be implicated in *our* violence. The hard truth is that human beings have committed deicide. (This is the real meaning of "the death of God."[50]) Our resistance to divine generosity can become so intractable that we would sooner murder God than welcome the stranger in our midst. This is the tragic blindness of our human situation to

146 Christ as Concentrated Creation

which the Gospel of John alludes ("and yet the world did not know him"), and it is why the image of the crucified Jesus, repellent as it is, bears a salvific anthropological truth: it unambiguously and graphically displays what is so often hidden to us, our sin and delusion, and it does so by drawing us into a face-to-face encounter with the human wreckage that our blindness produces.

What is so remarkable is the way we are drawn into this face-to-face encounter. It is not with the threat of apocalyptic revenge, nor with the bombastic display of a more extreme force. Instead, the condition of the possibility for this discovery—the "event" that casts all preceding events in a fundamentally new light—is the prior and totally gratuitous offer of forgiveness and eschatological peace from the risen victim himself. Such is the strange victory of Easter.

"The Resurrection," declares Girard, "is the spectacular sign of the entrance into the world of a power superior to violent contagion."[51] The reason for this superiority is because the return of the transfigured victim to his oppressors is at once the vindication of the unjustly accused Jesus of Nazareth and the sign of God's unconditional love for those swept up into the violent contagion culminating in Jesus's death. Both of these elements—justice and forgiveness—are constitutive of the Easter event, and together they manifest the non-violence of God in an eschatologically definitive way. This becomes strikingly evident in Peter's classic proclamation of the "good news" as depicted in the Book of Acts. Here is the first part:

> You who are Israelites, hear these words. Jesus the Nazorean was a man commended to you by God with mighty deeds, wonders, and signs, which God worked through him in your midst, as you yourselves know. This man, delivered up by the set plan and foreknowledge of God, you killed, using lawless men to crucify him. But God raised him up, releasing him from the throes of death, because it was impossible for him to be held by it. . . . God raised this man Jesus to life; of this we are all witnesses. (Acts 2:22–24, 32)

Notice the dramatic response of God to those implicated in Jesus's death. Whereas Jesus was handed over by Israel's leaders to be crucified by Roman imperial power—a routine practice of state-sponsored violence meant to terrorize an occupied population and quash any revolutionary impulse within it—God has vindicated this man by raising him from the dead, thus granting him eschatological life and revealing once and for all that he is God's "anointed one." Of this the disciples are witnesses. In what is aptly described as an improvised court scene, Peter reverses the verdict delivered by the Sanhedrin and Pontius Pilate. The judges have now become the judged and the entire apparatus leading to Jesus's death declared a sham. And what is the nature of this apparatus, according to Peter? "Indeed they gathered in this city against your holy servant Jesus whom you anointed, Herod and Pontius Pilate, together with the Gentiles and the peoples of Israel" (4:27).[52] No one is exempt from Peter's "structural" indictment, not even the apostle himself, who had previously denied knowing his master three times.[53] Jesus's prophetic ministry had threatened to disrupt a dominant social order, and that social order reasserted itself through a violent expulsion. The all-minus-one logic of such realpolitik is succinctly formulated in the Gospel of John, where the chief priest of the Temple, Caiaphas, declares to the maddening crowd: "It is better for you that one man should die instead of the people, so that the whole nation may not perish" (John 11:50). A clearer summary of the scapegoat mechanism cannot be found.[54]

But we must add right away that the theme of vindication does not exhaust the content of Jesus's resurrection from the dead. Critical though it is, without something else, without something more, it would be difficult to say how it reveals a power superior to violent contagion, as Girard claims it does. For what is to prevent the theme of vindication from merely reversing the roles between accused and accuser, with no end in sight to their rivalry? Might the rhetorical turning of the tables in Peter's resurrection kerygma be operating subtly with a logic of violence (or what amounts to the same thing, ressentiment) that looks to divine retribution for human transgression? Or, to frame the problem another way, does the entire drift of Peter's speech up to now only confirm that God's response to the death of Jesus is reciprocal, so that what has been done unto Jesus ("*You* have done this to God's anointed") will now be returned to his persecutors in kind ("*But* God has raised him up and. . . .")? And . . . and . . . what?

148   Christ as Concentrated Creation

At precisely this point Peter's speech takes a wholly unexpected twist. Instead of following the perhaps anticipated course of declaring imminent divine retribution, the speech shifts into a stunning offer of hospitality: an invitation to participate in a new kind of community founded upon the memory of the victim who *lives*; a community that is summoned to a way of human belonging that subsists from the welcoming of the stranger. No retribution, no retaliatory response, no tit for tat, the crucified-and-risen One is *given back* to those who expelled him with an utterly gratuitous offer of forgiveness: "Now when they heard this, they were cut to the heart, and they asked Peter and the other apostles, 'What are we to do, my brothers?' Peter [said] to them, 'Repent and be baptized, every one of you, in the name of Jesus Christ for the forgiveness of your sins; and you will receive the gift of the holy Spirit. For the promise is made to you and to your children and to all those far off, whoever the Lord our God will call'" (Acts 2:37–39).

What is crucial about this reversal upon reversal is that one does not annul the other. The offer of forgiveness in Christ does not obscure the injustice of exclusionary violence; it makes it truly visible for the first time. The gesture of divine pardon, which is just as unanticipated as it is unmerited, turns out to be the condition of the possibility for the recognition of guilt. The anteriority of divine hospitality, as communicated in the gift of eschatological pardon and peace, is what allows those who encounter it to perceive their implication in exclusionary violence. Mercy, not condemnation, lifts the veil of their *méconnaissance*. Through the bracing clarity of love's self-offering they are enabled to see, by extreme contrast and in retrospect, the darkness of those interpersonal and social mechanisms that construct identity through rivalry, reactivity, and expulsion.

Like the light that floods Saul's field of perception, blinding him for a time and calling to him with the voice of a victim, the self-communication of God in the risen Christ opens up a new self-understanding and summons him to a way of life that does not depend upon persecution: "On his journey, as he was nearing Damascus, a light from the sky suddenly flashed around him. He fell to the ground and heard a voice saying to him, 'Saul, Saul, why are you persecuting me?'" (Acts 9: 3–4). Having previously hounded the followers of

Jesus out of his zeal for ancestral customs (Gal. 1:13–14), the future apostle is confronted with the reality that his violence serves a false identity and is immediately beckoned to participate in a new way of life that is received from the One whom he persecutes. "He said, 'Who are you, sir?' The reply came, 'I am Jesus, whom you are persecuting. Now get up and go into the city and you will be told what you must do'" (Acts 9: 5–6).

James Alison draws out the significance of this new and strange presence among the earliest followers of Jesus and what it does to transform them: "The risen Jesus was not reciprocating anything done to him, but was a presence of love without condition. . . . Gratuity is experienced as the lack of retaliation where some sort of retaliation is to be expected, and then as the giving of something unexpected. This surprising nonreciprocation is what pulls the person experiencing it out of the reciprocating mode-of-being and enables that person to begin to receive and then transmit love as something simply given."[55] Love "simply given," a "presence of love without condition," "surprising nonreciprocation": one might say, "from nothing." This is the content of the Christian understanding of God, and such content is not an abstraction or a platitudinous assertion. It involves a claim, to be sure, but it is first demonstrated by its embodiment in the life, death, and resurrection of Jesus. The agapeic dispensation of God takes on a particular shape in our history, and its embodiment is a strange yet welcoming presence that gravitationally lures those who encounter it toward a way of life unbound by mimetic rivalry and reciprocity. It is a presence that gives itself to imitate, to trust without reserve, so that those who follow it may allow their desires to be purged and refashioned accordingly. To receive and transmit love as simply given is to participate in God's own pacific desire, and that desire is perfectly communicated in the crucified and risen Jesus, in whom there is no rivalry.

"I Have Overcome the World"

As important as the *imitatio christi* is in the New Testament, and the Christian tradition more generally, it would be anthropologically naïve and theologically reductive to assume that God's self-communication in Christ only amounts to the offering of a superior model for human beings to imitate. The content of revelation in Christian theology can hardly be summed up by pointing to Jesus as an unimpeachable guide for human behavior. To be sure, our engagement with Girard up to this point has given much greater depth to what the imitation of Christ implies. Given our understanding of mimesis as generative of human selfhood, and not merely a process of mimicking external behavior, we have already advanced well beyond superficial notions of the *imitatio christi* that present Christian life as the personal (read: individual) appropriation of Jesus's teaching and exemplary way of life, that is, as striving to the best of our ability to be "like" Jesus. We could do worse than this vaguely Pelagian view, but the Gospels convey to us a considerably richer and more dramatic account of revelation, one that shatters our assumptions about the prospects of individually redirecting our desires within an ambiguous social matrix. In short, God must break through *for us*.

One way to appreciate the dramatic quality of this inbreaking is by noting how often the New Testament characterizes the Christ-event in cosmic terms, as a world-making drama meant to subvert a dominant social imaginary. Modern readers might bristle at the ostensibly mythic features of the New Testament that portray Jesus's death and resurrection as a battle with the "powers and principalities," or Jesus's ministry as a contestation with "the Satan," the "father of lies," the "murderer from the beginning," and so forth, but perhaps we are in a better position now, having explored the structural and transpersonal dimensions of sacral violence, to understand why this might be phenomenologically on point. As we have seen, the kind of social order that exhibits the dynamics of mimetic antagonism and exclusionary violence, however implicit or sublimated at times, is a founding one in the sense that it frequently forms the default pattern of our imagination and social relations. Normally we do not perceive our involvement in rivalry and exclusionary violence, or the extensive human carnage that our possessive identity constructions produce. Our implication in them typically operates at a tacit level, as part of our social conditioning, and therefore something like a precognitive background that eludes direct detection or easy redirection. And yet

Strange Victory   151

it is precisely this tacit "world"—our pre-reflexive social programming, as it were—that Jesus was trying to shift.

Consider those sayings that contrast the Kingdom of God with "the world." When Jesus declares to Pilate, "My kingdom is not of this world [*kosmos*]," or when he warns his disciples, "Whoever loves his life loses it, and whoever hates his life in this world [*kosmos*] will preserve it for eternal life" (12:25), the point has nothing to do with a Manichean revulsion toward creation itself, as though the *kosmos* were roughly equivalent to "the physical universe." As Walter Wink points out, "the world" in such passages refers to "an alienating and alienated ethos," something like a destructive self-organizing "system" operating at a deep and pervasive level in the human life-world. It refers to a spiritual "world-atmosphere that we breathe in like toxic air, often without realizing it," and yet it "penetrates everything, teaching us not only what to believe, but what we can value and even what we can see."[56] Put differently, "the world" refers to *the human sociological realm that exists in estrangement from God.*"[57] The critical implication here is that creation itself is originally the work of a gracious creator, given "to be" as pure summons and gift, but at present colonized by interpersonal and social dysfunction to such a degree that we often take our dysfunction for granted, as though it were in some sense "normal," part of the natural order of things, perhaps even ordained by God (or the gods). For Jesus to tell his accusers, "You belong to this world [*kosmos*], but I do not belong to this world [*kosmos*]," is not to despise God's creation but to name the incommensurable "social imaginaries" out of which he and his interlocutors are operating. Such contrasts intend to thoroughly defamiliarize what "the world" might possibly mean. As with so many of Jesus's teachings, including his similes, parables, questions, denunciations, and creative exegeses, a space of cognitive surprise flashes forth so as to open fresh and liberating perspectives upon what the human life-world really *ought* to be, and therefore what God's intention for creation truly *is*. The original vocation of creation may be presently under siege, yet it is open to radical transformation. In this sense, the New Testament presents the drama of creation in "three simultaneous acts": the powers of this world are originally good, they are presently estranged or fallen, and they will be redeemed.[58]

Given the dramatic tension that these three acts generate when held together—and in general it must be said that they constitute the Christian sense of "salvation history," though not necessarily in linear fashion—the recurrent metaphor of Christ's "triumph" over the principalities and powers in the New Testament and the early church, however paradoxically formulated, conveys something essential about their tensive relationship. As Girard observes, Christ's triumph is by no means a violent conquest of the principalities and powers but instead an event of breathtaking irony that turns apparent strength into weakness—and apparent weakness into strength. "The victory of Christ has nothing to do with the military triumph of a victorious general: rather than inflicting violence on others, Christ submits to it."[59] Here is creative renunciation in its essential form. Commenting upon Saint Paul's seemingly absurd statement that the cross "despoils" the principalities and powers by making "a public spectacle of them, leading them away in triumph by it" (Col. 2:15), Girard notes that only by exposing the hidden mechanisms of sacral violence, while completely renouncing the means by which they operate, could their deceptive power be broken. By letting the powers do their worst, to fulminate so unreservedly against the innocence of the God-man, the duplicity and dissimulation by which such powers subsist could be brought out into the light and subverted through exposure.

"Christ does not achieve this victory through violence. He obtains it through a renunciation of violence so complete that violence can rage to its heart's content without realizing that by so doing, it reveals what it must conceal, without suspecting that its fury will turn back against it this time because it will be recorded and represented with exactness in the Passion narratives."[60] Girard is working here with one of the dominant soteriological motifs in the early church, which Gustaf Aulén dubbed the *Christus Victor* motif.[61] With many variations peppering the New Testament and patristic literature, the basic refrain is that the cross of Christ "represents" the convergent powers of sin, evil, and death in their most distilled form. Having lured them from their hiding places through his ministry of fierce compassion, Christ becomes the object of their

Strange Victory 153

reactive ire until finally they conspire to vanquish him in the most heinous way imaginable—through death on a cross. There is a larger-than-life dimension to this drama that lends itself to personification in the biblical and patristic literature, and not infrequently we will find "the prince of this world" or "the Satan" (i.e., "the Accuser") used to name what seems like a willful, transpersonal force bent upon Christ's complete annihilation. This is one reason why the motif seems to have fallen out of disfavor in subsequent centuries in the West, as various "ransom" theories of the early Church, such as we find in Irenaeus of Lyons and Gregory of Nyssa, seem to give too much power to satanic opposition to God. Nevertheless, Girard maintains that such personification of evil, while not to be taken literally, helps us to identify something of the perverse (because largely hidden) intelligence of mimetic contagion and violence. The motif of Satan being "duped" by the cross, while no doubt a metaphor, points to the way Jesus's ministry attracts the semiautonomous forces that keep human beings in bondage, which can only be overcome by a power quite superior to them.

What is peculiar about this "battle" is that it is won through apparent defeat. Precisely because Christ so fully displays the pacific reality of the Father—that is, because he is perfectly open to the unconditioned generosity of the Godhead, in whom there is no rivalry, aversion, deceit, or death—he not only attracts those forces in the human life-world that are threatened by such fullness of life; he "absorbs" them while exposing their mendacity. The great irony of this metaphor of military triumph, indeed, the extreme "foolishness" of it (1 Cor. 1:23), is that the "radical weakness" of God, which is not to be confused with divine incapacity, "defeats the power of satanic self-expulsion."[62] The fallen powers orchestrate their own demise by plunging into a generosity so abyssal and free, so "empty" of anything resembling force, treachery, and self-grasping, that they collapse under their own unstable weight.

The basic logic of this dramatic account is that any violence used against violence only reinforces it. Were God merely to *over*power the systemic forces that keep human beings in captivity, then God would in some sense be reciprocal to them, bound by an interminable cycle of mimetic contagion and retribution. Divine transcendence would thus be indistinguishable from the false transcendence produced by exclusionary violence, appearing in such a case as only a more impressive instance of it. On the other hand, were God totally impassive to the plight of human beings in their fallen and estranged condition, nonresponsive to the parasitical power that perpetuates itself through deceit, then it could hardly be said that God is the beneficent source and redeemer of creation, that is, the "God of life." Having abandoned human beings to their plight, such a God, to the extent the name could elicit any interest or devotion, would amount to something like a distant and vacant horizon—a No-thing which makes no difference at all. In the face of this seeming dilemma, the God of Jesus Christ enters into the very sinews of our mimetic rivalry and violence, and specifically the unspeakable horror and shame of a human execution, not to underwrite the forces provoked by his ministry but to defeat them through a self-giving so unrestricted and undeserved that they collapse from within. They "took the bait," as it were, and through the event of Easter were swallowed up by the abyssal compassion of God.[63] As Heim puts it:

> The trick, the startling reversal, is that this time simply by doing what it always does, the sacrificial process brings about its own demise. The divine power is neither deployed in violence against Jesus's persecutors nor shelved in empathetic helplessness. Through the resurrection the voice of the victim overcomes the silence of death, but without violence or retribution. The resurrection means that those who abandoned Jesus or turned against him need neither be punished as enemies nor confirmed in their sin. Instead they have the retroactive opportunity to cling to Jesus again. By taking up the place of the scapegoat, God has entered this human dynamic at one point where divine power may reveal and save simply by becoming the object of human sin. The double bind has been reversed. . . . It is evil's great triumph and its great mistake.[64]

This is the strange victory of God. Without mirroring anything of the violence leading to Jesus's death, God turns what would have been yet another killing in our history, destined to be forgotten, into

Strange Victory   155

a world-making reversal. With an "Aikido-style of judgment," God "uses" the self-organizing energy of violence against itself, allowing it to self-destruct in the infinite depths of divine justice and mercy.[65] The cross and resurrection thus represent God's great act of persuasion, as Irenaeus of Lyons puts it. God "did not use violence, as the apostasy had done at the beginning when it usurped dominion over us, greedily snatching what was not his own. No, He used persuasion, not violence, to obtain what He wanted, so that justice should not be infringed and God's ancient handiwork not be utterly destroyed."[66] In a similar vein, Gregory of Nazianzus refers to God's power as pedagogical and medicinal, not coercive. The transformational character of the entire Christ-event is "that we should be persuaded, not forced."[67] Salvation may indeed entail a shaking, in the sense that God providentially breaks through an oppressive situation, but the change it brings about cannot come by way of force, as this only would work *over against* creaturely agency. It comes through allurement. Like a schoolmaster or a doctor, God may well deprive us of certain illusions or coping mechanisms that stunt genuine growth, but such purgation means to free us for new patterns of intelligence and health that, because they elicit our will, are participable and self-generating. Neither impassive nor coercive, divine creativity in the world, as concretely enacted in the Christ-event, manifests the "third way" of persuasive love. Self-distributing, reconciling, and gratuitous, its christomorphic determination in human history, as with the summoning of creation itself, is characteristically agapeic.

The "Use" of Sin

"The story of Jesus is nothing other than the triune life of God projected onto our history, or enacted sacramentally in our history, so that it becomes story."[68] In making this statement, Herbert McCabe asks us to imagine a film projected onto a screen. If it is a smooth silver screen, we will see the film as it is, as the filmmaker intended it to be. But should the screen be distorted in some way, marred by blotches or twisted out of shape, the film will appear distorted, and all the more so if the film is projected on something other than a screen.

156   Christ as Concentrated Creation

The story of Jesus—which in its full extent is the entire Bible—is the projection of the trinitarian life of God on the rubbish dump that we have made of the world. The historical mission of Jesus is nothing other than the eternal mission of the Son from the Father; the historical outpouring of the Spirit in virtue of the passion, death and ascension of Jesus is nothing but the eternal outpouring of the Spirit from the Father through the Son. Watching, so to say, the story of Jesus, we are watching the procession of the Trinity. . . . That the Trinity looks like a story of (*is* a story of) rejection, torture and murder but also of reconciliation is because it is being projected on, lived out on, our rubbish tip; it is because of the sin of the world.[69]

McCabe's main point here is twofold. First, he wishes to underscore the inner relationship between the narrative shape of Jesus in our history and the eternal life of God. This is not to suggest that God is literally a story, as though there were successive moments in the Godhead, but only that when the eternal generation of the Logos is concretely enacted in our history, which is just what we mean by *incarnation,* it manifests as the life-story of Jesus Christ. McCabe warns that we not take the screen metaphor to imply that Christ merely "projects" God from a reserved distance. It is, rather, that Christ, through the Spirit, sacramentally *realizes* God in our history. Christ embodies and communicates what he signifies. Or, as Rahner puts it, "This man is, as such, the self-utterance of God in its self-emptying, because God expresses *himself* when he empties himself. He proclaims *himself* as love when he hides the majesty of this love and shows himself in the ordinary way of men."[70]

The second aspect of the film-screen metaphor means to illustrate why the life-story of God assumes the shocking features it does in our history. The rejection, torture, and murder that partly frame it are not internal of the Godhead as such, as though rivalry and exclusionary violence were expressive of trinitarian life. If the life, death, and resurrection reveal anything it is that "God is Light, and in him there is no darkness at all" (1 John 1:5). Jesus's resurrection entails "the definitive demythologization of God," as Alison puts it, for it reveals that God is "completely outside human reciprocity." God "is revealed not

Strange Victory 157

as partisan, interested in vindicating a particular group over against its enemies," but rather as the "self-giving victim" whose unconditioned generosity brings about reconciliation among rivals and eschatological life out of death.[71] Rivalry and exclusionary violence show up so vividly in Christ's story because they contrast so starkly with the goodness of God expressed in him. If God is Light, then when that light appears in unadulterated form in our ambiguous history, as it does in Christ ("I am the light of the world. Whoever follows me will not walk in darkness, but will have the light of life" [John 8:12]), it will illuminate the most hidden and refractory forms of darkness that disfigure our history. The "true God will reveal himself most clearly where the world of violence is most decisively contrasted to him," writes Raymund Schwager. "If the gods are the product of human mechanism, then he must appear most clearly in that world of violence as a person where this mechanism is most radically unmasked."[72] God's redemptive love goes to the heart of our darkness, infiltrates its secret recesses in order to expose and release its clutches from within. It reaches into those places where we are most vulnerable to rivalry, condemnation, alienation, shame, and the ravages of party spirit, even becoming victim to them, not in order to give them divine sanction but to unbind and transmute them with love's releasing power.

Here it is worth reflecting on the ambiguity that sometimes distorts Christian accounts of this releasing power as well as the reason why redemption in Christian theological terms is best understood as the conversion of mimetic desire rather than its condemnation. To speak of the former matter first, it is quite evident that the narrative pattern of Jesus's life, death, and resurrection has sometimes been interpreted in ways that suggest God's authorization of the very thing from which we are being liberated. In one of its most ironic forms, the sacrifice of Jesus on the cross is imagined as placating divine wrath toward sinful human beings, as though God required the sacrifice of an innocent victim in order to extirpate our sin. The self-offering of Christ, according to this view, reconciles us to God by mollifying the Father's righteous indignation toward us. Because God's honor has been offended against by human disobedience, and because we could never, through our own effort, make up for our offense against divine honor, God must exercise divine justice by having someone — in this case, the perfectly obedient Jesus—bear the brunt of our historically accrued penalty. Jesus, the exemplar of our faith, is also our redeemer in that he "assumes" our guilt. Jesus shields us from the wrath of God as our penal substitute. Jesus absolves us from sin, and thus from the eternal condemnation we rightly deserve, because the Father has found in him the perfect sacrifice whereby the age-old enmity between God and human beings (read: *rivalry* between God and human beings) is finally resolved. The sacrifice of Christ is thus the "payment" human beings needed but could never offer themselves, as the debt was just too great.

If there are elements in this compressed portrayal that sound familiar, or at least vaguely biblical, this should not surprise us. The "penal substitution theory" of salvation that I sketch here would not have gained an interpretive foothold in parts of the Christian tradition unless elements drawn from scripture seemed to support it. References to Saint Paul, for example, or Saint Augustine and Saint Anselm, can be assimilated in such a way as to buttress such an interpretation, as though we were reading off the plain testimony of scripture and tradition in articulating it. The theme of wrath found in Paul's letters, or the understanding of Christ as a perfect sacrifice in Hebrews, can be recomposed so as to portray God as somehow the agent of scapegoat violence rather than its ultimate *undoer*.[73] However providentially, God is imagined as deploying sacrificial violence toward an ultimately good end, namely, our redemption. Even if Christ's is the sacrifice to end all sacrifice, still, any atonement theory that implies God's implication in the very thing from which we are being liberated leaves us with an ambiguous image of God at best. More seriously problematic is the tendency to associate true Christian piety with a cult of suffering or victimization, as though God wills or looks favorably upon suffering or victimhood for its own sake. On such a view we must turn our freedom and dignity inside out, "stew up all [our] natural gifts into a beautiful guilt-complex," as Thomas Merton puts it, "and crawl towards God on [our] stomach to offer Him the results in propitiation."[74] What should be celebrated as the unconditioned source of human dignity and worth becomes clouded with a guilt-inducing, numinous presence whose "love" inspires in us obsequiousness, not freedom. The God who is unequivocally *for* us gets

Strange Victory 159

obscured by the human projection of God *over against* us. Such are the "strange ideas of conflict with God" that are really "born of the war that is within [and among] ourselves."[75]

Little wonder that recent decades have witnessed considerable unrest around atonement theories implying God's "need" for sacrifice. Liberation theologians, Black and womanist theologians, feminist theologians, and many voices in political theology rightly contest accounts of salvation that sacralize victimhood in any way. By isolating Christ's sacrifice in penal substitutionary terms, or seeing in it the solution of a problem on God's side, not only is the cross easily abstracted from the content of Jesus's ministry and resurrection, leading to a truncated vision of the Christ-event, but the socially and politically emancipative dimensions of Christian faith are distorted as well. Rather than emphasizing God's solidarity *with* victims in Jesus, and the call to transform unjust structural conditions that produce victims in the first place, certain accounts of atonement that portray Jesus's death on the cross as the placation of divine wrath too easily lend themselves to docile social obedience in the face of injustice. To isolate Jesus's death on the cross in the drama of salvation is to risk forgetting that Jesus did not just die. He was murdered. As Jon Sobrino makes clear, "He was killed like so many people before and after him—because of his kind of life, because of what he said and what he did." Jesus's death "was the consequence of his life and this in turn was the consequence of his particular incarnation—in an anti-Kingdom which brings death—to defend its victims."[76] This point of emphasis hardly means sidelining the redemptive dimensions of the cross in Christian imagination and practice, which would be just as reductive, but it does mean that we carefully understand in what way God can be said to "use" the cross for our redemption.

It was precisely for this reason that Girard adamantly insisted upon an "anti-sacrificial" reading of the atonement in the early part of his career. Christ's death "was not a sacrificial one. To say that Jesus dies, not as a sacrifice, but in order that there may be no more sacrifices, is to recognize in him the Word of God: 'I wish for mercy and not sacrifices'. . . . Rather than become the slave of violence, as our own word necessarily does, the Word of God says no to violence."[77] Here we see Girard laboring to articulate an understanding of Jesus's death as the subversion of sacrificial violence's generative power. While bearing the stereotypical marks of scapegoat violence found in many archaic myths the world over, the Gospels reveal a creative agency that, while becoming subject to the collusive powers of victimization, is revealed in their exposure and unbinding. An anti-sacrificial reading of atonement means to clarify that the efficacious protagonism at work in Jesus's life, death, and resurrection does not recruit violence in order to undo violence, as this would merely confirm its rivalrous logic. But neither does this protagonism fall headlong into its mechanisms with nihilistic abandonment, as this would do nothing to expose, much less transform, the imposing but ultimately deceitful powers of violence. Rather, the totality of the Christ-event steadfastly displays a third way: God's persuasive power of unconditional love.

Jesus's historical ministry on the margins of his society, his categorical renunciation of violence, his refusal to flee the gathering resistance around him, his faithfulness to the Father unto death, the irruption of eschatological life through his resurrection, the offer of forgiveness for human involvement in sin, the invitation to a new community animated by the Spirit, the summons to creative "we-centricity" in the midst of our frailties, wounds, and tendency toward rivalry: the entire arc of the Christ-event, its flow pattern and momentum, is God's great act to lure us (not strong-arm us) into its gracious unfolding. The generative power of God's self-giving, which is eminently participable, would free us from our self-imposed bonds and make us "heirs of God and joint heirs with Christ" (Rom. 8:17). It is for this reason that God became human: to reveal who God "really" is while revealing who the human being "really" is.[78] That this mutual revealing occurs in the midst of mob violence may be strange beyond telling, but this by no means suggests that God deploys violence in order to achieve some good end; it means that God was willing to undergo *our* violence in order to free us from it, so that we might have life. To imagine that God demands violence in any way is simply to project our delusive notions of wrath and justice upon God—a remarkably easy thing to do, it turns out. The truth is that *we* are the ones caught up in the mimetic rivalry that produces victims, even in the name of justice. As Alison observes:

We are the ones inclined to dwell in wrath and think we need vengeance in order to survive. God was occupying the space of *our* victim so as to show us that we need never do this again. This . . . turns on its head what has passed as our penal substitutionary theory of atonement, which always presupposes that it is *us* satisfying God, that *God* needs satisfying, that there is *vengeance* in God. Whereas it is quite clear from the New Testament that what was really exciting to Paul was that it was obvious from Jesus's self-giving, and the "out-pouring of Jesus' blood," that this was the revelation of who God was: God was entirely without vengeance, entirely without substitutionary tricks; and that he was giving himself entirely without ambivalence and ambiguity for *us*, towards *us*, in order to set *us* "free from our sins"—"our sins" being our way of being bound up with each other in death, vengeance, violence and what is commonly called "wrath."[79]

If we are crystal clear on this point—and this is exactly what the "demythologization of God" means in Girard's terms—then it becomes possible to say quite emphatically that Christ "died for our sins." Indeed, we can even begin reclaiming the language of sacrifice in accounting for Christ's death, that is, as "the one true sacrifice," or "the sacrifice to end all sacrifice." It was with this understanding that Girard began to reintroduce sacrificial language into his later work.[80]

Prompted in part by his ongoing dialogue with theological contemporaries, particularly Schwager, Girard came to recognize the fittingness of naming God's self-giving activity in Jesus as Love's great sacrifice—one that was freely willing to enter into our habitual patterns of exclusionary violence for our sake, to absorb them and ultimately dissolve them from within. By revealing God's *self* in the risen victim, and thus by offering forgiveness *from* the risen victim, God "used" our sin to save us from it. Jesus died for our sins in order to free us. Heim makes the point admirably clear:

> [Jesus's] death exemplifies a specific kind of sin we are all implicated in and we all need saving from, and acts to overcome it. Only the divine power of resurrection and revelation could do that. God was willing to be a victim of that bad thing we had

made apparently good, in order to expose its nature and liberate us from it. In so doing, God made the occasion of scapegoating sacrifice (what those who killed Jesus were doing) an occasion of overcoming scapegoating violence (what God was doing). It is the same event, but what is happening in that event for the people who kill or accept the killing or fail to oppose it (in short, for all involved) is not what's happening in that event for Jesus, for God, and hopefully for the church. God used our sin to save us from that sin. And the result, uneven but real, is that victims of such acts become harder to hide. They look too much like Jesus. The challenge, all too often failed, is to build another basis for peace than unity in violence. That is what the gathering around the communion table attempts to do.[81]

Here we begin to perceive with fresh eyes the distinctive character of Christian revelation, which is nothing if not historical, sacramental, and communal in character. For one thing, and to reiterate a point previously made, the grace of revelation in Christ occurs through the warp and woof of our history rather than imposing itself upon it. If revelation entails a dramatic breakthrough or reversal, in the sense that it disrupts emergent patterns that have cumulatively grown in our history to thwart true perception and threaten human flourishing, then this disruption will work not in a rivalrous manner with our created agency but in and through it. The God of Jesus Christ is the God of *creation*. The grace of salvation enlists our creaturely desires. It entices our participation, our cooperation. Any redemption *of* the human that does not fully embrace and work *through* the human could hardly be described as redemptive. What is not assumed is not redeemed, to intone the patristic theme. Even in the case of our learned tendency toward rivalry and exclusion—one that turns the inherent goodness of human desire in upon itself—God graciously reworks what had become an implacable obstacle for us into the means of our liberation. Instead of delivering an abstract fiat, which would merely override our human agency in interventionist fashion, the persuasive love of God enters freely and concretely into our humanity, precisely as human, in order to transmute what epitomizes our human brokenness, the cross, into the means of our liberation.

MEMORY, MERCY, AND CONTEMPLATION

If the story of Jesus is the triune life of God sacramentally enacted in our history, then it is also the story of creation as God wills it to be. Christ is concentrated creation. Just as the resurrection entails the definitive demythologization of God, so does it entail "the final demythologization of the idea of creation."[82] We have already encountered this theme in preceding chapters, but now I wish to conclude this chapter, along with part 2, by developing the theme in terms of the conversion of mimetic desire.

But first, what is meant by the demythologization of creation? Within the context of mimetic theory, it does not refer to an exegetical program, like Rudolf Bultmann's, that seeks to reinterpret various "mythological" (read: "premodern") themes in the Gospels with the help of existentialist philosophy. For our purposes, demythologization refers to a shift in imagination, an ongoing process of conversion whereby various forms of false transcendence are divested of their seeming ultimacy and exposed as illusory. Creation is demythologized when we come to perceive it as having its source and ground in original peace rather than strife; when we come to know that the creativity giving all things "to be" is not negatively structured by violence, death, or scarcity but is purely positive, free, and generous; when we come to experience our ontological dependence on God as opening up ever-widening circles of communion rather than ever-tightening knots of self-other reification. These are among the most liberating truths we will ever hear, and they are available to us not by dint of speculation, which has its place, but through the self-communication of God in our history. Because the resurrection of Jesus reveals God as having nothing to do with violence, and because the resurrection evinces a creativity bestowing life and reconciliation in the place of death and rivalry, we can know with utmost confidence that any so-called order rooted in rivalry and violence, whether framed in cosmogonic, naturalistic, or political terms, is not from God but merely a human projection and subject to eschatological dissolution.

Sebastian Moore describes this demythologization process as a "religious landslide."[83] Though not occurring all at once, demythologization allows for the telling and retelling of creation without any appeal to foundational conflict or violence. The Creator is the "non-discriminating cause of all out of nothing," one whose ungraspability, rather than inducing self-clinching anxiety or nihilistic despair, is totally trustworthy and to be "relaxed into."[84] There is a contemplative dimension to this relaxing, as we shall see, but Moore alerts us first to its social and ecclesial significance: "So the risen Jesus makes us think of God differently. God is all relationship, and this is the antithesis of solitary power. And when we begin to think of God in this different way, we begin to see why it is that the real God, the surprising God, shows up in our power-crazy world naked on a cross, tortured to death by the ruling power as a disturber of what it calls the peace. The disturbing, subversive nature of Christianity begins to appear."[85]

Moore makes clear that this subversive element assumes its most dramatic form in the Christ-event, though it is powerfully voiced by Israel's wisdom and prophetic traditions as well. The biblical traditions as a whole attest to a progressive "dis-identification" of God and worldly power, one that simultaneously radicalizes divine transcendence vis-à-vis our human projections (the "gods") while at the same time opening up a new way of being human, a new intimacy with one another.[86] "This shift into a God beyond the world is a shift that throws people together. It creates the consciousness of a people that, with our God-representing victim slain and risen, is *ecclesia*, the called-together, the new human polity—not of power and the force of rivalry and its uneasy resultants—but of love. The withdrawal of God into all-enclosing mystery and the throwing of people together is a single process, so that John, the most visionary of the evangelists, sees 'love one another' as the sufficient statement of the creation process brought to term."[87]

This is a remarkable insight, and there are three ways I wish to unpack its compact formulation. The first is by highlighting the commitment to justice and remembering history rightly. This, too, points to the conversion of desire, for it entails the opening up of memory and the recasting of our hopes. By raising Jesus from the dead, God makes graphically visible what so often remains hidden to us, with the effect that we might begin to remember differently. We are meant to see, even if in retrospect, how habitually we construe and cling to identities through mimetic comparisons and exclusionary othering.

Strange Victory   165

Surely this is a "dangerous memory," to borrow from Johann Baptist Metz, insofar as it provokes deeply uncomfortable truths about our human projects, in which we are so often dependent upon the reification of self-other as part of our identity formation, both personally and in groups. By foregrounding what usually remains background to us, the striking visage of the crucified-and-risen One would open our ears to hear the voices of those drowned out by our negligence, our deceit, our party spirit. This is a "critical anamnesis," for it beckons us to adopt a new historical consciousness: one that allows the dead, the vanquished, the excluded, and the stranger to disturb the present order of things.[88] The memory of the crucified-and-risen One prompts an unsettling shift in perspective. It means to interrupt patterns of history-making that mute the cry of its victims or that accept the production of victims in the name of imagined progress. But more than this, it means to inspire a practical engagement of solidarity with victims as well as creative resistance to the material, social, and spiritual conditions that continue to produce them. As Metz puts it, the "Christian *idea of God* is in itself a practical idea," for God cannot become a proper idea without "irritating and disrupting the immediate interests of the one who is trying to think it."[89]

This justice-focused approach to Christian discipleship is very much a spiritual discipline of conversion, for it means attending to an eschatological presence offering a path of discipleship for imagining and acting, and in this case on behalf of those who suffer on account of some unjust order of human belonging. Whereas so many of our self-protective strategies seem remarkably adept at screening out or rationalizing the sufferings of those rendered vulnerable, excluded, or simply invisible by our social constructions of reality, the memory of the crucified-and-risen One would thoroughly refashion how we remember by attesting to, and eschatologically amplifying, the voices of those who are its victims. "Consciously or unconsciously, history is defined as the history of those who made it, those who were successful and got to the present. There is hardly any way to talk about the vanquished and defeated, the repressed and the forgotten hopes of historical existence." What we need, Metz insists, is an "anti-history based on the memory of suffering."[90] In one respect, this is just what the biblical traditions afford us: a large-scale project of exhumation whereby readers are called to remember the stranger and the vanquished. From the exodus motif to the psalmist's laments, from the prophetic cry for justice to the apocalyptic refashioning of history, from the preaching of God's reign to the *memoria passionis, mortis, et resurrectionis Jesu Christi* threading the New Testament, the eschatological vision of the Bible calls us to remember against the grain of any patterning of human relations fashioned by dominating power and to work toward a future where strangers are welcomed and captives set free. Without this concrete, hope-filled orientation toward justice, biblical faith is dead (James 2:14–26).

No less important to Moore's formulation above is the way this dangerous memory is actually communicated to us: by way of a gratuitous, merciful love that invites us into reconciled relation with our victim, the crucified. However vital the justice orientation to biblical faith is, the fact that the crucified Jesus is "remembered" through an antecedent forgiveness—as the *risen* Christ—gives definitive testimony to the wider scope of mercy in God's redemptive dispensation. The appearance narratives in the Gospels unanimously attest to the anteriority of mercy, inasmuch as the risen Jesus is portrayed as offering peace and pardon to those whom he encounters. Without in any way obscuring the appalling injustice of the cross, or the challenging process of undergoing conversion in its light ("I am Jesus the Nazorean, whom you are persecuting" [Acts 22:8]), the Easter event exposes human involvement in sin through a prior and surprising summons to participate in a "new togetherness" born out of unconditional love.[91] By allowing us to trust entirely in God's compassionate embrace, in which there is no rivalry or death, the fuller extent of our involvement in sin is capable of being acknowledged. Trust is the enabling condition for growing into truth. As Rahner states, "The real truth about a person's guilt can come home to him only when he experiences forgiveness and his deliverance from guilt."[92] The implication here is that the recognition of our involvement in deceit and exclusionary othering—the "danger" of this recognition—can be received more deeply, more honestly and truly, because forgiving love is the condition of its possibility. Importantly, God's offer of forgiveness in the risen Christ is not acquittal from afar; it is the concrete "showing how" of a creative pattern of relating that, when experienced and received *from* the expelled other, begins to set us free from a conflictual pattern of relating—one we have hitherto deemed normal, or at least inevitable. As the luring presence of the risen Christ is felt and known in the midst of our mimetic compression, and as its nonreciprocal, nonvengeful, noncompetitive energy begins to demythologize our projections and unravel our tightly wound identities, we can begin to perceive more clearly that which we are being freed from—the bonds of sin.

The conspicuous role of mercy in the Easter event highlights the integral unity of justice and forgiveness in the Christian understanding of salvation. Along with its call to be in solidarity with the poor and the oppressed, the communal form of life that lies at the heart of authentic Christian discipleship is marked by reconciliation. To be *ecclesia*, as Moore observes, entails a process of being "relaxed into" a new kind of togetherness that depends upon God's love rather than "the mimetic glue that holds societies together but always on the edge of violence."[93] This is not to condemn mimetic desire as such, which is inherently good, but to redirect it according to divine desire. Indeed, Christian community at its best is a school of desire. Through its ritual and sacramental practices, its preaching and teaching, its fellowship and institutional forms, it serves to "rehearse" patterns of life marked by forgiveness and peace and thus offer a way of "relearning" desire together. The *ecclesia* cannot be a mere collective, nor an aggregate of individuals, but is called to be the ongoing, sacramental enactment of a way of togetherness in which "my" relatedness to God involves me directly with my neighbor. For ecclesial we-centricity to function healthily, for it to flow pacifically, those who participate in it must grow in their capacities to forgive one another, that is, to release one another from the projections, resentments, and dissimulations that are bound to come up in any shared form of life. Forgiveness does not substitute for truth-telling and justice, of course, and so great care must be taken to ensure that appeals to forgiveness do not devolve into "cheap grace." But in the midst of our ever-simmering tendency toward conflict and rivalry, which is mimetic desire's shadow side, there must be a shared set of practices, however imperfect and requiring of ongoing discernment, for forgiving and peacemaking that can release its members from the bonds of mimetic

168   Christ as Concentrated Creation

entanglement in grace. In this way, the *ecclesia* can be a leaven for the world—the "body of Christ."

Which brings us finally to contemplation. As Moore notes above, the discovery of God as "the non-discriminating cause of all out of nothing" is one into which we are invited to "relax." This suggestive phrasing has been partially clarified by adverting to communal practices of justice, forgiveness, and peacemaking, all of which mean to loosen mimetic desire from its tendency toward grasping. The conversion of desire from acquisitiveness to genuine creativity is a process into which we are being inducted by God, and such a process is necessarily *interdividual* in nature. This is one reason why community can never be the mere backdrop to genuine spiritual growth; it is its proper work. If our desires are interpersonally and socially mediated, then any individualistically conceived path of spiritual development can only amount to an abstraction. The self-other relation is "where God happens," insists Williams, and thus any appeal to contemplation as key to the ongoing process of relaxing into God means quite precisely that this shifts how we relate to one another. "You 'flee' to the desert not to escape neighbors but to grasp more fully what the neighbor is—the way to life for *you*, to the degree that you put yourself at their disposal in connecting them with God."[94]

Merton, also drawing upon the desert spirituality of Christian antiquity, writes that love is much more than a sentiment, "much more than token favours and perfunctory almsdeeds. Love means an interior and spiritual identification with one's brother, so that he is not regarded as an 'object' to 'which' one 'does good.' . . . Love takes one's neighbor as one's other self, and loves him with all the immense humility and discretion and reserve and reverence without which no one can presume to enter the sanctuary of another's subjectivity."[95] Notice here that the neighbor is not external to myself, as though we meet as two self-subsisting individuals. I am already deeply implicated with my neighbor, for we exist in a relationship of mutual dependence that binds us (and our desires) together, for both good and ill. Consequently, I do not love my neighbor merely by extending certain kinds of acts "toward" him or her, however good these actions may be. I love by discovering the neighbor as my "other self"—as the other who already indwells me, interdividually. Such we-centricity is

Strange Victory 169

emphatically not about making the other an extension of myself or expecting some kind of natural affection due to a common marker of identity (e.g., national, ethnic, religious, gender, familial). I do not love my neighbor because we are more or less "the same" or because we share common interests. Natural affection, itself a form of love, is not on the order of agape. The latter comes only by reverencing the other, by sensing his or her inherent beauty and holiness, by sharing in his or her sufferings, hopes, and fragility. The sanctuary of another's subjectivity is no matter of comprehension. No image or label can stand in for the neighbor's inviolable mystery. No idea "about" my neighbor coincides with the fullness of his or her reality. I cannot truly know my neighbor in any grasping sense, for such knowing is largely the function of projection, fashioned in the restless shuffle of mimetic proximity. But I may "unknow" my neighbor, as it were. I may "release" him or her from my preconceptions, from my convenient labels, from my overriding schemas, from my need to manage and defend my self-other perceptions. The humility of which Merton speaks is really about the holy mystery of the neighbor—this "other" who calls me to a certain way of attending and loving.

Martin Laird helpfully points out that contemplative practice is one way to gain skill in letting go of our habitual tendency to judge our neighbor, which only reduces the neighbor to a quasi-object. Contemplative practice invites us to witness our thoughts and desires dispassionately, or, as the monastic tradition emphasizes, with detachment (*apatheia*). We "release" our limiting thoughts of the other into silent awareness, without judgment or mental commentary. As contemplative practice becomes more consistent in our lives, it enables us to catch ourselves in the act of judging others in everyday circumstances. We practice, in prayer, the unbinding and unloosing of desire, and this allows us better to witness our desires and mimetic comparisons in real time, to let them go rather than getting caught up in their unending dramas. This is the practical and interpersonal wisdom of contemplation. When finding yourself judging another, Laird suggests, simply let the judgment become a reminder to return to silence, to an awareness that is deeper than any limiting thought or emotional reaction you may be having. Let it flow through you. Look over its shoulder. Meeting the temptation to judge in this way will open up remarkable depths for creative liberty and love for others. "The eye that sees all this is the eye of compassion that is born in silence."[96] Or, as he puts it elsewhere, "The Light that illumines the whole of our identity in God is at once the luminous ground of our solidarity in communal frailty and failure. Our hiddenness 'with Christ in God' (Col. 3:3) sustains no separate 'me' but a self-forgetful, self-giving 'we.'"[97]

Moore's account of contemplation and creation has just this unity of God and neighbor in mind. The "withdrawal of God" to which he refers by no means suggests a game of hide-and-seek, as though the living God were more present at an earlier time but has since retreated into some otherworldly plane. Moore is referring not to a change in God but to a "seismic shift" in human consciousness in relation to God. That shift has to do, in part, with a disidentification of God from human projection, and Moore is keen to highlight the role played by Israel's prophetic tradition in affirming God's radical transcendence vis-à-vis the human temptation to align God with any manipulable interest. God is not *a* god or the sum of gods, and neither is God "the Big Imagined Being—our big being as opposed to the beings of our neighbours, the best God." Another way of putting it is that God is the nondiscriminating cause of all out of nothing. God is "why we are at all, in whom we live and move and have our being, as Paul says."[98] We should not underestimate the extent to which this discovery of divine transcendence entails a purgative process, a certain demythologization, inasmuch as we must learn how to let go of various projections and agendas in our relatedness to God. Indeed, we may even wonder what difference remains between letting go of our projections—letting go of "the gods"—and letting go of God altogether. Such is the subject of the following chapter. But here it is needful to highlight how the discovery of God's radical transcendence, so far from resulting in dispirited distance or despair, opens up a new intimacy with God and neighbor.

"That which simply *is*, is to be trusted, relaxed into."[99] In making this observation, Moore is pointing out that the nondiscriminating cause of all out of nothing is not inert or abstractly remote but utterly simple, generative, all-pervasive, and beneficent. Though creation is not its own ground, and to this extent we must stress that the whole of creation is ontologically contingent, this lack of self-subsistence

Strange Victory 171

is not a matter to be a lamented or combated through self-grasping, as though we could finally stave off our ontological porosity. It is to be freely accepted and even cherished as the gift of a Creator who bestows us into being from nothing. Relaxing into God as the wholly trustworthy source of our being—as that which cannot be grasped or manipulated (Phil. 2:6)—is the deepest ground for relaxing into our relations with others. Because we can have confidence that the source and ground of being is self-bestowing love, the One in whom there is no rivalry or death, we can "sink" into this source and ground, as Eckhart puts it, and progressively release the projections, defensive mechanisms, and neurotic compensations that so often give mimetic desire an acquisitive edge. Contemplation is particularly restorative in this regard because, among other things, it proceeds by a long letting go. By deeply allowing whatever *is* "to be," itself an act of surrender and trust in the midst of creation happening, mimetic desire is allowed to stretch out and yield to silent awareness. In this way, contemplative prayer is kenotic. The agendas and self-preoccupations, the compulsive replaying of hurts and conflicts, the exhausting racket of comparing ourselves with others, the underlying anxiety that drives us to grasp at being, as though creation were a matter to be hoarded: all these patternings and mechanisms that distort our relationships with others are allowed to be emptied, poured out in the spacious availability of unbounded, luminous awareness.

Perhaps this luminous awareness will seem like nothing at all, or a "neutral empty space," but when truly relaxed into with all the trust with which we are capable, this "void" in fact engenders awe and deepest reverence. "This void engendering awe that arises from the dumping of all our gods requires only that we open to it," writes Moore. "That is what I pray in."[100]

PART 3

Purgation and Union

CHAPTER FIVE

On the Contemplative Consummation of Atheism

Two Atheisms

The previous two chapters form the middle panel of a triptych. Focused on Christ as "concentrated creation," and with specific concern for the inner relationship between *creatio ex nihilo* and the life, death, and resurrection of Jesus, part 2 sought to illuminate how Christ is at once the decisive enactment of God's saving intention in our history and the interpretive key that discloses the inmost character of the Creator-creature relation. This is not a static relation of natures, it turns out, but a dynamic, living process that achieves its definitive realization in a *person*. The hypostatic union of natures in Christ highlights, above all else, that the fullness of the God-world relation is not an abstract conjoining of opposable realities, nor the fusion of natures that renders all distinction illusory, but a mysterious relation of love that preserves while ceaselessly uniting difference. It is a noncompetitive relationship, to be sure, but more positively an ontology of communion whose invitation to others is infinitely expansive. "In my father's house there are many dwelling places" (John 14:2).

In the context of a human history maligned by broken relationships and violence, however, this creative love manifests itself as a kenotic presence that enters directly into the heart of our wounded nature in order to heal it. It "assumes" this nature, with all the onto-logical significance this implies, and enacts a form of life that sub-verts the power of sin and death from within. The spirit of rivalry, the pseudo-transcendences, the bulwarks against vulnerability, the illu-sory forms of solidarity, the exclusionary violence: such principalities and powers are unambiguously confronted by Christ, but without a whiff of mimicry, and exposed by a self-giving so complete that their seeming ultimacy in human affairs is shown to be groundless and subject to eschatological dissolution. The unconditionally generous God who gives all things "to be," and who therefore is not in rivalry with creation whatsoever, freely wills to become a creature in order to release the arthritic grip of disordered human desire and open it up to the pure positivity of divinizing love. Such is the self-implicating act of divine persuasion in our history, an activity that knows no envy or coercion. In its ultimate sense, the doctrine of *creatio ex nihilo*, along with the theology of the incarnation, is another way of affirm-ing God's unconditional love for creation—a love "from nothing."

I will further explore this theme of love from nothing in chap-ter 6, but in the present chapter I wish to dwell further upon the ongoing implications of desacralization discussed in part 2. In par-ticular, I am interested in exploring the liberating but also painful and sometimes ambiguous process of being purged of distortive concep-tions of God. This purgative process involves a kind of death, a relin-quishing of false securities and projective fantasies that set themselves up as ultimate, but which turn out to be suffocating self-enclosures. Genuine religious faith, especially one so cruciform as Christian faith, involves a thoroughgoing purification of all that blocks true percep-tion of God; in the context of Jesus's life, death, and resurrection, this unblocking entails a subversion of human projections so far-reaching that we may wonder whether Christianity implies a kind of atheism.

Reflecting upon René Girard's account of divine revelation as unmasking the false sacred, Scott Cowdell writes that the Gospels por-tray the figure of Christ as an "absence, silence, withdrawal, nonpres-ence . . . amid the world's mimetic clamor. This is why Christianity is closer to atheism than to anything resembling the archaic sacred, and why the secular imagination cut off from every sense of sacred power is actually *appropriately* underwhelming."[1] Cowdell suggests that

On the Contemplative Consummation of Atheism   177

because the pacific reality of God transcends any human ethos where mimetic rivalry and structural violence hold sway, that reality can only appear as a strange absence, a nonpresence by comparison. This hardly means that God does not in fact exist, or lacks creative agency to effect change in human affairs; rather, the nature of that creative agency is incommensurate with the machinations of coercive power and therefore seemingly underwhelming in its midst—a vanishing horizon, a hieroglyph, virtually "nothing." "This is why," Cowdell adds, "the dark night of Saint John of the Cross, named and celebrated at the onset of modernity, is actually the paradox of true divine presence and the dwindling to *nada* of false sacred power over us. Hence the silence of contemplation, also the nondramatic everydayness of eucharistic liturgy . . . and the existential homelessness that contributes a characteristic cast to authentic spirituality in secularity."[2]

This last point is quite significant, and I intend to develop it at greater length here. That is, I wish to explore the potential filiation between contemplative dispossession and the existential homelessness felt by many in our contemporary age—the sense of being in a spiritual desert, of being rudderless, hollow, or perhaps ontologically forlorn, abandoned to a time when God seems absent or barely noticeable. I have provisionally described this as the "nihilistic mood," not because of any overweening moralism that judges it to be without values, but because of the sometimes explicit (though often implicit) sense today that the world is all there is; that God, to the extent there *is* a God, is a distant and aloof deity, perhaps an impersonal force undergirding an impersonal universe; that if human beings have historically had a lively sense of God or gods, with many still believing today, we are increasingly suspicious of how much we construct our images of God/gods out of thin air based upon weakness, fear, and the need for consolation and control, leaving us to doubt whether there really is a "there" there. What constitutes the source and ground of all that is, if anything? Having become more aware of the projective tendency in our envisioning of God or gods, what happens when we follow our suspicions all the way down? Is there an end to them, a bottom? Can we have any confidence that "God" is anything more than our own hopes or neuroses writ large? Alas, is God dead?

178   Purgation and Union

In part, the present exploration will consider how negative theology and atheistic critique, while poles apart in obvious ways, nevertheless exhibit illuminating convergences around this projective tendency of human religiosity. Both cast a critical eye toward the human propensity to fashion God or gods in our own image, or what amounts to the same thing, the tendency to shelter ourselves from the feeling of existential insecurity with the superlative somethingness of divine substance. Indeed, the dialectical thrust of each may appear indistinguishable from the other at certain points, even if negative theology is ultimately linked to a cataphatic theology that affirms the pure positivity of divine life suffusing all of creation. Such will be the focus of the subsequent chapter, where I hope to show that the contemplative inhabitation of our creaturely "nothingness" coincides with the unqualified yes of epiphanic perception, that is, a loving return to manifestation and union with God. But here I shall dwell upon the negative side of this dialectic movement—purgation, absence, detachment, darkness, emptiness—and do so in sympathetic dialogue with the doubt, disenchantment, and existential rootlessness that seem so pervasive in our secular (or postsecular) age. I will maintain along the way that the path of contemplative dispossession is a far more patient and transformative inhabitation of God's apparent absence, and that while not yielding to cheap and easy answers to the above questions, it nevertheless sees in them a supremely spiritual task rather than any rejection of faith. As Simone Weil puts it, "There are two atheisms of which one is the purification of the notion of God."[3]

RETURN TO ZERO

In the preface to what would be his final completed manuscript, Thomas Merton writes that the contemplative today must inwardly discover the lostness that our modern age tends to foster. Stressing that the Christian contemplative path cannot flee from our shared human world but instead must enter ever more deeply into it, Merton maintains that the existential unease and spiritual disorientation felt by many today are not to be resisted as something alien to faith but rather experienced at its core. Contrary to any understanding of contemplation as an elitist enterprise preoccupied with esoteric knowledge, or the retreat to an inner citadel where the struggles of ordinary life do not reach, Merton insists that the emptiness, bewilderment, and insecurity felt by many today is at the heart of any contemplative life worthy of the name *Christian*. It interiorizes and metabolizes these struggles, not out of some misplaced martyr complex that hurls itself into manufactured crises, but because "underlying all life is the ground of doubt and self-questioning which sooner or later must bring us face to face with the ultimate meaning of our life."[4] While the existential homelessness characteristic of our age may have distinctive features to it, its deeper significance is not restricted to any particular era but confronts us with perennial questions of ultimacy, with the meaning of human life itself. In this sense it is ontological. It puts us in touch with our human condition.

But for that very reason it puts us in touch with God. Speaking of the monastic vocation, Merton writes, "This is an age that, by its very nature as a time of crisis, of revolution, of struggle, calls for the special searching and questioning which are the work of the monk in his meditation and prayer."[5] By plunging into the heart of the world, the monk plunges into his own heart, and vice versa, and both acts entail plunging into the searchless depths of divine freedom, in "direct dependence on an invisible and inscrutable God, in pure faith."[6] The contemplative vocation in the modern world, which, Merton adds, is by no means reserved only for monks, is to share in and fully inhabit our time of crisis, yet "in an altogether different and deeper way than does man in the modern world, to whom this disconcerting awareness of himself and of his world comes rather as an experience of boredom and spiritual disorientation." This different and deeper way is not the consequence of some special faculty with which especially pious persons are endowed, but because such a person "confronts his own humanity and that of his world at the deepest and most central point where the void seems to open out into black despair." The contemplative disposition is not a defensive reaction to this void but, paradoxically, an abiding with it and in it, of patiently allowing it to be. Contemplation does not fight the inchoate sense of "nothingness" that lurks within human consciousness, or simply declare it tragic, absurd, but entrusts itself to it with poverty of spirit. In this way, "the option of absolute despair is turned into perfect hope. . . . From the darkness comes light. From death, life. From the abyss there comes, unaccountably, the mysterious gift of the Spirit sent by God to make all things new, to transform the created and redeemed world, and to re-establish all things in Christ."[7]

The death-and-resurrection pattern at work in this compact summary—darkness/light, death/life, abyss/gift—is paradigmatic for Christian life, though by no means mechanically reproduced. It is not a formula. It must be lived in grace. And its lived variegations are expansive and inherently dynamic. Certainly, it does not imply that the contemplative vocation is the only (or even primary) way Christians ought to enter more fully into the struggles and joys of our world. There are many kinds of vocation we could stress here as manifesting christomorphic life, including the work of justice and reconciliation through sacramental ministry, family life, aesthetic creation, and political commitment. But at a time when the nihilistic mood seems especially prevalent among us—the haunting suspicion that perhaps "nothing matters" in the end, or that human life is lived in the face of an indescribable, indifferent void—the contemplative dimensions of Christian faith will have something indispensable to offer. At least this is what Merton wagers in his seminal essay "Contemplation in a World of Action":

> It is more and more usual for modern people to be afflicted with a sense of absence, desolation, and incapacity to even "want" to pray or think of God. To dismiss this superficially as experience of "the death of God" . . . is to overlook one significant fact: that this sense of absence is not a one-sided thing: it is dialectical, and it includes its opposite, namely presence. . . . [The] experience of the contemplative life in the modern world shows that the most crucial focus for contemplative and meditative discipline, and for the life of prayer . . . is precisely this so-called sense of absence, desolation, and even apparent "inability to believe." I stress the word "apparent," because though this experience may to some be extremely painful and confusing . . . it can very well be a sign of authentic Christian growth and a point of decisive development in faith, if they are able to cope with it. . . . One must, on a new

On the Contemplative Consummation of Atheism   181

level of meditation and prayer, live through this crisis of belief and grow to a more complete personal and Christian integration by experience.[8]

The contemplative path sketched here, which is one of crisis and growth, is commended to all Christians, and indeed to anyone who might wish to look more patiently and discerningly into the sense of divine absence that seems characteristic of our age. It means to deepen this sense of absence by radicalizing it, by going to its roots (*radix*). It means becoming open to the possibility that "emptiness" harbors a spiritual intuition of supreme importance, and that once recognized, it may be welcomed through an implicit act of trust—with a primal, wordless yes. To feel the underlying sense of our nothingness, with all the giddiness, confusion, and hopelessness this can stir up in us, is in fact to be in touch with our creaturely contingency—our *shared* contingency—and hence our immediate dependence upon God for being at all. To be awakened to this contingency, but more, to embrace it in freedom, is the first step toward radicalizing it, of living *into* and *from* this immediate dependence upon God as the source of our hope. Instead of resisting or buffering ourselves against this underlying sense of emptiness, or succumbing to it out of fatalism or despair, we may learn to relax into it and even be upheld by it, purified and transformed by it. Counterintuitive as it may seem, the mood of nihilism that in part characterizes our age is not so much a matter to be combated as one to be completed.

William Desmond, whose work we encountered in chapter 2, writes along similar lines, though in a more philosophical register. Referring to nihilism as the "devaluation of being," and seeing its contemporary prevalence as closely related to the modern drive toward instrumental reasoning (versus sapiential reasoning) and individual self-determination (versus relational interbeing), Desmond nevertheless asks us to consider whether there might be *some* truth to nihilism. "Suppose the origin is worthless, the world void of inherent value, our energy of being either reactive to or transformative of this worthlessness. What then?"[9] Framed as a philosophical-spiritual exercise, Desmond proposes that we allow ourselves to be sifted by the sense of nothingness, to enter more fully into it by way of purgation and release.[10] In an imaginative act of what he calls "returning to zero," Desmond invites us to touch base with our ontological porosity, to discover (or rediscover) our inmost vulnerability as creatures, and suspend for a while the habitual defenses we have accumulated against it. As a philosopher of the *metaxu*, or the "in-between" character of all life, Desmond proposes that such a meditation is not an exercise in morbidity, even if it may initially cause disorientation. Rather, it bears the potential for "unclogging" our capacities for aesthetic, ethical, and religious perception. "Suppose coming to nothing, 'being as nothing,' constituted a kind of ontological ordeal. Suppose in this there is both a deepening and a sifting: deepening, since we are thrown back on ourselves; sifting, in that we may be purged of impediments blocking our release to what is beyond."[11] What if instead of resisting this "being as nothing," or shielding ourselves against the ineradicable contingency and intermediation of life, we allowed ourselves for a moment—a moment that might turn into two, or three, or four ... — to give into it, to freely accept it, just as we must eventually accept our death? What if, with a basic clarity and an inside wink, a knowing smile, we recognize that we have nothing more (or less) to lose; that somehow it is deeply okay to let down all defenses, to drop all our mental-somatic clinging and just *be*? Might this apparent breakdown offer a breakthrough? Might there be a doubleness to the sense of "nothing" to discern here: one inciting a *reactivity* that only pings us back upon ourselves, the other prompting a *receptivity* that opens us up to what is beyond our grasp? Perhaps instead of diminishing our sense of wonderment in the midst of contingent existence, this return to zero can revivify it. Perhaps such an exercise can "hollow out a purer space" or even "prepare for a resurrected patience to ultimate transcendence, a new porosity to God."[12]

Anyone familiar with contemplative practice will recognize the basic disposition invoked here, but in several of his writings Desmond elaborates a distinctive philosophical exercise that serves as a variation on the ancient practice of memento mori, or meditation upon death. Here again there is no question of morbid fascination. Instead, there is a basic coming to terms and a potential rejuvenation. Dubbing it "posthumous mind," Desmond invites his readers to imagine themselves as having *already* died. "Suppose one were to die and then come back

On the Contemplative Consummation of Atheism   183

from the dead and now look upon what is there, beyond the instrumentalizing mind dominating so much of our first life, free of the will to power that endeavors to impose itself on being, or even affirm itself; free now to look on being as given in its otherness, loved for its otherness and not just for what it is for us."[13] Imagine revisiting our lives again, but from the point of view of having already lived them, from the other side of death, and with a capacious spirit that is no longer caught up with striving from the inside of "my" life. Whereas the first go-around with life entailed a great deal of exertion to affirm itself, to make a project of itself and acquire some identity vis-à-vis others that might prove lasting, stable, and significant, the posthumous return to life would be free from all such striving or even thinking of a life in terms of "proving" anything. All of that is over. Instead, posthumous mind would be generously present to the whole of its life, a welcoming witness to the fabric of relations out of which it emerged and in which it participated. Such a vision would not be isolated to the localizable space of punctiliar subjectivity, experienced only as "in here," with the world (and others) "out there"; instead its life would be perceived in its surprising givenness, as a "happening" within a comprehending, dynamic web of relationships. No longer driven by the fear of death, and no longer subordinate to the succession of time, it revisits its life from beyond death, beyond all succession, and takes it in whole—just as it is. It sees its life as such, as though for the first time, in its all its strange and wonderous thereness.

As unusual as this exercise may seem, its ultimate aim is to modulate our attention, to dislodge some of the accrued habits of mind that diminish our capacities for attending more deeply, here and now. "Contemplation, by contrast, introduces rupture into habitual seeing."[14] Like the return to zero, which invites us to look patiently into our ontological porosity, the cultivation of posthumous mind is really about reawakening us to the "intimate strangeness of being."[15] Like a splash of cold water on the face, or the striking of a meditation bell, it quickens our basic sense of aliveness, our being at all. As a "way of mindfulness," the exercise means to open up pores of awareness that go beyond the immediate need to engineer our lives. Its way of attending is agapeic. Beholding rather than seizing, welcoming rather than resisting, releasing rather than clasping, it allows for life to appear in its astonishing suchness. Posthumous mind is not the pretense to total objectivity or neutrality. Neither does it exclude creative agency. It is only the dropping of ulterior motives, of our tendencies to impose upon or egoically circumscribe. It is the simple willingness "to see what is good in being for itself, and not just for me."[16] Desmond suggests that if we allow ourselves to behold the givenness of things with this renewed innocence, with a childlike "first look," a "beginner's mind," then life will not appear as worthless in the least. It will not confirm the nihilist's outlook that "nothing matters." It will not be indifferent or suspicious of life's adventitious unfolding, as though "merely" or "absurdly" there. It will spontaneously marvel at life's appearance and tell of its inestimable worth. As with those who have been granted a second chance on life—like Fyodor Dostoevsky, who returned to life after being freed from a mock execution—seeing our lives again as though for the first time can awaken "agapeic mindfulness" and help reestablish a rapport with the inherent goodness of being, as lovable in itself. "For when we come back from the dead thus, we would do so to find again the things we loved for their intrinsic, indeed unfathomable, goodness. This here was loved for itself; what was beloved in it escapes beyond all categorial determination; we come back to life when we seek the unfathomable goodness of the elemental 'to be.'"[17]

As with Merton's account of contemplative renewal, there is a discernible pattern of death and resurrection at work in Desmond's return to zero. "The porosity of being is not a vacant emptiness but is endowed and empowered. It is a 'being nothing' which is the potency to open to everything. Describing it in terms of the return to zero implies a *fertile void*, not just a nihilating one."[18] Desmond is here pointing to a "born-again mindfulness," a "resurrection of astonishment" that is renewed in its capacities for beholding the intrinsic worth of being, its miraculous epiphany. Beyond the instrumentalizing mind that reduces being to calculation, and beyond the hyper-individuated mind that recoils from the inherent openness and intermediation of all things—the *metaxu*—there is an agapeic mindfulness that greets the present moment with simple gratitude, with a revitalizing yes. "The return to zero releases the energy of coming to be into a *new interface with creation*."[19] By "dying" to its objectifying gaze it perceives

On the Contemplative Consummation of Atheism   185

"the *givenness of creation* as an other, not there just for us, but having its being and value for itself."[20] Or again, in renouncing the will to dominate it discerns "being as perennial resurrection into thereness, out of nothing."[21]

The suggestion here, as always with Desmond, is that a certain way of mindfulness is necessary for beginning to appreciate just what *creation* (or *God*) might mean; that unless we are in touch with the original porosity of our being, or what he calls our *passio essendi*— our ontological receptivity that is open to all that is other, including ourselves as others—then not only will we be diminished in our capacities for discovering the elemental goodness of being, but we will likely be incapable of accepting that we are loved into being by God. Our "coming to be" is "agapeic origination": we come from an unconditioned and generously loving source, not for the aggrandizement of this source, but for the sake of creation itself. Why? "Because it is good."[22] Or, as Merton puts it, "We have no other reason for being, except to be loved by him as our Creator and Redeemer, and to love him in return. . . . It is love for love's sake."[23]

DOCTRINE AND MYSTAGOGY

Having limbered up our imaginations through the preceding spiritual exercises, I turn now to a focused inquiry into the potential convergences between negative theology and atheistic critique, particularly around the projective and reifying tendencies in the conceptualization of God. With an appeal to *creatio ex nihilo* as a doctrinal locus, I will suggest that the *via negativa* at work in this doctrine, along with the contemplative practice of dispossession it invites, provides a more patient and ultimately more transformative way to undergo such critique. Of course, I recognize that any appeal to doctrine in this context may seem disingenuous, since to some ears the mere mention of "doctrine" (and especially "dogma") suggests the end of questions and the short-circuiting of further discovery. Isn't a religious doctrine really a finished intellectual product and thus an obstacle to the spirit of open-ended inquiry? No doubt doctrines have at times functioned to blunt the questing spirit, but this hardly means that they have therefore performed *as* doctrine. On the contrary, the diminishment of wonderment and self-implicating risk are among the clearest signs that theological doctrine is not functioning properly at all.

In a searching essay dedicated to bringing contemplation and atheistic critique into dialogue, the late Michael J. Buckley writes that the "function of dogmatic stability is not to explain the mystery of God, but to lead into it and to safeguard its incomprehensibility. Dogma is to secure the inviolability of the mystery of the incomprehensible God."[24] Working closely with Karl Rahner's account of dogmatic formulae as mystagogical in character — as possessing "conceptual content" that refers "beyond itself and everything imaginable"[25] — Buckley maintains that dogmatic truths in the Christian tradition may indeed be committed to working with finite concepts to disclose something of the mystery of God, but only insofar as they point toward that which infinitely exceeds their capacity to grasp, and with the ultimate aim of inducting us *into* that mystery. Doctrines at their best are not impediments to discovery but facilitators of it. They are, as Mark McIntosh puts it, "a language for describing and participating in [the] encounter with God, as an itinerary giving an indication of the major landmarks along the journey."[26] This understanding of doctrine as mystagogical is by no means anti-intellectual or suspicious of discursivity, but neither is it without a vigorous sense of the dialectical nature of doctrine, which must "unsay" as much as it "says." "The self-disclosure of God, of One so infinitely Other," writes Buckley, "is finally only possible with the disclosure of the contradiction within finite concepts and human expectations that touch upon God. The darkness and its pain are here, but they are finally dialectical movements in which the human is purified from a projection by a 'no' which is most radically a 'yes,' a 'no' that is generated by the initial 'yes.'"[27]

Already in this statement we can anticipate how Buckley might develop correspondences between negative theology and atheistic critique, but we should notice first that this dialectical movement of yes and no is a basic feature of *creatio ex nihilo* itself. Indeed, it is hard to imagine a doctrinal formulation that is more affirmative *and* negative in its basic structure and meaning. To wit:

On the Contemplative Consummation of Atheism 187

- If, on the one hand, we find in the doctrine of *creatio ex nihilo* an unambiguous affirmation of creation as positively willed by God, as "coming to be" by an infinite Creator out of freedom and love, we find, on the other hand, a thoroughgoing denial of any mediating principle, whether material, causal, or conceptual, that allows us to grasp or somehow reach the bottom of that coming to be. We are forever mysteries to ourselves as creatures, as *given*, even as we may come to ever-more-refined understandings of the causes, processes, relations, emergent properties, and layered histories that are integral to our creaturely "becoming."

- Or if, on the one hand, "creation from nothing" affirms that the world of phenomena is not merely a vaporous illusion but in fact genuinely "other" than God, the integrity of the world, its otherness and dignifying distinction, is not self-subsistent or amenable to final comprehension but ontologically dependent upon an incomprehensible God for its existence. In simply *being* itself it is immediately referred to what is infinitely *beyond* itself. Creation is constitutively *ek-static*, a dynamic process of continual self-surpassing into divine mystery.

- Another gloss: if *creatio ex nihilo* points to the transcendent and pacific origin of all things, and thus the absence of any barrier or competitiveness between God and creation, then this lack of barrier means that the transcendent God is *inmost* to creation as its unconditioned source and ground, nearer to creatures than they are to themselves, the most immanent factor of their existence. Little wonder, then, that when we peer into the depths of our creatureliness we find no bottom, no graspable "thing" to objectify, nothing conclusively to represent or finally master. Deep calls upon deep.

Notice the rocking back and forth in these complementary statements, between yes and no, and the dialectical momentum that requires us to affirm *x* but also *y* through simultaneous acts of negation. Statements such as these (and many others that could be offered as corollaries) function as antinomies. "On the one hand 'x' and on the other hand 'y'" is a discursive attempt to hold apparent opposites in tension, to avoid collapsing poles of meaning into one another, to sustain paradox rather than conceptually enclosing it. Both/and, neither/nor, if/then: by saying and unsaying in this fashion we are establishing a kind of rhythm, a generative "play" of language that loosens up imagination and throws open spaces to keep mind and heart from clinching. Discursivity is not an enemy to contemplative inquiry, and yet too easily we get fixated on x at the expense of y, or vice versa, turning what should be a creative antinomy into flat contradiction, a lifeless binary. Contemplative inquiry of this sort may ultimately lead us into an "unknowing" beyond images and concepts, to a "dazzling darkness" where such antinomies are allowed to be in abiding awareness, but by no means does this movement involve any despair over images and concepts as inherently problematic, for such would only result in yet another stifling binary, a fixed opposition between word and silence, between kataphasis and apophasis. Hence the all-important "negation of the negation" in Pseudo-Dionysius the Areopagite: "Darkness and light, error and truth—[the supreme Cause of all] is none of these. It is beyond assertion and denial. We make assertions and denials of what is next to it, but never of it, for it is both beyond every assertion, being the perfect and unique cause of all things, and, by virtue of its preeminently simple and absolute nature, free of every limitation, beyond every limitation; *it is also beyond every denial.*"[28]

We cannot fail to notice the many words it takes to lead to this silence, and in fact the short treatise to which these lines serve as a fitting conclusion is intertextually related to other treatises in the Pseudo-Dionysian corpus brimming with content: cascading predications, biblical images, liturgical symbols, clashing metaphors, stressed analogies, doctrinal clarifications. As Denys Turner observes, "It is of the greatest consequence to see that negative language about God is no more apophatic in itself than is affirmative language. The apophatic is the linguistic strategy of somehow showing by means of language that which lies beyond language. It is not done, and it cannot be done, by means of negative utterances alone which are no less bits of ordinarily intelligible human discourse than are affirmations. Our negations, therefore, fail of God as much as do our affirmations."[29] Later in the same essay Turner remarks that the contemplative mood imbuing the works of Pseudo-Dionysius is correlated not with a simple lack of speech but the "self-subverting" of speech. Silence opens up from within language, just as language springs from what can never finally be said. This is why negations are never the end point of inquiry but must themselves be negated on account of their limitations. "It is on the other side of both our affirmations and our denials that the silence of the transcendent is glimpsed, seen through the fissures opened up in our language by the dialectical strategy of self-subversion."[30]

The recognition that our denials are as limited as our affirmations will become more significant as we proceed, but we should highlight how the self-subverting dynamic just described is operative in the doctrine of *creatio ex nihilo* as well. For although the language used here says something immeasurably positive about creation, namely, that its very being is gift—given "to be" by a God who lovingly wills and sustains creaturely difference out of God's own infinite liberty—we can never get to the bottom of what this gift entails or how it could ever be given. We do not quite know how to conceive of this "difference." By denying that God's creative act depends upon some extradivine principle or finite cause, whether preexistent matter, metaphysical necessity, or some need in God that creation seems to fulfill, we are deprived of any definable "whatness" that might secure our comprehension of the God-world relation. There is no mediating "thing" we might grasp here, no self-standing principle, no silhouetted "causal joint" that might render our relatedness to God conspicuous. Just what is the "stuff" of this relation? What does it consist of? Where is it located? What is its extension, its duration? The privative "from nothing" is quite the jolt. It uncaps questions while refusing to fill them in. It rejects every kind of "something" that might secure the God-world relation for comprehension, and thus it performs a self-subversion of language that opens up an unbridgeable fissure for thought. This fissure is endlessly thinkable, the source of never-ending wonderment, yet it is not finally circumscribable. *Creatio ex nihilo* forbids this encircling of thought, and so it keeps thought ever open to what exceeds thought. In this way it redeems thought and makes it holy.

The radical, qualitative distinction between God and creation can never show up as an item in the world, for it is just this distinction that gives creation "to be." We can never demarcate the divine difference that constitutes our existence. We cannot conceptually represent our "coming to be," even as we live it in the open fields of "becoming." Its hiddenness allows all things to manifest. Its distance is closest to us. Its nonavailability to representation makes every act of representation possible. Its non-obviousness is the most basic fact of our lives. Nothing "in" creation can be adequately compared to the origin "of" creation, and every attempt at any such comparison is made possible by the simply incomparable.

Even our attempts to account for God's distinction from creation can fall into the subtle trap of supposing that we know what *distinction* really means. If we assume, for example, that God's difference from creation is opposed to any similarity with creation, then we have only negatively defined divine transcendence as merely other-than-world. We end up defining the God-world relation according to a contrastive logic, quite despite ourselves. We cannot adequately describe God's difference from the world in the way we describe differences within the world. But then, neither can we describe God's similarity with the world in the way we describe similarities within the world. Rather, we must somehow attest to divine transcendence by pointing beyond the contrast of similarity and difference itself. Says Turner:

> We cannot know God's distinction from, and transcendence of, creation through any analogy with how anything at all differs from anything else, any more than we can know the intimacy of God's relation with the world in terms of how any things at all are similar to one another. For God transcends the difference between similarity and difference. . . . The divine transcendence is therefore the transcendence even of difference between God and creation. Since there is no knowable "distance" between God and creation, there is no language in which it is possible to state one. For all our terms of contrast state differentiations between creatures. There is none in which to state the difference between God and creatures. God is not, therefore, opposed to creatures, [and] cannot displace them.[31]

This last point is key. While the "negation of the negation" may appear excessive in its verbal gymnastics, such an exercise is salutary

On the Contemplative Consummation of Atheism   191

and consistent with the noncompetitive, noncontrastive logic we have been unpacking throughout this book. God's radical transcendence is not at all opposed to creatures, and neither does it displace them. God's "difference" from creation is what makes creaturely "union" with God possible. God's "distance" is the most "intimate" reality of our lives, so close that we cannot "see" it. God is the Other other, the non-Other, the *non aliud*, beyond all otherness and sameness. God "is neither named nor not named," writes Nicholas of Cusa, "nor is God both named and not named, but because of the excellence of God's infinity all that can be said disjunctively and unitively, whether by means of agreement or contradiction, does not correspond to God, for God is the one beginning prior to every idea that can be formed of God."[32] Through its discursive play and strategic self-subversions, such "learned ignorance" keeps language fresh to what most animates and transcends it. It prepares us for entering into that vast, open awareness wherein such antinomies as "otherness" and "sameness" are simply allowed to be.

This is the real aim of the Areopagite's mystical itinerary, notes Turner: to lead the reader to "the point where the mind has surpassed all discourse in which to state the contrast."[33] Or, as Vladimir Lossky puts it, "We must live the dogma expressing a revealed truth, which appears to us as an unfathomable mystery, in such a fashion that instead of assimilating the mystery to our mode of understanding, we should, on the contrary, look for a profound change, an inner transformation of spirit, enabling us to experience it mystically."[34]

FALLING IN LOVE WITH A BLANK

With this potential transformation in view, I return to Buckley's essay to consider how the mystagogical itinerary we are presently tracing shares important family resemblances with atheistic critique, at least insofar as both highlight the "radical finitude of religious ideas." I want to suggest here that both paths entail taking our suspicions seriously by subjecting to scrutiny the human tendency to fashion God (or gods) out of our own image, or what we might call "the self-projection inescapably present in religious ideas."[35] The recognition

192 Purgation and Union

of this deep-seated tendency can be quite disorienting, as it may shatter our original naïveté and threaten many of the personal and social patterns that depend upon such projections for their stability. We can even come to suspect that all our ways of imagining and speaking about God are *only* that—projections based upon the human need for security, consolation, or transcendent meaning in an otherwise brutal and indifferent universe. But the subversion of such projections can be tremendously liberating as well, since the images of God (or gods) to which we consciously or unconsciously cling can be stifling or even threatening to human flourishing, potent mechanisms of psychological repression and social coercion propagated under the guise of sacral authority. The recognition of this projective tendency is therefore by no means exclusively atheistic but in fact a theological insight of crucial importance. Any healthy tradition of faith will exhibit ongoing contestations of inadequate, contradictory, or oppressive images of God within it, and this is nowhere more evident than in the desacralizing thrust of the biblical traditions discussed in part 2. But it is also possible to see how this critically reflective spirit, once it gains sufficient momentum, can raise the question whether it is ultimately sustainable within the context of religious faith or finally inimical to any such context. Is it the beginning of a purified theism or the end of theism altogether? Or perhaps we find ourselves in a bewildering no man's land, an ambiguous "betweenness" where we feel the push and pull of both possibilities at once. As Buckley himself puts it, "If one admits that religious belief—to be authentic—must recognize its own set of projections, whether psychologically individual or social ... does this admission not indicate a destruction that constitutes the rejection of all divinity, the death of God, and the end of religion? Or can it equally indicate that this engagement with God must move dialectically into the stern demands of a life of contemplation, one moment of which is apophatic?"[36]

When Buckley refers to atheistic critique in this context he has specifically in mind such figures as Feuerbach, Marx, Nietzsche, Durkheim, and Freud. Noting the influence of Hegel on such figures more broadly, especially his understanding of religious symbols and ideas as the "objectification" (*Vergegenständlichung*) of Spirit, Buckley highlights the dramatic shift underway in Feuerbach from the broader scope of speculative idealism to a narrower and strictly atheistic interpretation of God as the product of the human mind. "God is the highest subjectivity of man abstracted from himself."[37] This abstraction is not only the objectification of human consciousness mediating itself through history but also, more significantly for Feuerbach, the fateful splitting of human consciousness from itself in alienation (*Entäusserung*). "Hence man can do nothing of himself, all goodness comes from God."[38] Though the symbol of God in human imagination might be a consoling, inspiring, and at times ennobling ideal, it is ultimately a reified projection of human consciousness that diminishes human self-understanding and capacity. Waking up from religion is thus like waking up from a dream. But more, it is the beginning of the maturating process of reintegrating disassociated projections back into ourselves, or what Feuerbach neatly summarizes as the reduction of theology to anthropology and the elevation of anthropology to theology.[39] Atheistic critique in this vein may involve a disorienting process that exposes human beings to uncomfortable truths, but it is ultimately humanizing for Feuerbach in the sense that it restores to human beings their rightful dignity as fully conscious, historical agents. No longer childlike in subordinating itself to fabricated entities, humanity may come of age and accede to its true potential through the conversion of all such objectifications into subjective form.

The general outline of Feuerbach's projection theory of religion was quite influential on the likes of Marx, Nietzsche, and Freud, however differently each developed it. Marx would famously declare, in his *Theses on Feuerbach,* "Philosophers have hitherto only interpreted the world in various ways; the point is to change it," a thesis that at once affirms and critiques aspects of Feuerbach's professed materialism. Nietzsche devoured *The Essence of Christianity* as a young student of theology and was especially drawn to Feuerbach's characterization of the Christian God as resulting in human self-denigration. Freud declared Feuerbach the philosopher he admired the most, although he viewed the personal God of Western monotheism as the infantile projection of a displaced father-figure rather than any idealized portrait of the human. Whatever the respective contributions of these masters of suspicion to political theory, genealogical critique, and psychoanalysis, all of them took the critique of religion as fundamental to their endeavors, and all of them developed their critiques with some variation on the projection thesis. That is, "They agree that what is believed in religion is a projection of the human, that the divine must be 'deconstructed' and disclosed as the human. The difference between them only underlines their agreement; whatever variances they exhibit lie with their understanding of the human."[40]

Such deconstructions of human projection are not only the province of atheism, however. Just as atheistic critiques of this sort were becoming a potent intellectual force in the late nineteenth and early twentieth centuries, so do we find theological movements that were no less forceful in their critique of the human tendency to envision God in its own image. One thinks of the surge in dialectical styles of theology after World War I (à la Karl Barth) that emphasize the paradoxical character of divine revelation and its subversion of human expectation. Barth was just as impressed by Feuerbach's projection thesis as Marx, Nietzsche, and Freud, although he sought to take theology through the "fiery brook" of atheistic critique in a Kierkegaardian way, with appeal to God's "infinite, qualitative distinction" and a relentless emphasis upon God's self-revelation that cuts across all our projective tendencies. Along with this strong theological response we can observe a somewhat different reaffirmation of divine transcendence in the groundswell of interest in negative and mystical theologies. Buckley remarks that, like atheistic critique, the remarkable renewal of contemplative traditions in the twentieth century shows a concern for "the proclivity of religion to become projection."[41] Both are critically alert to how readily human beings fashion images of God/gods in their own likeness and the need to correct that tendency. This is hardly to equate the two, of course, since the *via negativa* of contemplative discovery involves a purgative process of surrendering to That which surpasses all human understanding—of *undergoing* the infinite mystery to which the breakdown of all our discursive conventions point and to some extent participate. Atheistic critique may also involve a kind of purgative process, even a personally and socially transformative one, but it does not attest to any living faith in a God beyond all human projections, nor does it accept the possibility that the symbols, narratives, predications, doctrines, and embodied

On the Contemplative Consummation of Atheism 195

practices that make up a faith tradition are potentially truthful (if also limited) human responses to a self-disclosing reality. Nevertheless, the strongly dialectical thrust of negative theology, and the patient practice of nonconceptual awareness in contemplative prayer, are remarkable for the degree to which they insist upon the incomprehensibility of God and the radical finitude of religious ideas. "Contemplative authors and mystical theology at its finest have insisted that human experience is always and everywhere a finite modification of a finite subject, no matter what its intensity and extension, and that if it does not point beyond itself such an apotheosis of experience becomes idolatrous in any claim to represent the divine adequately. Mysticism and contemplation," Buckley insists, "are informed by a radical self-transcendence, a self-transcendence that is the polar opposite of self-preoccupation and narcissism, a transcendence that insists upon God as mystery above conceptualization."[42]

Buckley's main illustrations here are Pseudo-Dionysius, Gregory of Nyssa, and Saint John of the Cross. Regarding the latter, the sixteenth-century Spanish mystic displays a penetrating awareness of just how constructive human subjectivity is in all our experience, just as he provides a set of diagnostic tools for the transformation of that subjectivity as it opens itself to divine mystery in love. Frequently citing the medieval maxim "Whatever is received is received according to the receiver" (*Quidquid recipitur secundum modum recipientis reciptur*), John fully recognizes that our relation to God is mediated by sensory perceptions, feelings, imaginings, and concepts, all of which are necessary and good in their own way, however limited or subject to distortion they may be. The point is not to despair over these mediations, but neither is it to leave them uneducated by grace.

As classically outlined in *The Ascent of Mount Carmel* and *The Dark Night*, the Carmelite charts a mystagogical itinerary that highlights the transformative nature of maturing faith as it is purged of the tendency to cling to sensory perceptions, feelings, imaginings, and concepts in our relation to God. Far more self-implicating than the discursive gymnastics of affirming x or denying y, however needful at some level, the praxis of contemplative discovery assumes a protracted journey of sensory, affective, and intellectual dispossession, an ever-deepening yielding of the whole human person to God in

196 Purgation and Union

the "darkness" of faith. This dispossession is by no means antihuman or a matter of self-denigration, for its very essence entails our becoming free from the subtle mechanisms of clutching at life and the unconscious projections that bind us (and others) in webs of our own devising. There are ascetical dimensions of this journey that involve the disciplining of desire and the nonidentification of awareness with various states of mind in silent prayer, including thought patterns, moods, and feelings. The very "self" we imagine ourselves to be, and which is wrapped up in such identifications, mostly unconsciously, is relinquished in this "letting be" of gracious awareness, a process which John frequently refers to as our participation in Christ's death. But this relinquishing is not an act of nihilistic despair that resigns all agency to an impersonal void. It is a primal, naked trust of allowing ourselves to be slowly reconfigured, even "reborn," according to the loving freedom of divine life itself. Viewed in this way, renunciation of self is a movement toward wakeful union with God and the discovery of our true selves in God.

There is aridity in this journey. There is the desert. There is barrenness and the sense of nothingness when our needs and desires for satisfaction are suspended in prayer through the yielding of awareness to That which cannot be immediately seen, felt, or represented. "Preserve a loving attentiveness to God with no desire to feel or understand any particular thing concerning him."[43] Even if it is appropriate for beginners on this journey to find "gratification and satisfaction in the use of images, oratories, and other visible objects of devotion"—and to this we could add various intuitions and concepts about God that mediate something of the reality to which they point—eventually, as the spirit advances in its yearning for God (and not just what I want or imagine God to be), the gratification and satisfaction associated with these mediations begin to diminish and even become obstacles if clung to or conjured up out of boredom, frustration, or failing trust. Even the most sublime of spiritual experiences (e.g., subtle intuitions and resplendent visions, tears of compunction and tears of gratitude, inspiring ideas and rapturous recollections) must eventually be recognized for what they are—*creaturely* experiences—and allowed "to be" in open awareness. Neither indulging them nor pushing them away, it "turns only to interior recollection."[44]

On the Contemplative Consummation of Atheism 197

Abbot John Chapman memorably refers to this recollection as "falling in love with a blank." "Hence in 'contemplation,' the intellect is facing a blank, and the will follows it."[45] An influential twentieth-century spiritual director working in the Carmelite tradition, Chapman observes in his *Spiritual Letters* that the "great danger is that people love God for His gifts, and are always on the look out for them, and think all is lost when they have a little aridity; it is hard for them to learn to love aridity, to desire nothing so much as to be perennially dissatisfied with themselves, and full of an entirely vague and unsatisfactory longing for something unknown and unknowable. They have to learn this when they are plunged from time to time in the Obscure Night."[46] Chapman alternatively describes this longing as "absolute confidence in God," "wanting nothing but God," "attention to God, though without thinking of Him," "a sort of suspension," the "perception of your own nothingness," and the "very pure and indefinite and complete conviction that God is everything, and that nothing else is worth having," an "act of love" that "doesn't feel like it, because it isn't *felt* at all."[47] "What do I mean by God?" he asks in one letter. "I have no idea." Or, in another, "We are living in God—in God's action, as a fish in the water." "DO NOTHING. Let God act."[48] There is an elemental passivity in falling so completely into this boundless awareness, a nakedness and simplicity of spirit divested of all agendas, aims, and self-projections. "The great thing is to *accept*, but nothing more. Never mix your *self* up with God's work."[49] "God does everything." And yet this "ought not to produce passivity in other things," Chapman insists. No prescription for quietism here. "You should be as energetic, or more energetic, in all you do."[50]

The paradox between "nothing" and "everything" here can only be resolved by living it, as we shall have occasion to explore further below, but it is worth emphasizing that aridity is not itself permanent or a special state of mind to be sought. Contemplation is not about manufacturing feelings of emptiness with inward, vacant stares. Neither does it result in pessimism, obscurantism, or the inability to judge, act, or love. It is, rather, the accommodation of the whole human person to the gracious simplicity of God, and the slow, almost imperceptible discovery of that luminous awareness wherein all thoughts, feelings, and sensations arise and dissolve—the "simple intention" of the "real ME," as Chapman puts it.[51] There is indeed an unknowing in this discovery, but not a lack of *cognizance*. Although no discernible "what" avails itself for the mind to grasp, there is an unmistakable and utterly reliable "who" for the spirit to accept—a "pure *Who*," in the words of Merton. "He is the 'Thou' before whom our inmost 'I' springs into awareness. He is the I Am before whom with our own most personal and inalienable voice we echo 'I am.'"[52] If aridity accompanies this mystagogical journey, feeling at times like deprivation, doubt, or the absence of God altogether, even these can be eventually recognized as temporary subjective registrations of God's nonobjectifiable and unfailing presence. The darkness of faith is not something in itself—John does not mean to reify darkness as a kind of "thing" or "state"—but merely a function of "the divine light of contemplation" when it "strikes a soul not yet entirely illumined." Just as unadjusted eyes endure pain and disorientation when flooded by pure light, so does the soul experience "spiritual darkness" when struck by that which "surpasses the act of natural understanding. . . . This is why St. Dionysius and other mystical theologians call this infused contemplation a 'ray of darkness'—that is, for the soul not yet illumined and purged."[53]

Aridity is passage, not destination. It implies difficult growth, not permanent stagnation. As Buckley puts it, "Gradually out of this night arises a surrender to One whose incomprehensibility defies the immediate demands for conceptualization and satisfaction, and whose influence brings the person to a new kind of prayer that is peaceful, deeply loving, and without images."[54]

Beyond Every Denial

The deeper significance of this contemplative itinerary for our engagement with atheism is that it explicitly recognizes our habitual tendency to identify God with our human projections. Yet it does not stop there. True apophaticism does not conclude with a denial. It does not take our negations as absolute, which would simply turn our denials into implacable judgments, without any recourse to new experience or insight. "*It is also beyond every denial.*" The negation of

On the Contemplative Consummation of Atheism 199

negation in Pseudo-Dionysius is not finally atheistic in attitude, nor does it leave us in an intellectual lurch as to *whether* God exists. And although intriguing parallels may exist between them, neither is the negative theology of the Areopagite or John of the Cross or Thomas Merton the same as the deconstructionist's stance of "holy undecidability" between theism and atheism.[55] This is not to dismiss outright such stances or the possibility that they, too, may possess their own spiritual integrity, but only to point out that apophaticism in a Christian theological key takes the limitations of our concepts of God with utmost seriousness by commending a way of life leading to transformative *union* with the God who surpasses all comprehension.

As Lossky maintains, negative theology is not primarily a theory of ecstasy, nor a philosophical school of speculation, but "an expression of that fundamental attitude which transforms the whole of theology into a contemplation of the mysteries of revelation."[56] In this respect we should not relegate apophaticism or mystical theology to some special domain, esoteric or otherwise, separated from the very heart of Christian life. To oppose "spirituality" and "doctrine" in this way rests upon a fatal mistake, for it neglects the inherently mystagogical function of doctrine. "There is . . . no Christian mysticism without theology; but, above all, there is no theology without mysticism."[57] Like Buckley's contention that dogma serves to safeguard divine mystery while providing an itinerary for our induction into that mystery, Lossky regards *theosis* as the ultimate end of Christian life and thus dogma as pragmatic in nature.[58] Dogmas "constitute the foundation of mysticism."[59] Or again: "Apophaticism teaches us to see above all a negative meaning in the dogmas of the Church: it forbids us to follow natural ways of thought and to form concepts which would usurp the place of spiritual realities." This by no means denies concepts their orienting and disclosive function but rather points out their supporting role in "raising the mind to those realities which pass all understanding." To this end, the antinomic character of much doctrine, such as we find in the christological dogmas or in *creatio ex nihilo* — on the one hand x, on the other y, neither x nor y, beyond x and y, and so on — serve as markers for holding creative tensions together so that imagination and thought might be propelled beyond themselves into the living mysteries they portend. "It is not a question of suppressing the antinomy by adapting dogma to our understanding, but of a change of heart and mind enabling us to attain to the contemplation of the reality which reveals itself to us as it raises to God, and unites us, according to our several capacities, to Him."[60]

It should be obvious by now that the mystagogical path traced here is not fashioned principally as an "answer" to atheism, in the sense of adducing various arguments to meet intellectual challenges to theistic faith. There is a place for such an endeavor, and some of the best examples draw liberally from traditions of negative and mystical theology in order to highlight the limited nature of atheistic denials. To state the matter briefly, if somewhat provocatively, too often atheistic critique isn't atheistic *enough*. It is insufficiently rigorous in its denials, too confident in claiming to know what *God* actually means, as indeed it must if its denials are to stick. The main shortcoming with most arguments against theistic faith is the deep-seated habit of conceiving of God as *a* being among others, as some force or cause within the universe, an Intelligent Designer, perhaps a superlative being alongside (and therefore negatively defined by) the universe. Virtually every atheistic objection to faith presupposes some contrastive logic in its construal of the God-world relation, as though God and world were situated within a spectrum of being, within an encompassing horizon of potency and value, with God as the "highest" being acting upon "lesser" beings. Yet in all such cases we are really referring to something like a demiurge, to a godlike entity operating within a network of causes, a superior subject within an immemorial flow of becoming, not the inexhaustible, eternal wellspring of all that is—the eternal One who freely gives all things "to be." To begin speaking of God properly so that we might know what we are denying requires following a series of denials that go well beyond the usual compass of atheistic critique. This is why Turner describes modern atheism as a form of "arrested apophaticism." It denies, but only so far. By denying that God "exists," an atheist might find it surprising to learn just how readily a Pseudo-Dionysius, or a Thomas Aquinas, or a Meister Eckhart would agree, as all of them deny that God can be said to "exist" in any univocal sense, that is, as *an* existent among others.[61] "It falls neither within the predicate of nonbeing nor of being," writes Pseudo-Dionysius. "It is beyond assertion and denial."[62] Or the Angelic Doctor: "Now, because we cannot know what God is, but rather what He is not, we have no means for considering how God is, but rather how He is not."[63] Or Meister Eckhart with his typical homiletic daring: "For God is nothing: not in the sense of having no being. He is neither *this* nor *that* that one can speak of: He is being above all being. He is beingless being."[64]

To appreciate why such statements are not absurdities requires serious intellectual effort and not a little intellectual humility. But it also entails a self-implicating discipline to fully explore. Along these lines, David Bentley Hart complains that those who seem the most confident in their public denunciations of theistic faith, and who routinely demand knockdown proofs and empirical demonstrations, seem the "least willing to undertake the specific kinds of mental and spiritual discipline that all the great religious traditions say are required to find God."[65] Hart is referring here to various public intellectuals who have gained notoriety for their atheistic (or even anti-theistic) stances, couched usually within a naturalistic worldview. The point is applicable more broadly than to vocal polemicists, however. The invitation includes anyone with a sincere interest—atheist, agnostic, and theist alike—in discovering what *God* might really refer to or what it opens up for the genuine seeker. If truly serious in investigating the question of God from an experimental standpoint, and not only through argumentation, then one ought to be prepared to at least consult those practical traditions that are exquisitely attuned for just such an exploration. Though by no means the only appropriate discipline to commend in this respect, Hart suggests that contemplative discipline "is peculiarly suited to (for want of a better word) an 'empirical' exploration of that mystery." This is so because, as "a specific discipline of thought, desire, and action," it is "one that frees the mind from habitual prejudices and appetites, and allows it to dwell in the gratuity and glory of all things."[66] Far from being anti-intellectual, the practice of contemplative prayer "is among the highest expressions of rationality possible, a science of consciousness and of its relation to the being of all things, requiring the most intense devotion of mind and will to a clear perception of being and consciousness in their unity."[67]

The appeal to science here is meant in the ancient sense of the term—as practical wisdom (*phronesis*) rather than technical mastery.

For while there is an obvious sense in which contemplative practice is a discipline involving repeated acts of attending and discerning, often through the skillful coordination of body, heart, and mind, such repeated acts, as they become habitual, are not meant to acquire something special, whether peaceful feelings or discrete unitive experiences, but more simply to notice and gradually become released from the various compulsions to "have" or "do" or "be" anything at all. There is indeed a kind of activity here, but it is one of "un-doing," or perhaps "non-ado": the cultivation of that basic, wakeful receptivity whereby the habitual thought patterns and affective registrations normally conditioning experience begin to loosen up and become ever more transparent to the spacious luminosity of awareness itself. With seasons of practice, and with a learned patience for accepting the disorientation, ambiguity, doubt, failure, and boredom that likely accompany it—all of which may feel like the absence or darkness at various points— something in us begins to take root and silently declare itself:

> Something deeper begins to attract us, and this something deeper is more spacious, alluring, and silent than the tediously dramatic opera scores of inner chatter. The inner chatter will be present, but its grip on our attention loosens. It is as though this mass of thoughts and feelings was a brick wall that once obstructed our vision. But gradually we see that the sense of this wall's solidity is a creation of our identification with these thoughts and feelings. It is not a wall after all but a window. We can actually see through this mass of thoughts into something else in which they are immersed and saturated. This "something else" is untouched and free of all thoughts, even as it suffuses, and permeates, and knows how to do nothing other than be one with all. Something is being born of the practice of silence, and this leads us into Silence itself.[68]

Notice in Martin Laird's elegant summary that contemplative practice allows us to become witnesses to the flow of the discursive mind rather than identified with it. Such nonpossessive awareness notices thoughts without clinging to them. It allows feelings without indulging them. It "lets be" without pushing anything away. It

On the Contemplative Consummation of Atheism 203

welcomes without holding. It is fully present without overwhelming. It is detached but not avoiding. It is alert yet restricting nothing.

As we relax ever more deeply into this silent awareness, learning how to trust in it more than any particular object *of* awareness, yielding to awareness itself rather than requiring it to "do" or "be" any particular thing, gradually we discover that the thoughts and feelings constantly percolating through awareness are in fact grounded by a deeper awareness that remains pacific and free, wholly unassuming and unfailingly present in all our experience as its spacious ground. Thoughts and feelings do not necessarily cease to arise, nor are they rejected, but they become transparent to the basic luminosity of awareness itself. More and more we begin to "see" just how much we are constructively engaged in all our experience; how much our thoughts and feelings are disclosive of reality, yet also refracting or distorting of it, and in any case hardly exhaustive of it. We become more sensitive to the projective nature of our experience and how prone we are to reifying others, ourselves, and God, as though the discrete contents of our experience coincide with what they point to, stably and without remainder.

As this open awareness becomes more established in prayer, forming something like an inner climate, and as it begins to suffuse everyday life through the loosening up of feelings and thoughts from their typical reactivity, allowing us to grow more generous and freer in our encounters with others, less bound by mental habits that screen out the adventitious quality of things, then so do we become more freshly awakened to what *God* might possibly mean. God becomes less tethered to images and concepts, though not merely opposing them either. God becomes less and less substantialized, less thinglike, less identifiable with any particular object *of* awareness, whether in the form of affirmations or denials, and more and more like an unutterably felt vastness upholding and pervading our lives. Neither *this* nor *that*, as Eckhart says, and yet utterly reliable in its nonlocalizable unfolding. As St. Symeon the New Theologian writes, "When the mind is simple, or rather stripped of all concepts and completely clothed in the simple light of God and hidden within it, it can find no other object in which it is established to which it can direct the motion of its thought. It remains in the depths of God's light and can see nothing outside. This is what the saying means: God is light (1 John 1:5). God is the supreme light, . . . the repose of all contemplation."[69]

Passages such as these, which run throughout the Christian contemplative tradition like a golden thread, may not amount to any kind of "proof" for theistic faith in the face of atheistic critique—that is not the point—but they do refer us to an extensive body of testimony highlighting the experimental basis for some of its most fundamental claims. The assertion that God is not in any sense an object in the world, or the insistence that God's radical transcendence is the most immanent reality of our lives—the One *in* whom we live, and move, and have our being—is here given articulation on the basis of a living practice, not just speculation. No doubt formulated through a process of reflection that is conversant with, and informed by, theological tradition, there is a practiced way of life replete with a set of embodied skills, mental habits, and cultivated dispositions that provide something like a living "verification" of that tradition. As Sebastian Moore puts it, an "*experience* of 'without-whom-nothing' is replacing a *concept* of 'without-whom-nothing.'"[70] If the concept of God remains vitally important as a pointer, just as dogma more generally remains important as informative and expressive of this reality, concepts nevertheless do not substitute for the experience of the infinite. Just as important, contemplative realization does not render all conceptualization otiose. On the contrary, it "gives to that concept a peculiar validity, an edge of meaning, which it would not otherwise have."[71] There is a mutually informing relationship between conceptuality and nonconceptuality here. For if contemplative awakening infuses the concept of God with direct knowledge—an experimental knowing of the "absolute and all-conditioning quality that the mystic obscurely knows to be his who is embracing him"—then the contribution of conceptuality is, in turn, to affirm at the "level of rational philosophic wonder and discourse, that total mastery of God which the mystic obscurely knows at first hand."[72] Conceptuality gives something vitally important to such direct knowledge as well: practical orientation, communicability, the possibility of intersubjective agreement, and deepened understanding. Here we find an organic relationship between doctrine and experience, between conceptual articulation and nonconceptual realization, between dogma and mystery.

On the Contemplative Consummation of Atheism 205

The main contribution that a mystagogical understanding of doctrine makes for our purposes here is that the question of God is best understood as an outstanding invitation to explore rather than an intellectual problem to settle at arm's length. The question refers us to a mystagogical process that is inhabitable, repeatable, and in a certain sense verifiable by others. This is not to deny the inherently graced character of contemplative discovery, of course, which is by no means a matter of mechanical reproduction or technique, but rather to point to a living tradition of exemplars whose imitation and guidance opens up a path for giving the question of God an edge of meaning it would not otherwise have. No one is required to undertake such an exploration, but neither is it adequate to render definitive judgments about it without first having tasted it.

PATIENCE WITH GOD

Throughout this chapter we have been exploring the purgative dimensions of Christian faith. Beginning with the provocative suggestion that Christian revelation may imply some kind of atheism, at least insofar as the Gospels disidentify God from any "sacral order," we pursued the possibility that the purgative thrust of Christian faith shares surprising commonalities with atheistic critique as it concerns our tendency to fashion God (or the gods) in our own image. Both Christian faith and atheistic critique recognize this projective propensity, even if they arrive at significantly different conclusions as to its ultimate significance. Whereas atheism rejects the idea of God altogether, seeing in it a historically powerful but ultimately illusory projection of the human mind, mature Christian faith generally understands the critique of this projective tendency as the purification of the notion of God rather than its renunciation. To this extent, atheistic critique can be welcomed as a source of internal critique for Christian faith rather than dismissed as an enemy. As Rahner observes, the struggle with atheism "is foremost and of necessity a struggle against the inadequacy of our own theism."[73] This view is not unlike a crucial point made by Turner, which is that if atheisms are usually too limited in their denials, this may have just as much to do with the limited nature of many Christian theisms upon which they typically depend. Atheism and theism are often mirror images of each other, historically speaking, and so every opportunity a Christian has to engage atheistic critique is one that can be approached as potentially coming to a richer understanding of God. "Christians themselves need to be every kind of atheist possible in order to deny every kind of idolatry possible: for much atheism, as one knows it today, is but the negation of the limited features of a particular idolatry."[74]

Tomáš Halík has eloquently made a similar appeal in a more pastoral vein. A Czech Roman Catholic priest, sociologist, and theologian secretly ordained during the era of communist rule, Halík has garnered broad interest among those who find themselves pulled between theism and atheism, or, more precisely, those who feel moved by spiritual yearnings and barely articulate aspirations for human fullness, and yet who find no institutional or religiously communal space to call home. What Charles Taylor calls the "cross-pressures" at work in our secular (or postsecular) age fairly well captures the dynamic complexity and ambiguity out which Halík speaks:

> The striking fact about the modern cosmic imaginary is that it is uncapturable by any one range of views. It has moved people in a whole range of directions, from (almost) the hardest materialism through to Christian orthodoxy; passing by a whole range of intermediate positions. . . . [It] has opened a space in which people can wander between and around all these options without having to land clearly and definitively in any one. In the wars between belief and unbelief, this can be seen as a kind of no-man's-land . . . [or an] open space where you can feel the winds pulling you, now to belief, now to unbelief.[75]

For Halík's part, the point is not to expose atheism as a lie but to embrace it as an incomplete truth. It is "unfinished work, an unresolved matter, an uncompleted building." Atheism is (or at least can be) useful as "an antithesis to naive, vulgar theism," and to this extent it contributes to the purgative thrust of theism itself, even if "it is necessary to take a further step toward synthesis and mature belief."[76] This next step does not mean operating out of a combative spirit but rather deeply attending to, internalizing, and creatively responding to unresolved tensions through a more inclusive and generous spirit. It exhibits nothing of the retrenchment that is characteristic of more fundamentalist responses to secular modernity, but neither does it baptize secular modernity as historical destiny or renege on the obligation to criticize its excesses, contradictions, and ideological blind spots. Instead, it ventures into the gray zones of belief and unbelief, into the betweenness that many inchoately feel with respect to their ultimate attitudes toward God. With fraternal feeling and skillful patience, it offers itself as a living dialogue and as an openness to a faith yet to come. It is necessary to "live the faith also *from the standpoint of our profound solidarity with people who are religiously seeking, and, if need be, with those who experience God's hiddenness and transcendence 'from the other side.'*"[77]

This attitude of solidarity-in-seeking is not wishy-washy or lacking in theological conviction. It is not undecided as to whether it is theistic or atheistic. It is not cagey about religious doctrine. It grows out of a commitment to what doctrine implies. "God is mystery—that should be the first and last sentence of any theology."[78] This is the heart of Christian doctrine, as Buckley stressed above, and for Halík it is important to appreciate how faith and atheism can reflect two sides of this single mystery. Precisely because God is not an object in the world but radically transcendent to it, atheism can be interpreted as reflecting, however partially and negatively, something of that transcendence. "God definitely *is not* in the sense that *we are*, or things *are*, or the world *is*. It is that radical difference between His existence and our existence in the world that provides the scope for the existence of atheism and agnosticism—and also faith."[79] Here we see Halík making explicit appeal to the "the distinction" as a way to appreciate how both atheism and theism are possible as human responses to our ultimate situation. Because God is not ready-to-hand as a being *in* the world, then we should not be surprised, but rather come to expect, that atheism is an interpretive possibility as we reflect upon our ultimate situation. We need not say a necessary interpretation, but a genuine possibility. Perhaps this point is not sufficiently appreciated by those who categorically affirm or deny God's existence, as though its meaning were completely conspicuous to reason and finally resolvable with a simple yes or no. Of course there can be a yes to this mystery, even a passionate faith that commits itself unreservedly to living out its assent with hope and love, and yet it is never a thing to be grasped or fully comprehended, since the very "object" of faith is beyond all stable objectification, which is to say, no-*thing*. Faith is always on the way, a matter of pilgrimage, mystagogical.

Lest this account of divine transcendence be imagined as rendering God so remote as to become irrelevant or a mere riddle for human existence—a *deus absconditus* that seems only to frustrate the questing spirit or lead to permanent indecision—Halík, in classic contemplative fashion, insists upon the unrestricted intimacy of this mystery. "Yet God is not only hidden, He is also *watchful*—He reveals Himself and sees those who seek Him, as scripture says about divine wisdom."[80] God is not just some imagined end point of human seeking but the generative source *of* our seeking. God is *in* our seeking, the silent *aware-ing* behind and within our awareness, so to speak. "*He is in our openness.* Rather than our 'counterpart,' He is foundation, the fount not only of our existence but also of what our existence achieves. He is therefore also the foundation and fount of our seeking, our watchfulness, our openness, our self-transcendence."[81] Whereas typically we might be inclined to imagine ourselves as the origin of our seeking, the ground zero of our deepest aspirations and yearnings, it turns out upon closer discernment that all our seeking is in fact a response to an anterior call. "My" seeking, "my" openness, "my" yearning is really, and more fundamentally, something like an echo of a seeking prior to any "me" at all. The yearning arising within the self, which propels the self beyond itself, is in fact born out of an anterior movement that appears to have no discrete beginning and is by no means possessable or fully explicable by the self. Our seeking is a reverberation of God's own "self-pouring" in creation. "He 'pours Himself out' not only *into* our seeking; He is not in it simply as a *thing* we could look for—certainly we could never find Him among the 'things' and objective existences. God is present in *our very seeking*—and He is present in the world also through our seeking."[82] Put another way, the very dynamism of human self-transcendence, or what we might call the *eros* of human aspiration—the aspiration for ultimate meaning, for truth, for unconditional love and communion—is itself a participation in God's own life: God's own "yearning" in us, so to speak, which is immanent to creation as its source and ground. As Pseudo-Dionysius puts it, "The divine longing [*eros*] is Good seeking good for the sake of the Good. That yearning which creates all the goodness of the world preexisted superabundantly within the Good and did not allow it to remain without issue. It stirred him to use the abundance of his powers in the production of the world."[83]

This well-known passage concerning the self-diffusiveness of the Good foreshadows the main focus of the next chapter, but here it is worth highlighting, by way of conclusion, that contemplative discovery has potential for reframing theological engagements with atheistic critique altogether. The point is concerned less with offering intellectual defenses in the context of public debate, which have their place, and more with inquiring into the spirit of inquiry itself—its giftedness and unconditionality. The mere fact that we are moved by an ineffable yearning at all, moved by the search for truth, beauty, and goodness; the fact that we are creatures capable of wonderment and perplexity before the prospects of conditioned existence; the fact that we long for ultimacy in our lives, an abiding purpose and unrestricted acceptance of our being: all of this can be regarded as indirect (if still very real) testimony of a yearning radically prior to us, and which in fact is *given* to us, luring us beyond ourselves in *ekstasis*. Even though we are constantly tempted to "fill in" this longing with something finite and intermediate, perhaps attaching ourselves to ideas, forms of life, other persons, or collective causes that seem to harness what we are looking for, the path for fulfilling this longing, paradoxically enough, is learning ever more deeply to *allow* it. This longing is not something we "do" or "have" so much as it is something we *are*.

This is what I take, finally, to be the significance of Halík's suggestion that atheism is not so much wrong as it is insufficiently patient. This is not to deny that the sense of God's absence is not a real experience, or that the ambiguities and painful realities of life are not grave enough to lead some to the full-throated conviction that God is dead. And yet this felt absence is not a brute fact. It is an interpretable reality. "Hardly anything points toward God and calls as urgently for God as the experience of His absence." A mature faith in a secular (or postsecular) age is one that will have learned how to "incorporate those experiences that some call 'the death of God' or—less dramatically—God's silence."[84] It will have learned patience with God in the midst of this silence. And to do that, it will learn a great deal from the contemplative and mystical traditions of Christian faith, which, in their cruciformity, can help us learn what it means to live *into* that absence, purged and purified. "Crucified inwardly and outwardly with Christ," writes John of the Cross, "you will live in this life with fullness and satisfaction of soul, and possess your soul in patience (Luke 21:19)."[85]

CHAPTER SIX

Return to Love

THE INNER LAW OF LOVE

One of the refrains running throughout this book concerns the gratuity of creation—the sheer *fact* that anything exists at all rather than nothing, and the spontaneous sense of wonderment that arises when *recognizing* this fact. We have considered how the felt sense of creation's gratuity, in the sense of contemplatively "letting it in," is far more than an intellectual acknowledgment made in passing. It is a never-ending recognition, a boundless source of intuition we can never fully absorb or finally articulate. We can never think ourselves to the bottom of it, or lay exhaustive imaginative claim to it, for wonderment is the very wellspring of thinking and imagination. The upsurge of intuition that comes with recognizing the sheer givenness of things may induce astonishment in us, and perhaps a bit of vertigo, but we can also become mistrustful toward it, or just indifferent, jaded even, as the result of accumulated habits and preoccupations that blunt our perceptual, affective, and cognitive capacities. We can overlook what is right underneath our noses and grow cold to that basic sense of aliveness which is the precognitive condition for appreciating what *God* or *creation* might possibly mean. For while we may not be able to deduce from this intuition the existence of a creator God, at least in terms of rationalistic proofs, we will not even be attuned to the question of God, or to the possibility that all things are bestowed out of infinite freedom and love, unless we are open to the surprising *thereness* of everything we experience and know. The biblical affirmation that God is the eternal reality within whom all things live and move and have their being simply cannot be heard, much less believed, unless we first allow ourselves to be grasped by the fundamental mystery of our being at all—a mystery that, as Karl Rahner notes, is not provisional or negative but primordial and constitutive of our basic lucidity as self-aware beings, inmost to all our growth in knowing and loving.[1]

By highlighting the gratuity of creation in this way, and even referring to it as "good for nothing" or "without a why" (chapter 2), I do not intend to impute arbitrariness to God's creative act. It is not as though creation might as well not be, or that our agapeic origination makes no difference to God. Although we must consistently maintain that God does not create out of ontological lack, or on the basis of externally imposed necessity, there are deep reasons for creation we must discern if we wish to know just what "good for nothing" and "without a why" mean to convey—reasons that are internal to God, as it were, and expressive of God's inmost life and essence. Thomas Merton's statement from the previous chapter already suggests as much, insofar as love is the *reason for our being*. To put it this way affirms that love has its own reasons: that divine freedom is not an indiscriminate display of naked power but infinitely rich in content and inwardly determined by goodness for the other; that although unconditioned and ever-surprising in its prodigality, divine love is not something like a restless, primal urge of cathartic self-expansion but an inexhaustible fullness of creative self-donation, wholly luminous to itself and inherently inviting of participation. Though God lacks for nothing, it is entirely *fitting* that God creates and summons that which is other than God into being—for the sake of this other. It is *proper* that God shares the plenitude of divine life with that which is not-God, calling "into being what does not exist" (Rom. 4:17). It is so fitting and proper, in fact, that we can risk saying it is "necessary," not in the sense of compulsion, which would contradict everything we have insisted upon regarding divine freedom, but with *love's necessity*.

God is love (1 John 4:8). It is impossible for God not to be God. It is impossible for God not to be love. And while we can (and must)

Return to Love 213

affirm that love is actualized absolutely in intratrinitarian life, such that God need not posit a world in order to be this love in God's self, when we receive this love from the inmost depths of our being, and as we reflect further upon God's kenotic outpouring in history that ultimately assumes our humanity in the hypostatic union of natures—not just for a time but for eternity, irrevocably—then perhaps we might be excused for pressing the conceptual boundaries between freedom and necessity when accounting for God's creative act, or at least pointing beyond their binary opposition through complimentary acts of saying and unsaying. Perhaps we might even dare to say, along with Sergius Bulgakov, that God's love is so utterly free, so full in itself, that it could not fail to create the world; that creation expresses something of the "inner law of love."[2]

In this final chapter, I wish to draw out several of the themes developed throughout this book and bring them full circle, but now with a focus on God's summoning of creation as eternally ordered toward the incarnation. If the previous chapter highlighted the purgative dimensions of the mystagogical journey, inasmuch as it involves a long letting go of various ways we grasp at self, other, and God, this chapter emphasizes that all such ungrasping is fundamentally about receiving God's self-gift more deeply and living more fully into our capacities for communion with others. Taking seriously the purgative-unitive (death-resurrection) dynamic of the Christian faith, the spiritual path of dispossession must be shown as having nothing to do with transcending our creatureliness, as though aspiring for some pseudo-mystical plane abstracted from the world of phenomena and relationship. Rather, it orients us toward an ever-richer, ever-more-inclusive embrace of our creatureliness in all its fragility, concreteness, and interdependence. Growth in God implies growth in creatureliness and vice versa. As the great Flemish mystic John Ruusbroec puts it, the more we are drawn into God's "superessential unity," abiding therein "without intermediary in blissful rest," the more we will actively "flow forth" to all creatures in "common love."[3] Union with God entails a systole-diastole rhythm in which we are rendered ever more available for the "common life" of creation.[4]

This common life has its foundation in the all-embracing dynamism of the incarnation. In dialogue with Rahner, Bulgakov, and other theological figures who boldly explore the anthropocosmic character of God becoming flesh, this chapter proceeds by first unpacking the significance of *creatio ex nihilo* as an act of divine self-bestowal. It will then focus on the incarnation as the inmost reason and entelechy for the whole of creation's unfolding. The complementary insights of Rahner and Bulgakov will be our main guides throughout these first two movements. As will become clear, my approach to reading these two figures together is aimed principally at exploring their convergences on issues in incarnational theology. While Rahner has been a regular companion throughout this book, engagement with Bulgakov's more visionary style allows some of the daring aspects of Rahner's theology to emerge with greater force. At the same time, Bulgakov's ambitious (and at times idiosyncratic) approach to the theological tradition, while immensely generative, can gain further clarity and ecumenical flexibility through a sustained dialogue with Rahner. Meanwhile, their coupling provides a platform for synthetic and constructive work of my own, particularly as the chapter pivots to more recent developments in Christian theology that draw greater attention to the more-than-human world. Referred to as "deep incarnation," this paradigmatic shift in theology makes more explicit God's redemptive and divinizing love as inclusive of the entire community of creation, of which human beings are a precious part. This more inclusive vision is thoroughly biblical in spirit and content, and yet it represents a heightened awareness of the ecological crisis we currently face as a consequence of the human tendency to grasp at our creatureliness. In light of this tendency, the chapter concludes by suggesting ways a contemplative sensibility can help us recognize the inherent dignity of the nonhuman other and our interdependence with all creatures. In this way we share in God's own "letting be."

The Way of Antinomy

I begin by recalling the "ways of mindfulness" gestured at by William Desmond. As discussed in the previous chapter, the way of mindfulness characteristic of contemplative awareness, in contrast to the instrumentalizing mind that seeks control through technical manipulation and conceptual mastery, is nonpossessive. Delighting in paradox, patient with "betweenness," wide-eyed with wonderment, open to the felt sense of things, such awareness is attitudinally hospitable to the way things appear in their surprising *thereness*. Fully recognizing the situational need for more instrumental styles of mindfulness in human life, and by no means spurning the crucial, mediating role of conceptual activity, Desmond nevertheless maintains that because ours is an age increasingly dominated by calculative, bureaucratic, commodifying, and univocalizing ways of thinking—all of which present a clear and present danger to the value of human life in its ecological milieu—we are in great need of rehabilitating ways of mindfulness attuned to the "elemental affirmation of being at all." This is an "ontological yes" in that it is not determined by anything other than the primordial goodness of the yes itself.[5] The spontaneity of such yes-saying may take the mode of silent beholding, but no less important are exercises of imagination and language in their poetical, playful, and plurivocal modalities. Our whole field of imagination and language needs unclogging and recharging—in a word, "agapeic resurrection."[6]

It is with this rehabilitating work in view that I introduce Bulgakov into the mix. Arguably the greatest Orthodox theologian of the twentieth century, the entire thrust of Bulgakov's theology, his "Sophiology," could reasonably be described as exploring the "betweenness" of all reality—its *metaxic* character. Observing that Christianity has long sought to hold together contrary tendencies, the one more dualistic and the other more monistic, Bulgakov insists that Christian faith offers a path for envisioning and living into the dynamic *relation* of God and world, or what he broadly refers to as the Divine-humanity.[7] Noting the all-too-human tendency to fix reality according to a binary framework—"either God, or the world"[8]—but also admitting that Christian faith has variously succumbed to this tendency, oscillating at times between excessively "other-worldly" and "this-worldly" stances, the "fundamental dogma of Christianity concerning Divine-humanity" means to establish a more integral path that embraces distinctions in dynamic unity. "Divine-humanity represents a dogmatic call both to spiritual ascesis and to creativity, to salvation from the world and to a salvation of the world."[9] Neither dualistic nor monistic in bearing, a theology informed by the Divine-humanity reflects the wisdom of both-and. Attuned to relations and not just things, it perceives patterns of wholeness beyond the mere assemblage of parts. Prizing explicitness and uniqueness, it is even more sensitive to the implicit depth dimension from which all articulation arises. Welcoming of contrasts and never seeking their premature closure, it discerns the shared energies springing them forth in open-ended intermediation.

It is just this capacity for embracing tensions, or what Bulgakov regularly refers to as antinomies, that characterizes the highest vocation (but also the outer limits) of all theological reflection. Like Nicholas of Cusa's *coincidentia oppositorum*, and thus unlike any dialectical system which would conceptually enclose contradictions within itself, antinomic thinking in theology "is generated by the recognized inadequacy of thinking to its subject or its tasks; it reveals *the insufficiency* of the powers of human reason which is compelled to stop at a certain point, for it reaches a precipice and an abyss, while at the same time it cannot help but go as far as that point."[10] This last phrase is telling, for by no means does the recognition of reason's insufficiency in relation to its ultimate object (i.e., God) result in a lack of intellectual nerve. On the contrary, the activity of theology, which is as much an exercise of reason as it is of faith, is catalyzed by creative tensions that perpetually spring it forth in ecstasy. It does not resolve these tensions by finally synthesizing them, or by collapsing one pole into the other, but embraces them in their extremity, even highlighting their differences to the extent possible.

To take a chief example, Bulgakov insists that no logical bridge can resolve the ineradicable *difference* between God and creation. There is an "absolute hiatus, a bottomless abyss" that distinguishes divine transcendence from all we experience and know as creatures.[11] "The transcendent God is the eternally unknowable, inaccessible, unattainable, ineffable Mystery to which there exists no approximation."[12] In keeping with the Pseudo-Dionysian path of negation, including the negation of negation, God is referred to as "NOT-what (and NOT-how, NOT-where, NOT-when, NOT-why). This Not is not even *nothing*, insofar as a relation to some sort of *something* is connected with it . . . [but] is *Super-something*. NOT-what does not have any definitions of *something*; it is without qualities, or more precisely, super-qualified."[13] The alpha privative of negative theology is logically different from any philosophical or theological endeavor to conceptually link God with "nothing" in terms of pure potentiality or the "formless" ground of being, such as we find in the meontologies of Boehme, Schelling, and Hegel. It negates even these, insisting, "There is not and cannot be any natural transition from this NO-thing to SOME-thing that is accessible to understanding."[14] Before this "abyss of mystery" there can only be "sacred ignorance," which for Bulgakov, as in the Christian mystical tradition more generally, is registered with "a gesture, a surge, a motion, not a thought, not a word. It is music, inexpressible in word, an experience that cannot be thought out, an exit (*transcensus*) beyond one's very self." The NOT of the Absolute negates every expression, even negative expression itself, and demands the "fullest renunciation" of any pretense to comprehension, even as it invites our hearts and minds to loving self-surrender in its midst.[15]

Several of the themes developed in the previous chapter are crystallized here, for Bulgakov is quite sensitive to the projective aspects of human consciousness and our tendency to fashion God (or gods) out of our own image and needs. The purgative work of negative theology means to educate this projective tendency: not to reject it entirely, which would be inhuman, but to make us more critically aware of it by therapeutically opening our affective and intellectual horizons to That which infinitely surpasses them. There is no limit to this negation, in fact, not even when it comes to the "existence" of God. "One cannot say about the Absolute that IT exists, just as one cannot say that IT does not exist: here the human word falls silent, and remains only a taciturn philosophical-mystical gesture, a negation, a naked NOT."[16] With this gesture we are plunged into that "mysterious darkness of unknowing" of the Areopagite, who in *The Mystical Theology* writes of renouncing "all that the mind may conceive" and belonging "completely to him who is beyond everything. Here, being neither oneself nor someone else, one is supremely united to the completely unknown by an inactivity of all knowledge, and knows beyond the mind by knowing nothing."[17] All of our preconceived notions about the existence or nonexistence of God, and much else besides, are outstripped and purified through the release of our

218 Purgation and Union

habitual identification with conceptual markers and their contents. Such concepts are not disparaged or evacuated of all serviceable meaning, but neither are they are confused or synthesized into a definitive concept. Instead, they are released into the abyssal depths of awareness itself, allowing awareness to be recognized as unrestricted in its openness; empty yet luminous, a "free-flowing vastness and liberating peace that has no opposite," as Martin Laird writes.[18]

Lest this emphasis on unknowing imply that the Absolute is essentially impersonal and unlovable, unrelatable and forever anonymous, Bulgakov insists with equal diligence that the Absolute is epiphanic and self-communicative, not just within itself (as Trinity) but to that which is other than itself (as world). The Absolute does not just abide within unconditioned fullness but manifests itself as the "Absolute-relative," that is, as the Absolute *on behalf of* that which is not-God. The Absolute establishes what is not-itself and in doing so imparts itself. It summons the limited from its unlimited goodness and bestows itself as its inmost depths, allowing the relative "to be" while tarrying with the relative as its God. The "Absolute transcendent sets Itself as God, and consequently, accepts into Itself the distinction between God and the world, which includes the human being."[19] Without ceasing to be the Absolute, and without exhausting the resourcefulness of its illimitable reality, the Absolute nevertheless donates itself in establishing the relative, determining itself in relation to it, even becoming subject (or bound by covenant) to the relative out of love. Only on the basis of this self-communication can we say "God exists": "*He is*, HE is ON, The One Who Is, Yahweh, as he revealed himself to Moses. One cannot say this about the Absolute, for being is a correlative concept; God is *for* humankind or, more broadly, *for* the world. In order that God may be, the world must exist, and it likewise becomes the condition for the being of God. . . . The Absolute in the creation of the world or, to say it better, by the very act of this creation, generates God as well."[20]

We should not misunderstand Bulgakov here. By distinguishing the Absolute and God in this way, and by suggesting that the Absolute "generates" God in the act of creation, Bulgakov does not mean that there are two divine principles, one higher than the other, or that the Absolute is the undifferentiated, formless principle of being, whereas God is the emergent personhood of divinity, inextricably bound up with the world's becoming. There is no "Godhead behind God," as it were, and neither is the triune relationality of God imagined as subordinate to a prior reality, say, a *meonal* principle of "divine nothingness" out of which both God and creation emanate. Bulgakov conducts penetrating investigations into such views as they variously appear in philosophy and theology, both in their pure and mixed forms, including Neoplatonism, Gnosticism, and Cabbala, as well as German mysticism, Idealism, and early Russian Sophiology.[21] Sifting out what is valuable in these strands, but careful to avoid monism, pantheism, and dualism in its various guises, Bulgakov develops a trinitarian pan*en*theism, which is essentially the effort to embrace that most fundamental of antinomies, namely, the Absolute and the relative. We might summarize the matter this way: The Absolute (the Trinity in itself), without forsaking its absoluteness, summons forth that which is other than itself, the world, endowing this other with genuine integrity and a principle of vitality, that is, the opportunity and risk of creaturely self-actualization, a history of becoming. The Absolute thus relates to this other as its Creator and God, as an addressable Thou and covenantal partner in its creaturely sojourn. Creaturely "otherness" is introduced into the Absolute, by the Absolute, but for the sake of this other. "In the Absolute the distinction of God and world appears; it becomes correlative to its very self as to the relative, for God is correlative to the world. *Deus est vox relativa* [God is a relative voice] and in creating the world the Absolute places itself as God."[22]

The Absolute and God are not opposable realities but the coincidence of opposites. God *is not* the Absolute, and yet God *is* the Absolute as "existing for another—precisely the world."[23] There is a being-for-creation in the Absolute, and this we name "God" for the purpose of distinguishing (without opposing) this being-for-creation from the being-in-itself of the Trinity. This is what panentheism really means to signify, as opposed to pantheism or dualism. The created world lives, moves, and has its being in the Trinity, which is why various forms of pantheism (or monism) bear partial truths; and yet the Trinity qualitatively transcends the created world and remains radically Other to it, which is why some forms of dualism bear partial truths.[24]

"God" does not refer to a lesser being in a descending hierarchy, which would amount to ditheism, but is the Absolute *as it relates* to us. We do not know the Absolute as it is in itself, as *ousia*, to borrow Gregory Palamas's well-known distinction. We only know the Absolute in self-communication to us, as God, as divine *energei* establishing us and abiding with us, as participable, reconciling, and deifying.[25]

Bulgakov's distinction between the Absolute and God may pose some challenges to understanding, at least initially, but it expresses an enormously important insight regarding the nondual relation of divine mystery and divine self-communication, as well as the centrality of love in the doctrine of *creatio ex nihilo*. To further appreciate this, and the importance of embracing antinomies in theological practice, let us consider a significant passage from Rahner that carefully charts a parallel path:

> God is not merely the one who as creator establishes a world distant from himself as something different, but rather he is the one who gives himself away to this world and who has his own fate in and with this world. God is not only himself the giver, but he is also the gift. For a pantheistic understanding of existence this statement may be completely obvious. For a Christian understanding of God, in which God and the world are not fused but remain separate [i.e., distinct] for all eternity, *this is the most tremendous statement that can be made about God at all*. Only when this statement is made, when, within a concept of God that makes a radical distinction between God and the world, God himself is still the very core of the world's reality and the world is truly the fate of God himself, only then is the concept of God attained that is truly Christian.[26]

Although not verbally distinguishing God from the Absolute in the manner of Bulgakov, Rahner nevertheless articulates the same basic insight, which is that the ontological distinction between God and creation *is* God's self-bestowal. The genuine otherness of creation abides *within* God; or, what amounts to the same thing, God "gives himself away" as the inmost ground of creation. Creation itself bears the logic of love, of divine kenosis, insofar as God renders divine life wholly available to the eventualities of creaturely becoming, allowing creation to have its own integrity yet binding divine life to its ecstasies and travails, including its tragedies and "God-forsaken" moments out of compassion. Referring to the creativity of God in terms of "self-emptying," Rahner insists, as does Bulgakov, that nothing about this kenotic activity implies the diminishment of divine transcendence. Rather, it is the supreme testament to divine self-bestowal that God, "while remaining the absolute transcendent, nevertheless becomes the innermost principle, the innermost basis, and in the truest sense the goal of 'spiritual' creation. God is not only *causa efficiens* but also *causa quasi formalis* of that which the creature is in the truest and most concrete sense."[27] God is not just absolute reality in itself but the Creator whose summoning of the relative is the elicitation of that which may *receive* God's self-communicating love. Creation is not just *any* other, as it happens, but precisely that other whose being is dynamically oriented toward God. Creation may be ontologically distinct from God, but this difference is one of ontological capacity, of ecstatic openness. "The creature is really *capax infiniti*," which is to say, a finite reality capable of the infinite.[28]

Beguiled by Goodness

The specific character of the Christian understanding of the God-world relationship is coming increasingly into view, along with the incarnational logic that informs it. But before we consider the incarnation more explicitly, we should explore further how antinomic thinking in theological practice can help bring out the more sweeping implications of *creatio ex nihilo* as it concerns divine love. If we reflect further upon the fact that creation is not just *any* other but is constituted by God's self-bestowal, as a "giving away" of God, then we are immediately faced with the realization that creation, which need not be, nevertheless has everything to do with who God eternally *is* and thus may be "necessary" in another sense. That is, we can come at once to a double recognition: while God's creative act is wholly non-compulsory, since without the fullness of freedom it could not be the fullness of love, such love *cannot fail* to give itself away and establish that which is other than itself—precisely for the love of this other. Being what it eternally *is*, divine love cannot fail to "diffuse" itself, to share itself, to render itself participable, to distribute its own freedom and love and goodness to creatures according to their capacities. "In the insatiability of His love," writes Bulgakov, "which is *divinely* satiated in Him Himself, in His own life [as Trinity], God goes out of Himself toward creation, in order to love, outside Himself, not-Himself. This extradivine being is precisely the world, or creation." Such is "*the necessity of love*," adds Bulgakov, "which cannot *not* love, and which manifests and realizes in itself *the identity* and *indistinguishability of freedom and necessity*."[29]

Here we see Bulgakov deliberately pressing beyond the opposition of freedom and necessity, yet holding both together antinomically, paradoxically, in the *coincidence* of their opposition. Freedom and necessity are not dialectically synthesized into a new concept, but neither is their vital tension resolved by surrendering one or the other pole. Were we to synthesize them, we could not help but say that God is love *only* to the extent God posits a world. God would need the world in order to be love, which would essentially make creation the platform for divine self-realization, the cosmogonic projection of God's bid to *become* God. Bulgakov rejects this vampiric view of the God-world relation as biblically, doctrinally, and practically (ideologically) dubious. Instead he heralds the unconditionality of divine love *within* the Absolute, within the perichoretic giving and receiving of trihypostatic life. "God is absolute in His proper, divine life, and He does not need the world for Himself. For Him, the creation or noncreation of the world is not a hypostatic or natural necessity of self-complication, for *tri*hypostatizedness fully exhausts the *hypostatic* self-definition and closes its circle, whereas God's nature is *fullness* that contains the All in itself."[30] The Triune God is the absolute realization of relationship and unity, of personhood and nature, and therefore any relatedness to creation will have its eternal foundation *in* this realization, which is why only God can love in a truly free way, without any coercion or agenda, beyond all calculation and discrimination. "In relation to the life of Divinity itself, the world did not have to be."[31]

Return to Love 223

But this negative formulation of *creatio ex nihilo* is not enough. It is not sufficient to declare that creation did not have to be, however much we attest to its gratuity—the sheer wonderment that it *is* at all. We cannot relinquish the pole of necessity entirely in favor of contentless freedom, for otherwise we would have no way to fend off notions of divine caprice, as though creation were the product of arbitrary will, without any reason or meaning for *God*. To divorce freedom entirely from necessity leads to a deracinated understanding of creation and an impoverished sense of its deep structure, its raison d'être, which is why Bulgakov warns against this tendency as it shows up in nominalism, certain Reformed understandings of divine power, and eventually atheistic philosophies such as Schopenhauer's that interpret the world in terms of the manifestation of pure (i.e., blind) will. Against these tendencies, Bulgakov contends that if divine freedom points to the absence of any determinate necessity that requires the world for divine self-realization, such freedom does not mean that the world is not needed by God in a way that is *proper* to God. Hence the other side of the antinomy:

> God *needs* the world, and it could not have remained uncreated. But God needs the world not for Himself but for the world itself. God is love, and it is proper for love to love and to expand in love. . . . It is proper for the ocean of Divine love to overflow its limits, and it is proper for the fullness of the life of Divinity to spread beyond its bounds. . . . Consequently, God-Love *needs* the creation of the world in order to love, no longer only in His own life, but also outside Himself, in creation.[32]

Here we see Bulgakov walking an antinomic tightrope, perhaps at the very edge of incoherence. While he insists upon the fullness of love *in* the Absolute, he also insists that such fullness is inherently disposed toward the love of the relative, for what is not-Absolute. It pertains to the very character of divine love to love that which is other than itself. It is wholly *fitting* for divine love to pour itself forth in the elicitation of the relative, precisely for the cherishing of the relative. Being Creator is not something in addition to being God. "Rather, God is

224 Purgation and Union

the Creator by virtue of the inner necessity of His nature, divine love, because God is love, which is exhaustive and includes all its modes, and in particular love for creation. One can say that God is the Creator just as essentially as He is the Holy Trinity, the Father, the Son, and the Holy Spirit, that He is God having His nature, having his creation. God's self-determination as the Creator enters into the inmost depths of the divine being."[33]

References to the "fittingness" of creation, like the "fittingness" of the incarnation, are quite common in Christian theology, both Eastern and Western, yet Bulgakov is articulating here something more akin to considerations of the Good in Pseudo-Dionysius, whose *Divine Names* famously describes the Good as "self-diffusive." Indeed, Dionysius goes so far as to attribute "yearning" (or eros) to God's creative dispensation: "The divine longing [*theios eros*] is Good seeking good for the sake of the Good. That yearning which creates all the goodness of the world preexisted superabundantly within the Good and did not allow it to remain without issue. It stirred him to use the abundance of his powers in the production of the world."[34] Dionysius is quite aware of the audacity of this claim. That eros could be predicated of the self-subsisting Good seems contradictory on its face. Agape, sure, but eros? A bestirring movement that draws the lover beyond the self and toward the beloved, issuing from God? How could that which has no need in itself "yearn" for anything else? How could the inexhaustible be "stirred" into an ecstatic movement toward that which lacks self-subsistence? Such eros would seem the exclusive province of creatures, whose yearning for the Good is a self-transcending desire for union, for a fullness they presently lack, for the mutual belonging of creaturely differentiation in loving communion, animated by the One who draws all things unto itself. And yet Dionysius thwarts our expectations by claiming for *eros* a supreme role in God's creative activity, insisting that the very cause of the universe is the "superabundance" of eros. The Good is "carried outside of himself" in loving care for everything it creates. "He is, as it were, beguiled by goodness, by love [*agape*], and by yearning [*eros*] is enticed away from his transcendent dwelling place and comes to abide within all things, and he does so by virtue of his supernatural and ecstatic capacity to remain, nevertheless, within himself."[35]

Return to Love 225

Here again we see in play the greatest of antinomies, whose embrace stretches theology to its utmost limits—just where it belongs. For in the same breath that the Areopagite stresses the ecstatic outpouring of the Good into the multiplicity of creation, as though swept away in self-forgetful yearning for the beloved, so does he maintain that divine ecstasy is born out of eternal self-abidance, a resourcefulness that can never be diminished and which is inherently free. It is both wholly "beyond" itself and entirely "within" itself, without contradiction. If creation is "the divine *eros* in volcanic eruption," as Denys Turner puts it, and thus something like a "boiling over" whereby all creatures flow into existence, the Good nevertheless "retains its apartness in its self-possessed Oneness."[36] The Good remains indivisibly itself, just as it "diffuses" itself wholly for the other. "This essential Goodness, by the very fact of its existence, extends goodness into all things."[37]

When Bulgakov refers to the insatiability of God in the creative overflow of the Trinity, he clearly does not mean an acquisitive desire that requires a discrete object for its satisfaction. Such an understanding is more in the realm of wanting, which has a determinate goal in view. Wanting is fulfilled when its object is obtained, and thus motivated by a lack or appetitive need. Yearning, on the other hand, in the sense evoked by Bulgakov and Dionysius, suggests openness and positive distance, a desire for union that preserves and cherishes betweenness. It is reverberative and elastic, not targeting or enclosing. Yearning does not wish to cease yearning but delights endlessly in it. Its intimacy to the beloved is generous and accommodating. It is differentiating and nonpossessive, even as it seeks the "togetherness of everything."[38] If it "wants" anything, it wants only to give of itself, to lend its being to the other and be joined with the other. Yearning is thus the greatest of capacities—capacity for "unity, an alliance, and a particular commingling in the Beautiful and the Good." Such capacity in fact "preexists through the Beautiful and the Good."[39] Any creaturely yearning for the Beautiful and the Good ultimately comes *from* the Beautiful and the Good, and is preeminently realized therein. Divine yearning for creation is thus an overflow of fullness, not a lack. It is an ever-expansive movement of ecstasy and return: "through the Good, from the Good, in the Good and to the Good, unerringly turning, ever on the same center, ever in the same direction, always proceeding, always remaining, always being restored to itself."[40]

The Areopagite's suggestion that God is "beguiled by goodness," and that this is the reason for something rather than nothing, may seem quite hyperbolic—an "as though" speculation we needn't take too seriously, perhaps a bit of rhetorical indiscretion. But the discussion immediately adjacent confirms its serious intent. It is indeed hyperbolic, but in the richer sense of *huperballein*, which means to "throw above," or better, to "be thrown above." Hyperbole relishes in paradox, but not for its own sake. It is thrown into paradox by what is above it. "Throwing here suggests a metaphysical *exigency*," writes Desmond. "It is not an option. We are thrown towards transcendence by our being. The metaphysical hyperbole tries to name this process of being thrown above, that throws mindfulness into the *huper*, the beyond." It is "the way of excess," a beyondness of thought in which "paradoxical language is unavoidable."[41] The quintessential experience of excess to which Christian faith is heir inspires "its own special logic," claims Bulgakov, one that embraces paradox as it is drawn into "a living, immediate bond" with the One who inspires it. The way of excess is by no means irrational but hyperrational, transrational, a true knowing, yet with an "eye of noetic knowing that penetrates higher reality where neither the mental nor physical eye reaches."[42] Remarking upon Dionysius specifically, Bulgakov writes, "On the wings of Eros, in the surge of ecstasy, participation in and cognition of God happen—a surprisingly bold idea in an authoritative ecclesiastical writer. Such is the basis of the erotic gnoseology in Dionysius."[43] Bulgakov adds that this strongly positive theology is complementary to his equally robust negative theology, and that both are required in full measure for any theology "thrown above" itself. "With logical consistency Dionysius establishes the antinomy of religious consciousness that springs from this." On the one hand, "Divinity is *truly nothing*": the NOT-what, NOT-how, NOT-where, NOT-when, NOT-why, the unknowable in itself, beyond all creaturely cognition.[44] "No," insists Dionysius. "It is at a total remove from every condition, movement, life, imagination, conjecture, name, discourse, thought, conception, being, rest, dwelling, unity, limit, infinity, the totality of existence. *And yet,*" he adds, "since it is the underpinning of goodness, and by merely being there is the cause of everything, to praise this divine beneficent Providence *you must turn to all of creation*. It is there at the center of everything and everything has it for a destiny."[45] It is at once beyond all names, the Nameless One, the Name which is above every name, and yet it is epiphanic, self-positing, self-communicating, self-bestowing, engendering. "And so it is that as Cause of all and as transcending all, he is rightly nameless and yet has the names of everything that is."[46] The only reason why we can engage the self-transcending act of naming the Nameless One is because it has rendered itself knowable and lovable in creation. "Cognition of Divinity for a human being, and likewise for the ranks of angels and for every creature, is possible only by the path of the condescension of Divinity and the responding ascension of the creature, only through participation (*tais metochais monon*)."[47]

The most daring aspect of Dionysius's erotic gnoseology really comes to this: eros is not only from the side of creatures but is *from* the Good. Eros eternally preexists *in* the Good, that is, "superabundantly." "In short, both the yearning and the object of that yearning belong to the Beautiful and the Good. They preexist in it, and because of it they exist and come to be."[48] When referring to Saint Paul's "It is no longer I who live, but Christ who lives in me," or Ignatius of Antioch's "He for whom I yearn has been crucified," or the Proverbs' "Yearn for [Wisdom] and she shall keep you; exalt her and she will extol you; honor her and she will embrace you," we are meant to understand that for such sacred writers eros and agape have "one and the same meaning" as well as one source.[49] Creaturely responsiveness to God in the ecstasy of love is the reverberation of God's own ecstasy toward *us*, or better, the movement of God's ecstasy *in and through* us. To yearn for God, as Sebastian Moore puts it, is to "let God happen."[50] Divine yearning for the other is what causes us "to be." The "very cause of the universe in the beautiful, good superabundance of his benign yearning for all is also carried outside of himself in the loving care he has for everything." This is why we are never more attuned to the reason for creation, its inmost content and entelechy, than when we know ourselves as loved by God, as born out of divine yearning and permeated by God's all-embracing *energei*. Creation comes "to be" through divine beguilement. Wooed by the plenitude of divine goodness, swept beyond its absoluteness so as to render itself relative and participable, creation is God's ecstasy. The Good is just *too good* not to share!

When Bulgakov firmly rejects the notion that creation is a possibility God might not have exercised, as though it occurs to God through some deliberative process that the world is worth creating and loving after all, it is just this (hyperbolic) sense of necessity that most moves him. "Is love freedom or necessity? The answer is that it is, to the *highest degree*, both freedom and necessity, though not in their opposition or differentiation, but in their unity. For, truly, love contains both the greatest necessity and the greatest freedom."[51] Divine love is not compulsion or ontological lack. God has no need for creation in this sense. But because of who God eternally *is* — Love, Goodness — the world could not fail to be created. "Having in himself the power of creation, God cannot fail to be the Creator."[52]

The great mystery of God's creative love is that it is wholly free and wholly necessary. Or, to put it hyperbolically, it is *so* free that it *cannot help but* give itself away. It has not the slightest inclination to withhold itself, to resist offering itself to the created other, for rendering itself experienceable in loving "condescension." To create is just God being God. If the self-offering and self-receiving of love is realized *absolutely* in trihypostatic life, then precisely this absoluteness "desires" nothing more than that it be shared by the relative: differentiated and explored in all its modalities through the active self-transcendence of creaturely life. To one truly acquainted with divine love — not merely as a postulate but as *received*, recognized in one's own being — any construal of divine freedom that suggests the possibility of noncreation can only seem incoherent, "unfitting" in every sense of the word. That the Absolute might "hold back" the outpouring of its superabundant love into the relative as its God might be a conjecture of deliberative reason, which, as creaturely, reflects the tension between freedom and necessity, but it is inadequate as an account of divine freedom, which is only known to us in the pure positivity of self-revealing, self-emptying love. "*God is the Creator and the Creator is God*. That is the axiom of revelation."[53]

Return to Love 229

The "Becoming" of God

The Absolute Promise

Let us crystallize a few features of our inquiry thus far. We have sought in this chapter to open our imaginations to the wisdom of the between. Inspired by antinomic styles of theologizing, and alert to the intuition that arises when embracing (rather than enclosing) opposites, we are perhaps better poised for appreciating the extent to which our creaturely difference *from* God is in fact the self-bestowal *of* God. Without collapsing the distinction between God and creation (monism), neither should we construe this distinction in terms of separation or rivalry (dualism), but discern within it a dynamic *relation* in which creation's constitutive openness to God is grounded, empowered, and pervaded by God's self-diffusive love (pan*en*theism). Creation is the capacity for God (*capax infiniti, capax dei*). God is not only *causa efficiens*, as Rahner observes, but also *causa quasi formalis*. The boldness of this claim should not be missed. It is not that God endows creation with various properties that more or less reflect God from a distance, that is, extrinsically. Much less is the "let there be" of creation compatible with any deistic understanding, as though God set the world in motion only to withdraw from the scene. What quasi-formal causality means to convey is that God, the *living* God, bestows God's very *self* in the act of creation—without, however, ceasing to be sovereign, incomprehensible, and uncontrollable.[54] As with Bulgakov, but with appeal to the language of causality, Rahner's approach makes clear that God's ineradicable difference from the world is in fact God's gift of self to the world and thus the establishing of a *relation* by which creation is capacitated for ecstatic growth *in* God. God "gives Godself away" in order that creation might become.

Become *what*? With this question we sharpen our inquiry by considering more explicitly the inmost reason for creation at all. This is not to suggest that creation *is* incarnation, strictly speaking, or that becoming flesh is the inexorable working out of God's originally creative act. (There is an "extra," truly gratuitous dimension to the incarnation, as we shall see.) And yet both Bulgakov and Rahner share the conviction, notably patristic in sensibility, that the incarnation brings to completion the divine condescension inaugurated by the act of creation itself, just as it brings to fullest actualization the capacity of the creature for God. Most fundamentally, the incarnation is the *coincidence* of these two movements, their hypostatic union. It is that event in which God's self-communication reaches its climax, insofar as God becoming human entails the complete acceptance of creaturely reality. God "poses the other as his own reality," declares Rahner, and by this act God "gives himself away" out of love. "God himself goes out of himself, God in his quality of the fullness which gives away itself."[55] This is an astonishing claim, but we should take care to emphasize that this giving away is not the adoption of human reality as a divine prop. It is not a façade, somehow less human or strangely superhuman because of divine kenosis. It is *truly* human, *fully* human, so that in Jesus Christ we also see the climactic expression of the creaturely response *to* God. In Christ the human capacity for God is brought to its fullest fruition. In Christ the human capacity for loving freedom—for God—is so totally unimpeded, so "empty" of any grasping at all, that in him the "fullness" of God was pleased to dwell (Col. 2:9). In Christ the dynamic relation between God and creation—the *metaxic* character of all reality—achieves its definitive and unsurpassable articulation. The total, mutual acceptance of God and creation is just what the incarnation *is*. Jesus Christ is "the climax of God's self-communication to the world," the "absolute promise of God to spiritual creatures," because he is also the creature's total "acceptance of this self-communication" in freedom and love. What makes the incarnation unsurpassable and irrevocable, in Rahner's terms, is that this self-giving and acceptance occurs so totally "on both sides."[56] God and creation are not monistically collapsed in this mutual acceptance, but neither is there any lingering dualism in it. The unity of God and creation in Christ is not an extrinsic unity but is hypostatic.

> [The unity] must rather be understood only as an irrevocable kind of union between this human reality and God, as a union which eliminates the possibility of separation between the proclamation and the proclaimer, and hence a union which makes the really human proclamation and the offer to us a reality of God himself.

Return to Love 231

And it is just this that the hypostatic union means, this and really nothing else: in this human potentiality of Jesus the absolute salvific will of God, the absolute event of God's self-communication to us along with its acceptance as something effected by God himself, is a reality of God himself, unmixed, but also inseparable and therefore irrevocable.[57]

In light of this rich formulation, I cannot but agree with Rahner that "we should meditate on this centre of theology and of Christian life, and often speak less of a thousand other things."[58] In the spirit of such meditation, let us consider the enormous implication this affirmation has for understanding what "creation" really is.

To wit: creation is "a partial moment in the process in which God becomes world, and in which God in fact freely expresses himself in his Logos which has become world and matter."[59] Here we can begin to perceive that if the Logos becoming flesh is that event in which God's self-emptying love reaches its climax, then we have every reason to affirm the incarnation as the wherefore and why of creation itself. Creation and incarnation are not "two disparate and juxtaposed acts of God 'outwards' which have their origins in two separate initiatives of God. Rather in the world *as it actually is* we can understand creation and Incarnation as two moments and two phases of the *one* process of God's self-giving and self-expression, although it is an intrinsically differentiated process."[60] Notice that this understanding does not proceed on the basis of untethered speculation, as if we could deduce through pure reason the inner relationship between creation and incarnation. Though reason has an important role to play, what is *given* to reason to even think about is the living mystery of God's self-communication in our history. We are saved not by knowledge but by love, Rahner reminds us.[61] Nevertheless, on the basis of this self-communication in our history, and by deeply allowing its liberating truth to flood our hearts and penetrate our minds, we can say in ecstatic, reverberative response: *this* is why we were made. Retrospective of the incarnation we can raise reason to its highest vocation and say, at last, this is why we have come "to be." This is why anything is at all rather than nothing. This is the difference nothing makes. "It follows—and this truth is now situated on a profounder level than before—that the creature is endowed, by virtue of its inmost essence and constitution, with the possibility of being assumed, of becoming the material of a possible history of God. God's creative act always drafts the creature as the paradigm of a possible utterance of himself. And he cannot draft it otherwise, even if he remains silent. For this self-silencing always presupposes ears, which hear the muteness of God."[62] Or consider this "definition" of the human being: "We could now define man, within the framework of his supreme and darkest mystery, as that which ensues when God's self-utterance, his Word, is given out lovingly into the void of god-less nothing. Indeed, the Logos made man has been called the abbreviated Word of God. This abbreviation, this code-word for God is man, that is, the Son of Man and men, who exist ultimately because the Son of Man was to exist. If God wills to become non-God, man comes to be, that and nothing else, we might say."[63]

Such statements are as "hyperbolic" as anything one will find in all of Christian theology, and yet their radicalness points to a simple truth: we were made to be loved. "The spiritual essence of man is established by God in creation from the outset because God wants to communicate himself: God's creation through efficient causality takes place because God wants to give himself in love."[64] This comment comes very close to Pseudo-Dionysius's account of creation as the epiphany of divine longing (*theios eros*). Not that God "needs" the world in order to *be* love, but that the overflowing fullness of divine life "desires" nothing less than to bring forth that which is other than God so as to ecstatically share in this fullness. "God himself goes out of himself, God in his quality of the fullness which gives away itself. He can do this. Indeed, his power of subjecting himself to history is primary among his free possibilities. (It is not a primal must!) And for this reason, Scripture defines him as love—whose prodigal freedom is the indefinable itself."[65]

Regarding the inner relationship between creation and incarnation, it is obviously true that the actuality of the latter occurs within the contingent history of creation. The incarnation is an event in which the particularities of place, time, and persons are constitutively involved. It is emergent within a cosmic history as well, insofar as it occurs in a moment in which a self-aware creature of this universe

Return to Love 233

is capable of freely assenting to the creative impulses of the Creator. Nevertheless, we can look retrospectively *through* the historical actuality of the incarnation and affirm it as the inner reason and entelechy of all creation. Creation comes "to be," we might say, because God has willed to "become" a creature from all eternity. Creation thus constitutes "a partial moment in the process in which God becomes world, and in which God in fact freely expresses himself in his Logos which has become world and matter."[66] Rahner boldly maintains that the incarnation is "the asymptotic goal of a development of the world reaching out to God."[67] It is why there is a creation at all, even if the incarnation is by no means redundant with creation. By *asymptotic* Rahner means to signify that the whole of creation is oriented toward the incarnation as its climactic goal, while the historical actuality of the incarnation depends upon a new and entirely free initiative on God's part. The incarnation is not the inexorable outcome of creation's unfolding but a "new creation": the moment in which God's redeeming and divinizing grace breaks through so as to inaugurate the completion of the goal for which creation comes "to be."

Rahner is generally more amenable than Bulgakov to emphasizing the nonnecessity of creation along Thomistic lines, and yet in a notable departure from Aquinas, he orients the entire discussion of salvation around the incarnation, going so far as to claim, in company with the Scotist school of medieval theology, that God would have become incarnate had there been no fall.[68] The incarnation is the deepest reason for creation at all and thus more basic than any consideration of sin and death. Of course, the de facto condition of human existence reflects a cumulative history of sin, guilt, and evil, and so any incarnation in such a world would have a manifestly redemptive character. The focus of Jesus's ministry, along with his death and resurrection, bears this character out. The incarnation in its historical actuality, and not just as an idea, is liberating and pardoning. It has everything to do with setting captives free and bringing to realization the reign of God in all its personal and social significance. And yet for all of this, it is also (and most fundamentally) concerned with the divinization of *all* creation. Divinization is not just one among other understandings of what we call "salvation." *Theosis* includes (without being reducible to) its pardoning and liberating effects for

234   Purgation and Union

human beings. Taking the patristic axiom with utmost seriousness, Rahner maintains that God became human so that human beings might become God. Or, to put it in an anthropocosmic register—one that is inclusive of the more-than-human world—the life, death, and resurrection of Jesus is the "event in which God irrevocably adopts the creature as his own reality, by his own divine primordial act," and thus an event marking "the irreversible and embryonically final beginning of the glorification and divinization of the *whole* reality."[69]

From All Eternity

These are radical understandings, to be sure, but both Rahner and Bulgakov draw amply from ancient wisdom Christologies in formulating them. They also offer complementary perspectives on the same basic insight through the use of distinct idioms and philosophical-theological interlocutors. In Bulgakov, for example, we have already touched upon the theme of divine condescension in *creatio ex nihilo* and the understanding that our very being depends upon the "outgoing" of God from the absoluteness of divine love "into" the relative, which God establishes. This is appropriately described as condescension because, in needing nothing for itself, the Absolute freely determines itself in relation to the non-Absolute, "humbling" itself before that which "is not," and fully implicating itself in the adventurous becoming of conditioned existence. The Absolute *potentializes* itself, bestows itself as the ground of extradivine being, and invites that which does not exist—and which could never exist on its own—to issue forth with integrity and manifold possibilities. The positive foundation for creation is *in* divine life, or what Bulgakov refers to as the Wisdom (or Sophia) of God, and thus does the Absolute open up "another center" within itself. "It itself becomes thereby its own potency (or '*meon*') by giving in itself and through itself a place to the relative, but without at the same time forfeiting its absoluteness. Creation is the Absolute's sacrifice of its absoluteness, summoned by no one or anything and uncaused, rationally inexplicable."[70] This is yet another way to articulate *creatio ex nihilo*, which is not thinkable in itself, however much thought is drawn to it. God is not identified here as the first link in a finite causal chain, and neither is the world the result of some force on the same plane with it. Creation is "a leap," an act of "holy folly," "love for the sake of love," a gratuitous "let there be" whereby the Absolute freely and benevolently releases its all-sufficiency.[71] Inasmuch as creation is an overflowing from the inexhaustible resourcefulness of divine life, this self-diffusiveness is renunciative and kenotic, "a creative sacrifice of love" that is not only determined to "let be" the created other but to sojourn with this other to the very end. The Creator is revealed in the world and elects to "undergo" the world, without, however, displacing the world or ceasing to be its God. "Ignorant of envy, he wants to live in creatures and *become* in them. He honors the nature of the creature which is nothing, more than his own might, for he wants himself in creation, in it—in the other, although wholly indebted to him for its being."[72] By freely accepting the world of becoming in this way, but also tarrying with the world, God is "in process." God "flings himself into creation" and donates divine life to the potentializing of creation. God lovingly accepts the limits of creation while ceaselessly drawing creation forth into ecstatic fullness. Such is the humility of divine love. "God knows how to wait; for the consummation of the ages, when the Son will subject everything to the Father and God will be 'all in all,' is separated from the initial *let there be* by a lengthy historical process, which is the gift of God's omnipotence to creaturely freedom."[73]

Bulgakov's consistency in developing theology along antinomic lines brings him to say that God, as the Absolute, possesses the "fullness of life within Himself." God is "all-blissful and self-sufficient in the sense that this fullness cannot be completed by anything and does not have anything outside itself." There is "no place in God for any process," insofar as God cannot receive anything that God does not already have and supremely *is*.[74] This is one pole of the antinomy. But for reasons that can only be attributed to "love," "humility," "metaphysical kenosis," or "creation from nothing," the absolute fullness of God enters into relationship with not-God, the world, which God establishes, becoming "correlative to the world" and freely "thrusting Himself into the flux of the becoming of temporal, emerging being."[75] Creation is not the object of God's own fulfillment but the object of God's love—the love by which God becomes human for our sake. God does not need the world, yet in creating God "seeks" the world.[76] This is the other pole of the antinomy. What Bulgakov stresses here, above all else, is that while such becoming reaches its apotheosis in the incarnation, the whole of creation participates in the incarnation proleptically. Creation tends *toward* it and is included in it. "According to the direct testimony of Scripture, the coming of Christ into the world, the Incarnation, is predetermined before the creation of the world. That is, it is included in God's pre-eternal plan for the world, in His counsel concerning the world."[77] This is the "primordial grace" of creation. Even prior to the emergence of sin and its ramifying effects—its "fallenness"—God eternally wills to create the world for the sake of incarnation. "The Incarnation is not only the means to the redemption; it is also the supreme crowning of the world, even in comparison with its creation. In the Incarnation, God showed His love for creation."[78]

Bulgakov by no means underplays the redemptive character of the incarnation, which, on account of human sin, takes on a markedly different character than it would have had moral evil and spiritual dissipation not gained ascendancy in the world, choking its vitality and redirecting its growth. That sin and death could have ever achieved an adversarial, semiautonomous presence in the world is a possibility inherent to creaturely limitation and freedom, though in no sense an actuality rooted in God's positive will.[79] As with the broader Christian tradition that has consistently refused to attribute "substance" to evil, as if springing from an eternal foundation dualistically at odds with the Good, Bulgakov contends that evil is a perversion of the inherent goodness of being, a parasitical force and metastasizing sickness that threatens the integrity of creation. Envy and pride, sloth and self-loathing, devouring rivalry and hatred, deception and despair, malevolence and ravenousness, indifference and oppression: these are just some of the negative refractions of love's "absolute value."[80] They convert its purely positive energy into something else, as with a minus sign, something refused or misdirected, something corrupted and corrupting. Evil turns the creative energy of love into its opposite, with disastrous effects that can achieve self-organizing momentum in history like a weather system or a tectonic fracture. Given the ontological porosity between the human and the more-than-human world, between the anthropic and the cosmic, we can speak more broadly in terms a sickness of "the world" or of the "world soul" and thus well beyond the artificial confines of narrowly defined human existence. Bulgakov draws amply from scriptural and patristic resources in developing this anthropocosmic dimension of fallenness, in ways that can provide resources for imagining and responding to the ecological precariousness of our time, as we shall later see.

The redemptive thrust of the incarnation has sin and the ravages of death clearly in its view, and thus we are quite right to say that God became human *in order that* creation might be freed from the bondage of sin and death. As we saw in part 2, which focused on the death-dealing dynamics of acquisitive desire, mimetic rivalry, and exclusionary violence—a specific (but especially emblematic) strain of fallenness with far-reaching consequences—the content of Jesus's ministry and the narrative pattern of his life, death, and resurrection demonstrate that the incarnation is graciously interruptive, healing, and transformative. It reaches into the heart of human darkness. It plunges into the most recalcitrant regions of human brokenness, not least those interpersonal dimensions that twist what ought to be loving communion into division and violent exclusion. It "descends" into the hell of creaturely despair and those loveless regions of human experience (e.g., shame, fear, resentment, abandonment) in order that they may be brought out into the healing light of loving acceptance. The incarnation is a very particular enactment of divine self-bestowal, for it embraces the full gamut of human experience, including those patterns of existence that have become entangled and willfully resistant to the creative momentum of divine love.

> God comes even into the fallen world; God's love is repulsed neither by the infirmity of the creature nor by its fallen image. He is not repulsed by the sinfulness of the world but condescends to the point of taking upon Himself its sins: The Lamb of God, who takes upon Himself the sins of the world, comes into the world. God thus gives everything for the deification of the world and its salvation; there is nothing that is not given. Such is God's love; such is love. Such is love in the intratrinitarian life, in the mutual giving of the three hypostases; such is love in the relation of God to the world.[81]

Bulgakov maintains that if we understand the incarnation in this way, as redemptive *and* deifying, then it matters little to pose the speculative theological question whether the incarnation would have occurred had there been no fall. It is indeed liberating and redemptive, a restoration of the human condition from its woundedness, but it is also preestablished by God as the goal of creation itself, its inner entelechy and eschatological fruition. It is not possible for us to separate the soteriological meaning of the incarnation from its ontological significance. What we *can* say, based upon the content of revelation, is that God from all eternity seeks to "communicate His divine life to the world and to make His abode in the world; He wants to become man in order to make man god," but that the only world we know where this deifying self-communication takes place is one that needs salvation from all that imperils it. Here there is no either/or, only both/and. "The Incarnation was accomplished in all its significance as it was pre-eternally established in God's counsel, but it was accomplished for the sake of fallen humanity."[82] This is how Bulgakov adroitly glosses the Nicene phrase "for us *and* for our salvation."

Deep Incarnation

The Anthropocosmic Milieu

The doctrine of the incarnation confronts us with what only can be described as an ontological ultimate: in the unconditioned freedom that God *is*, God can "become" a creature and thus assume a finite, conditioned reality for God's self—without ever ceasing to be God. God can, and according to revelation has, become a creature of this evolving universe: flesh (*sarx*), a human being (*anthropos*), born of a woman (Gal. 4:4). As Rahner summarizes the matter, "God can become something, he who is unchangeable in himself can *himself* become subject to change *in something else*."[83] Similarly, Bulgakov: "God became *not* God without ceasing to be God."[84]

If this antinomic phrasing seems like an objectionable bit of nonsense, or a flat-out contradiction, we are perhaps on our way to perceiving just why it is the ontological ultimate Rahner and Bulgakov declare it to be. No philosophical ontology will arrive at such an affirmation without the impetus of revelation. No metaphysical speculation, however bold, will alight upon a fleshy Absolute without the gift of faith. And should we come to a point where we begin to allow our language to be hollowed out and reshaped by the peculiar pressure that God's self-communication in Christ exerts upon it, this will only amount to an initial, tentative step toward beholding the inexhaustible mystery of its content.

Astonishing and counterintuitive as the claim is, the doctrine of the incarnation is nothing less than the beating heart of Christian faith. It is singularly important for discerning the eternal character of God as Love, and it is determinative for arriving at a genuinely Christian understanding of the God-world relationship. If we can generally say that God's transcendence implies God's immanence and compassionate presence to the unfolding of creation, no less to its darkest travails than to its creative achievements, then here we must speak in a more concrete and particular manner, which is by affirming that out of unconditioned freedom and love God has elected to become a creature of this universe in order to share in, reconcile, and bring to fulfillment the whole of creation that has gratuitously come "to be." God has "pitched his tent among us" (John 1:14). In Christ, the eternal God has undergone the journey of creaturely becoming "with us" (Matt. 1:23), "recapitulating" in himself the history of that becoming (Eph. 1:10), passing even through the suffering and death of a horrific eventuality, the cross, for our sake (Rom. 4:25). By becoming a creature of this world, God has opened up the phenomenon of life from the inside out in order to shepherd it to its final fruition. Having accompanied creation throughout its sojourn, God assumes the inwardness and fragility of the creature, precisely *as* a creature, in order that God might truly be "all in all" (1 Cor. 15:28).

When the Gospel of John affirms that the eternal Word "became flesh," or when Paul declares that all things, whether in the heavens or on the earth, are "summed up" in Christ, the scope of the incarnation is expanded well beyond the destiny of human beings. Or, more precisely, because the incarnation embraces the *whole* of living human reality—its "deep nature," we might say—it necessarily includes as integral to that reality the broader cosmic history in which human beings are embedded. We cannot oppose the particularity of the incarnation and its all-encompassing breadth, as a binary logic is wont to do; we must discover how this particularity opens out unto, and is itself a unique manifestation of, the corporeality of creation as such. The "flesh" to which the Word is united in Jesus is inclusive of the entire phenomenon of life.

If it is true that both Rahner and Bulgakov are particularly alert to the anthropological significance of the incarnation, this should not be taken as evidence that they neglect its anthropo*cosmic* character. Even if we are justified in wanting to develop the more-than-human dimensions of the incarnation further, particularly in light of the ecological crisis in which we currently find ourselves, it is worth pointing out that both of their theological visions are bracing in their cosmicity precisely because of the kind of anthropology they develop. In Rahner's case, matter itself is understood as inherently creative and capable of developing "out of its inner being in the direction of spirit."[85] The entire created order is charged with the capacity for its divine source and ground. All creatures, no matter their degree of complexity and interiority, "bear the stamp of this one primordial ground of being," and thus does creation form an "ultimate unity and community" in its differentiated relatedness.[86] Because matter and spirit are intrinsically related, it is not despite materiality but in and through it that finite spirit comes to expression. This expressivity displays a dynamic history of emergence, of leaps into new horizons of being and relationship, so that in the broadest terms we can say that "the development of biologically organized materiality is orientated in terms of an ever-increasing complexity and interiority towards spirit, until finally, under the dynamic impulse of God's creative power, and through a process of self-transcendence of this kind, it becomes spirit."[87] It is true that this latter breakthrough in complexity and interiority, billions of years in the making, refers to the human being, who, on account of its capacity for self-awareness, is also, and by that very fact, capable of becoming conscious of its source and ground—the wherefore and why of its existence. This coming to consciousness is the birth of wonder, of that original experience of the mystery of existence, but also the capacity for growing freedom and responsibility. Rahner is not timid about highlighting the uniqueness of the human being in this "call" and "response" of the God-world relation. But he is no less insistent that human beings share in the corporeality of the world, such that any abstraction of the human being from our cosmic milieu is as much an anthropological mistake as it is a cosmological one: "The one material cosmos is the *single* body as it were of a *multiple* self-presence of this very cosmos and orientation towards its absolute and infinite ground. . . . For man in his corporeality is an element of the cosmos which cannot really be demarcated and separated, and he communicates with the whole cosmos in such a way that, in and through the corporeality of man as what is other to spirit, the cosmos really presses to this self-presence in spirit."[88]

If the human being is the cosmos come to self-awareness, and furthermore is that creature whose nature is assumed by the incarnation—the "event of God's free and forgiving self-communication," as Rahner regularly puts it—then it is crucial to grasp that the human being, precisely because it is the cosmos come to self-awareness, is interconnected with the whole community of creation, with every living being and every process that forms it, from bacteria, plants, insects, birds, and mammals to stars, planets, galaxies, black holes, quantum fields, and so-called dark matter. If there is a unique vocation in being human, such that God's self-emptying love comes to unprecedented expression in the idiom of our flesh, then this is hardly reason to abstract ourselves from the community of creation with which we share a cosmic corporeality. It is all the more reason to see our vocation as a summons to living responsibly *within* that community.

Bulgakov, for his part, regularly refers to the human being as a "microcosm" and creation as "a cosmo-anthropic world."[89] Drawing upon and expanding the wisdom theologies of the Church Fathers, and with particular indebtedness to Maximus the Confessor's account of the creaturely *logoi* whose ultimate prototype is found in the eternal Logos, Bulgakov's sophiological vision casts the multileveled manifestation of creation in evolutionary and integral terms.[90] The emergence of the human being represents a crucial mediatorial role between the realms of matter and pure spirit, and does so as a *complex unity* in which the inorganic, vegetal, and animal realms are recapitulated and brought to qualitatively new expression in human life. If humanity's capacities for rational freedom open up new horizons in the realm of creaturely becoming, this by no means eclipses the "extraordinary practical wisdom" implanted in the animal soul and exhibited throughout the world of instinct and complex social behavior, which we also share.[91] It is certainly true that Bulgakov's anthropology, like Rahner's, gives account of the human vocation in the world in terms of its distinguishing qualities. When referring to the human spirit as constituted by a "divine spark," or elsewhere as an "ontological *hiatus*" in which the human capacity for self-transcendence—the abyssal "I"—bears the "stamp of eternity," we are reminded of a long-standing view within Christian theology that the *imago dei* situates human beings *between* the animal and angelic realms, with all the dignity and risk this intense betweenness entails. In this way Bulgakov maintains that the human "encompasses creation within himself," and yet is "is something *new* in creation," that is, "a *transcensus*."[92]

If we are justified in wanting to nuance or reframe aspects of Bulgakov's strongly hierarchical positioning of the human being within the order of creation, particularly those places where the human vocation is depicted in terms of kingship more than kinship, we can draw further inspiration in this task by considering the remarkable depths to which his kenotic Christology reaches. The divine condescension of the incarnation is an enactment of God's "descent into creatureliness" as such, a feat of self-giving love whereby the Word "enters *inside* creaturely cosmic being."[93] In becoming human, God draws the full range of creaturely cosmic being "into His proper *life*; He humanized himself not from outside but from within, entering into the creaturely life of temporality and becoming."[94] The far-reaching significance of the communication of idioms (*communicatio idiomata*) in christological dogma means that the whole gamut of human experience, including the struggle, nescience, and vulnerability of creaturely being, is intimately known by God from the *inside*.[95] This includes the ordeal of felt separation from God, the experience of exclusionary violence at human hands, and the extreme hiatus of death itself—all of which converge at Golgotha.[96] Bulgakov insists that the fuller implications of the incarnation do not permit us to attribute such suffering only to the human "side" of the hypostatic union. A more penetrating understanding of God's self-giving love in Christ draws us into the most extraordinary of realizations, namely, that without ceasing to be the Absolute, the God of Jesus Christ became "subject" to the full range of creaturely experience, including all that seems the most contradictory to God, in order to redeem it.

> One must accept the full force of the fact that the God-Man suffered and tasted death not only in His humanity but also in His Divine-Humanity. One cannot separate, in opposition to Chalcedon, His humanity from His Divinity here, saying that He suffered not as God but only as man, since the death on the cross, just as His entire life, would then be only an appearance, in which His Divinity would not participate at all. On the contrary, the kenosis consists precisely in the fact that the Son diminished Himself in His Divinity and became the *subject*, the hypostasis, of the *Divine-Human* life, experiencing all that His human experienced.[97]

Intercorporeity

There is much more one might say about the anthropocosmic character of the incarnation in Rahner and Bulgakov's work, but here I wish to extend some of these contributions by considering more directly the implications of the incarnation for the more-than-human world. As mentioned at the beginning of this chapter, a number of Christian theological engagements with evolutionary sciences and ecology have recently coalesced around the highly fruitful notion of "deep incarnation."[98] Drawing upon the wisdom Christologies of the New Testament, along with major strains in patristic and medieval theology, this line of inquiry has sought to enrich our understanding of the incarnation by setting it within an evolutionary perspective and through a more direct dialogue with the natural sciences. Niels Henrik Gregersen summarizes the main thrust of this approach as follows:

> In this view, the Logos of God (the eternal Son) "became flesh" in Jesus, assumed a particular body and mind in him, and hereby also conjoined the material, living, and mental conditions of being a creature in any epoch. God thus became a human being (not

only a man), a social being who lived with and for others in a sinful world (not an autistic individual), a living being vulnerable like the sparrows and foxes (not just a member of *homo sapiens*), a material being made out of stardust and earth (not bringing with him a special heavenly flesh), thus susceptible to death and disintegration.[99]

At issue in this summary is what we mean by *flesh*. If the Gospel of John refers to the eternal Word becoming human (*anthropos*), it also declares that "the Word became flesh [*sarx*] and lived among us ... full of grace and truth" (1:14). The significance of this latter designation is that it includes the condition of corporeality that all finite and perishable beings share, thus uniting what may intuitively seem to us as opposed, namely the "glory" (*doxa*) of the imperishable God and the ontological vulnerability of all creatures. As numerous scholars have noted, there is a polemical aspect to the Johannine usage of the word *sarx*, which in its historical context serves as a rejoinder to any "docetic" tendency that would construe the incarnation of the Word as only "appearing" (without actually *becoming*) flesh. But more than polemics is at work here. To all those who cannot envisage the Logos actually suffering and dying in the flesh, whether because it seems to them intellectually objectionable or aesthetically offensive, the prologue of John stages something like a theopoetic intervention by crisscrossing and reframing the boundaries of what we imagine God to be. It presents us with a God whose bestowal of creation through the Word ("All things came into being through him" [1:3]) is intrinsically related to this same Word becoming flesh for our sake, thus sharing in the condition of material, biological, transient, vulnerable existence.

All of this is well within the scope of John's gospel, but we can appreciably expand our understanding of the incarnation's reach by reflecting upon our "deep nature" and the evolutionary dimensions of our corporeality. "In this context," observes Gregersen, "the incarnation of God in Christ can be understood as a radical or 'deep' incarnation, that is, an incarnation into the very tissue of biological existence, and system of nature."[100] "The divine Logos," he writes elsewhere, "does not enter only into the blood and flesh of Jesus as an individual body. The incarnation also extends into Jesus as an instantiation of the material universe and the frail flesh of biological creatures. The flesh that is assumed in Jesus Christ is not only the particular man Jesus but the entire realm of humanity, living creatures, and earthly soil."[101] Denis Edwards argues similarly, adding to his own account the immense timescale that spans the phenomenon of life: "Flesh [*sarx*] can be understood as involving the whole 3.7-billion-year evolutionary history of life on our planet, with all its predation, death, and extinctions, as well as its diversity, cooperation, interdependence, and abundance. Flesh involves all the interconnected ecological relationships that make up life on our planet." When affirming the Word becoming *flesh*, we are affirming God's "solidarity with *all* flesh, and this includes not only humanity but also the whole of biological life. The cross of Christ represents not only God's identification with suffering humanity and God's will to bring forgiveness and healing to human beings, but also God's identification with suffering creation and God's promise of new creation that will bring healing and fulfillment to all things."[102] Adding to the chorus, Elizabeth Johnson explains why the incarnation is a genuinely new event in God's relationship with creation and not at all redundant with the indwelling Spirit: "God's own self-expressive Word personally joins the biological world as a member of the human race, and via this perch on the tree of life enters into solidarity with the whole biophysical cosmos of which human beings are a part. This deep incarnation of God within the biotic community of life forges a new kind of union, one with different emphasis from the empowering communion created by the indwelling Creator Spirit. This is a union in the flesh."[103]

We can further enrich our understanding of this union in the flesh by drawing upon key phenomenological insights, particularly as they draw our attention to the hidden and interwoven depths of our corporeality. As Maurice Merleau-Ponty powerfully puts it, we are "inserted" into the flesh of the world, just as the world is "inserted" in us.[104] We do not just meet the world on the basis of a side-by-side encounter, as though the world were "out there" and we "in here." We are "intertwined" with the world, with others, in a chiasmic relationship, so that the flesh that I *am* is in fact the corporeality of the world lending a particular expression and stance *in* me.[105] Merleau-Ponty calls this "intercorporeity," by which he means the simultaneity of acting and being acted upon in any act of perception and bodily comportment. There is a "thickness of flesh" between perceiver and perceived, such that corporeity is not an obstacle but the very means of communication across distance and indeed for anything like perception and inwardness to occur at all. We "are the world that thinks itself," as he puts it. The "world is at the heart of our flesh."[106]

This reciprocal insertion of the body and world means that much—indeed, most—of what constitutes us remains in the background of our everyday experience. Our "body" is not just what we can see and sometimes feel within the vicinity of intentional awareness. There is a vast realm of corporeality from which we subsist and that makes possible any discrete act of perception and cognition—any sense of "self," "other," "world," or "we." Most of what constitutes us as psychosomatic beings is "absent" from our direct experience, and yet it is necessary for that experience to take place. Drew Leder provides an extraordinary account of this immense, interlaced, largely tacit realm of corporeality, and in a manner that can enhance our sense of the flesh to which God has become subject in the incarnation:

In addition to this perceptual communion of the flesh, I am sustained through a deeper "blood" relation with the world. It is installed within me, not just encountered from without. The inanimate, calcified world supports my flesh from within in the form of bones. A world of organic, autonomous powers circulates within my visceral depths. Science tells me that some ten quadrillion bacteria live within my body. I cannot even claim my own cells fully as my own. In all probability, they evolved out of symbiotic relations between different prokaryotic cells, one living inside another. My body everywhere bears the imprint of Otherness.

This encroachment of the world is renewed at every moment by visceral exchanges with the environment. In sleep I give myself over to anonymous breathing, relinquishing the separative nature of distance perception. Even waking perception is ultimately in service to the visceral. In the most basic sense, the animal looks around to find things to eat and avoid being eaten. . . . As I eat, the thickness of the flesh that separates self from the world melts

Return to Love 247

away. No longer perceived across a distance, the world dissolves into my own blood, sustaining me from within via its nutritive powers. I am not just a gazing upon the world but one who feeds on it, drinks of it, breathes it in.[107]

When we affirm that the Word became flesh, we are, of course, concerned with a particular body-person living in a particular historical context and a particular life-story whose events, relationships, exchanges, symbolic actions, and passivities are uniquely revealing of God. But the fact that the Word became flesh also means that God assumes the corporeality of world as this comes to particular expression in Jesus. Owing to our intercorporeity, there is no utterly buffered, isolatable flesh to which God becomes united in the incarnation; there is only deep interweaving and communion such that the entire sweep of the phenomenon of life—from the inanimate to the animate, from the metabolic to the symbolic, from the atomic to the biospheric, from the instinctual and passionate to the deliberative and reflexively aware—is implicated in him. This, I think, is one way to give fresh meaning to the Pauline expression that all things are "summed up" (or "recapitulated") in Christ. We need not force an interpretation that draws an exact parallel between ontogeny and phylogeny, as though the body-person of Jesus quite literally recapitulates every threshold or pathway of evolutionary history. If patristic or contemporary theologians refer to Christ as a microcosm that reiterates all of creation in a concentrated way, we do not have to appropriate this enduring insight by imagining that all the profiles and trajectories of cosmic, biological, and cultural history must be reproduced or enclosed in him. Given the intercorporeity of flesh we can say that while the physical, biological, and personal dimensions of the phenomenon of life are indeed implicated in the total body-person of Jesus—the microcosm metaphor is by no means nonsense—we can accentuate the relational dimensions of the incarnation and relieve the metaphor of undue anthropocentrism. Richard Bauckham makes just this point, noting that if it is important that Jesus "shares physicality with all creatures in this world, biotic life with all living creatures," this should be viewed as his participation in "the dynamic web of relationships that constitute the cosmos. It is not only his physical

248   Purgation and Union

solidarity with all other creatures that the risen Christ, by virtue of bodily resurrection, retains, but . . . also his participating in the interconnectedness of the created world."[108] A "christocentric universe," he adds, "is not an anthropocentric universe but a universe centered on the God who through incarnation participates in the interconnected life of all his creatures."[109]

A Cruciform Hope

God has taken on the flesh of the world and therefore "assumed," as an inner moment of divine life, the limitations and perishability that all creatures endure as a community of creation. It is in God's "co-suffering" with creation that the character of kenotic love is most clearly expressed. Though we have already touched upon this key theme with Bulgakov, Walter Kasper develops the point with an instructive emphasis on eschatological hope: "Here God's omnipotence is completely absorbed into outward weakness; here God takes the human condition, the human destiny, upon himself, with all its consequences. He enters into abandonment by God. There is no longer any human situation that is in principle cut off from God and salvation."[110] The great paradox of the cross is that it is the form God's power takes in human vulnerability: "riches in poverty, love in abandonment, fullness in emptiness, life in death."[111] Nothing within human experience is excluded from God's kenotic embrace, not physical agony, not the dregs of despair and social ostracism, not victimization and unjust death, not even the felt sense of abandonment by God in the hour of expiration ("My God, my God, why have you forsaken me?"). God's love for creation is such that God "allows the other to affect him; he becomes vulnerable precisely in his love. Thus love and suffering go together." This is not a "passive being-affected," Kasper adds, "but an active allowing others to affect one. Because, then, God is love he can suffer and by that very fact reveal his divinity. The self-emptying of the cross is therefore not a de-divinization of God but his eschatological glorification."[112]

The trinitarian dynamic of this self-emptying and glorification is crucial. Because God *is* Love—an eternal movement of self-emptying and self-reception, an overflowing fullness of ecstatic mutuality—God can be wholly for the creature, even becoming creaturely in the Word made flesh, without ceasing to be God. "The eternal intra-divine distinction of Father and Son is the transcendental theological condition for the possibility of God's self-emptying in the incarnation and on the cross."[113] What the doctrine of the Trinity crystallizes for us, and the reason why *ad intra* considerations bear directly upon concrete, *ad extra* realities, is that from eternity there is place in God for the *passio* of creation, "place also for a genuine sym-pathy with the suffering of human beings."[114] Because divine life is an eternal movement of *ekstasis* and *enstasis*, an infinitely relational spaciousness, the passion of creation to which God responds by way of self-communicating love is not an addendum to divine life but intrinsic to it. The divine "motive" for creation and incarnation is one and the same.

Appeal to the compassion of God does not, it is true, explain the wherefore and why of all pain, suffering, and death in our history, whether biological or cultural, and so it does not offer us an intellectual resolution to the aching perplexities that their pervasive presence raises for us. As discussed in chapter 1, there remains a nontheorizable surplus of negativity in our world which does not admit of tidy explanations or mollifying interpretations.[115] And yet the compassion of God "touches" us in the midst of those perplexities by manifesting in Christ how God relates and responds to them: with a love that opens up divine life to creation in all its travail, with a power that is able to heal and transform our weaknesses by giving them an eschatological future. This is core to the message of Jesus's resurrection from the dead. "God does not divinize suffering," writes Kasper, "he redeems it. For the suffering of God, which springs from the voluntariness of love, conquers the fateful character suffering, which attacks us from without as something alien and unintelligible. Thus the omnipotence of God's love removes the weakness of suffering. Suffering is not thereby removed, but it is interiorly transformed—transformed into hope. Kenosis and suffering now no longer have the last word; the last word belongs to exaltation and transfiguration."[116]

Kasper's account of divine love and eschatological hope, like Rahner's and Bulgakov's, focuses mainly upon the reality of human suffering, but we can likewise extend it by applying our previous considerations of deep incarnation. Gregersen points the way in the spirit of Martin Luther's *theologia crucis*: "The cross itself—the experience of biological death, physical pain, and mental anguish—is included in the identity of God. To the identity of God belongs also the humiliation. There is no longer any opposition between God's glory and the humiliation of Jesus. God's heavenly glory is stretched so as to encompass the soil of the cruciform creation."[117] Viewed in this way, the cross is "a microcosm in which the suffering in the macrocosm is both represented and lived out."[118] Or, again, "the death of Christ becomes an icon of God's redemptive co-suffering with all sentient life as well as with the victims of social competition. God bears the costs of evolution, the price involved in the hardship of natural selection."[119]

This latter statement highlights for us just how costly evolutionary processes really are. They do not just involve pain, suffering, and death as elements in the emergence and diversification of species; they involve struggle for resources, predation, high-stakes experimentation, meandering dead ends, and the extinction of species due to disease, famine, and other natural catastrophes. The costliness of evolutionary processes adds considerable poignancy to the problems associated with traditional theodicies, Gregersen notes, and for at least two reasons: first, because such costs cannot be accounted for with reference to human sin; and second, because they are so woven into the fabric of life processes that they appear part of the "package deal."[120] Whether or not the kind of creaturely diversity, sentience, beauty, and freedom that our world exhibits could have emerged without such costs is a perfectly legitimate (if probably unanswerable) question. What we can say—and herein lies the substance of cruciform hope—is that while such costs appear to be intrinsic to the only living world we actually know, they are borne by the Creator who freely becomes subject to them in compassionate love, and who in turn opens them up to eternal fruition *in* God.[121]

In addition to all the soteriological significance that Christ's death carries for human beings, it also means that the phenomenon of life of which Jesus is a part, including the evolutionary travail to which his (and our) corporeality is heir, is assumed by God. "The logic of deep incarnation," writes Johnson, "gives a strong warrant for extending divine solidarity from the cross into the groan of suffering and the silence of death of all creation. All creatures come to an end; those with nervous systems know pain and suffering. Jesus' anguished end places him among this company."[122] Such solidarity does not depend upon any explicit recognition for it to be efficacious, Johnson adds. It does not require, for example, that each creature have a concept or intuition that God is present in the midst of suffering and death. Even among human beings this would be true only some of the time. The efficaciousness comes from *God*. Even if silently, no creature possessed of sentience, however inchoate, is beyond God's loving embrace. "Seemingly absent, the Giver of life is silently present with all creatures in their pain and dying. They remain connected to the living God despite what is happening; in fact, in the depths of what is happening. . . . The cross gives warrant for locating the compassion of God right at the center of the affliction."[123]

This cruciform pattern of divine presence with creatures suggests that God's characteristic mode of action is not one of constant supervening upon natural processes or preventing all tragic eventualities from occurring. But neither is God impassive or incapable of responding to these eventualities. In keeping with the sacramental way God works through, rather than coercively upon, the web of created agency, the distinguishing form divine action takes is one of sustaining, compassionate presence that accepts and waits upon creaturely limitations, undergoing them with creation but also opening them up to new possibilities and ultimately their eschatological fruition in the Spirit. In sum, the whole of creation is addressed by God's promise of resurrection. "Given the personal presence of divine love to every creature in every moment, and the further revelation of the character of this love in the suffering and hope-filled story of Jesus Christ, there is warrant for holding that species and even individual creatures are not abandoned in death but taken into communion with the living God. Nothing is lost."[124] Or, as Johnson strikingly puts it, "Christ is the firstborn of all the dead of Darwin's tree of life."[125]

Here again the logic of deep incarnation serves to stretch Christian imagination well beyond the scope of human-centered aspirations. Put in eschatological terms, it informs a hope for "deep resurrection," by which Johnson means the extension of Christ's resurrection of the dead to the whole natural world.[126] This is a bracing affirmation that

252   Purgation and Union

takes the ontological implications of Easter seriously. Paul's reference to Christ as the "firstborn of all the dead" has already been cited (Col. 1:18), but we should add from this same passage the emphasis given to Christ's role of cosmic reconciliation. The "fullness of God" was pleased to dwell in him, and through his death all things, whether in heaven or on earth, have become reconciled with God (1:19–20). Christ is the firstborn of the dead, but he is also "before all things, and in him all things hold together" (1:17). Elsewhere Paul proclaims that Jesus's resurrection from the dead has broken through the finality of death, its seemingly invincible power, and subjected it to the Father so that God may be "all in all" (1 Cor. 15:28). The implication here is that by having freely undergone death, the risen Christ has breached death's power at its core. God graciously absorbs and even "uses" death, giving it a verbal structure in Christ so that what death consumes shall again be allowed to speak.[127] The sting of death has been "swallowed up in victory," and what is sown in perishability shall be raised imperishable (15:53–4). Paul can thus conclude his account with cosmic hope. "For in hope we were saved" (Rom. 8:24). Because Christ has been raised by the power of God, nothing, not even death, can separate creation from the love of God. If God is for us, who can be against us (8:31)? "For I am convinced that neither death, nor life, neither angels, nor principalities, nor present things, nor future things, nor powers, nor height, nor depth, nor any other creature will be able to separate us from the love of God in Christ Jesus our Lord" (8:38–39). If all of creation groans in travail, awaiting its fulfillment "as in the pains of childbirth," then the redemption made possible by Christ's death and resurrection—a redemption that Paul cites as corporeal and not just "spiritual"—is all-inclusive in its reach. It is a hope for *all* of creation.

Echoing the wisdom Christologies of the New Testament, but drawing also from the understanding of resurrection as *theosis* developed in much patristic theology, Rahner insists that corporeality is fundamental to Christian affirmations of resurrection. Because of this we can say that "a piece of the world, real to the core . . . is surrendered . . . to the disposition of God, in complete obedience and love. This is Easter, and the redemption of the world." The resurrection inaugurates a breakthrough, a decisive moment in which "God irrevocably adopts the creature as his own reality."[128] What is genuinely new with

Jesus's resurrection from the dead, and the reason why it is not redundant with the incarnation more generally, is that it is inclusive of, but also responsive to, Jesus's death. The resurrection is "of" and "from" the dead, meaning that it *goes through while transfiguring* death itself. Jesus's entire body-person, the full arc of his creaturely life, is transfigured by the creativity of God as the instantiating promise that corruptible creation is heir to eternal fulfillment in God. Both continuity and discontinuity mark the "new creation" of the risen Christ (2 Cor. 5:17). The resurrection concerns human destiny, to be sure, but it constitutes nothing less than "the irreversible and embryonically final beginning of the glorification and divinization of the *whole* of reality."[129] Giving expression to Easter's cosmicity, and thus to a Christ-mysticism without reserve, Rahner writes that "the world as a whole flows into his Resurrection and into the transfiguration of his body."[130]

It is with a cruciform hope like this that we can anticipate an eschatological future for all living creatures. "Based on the faithful love of God revealed in Christ," writes Edwards, "it can be said that God will not forget any creature that God loves and creates. Each is inscribed eternally in the divine life."[131] Recognizing that Christian theology has not often reflected upon the eschatological destinies of creatures other than human beings, Edwards proposes that we include in our eschatological imagination the communion of all sentient beings. "The God of resurrection life is a God who brings individual creatures in their own distinctiveness *in some way* into the eternal dynamic life of the divine communion."[132] Just how this could be may be well beyond our capacity to express, but it is not beyond our capacity to hope. "There is every reason to hope that the diverse range of creatures that spring from the abundance of the divine communion will find redemption in being taken up eternally into this communion in ways that are appropriate to each."[133]

RETURNING TO OUR SPIRITUAL SENSES

As previously noted, one of the driving factors for recent theological discussion around deep incarnation has to do with the growing sense of urgency regarding our shared ecological plight. In the midst of the most comprehensive crisis facing life on our planet, there is great need to bring the central affirmations of Christian faith to bear upon our common project of living justly, sustainably, and compassionately with our fellow creatures—not just human beings but the whole community of creation. This is not an exclusively Christian task, needless to say; humanity's diverse religious and secular traditions will need to learn richly from one another and cooperate on an unprecedented scale in order to respond appropriately. Nevertheless, it is out of the particularities of these traditions, not despite them, that such learning and cooperation must arise. As desirable as a shared ecological sensibility may be, it cannot emerge by bracketing out the unique content and motivational resources of humanity's diverse traditions but only by working through them. This suggests that while appeal to the central features of Christian faith cannot suffice as *the* answer to the issue of ecological crisis—and, indeed, we should be mindful of the ways the tradition has contributed to the crisis, even if indirectly, through its underdevelopment or misappropriation—such an appeal will be crucial as a contributing element for facing our crisis more squarely.

Hearing

Though specific treatment of ecotheology and environmental ethics is not possible here, I would like to conclude this chapter by indicating a few ways in which themes developed in part 3 can contribute to the discussion. The first is incarnational in character and follows from the preceding analysis. Having further inquired into what *flesh* means in deep incarnational perspective, we can more readily see how its all-embracing character guides a way of envisioning human flourishing as inextricably bound with the flourishing of other creatures. On account of our intercorporeity, and thus the inherently relational character of our being in the world—what Leder calls the "consanguinity" of all living bodies[134]—any understanding of our assumed human nature that excludes the more-than-human world results, ironically, in something less-than-human. Likewise, any ideal of spiritual transcendence that subtly implies a flight from our shared corporeality suffers from a malnourished incarnational imagination. The incarnation does not mean that God became flesh only to abscond from all embodiment upon Christ's death and resurrection. The affirmation of Christ's *transfigured* corporeality means that the only spiritual fulfillment proper to the God of Jesus Christ is one that fully embraces the whole of corporeal reality.

Christians are "the most sublime materialists."[135] In saying this, Rahner does not intend anything reductionistic. He means only to point out that material reality must be accorded the greatest possible significance, much more than any scientific or philosophical materialism can fathom, precisely because the world is an event of divine self-communication. The affirmation that God created all things out of self-emptying love, but more, that God became creaturely as the utmost expression of that love, subverts any binary thinking that casts "spirit" and "matter" as opposites, whether in the direction of spiritualism or materialism. A genuinely incarnational faith, if it is to shape how we perceive, feel, think, and act, directly challenges such contrastive thinking and throws open an alternative horizon in which the fulfillment of one implies the fulfillment of the other. "We neither can nor should conceive of any ultimate fullness of the spirit and of reality without thinking too of matter enduring as well in a state of final perfection."[136] Citing Tertullian's play on words, "the flesh (*caro*) is the pivot (*cardo*) of salvation," Rahner makes clear that Christian faith is one that loves the earth. Through Christ's death, the "divine heart" descends into the "center of the world," just as the world "sinks it roots into God's omnipotence."[137] Through his resurrection, Christ has "accepted the world forever. He has been born again as a child of the earth, but of the transfigured, liberated earth, the earth which in him is eternally confirmed and eternally redeemed from death and futility." There is a pronounced organicism to Rahner's Christ-mysticism here, as well as a strong sense of universal filiation in which the heart of God is found "in the midst of all the poor things of this earth," in the "wordless expectation of all creatures, which without knowing it, wait to share in the glorification of his body."[138] The empty tomb does not mean that God has left "the dark bosom of the earth empty and without hope. For he rose again in his *body*. That means he has already begun to transform this world into himself."[139]

The originally homiletic context of this account may have given Rahner license to express more poetically what he articulates elsewhere more philosophically and systematically, but it highlights the aesthetic rejuvenation that is central to any Christian contribution to our ecological moment. More basic than any problem-solving or technical solution, more fundamental than any ethical directive or policy goal, we need a renewal of perception: a return to our spiritual senses so as to behold the elemental beauty and inestimable worth of all creaturely reality. We need a *felt sense* of the intimacy of the God-world relation so that we know in a spontaneous way that the love of God leads directly to the love of creation and vice versa. Because God is at the heart of the world, "we children of this earth may love it, must love it." Without confusing God and creation, we must know at the level of affect, and not just through deliberation, that the way of genuine spiritual self-transcendence opens up an ever-greater love of creation in all its diversity, fragility, and interdependence. "If we seek the God of infinity," and if we seek "the familiar earth as it is and as it is to become," then we will discover that "one way leads to both."[140]

I will return to the importance of aesthetic rejuvenation momentarily, but I wish to draw out one feature of Rahner's homiletic appeal that requires specification in light of our accelerating ecological crisis. When Rahner refers to God as indwelling "the poor things of this earth," it is crucial to give this an added inflection by pointing out how vulnerable certain populations of human beings are as a result of our species' assault on the earth. We are not wrong to speak of the community of all creation, or the intercorporeity of all living beings, and certainly all forms of life are endangered by runaway deforestation and desertification, the depletion of groundwater and biodiversity, along with the alarming rate of climate change as a result of accumulating greenhouse gases. And yet the menacing consequences of these systemic changes are disproportionally felt by the most vulnerable in our society—the poor, the migrant, the displaced, the socially marginalized. While populations with economic and political means may be relatively buffered from the immediate impact of environmental degradation, at least in the short term, millions and millions of our brothers and sisters, billions even, live at the razor's edge of ecological disaster every day simply because they are poor. Environmental pollution, loss of green space, scarcity of food and water, the collapse of economic systems dependent upon healthy soil, fresh streams, stable coastlines, and biodiversity: these are just some of the numerous challenges many of our fellow human beings face with a level of desperation unfelt by the world's most privileged. For such brothers and sisters, the inter-corporeity of all life is not just an ontological fact worth pondering; it is a painful form of intercorporeity crying out for justice.

As Pope Francis urges in *Laudato Si'*, the first encyclical of his pontificate, "We have to realize that a true ecological approach *always* becomes a social approach; it must integrate questions of justice in debates on the environment, so as to hear *both the cry of the earth and the cry of the poor*" (49).[141] As the pope makes clear throughout his landmark encyclical, a true love of the earth cannot pit human and more-than-human reality against one another. The capacity to hear the suffering of our fellow human beings, especially the most vul-nerable, is intrinsically connected to hearing the cry of nature itself. Together these cries call for "ecological conversion" so that the work of justice for the most vulnerable is integrally united with ecological justice.[142] In an age in which unchecked anthropocentrism threatens the health of the very planet, any effort to heal social divisions, eco-nomic inequality, and political disenfranchisement within the *huma-num* turns out to depend crucially upon "care of our common home." Indeed, the pope insists that "we cannot adequately combat environ-mental degradation *unless* we attend to causes related to human and social degradation."[143] The point of this "unless" is not to reassert a form of anthropocentrism that prioritizes human over environmental concerns. It means to highlight how disordered relationships within the human family spill over and cause harm to our extended family. Love of our fellow human beings turns out to be fundamental to how we love the earth, and the greatest index for such love is how we love the least of these (Matt. 25:40).

Seeing

If *hearing* the cry of the earth and the cry of the poor represents one of the spiritual senses most needed during our time, the second I wish to highlight is *seeing* creation anew in the light of Divine Wisdom. Here we may take further inspiration from Bulgakov's visionary style of theology. Whatever critical engagements his theological project might encourage in the future, it is this visionary dimension that will be the most significant. As Andrew Louth rightly notes, Sophiology is not so much a matter of "thinking about a collection of truths" as it is a way of "looking" or "beholding."[144] A sustained spiritual exercise—one deeply rooted in the liturgical life of the church—it invites us to see creation sacramentally, as a great "showing forth" of God's invisible wisdom. Creation itself is an event of revelation, not merely its setting. Significantly, it was an encounter with Divine Wisdom in a natural landscape that proved decisive in Bulgakov's reconversion to his Orthodox faith. Traveling by train across the southern steppe, with the Caucasus Mountains spreading out in the early evening distance, the twenty-four-year-old Sergius was seized by a life-altering awakening:

> And fixing my avid gaze on the mountains that had opened before me, drinking in the light and air, I harkened to the revelation of nature. My soul had grown accustomed long ago to see with a dull silent pain only a dead wasteland in nature beneath the veil of beauty, as under a deceptive mask; without being aware of it, my soul was not able to reconcile with a nature without God. And suddenly in that hour my soul became agitated, started to rejoice and began to shiver: *but what if* . . . if it is not a wasteland, not a lie, not a mask, not death but him, the blessed and loving Father, his raiment, his love . . . ?[145]

Seeing creation as though for the first time ("Before me the first day of creation blazed") was not a matter of mental fabrication for Bulgakov. He was not trying to will his way to a new mode of perception. It was a matter of receptivity. He was newly *available* to what was always already there, but which had been obscured by a certain framing of the world. Bulgakov invokes the language of apocalyptic in this account; it *un*veiled what lay beneath years and years of habituation—not just his own but that of his intellectual milieu, which was largely beholden to atheistic materialism. With the veils to spiritual vision lifted, the "beauty of the primordial" was disclosed. It was Sophia, he would later recall, God's eternal Wisdom, whose

Return to Love 259

sheer innocence and unfailing splendor "told of another world, which I had lost."[146]

It was the first of several such encounters, and Bulgakov would accord enduring value to the felt sense of the God-world relation they opened up for him. There was enormous intellectual effort to follow, as the whole of his theological project can be viewed as an attempt to give such encounters systematic theological expression—its own kind of ascesis. And yet all of that disciplined effort flowed from a "lived experience of God" that he described in terms of a new "light," as "a completely different taste," as a "new sensation of being."[147] This is not a matter of sentimentalism, he would insist, or a reduction of faith to feeling, but an aesthetic rehabilitation capable of sparking and nourishing ongoing conversion in the moral, intellectual, and spiritual spheres.[148] It opened up for him an overwhelming sense of the inmost rapport between God and creation, and with it an immediate apprehension of creation's primordial unity *in* God.

If Rahner's account of Easter faith exhibits a theopoetic inclination toward organic images and metaphors, Bulgakov's extended treatment of the Divine-humanity is entirely suffused with a sense of organicism. This is not because he conjoins God and creature within an encompassing metaphorical frame, as this would undermine the way of antinomy previously discussed, but because he seeks creative reintegration of contrary tendencies that, when split off from one another, lead to desiccation and eventual pathology in their one-sidedness. Weaving together elements from scripture, liturgy, patristics, medieval mysticism, German Romantic philosophy, and nineteenth-century Russian figures (poets, mystics, novelists, and philosophers), Bulgakov characterizes the task of *wisdom* theology as healing the disenchanting effects of modern rationalism and materialism. If presently we find ourselves stuck in a cosmic imaginary that pictures the world in terms of mechanism, quantification, and instrumental control, what is most needed from Christian faith in our late-modern moment is not a pragmatic turn that reduces faith to policy but a sapiential turn that releases us from all objectifying tendencies so as to "see" the world in a new way—as *creation*.[149] Coordinated human action is of course quite crucial, but what inspires and sustains right action is a rehabilitation of vision, a renewal of perception, a shift in affect. True love for the world "can be accomplished only through a change in our conception of the world, and through a Sophianic perception of the world in the Wisdom of God. This alone can give us strength for new inspiration, for new creativity, for overcoming the mechanization of life and of human beings."[150]

Sophianic perception is akin to the vision of the artist. It does not require the accumulation of peak aesthetic experiences so much as it entails a sustained willingness to welcome and grow more sensitive to the beauty at the heart of created reality, just as it *is*. This implies an ascesis, a training of the "inner eye" whereby one becomes attuned to Divine Wisdom as "the intelligence of the world, its inexhaustible depths and the beauty of its forms."[151] In contrast to an objectifying gaze that looks at the world as something to manage, the inner eye of spiritual perception delights in the surprising excess of creation's unfolding, its penchant for novelty at all levels of organization, its mutually enfolding relationships. Because such perception is essentially welcoming rather than dominating, it already bears within it an ethic that values the "otherness" of creation. Rather than submitting the creaturely other to "my" interests, or according to pre-given frameworks of sensibility and comprehension, the ascesis of spiritual vision allows the creaturely other to show forth in its integrity, in its unsuspected beauty and distinctive intelligence, so as to overflow and even transform such limited frameworks. There is a self-emptying involved here, for Sophianic perception allows something new to appear through the renunciation of any claim over it. It sincerely wishes the other "to be," and in this way such perception shares in God's own creativity. Rowan Williams makes just this connection as he describes Bulgakov's Sophiology as a long-form recommendation for letting creation *happen*.

> The human calling to share the love and the liberty of God has to be in this perspective a calling to "let be." The paradox of real human creativity is that it is not the flexing of our human, our created will, the flexing of our muscles, the imposing of order, the dredging up of something new out of the depths of interiority; our creativity is most fully and freely expressed as humans when

Return to Love 261

we, as artists, stand back and let be. . . . The really creative work is a happening; it is the depth of the world occurring where the artist is because the artist has somehow exercised that asceticism of setting aside preferences and purposes and all the rest of it, so that something occurs.[152]

It may seem counterintuitive to emphasize such "letting be" in response to our ecological crisis, given that there is so much *to do* in terms of education, social protest, public dialogue, and policy-making. The suggestion that we "stand back and let be" may well appear like a recipe for indifferentism. But the contemplative attitude to which Williams refers is not at all opposed to ethical and prophetic action on behalf of social, economic, and ecological well-being. It nourishes such action by promoting that most basic mode of attention enabling us to "see" the more-than-human world as worthy of being, as valuable in itself, well beyond narrow human interests and designs. We are in need of "other ways of seeing and apprehending reality," writes Douglas E. Christie, ways that are "more subtle and more deeply rooted in our intuitive feeling for the whole." Drawing upon the ancient Christian contemplative tradition of *prosoche*, or being attentive, Christie notes that its recovery "may well be one of the most important contributions we can make to the work of ecological renewal."[153] Whereas instrumental styles of looking underwrite a fragmented vision of reality and thus feed the sense of human alienation from the living world, the cultivation of deep attention, of beholding all things through the wide eyes of wonderment, enables us to gain renewed access to the sense of wholeness and "help us heal some of the imaginative rifts that have prevented us from seeing and living in the world with a sense of its integrity, beauty, and mystery."[154] As with Bulgakov's conversion, it opens up our vision to another world—one we are in danger of losing.

Feeling

In keeping with this contemplative mood, I wish finally to appeal to the spiritual sense of touch, or more broadly feeling, in order to highlight the *felt sense* of our filiation with God and our fellow creatures—one that opens up the pores of an all-inclusive compassion in the midst of our ecological plight. This, too, entails ongoing conversion. Here the language of "letting go" or "letting be" that typically accompanies instruction in contemplative practice is highly suggestive. Such a disposition, it must be reiterated, has nothing to do with cultivating pleasant feelings or inuring ourselves from uncomfortable realities. "Contemplation is no pain-killer," insists Merton. It is not a "passive acquiescence to the status quo" or a kind of "spiritual anesthesia."[155] It is an opening, a purification and a freeing up of tightly wound identities, a welcoming of a fuller range of experience beyond narrow conceptual frameworks. Whereas often we grasp at being in the effort to secure identity for ourselves, whether individually or in groups, the contemplative path entails a process of releasing this tendency so as to grow in wisdom and love. Recognizing our propensity to cling to thoughts, desires, and emotional patterns as though our very existence depended upon them, contemplation relaxes our tenacious grip on the flow of experience and opens us up to the utterly spacious awareness within which all such experience arises. Such letting go is essentially kenotic. "To enter into the realm of contemplation one must in a certain sense die: but this death is in fact the entrance into a higher life." This higher life is not an abstraction or the mere blanking out of "lower" faculties. Indeed, Merton refers to contemplative awareness as a kind of *touch*. "It knows God by seeming to touch Him. Or rather it knows Him as if it had been invisibly touched by Him. . . . Touched by Him Who has no hands, but Who is pure Reality and the source of all that is real!"[156] Merton is clear that such language is metaphorical, and yet the intimacy of touching and being touched, as distinguished from grasping, suggests a quality of awareness that is at once intimate and capacious. Contemplation is a "gift of awareness." It is a "vivid awareness of infinite Being at the roots of our own limited being. An awareness of our contingent reality as received, as a present from God, as a free gift of love."[157]

Key to this characterization is the shift it denotes regarding our felt sense of contingency. While our ontological dependence as creatures is indeed a gift, we can nevertheless experience that dependence with a sense of unease. We are profoundly vulnerable by virtue of our creatureliness and thus ever on the lookout for safety, acceptance, and love. Myriad are the ways we might acquire what we seem to lack in ourselves, including strategies of self-buffering, self-aggrandizing, and self-dissipation, but underlying such strategies is the same basic feeling of disquiet that leaves us with a sense of perpetual displacement. We never really seem to be "at home." We never seem to be "at rest." We never seem to "fill in" the bottomless abyss from which we spring into being. Without seeking to overcome this underlying unease, as though our finitude were something to be combated, the contemplative approach simply turns *toward* this unease and, as it were, deeply allows it. It lets go of its defenses. It accepts the poverty of its being. It welcomes the fact that we are limited and ontologically on loan, interdependent with all other creatures in our shared corporeality. Rather than shielding ourselves against this apparent "nothingness," the contemplative gesture is one of unfolding the arms and unclasping the hands, of settling into the felt sense of our ontological dependence with an abiding trust in That Which Is. "We must 'empty ourselves' as [Christ] did," says Merton. "We must live by a power and a light that seem not to be there. We must live by the strength of an apparent emptiness that is always truly empty and yet never fails to support us at every moment."[158]

As we relax into our creatureliness in this trusting and nongrasping way, and as we grow more familiar with the pacific and nonobjectifiable depths of divine reality sustaining us in being, so will we discover deeper capacities for living freely and compassionately with our fellow creatures. The breath elongates. The shoulders drop. The eyebrows unfurrow. Awareness dilates. The heart opens. Sensing the inmost reality from which *all* creation springs—the pure source of all that is real, as Merton puts it—the contracted "self" with which we typically identify, and which seems set off from others and the world, becomes less determinative of the flow of experience, less partitional and weighty, less compulsive and clingy, increasingly porous and supple, perhaps receding altogether. The conceptual boundaries that seem to demarcate "me" from "you" (or "us" from "them," or "human" from "nonhuman") become increasingly permeable, more pliable for creative reimagining and living. The innate openness of awareness settles the body and allows the underlying affective tone of our being in the world to aerate. Less fixated by the whirling drama of the discursive mind, we learn to live more from the "heart-mind"—the inmost wellspring of awareness itself—and settle into the felt sense of God's unconditional love. Such love is not something acquired or earned. It is given in the very core of our being. It has only to be recognized and received. We need only to let it happen, to let it flow through us. To "let be." And although this unconditional love is something we are constantly forgetting or mistaking for something else, the sense of separation this misidentification generates, however real in its effects, is not real in an ultimate sense. As Laird writes:

> Because God is the ground of our being, the relationship between creature and Creator is such that, by sheer grace, separation is not possible. God does not know how to be absent. The fact that most of us experience throughout most of our lives a sense of absence or distance from God is the great illusion that we are caught up in; it is the human condition. The sense of separation from God is real, but the meeting of stillness reveals that this perceived separation does not have the last word. . . . The grace of salvation, the grace of Christian wholeness that flowers in silence, dispels this illusion of separation. For when the mind is brought to stillness, and all our strategies of acquisition have dropped, a deeper truth presents itself: we are and have always been one with God and we are all one in God (John 17:21).[159]

The sense of wholeness of which Laird speaks is the most fundamental basis for living freely and lovingly within the community of creation. So long as we are under the spell of separation we will be subject to the restlessness and acquisitiveness that so readily attach themselves to ersatz satisfactions. Laird points to our "consumer-driven entertainment culture" as a prime example.[160] The compulsive need for more, for the latest allurement, for the greatest convenience, for most revolutionary advancement, for the most status-bearing "thing": such endless aggregation results in a never-satisfying treadmill for those trapped by it, and yet we have premised so much of our late-modern economic and cultural life upon it. Easily the most dominant factor in our increasingly perilous relationship with the

Return to Love   265

more-than-human world, the compulsion for "more" is ultimately a spiritual sickness. It grasps at creation rather than letting it happen.

Contemplation "immerses us in the larger whole," writes Christie. It encourages "a quality of awareness that enables one to enter in and respond to both the seen and unseen dimensions of one's embodied life in the world."[161] Because of this sense for the whole—one that embraces our shared corporeality in its depths—contemplative practice can help nourish the "ecological conscience" we so desperately need today.[162] Through the "cultivation of a simple, spacious awareness of the whole," contemplative practice can "help us rediscover what it is to live in the world with purpose, meaning, and depth."[163] While not a substitute for other ways in which this ecological conscience must be developed and enacted, including artistic expression, scientific inquiry, education, public debate, and policy-making, the felt sense of wholeness that flowers in silence can restore our spiritual senses and renew our resolve by reconnecting us with the inmost source of our filiation of all creation. It is the return to love.

NOTES

ONE   The Difference Nothing Makes

1. Karl Rahner, "Current Problems in Christology," *Theological Investigations* 1, trans. Cornelius Ernst, O.P. (London: Darton, Longman & Todd, 1961), 151.

2. Ibid., 150.

3. Ibid., 152.

4. Janet Soskice helpfully characterizes *creatio ex nihilo* as a "recessive Christian doctrine." While not foregrounded in doctrinal discussions as often as the doctrine of incarnation or the doctrine of the Trinity, its importance "underlies much Christian thought and practice, devotional as well as systematic and apologetic, on the problem of evil, the possibility of miracles, the nature of religious language, grace, the efficacy of intercessory prayer, and God's loving presence to the created order" ("Why *Creatio ex nihilo* for Theology Today?" in *Creation* ex nihilo*: Origins, Development, Contemporary Challenges*, ed. Gary A. Anderson and Markus Bockmuehl (Notre Dame, IN: University of Notre Dame Press, 2018), 37. The recessive nature of *creatio ex nihilo* by no means indicates its relative unimportance. It only underscores that importance because its foundational role is presupposed in many other areas of Christian imagination, thought, and practice.

5. John D. Caputo, *The Weakness of God: A Theology of the Event* (Bloomington: Indiana University Press, 2005), 93.

6. Catherine Keller, *Face of the Deep: A Theology of Becoming* (London: Routledge, 2003). For a survey of recent critical approaches to *creatio ex nihilo*, see Thomas J. Oord, ed., *Theologies of Creation:* Creatio ex nihilo *and its New Rivals* (London: Routledge, 2014).

7. See Paul Copan and William Lane Craig, *Creation Out of Nothing: A Biblical, Philosophical, and Scientific Exploration* (Grand Rapids, MI: Baker Academic, 2004).

8. See Kathryn Tanner, *God and Creation in Christian Theology: Tyranny or Empowerment?* (Minneapolis: Fortress Press, 1988).

268 Notes to Pages 10–15

9. The specific sense of necessity rejected here has to do with any externally imposed exigency upon God. The nonnecessity of creation refers to God's unconditioned freedom, a freedom in which creation itself participates. Later, in chapter 6, we shall explore another sense of "necessity" (i.e., "fittingness") that proves crucial for elucidating the inmost "reason" for creation, namely, God's eternal nature as self-diffusive love.

10. Caputo, *The Weakness of God*, 59.

11. Ibid.

12. Ibid., 80, 85.

13. I agree with Caputo that *creatio ex nihilo* and divine omnipotence are correlative, but it should be pointed out that not all do. Jon Levenson, for example, affirms divine omnipotence while denying *creatio ex nihilo*. See his rich and challenging study, *Creation and the Persistence of Evil: The Jewish Drama of Divine Omnipotence* (San Francisco: Harper & Row, 1988).

14. Ibid., 87. Caputo cites John Cobb and David Ray Griffin, *Process Theology: An Introductory Exposition* (Knoxville, KY: Westminster John Knox Press, 1977) and Charles Hartshorne, *Omnipotence and Other Theological Mistakes* (Albany, NY: SUNY Press, 1983). Keller's extensive engagement with process theology, feminism, and deconstruction informs Caputo's assessment as well.

15. Caputo, *The Weakness of God*, 178.

16. Ibid., 180.

17. This either/or characterization is similar to Keller's summative assessment: "According to the logic of *ex nihilo*, one is either good or evil, corporeal or incorporeal, eternal or temporal, almighty or powerless, propertied or inferior" (*Face of the Deep*, 49). While Keller acknowledges that this "grid of dualisms" is not the necessary correlate of *creatio ex nihilo*, historically they have been closely associated. I think the point is highly debatable, but a fuller rejoinder would need to engage Keller's reading of theological texts on a case-by-case basis, which is not possible here. Keller does concede, however, (in a footnote, alas) that efforts to "radicalize" transcendence, such as we find in the work of Kathryn Tanner, serve commendably to disrupt such a grid (ibid., 254–55, n48). It is Tanner's lead I follow, though she is hardly alone in her commitment to engaging "classical" theological approaches in postmodern context.

18. Henri de Lubac, *The Discovery of God*, trans. Alexander Dru (Grand Rapids: Wm. B. Eerdmans, 1996), 94.

19. Kahled Anatolios neatly summarizes Athanasius's influential account as follows: "Creation's being from nothing is simultaneously its being in God" ("*Creatio ex nihilo* in Athanasius of Alexandria's *Against the Greeks—On the Incarnation*," in *Creation* ex nihilo: *Origins, Development, Contemporary Challenges*, ed. Gary A. Anderson and Markus Bockmuehl, 128).

20. Karl Rahner, *Foundations of Christian Faith: An Introduction to the Idea of Christianity*, trans. William V. Dych (New York: Seabury Press, 1978), 62.

21. Karl Rahner, "Immanent and Transcendent Consummation of the World," *Theological Investigations* 10, trans. David Bourke (London: Darton, Longman & Todd, 1973), 281.

Notes to Pages 16–22   269

22. Tanner, *God and Creation in Christian Theology*, 39.

23. Ibid., 41.

24. Robert Sokolowski, *The God of Faith and Reason: Foundations of Christian Theology* (Notre Dame, IN: University of Notre Dame Press, 1982), 19. We shall later have opportunity to qualify the statement that the world "might not have been." While obviously bearing the aspect of negation, *creatio ex nihilo* implies massive positive content. The more we explore that content, the more we will see that creation comes "to be" precisely because of *who* God is.

25. Ibid., 23.

26. Rowan Williams, "On Being Creatures," in *On Christian Theology* (Oxford: Blackwell, 2000), 74, 75–76.

27. I will significantly develop this connection between doctrinal insight and contemplative awareness in chapter 2.

28. Caputo, *The Weakness of God*, 45.

29. See David B. Burrell, C.S.C., "Creator/Creatures Relation: 'The Distinction' vs. 'Onto-theology,'" *Faith and Philosophy* 25 (2008): 177–89; with "Reply to Cross and Hasker," 205–12.

30. Tanner, *God and Creation in Christian Theology*, 46. For other works where Tanner develops this noncontrastive view of the God-world relationship in topically specific ways, see *The Politics of God: Christian Theologies and Social Justice* (Minneapolis: Fortress Press, 1992); *Jesus, Humanity and the Trinity: A Brief Systematic Theology* (Minneapolis: Fortress Press, 2001); *Economy of Grace* (Minneapolis: Fortress Press, 2005); and *Christ the Key* (Cambridge: Cambridge University Press, 2010).

31. Caputo, *The Weakness of God*, 39.

32. Tanner, *God and Creation in Christian Theology*, 47.

33. Ibid., 81–119. See also William C. Placher's discussion of divine grace and human initiative in *The Domestication of Transcendence: How Modern Thinking about God Went Wrong* (Louisville, KY: Westminster John Knox Press, 1996), 88–107.

34. Tanner, *God and Creation in Christian Theology*, 47.

35. Ibid., 46.

36. Wolfhart Pannenberg, *Systematic Theology*, vol. 1, trans. Geoffrey W. Bromiley (Grand Rapids, MI: Eerdmans, 1988), 416.

37. Richard Bauckham, "God Who Raises the Dead: The Resurrection of Jesus and Early Christian Faith in God," in *The Resurrection of Jesus Christ*, ed. Paul Avis (London: Darton, Longman & Todd, 1993), 136.

38. Ian A. MacFarland rightly observes that discussion of divine omnipotence cannot helpfully proceed without reference to *who* God is, which, for Christian theology, is possible only within a "christological matrix." If treated thus, most objections to *creatio ex nihilo* as a matter of "divine totalitarianism seem at the very least rhetorically misplaced" (*From Nothing: A Theology of Creation* [Louisville, KY: Westminster John Knox Press, 2014]), 23–24.

39. Caputo, *The Weakness of God*, 43.

40. Ibid., 53.

41. Ibid., 90.

270   Notes to Pages 23–27

42. William Placher characterizes the modern "domestication of transcendence," which took root in the seventeenth century, in three ways:

> 1. Many theologians came to think of God as one of the entities or agents in the world among the others, and of God's properties as differing from those of created things in degree rather than in kind. . . . 2. The effort to make God, and God's agency, comprehensible also leads to thinking about the relation of God to human freedom and responsibility as a zero-sum. . . . 3. Theologians who think of God as one thing in the world alongside others often then try to preserve some sense of divine transcendence by emphasizing that God is the most distant, most powerful thing in the world, at the peak of all the world's hierarchies of being and value. This often makes God the *enemy of transformative justice*, since God's place at the peak of hierarchies gives divine sanction to those hierarchies, and a God defined in terms of distance, power, and unaffectability gives such qualities the imprimatur of divinity. (*The Domestication of Transcendence*, 181–82)

Placher's study, which bears reading alongside several others providing comparable assessments (e.g., Charles Taylor, Louis Dupré, Stephen Toulmin, John Milbank, Hans Frei, Michael J. Buckley), concludes by arguing that many of the revisionist proposals in contemporary theology, including process theology, deconstruction, and functionalism, end up accepting the terms of modernity in their attempt to overcome them (183).

43. Placher, *The Domestication of Transcendence*, 190.

44. John Milbank, "Postmodern Critical Augustinianism: A Short *Summa* in Forty-Two Responses to Unasked Questions," in *The Postmodern God: A Theological Reader*, ed. Graham Ward (London: Blackwell, 1997), 267. As Milbank points out, much depends on how we characterize such relational differences. That they can be (and usually are) a mixture of agonism and peace, violence and harmony in our contingent history is undeniable. But whether we regard one or the other as "ontological" (or, anterior to creation) makes a very appreciable difference. Such is at stake in *creatio ex nihilo*, as I shall later explain.

45. Rahner, *Foundations of Christian Faith*, 105.

46. For more on this threefold narrative pattern in Paul's theology of "the powers," see John Howard Yoder, *The Politics of Jesus: Vicit Agnus Noster*, 2nd ed. (Grand Rapids: Eerdmans, 1994), 134–61; Hendrikus Berkhof, *Christ and the Powers* (Scottsdale, PA: Herald Press, 1962); Walter Wink, *The Powers That Be: Theology for a New Millennium* (New York: Doubleday, 1998).

47. William Placher, *Narratives of a Vulnerable God: Christ, Theology, and Scripture* (Louisville, KY: Westminster John Knox Press, 1994), 17.

48. Ibid.

49. Karl Barth, *Church Dogmatics* IV/1, trans. G. W. Bromiley and T. F. Torrance (Edinburgh: T&T Clark, 1956), 186–87.

50. Placher, *Narratives of a Vulnerable God*, 19.

51. Williams, "On Being Creatures," 72.

52. Ibid., 72–73.

Notes to Pages 29–34   271

53. Jean-Luc Marion, *God without Being: Hors-Texte*, trans. Thomas A. Carlson (Chicago: University of Chicago Press, 1991), 86.

54. Ibid., 101.

55. Williams, "On Being Creatures," 67–68.

56. Ibid., 68.

57. For an incisive summary of the relationship between *creatio ex nihilo* and major biblical themes, see Gary A. Anderson, "*Creatio ex nihilo* and the Bible," in *Creation* ex nihilo: *Origins, Development, Contemporary Challenges*, ed. Gary A. Anderson and Markus Bockmuehl, 15–35.

58. David B. Burrell, C.S.C., *Freedom and Creation in Three Traditions* (Notre Dame, IN: University of Notre Dame Press, 1993), 27. Burrell makes clear that the Genesis accounts do not affirm *creatio ex nihilo* in any strict sense, though he argues that such is a legitimate development of those accounts (16)—a development that was undertaken by all three Abrahamic faiths. These "respective communities came to realize that the divine action portrayed narratively must nonetheless be understood as that of causing the very being of things and indeed of all that is. This is what we mean by *creatio ex nihilo*, which intends to state that nothing at all is presupposed to his activity of creating" (25).

59. I am indebted to James Alison for this distinction as it relates to the resurrection. See his *The Joy of Being Wrong: Original Sin Through Easter Eyes* (New York: Crossroad, 1998), 100–102.

60. For this shift from metaphor to metonym in the evolution of resurrection language and belief, see N. T. Wright, *The Resurrection of the Son of God*, vol. 3 of *Christian Origins and the Question of God* (Minneapolis: Fortress Press, 2003), 129–205.

61. Pannenberg, *Systematic Theology*, 1:417.

62. Paul Ricoeur, "The Logic of Jesus, the Logic of God," in *Figuring the Sacred: Religion, Narrative, and Imagination*, trans. David Pellauer, ed. Mark I. Wallace (Minneapolis: Fortress Press, 1995), 281–82.

63. Markus Barth and Verne H. Fletcher, *Acquittal by Resurrection* (New York: Holt, Rinehart and Winston, 1964), 70. See also Rowan Williams's insightful discussion of "the judgment of judgment" in his *Resurrection: Interpreting the Easter Gospel* (Harrisburg, PA: Morehouse, 1994), 7–28.

64. Alison, *The Joy of Being Wrong*, 98. See also Alison's similar treatment in *Raising Abel: The Recovery of the Eschatological Imagination* (New York: Crossroad, 1996).

65. Ibid., 98–99. Similarly, Williams: "The creative life, death and resurrection of Jesus manifests a creator who works in, not against, our limits, our mortality: the creator who, as the one who call being forth from nothing, gives without dominating" ("On Being Creatures," 76). I will develop these themes of violence, forgiveness, gratuity, and demythologization at length in part 2.

66. Alison, *The Joy of Being Wrong*, 190.

67. James D. G. Dunn, *Christology in the Making: A New Testament Inquiry into the Origins of the Doctrine of the Incarnation* (Philadelphia: Westminster Press, 1980), 256. Raymond Brown also gives account of this retrospective movement in Johannine Christology in his *Introduction to New Testament*

Christology (New York: Paulist Press, 1994), 133–52. For a comprehensive account of retrospective Christology in the gospels, see Richard B. Hays, *Reading Backwards: Figural Christology and the Fourfold Gospel Witness* (Waco, TX: Baylor University Press, 2016).

68. Paul Ricoeur, "Thinking Creation," in *Thinking Biblically: Exegetical and Hermeneutical Studies*, by André LaCocque and Paul Ricoeur, trans. David Pellauer (Chicago: University of Chicago Press, 1998), 62.

69. Ibid., 63.

70. Ibid.

71. Ibid., 34.

72. Ibid., 63.

73. Gerhard May, *Creatio ex nihilo: The Doctrine of 'Creation out of Nothing' in Early Christian Thought*, trans. A. S. Worrall (London: T&T Clark, 1994), 177–78.

74. Ibid., 163.

75. Ibid., 161.

76. Ibid., xii.

77. Ibid., 111. Something similar must be said of the Christian gnostic Basilides, who, in the middle of the second century, formulated his view of *creatio ex nihilo* by "knitting together . . . common Christian and gnostic motifs" (84). While both Caputo and Keller point to May's examination of Basilides as evidence that gnostic tendencies are at root in *creatio ex nihilo*—Basilides precedes Tatian by a few decades—May himself argues that Basilides' formulation, which appears to have had no influence on Tatian, Theophilus, or Irenaeus, actually departs from usual gnostic views by declaring God the sole creator (83, 179–80). Moreover, whereas Tatian, Theophilus, and Irenaeus affirmed God's intimate involvement in history as a key corollary to *creatio ex nihilo*, Basilides limited God's role to a single, utterly remote act of creating the "world-seed" (180). Basilides' God is absolutely distant from and uninvolved with creation. This is what May means when he says that "the biblical ideas of creation and omnipotence are overstated in Basilides in a gnostic way" (84).

78. Paul Ricoeur, *The Symbolism of Evil*, trans. Emerson Buchanan (Boston: Beacon Press, 1967), 211–305. Also relevant is Ricoeur's discussion of the critical mutations decipherable in the biblical appropriation of Mesopotamian creation myths, particularly as relates to "chaos" (175–210). Evil is not a "necessary" feature of world order, which is "good from the first," but a scandalous rupture of that goodness that is historical (not cosmogonic) in character (203).

79. May, *Creatio ex nihilo*, 176.

80. Ibid.

81. As Tertullian memorably put it, the flesh (*caro*) is the pivot (*cardo*) on which salvation turns (*De resurrectione carnis*, par. 8). It is notable also that Tertullian drew explicit connections between *creatio ex nihilo* and the resurrection of the dead in this regard (par. 11).

82. Caputo, *The Weakness of God*, 87.

83. Placher, *The Domestication of Transcendence*, 211.

Notes to Pages 39–47   273

84. Edward Schillebeeckx, *Jesus: An Experiment in Christology*, trans. Hubert Hoskins (New York: Crossroad, 1985), 627.

85. Edward Schillebeeckx, *Christ: The Experience of Jesus as Lord*, trans. John Bowden (New York: Crossroad, 1990), 727, 728. Schillebeeckx draws explicitly from Thomas Aquinas's assessment of *creatio ex nihilo* in this formulation (*II Sent.* D. 37, q. 2, a. 1, ad 2).

86. Ibid., 729.

87. Ibid., 729–30.

TWO   Undergoing Something from Nothing

1. Sebastian Moore, "Some Principles for an Adequate Theism," *Downside Review* 95 (1977): 201.

2. Ibid., 203.

3. Ibid., 203–4.

4. Ibid., 203.

5. William Desmond, *God and the Between* (Oxford: Blackwell, 2008), 34.

6. Ibid.

7. Thomas Merton, *Thoughts in Solitude* (New York: Noonday Press, 1956), 43.

8. James Alison, *Undergoing God: Dispatches from the Scene of a Break-in* (New York: Continuum, 2006), 4.

9. Ibid., 5.

10. Denys Turner reminds us that it is a mistake to oppose contemplative silence and speech about God, just as it is false to oppose apophasis and cataphasis in general. With reference to the Pseudo-Dionysian corpus and its enormous influence in the history of Christian theology, Turner notes that all apophasis "presupposes the cataphatic 'dialectically' in the sense that the silence of the negative way is the silence achieved only at the point at which talk about God has been exhausted" ("Apophaticism, Idolatry, and the Claims of Reason," in *Silence and the Word: Negative Theology and Incarnation*, ed. Oliver Davies and Denys Turner [Cambridge: Cambridge University Press, 2002], 18).

11. Sarah Coakley, *God, Sexuality, and the Self: An Essay 'On the Trinity'* (Cambridge: Cambridge University Press, 2013), 41.

12. Ibid.

13. See Sarah Coakley, *Submissions and Powers: Spirituality, Philosophy, and Gender* (Oxford: Blackwell, 2002), esp. part 1. See also Sarah Coakley, "Dark Contemplation and Epistemic Transformation: The Analytic Theologian Re-Meets Teresa of Avila," in *Analytic Theology: New Essays in the Philosophy of Theology*, ed. Oliver D. Crisp and Michael C. Rea (Oxford: Oxford University Press, 2009), 280–312.

14. Coakley, *God, Sexuality, and the Self*, 45–46.

15. Ibid., 43.

274　Notes to Pages 48–55

16. Peter Harrison masterfully traces the shifting senses of theology as a "scientific" enterprise in his Gifford Lectures, showing that throughout antiquity and much of the medieval period it explicitly meant an ascetical and contemplative "way of life" involving a host of embodied virtues and mental habits rather than an independent body of knowledge. See his *The Territories of Science and Religion* (Chicago: University of Chicago Press, 2015).

17. See Pierre Hadot, *Philosophy as a Way of Life: Spiritual Exercises from Socrates to Foucault*, trans. Arnold I. Davidson (Oxford: Blackwell, 1995). See also his *What is Ancient Philosophy?*, trans. Michael Chase (Cambridge, MA: Harvard University Press, 2002).

18. Coakley, *God, Sexuality, and the Self*, 46.

19. Ibid., 343.

20. Williams, *On Christian Theology*, 76.

21. Belden Lane, *The Solace of Fierce Landscapes: Exploring Desert and Mountain Spirituality* (Oxford: Oxford University Press, 2007), 12–13.

22. Saint John of the Cross, "Sayings of Light and Love," from *The Collected Works of St. John of the Cross*, trans. Kevin Kavanaugh, O.C.D., and Otilio Rodriguez, O.C.D. (Washington, DC: ICS Publications, 1991), §88, 91.

23. The characterization of creaturely poverty as "sinking" into divine "nothingness" hearkens to Meister Eckhart. See *Meister Eckhart: The Essential Sermons, Commentaries, Treatises and Defenses*, ed. and trans. Edmund Colledge and Bernard McGinn (New York: Crossroad, 1981), esp. sermons 83, 207, and 208.

24. Rahner, *Foundations of Christian Faith*, 93–106; "Theology of Freedom," *Theological Investigations* 6, trans. Karl-H. Kruger and Boniface Kruger (Baltimore, MD: Helicon, 1969), 190–93.

25. Coakley, *God, Sexuality, and the Self*, 55–56.

26. Ibid., 112, 113.

27. Ibid., 57.

28. Ibid., 58.

29. Rahner makes a strong case for the resurrection of Jesus as providing a regulative role in uniting of transcendence and embodiment in Christian spirituality. See his "The Eternal Significance of the Humanity of Jesus for Our Relationship to God," *Theological Investigations* 3, trans. Karl-H. Kruger and Boniface Kruger (London: Darton, Longman & Todd, 1967), 35–46.

30. Thomas Merton, *New Seeds of Contemplation* (New York: New Directions, 1961), 13.

31. Ibid.

32. There is extensive literature concerning the status of "experience" in contemplative traditions, as well as a considerable range of positions one might adopt. At one extreme is the "pure consciousness" position that assumes something like a common core of ineffable, unitive experience standing behind all linguistic-conceptual expression. At the other extreme is the "constructivist" position that rejects any such common core, given the way language, culture, doctrine, and distinctive embodied practices construct experience, including

so-called mystical experience. Yet another position, trenchantly pursued by Denys Turner, is critical of any appeal to "experience" when analyzing mystical traditions of the apophatic variety, since it is the critique and breakdown of experience itself that most characterizes them (*The Darkness of God: Negativity in Christian Mysticism* [Cambridge: Cambridge University Press, 1995]). While I am generally sympathetic to Bernard McGinn's defense of experiential language when studying the Christian mystical tradition (see his review of Turner's book in *Journal of Religion* 77 [1997]: 309–11, and also his "Quo vadis? Reflections on the Current Study of Mysticism," *Christian Spirituality Bulletin* 6 [1998]: 13–21), I also agree with Turner that contemplative practice has to do with the crisis of experience and its critique and breakdowns, as well as the radical reframing of schemata *for* experience. Turner's essays on Meister Eckhart and John of the Cross are illuminating in this regard. Overall, while I tend to limit references to contemplative "experience" in this book — readers will notice that I typically prefer "awareness," "beholding," "wakefulness," and "practice" — my own view assumes the mutually informative character of contemplative awareness and the host of embodied, cultural, and discursive practices that give distinctive shape and texture to such awareness as actually *lived*. As this chapter attests, I am convinced that contemplative practice in the Christian tradition, while sharing a number of family resemblances with other traditions, will take on an irreducibly distinctive character as a result.

33. Teresa of Avila, *The Interior Castle*, trans. Kieran Kavanaugh, O.C.D., and Otilio Rodriguez, O.C.D. (Mahwah, NJ: Paulist Press, 1979), 71.

34. In one of his letters of spiritual direction from the 1920s, Abbot John Chapman makes the intriguing observation that whereas aridity in the spiritual life may have been interpreted in a former age in terms of divine reprobation, as though the sense of God's withdrawal were a matter of judgment, the "corresponding trial of our contemporaries seems to be the *feeling of not having any faith*; not temptations against any particular article (usually), but a mere feeling that religion is not true" (*Spiritual Letters* [London: Continuum, 1935], 47). For a rich study of how acedia has taken on many different hues in a secular age, including nihilism, yet in a way that still may speak to a religious imagination, see Michael L. Raposa, *Boredom and the Religious Imagination* (Charlottesville: University Press of Virginia, 1999).

35. Ibid., 74.

36. Ibid., 75.

37. Ibid., 74. For a rich, phenomenological study of the sense of "dilation" and "expansion" in prayer, including in Teresa, see J. L. Chrétien's *Spacious Joy: An Essay in Phenomenology and Literature*, trans. Anne Ashley Davenport (London: Rowman & Littlefield, 2019).

38. Ibid., 71.

39. Ibid., 78.

40. Raposa, *Boredom and the Religious Imagination*, 1–6, 136–66.

41. Teresa, *The Interior Castle*, 77.

42. Chapman, *Spiritual Letters*, 291.

276 Notes to Pages 58–68

43. As Moore observes, only within the climate of contemplative prayer can such language avoid becoming vague and pantheistic ("Some Principles for an Adequate Theism," 208).

44. Chapman, *Spiritual Letters*, 293.

45. Teresa of Avila, *The Interior Castle*, 82.

46. Ibid., 79.

47. Martin Laird, *Into the Silent Land: A Guide to the Christian Practice of Contemplation* (Oxford: Oxford University Press, 2006), 14.

48. Ibid., 17.

49. Ibid., 15.

50. On this point see Martin Laird, "The 'Open Country Whose Name is Prayer': Apophasis, Deconstruction, and Contemplative Practice," *Modern Theology* 21, no. 1 (2005): 141–55. Also relevant is his "'Whereof We Speak': Gregory of Nyssa, Jean-Luc Marion, and the Current Apophatic Rage," *Heythrop Journal* 42 (2001): 1–12.

51. Laird, *Into the Silent Land*, 8.

52. Ibid., 80.

53. Ibid., 9.

54. The first two volumes of Desmond's trilogy are *Being and the Between* (Albany: State University of New York Press, 1995) and *Ethics and the Between* (Albany: State University of New York Press, 2001).

55. It should be noted that Desmond's particular account of "representation" in this case has to do with calculative (predictive and controlling) knowledge. For an alternative and much expanded account of "representation" in language—one that bears many similarities to Desmond's project for its interests in metaphorical and contemplative styles of speech and knowing—see Rowan Williams, *The Edge of Words: God and the Habits of Language* (London: Bloomsbury, 2014).

56. Desmond, *God and the Between*, 242.

57. Ibid., 131.

58. Ibid., 129.

59. For a recent, engaging account of the existential vertigo such a question can arouse, one that, alas, concludes with tragic resignation bordering on nihilism, see Jim Holt, *Why Does the World Exist? An Existential Detective Story* (New York: W. W. Norton, 2012). For a helpful survey of philosophical and cosmological speculation concerning the question, see John Leslie and Robert Lawrence Kuhn, eds., *The Mystery of Existence: Why Is There Anything at All?* (Oxford: Wiley-Blackwell, 2013).

60. Desmond, *God and the Between*, 133.

61. Ibid., 248.

62. Ibid., 248–49.

63. Ibid., 96.

64. Ibid., 133.

65. Ibid., 202.

66. Ibid., 143.

67. Ibid., 43.

68. William Desmond, *Philosophy and Its Others: Ways of Being and Mind* (Albany: State University of New York Press, 1990), 236.

69. Desmond, *God and the Between*, 252.

70. Ibid.

71. Ibid., 253.

72. Ibid., 252.

73. Ibid., 254.

74. Rahner, *Foundations of Christian Faith*, 77.

75. Desmond, *God and the Between*, 255.

76. Sebastian Moore, *The Contagion of Jesus: Doing Theology As If It Mattered* (Maryknoll, NY: Orbis Books, 2007), 17.

77. Coakley, *God, Sexuality, and the Self*, 55–56.

78. Ibid., 331–32.

79. Ibid., 56.

80. Rowan Williams draws out the parallels between Paul and John on this score, noting how the role of the Spirit's "witness" is "not a pointing to the Son outside the human world, it is precisely the formation of the 'Son-like' life in the human world; it is the continuing state of sharing in the mutuality of Father and Son; it is forgiven or justified life" (Williams, *On Christian Theology*, 120ff.).

81. Coakley, *God, Sexuality, and the Self*, 111.

82. Ibid., 331.

83. Ibid.

84. Ibid., 112.

85. Williams, *On Christian Theology*, 74.

86. Hans Urs von Balthasar, *The Last Act*, vol. 5 of *Theo-Drama: Theological Dramatic Theory*. Trans. Graham Harrison (San Francisco: Ignatius Press, 1998), 81.

87. Ibid., 94.

88. Ibid., 105.

THREE   Jesus and the Non-Other

1. For two particularly clear presentations of this inner relationship, see Tanner, *Christ the Key*, and Rowan Williams, *Christ the Heart of Creation* (London: Bloomsbury, 2018).

2. Sokolowski, *The God of Faith and Reason*, 37.

3. Khaled Anatolios, *Retrieving Nicaea: The Development and Meaning of Trinitarian Doctrine* (Grand Rapids: Baker Academic, 2001), 286.

4. Karl Rahner, "On the Theology of the Incarnation," *Theological Investigations* 4, trans. Kevin Smyth (London: Darton, Longman & Todd, 1966), 117.

5. Ibid.

6. "The reason the pagans could not conceive of anything like the incarnation is that their gods are part of the world, and the union of any two natures in the world is bound to be, in some way, unnatural, because of the otherness that lets one thing be itself only by not being the other. But the Christian God

278 Notes to Pages 83–95

is not a part of the world and is not a 'kind' of being at all. Therefore the incarnation is not meaningless or impossible or destructive" (Sokolowski, *The God of Faith and Reason*, 36).

7. Williams, *Christ the Heart of Creation*, 63.

8. Edward Schillebeeckx, *Interim Report on the Books Jesus & Christ*, trans. John Bowden (New York: Crossroad, 1982), 128.

9. Stanislas Breton, *The Word and the Cross*, trans. Jacquelyn Porter (New York: Fordham University Press, 2002), 40.

10. I further develop this approach to atheism in chapter 5.

11. For more on this theme of unlimited dispossession in Stanislas Breton, see my "La puissance d'un dépouillement sans limites repenser: Repenser la *creatio ex nihilo* avec Stanislas Breton," trans. Claire Vajou, *Transversalités*, October–December, no. 135 (2015): 43–53.

12. Robert J. Daly, *Sacrifice Unveiled: The True Meaning of Christian Sacrifice* (London: T&T Clark, 2009), 220.

13. James Alison, "Oracles, Prophets, and Dwellers in Silence: Hints of the *'pati divina'* in the Theology That is Being Birthed," in *The Practice of the Presence of God: Theology as a Way of Life*, ed. Martin Laird and Sheelah Treflé Hidden (London: Routledge, 2017), 3.

14. Ibid.

15. Ibid.

16. N. T. Wright, *Jesus and the Victory of God*, vol. 2 of *Christian Origins and the Question of God* (Minneapolis: Fortress, 1996), 444.

17. Ibid., 251.

18. Martin Luther King Jr., *Strength to Love* (Minneapolis: Fortress Press, 2010), 11–20.

19. René Girard, *Things Hidden Since the Foundation of the World*, trans. Stephen Bann and Michael Metteer (Stanford, CA: Stanford University Press, 1978), 208.

20. Raymund Schwager, S.J., *Jesus in the Drama of Salvation: Toward a Biblical Doctrine of Redemption*, trans. James G. Williams and Paul Haddon (New York: Crossroad, 1999), 92.

21. Alison, *The Joy of Being Wrong*, 198.

22. Ibid., 199.

23. Girard first crystalized his insights on the mimetic character of human desire through an engagement with the modern novel, particularly Cervantes, Flaubert, Proust, Stendhal, and Dostoevsky. See his *Deceit, Desire, and the Novel: Self and Other in Literary Structure*, trans. Yvonne Freccero (Baltimore, MD: Johns Hopkins University Press, 1964).

24. Scott R. Garrels, "Human Imitation: Historical, Philosophical, and Scientific Perspectives," in *Mimesis and Science: Empirical Research on Imitation and the Mimetic Theory of Culture and Religion*, ed. Scott R. Garrels (East Lansing, MI: Michigan State University Press, 2011), 1–2.

25. Andrew Meltzoff, "Out of the Mouths of Babes: Imitation, Gaze, and Intentions in Infant Research—the 'Like Me' Framework," in *Mimesis and Science*, ed. Scott R. Garrels, 55.

Notes to Pages 96–99   279

26. Ibid., 68.

27. Andrew Meltzoff and Keith Moore, "Imitation of Facial and Manual Gestures by Human Neonates," *Science* 198, no. 4312 (1977): 75–78; Andrew Meltzoff and Keith Moore, "Imitation in Newborn Infants: Exploring the Range of Gestures Imitated and the Underlying Mechanisms," *Developmental Psychology* 25 (1989): 954–62.

28. Meltzoff, "Out of the Mouths of Babes," in *Mimesis and Science*, ed. Scott R. Garrels, 59.

29. Ibid., 61–62. See also Rechele Brooks and Andrew Meltzoff, "The Importance of Eyes: How Infants Interpret Adult Looking Behavior," *Developmental Psychology* 38 (2002): 958–66.

30. Michael Tomasello, *The Cultural Origins of Human Cognition* (Cambridge, MA: Harvard University Press, 1999), 62.

31. Meltzoff, "Out of the Mouths of Babes," in *Mimesis and Science*, ed. Scott R. Garrels, 64–66. See also Andrew Meltzoff, "Understanding the Intentions of Others: Re-enactment of Intended Acts by 18-Month-Old Children," *Developmental Psychology* 31 (1995): 838–50.

32. Tomasello, *The Cultural Origins of Human Cognition*, 61.

33. Ibid., 5–6.

34. Ibid. Tomasello describes the distinction between human and nonhuman primates in this way: "Perhaps surprisingly, for many animal species it is not the creative component, but rather the stabilizing ratchet component, that is the difficult feat. Thus, many nonhuman primate individuals regularly produce intelligent behavioral innovations and novelties, but then their groupmates do not engage in the kinds of social learning that would enable, over time, the cultural ratchet to do its work" (ibid.). For more on this distinction, see Michael Tomasello, Ann C. Kruger, and H. H. Ratner, "Cultural Learning," *Behavioral and Brain Sciences* 16 (1993): 495–552; Claudio Tennie, Josep Call, and Michael Tomasello, "Ratcheting Up the Ratchet: On the Evolution of Cumulative Culture," *Philosophical Transactions of the Royal Society* 364 (2009): 2405–2415.

35. Iain McGilchrist, *The Master and His Emissary: The Divided Brain and the Making of the Modern World* (New Haven: Yale University Press, 2009), 253.

36. For an important examination of the role of imitation in early hominid culture, see Merlin Donald, *Origins of the Modern Mind: Three Stages in the Evolution of Culture and Cognition* (Cambridge, MA: Harvard University Press, 1991).

37. Ibid., 251.

38. Vittorio Gallese, "The Two Sides of Mimesis: Mimetic Theory, Embodied Simulation, and Social Identification," in *Mimesis and Science*, ed. Scott R. Garrels, 102.

39. For good summaries of the research, see Marco Iacoboni, *Mirroring People: The New Science of How We Connect with Others* (New York: Farrar, Strauss and Giroux, 2009); Christian Keysers, *The Empathic Brain: How the Discovery of Mirror Neurons Changes Our Understanding of Human Nature* (Lexington, KY: Social Brain Press, 2011).

280 Notes to Pages 99–106

40. Vittorio Gallese, "The 'Shared Manifold Hypothesis': From Mirror Neurons to Empathy," *Journal of Consciousness Studies* 8, nos. 5–7 (2001): 33–50. See also Evan Thompson's comprehensive assessment in the same volume for its synthesis of cognitive neuroscience, phenomenology, and contemplative practice, "Empathy and Consciousness," *Journal of Consciousness Studies* 8, nos. 5–7 (2001): 1–32.

41. Gallese, "The Two Sides of Mimesis," in *Mimesis and Science*, ed. Scott R. Garrels, 100.

42. Charles Taylor, *A Secular Age* (Cambridge, MA: Belknap, 2007), 37ff.

43. McGilchrist, *The Master and His Emissary*, 249.

44. Girard, *Things Hidden Since the Foundation of the World*, 283ff.

45. James Alison, *Broken Hearts and New Creations: Intimations of a Great Reversal* (New York: Continuum, 2010), 163.

46. Jean-Michel Oughourlian, *The Genesis of Desire*, trans. Eugene Webb (East Lansing: Michigan State University Press, 2010), 34.

47. Ibid., 11.

48. Jean-Michel Oughourlian, "From Universal Mimesis to the Self Formed by Desire," in *Mimesis and Science*, ed. Scott R. Garrels, 46, 49.

49. Evan Thompson uses the term *neuro-nihilism* to describe certain neuroscientists and philosophers who deny anything like a "self" due to the lack of any such independent or indivisible reality in the brain. The "self" is only an illusion generated by mental processes. Thompson rightly points out that such a view is only shadow version of the Cartesian reification of the self, not a real alternative to it. See his *Waking, Dreaming, Being: Self and Consciousness in Neuroscience, Meditation, and Philosophy* (New York: Columbia University Press, 2014), 319–66.

50. Oughourlian, "From Universal Mimesis to the Self Formed by Desire," in *Mimesis and Science*, ed. Scott R. Garrels, 50.

51. René Girard, *The Girard Reader*, ed. James G. Williams (New York: Herder & Herder, 2006), 9.

52. Girard, *Deceit, Desire, and the Novel*, 81; Girard, *Things Hidden Since the Foundation of the World*, 296–97.

53. Augustine, *Confessions*, 1.11, trans. Henry Chadwick (Oxford: Oxford University Press, 1991), 9.

54. Ibid.

55. Girard, *Things Hidden Since the Foundation of the World*, 299.

56. René Girard, *Violence and the Sacred*, trans. Patrick Gregory (Baltimore, MD: Johns Hopkins University Press, 1977), 146.

57. Quoted in Girard, *Things Hidden Since the Foundation of the World*, 301.

58. Girard, *Deceit, Desire, and the Novel*, 100; *Things Hidden from the Foundation of the World*, 17.

59. The paradox of negative mimesis is nowhere more on display than in modern advertising. "Advertising promises originality. The consumer is supposed to believe that possession of the advertised product will guarantee the exceptional uniqueness embodied by those who model it. Only after purchasing

Notes to Pages 107–119   281

the product can human beings escape the mundane horde. However, this promise remains steeped in contradiction, for imitation and originality are mutually exclusive. Only by imitating the desire of our original models—the heroes of advertising—are we able to enjoy the pleasure of an autonomous existence" (Wolfgang Palaver, *René Girard's Mimetic Theory*, trans. Gabriel Borrud (East Lansing: Michigan State University Press, 2013), 69.

60. Girard, *Violence and the Sacred*, 148.

61. René Girard, *Battling to the End: Conversations with Benoît Chantre*, trans. Mary Baker (East Lansing: Michigan State University Press, 2010), 56–57.

62. Chris Hedges, *War Is a Force That Gives Us Meaning* (New York: Public Affairs, 2002), 21.

63. Ibid., 32.

64. Ibid.

65. Ibid., 64.

66. Ibid., 180.

67. Paul Dumouchel, "A Covenant among Beasts: Human and Chimpanzee Violence in Evolutionary Perspective," in *Can We Survive Our Origins? Readings in René Girard's Theory of Violence and the Sacred*, ed. Pierpaolo Antonello and Paul Gifford (East Lansing: Michigan State University Press, 2015), 20.

68. Aristotle, "Poetics," IV.

69. Dumouchel, "A Covenant among Beasts," 20–21.

70. For a compelling account of this retrospective hermeneutic at work, see Hays, *Reading Backwards*. See also Richard B. Hays, "Reading Scripture in Light of the Resurrection," in *The Art of Reading Scripture*, ed. Ellen F. Davis and Richard B. Hays (Grand Rapids, MI: Eerdmans, 2003), 216–38.

71. Gerhard Lohfink, *Jesus of Nazareth: What He Wanted, Who He Was*, trans. Linda M. Maloney (Collegeville, MN: Liturgical Press, 2012), 73.

72. Ibid., 76.

73. Ibid., 62.

74. Ibid., 62–63.

75. Girard, *Things Hidden Since the Foundation of the World*, 197.

76. Ibid.

77. René Girard, *When These Things Begin: Conversations with Michel Treguer*, trans. Trevor Cribben Merrill (East Lansing: Michigan State University Press, 2013), 47.

78. Girard first develops this theme in his *Deceit, Desire, and the Novel*, 307ff. For a helpful exposition and analysis of this theme, see Wolfgang Palaver, "'Creative Renunciation': The Spiritual Heart of René Girard's *Deceit, Desire, and the Novel*," *Religion and Literature* 43, no. 3 (2011): 143–50.

79. Girard, *Things Hidden Since the Foundation of the World*, 198.

80. Alison, *Broken Hearts and New Creations*, 165.

81. Ibid.

82. Ibid., 168.

83. Ibid., 165.

282 Notes to Pages 119–129

84. See Wolfgang Palaver, "From Closed Societies to the Open Society: Parochial Altruism and Christian Universalism," in *Can We Survive Our Origins?*, ed. Antonello and Gifford, 97–114.

85. Alison, *Broken Hearts and New Creations*, 166.

86. Ibid., 128.

87. Alison, *Undergoing God*, 30–31.

88. Alison, *Broken Hearts and New Creations*, 168.

89. Alison, *The Joy of Being Wrong*, 198.

90. Alison, "Oracles, Prophets, and Dwellers in Silence," 3–4.

FOUR   Strange Victory

1. Girard, *The Girard Reader*, 64.

2. Ibid.

3. Some critics have erroneously attributed to mimetic theory a fatalistic understanding of human desire, as though desire were essentially acquisitive and violence in human relationships inevitable. Were this true, mimetic theory would rightly be criticized for "ontologizing" violence and therefore incongruous with a theological vision that affirms the original goodness of creation. But this is not Girard's view, even if his tendency as an anthropologist, like the novelists and playwrights who have influenced him, has been to highlight acquisitiveness and violence in human relationships. For nuanced discussions of this issue in Girard's work, see Fergus Kerr, "Rescuing Girard's Argument," *Modern Theology* 8, no. 4 (1992): 385–99; Rowan Williams, *Wrestling with Angels: Conversations in Modern Theology*, ed. Mike Higton (Grand Rapids, MI: William B. Eerdmans, 2007), 171–85; Michael Kirwan, *Girard and Theology* (New York: T&T Clark, 2009), 132–42; Grant Kaplan, *René Girard, Unlikely Apologist: Mimetic Theory and Fundamental Theology* (Notre Dame, IN: University of Notre Dame Press, 2016), 46ff.

4. Girard, *Deceit, Desire, and the Novel*, 61–62, 108–12, 155–59.

5. Girard, *Battling to the End*, 31.

6. Girard, *Violence and the Sacred*, 146.

7. Girard, *The Girard Reader*, 12–13.

8. For an important study of the word *scapegoat* in scholarly and everyday discourse, see David Dawson, *Flesh Becomes Word: A Lexicography of the Scapegoat, or A History of an Idea* (East Lansing: Michigan State University Press, 2013).

9. Jean-Pierre Dupuy has worked to integrate Girard's thought with theories of self-organization to remarkable effect. See especially his *The Mark of the Sacred*, trans. Malcom B. DeBevoise (Stanford, CA: Stanford University Press, 2013). See also Pierpaolo Antonello's essay "Liminal Crises: The Origins of Cultural Order, the Default Mechanisms of Survival, and the Pedagogy of the Sacrificial Victim," in *Can We Survive Our Origins?*, ed. Antonello and Gifford, 25–47.

Notes to Pages 130–135   283

10. James O'Higgins Norman, "Mimetic Theory and Scapegoating in the Age of Cyberbullying: The Case of Phoebe Prince," *Pastoral Care in Education* 29, no. 4: 287–300.

11. For a Girard-inspired analysis of how modern states construct enemies or outsiders in the effort to maintain territorial systems, see Paul Dumouchel, *The Barren Sacrifice: An Essay on Political Violence*, trans. Mary Baker (East Lansing: Michigan State University, 2015).

12. Among the numerous places where James Alison has applied mimetic theory to understanding the social and ecclesial dimensions of homosexuality, see especially his *Faith beyond Resentment: Fragments Catholic and Gay* (New York: Crossroad, 2001).

13. James McBride, "Capital Punishment as the Unconstitutional Establishment of Religion: A Girardian Reading of the Death Penalty," *Journal of Church and State* 37, no. 2 (Spring 1995): 278.

14. Ibid., 287.

15. René Girard, *The Scapegoat*, trans. Yvonne Freccero (Baltimore, MD: Johns Hopkins University Press, 1986), 14.

16. Ibid., 18.

17. Ibid., 21.

18. In addition to Girard's own works, the extant literature applying mimetic theory to historical and contemporary events is quite large, though a few texts stand out for their breadth and interpretive agility. See especially Gil Bailie, *Violence Unveiled: Humanity at the Crossroads* (New York: Crossroad, 1995); Scott Cowdell, *René Girard and Secular Modernity: Christ, Culture, and Crisis* (South Bend, IN: University of Notre Dame Press, 2013); Palaver, *René Girard's Mimetic Theory*; Pierpaolo Antonello and Paul Gifford, eds., *Can We Survive Our Origins?*; and Marcus Peter Rempel, *Life at the End of Them versus Us: Cross Culture Stories* (Victoria, BC: Friesen Press, 2017).

19. Mirsolav Volf, *Exclusion and Embrace: A Theological Exploration of Identity, Otherness, and Reconciliation* (Nashville: Abingdon, 1996), 74.

20. Michael Kirwan makes the point precisely: "Just as metaphysical philosophy asks: 'why is there something, why not nothing?', so mimetic theory asks: 'why is there society, why not anarchy?'" (*Girard and Theology*, 25).

21. Rowan Williams, foreword to *Can We Survive Our Origins?*, ed. Antonello and Gifford, xii.

22. Girard, *Violence and the Sacred*, 93–99, 297–308. Girard is in dialogue here with Jacques Derrida's important essay "Plato's Pharmacy," wherein Derrida explores the undecidedly double meaning of the *pharmakon* in Greek thought. See Jacques Derrida, *Dissemination*, trans. Barbara Johnson (Chicago: University of Chicago Press, 1981), 63–171. For a study of Girard and Derrida in an explicitly theological vein, see Andrew J. McKenna, *Violence and Difference: Girard, Derrida, and Deconstruction* (Champaign: University of Illinois Press, 1992).

23. "What Otto described as metaphysical, Girard reveals as historical" (Cowdell, *René Girard and Secular Modernity*, 58). See Rudolf Otto, *The Idea*

284 Notes to Pages 136–141

of the Holy: An Inquiry Into the Non-Rational Factor in the Idea of the Divine and Its Relation to the Rational, trans. John W. Harvey (Oxford: Oxford University Press, 1923).

24. Girard, *Things Hidden Since the Foundation of the World*, 28.

25. Girard, *The Girard Reader*, 10.

26. Williams, foreword to *Can We Survive Our Origins?*, ed. Antonello and Gifford, xiii–xiv.

27. René Girard, *I See Satan Fall Like Lightning*, trans. James G. Williams (Maryknoll, NY: Orbis, 2001), 82.

28. Mircea Eliade, *A History of Religious Ideas*, vol. 1, *From the Stone Age to the Eleusinian Mysteries*, trans. Willard R. Trask (Chicago: University of Chicago Press, 1978), 70–72.

29. Girard, *I See Satan Fall Like Lightning*, 86. See also René Girard, *Evolution and Conversion: Dialogues on the Origin of Culture* (London: T&T Clark, 2007), 163.

30. G. H. de Radkowski, *Le Monde* (Oct. 27, 1972), quoted in Chris Fleming, *René Girard, Violence and Mimesis* (Cambridge: Polity Press, 2004), 111.

31. Paul Ricoeur, *Freud and Philosophy: An Essay on Interpretation*, trans. Denis Savage (New Haven, CT: Yale University Press, 1970), 32.

32. Robert Hamerton-Kelly, *Sacred Violence: Paul's Hermeneutic of the Cross* (Minneapolis: Fortress Press, 1992), 40.

33. For more on the specific meaning "secularization" takes in Girard's work, see Scott Cowdell, *René Girard and Secular Modernity*. See also Girard's illuminating remarks in his dialogue with Gianni Vattimo, *Christianity, Truth, and Weakening Faith*, ed. Pierpaolo Antonello, trans. William McCuaig (New York: Columbia University Press, 2010).

34. Girard, *I See Satan Fall Like Lightning*, 161. This statement hardly means that Girard is blithely optimistic about social "progress." Due to the volatility of mimetic desire and the contagion of violence, his view of our contemporary situation typically highlights the dangers and brutalities that lurk within it. The point of the above statement has nothing to do with a story of moral superiority but rather addresses the shifting default in our social imaginary that focuses on the status of the victim in a historically unprecedented way. Tremendous good comes from this shift, but there are many ironic mutations as well, such as claiming the status of victim in order to victimize others or extreme forms of "political correctness" that stifle open discourse and breed hostilities toward some social or political (and not infrequently religious) other.

35. James Frazer, *The Golden Bough: A Study in Magic and Religion* (New York: Macmillan, 1922).

36. Girard, *Things Hidden Since the Foundation of the World*, 154.

37. Ibid., 148, 151.

38. S. Mark Heim, *Saved from Sacrifice: A Theology of the Cross* (Grand Rapids, MI: William B. Eerdmans, 2006), 103.

39. See Girard's illuminating analysis of Oedipus Rex and the story of Joseph and his brothers in *I See Satan Fall Like Lightning*, 103–17.

40. As Jean-Michel Oughourlian succinctly puts it, in Exodus "it is the whole of the chosen people which is identified with the scapegoat, *vis-à-vis* Egyptian society" (Girard, *Things Hidden Since the Foundation of the World*, 153).

41. See Girard's book-length treatment in *Job: The Victim of His People* (Stanford, CA: Stanford University Press, 1987).

42. For extensive analysis, see Raymund Schwager, S.J., *Must There Be Scapegoats? Violence and Redemption in the Bible* (San Francisco: Harper & Row, 1987), 91–109.

43. Girard, *Things Hidden Since the Foundations of the World*, 157.

44. For a systematic study of this "dramatic" character of revelation in dialogue with Girard and Hans Urs von Balthasar, see Schwager, *Jesus in the Drama of Salvation*.

45. Girard, *Things Hidden Since the Foundation of the World*, 174–76. See also René Girard, "Is There Anti-Semitism in the Gospels?," *Biblical Interpretation* 1 (1993): 339–59, the bulk of which is reproduced in *The Girard Reader*, 211–21.

46. Girard, *Things Hidden Since the Foundation of the World*, 167.

47. Ibid.

48. Ibid., 169–70.

49. Williams, foreword to *Can We Survive Our Origins?*, ed. Antonello and Gifford, xvi.

50. For more on Girard's relation to death-of-God theologies, see my "Theology after the Death of God," in *T&T Clark Handbook of Political Theology*, ed. Rubén Rosario Rodríguez (London: Bloomsbury, 2020), 161–76.

51. Girard, *I See Satan Fall Like Lightning*, 189.

52. Note also the Davidic allusion to Psalm 2:1–2 in the same passage: "Why did the Gentiles rage and the peoples entertain folly? The kings of the earth took their stand and the princes gathered together against the Lord and against his anointed" (Acts 4:25b–26).

53. Rowan Williams, *Resurrection*, 8.

54. As Michael Kirwan notes, it is no exaggeration to say that Girard's anthropology reads like an extended reflection upon this single passage. See Michael Kirwan, *Discovering Girard* (London: Darton, Longman, & Todd, 2004), 72.

55. Alison, *The Joy of Being Wrong*, 74.

56. Walter Wink, *Engaging the Powers: Discernment and Resistance in a World of Domination* (Minneapolis: Fortress Press, 1992), 53.

57. Ibid., 51.

58. Ibid., 65. With reference to John's usage of "the world" more specifically, Wink summarizes as follows: "It is the good creation of a good Creator (John 1:10ab), it is estranged or fallen existence (John 1:10c and the vast majority of other references), and it is capable of redemption (John 12:47)" (Ibid., 51).

59. Girard, *I See Satan Fall Like Lightning*, 140.

60. Ibid.

286 Notes to Pages 152–164

61. Gustaf Aulén, *Christus Victor: An Historical Study of the Three Main Types of the Idea of the Atonement*, trans. A. G. Hebert (New York: Macmillan, 1969).

62. Girard, *I See Satan Fall Like Lightning*, 143.

63. See Gregory of Nyssa's use of this theme in his "The Great Catechism," in *Nicene and Post-Nicene Fathers of the Christian Church*, vol. 5, *Gregory of Nyssa, Selected Works and Letters*, ed. Philip Schaff and Henry Wace, trans. William Moore and Henry Austin Wilson (Edinburgh: T&T Clark, 1994), XXIV, 494.

64. Heim, *Saved from Sacrifice*, 164.

65. Gregory A. Boyd, *Cross Vision: How the Crucifixion of Jesus Makes Sense of Old Testament Violence* (Minneapolis: Fortress Press, 2017), 144.

66. Irenaeus of Lyons, *The Scandal of the Incarnation: Irenaeus against the Heresies*, ed. Hans Urs von Balthasar, trans. John Saward (San Francisco: Ignatius Press, 1981), 56.

67. Gregory of Nazianzus, Oration 31.25, in *On God and Christ: The Five Theological Orations and Two Letters to Cledonius*, trans. Lionel Wickham (Crestwood, NY: St. Vladimir's Seminary Press, 2002), 136.

68. Herbert McCabe, O.P., *God Matters* (London: Continuum, 1987), 48.

69. Ibid., 48–49.

70. Rahner, "On the Theology of the Incarnation," 116.

71. Alison, *The Joy of Being Wrong*, 98.

72. Schwager, *Must There Be Scapegoats?*, 134.

73. For helpful examinations of divine wrath from a Girardian perspective, see Schwager, *Jesus in the Drama of Salvation*, 1–25; Hamerton-Kelly, *Sacred Violence*, 88–119. See also Alison's subtle treatment of how penal substitution theories recompose various scriptural strands in problematic ways (*On Being Liked* [New York: Crossroad, 2004], 17–31).

74. Thomas Merton, *The New Man* (New York: Noonday, 1961), 41.

75. Ibid.

76. Jon Sobrino, *Jesus the Liberator: A Historical-Theological View*, trans. Paul Burns and Francis McDonagh (Maryknoll, NY: Orbis Books, 1993), 209–10.

77. Girard, *Things Hidden Since the Foundation of the World*, 210.

78. Ibid., 216.

79. Alison, *Undergoing God*, 62.

80. For helpful discussion of this shift in Girard's thought and its implications for some of the theological critiques of Girard's earlier work, see Cowdell, *René Girard and the Non-Violent God* (Notre Dame, IN: University of Notre Dame Press, 2018), 66–73; Chelsea King, "Girard Reclaimed: Finding Common Ground between Sarah Coakley and René Girard on Sacrifice," *Contagion: Journal of Violence, Mimesis, and Culture* 23 (2016): 63–73.

81. Heim, *Saved from Sacrifice*, xi–xii.

82. James Alison, *Raising Abel*, 52.

83. Moore, *The Contagion of Jesus*, 6.

84. Ibid., 5.

Notes to Pages 164–182   287

85. Ibid., 17.

86. Ibid., 12.

87. Ibid., 6.

88. Johan Baptist Metz, *Faith in History and Society: Toward a Practical Fundamental Theology*, trans. J. Matthew Ashley (New York: Herder & Herder, 2011), 68–69.

89. Ibid., 62.

90. Ibid., 107.

91. Moore, *The Contagion of Jesus*, 48.

92. Rahner, *Foundations of Christian Faith*, 93.

93. Moore, *The Contagion of Jesus*, 48.

94. Rowan Williams, *Where God Happens: Discovering Christ in One Another* (Boston: New Seeds Books, 2005), 33.

95. Thomas Merton, *The Wisdom of the Desert: Sayings from the Desert Fathers of the Fourth Century*, trans. Thomas Merton (New York: New Directions, 1960), 18.

96. Laird, *Into the Silent Land*, 125–26.

97. Martin Laird, *An Ocean of Light: Contemplation, Transformation, and Liberation* (Oxford: Oxford University Press, 2019), 56–57.

98. Moore, *The Contagion of Jesus*, 5.

99. Ibid.

100. Ibid., 11.

FIVE   On the Contemplative Consummation of Atheism

1. Cowdell, *René Girard and Secular Modernity*, 179.

2. Ibid. Grant Kaplan also offers an illuminating account of Girard's mimetic theory, secularity, and atheism in his *René Girard, Unlikely Apologist*, 153–200.

3. Simone Weil, *Gravity and Grace*, trans. Emma Craufurd (London: Routledge, 1987), 103.

4. Thomas Merton, *Contemplative Prayer* (New York: Random House, 2014), xxxii.

5. Ibid., xxxi.

6. Ibid., xxxiii.

7. Ibid., xxxiii–xxxiv.

8. Thomas Merton, *Contemplation in a World of Action* (New York: Doubleday, 1973), 177–78.

9. Desmond, *God and the Between*, 29.

10. For a brilliant study of Desmond's philosophy in the tradition of spiritual exercises, see Ryan G. Duns, S.J., *Spiritual Exercises for a Secular Age: William Desmond and the Quest for God* (Notre Dame, IN: University of Notre Dame Press, 2020).

11. Desmond, *God and the Between*, 30.

12. Ibid.

288   Notes to Pages 183–196

13. Ibid., 32.

14. Desmond, *Philosophy and Its Others*, 236.

15. Desmond, *God and the Between*, 119. See also William Desmond, *The Intimate Strangeness of Being: Metaphysics of Dialectic* (Washington, DC: Catholic University of America, 2012).

16. Desmond, *Being and the Between*, 37.

17. Ibid., 37.

18. Ibid., 31.

19. Ibid., 32–33. Italics original.

20. Ibid., 43. Italics original.

21. Ibid., 32.

22. Ibid., 253.

23. Merton, *Contemplative Prayer*, 61–62, 73.

24. Michael J. Buckley, S.J., *Denying and Disclosing God: The Ambiguous Progress of Modern Atheism* (New Haven: Yale University Press, 2004), 117.

25. Karl Rahner, "What is a Dogmatic Statement?" *Theological Investigations* 5, trans. B. Kelly (New York: Seabury, 1966), 18–19.

26. Mark A. McIntosh, *Mystical Theology: The Integrity of Spirituality and Theology* (Oxford: Blackwell, 1998), 40.

27. Buckley, *Denying and Disclosing God*, 117.

28. Pseudo-Dionysius, "The Mystical Theology," *The Complete Works*, trans. Colm Luibheid (New York: Paulist Press, 1987), 141. My italics.

29. Turner, *The Darkness of God*, 34–35.

30. Ibid., 45.

31. Ibid.

32. Nicholas of Cusa, "Dialogue on the Hidden God," *Selected Spiritual Writings*, trans. H. Lawrence Bond (New York: Paulist Press, 1997), 212.

33. Turner, *The Darkness of God*, 46.

34. Vladimir Lossky, *The Mystical Theology of the Eastern Church* (Crestwood, NY: St. Vladimir's Seminary Press, 1957), 8.

35. Buckley, *Denying and Disclosing God*, 100.

36. Ibid., 110.

37. Ludwig Feuerbach, *The Essence of Christianity*, trans. George Eliot (Amherst, NY: Prometheus, 1989), 31.

38. Ibid.

39. Ibid., xviii–xix.

40. Buckley, *Denying and Disclosing God*, 108. While Buckley is here more focused on projective theories of theism, his larger-scale study of modern atheism situates this particular form of critique within a much broader historical context. See his *At the Origins of Modern Atheism* (New Haven, Yale University Press, 1990).

41. Ibid., 109.

42. Ibid.

43. John of the Cross, "Sayings of Light and Love," *The Collected Works of Saint John of the Cross*, no. 88, 92.

44. John of the Cross, "The Ascent to Mount Carmel," *The Collected Works of Saint John of the Cross*, 39.1, 339.

45. Chapman, *Spiritual Letters*, 76.

46. Ibid., 125.

47. Ibid., 99, 290, 294, 98, 86, 59.

48. Ibid., 143.

49. Ibid., 87.

50. Ibid., 36.

51. Ibid., 85.

52. Merton, *New Seeds of Contemplation*, 13.

53. John of the Cross, "The Dark Night," *The Collected Works of Saint John of the Cross*, 5.3, 5.4, 402.

54. Buckley, *Denying and Disclosing God*, 115.

55. Caputo, *The Weakness of God*, 269.

56. Lossky, *The Mystical Theology of the Eastern Church*, 42.

57. Ibid., 9.

58. Ibid.

59. Ibid., 11.

60. Ibid., 43.

61. Denys Turner, "Apophaticism, Idolatry and the Claims of Reason," in *Silence and the Word*, ed. Davies and Turner, 16. See also Denys Turner, "How to Be an Atheist," *New Blackfriars* 83, no. 977/8 (2002): 1–22.

62. Dionysius the Areopagite, "The Mystical Theology," *The Complete Works*, 141.

63. Thomas Aquinas, *Summa Theologica*, I.3.1.

64. Meister Eckhart, *The Complete Mystical Works of Meister Eckhart*, trans. Maurice O'C. Walshe (New York: Herder & Herder, 2009), Sermon 62, 316–17.

65. Hart, *The Experience of God: Being, Consciousness, Bliss* (New Haven, CT: Yale University Press, 2013), 327.

66. Ibid., 321.

67. Ibid., 325.

68. Martin Laird, O.S.A., *A Sunlit Absence: Silence, Awareness, and Contemplation* (Oxford: Oxford University Press, 2011), 20.

69. Symeon the New Theologian, "The Practical and Theological Chapters," *The Practical and Theological Chapters and the Three Theological Discourses*, trans. Paul McGuckin (Kalamazoo, MI: Cistercian, 1982), 2.17, 67.

70. Moore, "Principles for an Adequate Theism," 203.

71. Ibid.

72. Ibid., 204.

73. Karl Rahner, "The Church and Atheism," *Theological Investigations* 21, trans. Hugh M. Riley (New York: Crossroad, 1988), 148.

74. Turner, "Apophaticism, Idolatry and the Claims of Reason," 19. This historical-dialectical relationship between atheism and theism is the main focus of Buckley's magnum opus, *At the Origins of Modern Theism*.

290   Notes to Pages 206–218

75. Taylor, *A Secular Age*, 351, 549.

76. Tomáš Halík, *Patience with God: The Story of Zacchaeus Continuing in Us*, trans. Gerald Turner (New York: Doubleday, 2009), 37.

77. Ibid., 18–19. Italics original.

78. Ibid., 45.

79. Ibid., 47.

80. Ibid., 53.

81. Ibid.

82. Ibid.

83. Pseudo-Dionysius, "The Divine Names," *The Complete Works*, 4.10, 79–80.

84. Halík, *Patience with God*, xiii.

85. John of the Cross, *Collected Works*, "The Sayings of Light and Love," nos. 87, 92.

SIX   Return to Love

1. Karl Rahner, "The Concept of Mystery in Catholic Theology," *Theological Investigations* 4, trans. Kevin Smyth, 40–41.

2. Sergius Bulgakov, *The Lamb of God*, trans. Boris Jakim (Grand Rapids, MI: William B. Eerdmans, 2008), 120.

3. John Ruusbroec, *The Spiritual Espousals and Other Works*, trans. James A. Wiseman, O.S.B. (Mawah, NJ: Paulist Press, 1985), 143–44.

4. Ibid., 151.

5. Desmond, *God and the Between*, 35.

6. Ibid., 43.

7. Sergei Bulgakov, *Sophia, the Wisdom of God: An Outline of Sophiology*, trans. Patrick Thompson, O. Fielding Clarke, and Xenia Braikevitc (Hudson, NY: Lindisfarne Press, 1993), 14.

8. Ibid., 15.

9. Ibid., 17.

10. Sergius Bulgakov, *Unfading Light: Contemplations and Speculations*, trans. Thomas Allan Smith (Grand Rapids, MI: William B. Eerdmans, 2012), 105.

11. Ibid., 110.

12. Ibid., 107.

13. Ibid.

14. Ibid., 154.

15. Ibid., 109.

16. Ibid., 108.

17. Pseudo-Dionysius, "The Mystical Theology," *The Complete Works*, 1.3, 137.

18. Laird, *A Sunlit Absence*, 91.

19. Bulgakov, *Unfading Light*, 109.

20. Ibid., 109–110.

21. See especially *Unfading Light*, 103–79. For Bulgakov's more extensive treatment, see his *The Tragedy of Philosophy: Philosophy and Dogma*, trans. Stephan Churchyard (New York: Angelico Press, 2020).

22. Bulgakov, *Unfading Light*, 184.

23. Bulgakov, *The Lamb of God*, 121.

24. See further discussion of the relative truths of pantheism and dualism in Sergius Bulgakov, *The Bride of the Lamb*, trans. Boris Jakim (Grand Rapids, MI: William B. Eerdmans, 2002), 3–7.

25. On Bulgakov's critical engagement with Gregory of Palamas on this point, see *Unfading Light*, 131–34, and *The Lamb of God*, 116, 122.

26. Karl Rahner, "The Specific Character of the Christian Concept of God," in *Theological Investigations* 21, trans. Hugh M. Riley (New York: Crossroad, 1988), 191. Italics mine.

27. Karl Rahner, "Immanent and Transcendent Consummation of the World," 281.

28. Rahner, "The Specific Character of the Christian Concept of God," 191.

29. Bulgakov, *The Lamb of God*, 120.

30. Ibid., 119.

31. Ibid.

32. Ibid., 120.

33. Bulgakov, *The Bride of the Lamb*, 49.

34. Pseudo-Dionysius, "The Divine Names," in *The Complete Works*, 4.9, 79–80.

35. Ibid., 4.13, 82.

36. Turner, *The Darkness of God*, 29.

37. Pseudo-Dionysius, "The Divine Names," 4.1, 71.

38. Ibid., 4.7, 77.

39. Ibid., 4.12, 81.

40. Ibid., 4.14, 83.

41. Desmond, *Being and the Between*, 218.

42. Bulgakov, *Unfading Light*, 7.

43. Ibid., 127.

44. Ibid., 126.

45. Pseudo-Dionysius, "The Divine Names," 1.5, 54. My italics.

46. Ibid., 1.7, 56.

47. Bulgakov, *Unfading Light*, 127.

48. Pseudo-Dionysius, "The Divine Names," 4.13, 82.

49. Ibid., 4.12, 81.

50. Moore, *The Contagion of Jesus*, 120–41.

51. Bulgakov, *The Bride of the Lamb*, 40. Italics mine.

52. Ibid., 31.

53. Ibid.

54. Karl Rahner, *The Trinity*, trans. Joseph Donceel (New York: Crossroad, 1997), 36–37.

55. Rahner, "On the Theology of the Incarnation," 115.

56. Rahner, *Foundations of Christian Faith*, 194–95.

292   Notes to Pages 230–242

57. Ibid., 202–3.

58. Rahner, "On the Theology of the Incarnation," 105.

59. Rahner, *Foundations of Christian Faith*, 197.

60. Ibid. My italics.

61. Rahner, "The Concept of Mystery in Catholic Theology," 43.

62. Ibid., 115.

63. Ibid., 116.

64. Rahner, *Foundations of Christian Faith*, 123.

65. Rahner, "On the Theology of the Incarnation," 115.

66. Rahner, *Foundations of Christian Faith*, 197.

67. Karl Rahner, "Christology in the Setting of Modern Man's Understanding of Himself and of His World," *Theological Investigations* 11, trans. David Bourke (London: Darton, Longman & Todd, 1974), 227.

68. Karl Rahner, "Christology within an Evolutionary View of the World," *Theological Investigations* 5, trans. B. Kelly (New York: Seabury, 1966), 184.

69. Rahner, "Dogmatic Questions on Easter," *Theological Investigations* 4, trans. Kevin Smyth (London: Darton, Longman & Todd, 1966), 128–29. Italics original.

70. Bulgakov, *Unfading Light*, 185.

71. Ibid., 186.

72. Ibid., 196.

73. Ibid.

74. Sergius Bulgakov, *Icons and the Name of God*, trans. Boris Jakim (Grand Rapids, MI: William B. Eerdmans, 2012), 30.

75. Ibid., 31.

76. Ibid.

77. Bulgakov, *The Lamb of God*, 168.

78. Ibid., 169.

79. Ibid., 171.

80. Bulgakov, *The Bride of the Lamb*, 157.

81. Ibid., 171–72.

82. Ibid., 170–71.

83. Rahner, "On the Theology of the Incarnation," 113.

84. Bulgakov, *The Lamb of God*, 213.

85. Rahner, "Christology within an Evolutionary View of the World," 164.

86. Karl Rahner, "Natural Science and Reasonable Faith," *Theological Investigations* 21, trans. Hugh M. Riley (New York: Crossroad, 1981), 34.

87. Rahner, "Christology within an Evolutionary View of the World," 164.

88. Rahner, *Foundations of Christian Faith*, 189–90.

89. Bulgakov, *The Bride of the Lamb*, 85.

90. Bulgakov, *Sophia, the Wisdom of God*, 64–65.

91. Bulgakov, *The Lamb of God*, 141.

92. Ibid., 136–37; *The Bride of the Lamb*, 174–75.

93. Bulgakov, *The Lamb of God*, 214.

94. Ibid., 232.

95. Ibid., 243.

Notes to Pages 242–250   293

96. Ibid., 312.

97. Ibid.

98. Some of the principal voices contributing to this area of Christian theology include Niels Henrik Gregersen, Elizabeth Johnson, Jürgen Moltmann, Celia Deane-Drummond, Denis Edwards, Christopher Southgate, Robert John Russell, Homes Rolston III, and Richard Bauckham. For a representative overview that includes these and other authors, see Niels Henrik Gregersen, ed., *Incarnation: On the Scope and Depth of Christology* (Minneapolis: Fortress Press, 2014). For a historical and systematic overview, see Denis Edwards, *Deep Incarnation: God's Redemptive Suffering with Creatures* (Maryknoll, NY: Orbis, 2019).

99. Niels Henrik Gregersen, introduction to *Incarnation*, ed. Niels Henrik Gregersen, 7.

100. Niels Henrik Gregersen, "The Cross of Christ in an Evolutionary World," *Dialog: A Journal of Theology* 40, no. 3 (2001): 205.

101. Niels Henrik Gregersen, "The Extended Body of Christ: Three Dimensions of Deep Incarnation," in *Incarnation*, ed. Gregersen, 233–34.

102. Edwards, *How God Acts: Creation, Redemption, and Special Divine Action*. (Minneapolis: Fortress Press, 2010), 124–25. My italics. See also Denis Edwards, "Incarnation and the Natural World: Explorations in the Tradition of Athanasius," in *Incarnation*, ed. Gregersen, 157–76.

103. Elizabeth A. Johnson, *Ask the Beasts: Darwin and the God of Love* (London: Bloomsbury, 2015), 198–99. See also Elizabeth A. Johnson, "Jesus and the Cosmos: Soundings in Deep Christology," in *Incarnation*, ed. Gregersen, 133–56.

104. Maurice Merleau-Ponty, *The Visible and the Invisible*, trans. Alphonso Lingis (Evanston, IL: Northwestern University Press, 1968), 138.

105. Ibid., 130–55.

106. Ibid., 136n2.

107. Drew Leder, *The Absent Body* (Chicago: University of Chicago Press, 1990), 65–66.

108. Richard Bauckham, "The Incarnation and the Cosmic Christ," in *Incarnation*, ed. Gregersen, 45–46.

109. Ibid., 51.

110. Walter Kasper, *The God of Jesus Christ*, trans. Matthew J. O'Connell (New York: Crossroad, 1984), 172.

111. Ibid.

112. Ibid., 196.

113. Ibid., 197.

114. Ibid.

115. Schillebeeckx, *Christ*, 725.

116. Kasper, *The God of Jesus Christ*, 197.

117. Gregersen, "The Cross of Christ in an Evolutionary World," 203.

118. Ibid.

119. Ibid., 205.

120. Ibid., 201.

121. I am influenced here by Johnson's framing of the issue of theodicy and evolutionary processes in her *Ask the Beasts*, 186–92. See also my "Does Darwin Have a Future? Pain, Suffering, and Death at Eastertide," *Theological Studies* 77, no. 2 (2016): 474–78.

122. Johnson, *Ask the Beasts*, 205. See also Elizabeth A. Johnson, *Creation and the Cross: The Mercy of God for a Planet in Peril* (Maryknoll, NY: Orbis Books, 2018).

123. Johnson, *Ask the Beasts*, 206.

124. Ibid., 231.

125. Ibid., 209.

126. Ibid., 208.

127. For more on this understanding of God "using" death by transmuting it, see John Behr's illuminating essay "Life and Death in the Age of Martyrdom," in *The Role of Death in Life: A Multidisciplinary Examination of the Relationship between Life and Death*, ed. John Behr and Connor Cunningham (Eugene, OR: Cascade Books, 2015), 79–95.

128. Karl Rahner, "Dogmatic Questions on Easter," 128.

129. Ibid., 129.

130. Karl Rahner, "The Resurrection of the Body," *Theological Investigations* 2, trans. Karl-H. Kruger (London: Darton, Longman & Todd, 1963), 213.

131. Edwards, *How God Acts*, 164.

132. Ibid., 165. See also Denis Edwards, "Every Sparrow That Falls to the Ground: The Cost of Evolution and the Christ-Event," *Ecotheology* 11, no. 1 (2006): 103–23.

133. Ibid., 166.

134. Leder, *The Absent Body*, 68, 159.

135. Karl Rahner, "The Festival of the Future of the World," *Theological Investigations* 7, trans. David Bourke (New York: Herder, 1971), 183.

136. Ibid.

137. Karl Rahner, "Easter: A Faith that Loves the Earth," in *The Great Church Year: The Best of Karl Rahner's Homilies, Sermons, and Meditations*, ed. Albert Raffelt, trans. Harvey D. Egan (New York: Crossroad, 1993), 194–95.

138. Ibid., 196.

139. Ibid., 194.

140. Ibid., 196.

141. Pope Francis, *Laudato Si'* (Vatican City: Vatican Press, 2015), 49.

142. Ibid., 117.

143. Ibid., 48.

144. Andrew Louth, "Sergii Bulgakov and the Task of Theology," *Irish Theological Quarterly* 74 (2009): 247, 252.

145. Bulgakov, *Unfading Light*, 8.

146. Ibid., 9.

147. Ibid., 12.

148. Ibid., 39–47.

149. Bulgakov, *Sophia, the Wisdom of God*, 16–17.

150. Ibid., 20–21.

151. Anastassy Brandon Gallaher and Irina Kukota, "Protopresbyter Sergii Bulgakov: Hypostasis and Hypostaticity: Scholia to *The Unfading Light*," *St. Vladimir's Theological Quarterly* 49, nos. 1–2 (2005): 38.

152. Rowan Williams, "Creation, Creativity, and Creatureliness: The Wisdom of Finite Existence," in *Being-in-Creation: Human Responsibility in an Endangered World*, ed. Brian Treanor, Bruce Ellis Benson, and Norman Wirzba (New York: Fordham University Press, 2015), 28–29.

153. Douglas E. Christie, *The Blue Sapphire of the Mind: Notes towards a Contemplative Ecology* (Oxford: Oxford University Press, 2013), 143.

154. Ibid.

155. Merton, *New Seeds of Contemplation*, 13.

156. Ibid., 2–3.

157. Ibid., 3.

158. Ibid., 62.

159. Laird, *Into the Silent Land*, 15–16.

160. Ibid., 16.

161. Christie, *The Blue Sapphire of the Mind*, 8.

162. Ibid., 20.

163. Ibid., 28.

BIBLIOGRAPHY

Alison, James. *Broken Hearts and New Creations: Intimations of a Great Reversal*. New York: Continuum, 2010.

———. *Faith beyond Resentment: Fragments Catholic and Gay*. New York: Crossroad, 2001.

———. *The Joy of Being Wrong: Original Sin through Easter Eyes*. New York: Crossroad, 1998.

———. *On Being Liked*. New York: Crossroad, 2004.

———. "Oracles, Prophets, and Dwellers in Silence: Hints of the '*pati divina*' in the Theology That is Being Birthed." In *The Practice of the Presence of God: Theology as a Way of Life*, edited by Martin Laird and Sheelah Treflé Hidden, 1–7. London: Routledge, 2017.

———. *Raising Abel: The Recovery of the Eschatological Imagination*. New York: Crossroad, 1996.

———. *Undergoing God: Dispatches from the Scene of a Break-in*. New York: Continuum, 2006.

Anatolios, Kahled. *Retrieving Nicaea: The Development and Meaning of Trinitarian Doctrine*. Grand Rapids, MI: Baker Academic, 2001.

Antonello, Pierpaolo, and Paul Gifford, eds. *Can We Survive Our Origins? Readings in René Girard's Theory of Violence and the Sacred*. East Lansing: Michigan State University Press, 2015.

Anderson, Gary A., and Markus Bockmuehl, eds. *Creation* ex nihilo: *Origins, Development, Contemporary Challenges*. Notre Dame, IN: University of Notre Dame Press, 2018.

Augustine, *Confessions*. Translated by Henry Chadwick. Oxford: Oxford University Press, 1991.

Aulén, Gustaf. *Christus Victor: An Historical Study of the Three Main Types of the Idea of the Atonement*. Translated by A. G. Hebert. New York: MacMillan, 1969.

Bailie, Gil. *Violence Unveiled: Humanity at the Crossroads*. New York: Crossroad, 1995.

Balthasar, Hans Urs von. *The Last Act.* Vol. 5 of *Theo-Drama: Theological Dramatic Theory.* Translated by Graham Harrison. San Francisco: Ignatius, 1998.

Barth, Karl. *Church Dogmatics IV/1: The Doctrine of Reconciliation.* Edinburgh: T&T Clark, 1956.

Barth, Markus, and Verne H. Fletcher. *Acquittal by Resurrection.* New York: Holt, Rinehart and Winston, 1964.

Bauckham, Richard. "God Who Raises the Dead: The Resurrection of Jesus and Early Christian Faith in God." In *The Resurrection of Jesus Christ*, edited by Paul Avis, London: Darton, Longman & Todd, 1993.

Behr, John. "Life and Death in the Age of Martyrdom." In *The Role of Death in Life: A Multidisciplinary Examination of the Relationship between Life and Death*, edited by John Behr and Connor Cunningham, 79–95. Eugene, OR: Cascade Books, 2015.

Boyd, Gregory A. *Cross Vision: How the Crucifixion of Jesus Makes Sense of Old Testament Violence.* Minneapolis: Fortress Press, 2017.

Breton, Stanislas. *The Word and the Cross.* Translated by Jacquelyn Porter. New York: Fordham University Press, 2002.

Brooks, Rechele, and Andrew Meltzoff. "The Importance of Eyes: How Infants Interpret Adult Looking Behavior." *Developmental Psychology* 38 (2002): 958–66.

Brown, Raymond. *Introduction to New Testament Christology.* New York: Paulist Press, 1994.

Buckley, Michael. *At the Origins of Modern Atheism.* New Haven, CT: Yale University Press, 1990.

———. *Denying and Disclosing God: The Ambiguous Progress of Modern Atheism.* New Haven, CT: Yale University Press, 2004.

Bulgakov, Sergius. *The Bride of the Lamb.* Translated by Boris Jakim. Grand Rapids, MI: William B. Eerdmans, 2002.

———. *Icons and the Name of God.* Translated by Boris Jakim. Grand Rapids, MI: William B. Eerdmans, 2012.

———. *The Lamb of God.* Translated by Boris Jakim. Grand Rapids, MI: William B. Eerdmans, 2008.

———. *Sophia, the Wisdom of God: An Outline of Sophiology.* Translated by Patrick Thompson, O. Fielding Clarke, and Xenia Braikevitc. Hudson, NY: Lindisfarne Press, 1993.

———. *The Tragedy of Philosophy: Philosophy and Dogma.* Translated by Stephan Churchyard. New York: Angelico Press, 2020.

———. *Unfading Light: Contemplations and Speculations.* Translated by Thomas Allan Smith. Grand Rapids, MI: William B. Eerdmans, 2012.

Burrell, David B., C.S.C. "Creator/Creatures Relation: 'The Distinction' vs. 'Onto-theology." *Faith and Philosophy* 25 (2008): 177–89.

———. *Freedom and Creation in Three Traditions.* Notre Dame, IN: University of Notre Dame Press, 1993.

Caputo, John D. *The Weakness of God: A Theology of the Event.* Bloomington: Indiana University Press, 2005.

Bibliography   299

Chapman, John. *Spiritual Letters*. London: Continuum, 1935.

Chrétien, J. L. *Spacious Joy: An Essay in Phenomenology and Literature*. Translated by Anne Ashley Davenport. London: Rowman & Littlefield, 2019.

Christie, Douglas E. *The Blue Sapphire of the Mind: Notes towards a Contemplative Ecology*. Oxford: Oxford University Press, 2013.

Coakley, Sarah. "Dark Contemplation and Epistemic Transformation: The Analytic Theologian Re-Meets Teresa of Avila." In *Analytic Theology: New Essays in the Philosophy of Theology*, edited by Oliver D. Crisp and Michael C. Rea, 280–312. Oxford: Oxford University Press, 2009.

———. *God, Sexuality, and the Self: An Essay 'On the Trinity.'* Cambridge: Cambridge University Press, 2013.

———. *Submissions and Powers: Spirituality, Philosophy, and Gender*. Oxford: Blackwell, 2002.

Cobb, John, and David Ray Griffin. *Process Theology: An Introductory Exposition*. Knoxville, KY: Westminster John Knox Press, 1977.

Copan, Paul, and William Lane Craig. *Creation Out of Nothing: A Biblical, Philosophical, and Scientific Exploration*. Grand Rapids, MI: Baker Academic, 2004.

Cowdell, Scott. *René Girard and Secular Modernity: Christ, Culture, and Crisis*. Notre Dame, IN: University of Notre Dame Press, 2013.

———. *René Girard and the Non-Violent God*. Notre Dame, IN: University of Notre Dame Press, 2018.

Daly, Robert J. *Sacrifice Unveiled: The True Meaning of Christian Sacrifice*. London: T&T Clark, 2009.

Davies, Oliver, and Denys Turner, eds. *Silence and the Word: Negative Theology and Incarnation*. Cambridge: Cambridge University Press, 2002.

Dawson, David. *Flesh Becomes Word: A Lexicography of the Scapegoat, or A History of an Idea*. East Lansing: Michigan State University Press, 2013.

Derrida, Jacques. *Dissemination*. Translated by Barbara Johnson. Chicago: University of Chicago Press, 1981.

Desmond, William. *Being and the Between*. Albany: State University of New York Press, 1995.

———. *God and the Between*. Oxford: Blackwell, 2008.

———. *The Intimate Strangeness of Being: Metaphysics of Dialectic*. Washington, DC: Catholic University of America Press, 2012.

———. *Philosophy and Its Others: Ways of Being and Mind*. Albany: State University of New York Press, 1990.

Donald, Merlin. *Origins of the Modern Mind: Three Stages in the Evolution of Culture and Cognition*. Cambridge, MA: Harvard University Press, 1991.

Dumouchel, Paul. *The Barren Sacrifice: An Essay on Political Violence*. Translated by Mary Baker. East Lansing: Michigan State University, 2015.

Dunn, James D. G. *Christology in the Making: A New Testament Inquiry into the Origins of the Doctrine of Incarnation*. Philadelphia: Westminster Press, 1980.

Duns, Ryan G., S.J. *Spiritual Exercises for a Secular Age: William Desmond and the Quest for God*. Notre Dame, IN: University of Notre Dame Press.

300   Bibliography

Dupuy, Jean-Pierre. *The Mark of the Sacred*. Translated by Malcom B. DeBevoise. Stanford, CA: Stanford University Press, 2013.

Eckhart, Meister. *Meister Eckhart: The Essential Sermons, Commentaries, Treatises and Defenses*. Translated by Edmund Colledge and Bernard McGinn. New York: Crossroad, 1981.

———. *The Complete Mystical Works of Meister Eckhart*. Translated by Maurice O'C. Walshe. New York: Herder & Herder, 2009.

Edwards, Denis. *Deep Incarnation: God's Redemptive Suffering with Creatures*. Maryknoll, NY: Orbis, 2019.

———. "Every Sparrow That Falls to the Ground: The Cost of Evolution and the Christ-Event." *Ecotheology* 11, no. 1 (2006): 103–23.

———. *How God Acts: Creation, Redemption, and Special Divine Action*. Minneapolis: Fortress Press, 2010.

Eliade, Mircea. *A History of Religious Ideas*, vol. 1, *From the Stone Age to the Eleusinian Mysteries*. Translated by Willard R. Trask. Chicago: University of Chicago Press, 1978.

Feuerbach, Ludwig. *The Essence of Christianity*. Translated by George Eliot. Amherst, NY: Prometheus, 1989.

Fleming, Chris. *René Girard, Violence and Mimesis*. Cambridge: Polity Press, 2004.

Francis (pope). *Laudato si'*. Vatican City: Vatican Press, 2015.

Frazer, James. *The Golden Bough: A Study in Magic and Religion*. New York: Macmillan, 1922.

Gallaher, Brandon Anastassy, and Irina Kukota. "Protopresbyter Sergii Bulgakov: Hypostasis and Hypostaticity: Scholia to *The Unfading Light*." *St. Vladimir's Theological Quarterly* 49, nos. 1–2 (2005): 5–46.

Gallese, Vittorio. "The 'Shared Manifold Hypothesis': From Mirror Neurons to Empathy." *Journal of Consciousness Studies* 8, nos. 5–7 (2001): 33–50.

Garrels, Scott R., ed. *Mimesis and Science: Empirical Research on Imitation and the Mimetic Theory of Culture and Religion*. East Lansing: Michigan State University Press, 2011.

Girard, René. *Battling to the End: Conversations with Benoît Chantre*. Translated by Mary Baker. East Lansing: Michigan State University Press, 2010.

———. *Deceit, Desire, and the Novel: Self and Other in Literary Structure*. Translated by Yvonne Freccero. Baltimore, MD: Johns Hopkins University Press, 1964.

———. *Evolution and Conversion: Dialogues on the Origin of Culture*. London: T&T Clark, 2007.

———. *The Girard Reader*. Edited by James G. Williams. New York: Herder & Herder, 2006.

———. *I See Satan Fall Like Lightning*. Translated by James G. Williams. Maryknoll, NY: Orbis, 2001.

———. *Job: The Victim of His People*. Stanford, CA: Stanford University Press, 1987.

———. *The Scapegoat*. Translated by Yvonne Freccero. Baltimore: Johns Hopkins University Press, 1986.

Bibliography 301

———. *Things Hidden Since the Foundation of the World.* Translated by Stephen Bann and Michel Metteer. Stanford, CA: Stanford University Press, 1987.

———. *Violence and the Sacred.* Baltimore: Johns Hopkins University Press, 1977.

———. *When These Things Begin: Conversations with Michel Treguer.* Translated by Trevor Cribben Merrill. East Lansing: Michigan State University Press, 2014.

Girard, René, and Gianni Vattimo. *Christianity, Truth, and Weakening Faith.* Edited by Pierpaolo Antonello. Translated by William McCuaig. New York: Columbia University Press, 2010.

Gregersen, Niels Henrik, ed. "The Cross of Christ in an Evolutionary World." *Dialog: A Journal of Theology* 40, no. 3 (2001): 192–207.

———. *Incarnation: On the Scope and Depth of Christology.* Minneapolis: Fortress Press, 2014.

Gregory of Nazianzus. *On God and Christ: The Five Theological Orations and Two Letters to Cledonius.* Translated by Lionel Wickham. Crestwood, NY: St. Vladimir's Seminary Press, 2002.

Gregory of Nyssa. "The Great Catechism." In *Nicene and Post-Nicene Fathers of the Christian Church*, vol. 5, *Gregory of Nyssa, Selected Works and Letters*, edited by Philip Schaff and Henry Wace, 471–509. Translated by William Moore and Henry Austin Wilson. Edinburgh: T&T Clark, 1994.

Hadot, Pierre. *Philosophy as a Way of Life: Spiritual Exercises from Socrates to Foucault.* Translated by Arnold I. Davidson. Oxford: Blackwell, 1995.

———. *What is Ancient Philosophy?* Translated by Michael Chase. Cambridge, MA: Harvard University Press, 2002.

Halík, Tomáš. *Patience with God: The Story of Zacchaeus Continuing in Us.* Translated by Gerald Turner. New York: Doubleday, 2009.

Hamerton-Kelly, Robert. *Sacred Violence: Paul's Hermeneutic of the Cross.* Minneapolis: Fortress Press, 1992.

Harrison, Peter. *The Territories of Science and Religion.* Chicago: University of Chicago Press, 2015.

Hart, David Bentley. *The Experience of God: Being, Consciousness, Bliss.* New Haven, CT: Yale University Press, 2013.

Hartshorne, Charles. *Omnipotence and Other Theological Mistakes.* Albany, NY: SUNY Press, 1983.

Hays, Richard B. *Reading Backwards: Figural Christology and the Fourfold Gospel Witness.* Waco, TX: Baylor University Press, 2016.

———. "Reading Scripture in Light of the Resurrection." In *The Art of Reading Scripture*, edited by Ellen F. Davis and Richard B. Hays, 216–38. Grand Rapids, MI: Eerdmans, 2003.

Hedges, Chris. *War Is a Force That Gives Us Meaning.* New York: Public Affairs, 2002.

Heim, S. Mark. *Saved from Sacrifice: A Theology of the Cross.* Grand Rapids, MI: Eerdmans, 2006.

Holt, Jim. *Why Does the World Exist? An Existential Detective Story.* New York: W. W. Norton, 2012.

302   Bibliography

Iacoboni, Marco. *Mirroring People: The New Science of How We Connect with Others*. New York: Farrar, Strauss and Giroux, 2009.

Irenaeus of Lyons. *The Scandal of the Incarnation: Irenaeus against the Heresies*. Edited by Hans Urs von Balthasar. Translated by John Saward. San Francisco: Ignatius Press, 1981.

John of the Cross. *The Collected Works of St. John of the Cross*. Translated by Kevin Kavanaugh, O.C.D., and Otilio Rodriguez, O.C.D. Washington, DC: ICS, 1991.

Johnson, Elizabeth A. *Ask the Beasts: Darwin and the God of Love*. London: Bloomsbury, 2015.

———. *Creation and the Cross: The Mercy of God for a Planet in Peril*. Maryknoll, NY: Orbis, 2018.

Kaplan, Grant. *René Girard, Unlikely Apologist: Mimetic Theory and Fundamental Theology*. Notre Dame, IN: University of Notre Dame Press, 2016.

Kasper, Walter. *The God of Jesus Christ*. Translated by Matthew J. O'Connell. New York: Crossroad, 1984.

Keller, Catherine. *Face of the Deep: A Theology of Becoming*. London: Routledge, 2003.

Kerr, Fergus. "Rescuing Girard's Argument." *Modern Theology* 8, no. 4 (1992): 385–99.

King, Chelsea. "Girard Reclaimed: Finding Common Ground between Sarah Coakley and René Girard on Sacrifice." *Contagion: Journal of Violence, Mimesis, and Culture* 23 (2016): 63–73.

King, Martin Luther, Jr. *Strength to Love*. Minneapolis: Fortress Press, 2010.

Kirwan, Michael. *Discovering Girard*. London: Darton, Longman & Todd, 2004.

———. *Girard and Theology*. New York: T&T Clark, 2009.

Laird, Martin, O.S.A. *Into the Silent Land: A Guide to the Christian Practice of Contemplation*. Oxford: Oxford University Press, 2006.

———. *An Ocean of Light: Contemplation, Transformation, and Liberation*. Oxford: Oxford University Press, 2019.

———. "The 'Open Country Whose Name is Prayer': Apophasis, Deconstruction, and Contemplative Practice." *Modern Theology* 21, no. 1 (2005): 141–55.

———. *A Sunlit Absence: Silence, Awareness, and Contemplation*. Oxford: Oxford University Press, 2011.

———. "'Whereof We Speak': Gregory of Nyssa, Jean-Luc Marion, and the Current Apophatic Rage." *Heythrop Journal* 42 (2001): 1–12.

Lane, Belden. *The Solace of Fierce Landscapes: Exploring Desert and Mountain Spirituality*. Oxford: Oxford University Press, 2007.

Leder, Drew. *The Absent Body*. Chicago: University of Chicago Press, 1990.

Leslie, John, and Robert Lawrence Kuhn, eds. *The Mystery of Existence: Why Is There Anything at All?* Oxford: Wiley-Blackwell, 2013.

Levenson, Jon. *Creation and the Persistence of Evil: The Jewish Drama of Divine Omnipotence*. San Francisco: Harper & Row, 1988.

Bibliography 303

Lohfink, Gerhard. *Jesus of Nazareth: What He Wanted, Who He Was.* Translated by Linda M. Maloney. Collegeville, MN: Liturgical Press, 2012.

Lossky, Vladimir. *The Mystical Theology of the Eastern Church.* Crestwood, NY: St. Vladimir's Seminary Press, 1957.

Louth, Andrew. "Sergii Bulgakov and the Task of Theology." *Irish Theological Quarterly* 74 (2009): 243–57.

Lubac, Henri de. *The Discovery of God.* Translated by Alexander Dru. Grand Rapids, MI: Eerdmans, 1996.

———. *Mystery of the Supernatural.* Translated by David L. Schindler. New York: Crossroad, 1998.

MacFarland, Ian A. *From Nothing: A Theology of Creation.* Louisville, KY: Westminster John Knox Press, 2014.

Marion, Jean-Luc. *God without Being: Hors-Texte.* Translated by Thomas A. Carlson. Chicago: University of Chicago Press, 1991.

May, Gerhard. *Creatio ex nihilo: The Doctrine of 'Creation out of Nothing' in Early Christian Thought.* Translated by A. S. Worrall. London: T&T Clark, 1994.

McBride, James. "Capital Punishment as the Unconstitutional Establishment of Religion: A Girardian Reading of the Death Penalty." *Journal of Church and State* 37, no. 2 (Spring 1995): 263–87.

McCabe, Herbert, O.P. *God Matters.* London: Continuum, 1987.

McGilchrist, Iain. *The Master and His Emissary: The Divided Brain and the Making of the Modern World.* New Haven: Yale University Press, 2009.

McGinn, Bernard. "Quo vadis? Reflections on the Current Study of Mysticism." *Christian Spirituality Bulletin* 6 (1998): 13–21.

McIntosh, Mark A. *Mystical Theology: The Integrity of Spirituality and Theology.* Oxford: Blackwell, 1998.

McKenna, Andrew J. *Violence and Difference: Girard, Derrida, and Deconstruction.* Champaign: University of Illinois Press, 1992.

Meltzoff, Andrew. "Understanding the Intentions of Others: Re-enactment of Intended Acts by 18-Month-Old Children." *Developmental Psychology* 31 (1995): 838–50.

Meltzoff, Andrew, and Keith Moore. "Imitation in Newborn Infants: Exploring the Range of Gestures Imitated and the Underlying Mechanisms." *Developmental Psychology* 25 (1989): 954–62.

———. "Imitation of Facial and Manual Gestures by Human Neonates." *Science* 198, no. 4312 (1977): 75–78.

Merleau-Ponty, Maurice. *The Visible and the Invisible.* Translated by Alphonso Lingis. Evanston, IL: Northwestern University Press, 1968.

Merton, Thomas. *Contemplation in a World of Action.* New York: Doubleday, 1973.

———. *Contemplative Prayer.* New York: Random House, 2014.

———. *The New Man.* New York: Noonday, 1961.

———. *New Seeds of Contemplation.* New York: New Directions, 1961.

———. *Thoughts in Solitude.* New York: Noonday Press, 1956.

———. *The Wisdom of the Desert: Sayings from the Desert Fathers of the Fourth Century*. Translated by Thomas Merton. New York: New Directions, 1960.

Metz, Johan Baptist. *Faith in History and Society: Toward a Practical Fundamental Theology*. Translated by J. Matthew Ashley. New York: Herder & Herder, 2011.

Milbank, John. "Postmodern Critical Augustinianism: A Short *Summa* in Forty-Two Responses to Unasked Questions." In *The Postmodern God: A Theological Reader*, edited by Graham Ward, 265–78. London: Blackwell, 1997.

Moore, Sebastian. *The Contagion of Jesus: Doing Theology As If It Mattered*. Edited by Stephen McCarthy. Maryknoll, NY: Orbis, 2007.

———. "Some Principles for an Adequate Theism." *Downside Review* 95 (1977): 201–13.

Nicholas of Cusa. *Selected Spiritual Writings*. Translated by H. Lawrence Bond. New York: Paulist Press, 1997.

Norman, James O'Higgins. "Mimetic Theory and Scapegoating in the Age of Cyberbullying: The Case of Phoebe Prince." *Pastoral Care in Education* 29, no. 4: 287–300.

Palaver, Wolfgang. "'Creative Renunciation': The Spiritual Heart of René Girard's *Deceit, Desire, and the Novel*." *Religion & Literature* 43, no. 3 (2011): 143–50.

———. *René Girard's Mimetic Theory*. Translated by Gabriel Borrud. East Lansing: Michigan State University Press, 2013.

Placher, William C. *The Domestication of Transcendence: How Modern Thinking about God Went Wrong*. Louisville, KY: Westminster John Knox Press, 1996.

———. *Narratives of a Vulnerable God: Christ, Theology, and Scripture*. Louisville, KY: Westminster John Knox Press, 1994.

Oord, Thomas J., ed. *Theologies of Creation: Creatio ex nihilo and its New Rivals*. London: Routledge, 2014.

Otto, Rudolf. *The Idea of the Holy: An Inquiry into the Non-Rational Factor in the Idea of the Divine and Its Relation to the Rational*. Translated by John W. Harvey. Oxford: Oxford University Press, 1923.

Oughourlian, Jean-Michel. *The Genesis of Desire*. Translated by Eugene Webb. Studies in Violence, Mimesis, and Culture. East Lansing: Michigan State University Press, 2010.

Pannenberg, Wolfhart. *Systematic Theology*, vol. 1. Translated Geoffrey W. Bromiley. Grand Rapids, MI: Eerdmans, 1998.

Pseudo-Dionysius, *The Complete Works*. Translated by Colm Luibheid. New York: Paulist Press, 1987.

Rahner, Karl. "Christology in the Setting of Modern Man's Understanding of Himself and of His World.? *Theological Investigations* 11, 215–29. Translated by David Bourke. London: Darton, Longman & Todd, 1974.

———. "Christology within an Evolutionary View of the World." *Theological Investigations* 5, 157–92. Translated by B. Kelly. New York: Seabury, 1966.

———. "The Church and Atheism." In *Theological Investigations* 21, 137–50. Translated by Hugh M. Riley. New York: Crossroad, 1988.

———. "The Concept of Mystery in Catholic Theology." In *Theological Investigations* 4, 36–73. Translated Kevin Smyth. London: Darton, Longman & Todd, 1966.

———. "Current Problems in Christology." In *Theological Investigations* 1, 149–200. Translated by Cornelius Ernst, O.P. London: Darton, Longman & Todd, 1961.

———. "Dogmatic Questions on Easter." In *Theological Investigations* 4, 121–33. Translated by Kevin Smyth. London: Darton, Longman & Todd, 1966.

———. "The Eternal Significance of the Humanity of Jesus for Our Relationship to God." In *Theological Investigations* 3, 35–46. Translated by Karl-H. Kruger and Boniface Kruger. London: Darton, Longman & Todd, 1967.

———. "The Festival of the Future of the World." In *Theological Investigations* 7, 181–85. Translated by David Bourke. New York: Herder, 1971.

———. *Foundations of Christian Faith: An Introduction to the Idea of Christianity*. Translated by William V. Dych. London: Darton, Longman & Todd, 1978.

———. *The Great Church Year: The Best of Karl Rahner's Homilies, Sermons, and Meditations*. Edited by Albert Raffelt. Translated by Harvey D. Egan. New York: Crossroad, 1993.

———. "Immanent and Transcendent Consummation of the World." In *Theological Investigations* 10, 273–89. Translated David Bourke. London: Darton, Longman & Todd, 1973.

———. "Natural Science and Reasonable Faith." In *Theological Investigations* 21, 16–55. Translated by Hugh M. Riley. New York: Crossroad, 1981.

———. "On the Theology of the Incarnation." In *Theological Investigations* 4, 105–20. Translated by Kevin Smyth. London: Darton, Longman & Todd, 1966.

———. "The Resurrection of the Body." In *Theological Investigations* 2, 203–16. Translated by Karl-H. Kruger. London: Darton, Longman & Todd, 1963.

———. "The Specific Character of the Christian Concept of God." In *Theological Investigations* 21, 185–95. Translated by Hugh M. Riley. New York: Crossroad, 1988.

———. "Theology of Freedom." In *Theological Investigations* 6, 178–96. Translated by Karl-H. Kruger and Boniface Kruger. Baltimore, MD: Helicon, 1969.

———. *The Trinity*. Translated by Joseph Donceel. New York: Crossroad, 1997.

———. "What is a Dogmatic Statement?" In *Theological Investigations* 5, 42–66. Translated by B. Kelly. New York: Seabury, 1966.

Raposa, Michael L. *Boredom and the Religious Imagination*. Charlottesville: University Press of Virginia, 1999.

Rempel, Marcus Peter. *Life at the End of Them versus Us: Cross Culture Stories*. Victoria, BC: Friesen Press, 2017.

Ricoeur, Paul. *Figuring the Sacred: Religion, Narrative, and Imagination.* Edited by Mark I. Wallace. Translated by David Pellauer. Minneapolis: Fortress Press, 1995.

———. *Freud and Philosophy: An Essay on Interpretation.* Translated by Denis Savage. New Haven: Yale University Press, 1970.

———. *The Symbolism of Evil.* Translated by Emerson Buchanan. Boston: Beacon Press, 1967.

———. "Thinking Creation." In *Thinking Biblically: Exegetical and Hermeneutical Studies*, edited by André LaCocque and Paul Ricoeur, 31–70. Translated by David Pellauer. Chicago: University of Chicago Press, 1998.

Robinette, Brian D. "Contemplative Practice and the Therapy of Mimetic Desire." *Contagion: Journal of Violence, Mimesis, and Culture* 24 (2017): 73–100.

———. "Deceit, Desire, and the Desert: René Girard's Mimetic Theory in Conversation with Early Christian Monastic Practice." In *Violence, Transformation, and the Sacred*, edited by Margaret R. Pfeil and Tobias L. Winright, 130–43. Maryknoll, NY: Orbis Books, 2012.

———. "Does Darwin Have a Future? Pain, Suffering, and Death at Eastertide." *Theological Studies* 77, no. 2 (2016): 474–78.

———. *Grammars of Resurrection: A Christian Theology of Presence and Absence.* New York: Herder & Herder, 2009.

———. "La puissance d'un dépouillement sans limites repenser: Repenser la *creatio ex nihilo* avec Stanislas Breton." Translated by Claire Vajou. *Transversalités* 135, no. 4 (October–December 2015): 43–53.

———. "Theology after the Death of God." In *T&T Clark Handbook of Political Theology*, edited by Rubén Rosario Rodríguez, 161–76. London: Bloomsbury, 2020.

———. "Undergoing Something from Nothing: The Doctrine of Creation as Contemplative Insight." In *The Practice of the Presence of God: Theology as Way of Life*, edited by Martin Laird and Sheelah Treflé Hidden, 17–28. London: Routledge, 2017.

Ruusbroec, John. *The Spiritual Espousals and Other Works.* Translated by James A. Wiseman, O.S.B. Mawah, NJ: Paulist Press, 1985.

Schillebeeckx, Edward. *Christ: The Experience of Jesus as Lord.* Translated by John Bowden. New York: Crossroad, 1990.

———. *Interim Report on the Books Jesus & Christ.* Translated by John Bowden. New York: Crossroad, 1982.

———. *Jesus: An Experiment in Christology.* Translated by Hubert Hoskins. New York: Crossroad, 1985.

Schwager, Raymund. *Jesus in the Drama of Salvation: Toward a Biblical Doctrine of Redemption.* Translated by James Williams and Paul Haddon. New York: Herder & Herder, 1999.

———. *Must There Be Scapegoats? Violence and Redemption in the Bible.* San Francisco: Harper and Row, 1987.

Sobrino, Jon. *Jesus the Liberator: A Historical-Theological View.* Translated by Paul Burns and Francis McDonagh. Maryknoll, NY: Orbis Books, 1993.

Bibliography 307

Sokolowski, Robert. *The God of Faith and Reason: Foundations of Christian Theology*. Notre Dame, IN: University of Notre Dame, Press, 1982.

Symeon the New Theologian. *The Practical and Theological Chapters and the Three Theological Discourses*. Translated by Paul McGuckin. Kalamazoo, MI: Cistercian, 1982.

Tanner, Kathryn. *Christ the Key*. Cambridge: Cambridge University Press, 2010.

———. *God and Creation in Christian Theology: Tyranny or Empowerment?* Minneapolis: Fortress Press, 1988.

———. *Jesus, Humanity and the Trinity: A Brief Systematic Theology*. Minneapolis: Fortress Press, 1992.

Taylor, Charles. *A Secular Age*. Cambridge, MA: Belknap, 2007.

Tennie, Claudio, Joseph Call, and Michael Tomasello. "Ratcheting Up the Ratchet: On the Evolution of Cumulative Culture." *Philosophical Transactions of the Royal Society* 364 (2009): 2405–2415

Teresa of Avila. *The Interior Castle*. Translated by Kieran Kavanaugh, O.C.D., and Otilio Rodriguez, O.C.D. Mahwah, NJ: Paulist Press, 1979.

Thompson, Evan. "Empathy and Consciousness." *Journal of Consciousness Studies* 8, nos. 5–7 (2001): 1–32

———. *Waking, Dreaming, Being: Self and Consciousness in Neuroscience, Meditation, and Philosophy*. New York: Columbia University Press, 2014.

Tomasello, Michael. *The Cultural Origins of Human Cognition*. Cambridge, MA: Harvard University Press, 1999.

Tomasello, Michael, Ann C. Kruger, and H. H. Ratner. "Cultural Learning." *Behavioral and Brain Sciences* 16 (1993): 495–552

Turner, Denys. *The Darkness of God: Negativity in Christian Mysticism*. Cambridge: Cambridge University Press, 1995.

———. "How to Be an Atheist." *New Blackfriars* 83, no. 977/8 (2002): 1–22.

Volf, Miroslav. *Exclusion and Embrace: A Theological Exploration of Identity, Otherness, and Reconciliation*. Nashville, TN: Abingdon, 1996.

Weil, Simone. *Gravity and Grace*. Translated by Emma Craufurd. London: Routledge, 1987.

Williams, Rowan. *Christ the Heart of Creation*. London: Bloomsbury, 2018.

———. "Creation, Creativity, and Creatureliness: The Wisdom of Finite Existence." In *Being-in-Creation: Human Responsibility in an Endangered World*, edited by Brian Treanor, Bruce Ellis Benson, and Norman Wirzba, 23–36. New York: Fordham University Press, 2015.

———. *The Edge of Words: God and the Habits of Language*. London: Bloomsbury, 2014.

———. *On Christian Theology*. Oxford: Blackwell, 2000.

———. *Resurrection: Interpreting the Easter Gospel*. Harrisburg, PA: Morehouse, 1994.

———. *Where God Happens: Discovering Christ in One Another*. Boston: New Seeds Books, 2005.

———. *Wrestling with Angels: Conversations in Modern Theology*. Edited by Mike Higton. Grand Rapids, MI: Eerdmans, 2007.

Wink, Walter. *Engaging the Powers: Discernment and Resistance in a World of Domination*. Minneapolis: Fortress Press, 1992.

———. *The Powers That Be: Theology for a New Millennium*. New York: Doubleday, 1998.

Wright, N. T. *Jesus and the Victory of God*. Vol. 2 of *Christian Origins and the Question of God*. Minneapolis: Augsburg Fortress, 1996.

———. *The Resurrection of the Son of God*. Vol. 3 of *Christian Origins and the Question of God*. Minneapolis: Augsburg Fortress, 2003.

Yoder, John Howard. *The Politics of Jesus: Vicit Agnus Noster*, 2nd ed. Grand Rapids, MI: Eerdmans, 1994.

INDEX

Abraham, 29
acedia, 55
Alison, James, 33–34, 44–45, 87–88, 92, 100, 118, 119, 120–22, 149, 156, 160, 271n59, 283n12
Anselm, 158
antinomy, 186–91, 212–13, 214–28, 235–36
apatheia, 58, 169
apophaticism. *See* negative theology
Aristotle, 16, 110, 135
atheism
    Christianity as a type of, 84, 176–78
    critiques of religion as projection, 176–78, 192–95, 200–201, 205–7, 217
    God's presence in human seeking for the divine, 207–9
atonement. *See* penal substitution
Augustine, 14, 15, 103–4, 158
Aulén, Gustaf, 152

Balkan wars, 108–9, 133
Balthasar, Hans Urs von, 76–77, 285n44
Barth, Karl, 26, 194
Basilides, 272n77
Bauckham, Richard, 21, 247–48, 293n98
becoming/coming to be, 62–67, 190

Breton, Stanislas, 84, 278n11
Buckley, Michael J., 186, 191–95, 198, 270n42
Bulgakov, Sergius
    on the Absolute and God, 215–20, 234–35
    on anthropocosmic character of the incarnation, 234–38, 241–43
    on antinomy of divine freedom and necessity, 213, 221–28, 235–36
    complements Rahner, 214
    on *creatio ex nihilo* as divine self-gift, 215–20, 234–38
    on Divine-humanity, 215–16, 243, 259
    Sophiology of, 215, 234, 241, 254–57
    trinitarian panentheism of, 219–20
Burrell, David, 30, 269n29

Cain and Abel, 106, 141
capital punishment, 130–31
Caputo, John, 6–8, 10–13, 18–19, 22–26, 272n77
causality, 22, 23–24, 39, 40, 221, 229, 234
Chalcedon, 3–4, 9, 82, 92, 243
Chapman, Don John, 57–58, 197, 275n34
Chrétien, J. L., 275n37

Christ
christological dogmas, 3–5, 9, 82, 92, 175, 199, 213, 230, 238, 243
as concentrated creation, 83, 163
cross of
—brings about reconciliation, 21, 33–34, 39–40, 147–49, 157, 166–68
—nonviolent victory over worldly power, 84–85, 145–55, 159–60
—penal substitution theories of, 157–62
—power appears as weakness, 70–73, 83–85, 88–91, 123–24, 145–55, 159–60
—redeems cosmic suffering and death, 248–53
—and scapegoat violence, 90–91, 112, 123, 143–55, 162
—"uses" sin to bring about freedom from it, 155–62
eternal Word from which creation originates, 35–37, 241
exemplifies freedom in creaturely dependence, 82, 89, 91–92, 123, 144, 232–33
hypostatic union, 72, 82, 175, 213, 230
imitation of, 111–14, 116–17, 143, 149–50
incarnation of
—affirms original goodness of creation, 86–87
—all of creation eternally ordered to, 229–38
—anthropocosmic character of, 238–53
—assumed full range of creaturely experience, 242–43, 248
—assumes creaturely flesh, 82, 238, 243–48, 250–53, 254–55
—deep incarnation, 243–53
—gratuity of, 229, 232–34
—manifests divine self-emptying love, 229–38, 248

—paradigmatic for God-world relation, 81–83, 86, 230, 239
—redemptive and deifying, 233–34, 236–38
Johannine Christology, 34, 83, 92, 239, 244
lack of rivalry with the Father, 91–92, 122
manifests triune divine life, 155–56
as microcosm of creation, 247–48
ministry opposed exclusionary violence, 88–91, 114–15, 143, 144–45, 159
Pauline Christology, 4–5, 32, 34, 83, 84, 239, 247
resurrection of
—and eschatological hope for all of creation, 251–53, 255–56
—Gospels written from perspective of, 111–13
—manifests both justice and forgiveness, 145–49, 164–68
—manifests divine creative freedom, 33–34, 85
—manifests nonrivalrous nature of divine power, 21–22, 28–34, 39–40, 85, 147–49, 153, 155–62
—as new creation, 73, 253
—and resurrection in the Old Testament, 28–31
—social and ecclesial implications of, 164–71
as strong protagonist/weak presence, 88–91, 123–24
teaching against reciprocal violence, 114–20
Christie, Douglas E., 261, 265
Coakley, Sarah, 45–49, 52–53, 74–75
contemplative prayer
aridity in, 55–57, 196–98, 202
and atheistic critiques of religion, 194–95, 209
and Desmond's "ways of mindfulness," 181–85, 214–15

as discipline of deepening awareness, 201–5, 261–65
and ecological renewal, 261–65
experience of creaturely contingency, 17–18, 42–44, 49–53, 62–63, 170–71, 179–81, 262–64
and modern "nihilistic mood," 178–85, 214–15
nonconceptual awareness of God, 41–42, 45, 49–51, 53–54, 58–61, 196–98, 204–5
purgation of distorted conceptions of God, 194–98, 203–5
relation to doctrine, 185–91, 199–200, 204–5, 207
relation to systematic theology, 43–48
as transformation of desire, 57–58, 168–71
trinitarian aspect of, 48, 53–54, 73–74
conversion, 143, 163–71
Cowdell, Scott, 176–77, 283n18, 283n23, 284n33, 286n80
creatio ex nihilo
antinomic character of, 186–91
biblical traditions of creation, 8–13, 28–34, 69
Christ's incarnation paradigmatic for, 81–83, 86, 230, 239
and contemplative experience of creaturely contingency, 17–18, 42–44, 49–53, 62–63, 170–71, 179–81, 262–64
as divine self-gift, 176, 212–13, 215–21, 229
doctrine of hope for creation, 38–40, 87, 248–53, 255–56
eschatological as well as protological, 10, 28, 31, 34, 111
grammar for speaking of, 7, 10, 15, 18, 19–21, 22
objections to, 5–8, 10–13
origin of doctrine, 4–5, 64
sustaining/ongoing nature of, 71
See also Christ; God; love; power

creation
agapeic origination of, 67–73, 155, 185, 212
and anthropocosmic dimension of the incarnation, 238–53
in Bulgakov's Sophiology, 215, 234, 241, 254–57
and creaturely capacity for God, xv, 221, 229
drawn into trinitarian life, 73–77
eternally ordered to the incarnation, 229–38
gratuitousness of, 17–19, 26–30, 34, 36–38, 62–73, 121, 155, 181–85, 187, 189, 211–12
incarnation paradigmatic for God-world relation, 81–83, 86, 230, 239
noncompetitive/nonrivalrous relationship with God, 7–8, 10–26, 32–34, 36–37, 49, 51, 59–61, 81–83, 120–24, 187–91
original goodness of, 37–38, 68, 86–87, 150–55, 282n3
originates from eternal Word, 35–37, 241
See also *creatio ex nihilo*
cross. *See* Christ: cross of

Daly, Robert J., 85
Dawson, David, 282n8
Day of Atonement, 128
death, 248–53
death penalty, 130–31
deep (*tehom*), 6–7, 12–13
deep incarnation, 243–53
demythologization
of creation, 163–64
of God, 28, 33–34, 156–57, 161, 163
Derrida, Jacques, 6, 283n22
desire
divine eros, 120, 224–28
transformed in contemplation, 57–58, 168–71
See also mimetic desire

Desmond, William, 63–72, 111, 181–85, 214–15, 226
Dionysius. *See* Pseudo-Dionysius
discipleship, 111–14, 116–17, 143, 149–50
Divine-humanity, 215–16, 243, 259
divinization. See *theosis*
doctrine
  and antinomy, 186–91, 212–13, 214–28, 235–36
  history of, 3–4
  relation to contemplation, 43–48, 185–91, 199–200, 204–5, 207
Dumouchel, Paul, 110, 283n11
Dunn, James D. G., 34
Dupuy, Jean-Pierre, 282n9
Durkheim, Émile, 192

Easter. *See* Christ: resurrection of
Eckhart, Meister, 70, 171, 201, 203, 274n23
ecological crisis, 214–15, 237, 240, 253–65
Edwards, Denis, 245, 253, 293n98
Eliade, Mircea, 137
empathy, 99
eros, 224–28
evil and suffering
  Christ redeems suffering and death, 248–53
  evil as perversion of goodness, 236
  gnostic view of, 37
  and non-human creation, 38–40, 248–53
  Satan personifies evil, 153
  theodicy, 6–7, 8, 23, 38–40, 248–53
evolution, 98, 134, 136–37, 243, 245–48, 250–51
exclusionary violence. *See* violence

Father, 91–92, 117, 122, 157–58. *See also* God; Trinity
Feuerbach, Ludwig, 192–94
fittingness, 212, 223–24
flesh, 82, 238, 243–48, 254–55
Francis, Pope, 257

Frazer, James, 139
freedom
  antinomy of divine freedom and "love's necessity," 212–13, 221–28, 235–36
  of Christ, 82, 89, 91–92, 123, 144, 232–33
  interplay of divine and creaturely freedom, 20–21, 23–24, 38
  unconditioned nature of divine creativity, 20–21, 26, 33, 36–40, 85
  and vulnerability in contemplative prayer, 49–50
Freud, Sigmund, 95, 108, 138, 192, 193

Gallese, Vittorio, 99
Garrels, Scott, 95
gift. *See* creation: gratuitousness of
Girard, René
  account of mimetic desire, 92–95, 100
  account of scapegoat violence, 34, 127–29, 131–32, 134–38
  on biblical revelation, 90–91, 138–45, 176
  on Christ's sacrificial death, 159–62
  on creative renunciation, 117
  on mimetic rivalry, 102–7, 118, 127–29
  "phenomenology of redemption," 85–86
  on the victory of Easter, 146, 152–53
  See also mimetic desire; scapegoat violence; violence
gnosticism, 6, 37, 219
God
  apophatic language about, 186–91, 200–201, 216–18, 226–27
  "death of God," 145, 180, 192, 209–10
  encountered in contemplative prayer, 41–42, 45, 48, 49–51, 53–54, 58–61, 196–98, 201, 204–5

freedom of
—gratuity of the incarnation, 229, 232–34
—interplay of divine and creaturely, 20–21, 23–24, 38
—and "love's necessity," 10, 17, 212–13, 221–28, 235–36
—unconditioned nature of divine creativity, 20–21, 26, 33, 36–40, 85
goodness of, 6–7, 23, 209, 224–28, 235
noncompetitive/nonrivalrous relationship with creation, 7–8, 10–26, 32–34, 36–37, 49, 51, 59–61, 81–83, 120–24, 187–91
nonviolence of, 25–26, 34, 88, 117, 138–49, 164–66, 176
power of
—appears as weakness in Christ, 70–73, 83–85, 88–91, 123–24, 145–55, 159–60
—Caputo's critique of omnipotence, 6–8, 10–13
—and creaturely freedom, 20–21, 23–24, 38
—incompatible with violence, 25–26
—and noncompetitive/nonrivalrous relationship with creation, 19–26
—persuasive rather than coercive, 155, 160
—resurrection manifests pacific nature of divine power, 21–22, 28–34, 39–40, 85, 147–49, 153, 155–62
—strong protagonist/weak presence, 88–91, 123–24
—and vulnerability, 19–26, 248
—"weak God" theologies, 6–7, 11–13, 23
present in human searching for the divine, 207–9
and projection theories of religion, 176–78

purgation of distorted conceptions of, 176–78, 186–92, 194–98, 200–201, 203–5, 216–18
self-emptying love of
—agapeic origination of creation, 67–73, 155, 185, 212
—in *creatio ex nihilo*, 176, 212–13, 215–21, 229
—divine eros, 224–28, 232
—divine freedom and "love's necessity," 10, 17, 212–13, 221–28, 235–36
—in the incarnation, 229–38, 248
—as self-diffusiveness of the Good, 209, 224–28, 235
—trinitarian nature of, 222, 237, 248–49
transcendence and immanence of
—atheism as response to, 207
—classical account of, 14–19
—and *creatio ex nihilo* as divine self-gift, 212–13, 215–21, 229
—and the cross, 39–40, 145, 153
—and demythologization of God, 28, 33–34, 156–57, 161, 163
—experienced in contemplative prayer, 17–18, 49–50, 62, 204
—and noncompetitive relationship with the world, 7–8, 10–19, 82–83, 120–24, 187–91
unity of God and neighbor, 170–71
See also Christ; Father; Spirit; Trinity
God-world relation. *See* creation; God
goodness
divine, 6–7, 23, 209, 224–28, 235
of mimetic desire, 125–26, 167
original goodness of creation, 37–38, 68, 86–87, 150–55, 282n3
Gregersen, Niels Henrik, 243–45, 250
Gregory of Nazianzus, 155
Gregory of Nyssa, 14, 76, 153, 195, 286n63
Gregory Palamas, 220

314 Index

Hadot, Pierre, 48
Halík, Tomáš, 206–10
Hamerton-Kelly, Robert, 138
Harrison, Peter, 274n16
Hart, David Bentley, 201
Hedges, Chris, 107–9
Hegel, G. W. F., 192, 217
Heim, Mark, 141, 154, 161
Holocaust, 132–33
homosexuality, 130
hope for creation, 38–40, 87, 248–53, 255–56

imitation. *See* mimetic desire
immanence. *See* God: transcendence and immanence of
immigrants, 130
incarnation. *See* Christ: incarnation of
infants, 95–99, 103–4
instrumental thinking, 63–64, 66, 68, 181, 214–15
intercorporeity, 243–48, 254, 256–57
Irenaeus of Lyons, 9, 36, 37–38, 153, 155, 272n77
Israel, 29–30, 89, 114, 128, 141–42

James, William, 95
Jesus. *See* Christ
Jews, violence against, 132–33. *See also* Israel
Job, 142
John of the Cross, 51, 177, 195–96, 198, 199, 210
Johnson, Elizabeth, 245, 250–51, 293n98
Justin Martyr, 9

Kaplan, Grant, 282n3, 287n2
Kasper, Walter, 248–49
Keller, Catherine, 6, 10, 268n14, 268n17, 272n77
kenosis. *See* love

Laird, Martin, 59–61, 169, 202, 218, 264

Lane, Belden, 50
Leder, Drew, 246, 254
Levenson, Jon, 268n13
Lohfink, Gerhard, 113
Lossky, Vladimir, 191, 199
Louth, Andrew, 258
love
    agapeic origination of creation, 67–73, 155, 185, 212
    for all of creation, 213, 256–57, 260
    divine eros, 224–28, 232
    divine freedom and "love's necessity," 10, 17, 212–13, 221–28, 235–36
    evil as perversion of, 236
    felt in contemplative prayer, 264
    God's self-giving love in *creatio ex nihilo*, 176, 212–13, 215–21, 229
    God's self-giving love in the incarnation, 229–38, 248
    as self-diffusiveness of the Good, 209, 224–28, 235
    trinitarian nature of divine love, 222, 237, 248–49
Lubac, Henri de, 14
Luther, Martin, 250

MacFarland, Ian, 269n38
Marion, Jean-Luc, 28–29
Marx, Karl, 192, 193
matter
    creation from preexistent matter, 9, 35–36, 66
    eschatological transformation of, 240, 255
Maximus the Confessor, 241
May, Gerhard, 35–36, 272n77
McBride, James, 131
McCabe, Herbert, 155–56
McGilchrist, Iain, 98
McIntosh, Mark, 186
Meltzoff, Andrew, 95–96
Merleau-Ponty, Maurice, 245–46
Merton, Thomas, 43, 54, 62–63, 158, 168–69, 178–81, 185, 198, 199, 262–63

Metz, Johann Baptist, 165
Milbank, John, 24, 270n42
mimetic desire
  in cognitive and behavioral sciences, 95–99
  and contemplation, 168–71
  conversion of, 163–71
  Girard's account of, 92–95
  and identity
  —group identities, 87–91, 118–19, 121, 122
  —individual identity, 101, 105–6, 118–19
  —relational nature of the self, 93, 99–101, 118–19, 150
  — "we-centricity," 93, 99, 101, 123, 160, 167, 168
  inherent goodness of, 125–26, 167
  and Jesus's call to discipleship, 114, 118–20, 143
  leads to reciprocal violence, 102–4, 107–10, 115–16, 126
  and rivalry, 101–10, 116, 118, 126, 127–29
  See also violence
mirror neurons, 99–100
monasticism, 179
Moore, Sebastian, 41–42, 72, 121, 163–71, 204, 227

necessity, 10, 17, 212–13, 221–28, 235–36. See also fittingness
negative theology
  commonalities with atheistic critiques of religion, 176–78, 192–95, 200–201, 205–7, 217
  and human searching for God, 207–9
  purgation of distorted conceptions of God, 176–78, 186–92, 194–98, 200–201, 203–5, 216–18
  relation between doctrine and mysticism, 185–91, 199–200, 204–5, 207
  See also atheism; contemplative prayer

Nicaea, 9, 238
Nicholas of Cusa, 14, 62, 120, 191, 216
Nietzsche, Friedrich, 85, 138, 192, 193–94
nihilistic mood, 178–85, 214–15

omnipotence. See power
onto-theology, 10, 19, 23, 27, 28, 36, 46
Otto, Rudolf, 135
Oughourlian, Jean-Michel, 100–101, 285n40

Palaver, Wolfgang, 280n59, 281n78, 282n84
panentheism, 219–20, 229
Pannenberg, Wolfhart, 20–21, 32
Paul (apostle)
  Christology of, 4–5, 32, 34, 83, 84, 239, 247
  conversion of, 148–49
  on eschatological new creation, 73, 87, 252
  on the power of the cross, 21–22, 25, 72, 84, 152
  on the Spirit, 52–53, 75
peace, 21–22, 28–34, 39–40, 72, 85, 86, 135–36, 147–49, 153, 155–62
penal substitution, 157–62
Piaget, Jean, 95
Placher, William, 23, 25–26, 269n33
Platonism, 6, 16, 35–36, 66
posthumous mind, 182–84
power
  appearing as weakness in Christ, 70–73, 83–85, 88–91, 123–24, 145–55, 159–60
  Caputo's critique of omnipotence, 6–8, 10–13
  Christ as strong protagonist/weak presence, 88–91, 123–24
  divine power and creaturely freedom, 20–21, 23–24, 38
  and divine vulnerability, 19–26, 248

power (*continued*)
  incompatible with violence, 25–26
  and nonrivalrous relationship
    between God and creation,
    19–26
  persuasive rather than coercive,
    155, 160
  resurrection manifests pacific
    nature of divine power, 21–22,
    28–34, 39–40, 85, 147–49, 153,
    155–62
  "weak God" theologies, 6–7,
    11–13, 23
  See also violence
prayer. *See* contemplative prayer
process theology, 6–7, 12–13
projection theories of religion,
    176–78, 192–95, 200–201,
    205–7, 217
protagonist, God as, 88–91, 123–24,
    160
Pseudo-Dionysius
  and apophaticism, 188–89, 191,
    195, 198, 199, 200, 216, 217,
    273n10
  on divine eros, 209, 224–27, 232
  and divine transcendence/imma-
    nence, 14
  and vocation of theology, 45

Rahner, Karl
  on anthropocosmic character of
    the incarnation, 229–34, 238,
    240–41, 252–53
  on atheism, 205
  complements Bulgakov, 214
  on contemplative prayer, 52
  on *creatio ex nihilo* as divine self-
    gift, 15, 24, 220–21, 229–34
  on guilt and forgiveness, 166
  on history of doctrine, 3–4, 186
  on the incarnate Christ, 82, 92,
    122, 229–34
  on the incarnation as God's self-
    emptying love, 156, 220–21

  on mystery of being, 212
redemption. *See* Christ
representational thinking, 63–64, 66,
    68
ressentiment, 85, 105, 147
resurrection. *See* Christ: resurrection
    of
return to zero, 181–85
Ricoeur, Paul, 32, 35, 37, 138
rivalry
  alleviated by a scapegoat, 127–29
  and mimetic desire, 101–10, 116,
    118, 126
  nonrivalrous relationship between
    God and creation, 7–8, 10–26,
    32–34, 36–37, 49, 51, 59–61,
    81–83, 120–24, 187–91
  not present within the Trinity,
    91–92, 122
  resurrection manifests nonrival-
    rous nature of divine power,
    21–22, 28–34, 39–40, 85, 147–49,
    153, 155–62
  See also mimetic desire
Romulus and Remus, 106
Ruusbroec, John, 213

sacrifice. *See* scapegoat violence
salvation. *See* Christ
Satan, 153
scapegoat violence
  examples from historical events,
    131–33
  examples from modern culture,
    129–31
  Girard's account of, 127–29,
    131–32
  Jesus as scapegoat, 90–91, 112, 123,
    143–55, 162
  Jesus's victory over, 150–55
  mechanism to alleviate cyclical
    violence, 131, 134–38, 139–40,
    144
  and penal substitution theories,
    157–62

reinforces group identity, 129–33
scripture exposes injustice of,
 138–45, 164–66, 176
Schillebeeckx, Edward, 39–40, 83
Schwager, Raymund, 91, 161, 285n42,
 285n44
selfhood, 93, 99–101, 118–19, 150
Sermon on the Mount, 115–20
sin
 anthropocosmic dimension of,
 236–37, 248–53
 in history of human evolution,
 136–37
 mimetic rivalry as, 126
 redeemed by Christ, 155–62,
 233–34, 236–38
Sobrino, Jon, 159
Sokolowski, Robert, 17, 27
Sophiology, 215, 234, 241, 254–57
Soskice, Janet, 267n4
Spirit, 52–53, 74–77, 180, 245
spiritual senses
 and the ecological crisis, 253–54,
 256–57, 259–61, 264–65
 feeling, 261–65
 hearing, 254–57
 seeing, 257–61
suffering. See evil and suffering
Symeon the New Theologian, 203

Tanner, Kathryn, 10, 16, 19, 22,
 268n17
Tatian, 9, 36, 272n77
Taylor, Charles, 100, 206
Teresa of Avila, 55–57, 68
terrorism, war on, 109–10
Tertullian, 9, 255, 272n81
theodicy, 6–7, 8, 23, 38–40,
 248–53
Theophilus of Antioch, 9, 36, 37,
 272n77
theosis, 176, 199, 214, 233–34, 236–38,
 252
Thomas Aquinas, 14, 23–24, 45, 201,
 233, 273n85

Thompson, Evan, 280n40, 280n49
Tomasello, Michael, 96–98
transcendence. See God: transcendence and immanence of
Trinity
 Bulgakov's trinitarian panentheism, 219–20
 and contemplative prayer, 48,
 53–54, 73–74
 creaturely otherness reflects, 73–77
 and intradivine divine self-
 emptying, 222, 237, 248–49
 manifested in life of Jesus, 155–56
 no rivalry within, 91–92, 122
 and penal substitution theories,
 157–58
 See also Christ; Father; God; Spirit
Turner, Denys, 188–89, 190, 191, 200,
 205, 225, 273n10, 274n32,
 289n61

victim. See scapegoat violence
violence
 creative renunciation of, 114–20,
 126, 152
 cross as nonviolent victory over
 worldly power, 33, 84–85, 145–
 55, 159–60
 God not implicated in human violence, 34, 88, 117, 141–42,
 145–49
 Jesus's ministry opposed exclusionary violence, 88–91, 114–15,
 143, 144–45, 159
 and mimetic rivalry, 102–4, 107–10,
 127–29
 reciprocal
 —in account of mimetic desire,
 115–16, 126
 —alleviated by a scapegoat, 131,
 134–38, 139–40, 144
 —Christ's teaching against, 114–20
 —subverted by the cross, 33, 145–
 55, 159–60
 See also scapegoat violence

Volf, Miroslav, 133
vulnerability, divine, 19–26, 248. *See also* power

war, 107–10
weakness
  power appears as, in Christ, 70–73, 83–85, 88–91, 123–24, 145–55, 159–60
  "weak God" theologies, 6–7, 11–13, 23

"we-centricity," 93, 99, 101, 123, 160, 167, 168
Weil, Simone, 117, 178
Williams, Rowan, 17–18, 28–30, 49, 63, 76, 134, 145, 168, 260–61
Wink, Walter, 151
Wisdom, Divine. *See* Sophiology
world, 150–55. *See also* creation

BRIAN D. ROBINETTE is an associate professor of theology at Boston College. He is the author of *Grammars of Resurrection: A Christian Theology of Presence and Absence*.

Ingram Content Group UK Ltd.
Milton Keynes UK
UKHW020205230523
422194UK00003B/71